A HISTORY OF ENGLISH

A HISTORY
OF ENGLISH

Barbara M. H. Strang

METHUEN & CO LTD

First published in 1970
by Methuen & Co Ltd
11 New Fetter Lane, London EC4P 4EE

First published as a University Paperback in 1974
Reprinted twice
Reprinted 1979

© *1970 Barbara M. H. Strang*

Printed and bound in Great Britain at
William Clowes & Sons Limited
Beccles and London

ISBN 0 416 16820 5 (hardback)
0 416 80660 0 (paperback)

For C. S. and C. J. S.

Boots it to know how our forefathers spoke
Ere *Danish, Norman,* or this present yoke
Did gall our patient necks? or matters it
What *Hengist* utter'd, or how *Horsa* writ?
Last, think'st that we, who have destroy'd whate're
Our Grandsires did, will with their language bear?
That we (who have all famous Monuments
Raz'd, and defeated thus all good intents
Of former Piety:) will honour give
To antique Characters? shall Paper live,
And Inke, when Brasse and Marble can't withstand
This iron ages violating hand?

Ioannes de Bosco to William Somner, 1659

How can a lively mind *not* want to know something
of such things, if anything can now be known?

J. W. Clark, 1957

Analytical Contents

PART TWO: THE CHRONOLOGICAL SEQUENCE

Chapter I: *1970–1770*

Analytical contents

Chapter II: *1770–1570*

ix

Chapter IV: *1370–1170*

Preface

The production of yet another outline history of English may seem to be presumptuous and pointless. To me it is a sufficient justification that, by producing at this point in time a work which does not simply echo others, one can suggest something of the inexhaustible richness and variety of the subject.

This is a book for beginners in linguistic history, but it does assume analytic knowledge of the structure of present-day English and some familiarity with the tools of linguistic study. Without such assumptions it would have had to be either much longer and more repetitive or uselessly vague.

Unlike structure, history has generally been taught in England wherever, at university level, the English language is an object of study. Over some twenty years of personal involvement in this teaching I have been struck by the fairy-tale – not to say nightmare – quality the subject has for most students. Grimm's Law, Verner's Law and the Great Vowel Shift seem to operate in a world strangely mutated from that in which they converse. For this reason it has seemed important to lay considerable emphasis on two things: first, variation and change observable at the present time as living evidence of the ceaselessly, oceanically, heaving, swelling, flowing, ungraspable mass that historians corset into manageable chunks on to which quasi-scientific labels can be stuck; second, the operation in the modern world of factors which make linguistic change much more complex than in the medieval world. Language is tied to personality, from which it derives unalterable characteristics, but personality is tied to society, which changes. Linguistic change, as well as language, has a history. It is more complicated now than ever before. If I have presented a picture which seems confusing, especially in the treatment of recent centuries, I do not regard this as failure. Those who find the account of post-medieval English too difficult may prefer to go from the opening chapters to the medieval ones, and fill in the gaps later. In the long run they should not rest content with less than an understanding, so far as it can be achieved, of how the present situation has come about.

As a whole, I believe this book has something new to say. In many of its parts it draws heavily on the work of numerous scholars. I have not tried to disguise its derivativeness, and I am humbled by the splendour of the scholarly tradition on which, in pathetically small measure, I have been able to draw. The time is long since past when one writer could depend on close first-hand knowledge of all primary and secondary material from all periods (I am, however, well enough aware that it is possible to know more about the history of English than I do). Yet the subject has a unity, and a single perspective still, I believe, has a value different from that of a group-study by a team of specialists. To me, at least, what I have written raises countless issues for enquiry and discussion, and I should hope it might serve others as a springboard rather than a textbook.

Acknowledgements

The writing of books is a solitary activity, but the author is only in a position to write as a result of the activities of others. It is now twenty-eight years since the late Professor C. L. Wrenn first opened my eyes to the absorbing questions there were to ask about the English language, and the detective care needed to interpret the evidence from which answers might be constructed. The excitement of such enquiries is with me still. When I began to teach the subject myself I came under the tutelage of Miss B. M. Daunt, and of the many things she taught me, the most fundamental, which has guided my teaching and writing ever since, was that for the reconstructed language of the past we must never postulate states or changes that we cannot exemplify, or at least understand, from the evidence of the present. Twenty years of University teaching in Newcastle, and a standing interest in the urban speech of Tyneside, have made me acutely conscious of the complexity of the processes of linguistic urbanisation, and of their relevance to the history of English in the last eight hundred years. From the published work of those I was not privileged to meet I have learnt far more than the sketchy acknowledgements within my text indicate – above all from Sweet, Jespersen, Wyld, Mossé, Mustanoja, Meillet. In the field of historical, as of structural, linguistics the roll of honour predominantly consists of foreign names. And it has been my students who have provided a constant supply of fresh questions to examine, and who, refusing to be blinded by science, have helped me to discriminate which are the presentable answers.

I should not have been able to set down this account without more direct help. First the Council of the University of Newcastle upon Tyne granted me study leave for the Michaelmas Term of 1968, and in the (for me) tranquillity of Cambridge, Massachusetts, with the magnificent library resources of Harvard at my disposal, I completed the first typescript in twelve weeks. My friends, colleagues and research students have assisted in many ways, and I should especially like to mention the late Professor Peter Ure, Dr Yngve Olsson, Mr John Frankis, Mr Richard Bailey, Miss Anna Baker, Mr John Pellowe and Mrs M. E. Shepherd, for help in the re-arrangement of departmental duties and in

Acknowledgements

the reading, preparation and improvement of the final draft. Lord Strang and Professor Randolph Quirk gave a quite disproportionate amount of their time to reading and commenting on the entire type-script, and Professor Angus McIntosh has given generous help in consultation and in access to his unpublished material on ME dialec-tology. My family have supported me in countless ways, culminating in a proof-reading by my husband, which, despite four previous readings, brought to light a large number of slips which would otherwise have remained undetected.

To all those I have mentioned I gladly offer my thanks. The greatest splendour of the life of scholarship is the generosity of its traditions. I have called upon them to the full, and I have never been disappointed.

Abbreviations

Apart from a few abbreviations in common use, or occurring in this book only in quotations from other writers, the following short forms are used. Certain abbreviations render more than one full form, but in context no ambiguity should arise. Some have alternative forms, the longer for use in contexts that might otherwise be of doubtful interpretation.

A(cc)	Accusative
adj	Adjective
adv	Adverb
AS	Anglo-Saxon
AV	Authorised Version
BBC	British Broadcasting Corporation
Br	British
C	Cardinal vowel (in description of sounds)
c	Century (in chronological statements)
C	Common (especially in combination, as CG = Common Germanic)
C	Consonant (in phonological analyses)
D(at)	Dative
dem	Demonstrative
E	Early (especially as the first element of three-term combinations, as ENE = Early New English)
E	East (especially in combinations, as EG = East Germanic, SE = South-eastern)
E	English (especially as the second element of combinations, as OE, ME, etc., q.v.)
EPNS	English Place-Name Society
F	Feminine
F	French
G(en)	Genitive
G(mc)	German(ic) (especially as the second element of combinations, as NG = North Germanic)
Go	Gothic

Gr	Greek
I	Instrumental
IE	Indo-European
imp	Imperative
ind	Indicative
inf	Infinitive
J	Judgement
Kt	Kentish
L	Latin
M	Masculine
m	Million
ME	Middle English
Mid	Midland(s)
MS(S)	Manuscript(s)
N	Neuter
N	North(ern) (also in combinations, as NE, NW, NG)
N	Noun/nominal
N(om)	Nominative
NE	New English
Nhb	Northumbria(n)
NP	Noun Phrase
NWS	Non-West Saxon
O	Operation
O(bj)	Object
OE	Old English
OED	*Oxford English Dictionary*
OFris	Old Frisian
OHG	Old High German
ON	Old Norse
Part	Participle
PE	Present-day English
PF	Periphrastic Form
pl	Plural
pres	Present
RP	Received Pronunciation
RS	Received Standard
S	Selection
S	South(ern) (also in combination, as SE, SW)
S(ubj)	Subject
sb	Substantive

Abbreviations

Sc	Scots, Scottish
sg	Singular
T	Tail
UK	United Kingdom
US(A)	United States (of America)
v	Verb
V	Vowel
W	West (also in combination, as SW, NW, WG)
WF	Word-formation
WS	West Saxon

Capital roman numerals are used for reference to periods and to chapters dealing with those periods, as follows:

I	= 1970-1770
II	= 1770-1570
III	= 1570-1370
IV	= 1370-1170
V	= 1170-970
VI	= 970-770
VII	= 770-570
VIII	= 570-370
IX	= Before 370

List of signs and symbols, mainly phonetic

a Cardinal Vowel no. 4 (approximately as in F *patte*); used for first element of E diphthong [aɪ]

æ Front vowel between open and half-open (E vowel in *cat*)

ɑ Cardinal Vowel no. 5 (approximately as in F *pas*); used for first element of E diphthong [aʊ], and for E [ɑː] in *car*

ɒ Open rounded Cardinal Vowel no. 5 (E vowel in *dog*)

b Voiced bilabial plosive (E *b* in *labour*)

β Voiced bilabial fricative

ç Voiceless palatal fricative

ɔ Cardinal Vowel no. 6 (approximately as in G *Sonne*); used for E [ɔː] in *saw*, and first element of diphthong [ɔɪ]

d Voiced alveolar plosive (E *d* in *lady*)

ð Voiced dental fricative (E *th* in *other*)

e Cardinal Vowel no. 2 (approximately as in F *thé*); used for first element of diphthong [eɪ]

ə Unrounded central vowel (E initial and final vowels in *another*)

ɛ Cardinal Vowel no. 3 (approximately as in F *père*); used for first element of diphthong [ɛə]

ɜ Unrounded central vowel (E vowel in *bird*)

f Voiceless labio-dental fricative (E *f* in *four*)

g Voiced velar plosive (E *g* in *eager*)

h Voiceless glottal fricative (E *h* in *house*)

i Cardinal Vowel no. 1 (approximately as in F *si*); used for E [iː] in *see*

ɪ Centralised unrounded half-close vowel (E vowel in *sit*)

j Palatal unrounded approximant (E *y* in *you*)

k Voiceless velar plosive (E *c* in *car*)

l Voiced alveolar lateral continuant (E *l* in *lay*)

ɫ Voiced alveolar lateral continuant with velarization (E *ll* in *ill*)

m Voiced bilabial nasal (E *m* in *me*)

n Voiced alveolar nasal (E *n* in *no*)

ŋ Voiced velar nasal (E *ng* in *sing*)

o Cardinal Vowel no. 7 (approximately as in F *eau*)

ø Rounded Cardinal Vowel no. 2 (approximately as in F *peu*)

θ Voiceless dental fricative (E *th* in *thing*)

p   Voiceless bilabial plosive (E *p* in *pea*)

r   Linguo-alveolar roll (Sc, It *r*); also used for E *r* in *red*

ɹ   Voiced post-alveolar frictionless continuant

s   Voiceless alveolar fricative (E *s* in *see*)

ʃ   Voiceless palato-alveolar fricative (E *sh* in *she*)

t   Voiceless alveolar plosive (E *t* in *tea*)

u   Cardinal Vowel no. 8 (approximately as in F *doux*); used for E [uː] in *do*

ʊ   Centralised rounded half-close vowel (E *u* in *put*)

v   Voiced labio-dental fricative (E *v* in *ever*)

ʌ   Unrounded Cardinal Vowel no. 6; used for E vowel in *cup*

w   Labio-velar approximant (E *w* in *we*)

ʍ   Voiceless labio-velar fricative (sometimes E *wh* in *why*)

χ   Voiceless velar fricative (Sc *ch* in *loch*)

y   Rounded Cardinal Vowel no. 1 (approximately as in F *du*)

ɣ   Voiced velar fricative

z   Voiced alveolar fricative (E *z* in *lazy*)

ʒ   Voiced palato-alveolar fricative (E *s* in *measure*)

ʔ   Glottal plosive (stop)

:   Indicates full length of preceding vowel

ˈ   Main accentual stress of pitch prominence on following syllable

ˌ   Secondary accentual stress on following syllable

~   Nasalisation, e.g. [õ]

¨   Centralisation, e.g. [ö]

˳   Devoiced lenis consonant, e.g. [z̥]

ˌ   Syllabic consonant, e.g. [n̩]

[ ]   Phonetic transcription

/ /   Phonemic transcription

◡   Short (in syllabic or metrical length)

—   Long (in syllabic or metrical length)

⌒   Half-long (in syllabic length)

>   Becomes

<   Develops from

Ø   Zero

*   Hypothetical, reconstructed, not recorded

+   Presence of a specified feature

−   Absence of a specified feature

±   Regardless of whether a specified feature is present or absent

/, \, ×   Stress, half-stress, unstress, in cases where unstress requires marking.

PART ONE

Introductory

Synchronic variation and diachronic change

§ 1   The prevalence of linguistic change is something widely forced on our attention. Very often the notice it receives is unfavourable; these comments from the press represent points of view held by many educated and thoughtful English-speaking people:

I

Sir,–May I utter a protest against the currently fashionable abuse of the word sophisticated as applied to weapons or nuclear and electronic devices of advanced design?

The Oxford English Dictionary (Vol. 10, page 436) gives three meanings for sophisticated: (i) adulterated, not pure or genuine; (ii) altered from, deprived of, primitive simplicity or naturalness (generally, it seems, in a perjorative sense, implying artificiality); (iii) falsified in a greater or less degree; not plain, honest or straightforward.

None of these definitions fits the meaning now given to the word by the scientific and strategic pundits and radio and television commentators when they talk of sophisticated weapons or machines. On the other hand, there is a range of simple terms that are perfectly adequate for the purpose.

I suggest complex, elaborate, highly refined, or highly developed. Some of these terms are shorter and none contains more syllables than sophisticated.

Let this word, therefore, be saved from deteriorating into pseudo-learned jargon.

Yours faithfully,

II

Sir,–In *The Teacher* dated June 16 a correspondent wrote of 'the clumsy efforts of we anglers'. In *The Times* dated June 17 a correspondent writes 'Let we in the West make sure that we do all we can ...'

Does this mean that the word *us* is about to disappear from our language? Or that normal English usage is now ignored in papers which previously set high standards?

Yours faithfully,

3

III

Sir,–Is it not regrettable that a headline in *The Times* 'The lesser known side of a great collection' (September 20) should lend authority to the increasing practice of treating 'lesser' as an adverb, a usage which the O.E.D. tells us has been obsolete since 1625 ?

One is helped to keep the distinction clear by remembering that the Lesser Spotted Woodpecker is *more* spotted, not *less* spotted, than the Greater Spotted Woodpecker.

Your obedient servant,

IV

Sir,–Every so often a familiar word takes on a new and senseless life. *Superb*, for instance, is now commonly abused. *Literally* – 'he literally exploded with rage' – seems to be on the way out, but *virtually* has taken its place. In the course of a day influenza-bound recently I heard speakers on various B.B.C. programmes use this adverb improperly nine times.

With superb diffidence, I am, Sir, virtually yours,

Sir,–Can anything be done to stop the appalling new word 'escalate' from escalating into the next edition of the Oxford Dictionary ? The hope is being expressed that the Viet-Nam business may not 'escalate' into a major war. What's wrong with the simple word 'develop' ?

Your obedient servant,

Sir,–It is with regret that I read in your columns of the passing of the word 'literally' from our vocabulary.

I have had an affection for its misuse ever since I read that Squeers had literally feasted his eyes, in silence, upon the culprit (Smike).

Yours faithfully,

V

Sir,–I am also one who fears for the state of the English language. Care for its development, propagation and standardisation needs to be made more of a political issue, as in France, Norway and the USSR.

In particular, let there be care over the formation of new words, 'Television,' 'auto-mation,' and 'hyper-sonic' are of mixed linguistic origin.

Also, consider this sentence: 'I've got to get there to get rich.' Such usage is common now.

In English this becomes: 'I need to arrive there to become rich.'

Moreover, 'Ae've getten a one' sounds better than 'I've got one.' Most curious !–

Yours faithfully,

4

On the other hand, a more tolerant view is also expressed

VI

Sir,–English is a living language. Meanings change, and dictionaries cannot always keep pace with current usage.

If the majority of English-speaking people use the word sophisticated to describe something which is highly refined, then that *is* its meaning.

Yours faithfully,

Familiarity with the concept of change should not blunt the edge of curiosity about it. It is not immediately obvious that language should change; indeed, many have thought, at various periods, and some still think, that change could be halted, or at least brought under control. Animal cries, for example, may change a little from era to era, but there is some reason to think they do not change nearly as much as language. The sound made by sheep was represented by the Ancient Greeks as *bē*, *bē* (approximately /bɛː/ /bɛː/), and much the same sort of sound can be heard from English sheep at the present day. But the Modern Greek equivalent of the linguistic form is pronounced /viː/; it has lost all connection with the natural sound to which it was originally related. Why should speech be more subject to change than animal cries? Before we answer that question, we should put beside it another, even nearer home. Ancient Greek also had a representation for the sound of a sob, *pheu*, which would have been something like /phɛʊ/, with a clearly echoic character, presumably then, and certainly in relation to sobs as we now know them. Yet this in present-day Greek has become /fɛf/, a sound which emerges rather ludicrously from the lips of a tragic actress. Evidently, even among human vocalisations linguistic ones are more subject to change than non-linguistic ones. Why should this be?

§ 2   The brief answer to these questions may sound paradoxical. Language changes because of the element of imitation inescapable in the learning and practice of it. The lamb does not bleat in deliberate imitation of the sheep-community into which it is born; it bleats as its genetic blueprint lays down for it. The human baby has a genetic blueprint, too, relevant to language, a blueprint which enables it to become a learner of language. But nothing in its inheritance specifies which language it will learn; a normal human baby, of whatever parentage, will acquire the language or languages of the particular speech-community in which it is raised. Many types of activity go into this long process of acquisition, and all the activities are dependent on the genetic capacity; we cannot say that a baby learns a particular language just by imitating. But we can say that imitation is one kind of activity which is indispensable. And it is precisely because of the two factors, absence of genetic conditioning towards a specific language, and presence of imitation, that language is always and everywhere subject to change, while 'natural' (non-linguistic) sounds, in animals and humans, are not.

§ 3   Let us examine this assertion. First a point of clarification. Not only pronunciation, but language as a whole, is always subject to change. In comparing non-linguistic vocalisations one can only give specific examples from pronunciation; non-linguistic vocalisations are, by definition, sounds, but they have neither words nor grammar. The main levels of organisation in language – sounds (phonetics–phonology), words or vocabulary (lexis) and grammar (morphology–syntax) are all three subject to the universal condition of mutability. The change takes various forms, and varies in pace, but operates at all levels. It could not be otherwise, since the levels are interrelated at many points. The absence of telling comparisons with non-linguistic material makes us fall back on other kinds of evidence, but we must not conclude that changes in pronunciation are somehow unavoidable in a way that other changes are not.

§ 4   All the same, it is easy to begin with sounds in showing how imitation results in change, and the problems of constructing an example can serve as a reminder that sounds do not function in isolation. A baby's vocal activities are steps on the road towards language long before he produces anything his parents seize on as his 'first word', but the parents' recognition of his activities is a milestone, because once they begin to accord linguistic status to certain vocalisations they reinforce these vocalisations by isolating, repeating and encouraging. From that point the rate of progress snowballs. Very often the items that usher in this phase of development take, in our society, such forms as /mʌmɪ, mama, dæd, dædɪ, dada/, etc. The qualification *in our society* is needed, not because English babies start their language-activities differently from other babies, but because both the targets of their imitation and the efforts most likely to be crowned with recognition by their parents, are English.

The sound-sequences I have given as examples involve complex continuous muscular movements – as do all linguistic vocalisations.

6

They are so complex that exact repetition cannot be guaranteed, indeed, is so exceptional as to be a fluke. But once a sequence has been recognised and responded to the baby has a strong incentive to try to repeat it; how far this imitation is dependent on the parents' speech, and how far it is directed towards the child's own remembered vocal activity we do not know. There is no reason to think the mix between the two is the same for all children. The unit which sparks off this cycle of recognition, response and reproduction is one that from the viewpoint of adult language we call a word (though perhaps from the baby's viewpoint it could better be called a sentence, and even for adults it functions as a one-word sentence). To this, therefore, in the first instance, the child's efforts are directed. He aims to produce word-sentences, functioning in an activity where word and sentence are not yet discriminated as distinct types of structure.

These sequences which become the goals of conscious imitation are preceded, accompanied and even followed, by rudimentary syllables practised in the activity called babbling, the later phases of which clearly suggest a sense of speech-sounds as discrete. In /pa, ma, ta, da/, etc. we have two-place syllables, in which substitution regularly occurs in the first, i.e. consonantal, position. This already indicates the functional discreteness of the speech-sounds which in mature speech are to become phonemes. That is not, of course, to say that the baby thinks of two positions in such syllables as each constituting the domain of a range of substitutions.

When we turn to the discrete, or at least isolable, speech-sounds, we find a difference between the fillers of the two positions in our examples. The relevant characteristic is more clear-cut, and easier to describe, in the fillers of our second position, i.e. vowels, and it is the conditions for vocalic change we should examine first. When we aim to repeat a vowel sound, such as the /a/ of /pa/, we have normally two kinds of reference-standard to go by. We have our memory for muscular movement – for what it was like to place our jaw, tongue and lips in a certain posture, to create the resonance chamber, modified uniquely according to the peculiarities of our own oral-pharyngeal anatomy, in which a vibrating air-column will produce a sound of /a/-like character and no other. As this involves a sense of the placing of mobile parts of the body it may be called kinaesthetic, though in a somewhat specialised sense. Secondly, we recall the effect of the sound itself; we have an acoustic standard of appeal. But both the kinaesthetic and the acoustic references involve memory. We have in the ordinary way no objective realisation to refer to. Nowadays we are so familiar with an abundance of recording devices that the qualification 'in the ordinary way' is needed. However, the qualification has no bearing on how we become proficient in the making of speech-sounds or maintain our unthinking proficiency as adult speakers. Throughout the history of mankind language has been transmitted from generation to generation without recording devices, and now that we have them we do not attempt to transmit our language by giving infants a recorded standard to imitate.

§ 5   Therefore, without going into the stages by which, or the developmental phases at which, the child builds its repertoire of distinctive speech-sounds, we may safely assert that the building process depends, *inter alia*, on memory, on kinaesthetic sense, and on acoustic perception. With these three aids the incoming member of the speech-community aims at the reproduction of what he has isolated as being a speech-sound functional in that speech-community. If we think of the goal he aims at as the bull's-eye of a target, and if we bear in mind the rarity of exact repetition of complex muscular movements, we realise that most of the time he will not hit the bull's-eye; most shots will be, at best, near misses. As long as they are near-enough misses, he will not be corrected by a senior member of the speech-community, and every near miss left uncorrected will contribute in a very small way to the linguistic history of that individual, and in an even smaller way to the history of the language concerned. For a near miss will create its own memory, of movement and acoustic perception, and will tend to shift the bull's-eye ever so slightly into a new position.

But the situation is more complicated than this. For not only learners, but also mature speakers, vary in their realisation of the norm they aim at. The remembered bull's-eye is shifted not only by the speaker's own variable shots, but by the constant fluctuations in the evidence about the target pouring in from surrounding speakers. The target, the norm for, say, an /a/ sound in a given variety of present-day English, is never still. Notice two important points:

(1) The interdependent movements of target and aim can take two forms. They may simply fluctuate or oscillate around the same point; or they may begin to move in a given direction – a movement that, once begun, is bound to accelerate because of the reinforcing mutual influences of target and aim. It is this directional movement that builds up in time to a sound-change. That it must happen from time to time and from sound to sound is a necessary property of language;

but which sounds are affected at a given time is entirely random, and no specific cause can or should be given. There are, as we shall see, sound changes with specific causes; at present we are concerned with those necessary changes whose existence, in general, is conditioned by the circumstances of language use and transmission, but whose precise form and incidence have no specific causation.

(2) Though the necessity of this kind of fluctuation and change in pronunciation can most clearly be demonstrated from the patterns of language acquisition, variation in pronunciation is equally inevitable in adult speakers; their habits are more fully formed, but they do not have (or at least do not use) an objective standard of reference to check the day-by-day maintenance of their norms.

§ 6   In §4 we spoke of a difference of kind between consonants and vowels. We are now in a position to specify this difference. The positions of the vocal apparatus in producing vowels are infinitely variable; the tongue is more or less raised or fronted, the lips are more or less rounded or retracted; there is no fixed number of possible positions. by contrast, consonants approximate more to a yes–no kind of classification – they are or are not stops or fricatives, labials or dentals, voiced or voiceless. As a matter of fact, the differences are not so clear-cut as elementary manuals may suggest, but yes–no decisions are more relevant to consonants than to vowels. The distinction has a bearing on the way sounds are realised, and so on the way they characteristically change. A vowel can move (i.e. vary) quite a lot; generally we will not notice the difference unless it begins to impinge on the territory of a neighbouring vowel. The variation will tend to be checked as difficulties of communication arise – we find ourselves, for example, saying: 'Was it *pat* or *pet*? *sat* or *set*? *gnat* or *net*? *bat* or *bet*? *mat* or *met*? *vat* or *vet*?' This tends to create a no man's land between adjacent vowels, leaving them free to move on either side of the disputed territory (I speak only of a tendency; the distinction can be lost altogether even where it is semantically load-bearing, as it is between /æ/ and /ɛ/ in British English, levelled under one phoneme in New Zealand English). But in general we are entitled to expect two kinds of pattern in the realisation of vowels in any variety of a language (and the same in their history). The first kind of pattern is that single vowels will oscillate or drift about according to the amount of elbow-room their neighbours leave. If they have a lot of elbow-room they may shift about considerably; otherwise much less. The second kind of pattern is that whole groups of vowels shift around together, keeping the distances between them the same. Either way, vowels change readily even without special influence from their environment in a word, which can result in further kinds of change. But the nature and limitation of variation are controlled by a factor additional to the three we have already mentioned (memory, articulatory movement and acoustic perception); namely, their role in communication, as distinctive elements in a system of contrasting sounds on which we depend for the formation of words and sentences.

By comparison, consonants can be expected to vary less in their realisations, and to change less through time. They are much affected by their environment in words, i.e. are subject to conditioned changes of various kinds; but unconditioned changes, those arising randomly out of the nature of speech, and lacking specific causation, are characteristically vocalic and more rarely consonantal.

§ 7   We see that there is an interrelationship between the variation acceptable in concurrent realisations of distinctive sounds (synchronic variation) and the variation occurring through time and traceable as historical change (diachronic variation). In both cases human imperfection in exact reproduction lies at the root of variation, but in both cases the function of language imposes a limit on variation. In other words, though we can in academic study isolate single sounds to see what becomes of them, they do not exist in isolation when they function linguistically. Their relationship to other sounds, and indeed to other levels of linguistic organisation, is relevant along two dimensions of relationship, which will concern us in all branches of historical and structural linguistic study. Sounds occur in sequence, followed, preceded, or both, by other sounds in the language. This dimension is syntagmatic, occurring through time, and accounts, as we have said, for conditioned variation. For example, in the word *Tuesday* the opening sequence /tj/ can readily assimilate to /tʃ/; at the present time we observe this tendency in variable realisations, but eventually only /tʃ/ may survive (such a development underlies the /tʃ/ now general in words like *picture*, *feature* /pɪktʃə, fiːtʃə/). Syntagmatic variation is not, however, due only to neighbouring segmental sounds, but can result from syllable position or stress, or from factors of word or morpheme function.

Secondly, the relevant environment for a linguistic sound consists of its paradigmatic position, i.e. of its relationship to what could occur in the same position, but is for the moment excluded. Thus, in selecting /æ/ as the vowel for the word /pæt/ we are excluding other sounds which

10

might occur such as /ɛ/ *pet*, /ɪ/ *pit*, /iː/ *peat*, /ʊ/ *put*, /ʌ/ *putt*, /ɑː/ *part*, /aʊ/ *pout*, /ɜː/ *pert*, /ɔː/ *port*, /ɒ/ *pot*. Although in a special sense we are selecting the /æ/ of *pat* as against the other vowels which would yield actual English words in the environment /p-t/, we are also in a real, though more general, sense, excluding other vowel sounds which could make real English words in this environment, but happen not to, such as /uː/, /ɛə/, /əʊ/; and there would be uncertain cases, such as /ɪə/ which occurs only in the proper name *Peart*, and /aɪ/ which occurs only in the rather archaic poetic word *pight*. All these constitute 'items at risk' in the environment /p-t/, while consonants like /b/, /g/, /f/, could not fit in that frame.

Since at the moment we are concerned with necessary linguistic change, it is the paradigmatic environment which is most relevant to us. Where we select one item in sequence to the exclusion of all other possible ones, we are entitled to recognise the existence of a system; each possible item, each item at risk at that point of the sequence, is a term in the system. What characterises a system is that it has a fixed number of terms, each one excluding all others on any occasion of selection. The definition, therefore, applies to the sounds of a language as a whole. In the second position of a sequence beginning /p-/ we may select a vowel (/peɪ/ *pay*) or a consonant (/preɪ/ *pray*). But the broader system (of English sounds in general) contains more specific sub-systems within it. Thus, in many circumstances, as in the case of the /p-t/ words, we need to distinguish vowel positions from consonant ones, and to treat vowels and consonants as separate systems. In other cases, we find that the short vowels on the one hand form a distinct system as against the long vowels and diphthongs, which form another; or the vowels of stressed syllables as against those of unstressed syllables. There is, to use one metaphor, a hierarchy of systems; or, to use another, there are concentric circles of relevant contrast (selection and exclusion). Language is systemic in the sense that it tends towards the organisation of items into systems; however, it is not mono- but polysystemic. The analyst of a language has the responsibility of deciding at any point in his description what is the relevant system.

We are now in a position to formulate the factor which, in the daily use of language, operates as a restriction on the extent of variation. A sound varies freely as long as it does not get too close (too close for communicative comfort) to its neighbours in the system. A simple example of the operation of this factor can be found in present-day English. In the non-localised accent of Standard English known as

Received Pronunciation (RP), the low short vowel /æ/ is traditionally described as front – a quality which, indeed, it regularly has among middle-aged and older speakers. But there is no back vowel corresponding to it; no communicative problems arise if it drifts backwards, though considerable problems arise if it drifts upwards. And in fact it is now drifting backwards, and in many young speakers of RP a back variant can be heard. It is all the more remarkable that such drifting between the front and back positions can be observed at many points in the history of the language (which has always had a system of the same 'shape' at this point). By contrast, other short front vowels are paired with corresponding back vowels in the same system, and do not drift (indeed, have never drifted) in quite the same way (cf. /ɛ/:/ɒ/; /ɪ/:/ʊ/). It is true that in physical terms the size of the front-back space increases higher in the mouth, but the persistence of these tendencies to drift or not drift strongly suggests that systemic control is also involved. In addition to this negative or restrictive influence, we can expect to find the system exerting a positive or formative influence.

§ 8   We need to distinguish, both in structural and in historical linguistics, the study of sounds (*phones*) as such, i.e. *phonetics,* from the study of sounds as points of contrast in a system (*phonemes*), i.e. *phonology.* The distinction is not always relevant, even in structural study, and in such cases it is convenient to speak in phonological terms, and to transcribe phonemically, between slant lines, rather than phonetically, between square brackets. But historical study, for which the foregoing also holds, adds a further complication. Development through time involves us in distinguishing various senses of *phonological.* Phonological change may affect one or more phonemes, changing their phonetic realisation or their distribution in words, but leaving the number of contrasts unaltered. This is true of the following group of changes, which began in the 15c:

> ME /iː/>NE /aɪ/ in such words as *white*
> ME /eː/>NE /iː/ in such words as *meet*
> ME /ɑː/>NE /eɪ/ in such words as *name*
> ME /ɔː/>NE /əʊ/ in such words as *home*
> ME /oː/>NE /uː/ in such words as *doom*
> ME /uː/>NE /aʊ/ in such words as *house*

Or it may change the structure of the system, reducing the number of terms in it. The list of ME vowels just given omits the item /ɛː/, whose history shows a further complication. After the vowel-changes just quoted, the descendants of ME /ɛː/ were redistributed between /iː/, as in *meat*, and /eɪ/ as in *steak*, with loss of one contrast. By a sub-variety of this system-modifying change, developments may affect phonemes in sequence, as when post-vocalic /r/ is lost in words like *part*, resulting in the compensatory lengthening of the preceding sound, and so producing a long vowel new to the system. All these developments are in some sense phonemic or phonological; the term *phonetic change* should be reserved for changes in the realisation of a phoneme in a specified environment, without any consequent change at phonological level.

§ 9 In everything said so far we have taken spoken forms as our starting-point and correlated them with written forms. That speech is prior, both phylogenetically, in the history of mankind, and ontogenetically, in the history of the individual, is obvious. Any study of how a language functions, structurally at a given point in time, or historically through time, must make sense in relation to speech. But writing, having once started as a durable record of speech, can take many forms, bear many different relationships to speech, and finally, can take wing as an independent factor in structure and history. Until the invention of recording devices, however, our only access to the speech of the past is by reconstruction, directly or indirectly, from written forms – and the history of effective recording devices is not older than the oldest living speakers of whom we can have direct experience. Effectively, therefore, studying the history of the language means using written evidence. It is natural and proper to try to determine what spoken English was like throughout its history, but the starting-point must be written evidence assessed in its own right. Even on the question of what the relationship between writing and speech was at any period we have to depend on inference from what is written. In practice, therefore, historical study is bound to recognise two different sorts of priority ordering writing and speech relative to one another. A particular emphasis on reconstruction of pronunciation has developed because one of the principal motives for studying language history has been the desire to restore to early works of literature a pronunciation which enables their 'outer harmony', even, sometimes, their literal meaning, to be appreciated.

§ 10 We have not been able to separate phonological issues from considerations of larger linguistic units. These units, which we may

13

think of as represented by two main kinds, words and grammatical patterns, are much like sounds in their characteristic variations, synchronically and diachronically, but one difference of function is crucial. Individual sounds, as we have seen, contribute to meaning, or difference of meaning, in higher-ranking units; but they are not themselves meaningful. Semantic function affects the patterns of acquisition and variation for words and larger structures.

There are, no doubt, many factors which play a part in an infant's early acquisition of words. The following, even if not exhaustive, must be taken into account. First, the child is exposed to the use of words and structures by more mature, often fully mature, speakers. Secondly, he has to make a set of inferences – isolating particular stretches as in some sense the same, despite differences of realisation. What he isolates is therefore a composite of form and meaning (this distinguishes him in his role as language-user from the parrot, who copies the form and produces it even when it is semantically inappropriate). But the meaning component requires further attention. The infant does not understand the meaning in the sense that he can explicitly or implicitly paraphrase – to begin with, he has no other linguistic repertoire to relate an item to, by paraphrase or contrast. He identifies semantic function as being a role played in a particular situational context. This may be a simple labelling situation, as when he says *Mummy*! on seeing the person to whom he attaches that label; or a more complex situation in which he recognises a change in his environment by such a remark as *All gone! Gone now!* Over and above any inference about sameness of linguistic forms to which he has been exposed, he is therefore also making a double semantic inference – an inference about sameness of function for the form, and an inference about sameness of the situation in which the form is appropriate. Neither of these 'samenesses' are cases of simple identity. If a baby says *Gone now*! on three occasions – when his mother leaves him, or the television-screen goes blank, or his dinner-plate is empty – he is singling out divergent features of his total situation as having enough in common to constitute a fit setting for the same comment. The more his efforts are reinforced by success – recognition and response – the more he extends his range. Notice, however, that likeness is a tricky property, since things can be alike and different in an infinite number of respects; we extend our linguistic repertoire by hitting on what seem to be crucial likenesses, trying out a new usage, and adjusting to the response it it evokes. The example *Gone now* is an unusually simple one, since it involves a single principle of resemblance; commonly, variation in word-usage will exploit different, independent principles of likeness. The consequence of this for word-history through the centuries can be traced by looking up the *OED* entry for such a noun as *term*. This pattern in language-acquisition is like that of the acquisition of sounds in the sense that there is never an objective standard to refer to; we infer, check, adjust and reproduce on a subjective basis – to some extent all our lives; and wholly until we are mature enough to use a dictionary. But it is different from the acquisition of sounds in that more than formal sameness has to be identified; the two senses of functional sameness are a new factor in the situation.

A further kind of variation in words is related to the structure of vocabulary as contrasted with the structure of a sound-system. As speakers of English we are not free to make conscious additions to its sound-system; but vocabulary does not constitute a system. When we learn it, we not only learn items, but learn that, within certain constraints, we can form new items. The restraints are considerable, and in a single lifetime the number of new simple words formed constitutes a finite list (consider *radar, laser, maser, quasar, moped, motel,* to take some recent examples). But with compounds there is much greater freedom, and the variety of principles of resemblance drawn on in making the new formations is very great (consider *automobile/autocode/ automania, non-proliferation/non-talent, fail-safe,* as recent examples). At this level, learning is not just acquiring control of a repertoire of existing items, but also learning the conditions for creating new ones. As always, the characteristics of language-acquisition and use have their counterpart in language-history.

§ 11   The levels of abstraction, inference and application are even more complex when it comes to grammatical patterns. As with vocabulary, children's 'mistakes' may show the process at work, when they apply analogical principles to produce such forms as *buyed* and *couldn't of.* The child traces a composite functional – formal resemblance between, say, *love: loved, hug: hugged,* and infers that to the same functional contrast the same formal contrast will correspond when the first term is *buy.* Or he observes that to unstressed /əv/, *of,* corresponds stressed /ɒv/ *of,* and he extends the correspondence to all instances, ignoring the distinction mature speakers make between the correlation /əv/:/ɒv/ and /əv/:/hæv/. Broadening experience diminishes the range of such easily detectable false inferences from true resemblances. But in divided usage amongst adults we can still trace the effects of divergent principles

15

of resemblance. This may appear in, for example, uncertainty over the use of *who/whom* (by no means a recent issue, cf. *Whom do men say that I am?* in the Authorised Version); or of concord (also a long-standing difficulty, cf. Swift 'The common weight of these Halfpence are' 1724 = *is*, in editions from 1725) and in many other usages. On the influence of conflicting analogies Randolph Quirk has written forcefully (1968, 176–7):

> The uncertain properties of *regard* (readily attested in everyday examples of speech and writing as well as in the vociferous complaints of purists) provide a good illustration of the usefulness of plotting serial relationship, not least in that it provides 'an insight into the dynamic synchrony of language' which, as has recently been insisted, 'must replace the traditional pattern of arbitrarily restricted *static* descriptions'. Despite the continuing membership of *regard* in a subclass of particle-associated verbs (*regard* N *as, describe* N *as, look upon* N *as, take* N *for*, etc.), there are constantly operating tendencies to give it the properties of such verbs as *think* (cf. OED s.v. *regard*, v., 6); it is significant that *consider* shares more firmly than *regard* the properties of *think* and of the particle-associated verbs. This 'is simply an expression of the fact that relationship is an infinitely variable quantity', that 'there are many cross-relationships between very diverse families', and that, above all, 'similarity is multi-dimensional'.

As we have come to expect, the kinds of variation found in concurrent usage have their counterparts in history. In course of time, for example, many verbs have been attracted into the class forming the past by addition of *-ed* without vowel change, cf. NE *help, helped* beside OE *helpan*, inf, *healp*, past sg, *hulpon*, past pl. There are also examples in larger syntactical patterns, where, for example, the force of the common presence of subject before predicate creates a sense that this is a subject-position which must be filled out by something, even if no meaning or form is appropriate; accordingly, we witness the growth of the so-called introductory subject forms *it, there*. In the 9c King Alfred can write 'Swǣ (*so*) fēawa (*few*) hiora (*of them*) wǣron (*were*); but to translate this we need to supply the subject spot-filler 'there' – 'so few of them there were' or, more naturally, 'There were so few of them'. In fact it is in syntax, the level of sentence-formation, that our linguistic originality has greatest play. Most of the sentences we produce or grasp are sentences we have never heard before, and on the relatively rare occasions when we have done so we do not produce the sentences (except for purposes of quotation) *because* we have heard them before and have learnt them from experience. The patterns are familiar, but their exponents vary literally infinitely. Relatively speaking, the patterns are stable through time, but even they, as we have seen, undergo gradual change as changing analogies come to be dominant.

§ 12 Language is human behaviour of immeasurable complexity. Because it is so complex we try to subdivide it for purposes of study; but every subdivision breaks down somewhere, because in practice, in actual usage, language is unified. The levels of phonology, lexis and grammar are interrelated, and so are structure and history. There remains a further dichotomy, implicit in much of our discussion, but not yet looked at in its own right. Language is both individual and social. Acquisition of language takes place in the individual, and we have stressed that he is an active, even a creative, participant in the process. Yet what he learns from is exposure to the social use of language, and although cases are rare there is reason to think that the individual does not master language if he develops through the relevant stages of infancy without such exposure. And if he does have normal experience of language as a baby the speaker's linguistic creativeness is held on a fairly tight rein by the control of social usage – he cannot be too idiosyncratic if he is to be understood and accepted. The governing conditions come from society, though executive language acts (speaking, writing, etc.) are made by individuals. Here, too, then, we have not so much a dichotomy as an interplay of factors distinguishable for certain purposes.

§ 13 Now the way a language is used in a human community is one aspect of its structure, an aspect with a history of its own. This aspect of the subject is sometimes referred to as the external history of a language, to distinguish it from the internal (structural or systemic history). Again, the two are interrelated, but they can usefully be distinguished for certain purposes.

At the present time, for instance, English is spoken by perhaps 350 to 400m people who have it as their mother tongue. These people are scattered over the earth, in far-ranging communities of divergent status, history, cultural traditions and local affinities. I shall call them A-speakers, because they are the principal kind we think of in trying to choose a variety of English as a basis for description. The principal communities of A-speakers are those of the UK, the USA, Canada, Australia, New Zealand and South Africa. There are many millions more for whom English may not be quite the mother tongue, but who learnt it in early childhood, and who lived in communities in which

English has a special status (whether or not as an official national language) as a, or the, language for advanced academic work and for participation in the affairs of men at the international, and possibly even the national level. These are the B-speakers, found extensively in Asia (especially India) and Africa (especially the former colonial territories). Then there are those throughout the world for whom English is a foreign language, its study required, often as the first foreign language, as part of their country's educational curriculum, though the language has no official, or even traditional, standing in that country. These are the C-speakers.

The numbers are certainly very large, but I have not been able to be precise about them. There are two reasons for this. One is that 'being a speaker of a language' is not a cut-and-dried yes-or-no issue. We might be able to determine it to our satisfaction as regards A-speakers, but there are no agreed criteria to apply to B- and C-speakers; however, even among A-speakers it is intuitively evident that not all members of the community have equal mastery, and measures of this are just beginning to be devised. The second reason is that even if we had reliable measures for rating people as speakers of a given language, the statistics do not exist for applying these measures. It has never been true that all UK citizens were English speakers, and it is becoming less nearly so than in the recent past. Similarly, the USA has millions of residents for whom English is not their mother-tongue, though the numbers of those without reasonable competence in it are unknown. The equation of 'population of English-speaking country' with 'size of English-speaking community' cannot be made without important qualifications.

However uncertain, the figures point to a speech-community so large that we anticipate in it not merely the individual, idiolectal variations already referred to, but also the existence of distinct institutionalised varieties. And, of course, we are accustomed to recognising such varieties – we know that American English is different from British English and within the two, US English from Canadian, Boston from Brooklyn, Southern, Mid-Western or West Coast, or Edinburgh from Liverpool, Leeds or Newcastle. These examples introduce us to an important principle in the classification of varieties. In fact, in all the communities containing A- and B-speakers a special variety of English has developed, used for all public purposes, Standard English. By and large, with rather trivial exceptions, this kind of English is the same wherever English is used, except in one area of its organisation – the accent, or mode of pronunciation. Different accents characterise the spoken standards of say, England, Scotland and the USA. In England special status is accorded to an accent characterised by its having no local roots, namely RP. Communities with only C-speakers are characterised by having no fully developed indigenous Standard so that they model themselves largely on the Standard (including accent) of one of the major English-speaking communities. In addition to the distinction between Standard and non-Standard varieties of English we have to take account of local varieties or dialects, noting that in English English the complication resulting from the status of RP yields a different relationship between dialect and Standard than that found in other communities. There are other dimensions of variation dependent on the medium – whether, for example, language is spoken or written; and on register, the use to which the language is put on a given occasion.

In this large, socially, politically and culturally complex speech-community, the dimensions of linguistic variation are, not surprisingly, also complex. We cannot expect to describe English within a framework suited for the analysis of a language spoken by, say, a few hundred illiterate Amerindians of a single tribe living in close cultural unity. At every stage the history of the language must be studied in the light of its use in the world.

§ 14 Another aspect of the relations between individual speaker and society is relevant, one which takes us even further from the considerations usually thought of as belonging to linguistic history. For the society that conditions our individual usage also has a history. Try to list the varieties of English you are exposed to in a single day. You will hear, perhaps, the English of your family, localised or non-localised; of shopkeepers and bus-conductors, probably localised; if you are a student, you will hear lecturers using different Englishes, probably at least one of them having a foreign accent; you will read books and newspapers in international Standard; hear television news programmes, probably incorporating at least one American report; see a film using, perhaps, one or more varieties of American English; listen to pop-records, which may be genuine transatlantic, mid-Atlantic, Mersey-side, Midland (but probably not RP); and chat with friends using different sorts of English. It goes without saying that the language-exposure of an Anglo-Saxon villager was not like this. Part of the reason for the change we have already identified in the increasing diffusion of the language throughout the world. But there are non-linguistic factors which also have a traceable history. Consider the difference in the range of the individual's exposure to such divergent varieties of English as there were:

(a) before the development of radio, telephone, sound-film and television, and after;
(b) before the introduction of universal education (with near-universal literacy), and after;
(c) before the invention of railways (the first faster-than-horse-land-transport) and after;
(d) before the introduction of printing, and after.

We may call such historical factors technical; they are external to language, but influence its development in the individual and in society.

§ 15 These discussions indicate something of the range of questions needing to be asked in relation to any period. It will not be possible to answer all questions at every period; on the other hand we have learned something about the difference between acceptable and unacceptable answers. An answer will not do unless it supposes a process, or a state of affairs, we find plausible for language today, or preferably can exemplify from the present condition of some language extant at the present time.

The greatest problem of presentation is due to the unity of English, from level to level, from variety to variety, from generation to generation. There are distinctions, but no clear-cut divisions; yet in a verbal account presentation must be successive. No mode of subdivision designed to produce this successivity is wholly acceptable; we have to look for the least evil. The two main principles of subdivision would be by theme or by time. We might trace the history of varieties of English, of grammar, vocabulary and phonology. This would make an interesting series of essays, but it would not at any point convey the sense that these levels of structure were interrelated in a functioning whole. If we follow through the time dimension we do gain on this point, though the tracing of single variables in our account becomes more difficult.

The principle of chronological sequence once adopted still leaves a choice – to move forward from the earliest records to the present day, or back from the present day to the earliest records. Most historians have preferred to move towards the present day. Yet this is an enterprise in which it is doubtfully wise to 'Begin at the beginning and go on till you come to the end: then stop.' The most important reasons for this are clear in the very formulation of the King's directive to the White Rabbit, in the implication that there is a beginning and an end. Something begins, of course; the documentation of the language. But, however carefully one hedges the early chapters about, it is difficult to avoid giving the impression that there is a beginning to the English language. At every point in history, each generation has been initiated into the language-community of its seniors; the form of the language is different every time, but process and situation are the same, wherever we make an incision into history. The English language does not have a beginning in the sense commonly understood – a sense tied to the false belief that some languages are older than others.

At the other terminal it is almost impossible to free oneself from the teleological force of words like 'end'. The chronological narrative comes to an end because we do not know how to continue it beyond the present day; but the story is always 'to be continued'. Knowing this perfectly well, one is yet liable to bias the narrative in such a way as to subordinate the question 'How was it in such a period'? to the question 'How does the past explain the present?' Both are important questions, but the first is more centrally historical.

In addition, the adoption of reverse chronological order imposes on us the discipline of asking the same questions of every period; this is salutary even where it does no more than force us to acknowledge our ignorance. This, therefore, is the arrangement we shall follow.

§ 16 At any period the maximum age-spread of speakers is about a hundred years. This is not to say that the youngest speakers can know what the language of a century before was like; there is evidence that the adjustment of the individual to the social norm continues through life, though there is insufficient knowledge of how full this adjustment normally is. Intuitively we are aware of differences at every level between the speech of the old and the speech of the young. We are now in a position to make exact measurements, but except for isolated speakers the task has not been done. All the same, it is not unreasonable to assume that normal experience makes us aware of about a century-span of linguistic change. The differences are on a scale by no means unimportant, but doubtfully large enough or sufficiently clear-cut to make one-century steps adequate for our backward march. Indeed, it follows from the co-existence of speakers covering a span of a century that some developments will not be clearly established within a century. Doubling this span gives a meaningful stretch of time, but one not too complex

21

to account for in a reasonably unified way. Chapter by chapter, therefore, we shall move back two hundred years, centring as far as possible on the exact date, but bearing in mind that at any date, if we take fifty as representing middle age, members of the community will be fifty years above or below this age, representing a century span at any point in time. Starting from 1970, and assuming a state of English more or less as I have described it in *Modern English Structure*, we shall ask what would strike us as different in 1770, 1570, 1370, 1170, 970, 770, 570, 370, and finally, what can be traced behind that date. We shall refer to the conventional divisions into OE (settlement to 11c), ME (11c to 15c), NE (15c to the present day), without making that tripartite division the framework of exposition.

However, this book aims to give an introduction not only to what can be shown to have happened in the history of a single language, but also to the kinds of thing that can happen; to the evidence available and the methods of using that evidence. We cannot consider all these aspects for every period, but we can ensure that they all arise somewhere in the historical survey. The chapters will differ, therefore, not merely in dealing with different periods, but also in their focus, according to the nature of the issues and the evidence best illustrated in each period.

Changes within living memory

§ 17 In addition to types of change dependent on factors below the level of consciousness, and inaccessible to deliberate control by speakers, there are other kinds of change, widespread and perhaps even universal, which are progressively more conscious and even deliberate, involving adaptation to external conditions. These conditions fall into two main classes – those having to do with the exposure of speakers to varying types of experience, and those having to do with the speaker's image of himself *vis-à-vis* his language. For both types our own lifetime has been a period of unprecedented complexity, and of relatively full documentation.

§ 18 It is not necessary to demonstrate that our life differs more from that of our ancestors in 1770, or even 1870, than has ever happened in any comparable period. For new objects and new experiences speakers have to devise forms of expression. The wealth of word-formation (WF) developed in face of this challenge is not spread evenly across the face of the grammar. For the most part it is new objects, processes, states, experiences that are identified (*penicillin, quasar*) or invented (*cyclotron, sputnik*). The principal domain of the new forms is not, however, merely the noun, but nominal structures more broadly considered. The old descriptive adjectives remain, though they may emerge in special relationship with their head to designate something new (*cold war*; contrast *a long, cool look* with *a long cold war*); but the modifiers which have been most active are those which relate to sub-classification of the head and are most commonly realised, like the head, by nominals (*credit squeeze, disc brake*). The new or newly identified activities are secondary (*escalate, to hoover*) and new verb forms are nothing like as common as new nominals, though commoner than new adverbs. None of these forms are recorded in *OED*, even in the *Supplement* published in 1933, and covering items brought into use as late as 1928. The dictionary is not completely exhaustive or accurate in dating, but absence of a word from the *Supplement* is a strong pointer to its having come into use in the last forty years. Items of this kind are to be counted

23

not in tens or hundreds, but in thousands, though some have been mere transients.

§ 19   In creating forms to meet new situations speakers have a range of devices open to them. Much the rarest is sheer invention out of the blue. In the whole history of English there are very few certain examples, though probably the clearest case is the trade-name *Kodak*. This was invented by George Eastman on phonological principles as the name for a type of camera also invented by him. Mencken cites two original sources for the formation of this word:

> To the history of *kodak* may be added the following extract from a letter from its inventor, George Eastman (1854-1932) to John M. Manly Dec. 15, 1906: 'It was a purely arbitrary combination of letters, not derived in whole or in part from any existing word, arrived at after considerable search for a word that would answer all requirements for a trade-mark name. The principal of these were that it must be short, incapable of being mis-spelled so as to destroy its identity, must have a vigorous and distinctive personality, and must meet the requirements of the various foreign trade-mark laws, the English being the one most difficult to satisfy owing to the very narrow interpretation that was being given to their law at that time.' I take this from George Eastman, by Carl W. Ackerman; New York, 1930, p. 76n. Ackerman himself says: 'Eastman was determined that this product should have a name that could not be mis-spelled or mispronounced, or infringed or copied by anyone. He wanted a strong word that could be registered as a trade-mark, something that everyone would remember and associate only with the product which he proposed to manufacture. *K* attracted him. It was the first letter of his mother's family name. It was "firm and unyielding." It was unlike any other letter and easily pronounced. Two *k's* appealed to him more than one, and by a process of association and elimination he originated *kodak* and gave a new name to a new commercial product. The trade-mark was registered in the United States Sept. 4, 1888.'

It was rapidly borrowed from American into British English and used from 1890 (see *OED*) in ways which are ambiguous between trade-name and common noun. But that it was felt to be a common noun (like *hoover* today) is shown by the use of the verb *kodak* recorded from 1891. *OED* also records from the 1890s *kodaker*, *kodakist* and *kodakry*. In my own English this word, unlike *hoover*, is purely a trade-name, and I am not conscious of having heard it used as a common noun, or its derivatives used at all. It is my impression, though claims on this subject are difficult to substantiate, that its life in common use was very short and has long been over. Whether this holds in the present instance or not, it is certainly the case that the history of the language is not a steady stream flowing in one direction, picking up new resources as it goes; there are many false starts and minor eddies which never come to be incorporated in the main current. This property can best be illustrated from recent history, for which we have abundant documentation and our own competence as native speakers to refer to.

It has recently been established, as laymen have always suspected, that sound symbolism exists, across the boundaries of languages and cultures; and we may reasonably suppose that it plays a part in winning acceptance for successful formations of this kind. Another invention in which analogy's role is, at best, minimal, is *nylon*, selected by the Du Pont company from some 250 proposals; it has no etymology, but is easily remembered, redolent of Greek on the one hand and of the (equally invented) *rayon* (1924) on the other. Once these two existed, they created a precedent for the virtual morpheme *-on* = (variety of) synthetic fibre/fabric, as in *orlon, perlon*; cf. the pattern *-(vowel) + n* echoed in *terylene, acrilan*. This family of words illustrates a range of analogies that can operate in word-formation once a model, however arbitrary, comes into existence.

§ 20 By contrast with the rare extreme of pure invention, many, probably innumerable, formations exploit the principle of analogy, of developing the new on the basis of what is already familiar. Since likeness is an infinitely variable relation, in degree and in kind, many different sorts of likeness can underlie a new development. Yet a development is only new if it involves difference as well as likeness.

One kind of likeness involves relationship between languages. When, through cross-cultural experience, speakers of one language are conscious of an 'empty slot' in their language which is filled in another language they are acquainted with, they may, on the basis of likeness of function, fill the gap by borrowing the filler, as happened in the English adoption from French of *couture, collage* (not in the *OED* Supplement). Borrowing may also rest on a more limited basis when, for a common function a common pattern is used, but its component parts are native, as in English *power politics* on the model of German *Machtpolitik*, and, with greater concessions to the English form of component parts, *wishful thinking* on the model of German *Wunschdenken* (all post-*OED Supplement*). Borrowings of the *couture* type are called *loan-words* (itself formed on the model of German *Lehnwörter*, but recorded in English from 1874) and of the *wishful thinking* type *loan-translations* or

25

calques (itself a loanword from French, and post-*OED Supplement*). More interesting, and less discussed, examples are *trousseau* and *allure*. *Trousseau* in its French sense of 'bundle' (especially 'bunch of keys') has been recorded in English in c1225, where it appears to be a genuine but short-lived loan, and 1847, when it appears to be a deliberate Gallicism. In its present English sense, which has no French analogue, it is first recorded in 1817, in italics, as if it were French, and apparently through misunderstanding; yet it fills a gap, and has caught on. *Allure* as a noun in approximately the present sense is recorded from 1548 to 1758, but marked by *OED* as obsolete. In the French sense ('gait') it was introduced to English in 1882, and in *OED* is not said to be obsolete, though my belief is that it has now become so. Finally, *OED Supplement* notes from 1901 the (re-)introduction of the present sense, no doubt arising by conversion (§ 31) from the long-established English verb.

Other fairly recent English adoptions involving similar principles are *rôtisserie*, and *papier mâché*, in which the component words are genuinely French but the special meaning of the phrase does not exist in French (cf. the French, and widespread European, use of *smoking*, a genuine English word, with the meaning *dinner jacket*, which it does not have). The rarity of this kind of development depends on the rarity of a situation of knowing the form of a foreign word, and having occasion (of whatever kind) to employ this model in one's native tongue while not knowing, or not caring to adopt, the meaning of the source language.

§ 21   Borrowing from dead languages may involve different principles from borrowing from living ones. Though whole words are taken over, this has not of late been the dominant type of borrowing, and the application is characteristically different from that found in the ancient language. Thus, *nucleus*, from Latin *nucleus*, 'kernel', is recorded in English from 1708 (1704 in a quotation of the Latin use), but its use in reference to the 'kernel' of atoms is understandably not yet recorded in *OED Supplement*.

Overwhelmingly the dominant kind of borrowing from dead languages in recent English has been the borrowing of parts of words–*affixes*, of which some are *prefixes*, some *suffixes*. Thus the Latin prefix *non-* is common from about 1500 in a negative sense (its ME predecessor seems to be more usually of immediately French origin, only indirectly Latin); but in the special sense of indicating 'failure of to be what it sets out to be', as in *non-event*, *non-talent*, it belongs to very recent years. Among suffixes, *-ise* may be considered. In ME *-ise* words, such as *baptise*, are

26

borrowed as wholes, but from the 16c *-ise* operates independently as a formative, as in *womanise*, where it is attached to an English base; even where both components of the word are Greek the whole formation may be English, as in *monopolise* (Greek *monopoleo*). 20c coinages show both the continuation of well-established functions (*publicise, Sanforise, de-Stalinise*) and the development of new ones, *hospitalise, motorise.* The divergent spellings, *-ise, -ize* associate these forms etymologically with respectively, a directly French (ultimately Greek) source, and a directly Greek source; some are demonstrably one or the other, but for many the immediate source cannot be identified and it is usual to adopt one or other spelling consistently for all forms of the type. Some publishing houses favour *-ise*, others *-ize*. The uncertainty demonstrates the extent to which the suffix has taken wing as an independent formative in English. Exactly the same point is demonstrated by the use of elements such as *tele-* with *vision* (which is not from Greek), in an application only conceivable as a result of recent technical developments; *tele-* here is etymologically Greek, but functionally English; cf. also the so-called hybrid *sociology*, in which *-(o)logy* is functionally English, not Greek. *Television* is recorded (as a term for an unrealised objective) in 1909; *sociology* from 1843.

Especially, but not exclusively, in the fields of science and technology, abundant new formations depend on processes more akin to *compounding* (see § 29) than *affixation*. This large class of forms exploits items akin to whole words in their capacity to function independently, but sometimes differing from whole words in having a special form when functioning below the rank of the word (i.e. morphemically). Very often a string of such *compounding forms* builds a word, only at most the terminal one appearing in the shape it would have as an independent word. A familiar example is *trichlorophenylmethyliodosalicyl* ('A solution of halogenated phenolic bodies in water, made from the following ingredients–Chlorine 0·4%; Iodine 0·11%; Bromine, a minute trace; Phenol 0·63%; Salicyclic Acid 0·045%; with the partial elimination of the ionisable halides.'). Since English is not one of the languages in which such forms are readily accommodated in everyday use, the normal term for this substance is T.C.P. (illustrating a principle of formation discussed below, § 31).

§ 22 Evidently, as a component, whatever its origin, establishes itself as an English formative, we become increasingly uncertain about tracing and accounting for its history. It is again mainly, though not exclusively, in the field of science and technology, that whole words, usually of classical or quasi-classical type, are current so internationally in developed countries that it is difficult or meaningless to say what their source is. Latin *complex* has been established as a noun in English since the 17c. Its psycho-analytic use was established by Jung, writing in German, in 1907 (though it had been used by Neisser in the previous year). This extension of sense in English should therefore, historically, be regarded as a German sense-borrowing, introduced to the language by Ernest Jones in 1910, but it is now felt to be internationally valid to such an extent that we have lost all sense of its German origin–the more so as it is not Germanised in form.

§ 23 All types of borrowing from foreign languages, living or dead, naturally depend on two preconditions. One must be exposed to experience of the foreign language, and one must see a role for the alien item in one's native language. During the lifetime of English speakers living now there have been several important situations involving exposure to foreign language experience. The first two, school language-study and foreign travel, are alike in that they both represent a type of experience not open to the whole population, and tending to carry with it a sense of prestige. The first does not seem to have been a rich source of borrowing, but it has been influential. Since most young people now learn Latin in one of the 'new' styles of pronunciation, long assimilated Latinisms have often been re-styled, so that, for example, *re* is heard as /reɪ/, beside traditional /riː/, *nisi* as /niːsiː/ beside traditional /naɪsaɪ/, *a priori*, /ɑː priːɔːriː/ beside older /eɪ praɪɔːraɪ/. One might question whether these should be regarded as phonological changes, affecting pronunciation of an existing word, or as re-borrowings. The distinction between school and travel as matrix of experience is not so clear when the source of a form is a language normally taught in school but also spoken in a country often visited by English tourists or travellers. The phonological re-styling of words is also found to affect loans from living languages, not because of changes in the mode of pronunciation for the source language, but either from a sense that a word should not be fully anglicised when one is conscious of its alien origins, or from a sense that demonstrating one's knowledge of its foreign antecedents is commendable. The re-shaping does not affect old-established basic everyday words, but even very ancient loans may be altered if they are not too common. For instance, *chivalry* has been in the language since about 1300, and as in all medieval loans from French its *ch* had the value /tʃ/ (cf. *champion, choice*); but in the past century the pronunciation with initial /ʃ/ has come in, on the analogy of the current French pronunciation, and of more recent English loans from French (*champagne, chic*). The *OED* C volume records the /ʃ/ form as the first, /tʃ/ as the alternative, pronunciation; but nowadays /tʃ/ is heard rarely, usually from elderly speakers. Other established words liable to remodelling are *coupon* (1822), with a variant in final /ɔ̃ː/, which is not an English sound at all, and *envelope* (recorded 1715) (with initial /ɛn/, /ɒn/, more rarely /ɑ̃/). For *turquoise* the re-Gallicised form /tyrkwaz/ is sometimes heard; this has already been re-modelled (on the basis of spelling rather than etymology) from the 17c /tʊrkəs/ witnessed by Milton's spelling *turkis* (still current with Tennyson); the presence of /w/, as in the common present-day pronunciation (tɜːkwɒɪz/ is not recognised by *OED* T–U, but is quoted there from Webster's (American) Dictionary of 1911. Cf. also *valet* /vælət/, /væleɪ/ (from 1567) and *amateur* (various pronunciations, from 1784).

The development of a recent loan is particularly revealing. *Garage* is recorded from 1902 (*OED Supplement* only), and accorded, at that date, pronunciations apparently equivalent to /gæˈrɑːʒ/, /ˈgærɪdʒ/ (in that order). The 1960 reprint of the 1956 edition of Jones's *English Pronouncing Dictionary* gives priority to /ˈgærɑːʒ/. A recent comment is: 'Owing to the rapid development of the internal combustion engine the word has become so familiar that, although more conservative speakers still prefer a quasi-French pronunciation of the final syllable, a fully anglicised pronunciation is now probably more common and will certainly eventually prevail' (Bliss, 1966, 7). Bliss is clearly writing from impression, and I can only counter with a different impression: that in my childhood both an anglicised and a more or less French pronunciation were widely current among standard speakers, but that now the French pattern of stress and phonemes for the second syllable are the norm amongst standard speakers, the fully anglicised form remaining numerically quite common, but mainly relegated to non-standard use. Here we introduce a factor of currency in different varieties of English, a complicating factor that will recur very often. Meanwhile, the Americans have retained a markedly French overall pattern for the word, with a characteristically English reduction of the first vowel, /gəˈrɑːʒ/.

There has also been abundant re-shaping or re-borrowing of foreign place-names. As usual, the most everyday items (e.g. *Paris*) remain, but others are altered – anglicised pronunciations of *Marseilles, Lyons,*

Orleans, are much less common now than in my childhood. Only, in my experience, a few elderly speakers give *Milan* the first syllable stress and second-syllable reduction it had when it became the base of *millinery*) (from 1529), though *OED* L–M only records the /ˈmɪlən/ form; here, the de-anglicisation has affected only stress-placement and its consequences. Re-borrowing has also affected the name of *Rome* (which for Shakespeare was homophonous with *room*); in this case *OED* Poy–Ry records only the present form, but notes that some educated speakers in the 19c still said /ruːm/. One of the oddest kinds of de-anglicisation has affected the name of *Munich.* In this case the German is *München* and the English /mjuːnɪk/, but because of a general sense of the German speech-value of the *ch* grapheme, a variant /mjuːnɪχ/ has become quite common, though it is neither English nor German.

An interesting case of re-modelling that does point to international contacts rather than the schoolroom as its situational matrix, is *ski.* In my childhood the principal form was the approximately Norwegian /ʃiː/–indeed, *OED*'s first example (1854) occurs in the form *she-running*; through the English the activity and its terminology were introduced into Alpine, and later other, areas, and the General European form, suggested by the spelling, evolved as /skiː/; this then became dominant in English (*or*: was borrowed and displaced /ʃiː/), and is the only form I have heard for many years. A word may end up, in speech and spelling, part English and part from two different foreign languages. *Pistachio,* for which, it seems to me, the most usual current pronunciation is /pɪstɑːʃɪəʊ/, has features derived from both Italian and Spanish. In both pronunciation and spelling it is rather dissociated from normal English than affiliated to any foreign source.

In all these cases phonology and lexis are intermingled, but of course there are numerous clear-cut instances of word-borrowing in the post-war period, and in some cases travel is pretty clearly the relevant situational factor. Examples (of post-*Supplement* date), are *bistro, carnet, couchette, pasta, croissant* (and the names of foods using *pasta,* e.g. *minestrone, ravioli, lasagne*), *pizza, riviera, patio, schnitzel, tournedos, zabaglione.*

NOTE: The division of entries for food-items between this and the subsequent paragraph may seem arbitrary. I have included here prepared foods which, by the nature of the preparation seem likely to have been encountered *in situ*; and in the later paragraph those unprocessed, or sold ready prepared, for which a first meeting in this country is at least equally probable.

§ 24 While the items just listed 'pretty clearly' entered British English usage as a result of travel, other channels could, in some cases, have been contributory. One is trade, another written material, a third, American English. Obviously these are not mutually exclusive, since, for example, an item entering as a result of trade may be spread through written advertising copy; this is probably the case with *copita* (which has a more restricted sense in English than in Spanish). In considering the next batch of examples, therefore, I shall not try to distinguish whether it was first the object or advertisement for the object, that resulted in English use of a new lexical item. Nor is the possibility that travel, language-study or inter-variety borrowing, was the, or a contributory, channel, to be excluded. Our language-experience includes many interwoven strands that can be distinguished but not always unravelled. Examples belonging here, and all post-*Supplement* in date, are: *anorak, bidet, boutique,* (and a large number of terms from the world, broadly speaking, of fashion, such as *après-ski, bouclé, cloqué, dirndl, en brosse,* [*haute*] *couture*), *espresso, marron glacé, scampi* (formerly *Dublin Bay Prawns*), *marijuana, sauna.*

Some of these may begin to suggest other channels – notably journalism and literature – and the operation of factors not due to special links between English and another language, but rather to particular cultural dominance in one country acting as a channel by which its terms come to be accepted very widely in numerous languages, or to the universal association of institutions or activities with a particular country. As recent examples in varied spheres of activities consider *apartheid, ombudsman* (rejected in favour of *Parliamentary Commissioner* in official language, but clearly dominant in everyday use), *pied noir, maquis, enosis, bonsai, baguette,* (*en*) *cabochon, afficionado, cavalletti, dressage, palomino, sputnik, autobahn, autostrada, concours d'élégance, écurie, équipe, deux chevaux, courgette, fines herbes, danseur* (*noble*), *zapateado, déjà vu, schizophrenia* (and its derivatives), *voyeur, cinéma vérité, explication de texte, haiku, Noh, festschrift, fauve* (and its derivatives), *tachisme* (and its derivatives), *objet trouvé, régisseur, répétiteur, piton, sherpa, tronc, karate, zombie.* Qualities as well as objects may be identified through exposure to foreign cultures, and this identification may be the matrix for borrowing, as with *echt, Gemütlichkeit, dolce vita,* and with a very important group of items to be discussed in § 82. *Discothèque* is French in form, but is an innovation of the 1960s in both French and English. Dominance in an activity, as of the Italians formerly in music, may lead to so great a proportion of foreign terms that new terms are

31

invented to sound as if they belonged to a particular language; this is the case with *glissando*, which has a French stem 'Italianated' in English, but for which there is no Italian source. But in fact so many formatives and patterns of formation now have multilingual currency that a word may be accepted in many languages in a linguistic form which makes its origins unidentifiable. Thus we know on non-linguistic evidence that *mo-ped* originated in Europe, but its component parts could equally have arisen by shortening in English. The role of written mediation is certain in cases where great uncertainty is manifested about pronunciation, as with *apartheid*.

The abundance of borrowing should not lead us to think of English as a sponge sucking up material extraneous to it and yielding up nothing but what it has absorbed. There are very many areas of human activity in which Anglo-American influence dominates the world; ideally, part of the history of the English should be loans from as well as to, the language. In a short volume we cannot undertake the task, but will simply draw attention to the need for the French item *franglais* (which has some currency as a loan in English), as evidence of the pervasive influence of English abroad.

§ 25 Another matrix of exposure to foreign speech is the presence of foreign speakers in England. In this connection it is worth recalling that English has never been the only language spoken in Britain. Linguistic contacts with native speakers of languages other than English have born remarkably little fruit, and will mainly be the concern of earlier periods, though the borrowing by geologists of Welsh *cwm* (as, in English, a technical term), is post-*Supplement*. The currency of *goy* may be due to the Jewish community in our midst (but see also § 28), and newly adopted terms for foreign items may be due to the presence of immigrants in England. This is particularly likely with culinary terms such as *shish-kebab*, *poppadum*, *risotto* (and perhaps some mentioned in § 23). Perhaps the most striking example is *au pair* (in its original adverbial function, but also peculiarly English in adjectival function). In relation to the number of contacts the borrowings are few, and this reflects, as in previous centuries, the relative esteem and practical valuation in which the culture of immigrant communities is held; on the whole English people have not bothered to learn the non-English languages of newcomers or traditional inhabitants in Great Britain and have found no occasion to parade isolated items picked up from them.

§ 26 No language shows a more developed form of institutionalised differentiation of varieties than English. Concomitant with it is the possibility of borrowing from alien varieties of English; and for this, as well as for borrowing from obviously foreign languages, 20c experience provides numerous occasions.

Rather a special case is the differentiation between spoken and written forms of the language, but this difference has been so productive in the past century that it must be mentioned without delay. Written English is, of course, taught to us all, according to pretty settled rules, from early years. The rules and models for spoken English are, as we have seen, far less cut and dried. Spelling 'as one speaks' produces forms which are dismissed as spelling mistakes. Influence the other way, from writing to speech, is often regarded differently. The first legal requirement of universal education in English dates from 1870; a major linguistic consequence of this is that for a century we have been producing young people who through written material are exposed to a far wider range of linguistic experience than their familial background (their speech tradition and environment) afforded. Reinforcing the tendencies which result is a general sense of the authority of written forms, and this sense in turn was strengthened by the authority of the vast number of first-generation teachers who had to be produced to put each new phase of educational development into practice. This, more than any other, has been the century of the spelling-pronunciation, in which the writing-model has prevailed over spoken tradition. Examples, with the spelling-pronunciation first in each case, are *forehead* (/fɔːhɛd, fɒrɪd/), *often* (/ɒftən, ɒfn/), *towards* (/tʊwɔːdz, tɔːdz/), *again* (/əgeɪn, əgɛn/), *conduit* (/kɒndʊɪt, kʌndɪt/), *comparable* (/kɒmpərəbl, kʌmpərəbl/), *waistcoat* (/weɪstkʊt, wɛskɪt/), and in proper names *Ralph* (/rælf, reɪf/), *Coventry* (/kɒvəntrɪ, kʌvəntrɪ/).

§ 27 What is more usually meant by internal borrowing (borrowing between varieties of the same language) is the passage of items between dialects; for our purposes borrowing from local dialects and the diction of special groups into the standard language is particularly relevant, and it is not very common. *Gormless* (*gaumless*), *gaup* and *blether* have recently attained some currency outside their region of origin, as have *dour* and *Scots* (the latter not in *OED* S–Soldo or *Supplement*), but are perhaps not fully established in the standard language; the same is true of *scrounge* and *buzz* (of aircraft) from army/R.A.F. usage, and items from Cockney rhyming-slang. The new status of teenagers is reflected in the tendency of older groups to pick up their vogue-words – and with accelerating pace, so that the gap between teenage and general currency of recent items like *flower-power* and *scene* has been shorter than the gap for earlier items such as *square*, *hep*, *with-it* and *switched-on*. An interesting aspect of this form of internal borrowing is the prestige of provincial behaviour patterns, which has led to the transmission of originally local dialect words (used by teenagers because of regional tradition) through teenage vogue-diction into more general currency, where all awareness of their local origins has been lost. Examples are *gear* (Merseyside) and *king* (Tyneside) as general predicatives of approval.

The limited exploitation of these possibilities focuses attention on another factor which is crucial for the consequences of exposure to varied linguistic experience, namely the speaker's self-image and image of the culture from whose language it is open to him to borrow. We have mainly regarded him as borrowing for convenience, using the resources of a different language or dialect from his own to handle new experiences or ways of looking at experience. But some examples will already have suggested that borrowing can result from other motives, for instance, from the desire to associate oneself with a prestige group (teenagers [the word itself is post-*Supplement*], or the well-travelled and well-read). Shrewd insights and admonitions on this subject are found in Hope (1962-3, 1 and 2), with examples drawn mainly from borrowing between French and Italian. As part of an answer to the question 'Why are words borrowed?' he stresses the importance of factors other than the need to fill a gap in one's lexical repertoire. The psychological climate of borrowing varies; there are times and places in which exceptional prestige attaches to loanwords, and special sympathy is felt for one or more languages. These attitudes and feelings have negative counterparts – speakers may try to purge their speech of words they feel to be foreign, and particularly may show antipathy to loans from certain languages. However, it will not do to class some loans as necessary and others as bids for prestige or expressions of snobbery. It is people who use words according to pressures from within or without, and as their tastes and knowledge permit. On the one hand it is foolish to suppose that all borrowings are necessary in the sense that they fill gaps in the lexical repertoire; on the other hand it is foolish to class as unnecessary the borrowings which depend on the gratification of human feelings no less profound than the desire for adequate expression of message-content.

34

In this sense every borrowing is a necessary one, but the necessity may arise from developments sometimes thought of as dispensable, 'new human aspirations, shifts of moral, spiritual and aesthetic values and the like' (15, 37).

§ 28 The major participants in the movement of words through internal borrowing are British and American English. This has not always been a one-way movement, but in recent years it has been dominantly a west–east one. In 1927 Sir William Craigie wrote:

> For some two centuries, roughly down to 1820, the passage of new words or senses across the Atlantic was regularly westward; practically the only exceptions were terms which denoted articles or products peculiar to the new country. With the Nineteenth Century, however, the contrary current begins to set in, bearing with it many a piece of driftwood to the shores of Britain, there to be picked up and incorporated in the structure of the language. The variety of these contributions is no less notable than their number.

He listed examples under four main headings:

1. 'There are terms which owe their origin to the fresh conditions and experience of the new country,' e.g., *backwoods, blizzard, bluff, canyon, dug-out, Indian-file, prairie, squatter.*
2. 'There are terms of politics and public activity,' e.g., *carpet-bagger, caucus, gerrymander, indignation-meeting, lynch-law.*
3. 'There are words and phrases connected with business pursuits, trades, and manufactures,' e.g., *cross-cut saw, elevator, snow-plow, to corner, to strike oil.*
4. There is 'a large residue of miscellaneous examples,' e.g., *at that, to take a back seat, boss, to cave in, cold snap, to face the music, grave-yard, to go back on, half-breed, lengthy, loafer, law-abiding, whole-souled.*

With few exceptions these are now so fully assimilated that British speakers hardly think of them as American. Borrowing between closely related languages, or dialects of the same language, differs from borrowing across a greater gulf. The channels of communication are wider; speakers may even be unaware of which variety is being used by their interlocutors; and new items that crop up can be absorbed without reflection on which variety they belong to. American loans into British English do not, by and large, proclaim their origins by distinct formal properties, as foreign-language loans do. They can be instantly absorbed – though if they are spotted (sometimes even when they are falsely identified)

35

they may give rise to howls of protest. There are many parallels between the relations of American and British English in the 20c and those of Norse and English in the late OE, early ME period. One of the resemblances is the larger number of doubtful cases, cases in which it cannot be finally determined whether a loan is involved or not.

Though there are abundant source-materials for the analysis of Anglo-American lexical relations, and though studies have been made of large areas of the subject, we lack a general history, from full knowledge of both sides, of the relations between these two great varieties of English. There are certainties, but also areas of doubt. We can direct attention at both by focusing on some developments of recent years. Mencken (Supplement 1, 443) lists *chain-store, to rattle (somebody), to put across, back number, boom, crook (sb), to feature, filling-station, O.K., mass-meeting, up against* and *up to* as fully assimilated Americanisms in 1945, and on pp. 444-5 he quotes a 1935 list of some 130 items between H and O, including *half-baked, handy, headlight, hike(r), hunch, influential, jeopardise, kitchenette, to lobby* and *mileage.* He also quotes a comment by W. H. Horwill in 1935:

> The naturalization of American usage in England . . . is a process that never slackens . . . (1) The use of adverbs to intensify the meaning of verbs, e.g., *to close down, to test out,* has made rapid headway among English writers and speakers since the beginning of the present century. (2) There is an increasing tendency to adopt those combinations of verb and adverb which Americans prefer to a single verb or a more roundabout expression, e.g. *to turn down* rather than to reject, and t*o put across* rather than to secure the adoption of. (3) Those sections of the English daily press which have been becoming more and more Americanized in other respects are following the American example in the choice of short words for headlines. (4) Certain uses of familiar words, which at the beginning of the century (or, at the outside, fifty years ago) were peculiar to the United States, are now either completely naturalized . . . or evidently on their way to naturalization. (5) . . . Many words and locutions invented in America . . . have become so thoroughly incorporated in the language that few of us are aware that they are actually American coinages. Every one recognizes, of course, that such terms as *banjo, blizzard, bogus, bunkum* and *lynch law* came to us from across the Atlantic, but it would surprise most Englishmen to be told that they owe to American *to belittle, boarding-house, business man, governmental, graveyard, hurricane-deck, law-abiding, lengthy, overcoat, telegram.*

During the Second World War the American War Department found it necessary to include in its 'Short Guide to Great Britain' a glossary listing many items that American servicemen would find to be unfamiliar to British interlocutors; I give some examples (American on the left, British on the right) which show how far the items have been absorbed in the last quarter-century. I have also marked † items which, from my recollection, were already in British usage during the war years (not necessarily to the exclusion of the British equivalent listed):

ad	*advert*
advertising manager	*advertisement manager*
atomizer	*scent-spray*
bakery, grocery	*baker's shop, grocer's shop*
banked (*curve in a road*)	*superelevated*
†*battery* (automobile)	*accumulator*
bingo	*housey-housey*
bowling-alley	*skittle-alley*
†*brief-case*	*portfolio*
car (of a train), *dining car*	*carriage, restaurant-car*
†*cheese-cloth*	*butter-muslin*
clipping (newspaper)	*cutting*
commuter	*season-ticket holder*
cone (ice-cream)	*cornet*
†*dessert*	*sweet course*
†*farm-hand*	*agricultural labourer*
†*junk*	*rubbish*
landscape architect	*landscape gardener*
long-distance (telephone)	*trunk*
†*peanut*	*monkey-nut*
porterhouse (steak)	*sirloin*
radio	*wireless*
raincoat	*mackintosh*
run (in a stocking)	*ladder*
†*scrambled eggs*	*buttered eggs*
soft drinks	*minerals*
straight (of a drink)	*neat*
†*sweater*	*pullover*
thriller	*shocker*
toilet	*lavatory*
weather man	*clerk of the weather*

I do not pretend that my own recollections are sufficient to correct inaccuracies in this list; I put them in to show the uncertainties clustering round even a topic in the linguistic history of our own times. Entries in the British column will raise queries in many minds. Even so, the list (and for further details see Mencken, op. cit., 457–87) indicates formidable changes in the last twenty-five or so years.

There are certain American usages that are constantly quoted as points of difference – *fender* and *hood* of a car, *elevator*, *suspenders*, etc.; these items are almost as familiar in Britain as their traditional British counterparts, but they do not seem to make headway in usage. On the whole it is the less noticeably American Americanisms that are most readily assimilated.

One further point: American English speakers have been far more hospitable than their British counterparts to words encountered in the speech of their foreign-language fellow-countrymen – items from Amerindian languages, from the languages of early and late European settlers, are extremely numerous, and at earlier periods many of these have been channelled through American English into British English. How far this has happened in recent years is impossible to establish because the lines of communication are so multifarious, but it could well be that, for instance, *sauna* is in British English a loan from American rather than, or as much as, directly from Finnish. However, there is one group of words, recently acclimatised to varying degrees, for which American English has probably been at least in part, the intermediary. There are terms from Yiddish, such as *goy*, *kibbutz*, *kitsch*, *schmaltz* and *schmuck* (all post-*Supplement*). The group also illustrates the impossibility of regarding the assimilation of loans as a yes–no question; there are infinitely variable degrees of acceptance, in different circles, for different purposes. Not only the colour, but also the truth, fades from the picture if we portray only what is, or comes to be, accepted by all of the people for all purposes all the time.

§ 29   In each area I have mentioned only a few of very large numbers of relevant examples. Both the wealth of occasions for new words, and the abundance of matrices of exposure to alien linguistic experience, account for the enormous scope of borrowing in our lifetime, and for the many unsolved, even insoluble, problems connected with it. The pace and scale, we may guess, are unprecedented, but we must expect that they were much greater in the past than either written records, or dictionaries derived from them, disclose. Naturally, the unanswered questions can be expected to be more numerous.

However, the kinds of innovation explored so far are less pervasive than exploitation of existing resources of the language, by WF and by extension of meaning.

In his classic study of English WF, Marchand (1969) identifies six types of formation. The most abundant and most varied, is compounding. For this I follow Marchand's definition: 'When two or more words are combined into a morphological unit, we speak of a compound'; the requirement that the components should be words does not rule out components which in compounding take on special forms, but it excludes formations using morphemes which only operate at sub-word rank; on this point I have been rather more inclusive than Marchand. The lay-out of the formation in writing is not necessarily a reliable indication of whether it constitutes a 'morphological unit'; hence, some examples quoted are spaced as two words, others are hyphenated, others again are run into a single sequence. Of thousands of forms introduced (so far as can be traced) in the post-*Supplement* period I mention only a few taken from a single 1965 issue of the *Sunday Times* and one of *The Observer* (chosen blind, i.e. in advance of publication): *aerotrain, after-sales* (adj), *air-dried, bathrobe-belted, between-agers, camera shift, chemophobe (-ia), chromatography, class-jealousy, contingency planning, convenience food, cost effectiveness, credit squeeze, cross-court, dawn-chilled, (-power), disc brake (-ing), drop goal, drum brake, easel-painter, equine flu, eye bank, face-devouring, factory beef, (-farmed, -farming), fail-safe, flavour flattening* (adj), *free form, (-range), front-wheel (drive), front traction, functional costing, grassroots* (in a figurative sense), *hair-sculpture, host mother, market research (-er), middle distance (attrib.) mini-comedian (-comic), motor-way, mystagogue, New Wave, pea-pricker (-ing* [used in deep-freezing peas]); *people trap; pinko-grey; rib-tickling, road-clogging, sex-battle (-joke), side-mirror, sit-down (attrib), standing ovation, stodge-filled, stop-go, story-line.*

From this list I have excluded several items that are probably better regarded as derivational (see §30) (such as *chatter-up, low-keyed*) and a number that could be regarded as minor extensions of familiar patterns (such as *self-generating, semi-invalided, Boccacio-style*), even though extensions of this scope have been recorded by earlier lexicographers. I have also excluded larger structures of a type freely formed, though the principles of their formation have yet to be stated: *hand-on-heart, larger-than-life, straight-from-the-shoulder, sealed-for-life, steam-or-dry, clean-shirt-every-day (fiend), much-talked-about, all-too-accurate, blow-by-blow, mile-and-a-half (horse), swathed-in-a-rich-sauce (prose), neo-après-Waterloo, difficult-to-reach, 100-m.p.h.* (all attributive, though I have included the head where it would be difficult to supply one by guesswork); there are also nominals, such as *oratorio-stage-documentary* and *what-would-have-happened*. However, a number of comments immediately suggest themselves. First, an item may belong under the heads of both derivation and compounding (*between-agers*). Second, items recently regarded as purely American crop up quite unselfconsciously (*bathrobe* is an element of a compound, though it was on the wartime list of items not familiar in England, cf. §28). Third, what counts as a lexical item is by no means self-evident; my inclusions and exclusions imply principles which it would be tedious to set out at length, but one of the criteria usually adopted, namely *uninterruptability*, shows up individual differences amongst contemporary speakers (the same issues of the papers included *hardest-working* and *top cultural brass*, with interruptions of what, in my speech, must occur in unbroken sequence). What is a word is a question on which there are different empirical as well as theoretical answers. Fourth, almost all the items are meaningful even at first encounter, and stripped of their context – in fact, they are so unobtrusively new that in many cases we might not think to enquire whether they were in the lexical record, and in some cases their absence might make us doubt the accuracy of the lexical record. And this brings us to the fifth point: in at least one case (*pinko-grey*, introduced by E. M. Forster in *A Passage to India*, 1924) we can demonstrate that there is an omission from the lexical record. Our understanding of lexical productiveness in English during the post-*Supplement* years will be greatly clarified when the second *Supplement* appears in 1975, though even this will not tell us which formations have been used, but only which have established themselves, and from what dates. The scale of recording is indicated by the fact that in 1967 readers for the second *Supplement* produced 42,000 quotations, a rate which the Editor, Mr. R. W. Burchfield, expects to continue 'more or less indefinitely' (private communication). Naturally, not all the quotations are for new items, but many are. Sixth, the grammatical area of dominant productiveness is the nominal group, especially its head (nouns and noun-like words). Finally, the list illustrates many different degrees of newness, many different degrees of currency, acceptability and promise of becoming a lasting element in English vocabulary. When we speak of new compounds as running, over a few years, into thousands, the vagueness of the expression is not due simply to indolence or ignorance, but also reflects the impossibility of knowing exactly what to count in a numerical assessment of the extent of innovation.

§ 30   Derivation is a mode of WF using formatives which are not words with an independent existence, and falls into two main types, prefixation and suffixation. It may combine with compounding. Innovation is even more difficult to detect in derivatives than in compounds, since prefixes and suffixes are limited in number, generalised in meaning, and formations using them tend to be covered by dictionaries at least in part by general rules rather than by exhaustive listing. Nevertheless, some new items, and new trends, can be distinguished. Marchand records only a handful of new prefix-formations from the 20c, and none of them involve new types; by contrast, the 19c was rich in new types. Suffixes have been slightly more productive in recent years, at least on a definition which includes as suffixes formatives like *-burger* in all words modelled on *hamburger* (itself recorded from 1902); and there are very many new formations within established types. Derivational examples from my newspaper analysis, not covered by *OED* or *Supplement* (through direct entry or general rule), include *altoist* (= *player of the alto saxophone*), *audio-cliché, chatter-up, collectivitis, entrepreneurial, gardenscape, genteelism, gimmicky* (*-ry*) (*gimmick* itself is borrowed from American English in the post-*Supplement* period), *hypercalcaemia, improvisational, low-keyed, novacentenary, pinnacular, post-utility* (where *utility* has its Second World War sense), *tenorist* (= *player of the tenor saxophone*).

In certain cases we may be dealing with a newly developed meaning in a whole formation or in one of its formatives. My material includes *handicapper* (of a horse: *that runs in handicap races*; but in *OED* only of a person: *one whose task it is to assess or impose handicaps*); the new sense of *non-* in *non-talent* (see § 21 above) has not yet found its way into British English dictionaries.

Two interesting formations in my material are *automania* and *autobar*, in both of which *auto-* has the value *automobile* (though this form is not in general British English use), and even at first encounter is so understood, though *automania*, in particular, has the appearance of being a formation of *auto-* (= *self*), as in *autosuggestion, autohypnosis* (and, indeed, in *automobile* itself). This kind of formation is a *clipping compound*; *-burger* formations and *drop goal* (= *goal resulting from a drop kick*) might also be placed under this head.

§ 31   My material did not include examples of other kinds of formation productive (in varying degrees) in the post-*Supplement* period. *Back derivation* accounts for such recent forms as *televise* (from *television*) and *stagemanage* (1906); *burgle,* v, is said in *OED* to be very recent, colloquial or humorous (a comment not varied by the *Supplement*), but it seems to me to have been in perfectly normal use as far back as my memory goes, and I am assured that this holds a generation further back. *Derivation by zero-morpheme* is what used to be called *conversion*. As recent de-nominal verbs formed in this way Marchand gives *contact* (1929), *audition, date* (1928), *pressure*, which are not in *OED* or *Supplement*. Though English has a long tradition of making de-adjectival, de-adverbial and de-interjectional verbs ('conversions', e.g. *to idle, to thwart, to hail* [= *greet*]), there have not been instances of recent formations of these types establishing themselves; de-verbal nouns also mainly characterise the WF of earlier periods. *Rhyme-motivation* is not strong, but is probably a more important element than brevity in the preference for *hi-fi* over *high-fidelity*, and is no doubt the dominant factor in *walkie-talkie*. *Blending* accounts for *smog* (1905) and *brunch* (1900); *word-manufacturing* for *radar* and *Nato*. Examples are not wanting, but all other types together do not account for so much activity as either compounding or derivation.

§ 32   WF necessarily gives rise to some considerations of semantic change within well established items, but that is also a topic calling for separate treatment. An example which attracted a good deal of attention when first recognised by a dictionary (Webster's *Third*) is *anthropoid*, with the meaning *ape-like* in such collocations as *anthropoid mobster* (not yet recognised by a British dictionary). *Redundant, redundancy* have been changing rapidly, the latter having developed the sense (as a count-noun) 'dismissal'. So have *disc, flip* and *commercial* (the last used of entertainment, with strong connotations of approval or disapproval, according to one's viewpoint).

Finally there is the complication that this kind of change operates any time, anywhere, on words of any origin – even recent loanwords. For example, *commute* entered English in the 17c. It already had an odd, mixed history, since its source was Latin *commutare*, which would ordinarily yield *commutate*, a form which indeed entered English at the same time, but only as a rare intransitive verb, which never succeeded in putting down roots (though American English has recently renewed it as a transitive verb with a technical sense in the field of electricity). The *commute* form derived from the analogy of *-mutare* verbs which had reached English via French (e.g. *transmute*), though *commute* itself did not exist in French. The earliest English senses (both recorded in 1633) were, according to *OED*:

42

1. *trans.* To give (one thing) in exchange for another...
2. ... to change an obligation, etc. into something lighter or more agreeable....

A few years later (1642) a closely related sense is found:

3. To change (a punishment, or a sentence) for (*to, into*) another of less severity, or a fine...

And in 1645 (an unreliable dating, but there is a further instance in 1653):

5. *intr.* To make up, compensate, compound *for*.

This family of senses paved the way for the next major development, recorded for English in 1795:

4. To change (one kind of payment) *into* or *for* another; *esp.* to substitute a single payment for a number of payments....

Meanwhile, a somewhat similar semantic course had been traced by the noun *commutation* (first recorded in 1509). However, it was only in the US that this entered into the compound *commutation-ticket* (1849) for what in Britain was, and is, called a *season-ticket* (first recorded from Dickens in 1835). The verb *commute* in the sense 'to use a commutation-ticket' is entered by *OED* as *US*, but without date or example; both Mathews' *Dictionary of Americanisms* (1951) and Craigie and Hulbert's *Dictionary of American English* (1938) have an instance from 1889. Actually, they both state that this use is implied by the existence of *commuter* in 1865, but since that noun is used in the collocation *commuter's roads* the inference is doubtful. It is at least equally possible that the sequence was:

1. *Commutation ticket;*
2. *commuter,* i.e. user of a commutation-ticket, and, by extension, any regular traveller over a short distance, typically between suburb and business quarter in a conurbation.
3. *commute,* as a back-derivation from a *commuter,* to travel as in 2.

Further, both these American dictionaries specify that the travel is by public conveyance or by ticket, though at any rate by 1951 this element in the meaning was by no means indispensable. The first major dictionary to record this further development of meaning seems to have been Webster's *Third New International* of 1961, which adds, 'travel back and forth regularly or frequently (*commuting* between London and New York).'

Commuter is clearly a loan from American to British English, but the latest extension in meaning of the verb *commute* seems to have been virtually simultaneous in the two varieties of English; why this should be so is clear enough from the nature of the instance quoted by Webster. There is much to reflect on in this development. Above all, the complexity and uncertainty of one tiny area of recent history must stay in our minds as we attempt to unravel what happened further back in the history of our language.

§ 33 Lexical change is a subject particularly well suited to demonstrate what can be observed, and the limitations of understanding, in our own linguistic experience. In grammar and phonology change is not always so easy to detect, nor can the establishment of a trend be so readily determined from short-term observations. But it would be wrong to pass over these topics in silence, as if they were different in kind. Indeed, we have already seen evidence of their interconnection.

Under the broad heading of phonology I want to include all material relating to pronunciation and change of pronunciation – not only changes in the phoneme system or in the phonetic realisations of its terms, but also changes in the distribution of these terms in lexical forms and changes occurring along the syntagmatic sequence of items frequently juxtaposed to one another. The difficulties of investigating such matters, even in our own lifetime, are very great. In a brief study we are bound to focus attention on a single variety of English, with only occasional glances at other varieties; but when we attend to people talking we find the notion of 'a variety' greatly in need of clarification. Some of this clarification could come from research, but some difficulties are ineradicable. Customarily in the discussion of *accents* (modes of pronunciation) in British English, a distinction is made between RP and the rest. This distinction rests upon the concept of *localisation*; an RP speaker is usually an English English speaker, but his speech does not reveal what, within England, his local affinities and origins are. Other speakers, speakers of localised varieties, do carry in their speech indications of their local affinities. Most of us have some idea how to apply this distinction, but in many cases it does not yield a clear-cut classification of speech varieties. For one thing, localising characteristics are differently identified by various hearers; even professional linguists differ in particular cases as to whether an individual is using RP; for another, types of non-localised speech are various, not single. Furthermore, all who have described RP have recognised concurrent variations in it. And, of course, individual speakers alter their mode of speech from occasion to occasion; being an RP speaker, as far as that expression has meaning, is not an all-or-nothing, once-and-for-all, status. If we can agree to use RP for the variety of speech heard from British-born national newscasters on the BBC we shall have a general idea of the kind of accent we are talking about, though we shall not have settled completely doubts about how far variation arises within RP and how far because a normally RP speaker is departing from RP.

§ 34 As part of a general study of English pronunciation, Professor A. C. Gimson has investigated current developments in RP. He draws attention to the manner in which the span of concurrent variants indicates in one dimension the variations that will eventually be spaced in another dimension, that of time, as historical developments:

> At any given moment, therefore, we must expect several pronunciations to be current, representing at least the older, traditional, forms and the new tendencies. . . . The speech of any community may therefore, be said to reflect the pronunciation of the previous century and to anticipate the next. (1962, 65 and 69)

Various types of change can be illustrated within the range of RP at the present time. The system itself is being re-shaped. This is most noticeable amongst the vowels, but can be seen even among the consonants. The contrast of /w/ and /ʍ/ has characterised northern speech at all periods, but has been largely absent from southern English since the Norman Conquest. It hardly, therefore, belongs in RP. Yet English spelling enshrines the memory of it, and so great is the authority of the written form, especially in recent generations (cf. § 26), that it has to some extent been re-introduced, especially in careful and public styles of enunciation. Nevertheless, in recent years the /ʍ/ phoneme seems to have been declining; we do not know what is happening in the population as a whole, but each year I examine the incidence of it among my incoming students, and every year a smaller proportion use it. Both the historic and the contemporary tendency to abolish this distinction can be related to the light functional load it carries. It does differentiate pairs of words which are otherwise homophonous (e.g. *watt, what; wye, why; witch, which*), but these words tend to be so distinct in grammatical function that they rarely need disambiguating. The system's threshold of resistance to change is therefore lowered, and this situation cannot be understood if phonology is treated in isolation from lexis and grammar.

A similar, but purely recent, conflation of two distinct phonemes can be seen in the case of vowels between /ɔ:/ and /ɔə/. The second of these is again found, by the primitive sampling based on my students, to be in rapid decline. Once again, the potential homophones differentiated by this distinction (e.g. *maw, more*) do not give rise to sufficient ambiguity to constitute a powerful defence of the older system. The change has had interesting repercussions on the rest of the vowel system. Professor Gimson writes:

/ɔə/ having coalesced with /ɔ:/ for most RP speakers, the pattern of centring diphthongs is rendered asymmetrical, there being only one back glide of this type opposed to the two front glides. As a result, the 1st element of /ʊə/ can be lowered considerably without risk of confusion. Thus several words with /ɡə/, which have a pronunciation [ʊə] for some RP speakers, are given by others a glide [ɔə], e.g. in *poor, sure*. This glide [ɔə] may in turn be levelled with the realization of /ɔ:/. Thus, *Shaw, sure, shore*, still pronounced by some /ʃɔ:, ʃʊə, ʃɔə/, are levelled by many others to /ʃɔ:/ for all three words; or again, *you're* (most frequently with /ʊə/) may be realized as /jɔ:/, i.e. identical with *your*. It is to be noted, however, that such lowering or monophthongization of /ʊə/ is rarer in the case of less commonly used monosyllabic words such as *moor, tour, dour*. (139–40)

This illustrates a type of development which has considerable importance for linguistic history – one in which a phonological change developing for phonological reasons, spreads patchily, word by word, and does not steamroller its way through all relevant forms. The 'lost' phoneme /ʊə/ is much the rarest among English vowels (Fry, 1947, 106); it is vulnerable because it is not used often enough to keep it familiar, and because its functional load is light. The two related reasons reinforce each other in squeezing it out. Note that the consonant in the most nearly analogous position, /ʒ/, tends to be squeezed out in uneducated speech, but is preserved in RP because it is associated with a special quality ('Frenchness' in certain alien words), which it is prestigious to distinguish in one's speech. The role of social prestige in phonological change will be discussed further at § 99.

However, one must not set up 'the system' as an almost personified all-seeing force acting in the best interests of clear communication. Commonsense tells us that it will generally do so, not because it is like a person, but because people will more or less consciously adapt their behaviour to bring about this end. Yet there are changes in the system which produce adverse effects. Recent years have seen a tendency to drop the anomalous three-vowel sequences /aɪə/, /aʊə/, reducing both of them independently to the centring diphthong /ɑə/, which is more in line with the typical patterns of English vocalic pronunciation. Here it is not a question of subsuming one phoneme under another, but of bringing unused types into line. In this situation system-constraint is weakened, even in face of new homophones, such as *tyre, tower,* belonging to the same form-class. But the consequent /ɑə/ form was no sooner formed than it became anomalous, since, as we have seen, the tendency is to drop centring diphthongs with a back first element, absorbing them into the corresponding or nearest available long back vowel. In line with this aspect of patterning in the system, /ɑə/ has further tended to give way to /ɑː/. In many RP speakers, therefore, the three forms *tar, tyre, tower,* are now homophonous, even in careful speech (e.g. scripted English as used by newscasters).

§ 35 Phonetically, the realisations of phonemes tend to range or wander quite extensively. This is especially true of vowels, which characteristically depend for their identification on more–less qualities (high, low, front, back, rounded, retracted, etc.) rather than consonants, which are characteristically identified by yes–no qualities (labial, dental, palatal; stop, trill, etc.); though the distinction is not absolute. In 7.09–7.28 of his book, Professor Gimson has carefully diagrammed within the 'vowel-box' the range of normal realisations, in RP and closely related varieties of English, of the vowel phonemes. These diagrams deserve careful study, and I want to draw attention to three points which emerge from them.

1. The range of realisations of a single phoneme may cover a far wider 'spread' within the vowel-box than the distance between central realisations of two distinct phonemes.

2. The limits of tolerance for realisation for any single phoneme are affected by the amount of elbow-room allowed by its nearest neighbours; /ɜː/ has great up–down freedom, but virtually none in the front-back dimension; /iː/ can vary mainly by diphthongisation; /ɪ/ has, context for context, rather little freedom, but does vary according to the degree of stress on syllables it occurs in, since it frequents weak syllables where it has fewer rivals than in strong syllables (cf. § 38). By contrast with all these, the diphthongs have much greater tolerance of diversity. For these points consider the diagrams reproduced below:

/ɜ:/ (Gimson, 116)

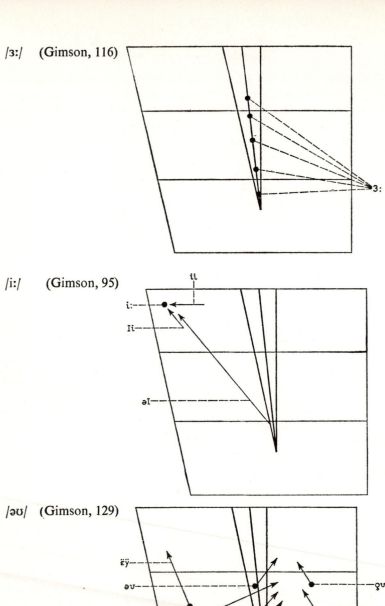

/i:/ (Gimson, 95)

/əʊ/ (Gimson, 129)

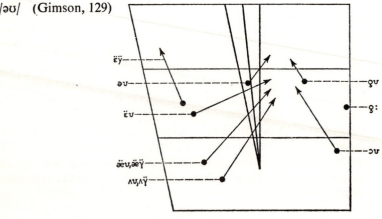

48

Final /ɪə, ɛə, ʊə/
(Gimson, 136)

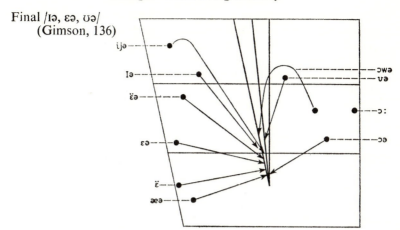

3. Constraints on variation arise not only from the structure of the sound-system, but also from the social meaning of the realisation. Gimson writes:

> In RP the only diphthong in the front region (other than the diphthongized version of /i:/–[ɪi]) with which /eɪ/ is in contrast is /aɪ/. The 1st element has, therefore, considerable latitude of articulation (especially between the half-close and half-open positions) before it risks confusion with the fully open 1st element of /aɪ/. In general RP, starting points of the type *C* [e, ẹ, ɛ, ɛ] and a centralized [ɛ̈] are all found. In some regional speech, however, especially in popular London dialect, the 1st element may be as open as [æ] or *C* [a] or a sound similar to that used for RP /ʌ/. In such cases, since confusion with RP /aɪ/ would be likely, the realization of /aɪ/ has a more retracted 1st element (*C* [ɑ] or [ɒ]), so that *fate* [faɪt] is kept distinct from *fight* [fɑɪt], [fɒɪt]. The use of such a 'wide' diphthong as [aɪ] or [æɪ] for RP /eɪ/ is considered unacceptable for social reasons. Many RP speakers react against the popular 'wide' realization by using the closest and 'narrowest' variety of /eɪ/. In advanced RP, however, there may be little or no vocalic glide in the realization of this phoneme, especially in the fully long allophone, e.g. *day, game, made,* with [ɛ:], or [ẹ:]; this monophthongized form may also be heard in cases where, for rhythmic reasons, the quantity is somewhat reduced, e.g. *lady, nature, relation,* with [ɛ]. (122–3)

And again:

> The RP diphthong /aʊ/ is in opposition in the back region with /əʊ/; if the latter has a starting point in the central area below half-close, the starting point of /aʊ/ cannot be raised to any extent without the possible loss of contrast

between such words as *tone* and *town*. RP variants, therefore, involve particularly the fronting or retraction of the starting point rather than its raising. Considerable latitude is permitted between the values *C* [ä] and *C* [a]. Since, however, several popular regional forms of speech (especially a modified popular variety of the London region) have typically a 1st element in the *C* [a] or [æ] areas, reaction amongst careful speakers causes the diphthong to have a more retracted starting point, sometimes reaching *C*[a]. (131)

The variation acceptable within these constraints may at any time change from random fluctuation to a drift in a particular direction, and once started, will snowball. A phoneme which shows such change very clearly during our own lifetime, and which appears to be continuing its progress in the same direction, is the one represented till recently as /oʊ/, but transcribed since Gimson as /əʊ/. Earlier /oʊ/ was vulnerable for a number of reasons; the [o] did not function elsewhere in the language, and there was only /aʊ/ to check the range of the first element forwards or up–down. Of the sound and its variants, Gimson writes:

Description – The glide of RP /əʊ/ begins at a central position, between half-close and half-open, and moves in the direction of RP /ʊ/, there being a slight closing movement of the lower jaw; the lips are neutral for the 1st element, but have a tendency to round on the 2nd element. The starting point may have a tongue position similar to that described for /ɜː/.

Variants – A number of variants of this narrow diphthong are to be found within RP. The type described above is that which has in recent years become general. A more conservative diphthong, however, has its starting point in a more retracted region, [ɔ̞], or [ö] and the whole glide is accompanied by increasing lip-rounding. Another variety (of an advanced kind and usually characterized as an affectation) has a starting point more forward than the central area, (i.e. [ɛ̞] or [ɛ̈]). It is also to be noted that, in the speech of many speakers of general RP, the 1st (central) element is so long that there may arise for a listener a confusion between /əʊ/ and /ɜː/, especially when [l] follows, e.g. *goal*, *girl* (the [ʊ] element of /əʊ/ being confused with the glide on to [ɫ]). Though this may be a source of possible confusion for a listener, the speaker will often retain a qualitative distinction between /əʊ/ and /ɜː/, the latter being realized with a very open type of central vowel.

§36   Variation may also arise from the physical conditions of getting from one articulation to the next. This may result in variable presence or absence of the realisation of a phoneme, or in a sub-phonemic glide. Consider the examples of *length*, *empty* and *milk*. In /lɛŋ(k)θ/, the transition form /ŋ/ to /θ/ involves two main articulatory movements;

the tongue goes from velar to dental position, and the velum from lowered to raised position. If the two are perfectly synchronised, or if the tongue moves first, the sequence will produce audible articulations realising two phonemes. If, however, the velum moves earlier than the tongue there will be a /k/-like release as, with the velum raised, the tongue moves from its /ŋ/ position to its /θ/ position. Note that a third variable is involved here – the on-off mechanism of vocal cord vibration. This generally seems to be timed to stop early, in anticipation of /θ/, so that if a transitional phoneme is realised it is usually /k/ rather than /g/. In this case spelling does not indicate the very common presence of such a transitional phoneme, but in *empty* it does. At an earlier stage the medial consonant sequence was /mt/, as in *Umtali*. Here again (apart from voice) two major articulatory changes are involved – from bilabial to alveolar articulation, and from nasal to oral (velum lowered to raised); and once again, a tendency to time the velar movement before the lip-tongue movement results in the audible realisation of a glide phoneme. As the voice mechanism switches off, and the nasal passage is closed, the speech-organs are left in position for a /p/, and the release of that position on the way to the /t/ position results in a /p/-sound; the presence or absence of this sound, except in careful spelling-pronunciations, depends on unreflecting habits of articulatory timing rather than on spelling-differences between forms such as *empty* and *Umtali*.

The case of *milk* is different, because it is sub-phonemic. An /l/-sound can in principle take on the colouring or timbre of any vowel-sound, and there are two main ways of exploiting this variation. An /l/ may assume the colouring of a vowel in its environment (be conditioned by its phonetic context), or it may be assigned a particular quality according to its place in a larger structure, such as syllable, morpheme or word (be conditioned by its position); moreover the preferred type of condition can change, through time or across varieties. As far as vocalic colouring is concerned, RP selects two qualities, that of /ə/ ('dark l') and /ɪ/ ('clear l') and distributes them positionally – dark *l* post-vocalically, and clear *l* pre- or inter-vocalically. Positional conditioning, obviously, can lead to a considerable articulatory gap, if, say, a high, front vowel is followed by a dark *l*. As the mouth is re-shaped and the tongue moves from the /iː/ of *feel* or the /ɪ/ of *milk* to the dark *l* position articulation is continuous, and a glide vowel can be heard. In popular London speech, where post-vocalic *l* has a positively back quality, /ɒ/ or /ʊ/, the glide is even more noticeable; but in other local

51

speech, such as that used on Tyneside, the *l* is conditioned by phonetic environment – after a front vowel /l/ is clear, and no glide is heard. Where the glide is present it constitutes a phonetic variant whose contrast with the phonemic norm may eventually give rise to a distinct phoneme.

Developments arising from the sequence of articulations need not involve addition. On the contrary, what in careful articulation is realised as /tjuː/ in words like *Tuesday* is often, in colloquial utterance, assimilated to /tʃuː/ (where /tʃ/ is partly like a succession of phonemes, but has more of the properties of a single phoneme and is generally so identified by native speakers). Variation seen here between different concurrent realisations is parallelled historically by the regular development of /tʃ/ from earlier /tj/ in such words as *feature, fortune*.

§37 Variation related to the lexical distribution of phonemes has already entered the discussion in relation to /ʊə/, /ɔə/, /ɔː/. But it also occurs when all the phonemes in question are fully established in the language. An example is the replacement of /ɔː/ by /ɒ/ in such words as *often*, *cross* (and even earlier in *God*, where the historically developed /ɔː/ came to be felt as sub-standard). Currently /æ/ and /ɑː/ are in rivalry in the second syllable of *elastic* (and in other similar words), but /æ/ looks like emerging victorious. Many factors, not all phonological, may contribute to the distributional history of phonemes. For instance, morphemic status was involved in the now dying use of /ɪn/ for /ɪŋ/ (this is not, as is often said, a matter of dropping a sound, but of substituting one phoneme for another); thus, *hunting* would have the form /hʌntɪn/ or /hʌntn/, but *sing* would not be made homophonous with *sin*. At many points in the history of the language we find phonemes coming, going or changing, not for any phonological reason but because one sequence makes a more familiar shape of word than another. Though these tendencies can readily be illustrated from uneducated speech at the present day (e.g. in /mɪsˈtʃiːv(j)əs/ for *mischievous*), high standards of literacy tend to check them in contemporary RP; in the past they have accounted for such items as the *-d* of *sound*, the *-ing* of *nightingale* and the *-l* of *Bristol*. The use of (genuine or bogus) alien phonemes is also relevant here (cf. §23).

Another connection with words is seen in the strong tendency for disturbances of phoneme realisation at word boundary. For instance, what in isolation is pronounced /kɑːnt/ becomes, in colloquial utterance, /kɑːŋ/ in the sequence *I can't go* and /kɑːm/ in the sequence *I can't possibly go*. Phonologically, word-boundaries may shift or vanish in sequences which often occur together. Thus, *a great deal* may be realised as /ə greɪt diːl/, /ə greɪddiːl/ or even /ə greɪdiːl/; the same processes account for the phonology underlying numerous recent jokes about the *Pry Minister*. Many examples are given by Gimson, op. cit., 266 ff. Word-boundary disturbance has been a factor in the development of English.

The word also seems to be, and to have been, influential as a unit over which phonemic patterning operates. A common change of this kind is *assimilation*, that is the attraction of one segment to a form more like another. It may occur between adjacent phonemes, as in the word-boundary examples already considered; or between separated phonemes with corresponding syllable position. Thus, one often hears from children /əmɛməniː/ for *anemone*, and I have heard /fɪmomɪnə/ for *phenomena* from an undergraduate. Or a phoneme may be added rather than changed to give analogous syllable patterning within the word, as in the pronunciation /ælɪluːlje/ for *alleluia*, common especially among children. In some cases that could be accounted for in this way, one suspects a further influence from a word the affected word is commonly paired with – notably in the very widespread pronunciation /lɒŋdɪtjuːd/ for *longitude*, cf. *latitude*.

§38 Phonological variation also involves and depends on phonological systems above the level of the segmental phoneme. Of these in English by far the most important is stress. The analysis of stress in English is still controversial, but all will agree that there are at least two functionally distinct degrees, that further degrees are easily recognisable, whatever interpretation we give them, and that throughout the traceable history of English stress-contrast has been of great inherent importance and a profound influence on development in every area of linguistic organisation. I shall adopt the view that there are two phonemically distinct degrees of stress, yielding syllables that may be described as *strong* and *weak*; and that both may be *reinforced*, giving a heightened variant of strong or weak, while at least the strong may also be *reduced*. The normal form of strong syllables affords a canonical form which is what we usually utter if asked to produce a syllable in isolation, and what naturally forms a starting-point for describing the language. But in a language with so marked a stress-system as English it is no more than a starting-point. Certain consequences of the stress-system seem to be particularly important for variation through space and time. One is that certain monosyllables are, because of their grammatical function, habitually weak and only in special circumstances strong. They include the articles *a(n)*, *the*, some modals (*shall, will, can, must, should, would, could*), forms of *be* and *have*, some personal pronouns, a number of prepositions and conjunctions, and a few other forms. A detailed list, with transcriptions of the weak and strong forms, is given by Gimson, op. cit., 240–2. The familiar pairing of strong and weak forms may lead to the analogical creation of strong forms. Thus, /əv/ is the weak partner corresponding to both *of*, /ɒv/ and *have* /hæv/; when its strong form is supplied it may take the form most usual in a particular position. Hence the now familiar 'you shouldn't *of*'; strong *of* in final position is common (*What are you thinking of?*) and takes precedence over historically correct *have* (cf. § 11). The distribution of weak forms varies in different kinds of English (cf. RP *difficulty* /ˈdɪfɪkəltɪ/ with some dialects /ˈdɪfɪˌkʌltɪ/), and weak forms have both had a special history and played an important part in the development of the language.

A second important consequence has to do with the distribution of vowel-phonemes. RP (unlike some English dialects) has a special vowel confined to use in weak syllables, /ə/; it is far the commonest vowel, accounting for 10·74% of the vocalic realisations in colloquial RP, though there are over twenty to choose from. The second commonest is /ɪ/ (8·33%); though there are marked differences between the realisations of /ɪ/ in strong and weak syllables (consider the various /ɪ/s of *kitchen, civility*). If we are to separate weak /ɪ/ from strong /ɪ/ we might come near to saying that the presence of either /ə/ or weak /ɪ/ signals a weak syllable, and that weak-syllable nuclei should be regarded as forming a different system from strong-syllable nuclei.

Finally, concurrent word-forms show some rather surprising segmental consequences of stress over and above the vocalic ones already mentioned. In the articulation of consonants a distinction is made between *fortis* and *lenis*, i.e. between greater and lesser degrees of force of articulation. The pairing of English consonant-series, voiceless and voiced, as in /p/, /t/, /k/, /f/, /θ/, /s/, against /b/, /d/, /g/, /v/, /ð/, /z/, etc., is accompanied by contrast in the fortis–lenis system. The fortis quality goes with voicelessness, the lenis one with voice; for this reason a voiced /p/ is not the same as /b/, and a voiceless /z/ is not the same as /s/. The language of linguistic description is somewhat misleading here, since it makes us think that voicing a sound is adding something to it. In a sense this is true, but it is far outweighed by the effort of fortis articulation that accompanies voiceless consonants. Consequently, in weak positions there is a tendency for consonants to become voiced. This is most noticeable for consonants at syllable-boundaries where they are not immediately preceded by stress, as in *absolve*, /əbˈzɒlv/, compared with *absolute*; /ˈæbsəluːt/, *exert* /ɪgˈzɜːt/, compared with *exercise* /ˈɛksəsaɪz/. What is by origin the same word may have strong and weak forms according to its grammatical function (cf. *some*, *there*), and in such cases may develop a voiced syllable-closing consonant in the weak form; it is in this way that *of* has separated from *off*, the distinction between the two now being enshrined in a difference of spelling, and paired with a difference of grammatical function, since prepositions are normally unstressed, adverbs stressed.

§ 39 At first sight the distribution of stresses in words of more than one syllable appears chaotic. There are full analyses in Kingdon (1958) and Gimson (1962). To put it in other words, there is a bewildering variety of conflicting models or analogies. Many of the commonest words conform to a pattern in which the first integral syllable (viz. the root syllable, the first after any prefix) is stressed; this pattern is very ancient, and its strength as a model depends not so much on the number of words involved as on their frequency. Divided usage at the present time will therefore often show itself as a tendency to move the stress toward the beginning of a word, as in; /ˈædʌlt/ beside /əˈdʌlt/, /ˈækjʊmɪn/ beside /əˈkjuːmɪn/, /ˈsɒnərəs/ beside /səˈnɔːrəs/. In some examples the shift may be on to what has been a prefix, but is now doubtfully perceived as one, as in /ˈɛkskwɪzɪt/ beside /ɪksˈkwɪzɪt/. In four-syllabled words there are many cases of divided usage, e.g. as *controversy*, *hospitable*, *despicable*, *formidable*, *metallurgy*; and some among five-syllabled words (*inexplicable*). Clearly, stress-placement controls other features of phonological realisation (for example, different vocalism). What ordinary transcriptions do not indicate, though it can be clearly heard in the pronunciation of these examples with different stress-patterns, is that rhythm and tone are related, in a dependent way, to stress placement (see § 40).

Variable stress-placement is exploited for grammatical purposes, in a series of items with root stress in nominals (usually nouns and substantival modifiers) and second-syllable stress in verbs, e.g., *absent*, *concert*, *desert*, *perfect*, *record*, *subject* (again, there are consequential variations of segmental realisation). Here, the pattern of contrast may become an analogical influence, as is happening in the growing tendency to use *dispute* as a noun with first-syllable stress (in contrast with regular second-syllable stress on the verb); or there may be instability because of conflicting analogies, as with *contact, confine.*

Contact, which is recent as a verb, shows the third main type of analogical pull, that of the word-family an item belongs to. Since *contact* is best established as a noun, in first using it as a verb one might conform to the precedent that *contact* has first-syllable stress, or the precedent that de-nominal verbs have second-syllable stress. Word-analogy is responsible for variations such as *applicable, subsidence* (first-syllable stress, or a variant with a second-syllable stress on the model of *apply, subside*). *Secret,* borrowed in ME with second-syllable stress, has shifted to first syllable stress; its derivative *secretive* (a 15c formation), kept the older stress as late as *OED,* but is now tending to follow the example of the commoner *secret,* with first-syllable stress.

There is no agreed frame of reference for the analysis of stress in present-day English, and there is widespread awareness of variation in usage. The types of variation are ancient, but the system (if that be the right term) within which they occurred is *a fortiori* not clearly identifiable in previous centuries. Its relationship of 'government' to other parts of the phonology does, however, seem to persist at all periods.

NOTE: Placement of stress early in the word is often called *front-stress(ing).* Though the term is convenient for its brevity, it can give rise to confusion, since it identifies the beginning of a word as its front, and movement towards it as frontward or progressive movement. However, in another branch of phonology, the study of assimilations, what follows in sequence is taken to be 'ahead', i.e. assimilation towards a following sound (as in /kɑːŋgəʊ/, *can't go*) is called *progressive assimilation.* Thus, the figures of speech derived from direction have opposite meanings in these two branches of study. For this reason I prefer to avoid both usages though both may be encountered in further reading.

§ 40 The stress system is closely related to, and in some sense governs parts of, the systems of rhythm and intonation. These are systems with realisations, and, like any other, they change through time. Already in dealing with stress we were moving into an area whose history is difficult to reconstruct, since all evidence comes from writing, and English writing has never systematically represented phonological systems above the level of the segmental unit. But of course we have a great deal of more indirect evidence about stress from the metre of extant verse from earlier periods. The same kind of evidence assists us, though even more indirectly, about rhythm.

The best analysis of present-day English rhythm comes from David Abercrombie. Briefly, the crucial features (for our purposes) are the following. Rhythm characterises all spoken English (not only verse), its operative unit being the *foot*, which lasts from the onset of one stress to immediately before the onset of the next, and is realised over one or more syllables. The feet are perceived as isochronous; that is, they are felt as being equally spaced in time, though, like phonetically distinct realisations of phonemes, they may be measurably different. The foot-unit is in triple time, and may be thought as akin to a three-beat bar. It does not follow that syllables are without inherent length or quantity; indeed there is a sense in which they have just this property. The position is complex because context in the foot is only one of three variables governing syllable-length on any given occasion of use. It is the overriding one – for instance, a syllable standing alone in a foot will take up the whole of its three beats. But it provides a framework within which other conditions operate. They involve, not absolute length, but a fixed proportion of the total time of the foot. The situation is clearest in the disyllabic foot – the paradigm foot, consisting of a stressed syllable followed by an unstressed one. Disyllabic feet use syllables of three lengths–short, ♩, ∪; half-long, ♩., ∩; and long, ♩,–, (i.e. the ratios are 1, 1½, 2). The second set of conditions is imposed by word-structure. If a word-boundary occurs within a disyllabic foot, the rhythm will be ♩ ♩,– ∪, as in the first two syllables of /*tea for*/*two*, /*tit for*/*tat*. Such feet are called Type C feet. This condition is secondary to foot-structure in that it operates once the foot-boundaries are established. The third condition is tertiary in the sense that it only operates if no word-boundary occurs within the foot. The third condition has to do with the phonemic structure of the syllables in the foot, and governs the choice between a pattern ♩♩, ∪– (Type A) and ♩. ♩., ∩ ∩ (Type B). The distinction depends on the vocalic nucleus and consonant closure of the first syllable. If there is length in either of these positions – by virtue of a long vowel or a diphthong, or through the presence of more than one consonant – the foot will be of B type; if there is no such feature, it will be of A type. This accounts for the rhythmic difference between such forms as *orchard, moaner, only* (B) and *meadow, silly, record* (A). The phonemic structure of other parts of the foot is immaterial. The same criteria of syllable structure operate as far back as the pre-history of English.

In this system, too, there is variation at the present time. Abercrombie notes that some RP speakers lack Type A and have difficulty in recognising it; I have found this to be true of some speakers of localised varieties of English. There seems also to be fluctuation in cases where the first syllable has no consonant closure. Abercrombie lists *drawing* as B, though for me the second syllable is markedly shorter than the first; in a word like *drawer* there may even be variation between one- and two-syllable realisations. On the whole, however, the system is remarkably stable.

The intonational systems of English are at present complex, and to some extent controversial in analysis. It is, however, plain that they vary – as between British and American, RP and localised dialects, for example. No doubt they have also changed through time – indeed we cannot explain the present range of varieties in any other way. The problem is to obtain evidence about what has happened, since in this matter even verse is of no assistance. Some clues have been found, and tentatively interpreted, but it remains generally true that this is the branch of linguistic history in which there is least possibility of reconstructing the voice of the past. The extensive silence on the subject in later chapters does not mean that it has been forgotten, but that little can be said about it. What evidence there is points to continuity for a thousand years in the principal patterns.

§41 It is very much more difficult to show how synchronic variation in grammar provides a model for variation through time. A recent book on *Linguistic Change in Present-day English* (Barber, 1964) has substantial sections on pronunciation (33–76), and vocabulary and meaning (77–128), but a much shorter one on grammar (129–45). About the developments mentioned in the chapter on *Grammatical Changes* some people might have reservations – for instance, under the heading 'loss of inflections' Barber discusses the distribution of *who* and *whom*, though uncertainties in this area of usage can clearly be traced back to the time of Shakespeare, and sequences like *he gave it to my brother and I*, though many will feel this is non-standard (i.e., not a change in the variety of English under discussion). Barber thinks there is an increasing use of *more, most*, rather than *-er, -est*, in comparison, in keeping with a trend which again goes back at least four hundred years; he may be right, but we lack precise numerical information on the subject.

In a contrary direction he seems to detect a shift towards *-'s* genitives and away from *of*-constructions; also a revival of subjunctives. Once again, we lack figures to confirm these trends; in any case it is not wholly clear how far the special varieties of English favouring these tendencies (newspaper writing and formal American) are simply becoming more preponderant, and how far their preponderance is influencing standard British usage. Indeed, the concept of 'a variety', though indispensable,

Barber
aux.

is itself getting less and less clear as our linguistic exposure grows more complex and diversified. Similar comments could be made about his observations on auxiliaries – the alleged trespass of *will* on *shall*-territory, and growth of *get, want, ought (to), better,* and *of* auxiliaries cf. § 38), the tendency to lose unstressed *have* and *do.* He notes increasing tolerance of *like* as a conjunction, of tentative modifying *sort of, kind of,* and of zero-relatives in object function; the tendency to drop *that* after *now, so,* and to introduce it as a quantifier (*that good*); the shift of participial *interested, surprised,* in an adjectival direction, witnessed by the use of modifying *very;* and some tendencies to discard the definite article (though these, too, have a long history). The strong trend towards formation of verb-particle structures (*look up a friend, run down a rival*), notable since the 12c, is said to be accelerating, and so are analytic constructions of the *have a look* type. An important matrix of change is contamination of one construction by another (where conflicting analogies are relevant); this tendency has no doubt existed since the beginnings of language. Recent examples are said to be the *between 35 to 40 degrees* type of construction (blending *between A and B* with *from A to B*) and *be comprised of* (blending *consist of* and *comprise*). Finally, Barber gives examples operating in the borderland between syntax and style.

These instances of change may seem both peripheral and trivial in comparison with the phonological and lexical material, and we may be much less willing to agree that they are relevant. We cannot conclude that Barber's material on grammatical change is thin and sometimes questionable because he is a poor observer or because there is generally rather little grammatical change. As a matter of fact his grammatical chapter contains an unusual proportion of first-hand observations. And though some areas of grammar, like some of phonology and lexis have remained unchanged since our earliest records, it might be held that the most profound overall changes have been in grammar; indeed, linguists who classify the languages of the world into types based on grammatical structure would place Old and Modern English in different typological classes. A third possible explanation can hardly be proved false, but should be entertained only as a last resort: namely, that although there has been considerable grammatical change in the past, English grammar in our own lifetime is somehow uniquely stable and free from change.

The most promising direction of search for an explanation would seem to lie in the assumption that there is grammatical change in progress at the moment, as in the past, but that we are considerably less

59

perceptive of it than of other kinds of linguistic change. I think there are at least four factors relevant to this 'blindness':

1. Grammar deals with observed rules of a middle degree of generality. The rules of grammar are more numerous than those of phonology and less specific than those of lexis; consequently they are difficult to spot and formulate, even for that minority of speakers who pay attention to their own, or other people's, usage. The level of generality, then, tends to shield grammatical rules from observation; they constitute an area in which our frame of reference is particularly vague and ill-formed, so that departures from precedent are difficult to identify. Perhaps from the same feature derives the particular problem of noting gaps in usage – for example, that older people, or young ones, or non-standard or superior speakers, never employ a construction which we ourselves accept as commonplace.

2. The second factor relates not to the language itself but to the way we have been habituated to thinking about it. The amount of attention paid in school to phonology and lexis is slight in comparison to that paid to grammar. The grammar-teaching we are nearly all exposed to is not (see 4 below) based on knowledge, and it highlights issues selected for reasons which have often little to do with grammar as a level of linguistic organisation or grammar as an academic discipline. Several features in the orientation of this teaching encourage the development of a blind eye, but all may be related to the concept of correctness which informs it. In the first place, emphasis is on areas where pupils might be inclined to use forms of constructions regarded as incorrect; the great mass of grammatical usage on which all agree and which none could get wrong, the very mechanism which enables us to talk together, is almost entirely disregarded. Then, having had his focus thus narrowed, the pupil is often taught that usages are never employed, or never employed by educated people, though he can hear them around him every day, and from people who, on any but a circular definition, are educated. (I still find that more than half my incoming students each year have been taught that 'there's no such word as *get* in the English language', though I can think of few approaches better calculated to persuade a student that grammar has nothing whatever to do with grammar as used.) Thirdly, the assumption is that there is one standard of correctness for all purposes, and departures from it are errors. In view of all this, grammar tends to escape attention save where a shibboleth is vio-

lated, and any variation that is noticed will by definition be a lapse.

3. Closely related to the pedagogic factor is a historical one. We are in a position to be acutely aware of the special ring of grammatical variations in our own day – to identify journalistic usages, colloquial and slang constructions, Americanisms, and so on – and to exclude them from the charmed circle of accepted structures. In looking at the language of the past we only rarely, by chance and scrappily, have so acute a discrimination. We observe a new pattern coming into use and gradually establishing itself in preference to an old one, but we can seldom, and then only in recent centuries, observe this as anything but a chronological sequence. The social turmoil which may have accompanied its rise to general acceptance is usually concealed from us. This means that in trying to trace the lineaments of variation through time in variation now current we need to pay attention not only to divided usage, but also to divided standards of acceptability.

4. The fourth class of factor in our grammar-blindness is purely academic. Though, as I have acknowledged, our descriptions of the variation in pronunciation are imperfect and our descriptions of present-day lexis highly imperfect, the studies in these two areas, for English both present and past, are far superior to the existing descriptions of English grammar, especially at the present day. Probably this factor should be sub-divided. There is a descriptive weakness, as Quirk said in 1960:

It may seem strange to hear of plans for a survey of English usage when one reflects for how long and by how many and with what degree of attention the English language has been studied. The position is, however, that the masses of material compiled over the years prove quite inadequate to serve as the basis of even elementary teaching-grammars, a fact which has emerged rather suddenly and with particular starkness in recent years, when increasing attempts have been made to improve and extend the teaching of English as a foreign language. . . . For no period in its history has the grammar of English been described with anything approaching systematic accuracy and completeness, and the writers of practical teaching manuals in consequence have no body of full and objective data from which to draw materials or on which to build a structural approach or base dependable rules, and the inadequacy of current teaching-grammars used both at home and overseas is often recognized by none more clearly than by those who write them. These writers have still to rely upon their own uncertain impression of what is normally written or spoken by the educated (and therefore safely imitable) native speaker, and some are emboldened by the lack of reliable information to continue prescribing according to their own predilections. The extent to which prescription is seriously or pathologically at variance with actual usage (a matter which itself needs investigation) is in large measure a direct result of the continued absence of proper information, and it is at the same time a rebuke and a challenge to linguists.

There is also a theoretical weakness. Linguistic theory gives us a frame of reference in terms of which we can compare and notice differences. Even amongst linguistic laymen such a frame of reference, however subliminal, prevails in phonology and lexis. Everyone has had the experience of reacting to speech with such reflections as 'That's not the vowel I use in *but* or *castle*' or 'That's not how I use the word *disinterested*' (or 'That's not the right pronunciation or use . . . '). But except for the shibboleths on which attention was focused at school our grammatical frame of reference is very weak, and we are much less well equipped to compare, identify and distinguish, because we do not really know what constitutes 'the same' grammatical use or construction.

§42 Now, it is clear that linguists cannot directly do anything about factors 1, 2 and 3, but 4 remains, in Quirk's words, 'a rebuke and a challenge to linguists.' This is not to say that linguists have remained idle in the sixties; they have been active in both theoretical and descriptive work. But the omissions of centuries are not made good in one decade. There are two chief ways into the descriptive problem, and both are permeated with theoretical issues. One is to draft a grammar, programme a computer to generate sentences from a stored lexicon according to the rules of the grammar, and gauge, from the acceptability of the resulting sentences, how accurate the input has been. The inherent strength of this approach lies in its rigorous testing of the accuracy of the rules, leading to their progressive refinement. Its inherent weakness lies in the impossibility of checking the exhaustiveness of the rules; whole ranges of possible constructions may be overlooked. There is at present another weakness, not inherent but accidental, in that decisions about acceptability are wrongly assumed to be clear-cut, and therefore are not investigated.

The other approach works in the opposite direction. First, a variety is selected for investigation (e.g. educated British English); then a large sample of its use in various media, registers and styles is collected and subjected to an analysis required to account for everything in the sample. The inherent strength of this is the inclusiveness of its findings (granted only that the sample has been well chosen). Its inherent weakness is that corpus-based rules might be framed too broadly, and lack the refinement that testing by machine-generation of sentences would provide· They might, for instance, be framed in such a way as to allow the generation of such notorious sentences as 'Colourless green ideas sleep furiously' (Chomsky) or 'The molten postage feather scored a weather' (McIntosh). In the principal investigation being conducted on these lines, Quirk's *Survey of Educated English Usage*, there is a further, non-inherent, strength, since the selection of variety has imposed an enquiry into what is Educated English Usage; in other words, a systematic investigation into acceptability.

There is, of course, no reason why the two methods should not be combined, in which case the proper sequence would seem to be first to account for a corpus and second to test the refinement of one's formulations by machine-generation, but that stage of work has not been reached, though important parts of it are covered in recent work using a computer to simulate the recognition of syntactic structure by human speakers (Bratley, Dewar and Thorne, 1967).

If we seem to have strayed far from the simple classification of types of change, mention of investigating linguistic acceptability brings us right back to our subject. For to get more than the rather random observations already mentioned we need a check on the issues concerning which opinion and usage are currently divided. It has long been known that reliable information cannot be obtained simply by asking direct questions about acceptability, but recent work has shown that meaningful answers arise from the correlation between such views and the capacity to carry out simple operations upon sentences. In a continuing series of experiments, Quirk and his colleagues have applied these techniques. First, an Operation Test (O) requires the informants (seventy-six undergraduates reading English or Geography) to carry out a simple operation on each of a battery of sentences – making it negative, interrogative, past, present, pluralising its subject, etc. The 'problem sentences', the focus of interest, must be well concealed in a battery containing many 'straightforward' ones. Next, informants are submitted to a Judgement Test (J) in which they have to score sentences as *Yes* (wholly natural and normal), *?* (marginal or dubious), or *No* (wholly unnatural and abnormal). The unreliability of J alone is shown by the fact that it produces only a small degree of higher acceptability for 'Not if I have anything to do with it' than for 'Label break to calmed about and'. But what emerges clearly is the positive correlation between O and J results. Finally, in Selection Tests (S), informants could be asked to choose between alternatives of the form:

'Neither he nor I $\begin{cases} \text{know} \\ \text{knows} \end{cases}$ the answer'. The experiments led to construction of a framework of classifications for acceptability with these terms:

I. LEXICAL	II. GRAMMATICAL
(a) congruous	(a) established
(b) obscure	(b) divided
(c) incoherent	(c) ill-established
	(d) dubious
	(e) unacceptable

Our main concern is with column II [though the columns are related – a sentence cannot be established as II(a) unless it is also I(a)]. II(a) includes such sentences as 'They always come here' and its corresponding inversion-question, 'Do they always come here?' II(b) includes competing forms of roughly equal acceptability; to it belong *who/whom* in the sentences 'Whom did you see?' (O: *put into the present*) and 'Who did you want?' (O: *put into the present*). II(c) 'embraces structures of various types brought together only by the fact that rules governing their form and use appear not to be well established among users of the language' (Quirk and Svartvik, 1966, 102), e.g. 'It's in the front of the station,' 'The old man chose his son a wife,' 'They aren't, but they claim so,' 'Neither he nor they know the answer' (O: *make into an inversion question*); 'Neither I nor he felt a thing' (O: *put into the present*). II(d) includes items for which the O-success rate is only fair and the acceptance rate is low in J, but nevertheless there is not a majority of rejections, though there are many queries. Examples are 'He isn't much loved' (O: *put into the positive*) and 'I regard him foolish' (O: *put into the plural*). 'Some food was provided the man' (O: *put into the present*). Rather a wide range of acceptability is covered here. II(e) includes the limiting cases for our interest, e.g. 'A nice little car is had by me' (O: *put into the negative*); this showed an O-success score of 36 (the maximum being 76 and the minimum 23) and a J-score of *Yes* 1, *?* 2, *No* 73.

The techniques reported in this work, in Quirk (1966), Davy and Quirk (1968), Greenbaum (1968) seem to show the way to an understanding of those areas in which grammar, like phonology and lexis, is divided and in transition at the present time.

§ 43 However, acceptability-tests are limited by the grammarian's intuitions about where divided usage and opinion lie. It is a great advance to have a means of measuring acceptability, but it is by no means the end of the road. And it is noticeable that few, if any, of the usages now rating as II(b), (c) or (d), involve innovations; by and large they have been problem areas for at least a couple of centuries.

Therefore, though I can be no more than impressionistic and random in my observations, I would like to point to areas where change may be in progress, but where comment is scarce. The traditional view that the central structure in language and the central concern of the linguist is the sentence, has recently justly received powerful support. But the centre is not the whole. Attempts to study sequences above the sentence are still in their infancy (Harris, 1952), but this is a level at which many signs of innovation are to be found. The signs may be misleading; the ready availability of recording machines has made us much more aware than most of our predecessors of the actual structure of spoken continua. Nevertheless, without prejudice as to how old some of the structures may be, we ought to record some of the now widely current practices which depart from the norms described in such grammars as we have.

First, within the sentence, there is the matter of S–V concord, considered by Quirk and his colleagues only in cases where there is no one clearly right answer. To their kind of test-sentence might be added one of the kind heard this week (April, 1968) on the radio: 'All policemen and every special constable is on duty'. But even where there is a solution, departures from the accounts given by grammarians are startingly common, and seem to show that a new grammatical contrast has established itself. In a sentence such as 'This increasing complexity and differentiation which causes a deeper and more complicated response . . . is found . . . in the early comedies', the singular signals the unitary nature of the subject; it is not

'1. This complexity . . . causes and is found'
'2. This differentiation . . . causes and is found'

but 'This [combination of] complexity-and-differentiation'; the sentence is in contrast with one which might read: 'This complexity and this differentiation cause . . . and are found . . .'. A corpus-based study of concord shows not only a looseness of the S–V bond, but also that apparently remote factors in the total structure of the sentence favour or disfavour certain types of linked patterning. Grammatical complexity (which can at present be only roughly defined) is a loosener of bonds; number-restricted pre-modifiers, such as *each, this*, less potent preservers of them than one might think. Thus one finds in a present-day

65

sample 'This country house group divert themselves in genteel ways' and 'Each set of concrete examples tend to hang together'; and if one retreats two-and-a-half centuries one finds in the grammatically-obsessive Jonathan Swift 'This October Club renewed their usual meetings, but were now . . .' (Strang 1966, 1967). There is room for far more investigation of total patterns rather than of bits of sentences.

The sort of issue that is raised, and the difficulties of description in the absence of a well-formulated grammatical theory, can be demonstrated from recordings of actual speech, and from the work of recent novelists who try to copy the structures of actual speech and inner monologue. Of the vast range of material that might be used in this way I shall take some instances from a single work by a novelist specially skilled in such portrayal, and one whose style is not affected by certain distorting factors which may enter the work of the more 'serious' writer. The book is *Greenmask*, by Anne Blaisdell (also known as Elizabeth Linington [her actual name], Lesley Egan, Dell Shannon); this, like the novelist's many other works, is rich in accurate observation of colloquial structures. It has the advantage over direct material of being accessible in the same form to all readers. The examples should be read not in the light of a norm of correct usage or good style, but in terms of effectiveness of communication. That they are successful in these terms is shown by the popularity of the novels. I have sometimes used for comparison familiar colloquial structures not exemplified in this one book; such instances are given without source-references.

There is abundant evidence not only of the development of new modals and auxiliaries, but of the loss of old ones:

'Well, what the hell you want with me?' (155).
'Monday – what you think you got. . . .' (155).
'No reason, he muttered, you got no reason – ' (156).
'What you people think you're playing at. . . . ?' (177).

These structures cannot be accounted for in terms of ellipsis but call for a new description of the verb-phrase. Very often the subject goes too. This may be in patterns where formal speech would have *It is, it was; They are, they were; There is, there are; There was, there were.* For example:

'Pity to spoil your day off' (5).
On the whole, a very nice one to handle (6; a structure, as often happens, requiring material from neighbouring sentences for its interpretation: the

grammatical need to look beyond the sentence is perhaps on the increase);
Just the cross he had to bear, he thought, 5; if so, her bad luck, 66.
Because – he used to make a little joke about that – not his kind of place
that gets held up, 16.
A waste of time. Never any prints, 102.

The 'understanding' of the omitted elements already involves the
neutralisation of several contrasts that would have to be made in full
discursive syntax; and perhaps a further neutralisation is involved in:
'"Reason you haven't made sergeant"' (11); (cf. also the material on
article-deletion below); there is clear *that is* deletion in: 'I did some
secretarial work for him, how we met,' 161. But so far the structures
might have been found over a thousand years ago (see King Alfred's
Preface to the Pastoral Care), though they have not often figured in
literature, and less in 'grammar' during the intervening centuries.

What cannot be traced so far back, though I should not venture to
assert that they are new, are structures of this kind in which there may
or must be a conditional component 'suppressed', as in:

At the side of the yard in that direction was a low cement wall with some
kind of vine growing up it. Darker over there, the lights not reaching so
far (81);
Anybody'd know – a little place like that – not an awful lot to take (16);
She looked delighted. This kind, he thought. Holds hand with a gorilla
as long as it had pants on (78);
Silly little bitch on the make, delay him for nothing (93);
Sergeant Ellis was working Edward Halliday; interesting to see what
he'd got there (163).
'Like to talk to you some more, Mr. Welbert' (180).

The last also involves a first person subject. And the second person may
also be lost, as in:

'You cold-blooded little bastard. Wait around for somebody else to get
killed,' 14.

Sometimes 'suppression' comes near to neutralising the contrast between
imperative and indicative (consider the series, '"See, she called in . . . ."
68; 'Talk about off beat. . . .' 4, etc, compare and contrast colloquial
'You dare!', which is neither indicative nor imperative; 'She seemed
like a nice girl: wish D'Arcy luck,' 68; 'Come to think. . . . ' 80, etc.;
'Come down to it. . . . ', 88, etc.) though this is not involved where the
subject goes and a modal remains ('"Will do,"', 73).

But in some of these cases it would seem that some sort of conditional
or *if*-element was understood, and this is clearly the case elsewhere:

'"Blessing in disguise, ask me,"', 112; or with subject: '"You're brought up a certain way, you don't walk out on it"', 183. Meanwhile, though traditional *if* remains *de rigueur* in some functions with expressed or assumed apodosis ('If it had been Edward,' 190), in others there is a pseudo-apodosis ('If you'd like coffee, there's some in the pot'). Very commonly *if*-clauses with second person subjects and without apodosis are used with no conditional meaning at all, but as polite requests:

'So if you'd just close an eye occasionally–' 4. 'If you'd tell me generally, you know', 17 (cf. If you'll [just] come this way....).

Another variable domain is that of relative constructions. Zero-relatives in object function (e.g. 'The man I saw is your uncle') have long been prevalent (though not always accepted with sang-froid). Grammars do not generally acknowledge the zero-relative in subject function, but *Greenmask* provides (even if in sentences peculiar in other ways) a number of plausible instances:

It was the anonymous ones like this were the tough ones (14);
It was Carter remembered it, 35.
'Oh, no, I expect it'd be different police came ?' 40;
'What I do think is that it was the press stories on that gave him her name', 66;

and with deletion of the entire relative construction in complement function:

'Well, it's not the kind just so easy to break', 89.

A famous crux in 14c poetry has the same sort of zero-subject-relative:

Prayses þe (*the*) porter bifore þe (*the*) prynce kneled (*Sir Gawain and the Green Knight*, l. 2072).

Deletion of *that* as a conjunction, noted by Barber, is also common in the text of *Greenmask*.

Various structures have zero-article in patterns where an article form is customarily said to be obligatory:

'List of all he's got on him, please,' 97 (note that we cannot say whether a whole S–V structure is deleted before this; it might be taken as approaching a nominal imperative).

Opening of second sentence:

'Well, our Edward's very stiff-necked and upstage about my poking around. Dumb cop wasting time asking silly questions when obviously it's this homicidal maniac,' 166.

Changes within living memory

And in a correlative comparative construction:

'Longer it is, the harder it is to say, you know', 33.

Conversely, there is a contrastive-stressed use of what I would class as an indefinite article rather than a cardinal numeral in:

Maddox thought D'Arcy certainly showed good taste – one very good-looking girl, 178.

There are newish patterns of adjectival modification in:

'Very damned awkward', 4; 'Very damn embarrassing', 69; 'For pretty certain', 15.

There is one example of what I believe to be a growing loosening of the bonds between tense and temporal adverbials:

So they notice it when he doesn't come home the usual time last night, 6.

In several instances already quoted particles might have been expected but are not present; absence of particles (sometimes in conjunction with other factors) accounts for the sense of 'heightened absoluteness' in a miscellany of other examples, such as:

'I think he's a stockbroker, something he said,' 41;
'All the schools getting so crowded now, they've got quite a student body,' 53;
Because, people living alone – Number Three might have been done last night. . . ., 67.

With additional deletion of object, and of second-clause verb:

Come to think, a movie theater such a nice anonymous place, 103.

Evidently the possibilities of variation, the matrix of change, in grammar, are very great indeed. The haphazard nature of the examples we find is partly a consequence of our lack of any formulated standard of reference.

PART TWO

The chronological sequence

CHAPTER I

1970 – 1770

§ **44** The past two centuries have witnessed greater changes in the structure of the speech-community, of the audience and experience of English-speakers, than any period in the history of any language. The community is of unprecedented size (cf. § 13), and the language has developed a unique role in the world. Marckwardt (1958, 172) quotes an estimate that three-quarters of the world's mail is in English. More important than the size of the figures is the spread of English-speakers over the continents – only South America lacks a large community of people for whom English is the first language. This extension naturally brings variation in its train, as studies of English in America, Australasia and elsewhere have repeatedly stressed (see note on p. 76). The variation is superficially obvious in vocabulary, especially in the naming of plants, animals, topographical features, customs and institutions. But it has equally important covert features. Australian English, spoken in a country of nearly 3m square miles, and even American English, in a country of over 3½m square miles, are notoriously more uniform than English English, spoken in an area of just over 50,000 square miles. For the most extreme case, that of Australia, this is particularly relevant for our purposes; since, though the first English was spoken in Australia in 1688, Cook's first major exploration dates from 1770. G. W. Turner (1966) writes:

> The homogeneity of Australian English is remarkable. It would be difficult to find elsewhere a geographical area so large with so little linguistic variation. The same accent is heard through widely different climates and there is little variation in vocabulary. Even if we include New Zealand, differences are hardly more marked than those found within the eastern United States (163).

The relative uniformity is accounted for by several factors, notably the tendency to explore the interior from urban coastal bases, whose speech remained a norm, high mobility from the early days of settlement, social insecurity leading to linguistic conformity (with strong influence from the literary language), and the mixed dialect origins of early settlers,

73

which would tend to favour the dropping of noticeably local and restricted usages (Turner, 10–15). The mobility factor needs to be broken down further. In the earliest days it refers to a nomadic way of life. But it is linguistically relevant that hard on the heels of extended inland settlement followed the first of the modern aids to speed in travel – the steamship and the railway. Moreover, the extreme smallness of the population militated against the formation of subgroups – in 1834 the population was only about 36,000, and 'new chums' felt a strong pressure to conform. In part this pressure derived from each new arrival's sense of joining a group–Australian or New Zealand; if the first English-speakers in England had such a sense, it related to a much smaller group. English had a history of several centuries in this country before the speaker's self-identification was with a national rather than a locally restricted community (cf. §210).

The uniform development of Australasian English has, by and large, proceeded at the cost of divergence from British English; here again, we must distinguish two factors – difference of 18c source, and difference in the evolution of the source-language. The basis of Australasian English is a mixed, predominantly London, urban dialect of lowish class – all its elements are found in England, but did not necessarily constitute a variety there, and certainly not a variety identical with the prestige English underlying what is now called RP. The second difference depends on independent development, directly related to the isolation of the communities from one another. In early days this was in one sense very great, and progressively reduced: the opening of the Suez Canal in 1869 and the Panama Canal in 1914 reduced 'linguistic distances' (Turner, 23); later, flying shrank them drastically. In another sense, they increased – not until the close of the 19c were most Australians born in the country; in earlier years most spoke an English brought from 'home'.

The more diversified and complex character of American English, and the greatly more diversified and complex history of British English, are related to their greater antiquity. But diversification is not simply a function of time; we should not envisage a future in which all speakers in Britain speak a different dialect, and when American English has overtaken British, and Australian has overtaken American, in diversity. Nor should we postulate a lost period of unity which has given place to the fragmentation long familiar to us. There is a complicated interaction between time and the sense of community-identity resulting from shared linguistic experience.

In the history of the sense of community-identity a period beginning around 1770 may be taken as a watershed, a division unique in history between before and after. Before, movement between groups was limited to the range and speed of horse or human foot by land, and of sail by sea; the man who moved between communities was the exception. After, the development of steamship (effectively from 1790), railway (1825), car (steam-driven 1763, petrol-driven 1886), planes (1903), made the mobile man the norm, above all in the US. These developments are commonly thought of in terms of shrinking the world; we also need to look at them from the contrary viewpoint, as extending our linguistic exposure, experience and influence. Even more radical have been the technical developments of the past century, which have enabled this extension to take place without our stirring from our seats: spoken communication without mutual confrontation and over large distances is a new factor in linguistic history. It starts almost one century ago with two-way communication when A. G. Bell invents the telephone in 1876, but continues with one- and two-way communication in radio (first transmission 1895), sound-film (1925), and television (experimental transmission 1939). Both in invention and in early public exploitation these facilities originated almost entirely in the English-speaking world. The past two centuries, in these respects, are a period of increasing convergence throughout the English-speaking world, above all, between the American branch of the community and all others centred upon it for much of their educational and entertainment material. We now hear so much of what are traditionally thought of as different varieties of English that we find it very difficult to recognise an Americanism when we see one. The very conception of 'a variety of English' is waning in value.

Of course, before 1770, not everyone was confined to the English of his town or village unless he hiked or hacked to another; many were exposed to the highly prestigious and influential written form. But this has also assumed new roles in the last two centuries, especially that immediately past; universal education since 1870 (cf. §26) has enhanced respect for it, and for a naive concept of correctness derived from it. Education has had another kind of standardising effect during the past century. The Public Schools Act, 1864, enumerated nine schools of this type; they were relatively small and retained considerable local connections. Subsequently they have vastly increased in numbers and in size and correspondingly have reduced their local connections. They became important agencies in the transmission of a non-localised variety of

English as the form with highest prestige; the adoption of this variety by the BBC in its early days naturally extended the influence of this model.

NOTE: There is a long and distinguished tradition of the study of American English, a considerable body of important work on Australasian English, and recent years have seen growing interest in other overseas varieties. Indeed, though the English of Britain has often been described, one of our main deficiencies is a general account of what is English about English Standard English. I do not attempt to describe overseas varieties but merely to point to their bearing on the history of our own kind of English. The following are excellent treatments with good bibliographical information: Markwardt (1958), Mencken (1935), Krapp (1925, reprinted 1960), Turner (1966), Cassidy (1961); for a limiting case, see Hall (1943).

§45 Recent technical and social developments, then, have restrained the fragmentation of the speech-community, leading to a variety of internal developments in new Englishes as compared with older Englishes. Another dimension of difference lies in the size and location of components of this community. In 1770 the population of England and Wales was perhaps 7½m and there were 1,500 in place of the present 14m Australasian English population. We cannot give exact figures for English-speakers, but we can note the subtraction of the whole range of African English communities (Kenya 1890, Rhodesia 1888, Nigeria 1861, Ghana 1821, South Africa 1795, Sierra Leone 1788). In Asia, Malaya would be missing (1786), and although the English had been in India since the early 17c there was no substantial indigenous English-speaking community before the 19c; Malta was not yet British (1814); indeed, outside the British Isles only three major areas would remain – the West Indies, and what are now Canada and the United States of America. Both in numbers and territory the North American communities would, however, be much reduced. In all the (present) US lands west of the Mississippi the major developments are post-1850. The centre of population gravity has been calculated as lying near the Atlantic Coast in 1790 and in Illinois, some thousand miles to the west, in 1950; but the greatest movement in a single decade was between 1850 and 1860. The population is now given as 192m (not all of whom are English-speakers, see Fishman 1966, and my §13); in 1790 as about 2m in a narrow east coast strip, by no means all of them English-speaking. The War of Independence (1775-83) obviously marks an important break with the sense of Britain as the centre from which linguistic and other standards emanate – though there is evidence in the adoption of /ɑː/ in words like *aunt, dance,* in some east coast speech that English influence did not terminate abruptly; and in the evolution of Canadian English evidence that geographical and economic ties can be more important than political ones in determining the main centres from which linguistic influence shall emanate. Canada has a present population of 18m (in an area substantially larger than the US), of whom 67% are purely English-speaking and a further 13% bilingual in English and French. The cession of the country to England dates from 1763, but at the beginning of our period the population was confined to the Atlantic provinces and numerically (as well as politically) formed part of the American colonial population already mentioned; the number of English-speakers was exceedingly small. The West Indies was pre-eminently a linguistically mixed area, the centre of the Slave Trade. The size of the late 18c population is unknown; it is now about 2m. It must be remembered that Britain itself, never entirely English-speaking, was even less nearly so in 1770, when Gaelic and Welsh were considerably stronger, Manx still flourished and Cornish had not quite died out. In Ireland in the mid-19c 4m out of 7m were Irish-speaking, 1m of them knowing no English; presumably the extent of English was less around 1770.

§46 Looking back two hundred years we find, accordingly, an English-speaking community amounting to less than one-twentieth of its present size, less extensive in geographical range, at once more focused on a single centre of standardisation and less open to intercourse with it; virtually stripped of its present international roles, but already in contact with a great number of other speech-communities. We have seen that the mark of varieties developed since 1770 has been internal uniformity, and that we cannot extrapolate from past tendencies to diversification. Since the wish to extrapolate is deep-seated, we must now safeguard against the equally false inference that English is on the way to becoming entirely uniform. This is, in principle, impossible. Marckwardt says:

> It goes without saying that no two persons ever have an identical command of their common language – If this be true of but two persons, the potential of difference resident in a language spoken by more than 200 million truly staggers the imagination (1958, 3).

It follows that variation in English will be greater now than in 1770, and will increase, if not exactly *pari passu* with the speech-community.

What has changed is the alignment of speakers into groups. The over-riding importance of geographical factors has given way to a dominance of cultural and socio-economic factors. 'There is more contact, linguistic and otherwise, between Australia and England now than there was between Northumbria and Kent a thousand years ago' (Turner, 1966, 23). The characteristic of the past two centuries is the extent to which a man can choose the group with which he will linguistically associate himself. He is still not entirely free in this respect, even in American society (Labov, 1966). But in a broad sense, fluctuating, self-electing, social groups are the main determinants of the variations within English today. The conception of linguistic varieties as existing in multi-dimensional socio-economic space, a conception relevant to English since at least the 14c, overtakes the conception of dialects in geographical space during recent generations. The old country shows both types of variation in rivalry; English abroad shows the direction of the future.

So far the spread of the language has led only to peripheral misunderstandings, but it is easy to imagine a language stretched to the point where its varieties became mutually incomprehensible and would need naming as new languages. This happened to the linguistic heritage of the Roman Empire, with the fragmentation of Vulgar Latin into French, Spanish, Portuguese, Rumanian, Romansch, etc., and yet further back, to the ancestors of the language-families we know as Italic, Germanic, Celtic, etc. Divergence and fragmentation characterise an expanding world – one in which peoples explore, conquer, colonise and settle; convergence characterises a shrinking world such as our own, where geographical distance has been subordinated to more abstract conditions. There must in principle be a limit to the number of speakers who can be mutually intelligible to each other, but the cut-off is gradual.

§47 Let us now focus attention on the internal development of what we can in a very broad sense recognise as standard usage in English English, looking first at its phonology. Some short histories of English give the impression that change in pronunciation stopped dead in the 18c, a development which would be quite inexplicable for a language in everyday use. It is true that the sweeping systematic changes we can detect in earlier periods are missing, but the amount of change is no less. Rather, its location has changed; in the last two hundred years changes in pronunciation are predominantly due, not, as in the past, to evolution of the system, but to what, in a very broad sense, we may call the interplay of different varieties, and to the complex analogical relationship

78

between different parts of the language. These tendencies are old, but are not until recently predominant. H. C. Wyld writes of the usages which have surfaced during this period as 'the new English', 'new-fangled English' and 'improved English'. Of developments in pronunciation, viewed generally, he says:

> The process of 'improvement', so far as one can see, but it is absurd to attempt great preciseness in these matters, began roughly in the third quarter of the eighteenth century, and has gained in force and volume ever since.
> But if the triumph of the pedagogue is thus unquestionable, the success ... must be set down rather to social causes than to a sudden capacity on the part of the Orthoepist to persuade those to whom he had so long preached in vain. It was assuredly not the [aristocrats] who first adopted the new-fangled English. These and their like, and long may they flourish, have hardly done so at the present time. It was the new men and their families, who were winning a place in the great world and in public affairs, who would be attracted by the refinement offered by the new and 'correct' system of pronunciation which they learnt from their masters of rhetoric, or from their University tutors. That this new, wealthy, and often highly cultivated class should gradually have imposed upon society at large the gentilities of the academy of deportment ... would have seemed incredible to Lady Wentworth and her friends. But so it has come about. . . . It is not wholly fanciful to attribute in no small measure to the personal prestige of Johnson [d. 1784, B.S.] ... the very marked reaction in favour of a certain type of 'correctness' which set in about this time, and which has continued ever since to make fresh inroads upon established tradition. But even so mighty a force as Samuel Johnson required suitable social conditions in which to exert his 'influence'. (1920, quotation from the 1936 edition, 285).

These are not the only changes, but they are the most noticeable. What the 'new English' amounted to will emerge from the specific developments now to be considered.

§ 48 The consonant-system has undergone very little change not only in the last two centuries, but throughout the recorded history of English; so slowly does the system change that those consonant phonemes which have come into existence during the past fifteen hundred years still exhibit differences from older items. There is, however, some loss, and a great deal of alteration in the distribution of items through time.

The sound /ŋ/ now appears medially and finally in stressed and unstressed syllables, as in *singing*; it has never been accepted in initial position. Its extension to unstressed syllables is quite recent, and has spread from middle class into general usage under the influence of spelling (or so the expression 'dropping the g', for the older pronunciation, indicates). As recently as 1936 Wyld retained his 1920 comment that the older pronunciation (/ɪn/, /ən/) was 'still widespread among large classes of the best speakers, no less than among the worst' (op. cit., 283). He describes these forms as 'of considerable antiquity' and 'at one time apparently almost universal in every type of English speech', he notes that Swift had objected to them in the early 18c, and in 1801 Walker ambiguously remarks that the best speakers use 'g-less' forms, but yet these forms savour of vulgarity (ib., 289). During the same period unease about the pronunciation was shown by hyper-correct 'reverse forms' in -*ing* where it had no place historically – as in *lupin, chicken, children.* The movement towards -*ing* gained momentum in the 19c:

> Apparently in the twenties of the last century a strong reaction which set in in favour of the more 'correct' pronunciation, as it was considered, and was in reality an innovation, based upon the spelling, was so far successful that the [ŋ] pronunciation . . . has now a vogue among the educated at least as wide as the more conservative one with -*n* (Wyld, loc. cit.).

Nowadays, except in non-standard speech, the old form is hardly more than a slightly comic memory.

In 1770, then, /ŋ/ in unstressed syllables was hardly known. The sound was used in stressed syllables, but only before a velar stop, as in the now dialectal pronunciation /sɪŋg/; in such positions it had been an allophone (a variant conditioned by a neighbouring sound) of the /n/ phoneme. As an independent phoneme it is new, noted by some 17c observers, but not generally accepted even at the close of the 18c; it depends on the loss of the following velar in morpheme-final stressed position, and on spelling-pronunciation in unstressed syllables. Its restricted distribution still reflects these origins.

§ 49 A sound commonly regarded as a consonant is /h/, which complements /ŋ/ in that it can only occur (now, and throughout the history of English) in initial position – the position from which /ŋ/ is excluded. It also shares with /ŋ/ the characteristic that its history is closely related to stress. If we go back to 1770 we find that in educated usage /h/ is normally present at the onset of appropriate stressed syllables and absent in unstressed ones – a distinction of which we find traces today, despite much comment on 'dropping of h' as a vulgarism. The distinction had by 1770 been present in the language for many centuries, with the consequence that speakers had come to think of /h/ as a marker for the onset of a stressed syllable which would otherwise begin with a vowel. Putting this inference into practice, they commonly introduced unhistorical *h*'s, and were equally commonly condemned by purists for doing so. But not till the close of the 18c does explicit condemnation of 'dropping h's' begin. With the spread of education a new view about *h*'s comes to dominate usage, at the expense of traditional pronunciations – the view that if it is in the spelling it must be pronounced; of course, this view can only prevail where spelling itself is highly regularised, and this regularisation reached an advanced stage after the publication of Johnson's *Dictionary* (1755).

So, as with /ŋ/, the highest classes, in their self-assurance, remain traditional, and so do those untouched by education, but the new correctness catches on throughout a broad social spectrum between these extremes. Two classes of *h* must be distinguished. In native words such as *he, heaven, heart*, the prosodic distribution began to give way to a lexical one. But in words of French origin such as *honour, herb*, the *h* spelling had never indicated a sound in English, even when stressed. It is a secondary, and on the whole later, extension of the spelling-pronunciation to use *h* in French words; Uriah Heep, not otherwise an *h*-dropper, says *umble* (*David Copperfield* was published 1849-50), and fifty years ago *humour, hotel, hospital*, and *herb* without *h* were much commoner than they are today.

On the /w/, /ʍ/ contrast cf. §34.

§ 50   However, most of the differences in consonants we should notice if we were transported back to 1770 would be of a much less systematic kind. Wyld's general comment on the situation is this:

> If we could recall speakers from the seventeenth and eighteenth centuries it is probable that what would strike us most would be the pranks that even the most refined and well-bred persons would play with the consonants. From this point of view the English of these periods would appear to us with our modern standards as a mixture of rusticity, slipshodness and vulgarity (ib., 283).

From the mid-19c dates a tendency to restore /w/ forms in such words as *woman, swore, swollen, quote*, and (in unstressed syllables) *Edward, upward, Ipswich*; note present educated *towards*, /tɔːdz/ beside increasingly frequent /tʊwɔːdz/). Other labials have not been much affected, but spelling has restored the /b/ of *Lambeth* and its authority has removed the /p/ of *mushrump*, 'mushroom', except jocularly. From the same period we have a tendency to restore a traditionally silent *d* indicated in spelling, in such words as *husband* (finally) and *London* (medially); note present *Wednesday*, /wɛnzdɪ/ beside extra-precise /wɛdnzd(e)ɪ/. Conversely, an unhistorical final *d* has been removed, except in the most uneducated speech, from such words *gown(d)*, *scholar(d)*, *vil(d)e*; but remains in *visard*, which is not used often enough to keep generally alive a sense of traditional sound-spelling relationship, and in *sound*, where the spelling already followed the pronunciation. The corresponding voiceless sound has had a similar history – restored on the authority of spelling in words which formerly lacked it, such as *pageant*, *respect*, *strict* (but medially it is still not regularly restored in *mostly, lastly, often*, and only exceptionally is it heard in *Christmas*); and removed where it was unhistorical as in *vermin/varmint* (the latter already vulgar in the late 18c; but note that *margent* beside *margin* is felt to be poetic, and that the *-t* has established itself in sound and spelling in *graft*, earlier *graff*). Final *f* has been restored in *mastiff*, *(hand)kerchief*; but the *f*-less form remains in *hussy*, also differentiated semantically from both /hʌsɪf/ and *housewife*. Medial /l/ has generally been restored during the same period in such words as *soldier, falcon(ry)* (but in *fault* the restoration began earlier), and medial /v/ in *seventy, pavement, Devonshire* (but as a technical term in agriculture, *Denshire*, vb); *Daventry* now varies between traditional /deɪntrɪ/ and a spelling-pronunciation. Finally, among individual sounds, the glide /j/ has undergone the double process of restoration and removal. Early NE had assimilated /dj/ to /dʒ/ and /tj/ to /tʃ/; the 19c largely removed the /dʒ/ from such words as *immediate, idiot, odious* and *Indian* (but cf. *Honest Injun!*), though *duty* can still be heard as /dʒuːtɪ/ beside /djuːtɪ/, and /tʃ/ in such words as *feature, nature* has proved more durable. /ʃ/ by assimilation from /sj/ was common in *sewer, otiose, halcyon, nauseous*, in which we have removed it; we keep it fairly often in *associate*, and regularly in *sure, nation*, etc. In this case, the corresponding voiced sound has survived better (*vision, enclosure*), but /zj/ is sometimes restored in *casual*, and generally in less common words such as *brasier, osier, hosier*. Removal of /j/ occurs between a velar stop and a front-vowel – *can, girl*, were regularly /kjæn/, /gjɜːl/ till well on in the 19c, and analogous forms occur in New England.

Of a more general kind is the tendency in early NE to voice consonants in a voiced environment, a tendency also reversed in the 'improved' English. By the close of the 18c such forms as *deputy* with /b/ for /p/ and *protestant* with /d/ for the first /t/ were already regarded as vulgar and they are now unknown in Standard; the converse tendency to unvoice (as in *optayne* for *obtain*) may never have been Standard, though instances may still be heard quite often.

One example must suffice to show that spelling-pronunciation is not the only villain of the piece. In the word *stomacher*, which is no longer in daily use, the traditional pronunciation with /tʃ/ recorded as late as 1909) has given way to one in /k/ on the analogy of the much more frequently used base-word, *stomach*.

§ 51 Apart from the very recent changes discussed in § 34 the only development affecting a vowel-phoneme as a whole is a long-standing downward and forward drift of /ʌ/ (as in *love, come*) which has had no close neighbours.

The more scattered vowel changes reflect, as do those in consonants, the conflict between varieties and between principles of analogy, with the model of the written form of the language dominant as a source of influence. Again, because they are scattered, they can be exemplified rather than described exhaustively; and they are still going on. The words *sausage, sauce, saucy* normally had the stem-vowel /æ/ in the 18c, but towards its close the present /ɔ(:)/ pronunciation was coming into use, and in 1791 was thought more educated. There has been a steady growth of /ɒ/ replacing /ʌ/ in such words as *dromedary,* and *bomb, bombard, bombast*; compare the present divided usage in *combat, conduit, constable, comrade, Lombardy, accomplish,* etc. In *coney* the replacement of traditional /ʌ/ has been /əʊ/. In *yeoman o* was 'mute' but the present spelling-pronunciation is recorded from 1791. The current pronunciation /ɔ:/ for *au* before *n* is due to the spelling; in the late 18c /ɑ:/ would have been normal in *jaundice, Maundy*; it survived in *haunch* until the late 19c, and in *launch, laundry* can still sometimes be heard from elderly speakers. In other *au* words such as *daughter* /ɑ:/ was considered affected at the close of the 18c. Even after *w*, though /ɔ:/ was usual, some speakers kept /ɑ:/ till about 1800 in such words as *war, quart* (cf. current variation, but generally /ɑ:/, in *qualm*). Turning to unstressed syllables, we find the restoration of /aɪl/ for *-ile*; /əl/ was normal in the 18c (and is the source of the syllabic *l* in such words as *fertile* in the US). But the spelling-pronunciation had developed in three words – *exile, edile, infantile* by 1795; in 1909 Jespersen records that both pronunciations are current in educated British usage, though schoolmasters prefer /aɪl/, which, he says, has already prevailed in words of more than two syllables. Born in 1925, I have never heard the historic form from a British speaker.

Sometimes a pronunciation which could be suggested by spelling could also have arisen in another way. An example is /oʊ/ (see note on p. 86) in *gold*, which had /uː/ in the 18c; (-)*old* is not normally pronounced /uː/, so spelling may be a factor, but an /oʊ/ form could also result from the analogy of derived or compounded forms. *Waistcoat* (cf. § 26), is a similar case – influence from spelling, or from the independent words *waist* and *coat*, or both? Jespersen notes in 1909 that the form now general is being introduced into currency by ladies, though the traditional form remains normal. Reformation on the model of related words certainly accounts for many changes – for the long vowel or diphthong in the first syllable of *barefoot, farewell, Shakespeare, housewife, fivepence* (/ɪ/ 'now giving way' 1909), *cheerful* and *leapyear*. The stressed vowel of *parentage, occasional*, was /æ/ till the close of the 18c, but this has given way to /ɛə/, /eɪ/ from the base-forms during the 19c. The second element of a compound has been reformed in *fortnight*, earlier /-nɪt/, but with the present form from 1780. The old short form may survive beside the new long one with differentiated functions, as in *utter/outer, cleanly* (/ɛ/ adjective, /iː/ adverb). The re-formation does not always survive: *knowledge*, traditionally with /ɒ/, developed an /oʊ/ form from *know*, recorded from 1791 to 1909 in solemn and public use (Tennyson preferred it).

Contrariwise, a simple form may substitute for its older long vowel a short one borrowed from derivatives. This accounts for /ɛ/ in *friend* (contrast *fiend*, which has few derivatives); the long vowel is recorded till 1791, but a short alternative occurs from 1621. Similarly in *guild* (/ɪ/ first recorded in 1791), and in *wind*, sb, whose older form in /aɪ/ was described as 'solemn' in 1787 and remained in declamatory style during most of the 19c. A complex of analogical ties accounts for the present variables of *threepence* (notably /θrɪpəns/, /θrɛpəns/, /θrʊpəns/); probably all have co-existed since the late 18c.

Indeed, the presence of alternative forms accounts for a number of developments. In *again(st)* a second syllable in /eɪ/ is increasingly felt to be more 'correct'; but /ɛ/ seems to have been dominant until recently, with the two forms in rivalry for at least three hundred years. In words of the type *leisure, pleasure, treasure* the stem vowel could be long or short in the 18c (cf. current US /liːʒər/); of two commentators writing almost simultaneously one, in 1787, describes the long vowel as 'affected', the other, in 1791, prefers it; but in Britain it has gone. Doublets are particularly likely to arise in monosyllables commonly used with weak sentence stress, such as personal pronouns and operator or auxiliary

84

verbs. In the 18c *were* had a strong form, /wɛə/, beside a weak form much like our own. Since the weak form is much commoner, it has prevailed, and when the item is stressed a new strong form is developed by lengthening and making more tense the vowel of the weak form (/wɜ:/ versus /wə/). The last speaker I heard regularly using /ɛə/ from the old strong form was my mother (b. 1894).

It is difficult to know how far the recent history of words of the type *cloth, lost, cross, off* represents sound-change, and how far conflict of analogies and varieties. At the close of the 18c the vowel was /ɔ:/ in words in *-st* (*frost, cost, lost*), *-ss* (*dross, cross, loss*), *-sp* (*hospital, prosper, prospect*), *-th* (*cloth, loth, cloths, broth, moth*); in some speakers also before /-f/ (*often, soft, cough, coffee, office, officer*), but others had /ɒ/ before /-f/. In some cases the /ɔ:/ had arisen by lengthening not much earlier, which makes a theory of phonological shortening suspect. As usual, before 1800 social consciousness is at work on the distribution of the forms, and in 1791 the long vowel before /-s/ is declared vulgar. Also as usual, it persisted not only among the vulgar, but also among the most assured. It is now comparatively uncommon in educated speech, and often provokes a strong reaction. It is noticeable that in the Queen's broadcast speeches /ɔ:/ has given way to /ɒ/ in the few remaining disputed words in this class.

Also difficult of interpretation is the relation between the sounds /ʊə/ and /ɔə/ during our period (cf. § 34). Left to themselves, they would no doubt have coalesced under /ɔə/, the form in which speakers as unimpeachable as Byron and Tennyson rhyme *more* and *poor*; more recently, the anecdote that George Bernard Shaw, when asked 'Are you Shaw?' answered 'Positive', even if apocryphal, points in the same direction. But purists have not left them to themselves, and increasingly /ɔə/ in *sure, poor, moor*, is felt to be vulgar or slipshod. So the phoneme-system, for most speakers, remains intact, but ever fewer individual items are left employing /ʊə/ except in the most careful utterance. *Whore* has gone over entirely to /ɔə/ (presumably most pupils gave their teachers no opportunity of correcting their pronunciation of it); and the same process may account for the rather puzzling vowel of *door*. I know one speaker who uses /ʊə/ in *mourn*, but I have never heard the usual /ɔə/ reprimanded, as in *during* it would be.

Of course, the separation of changes into two heads, those affecting vowels and those affecting consonants is a convention to help exposition; in many words (cf. *Daventry* and *hussy* above) both may be affected;

in these and other words (e.g. *Leveson* in spelling-pronunciation as against /l(j)uːsən/) the two may be inextricable.

§ 52   Concerning the stress system I take the view that at present there is a single contrast, stressed and unstressed, and that the recognisably distinct intermediate grades should be classified as either weak variants of stressed syllables or strong variants of unstressed ones. The decision is not random; when we place a syllable in sequence into a metrical environment we immediately recognise it as functioning as a stressed item, however weak, or an unstressed one, however strong. This system is a dominant one in English, in the sense explained in § 39. Two centuries ago the system was basically the same, but different in an important respect in the distribution of elements. Intermediate grades (there was possibly then only one distinct intermediate grade, commonly known as secondary stress) were invariably satellites of the strong grade. This is what is meant by saying that secondary stress was 'more important' in the 18c – a status it has preserved more in Australasian and US speech than in this country (cf. words such as *secretary, dormitory*; for a contrary development in such words as *fertile* cf. § 51). The rhythm is often said to be slower or more ponderous; this follows from the presence of extra syllables functioning as stressed, and is not an independent change in the rhythm of the language. Similarly, the vowels of syllables with secondary stress conform to the pattern for vowels in stressed syllables, not for those in unstressed syllables.

Not only the system, but the location, of stresses is difficult to describe in PE because many conflicting principles seem to be at work (cf. § 39). The same applies to the 18c. So many independent principles are at work that we would expect a great deal of stress-shifting to have taken place, especially during the last two centuries when people's views about their language have had unprecedented influence on their usage. On this occasion, however, we find not merely haphazard movements between forms, but in at least one case the exploitation of the stress variable for a new grammatical purpose.

Overall, we would expect stress-shift back to the first syllable of a word to be the commonest change; and overall it is, but not necessarily in the last two centuries, since so many movements of this kind had already happened before 1770. Still, there are abundant recent examples, such as *compensate, concentrate, contemplate, balcony,* with second-syllable stress well on into the 19c; *reconcile* had first- or second-syllable stress in the 19c, and in the late 18c *comparable, acceptable* differed in meaning according to the position of the stress on the first or second syllable. Some words which put the stress on to the first syllable have not kept it there (*accessory,* and usually *peremptory*); there is still controversy about *controversy.* In a number of items the present distinction between form-classes, as in ˡ*subject* sb, subˡ*ject,* vb, has only been regularised in the past two centuries (in addition to *subject, survey* and *record* are examples); this grammatical exploitation had begun in earlier centuries, but what was exploited was a variation arising in an entirely different way (cf. § 129). We find many examples of such linguistic opportunism – some lasting and profound in their effects, some transient and undeveloped (cf. *comparable,* above).

To some extent the regularisation of the noun-verb contrast involved movements counter to the shifting of the stress towards the first syllable. Other words, for a variety of reasons, share in this counter-movement. Wilde still uses the traditional first-syllable stress on *Trafalgar,* and ˡ*successor* is used till the close of the 19c.

A new type of compound characterises the NE period, using, instead of the traditional / x pattern, as in *wisdom, bookshop,* a level-stressed pattern / /, as in *gold watch, mince pie.* First noted in the 17c, the type becomes fully established and highly productive in the late 18c and 19c; the relative newness of it is still shown by the marked fluctuation amongst speakers in the use of level stress – a factor which makes generalisation impossible.

§ 53   The correlation between language and experience is most directly reflected in lexical changes, and we have already glanced at the ferment of innovation going on in the 20c. We have experience of new objects, new ways of regarding the world, new things to do and new thoughts to think in comparison with people two, or even one, hundred years ago. The terminology of new ranges of science and technology has come into existence, and to a remarkable extent has passed into daily, or at least daily newspaper, use. In their more highly developed forms these terminologies represent special or restricted languages on a scale previously unknown (though the principle is ancient). There is no point in listing examples of tendencies so pervasive and well-recognised. But there is a good deal of confusion about the interpretation of the material. Many of the elements combined into new terms are Greek or

Latin in (ultimate) origin, medieval Latin in immediate source; but it is unreasonable to suppose that they must therefore be combined in modern English according to the rules of classical Greek or Latin (on so-called hybrids cf. § 21).

Detailed evidence about the adoption of formatives and patterns belonging to, or at the fringes of, technical usage, can be found in Marchand (1969). Towards the end of the 18c patterns of the type *de–verb–ise* (as in *deodorise*) and *de–verb–ate* (as in *dehydrate*) are established (op. cit., 153, 155), and *mono-* establishes itself as an English formative (178). 19c are *epi-, hypo-, intra-, meta-, micro-, multi-, neo-, retro-, ultra-* as productive elements in English (though usually there are earlier loans incorporating these forms; cf. op. cit., 164–201); at the same time, many new uses of old formatives develop. During this period prefixes are much more mutable than suffixes, which were, broadly speaking, already established in their present functions by 1770.

The second general comment called for by this terminology concerns its status as English. The more technical a term, the more esoteric its use; negatively, the more numerous the competent speakers who do not know it. And, of course, 'knowing a word' is not as clear-cut as knowing how to knit; I know the words *isotope* and *siskin*, but I would score myself much lower for them than for the words *labial* and *halter*. It has often been noted that languages have a 'core' vocabulary shared by all speakers, and a lot of more restricted vocabulary, though the dividing-lines and the quantification have not been established. Technical terms, for the most part, do not belong to the core vocabulary; in terms of affiliation they are therefore less English than words like *apple* and *father*. Equally, in terms of range, they extend far beyond English and have, with varying degrees of modification, extensive international status. Just as recent cultural developments, in a broad sense of cultural, have blurred the distinctions between varieties of English, so have they, still in a broad sense of cultural, called into question the difference between being, and not being, English. The difference was, in any case, never as clear-cut as non-specialists have thought.

§ 54 Finally, it should be noted that the innovations in this area are, above all, in the form-class noun; and that the favourite methods of WF have restored the processes of compounding and derivation to a dominance they had not enjoyed since the OE period. Naturally, WF is not confined to terminology. By the beginning of our period English already had a stupendous range both of compounding types and of affixes for use in derivation. The subject does not lend itself to summary, but the present position and its history are ably treated in Marchand (1969) on which this sketch is heavily dependent. Many old formative patterns have remained productive, but the range of patterns was so extensive as to permit only limited further development, accompanied by some rationalisation between competing forms. Some well-established formatives illustrate general principles by the way they become particularly active. WF depends on the speaker's sense of overall pattern and relationship in his own language, and accordingly, there can be much scope for individual variation, long intervals of apparent dormancy before a pattern becomes active, and an explosive rate of increase when the period of productivity sets in. OE *-ig*, later *-y*, was added to nouns to form adjectives, many of which survive alongside their noun bases, as in *blood: bloody, craft: crafty, ice: icy*. But in *crafty* there is a considerable shift in the semantic relationship between base and derivative, and in another pair, *naught: naughty* this process has gone so far that most speakers do not associate the two. In other cases the noun has died out, leaving the adjective isolated (*dizzy, giddy, empty*). There is enough to keep alive the sense that *-y* is a way of forming adjectives, but the sense of what they are formed from is weakened. So, mainly in the 16c, redundant formations on adjective stems are produced – *hugy, moisty*; but the type does not catch on except with colour-adjectives, where it enables speakers to make a distinction between *-ish* ('rather', as in *blue-ish*) and *-y* (often with the sense 'partaking the character of two colours', as in *bluey-green*). And it is added to verbs – *catchy, drowsy* – which establish themselves, but do not become very productive as a type; or to plural nouns, as in *tricksy, folksy, tipsy*, of which the same observation holds (but note the addition of a depreciatory tone). This diversification weakened the original clear-cut relationship for a time, but the sense of it never died. Suddenly, after 1800, the type, in its original de-nominal use, became highly active again, but very often in stylistically-marked formations of a highly colloquial or even slang(y!) character, as in *dotty, nervy, shirty, jumpy, Christmassy, classy, arty, sexy*. The suffix *-ish* seems to have shown a similar recent spurt. It is a very ancient element, already in the language when the English came to this country, and, as in *English*, was mainly used to form tribal or national names, but was also added to other nouns to form adjectives, as in *childish*; when this use came into conflict with the formations in *-like* the rivalry was resolved by restricting the *-ish* form to a somewhat derogatory use. It was first extended to adjective bases in late ME with colour-words, which are syntactically more noun-like than other adjectives. So matters stood until the last century, when it came to be used extensively in colloquial formations on other adjective stems 'when the speaker does not wish to be too categorical' (Jespersen, 1909, etc., VI, 324). Thus, *baddish, biggish, dullish, largish, tallish* (but *more-ish* is already in Swift as a long-standing colloquialism, and the more colloquial a word or formation is, the greater is likely to be the time-lag between its inception and its appearance in our written records).

Another principle in the ecology of formatives and formations is illustrated by the related group *-ion, -sion, -tion, -ition, -ation*. The variant forms are accounted for by historical factors, often in the source-language, Latin, rather than English, and in the source-language the *-a-* type tends to be commonest; it has certainly given most forms to English; consequently it becomes the most productive, and is the only type to be used with native stems, the conclusive sign of acclimatisation. This stage is reached just before our period, with *flirtation* (1718) and continues into it with *starvation* (1778); the 19c yields *botheration* and the 20c *flo(a)tation* and *Westernisation*.

How a formative can extend its range is shown by *-less*. In OE this was only attached to nouns, as in the antecedents of the modern words *lifeless, breathless, homeless*. But from the ENE period many nouns were identical in form with verbs, and such formations as *fearless, needless, countless* could be felt to provide models for *-less* formations on purely verbal stems. Formations acting in this way may be called *matrix-formations*; they give birth to new types. So we find the development of verb-based formations, in an exploratory and peripheral way, in the 16c (*opposeless, resistless, staunchless*), but as part of the core vocabulary mainly in the 19c (*dauntless, fadeless, tireless*).

From the 14c English had a number of French loanwords – *hamlet, gauntlet, frontlet*, etc. – which suggested that *-let* was a diminutive formation (historically, it is a reduced form of two French suffixes, *-el* and *-ette*). At first, applications of this supposition were rare – *kinglet, princelet, ringlet* are 17c; but in the 19c it became highly productive in such formations as *starlet* (at first in the sense *starfish*!), *booklet, leaflet, flatlet*, with innumerable nonce-formations besides. Other formatives newly and highly productive in the 19c are *-ette* and *-ite*, and in the 20c *-proof*. By contrast with most of the instances we have considered, it can happen that a single word is so analysed by speakers as to become productive without any time-lag: this was the case with the late 19c American loan from Spanish, *cafeteria*, and the many subsequent

-teria formations; cf. *hamburger*, with numerous metanalysed forms in *-burger*.

The more strongly a correlation establishes itself the greater is our tendency to bring into use forms that occupy what would otherwise be gaps in the pattern; as if, from the correlation *crafty: craft* we were to form from the adjective *dizzy* a noun – **dizz*. This process of *back-derivation* (cf. § 31) has naturally been on the increase in recent centuries. It is known from 1300 (*backbite*), and there are a few examples up to 1600, but only in the 19c do instances become abundant and central, as in *caretake* (1893), *eavesdrop* (1906), *gate-crash* (not in *OED*), *house-hunt* (1888), *housekeep* (1842), *manhandle* (1865).

§ 55 Formation of new words by *clipping*, i.e. cutting off part of the word, is also mainly characteristic of recent times, though it was more established before 1770 than back-derivation was. It has always tended to belong to colloquial language, and this may have retarded its appearance in our records. From our period come such examples as *lab, pub, exam, gym, memo, phone*; some have established themselves as the normal, not merely casual, form, e.g. *cable, zoo, bus, lino*.

Blending and word-manufacturing, as in *chortle, smog, brunch*, and *Nato, radar, Benelux*, are almost confined to recent English. Before the mid-19c the types are rare in the records of standard English, but there are some possible examples in 14c regional poetry and it is noteworthy that *glaze* (combining *glare* and *gaze*), familiarised by Shakespeare's use in *Julius Caesar*, is subsequently recorded from dialect use; the type may have a richer history than the evidence shows. Miss Valerie Adams is at work on the first full-length study of blends in English.

Certain ancient types of formation have waned in importance. Ablaut-combinations (in which two elements are repeated with vowel change) are almost all old – except *crisscross* (1846), *clipclop* (1863), *pingpong* (1900) and a few forms of hardly more than nonce standing. There has been a notable failure of new forms in the dominant *i/a* pattern (*chitchat, shilly-shally*) to gain a footing in recent English. The complementary type, rhyme combinations, in which only the initial consonant or cluster varies, is rather stronger, though most formations are old. *Fuddy-duddy, fuzzy-wuzzy, ragtag, hanky-panky, walkie-talkie* and *brain-drain* are recent.

Naturally these are not the only means of extending native and acclimatised resources. The meaning of a word is not something clear-cut, settled once for all, referable to an objective standard; new applications come into use, old ones drop out. Of the many novelties during our period that have made new demands on the language, the terminology of railways can stand as an illuminating example. They came into use rather earlier in England than in America; conversely, American landsmen exploited steampower for inland waterways before the English. This is reflected in such American uses as *all aboard, caboose* and *berth* in railway contexts; but other differences (*conductor/guard, freight train/goods train*, etc.) are a matter of chance (Krapp, 1925, 138–9).

§ 56 Throughout its history, English has absorbed large numbers of loanwords, a practice that Jespersen calls 'linguistic omnivorousness' (1909, etc., VI, 139). This voracity is commonly, but not altogether rightly, thought to date from after the Norman Conquest. Loanwords are interesting in themselves, and for the light they throw on cultural relations, but on the second point it is easy to be misled. Languages do not only borrow what they need, in the sense of what is missing from them, and the circumstances of borrowing can be far more complex than is commonly supposed [as when the English transmitted the word *kangaroo* to one group of Australian aborigines, having learnt it from another – the English thinking the word belonged to the new group of natives and the aborigines thinking it was English, Turner (1966, 199)]. Since no one is in danger of overlooking the significance loans do have for cultural history it seems well to begin by pointing out pitfalls. That said, it must be added that in the past two centuries, to a large extent, loans do have the cultural meaning they seem to.

During that period much the largest group are French. One group can be traced to the Revolution and the Napoleonic Wars – *émigré, guillotine, régime, tricolour, fusillade, epaulette, coup*. The late 18c also reflects traditional links in cuisine, with *aubergine, aspic* and *cuisine* itself; in fashion, with *bandeau, chignon, corduroy*; and in travel, especially the Romantic love of mountains, *avalanche, crampon, moraine*. The new ease of communication (not only by physical travel) is shown by the number of 19c loans, greater than at any period since ME (cf. Serjeantson, 1935, 165). These continue the same areas of contact with *barrage, communiqué, chassis* (borrowed in reference to a gun-carriage); *café, à la carte, gourmet, restaurant, menu, chef, sauté, soufflé; fichu, moiré, crepe, blouse, crinoline, trousseau, lingerie, guipure, beret, piqué, tricot, layette, chiffron, suede; crevasse, massif, ravine*; and represent many other fields in which the English looked up to the French – *parquet, passe-partout; chassé, glissade; acrobat, can-can; croquet, bezique;*

rococo, renaissance; nocturne, baton; matinee, première; glycerine, pipette; communism, entente; dossier, gendarme – as well as fields where this consideration did not hold, but where French terms were felt to lend a certain glamour: *planchette, seance; chauffeur, coupé.* In the 20c loans have been fewer (it is well known that they have been repaid with interest), and in similar fields, including *revue, vers libre; garage, limousine, hangar, camouflage; enfant terrible; pied-à-terre.*

In the late 18c relatively few loans come direct from Italian – within our period examples are *falsetto, bravura; maraschino, semolina; lotto; torso, condottiere.* Direct influence is greater in the 19c, with three strains in it – words for objects or institutions associated with Italy (*vendetta, mafia, salami, risotto, gorgonzola*), words belonging to fields in which Italy had real or imputed leadership (*magenta, studio, replica, tempera; piccolo, prima donna, sonatina, intermezzo, cadenza*), and a miscellaneous group (*scarlatina, tombola, inferno*). Among other Romance languages, Spanish is progressively strongly represented, to a very large extent by loans to American English. Strictly, American English rather than Spanish is the immediate source of many of these words in British English, but the distinction is not always clear, and the Spanish form of the words tends to make them felt as aliens. In the late 18c we have *albino, merino, alpaca,* and in the 19c *silo, guerilla, pronunciamento, pelota, tilde, lasso, mustang, bronco, bonanza, patio, cafeteria, tango;* and in reference to Spanish or Spanish American institutions *picador, rodeo, pueblo, adobe,* etc.

From the Germanic languages, which are genetically more closely related to English, the yield is smaller – from Continental Dutch *scow, mangle, taffrail, flense;* from South African Dutch *eland, hartebeest, veldt, commando, trek, spoor, commandeer* (and from Dutch through American English, *spook, waffle* sb, *boss, dope*). From High German come such words as *iceberg; lammergeier; poodle, dachsund; schnapps, lager, kirsch, kummel, marzipan, zither, leitmotiv; alpenstock, edelweiss, rucksack, yodel; kindergarten, semester, seminar, protein, ohm, hinterland, zeitgeist.* Note that there are musical terms, but the distinction of German musical life in the 19c has not sufficed to displace Italian as the language for musical terms, though the period of Italy's authentic musical leadership was past. Scandinavian loans are few, the main ones being *vole, floe, nag* vb, *ski* (in the form /ʃiː/), *rorqual,* and very recently, *ombudsman.*

One of the most surprising facts about the history of English is the resistance of the language to Celtic loans, though the communities have adjoined and overlapped, and their members have intermarried, throughout the period when English has been spoken in this country – and even before. This resistance is usually discussed in relation to the period of initial settlement, and explained by the reluctance of conquerors to learning from the conquered. Perhaps the pattern of non-borrowing was set then, and relations between the communities have conformed in subsequent centuries. At all events, the facts are more remarkable than has generally been realised. Borrowings since 1770 have still a strong flavour of their land of origin and have hardly entered the mainstream of the language. From Irish we have *banshee, shillellagh, spalpeen, blarney, colleen, keen* vb; from Scots Gaelic *claymore, cairngorm, corrie, sporran, glengarry*; from Welsh *eisteddfod*; perhaps from Breton *menhir*, and directly or indirectly from Cornish *dolmen*.

The more distant European languages have naturally given less, and many of the words are still strong in narrowly local associations. Examples from Russian are *vodka, droshky, samovar, tundra, troika, polka* in the 19c; *pogrom, soviet, bolshevik, intelligentsia* in the 20c. From Polish *mazurka*, and from Czech only *robot* (the English version of Capek's play dates from 1923). Hungarian affords *czardas, goulash, paprika*.

Outside Europe, loans mainly reflect imperial expansion on the remaining continents. In the Middle East, Arabic is the source of *wadi, alfalfa, yashmak, loofah, safari* (this mediated by Swahili); Persian of *purdah*, and other words of purely Persian reference; Turkish gives *fez, bosh, Kismet, macramé*, and Hebrew *kosher*. Further east, we have from the Indo-European languages of India, Hindustani *sari, cheetah, howdah, chit, bangle, thug, puttee, khaki* (which Hindustani borrowed from Persian), *cashmere, pyjama, chutney, dumdum, gymkhana, polo*, etc.; from Sanskrit *suttee, yoga, nirvana* and *swastika*; from the non-Indo-European Dravidian languages *mulligatawny*, and from Romany *rum* (adj = *queer*). Tibetan gave *yak*, Chinese *chin-chin* and *kowtow*; Japanese *hara-kiri, tycoon, geisha, ju-jitsu*; Malay *sarong*; the languages of various Pacific Islands *taboo, tattoo, kiwi, ukulele*. From Australia there is a rather larger group, including *kangaroo, dingo, corroborree, wombat, boomerang, budgerigar*. The African group is remarkably small, though *gorilla, okapi, tsetse* should be mentioned. South America is represented mainly by words of strong local associations – *puma, curare, angostura, curacao, sisal, coyote*, from various languages, and with some mediation from North American English. Finally, Amerindian languages in the north contributed to general English (over and above items that entered British English from American

English) *pemmican, toboggan*; Eskimo *oomiak, igloo*, and very recently, *anorak*.

While this completes our round-the-world tour of evidence in loans of contact between speech-communities, a further type of loan occurs independently of such contact. I refer, of course, to loans from Greek and Latin (already mentioned under the heading of technical terminology, but occurring in other fields). They include, since 1770, *bonus, extra, prospectus, via, deficit, tandem, habitat, humus, ego, stet, omnibus, sanatorium, aquarium, consensus, referendum*; and from Greek *phase, pylon, corm, myth, agnostic, therm.*

A half-loan, loan-formation or loan-translation is represented by a type, usually derived from a complex form in the source-language, in which the elements are rendered into corresponding ones in the borrowing language; there is no outer similarity of form, but the structure and function are alike. Borrowings of this type are sometimes known as *calques*. They have rarely been as frequent as other types of innovation in English, and are thinly represented in the last two centuries, though one familiar example is *Superman*, formed by George Bernard Shaw on the model of Nietzsche's *Übermensch.*

§ 57 The introduction of new words can often be given a semblance of dating, however well we may realise that the first recorded instance may not be the first use, and the first use may be far removed from the first time at which a word has any significant standing in a language. Even this semblance of dating is absent in the case of words lost; as we read authors back to 1770 we may notice elements in their vocabulary which strike us as old-fashioned, or not quite the word we would choose now; we may sense that particular items are nonce-formations or deliberate archaisms. But we do not identify words as being everyday items for, say, Wordsworth, and now wholly lost. The process of decay is in principle more protracted than that of inception. That through time, over a broad front, there is loss, we know; but except in periods of abrupt cultural revolution, it can hardly be traced over a period of two centuries. We may be sure that some losses correspond to these immense gains in vocabulary, but we cannot put a finger on them; my belief, which not all linguists share, is that on balance there is a great increase. If we were to try to converse with an Englishman of 1770, we should, I think, have to be much more selective about our choice of words than he would about his. The areas in which vocabulary was poorer, less sophisticated and cosmopolitan, two centuries ago are sufficiently indicated by the examples already given. The most general characteristic of the innovations from all sources is the extent to which they belong to the form-class noun. New objects and concepts lead the field; new qualities and activities are far behind, though both, as reflected in linguistic innovation, are far ahead of what has been known in earlier periods.

§ 58 Grammatical change, too, is often manifested over an extended period, with long stretches of dormancy; it does not always fit conveniently into periods of two hundred years, or even longer ones. A measure of arbitrariness in the placing of particular changes is the price we pay for trying to give some impression of what it would have been like to speak English at points of time not too widely separated from each other; and I think the price is worth paying. Generally speaking, we may look at grammatical changes under the heads: changes in the NP; changes in the VP; and changes in the relations between them; changes in relational elements lacking primary association with either the NP or the VP; changes in the structure and function of clauses, and in the modes of relating clauses. Not all these headings will be relevant at every period, nor will the same order of treatment always be the best; moreover, the distinctions are less clear-cut than might appear.

NOTE: By NP I mean here such structures as serve as subject, object or complement in simple sentences; by VP, such structures as serve as predicators.

The general principles governing the structure of NPs have been unchanged since late ME, and many of the complex rules for the ordering of elements go back to the first recorded evidence. One important feature, peculiar to English, is, however, of recent development, namely the phase in the evolution of the 'prop-word' *one* in which it can function directly after articles and the like. The term *prop-word* was coined by Sweet for those uses of *one* in which it replaces a noun – 'two green balloons and a red one': what is notable about English usage is not the avoidance of repetition, but the urge to fill the spot which is felt to exist after *red*. Such 'fillers' have come to contribute in several ways, at several periods, to the familiar shape of the English sentence. Prop uses of *one* have been developing for perhaps a thousand years, but it is only since about 1800 that the use of determiner directly followed by non-numeral *one* has come into use; Jespersen (1909, etc, II, 256–63, 503) quotes examples with post-modifiers – from Jane Austen *the one preferred*, and from Kipling *all the ones in fat grey envelopes*, where the plural form demonstrates the separation of the prop-use from the numeral use of *one*; post-modification is often by relative clause (Thackeray, *the one I like best to talk to*; plural more recent, Shaw, *the ones that concern me*). To such uses in former times corresponded *that* or *those* – forms which are still usable, though decidedly stiff. The extension of *one* at the expense of *that* seems to be continuing somewhat hesitantly before *of*-constructions and modified genitives (Jespersen quotes *the one of duty* and *the one formerly Guizot's*, which are both fairly unnatural to my ear). Jespersen also records (1913) from conversation a usage now extremely familiar in which, without modification, *the one* = *the right one: That's the one*; he had not found the expression in writing and it was not in *OED*, so we may conclude that it was very recent. On the other hand, *a one* is depreciatory; it is recorded from the mid-19c (in literary representations of colloquial speech). *This/that one, those ones*, of animates and inanimates, are both 19c; by 1913 Jespersen had not found examples of *these ones*, though by now it seems to me normal in a context of selection, less so in a context of identification. *What one* and *which one(s)* are well authenticated at the same period, but for Jespersen *one* after a possessive pronoun is a novelty ('even beginning to be used . . .'); his quotation from Anthony Hope, 'While he attacked his pile, she began on her one' now seems perfectly normal. After a noun genitive the usage is even more recently established. Jespersen writes:

> I once heard a lady say 'Her parasol is finer than *her sister's one*' [*one weakly stressed*]; but a friend whom I asked about this told me that to him the combination would sound much more natural in such a sentence as this: 'Her parasol is fine, but her sister's one is finer.'

Has usage changed, or was Jespersen's friend pompous in his generation? Probably both. Only in the Appendix is Jespersen able to exemplify *ones* without modification and followed by a relative clause ('ones that convey precisely the same meaning . . .'). The weak form of this *one*, /(ə(n/, written *'un*, was colloquial in earlier centuries, but is now only vulgar, belonging perhaps more to formulas and to parodies of vulgar speech, than to any productive usage. It can probably be interpreted as preserving the older form of *one* – the form current before initial /w/ developed in stressed uses.

These developments in the use of the prop-word are merely the logical extensions of usages begun centuries earlier, but they deserve attention as being to native speakers so normal as to be virtually unnoticeable, whereas on a comparative view they contribute to one of the most unusual features of English nominal usage.

One problem in NPs was solved by a pattern introduced in the 18c and now widespread. The ancient rules of patterning require the making of a choice between definite and indefinite and the use of not more than one item from the determiner system. This is simple when determiners like *a*, *the*, *some*, are chosen, since they offer a choice of definiteness; but the possessive pronouns do not. When we use an expression like *my friend*, the *my* carries definiteness with it. The solution is the dispersion of the strands of meaning into more elements in such structures as *a friend of mine*.

§ 59   In verbs, English is most remarkable for the grafting on to its historic two-tense inflectional verb-system of an elaborate network of modal, aspectual and clause-contrastive systems mainly signified by separate words (operators or auxiliaries) rather than by inflections. The evolution of this complex will attract our attention at every period. Among the modals, the overlapping uses of *shall and will* suggest that the relationship between them has been changing and will change further, but one cannot, over two centuries, identify clear-cut changes; nothing that was normal in 1770 would be unacceptable now, and vice versa. In a much more general spirit we can note (with Jespersen, 1909, etc., IV, 296-7) that *will* has been expanding at the expense of *shall*; the tendency has gone further in Scottish, Irish and American English than in English English, but it has not wholly added, or wholly removed, any single function. A rather clearer pattern will show up over a four-hundred-year time-span. *Would and should* are pulled hither and thither by their inescapable but asymmetrical relations with both *will* and *shall* and with each other. For all four modals many speakers (or rather, writers, who provide our evidence) have censored their usage in an attempt to conform to rules first set out by John Wallis in 1653. Although individuals do reflect certain trends involving these modals there is considerable evidence that the main outlines of present usage were established by the 16c.

Outside the modals we find developments tending to make the whole system of verb-contrasts more regular and symmetrical. Thus, as the simple tenses show formal active/passive contrasts (*The man builds the house; the house is built by the man*) so a deficiency is felt in the periphrastic (continuous, durative) forms which, at the beginning, lacked such contrast of form (*The man is building*, active; *The house is building*, passive). The sense of pattern was linked with a semantic need, for serious ambiguity could arise. The ambiguity could be avoided by omitting the aspectual component (Macaulay is said to have written 'while brave men were cut to pieces' to avoid *were being* in a structure where *were cutting* could only confuse); but speakers naturally came to prefer a single pattern for what the symmetry of the verb-system suggested was a single function. The tendency is also part of a growing use of periphrastic forms which can best be traced over a four-century period. No less a man than Dr Johnson took the lead in objecting to *is -ing* used passively, though he was unable to avoid such uses himself. In the closing years of the 18c the *being built* type makes an appearance; it faced a century of attack from purists who took the opposite view from Johnson (i.e. held that innovation is unpardonable even for the sake of clarity), but is now, of course, completely established. Perhaps the solution once seemed less inevitable than it does to us because it antedates the use of *is/was/were being* with a predicative (as in 'she was not being very successful'); this followed hard upon the other. The possibility of adding perfective to durative and passive in non-finite structures such as *having been made*... is also 19c. The process of 'levelling up' the passive duratives apparently still continues; Jespersen finds *has/had been being ---d* 'practically impossible' and some recent grammarians support him. To me these forms are quite normal, but, contrary to what might be supposed, they belong more to spoken than to written English. On the whole subject see Jespersen 1909, etc., IV, 210–14, 225; V, 57.

This topic naturally leads on to two others – further developments of the passive, and further developments of *-ing*, which we will look at in that order. Clauses with both indirect and direct objects have, during the NE period, developed alternative passivisations. In 1927, commenting on the limitation of these developments, Jespersen wrote:

> It would probably be difficult to find examples like these: he was *written* a letter, *sent* a note, *telegraphed* the number, or she was *got* a glass of wine, or *done* any injustice (op. cit., III, 309).

I currently find them all normal, except the third, which is not only grammatically improbable.

It is from the middle of the 19c that *be/is/was/were having* come into use ('whenever they happened to be having meals'). In 1931 Jespersen notes the durative form with *have to* (supplying the non-finite forms of *must*) as 'comparatively rare', and quotes only from 1927 and after ('he's having to sell his house'); to me this is a completely established usage. He quotes 'getting to be' from 1912 as 'rare', but it is now quite at home (op. cit., IV, 168–231). In the use of gerundial -*ing* or the *to*-infinitive after other verbs there is at present some divided usage; generally, the gerund has been gaining ground, and two centuries ago would not have been found in a number of structures where it is now required –*fell to eat(ing), with a view to prevent(ing)*; the trend goes back into earlier centuries.

The tendency to regularise verb-forms also appears in the use of *has*, etc. to form perfectives. The development as a whole might be regarded (like the article-system) as a European phenomenon, since the two major language-families underlying most present European languages, Germanic and Italic, originally lacked perfective operators, and the descendants of these languages developed them, typically by exploiting the full verb equivalent of *have* with transitives and of *be* with intransitives. English has long tended to generalise *have*. The only verb commonly using *be* until the early 19c is *become,* and even this has since generalised *have*. Other superficially similar structures with *be* usually involve a copulative clause with predicative (*their parties are grown tedious*) rather than a perfective (*their parties have grown bigger every year*). *Be done* (*with*), *be finished* (*with*), on the contrary, which might be interpreted as predicative or perfective, only arise in the 19c. *Get/got* in various senses has been expanding its grammatical functions for a long time, a recent stage being the development of *'ve got to, am obliged to*.

Perhaps it is the growing symmetry of the verb-contrasts which has given rise to another group of tendencies usually treated in isolation, but clearly related to one another. I would characterise them as involving a sense of the VP, even of the sequence subject + verb, as a unity within which certain choices have to be made; the forms indicative of these choices then tend to be placed in conventionally determined positions, even if in a particular instance this placing is contrary to the logical function of the item in question. Thus, in the placement of the perfective, we find a growing preference for *I should like to have (seen)* as against *I should have liked to (see)* (more recently, also, *I should have liked to have* [*seen*]); cf. also the 19c development *He has been known to* (*write*); with modals, *I shall hope to (see)* beside *I hope I shall (see)*; with negatives, *you mustn't (go),* which logically negates the *go*, and not the *must* (and very recently, *you hadn't better* [*go*] beside *you'd better not* (*go*), where *had* is a 'false expansion' of *'d = would*, and occurs from the 18c). On the distribution of indicators between S and V, note *he seemed as if . . .* (= *it seemed as if he . . .*); *he seemed certain, likely,* etc. . . . (= *it seemed certain, etc., that he would*); note that objections have been raised aginst *he ought to be punished* but they have not prevailed.

A type of structure now of great importance in the language (see Olsson, 1961) – *have a try, take a look,* etc. develops rapidly from about 1800; beside it we may mention somewhat similar patterns in which the verb is of fuller meaning – *laugh one's thanks,* recorded from about the same date, though one might expect it to be the antecedent, and *grope one's way,* starting a little later. Structures with what Jespersen (III, 383) calls 'quasi-predicatives', such as *fall flat, come in useful,* now very common, also appear from about 1800.

Areas of divided usage today often show many centuries of rivalry – as between *who* and *whom* in various functions, *wh-* and *that* relatives (though *that*, over several centuries, tends to abandon non-restrictive clauses, in which it is now very rare), and *dare/need* as operator and full verbs. Though, with more sophisticated means of quantification than we possess, it might be possible to show gains or losses, it is not the case that any usage now possible was not so in 1770, or even 1570, in these areas. The circumstances which now make for the slackening of concord between S and V (cf. Strang, 1966) are of equal, and often greater, antiquity.

Finally, we must record the growing regularisation of order within the clause. The unmarked order of elements, the order followed unless there is reason to depart from it, is SVO. The evolution of this pattern (making allowance for the fact that literary material may not be wholly representative) is clearly shown by figures for relevant clauses from Jespersen. In an OE poetic text it occurs in 16% of clauses, but in later prose in 40%; the percentage grows through the ME and ENE. periods, reaching 93% in Shakespeare's prose, and 86% in his poetry. The gap between prose and verse persists, and in the remaining centuries the figures for prose climb steadily the small remaining distance, reaching 99% in Shaw. Jespersen comments:

> English shows more regularity and less caprice in this respect than most or probably all cognate languages, without, however, attaining the rigidity found in Chinese, where the percentage in question would be 100 (or very near it) (VII, 59–61).

§ 60 For periods not otherwise illustrated by transcribed passages, each chapter will conclude with a transcribed annotated passage written within a decade of the earliest date it deals with.

The good old monk was within six paces of us, as the idea of him
/ðə guːd oːld mʌŋk wəz wɪðɪn sɪks peːsɪz əv əs əz ði: aɪdɪər əv ɪm/
crossed my mind,   and was advancing towards us a little out of the
/krɔːst mɪ maɪn(d), ən wəzədvaːnsɪn tɔːdz   əs a lɪdl aʊt əv ðə/
line, as if uncertain whether he should break in upon us or no. He
/laɪn, əz ɪf ʌnsɜːtn weðər iː ʃəd   breːk ɪn əpɒn əs ə noː iː/
stopped, however, as soon as he came up to us, with a world of
/stɒpt   aʊɛvər   əz suːn əz iː keːm ʌp tʊ əs wɪð ə wɜːld əv/
frankness: and having a horn snuff-box in his hand he presented it
/fræŋknɪs ənd ævɪn   ə hɔːn snʌfbɒks ɪn ɪz ænd iː prɪzɛntɪd ɪt/
open to me. 'You shall taste mine,' said I, pulling out my box
/oːpn tə mi: ju: ʃəl teːs(t) maɪn sɛd aɪ pʊlɪn   aʊt mɪ bɒks/
(which was a small tortoise one), and putting it into his hand. 'Tis
/wɪtʃ wəz ə smɔːl tɔːtəs ən   ən pʊtɪn ɪt ɪntʊ ɪz ænd tɪz/
most excellent,' said the monk. 'Then do me the favour,' I replied,
/moːst ɛksələnt sɛd ðə mʌŋk ðɛn   du: mi: ðə feːvər   aɪ rɪplaɪd/
'to accept of the box and all; and when you take a pinch out of it,
/tʊ əksɛp əv ðe bɒks ən ɔːl ən wɛn ju: teːk ə pɪntʃ aʊt əv ɪt/
sometimes recollect it was the peace-offering of a man who once
/sʌmtaɪmz rɛkəlɛk ɪt wəz ðə pi:s ɒfrɪn   əv ə mæn u: wʌns/
used you unkindly, but not from his heart.'
/ju:zd jʊ   ʌŋkaɪndlɪ bət nɒt frəm ɪz ha:t/

Sterne, *Sentimental Journey*, 1768, The Snuff-Box.

The differences from modern usage here are very slight. Judgement of where /h/ is strong enough to be pronounced is subjective. The /uː/ of *good* would be old-fashioned, but the passage, after all, was written at the close of Sterne's life. An old man at this date might have had a trace of post-vocalic /r/. The sound transcribed /ŋ/ in medial position would at this date be, not a phoneme, but a conditioned variant of /n/; phonetically /ʌ/ would be more high and back than now. A pronunciation roughly corresponding to RP has been assumed, regardless of whether Sterne actually used such a variety.

Grammatically we note aphetic *tis*, later expanded to more 'correct' *it is*, and newly shortened, on the analogy of other weak pronoun + verb sequences, to *it's* (cf. *I'm*, *he's*). *Favour* is constructed with *to* + inf.

rather than with *of* + *-ing*: the rivalry between these constructions has lasted for several centuries, with a growing tendency for *of* + *-ing* to extend its range. *Accept* is constructed with *of*; such constructions were frequent in the 17c and 18c but the dominant tendency has been preference for the simple form. For a similar conflict actually in progress cf. the discussion of *regard*, § 11, and for the 18c developments cf. Strang (1967).

Lexically, there is little to surprise us except the use of *tortoise* = *tortoiseshell* (in *OED* from 1654 to 1902). A subtler aspect of lexical change is exemplified by *horn snuffbox*, since, though the term is perfectly familiar, we have far less frequent occasion to refer to the object than did 18c speakers. But since the main lexical differences in Period I are additions to the repertoire we find less to comment on in the lexis of an 18c writer than he would in ours.

CHAPTER II

1770 – 1570

§ 61 In 1770 English was spoken by virtually the whole population of England, with further communities in Lowland Scotland, Wales, Ireland, North America, the West Indies and India. When we have moved back as far as 1570 we find it spoken to the same extent in the British Isles, but by a population of about four and a half million, and lacking all overseas branches. The geographical and political differences in the structure of the speech-community are at least as important as the change in size, for in 1570 English is essentially the language of a single community in a single environment. Throughout these two centuries oral communication, and therefore exposure to the speech of others, is limited to pedestrian (and sail-power) range, i.e., on land, to journeys made on foot or by horse transport; and of course this will remain true for the rest of our history, though at no other period shall we find travel, despite these restricted means, so powerful an element in linguistic history.

These two centuries (henceforth to be referred to as II), though they were technologically static by comparison with I, witnessed major social changes which had a great bearing on the language. From the opening years of the 17c the language was planted on the North American Continent, and very shortly afterwards in the West Indies. Thus the most important bifurcation of the community, the establishment of what became the two largest groups of speakers, characterised by the two main varieties of standard, falls within II. In both communities the closing years of the period saw the beginning of another profoundly influential change. In 1570 only London, and to a very limited extent Oxford and Cambridge, Bristol, Edinburgh and the other Scottish University cities, had attracted a substantial community of long-term residents, families and founders of families, of mixed local origins, that is, of people for whom the acquisition and use of language within the social group meant something other than fitting into relatively uniform speech-ways passed from generation to generation throughout the whole relevant group. Around 1570 the population of London was about 200,000, i.e.

about one in twenty Englishmen lived there, and many more must have had to do business with its citizens; but there is no reason to think that urbanisation was a significant factor in language-development anywhere else. Our knowledge of urban speech-varieties and their origins is very limited, but it does seem to be a usual consequence of the mixing in an urban community that social stratification develops as geographical affiliations are blurred. It is, after all, natural for speakers exposed to different types of speech to wonder about the meaning of the differences, and for English speakers, at least, to try to correlate these differences with a scale of correctness or social prestige. Such an attempt is always in some measure self-fulfilling – that is to say, the view that a usage is 'the best' naturally leads to its adoption by those who want their speech to be 'the best'. Thus a consequence of urbanisation is subordination of the old local structuring of language-varieties to a new social structuring, until eventually the whole fabric of 'dialects' is altered. In its maturity this process leads to so much inter-variety borrowing that the course of events has to be explained in terms quite different from those appropriate to the pre-urban phase. It is broadly true that urbanisation, with all its consequences, was minimal in the speech exported to North America, because the London element among the earliest emigrants was not particularly strong, but at the end of II urbanisation had reached an advanced stage in the language exported to Australia, both because by then it had proceeded much further in the whole country, and because there was a strong London element among the early emigrants. By 1770 all regions of the country had witnessed some measure of urban concentration; the movements of population at the Industrial Revolution brought about a situation in which the norm for speakers was experience of a geographically mixed rather than an unmixed local community. Of course the inherited character of local dialects was still extremely marked, and had a special emotional status, but it was no longer the only kind of speech experienced by the majority of speakers.

Nevertheless, to understand the ways in which American and British English have diverged we should bear in mind a characteristic of English at the beginning of II which will be fully documented in following pages, namely, its tolerance of diversity. If the source-language had been more uniform the two varieties might not differ so markedly today. We can readily find usages in which American English is more conservative than British English, and we can readily find counter-examples. But we can find many other points on which both, though divergent, go back to perfectly standard late Elizabethan or early Jacobean precedents. A. H. Marckwardt writes:

> The earliest English colonists in the New World were speaking Elizabethan English . . . when they came to America – not the measurably different English of Dryden, Defoe, and Bunyan. . . . Since the earliest American settlers employed Elizabethan English, it is the highly variable and complex character of that medium that provides us with an explanation of the beginning of the divergences in the two great streams of our language (1958, 10–11, 20).

By the end of the period the feeling that there ought to be one correct usage, no more, no less, on every point, was highly articulate, though its effects were fully felt only in I; at the beginning of the period we hardly even meet the feeling.

The increase of population within the branches of the speech-community inevitably brought changes in its wake. It is also of some importance that the increase in population did not proceed steadily; growth was relatively slow until the 18c and very fast from the time of the Industrial Revolution (as, indeed, it continued to be throughout the 19c). Our own experience is of an age-structure in which the old preponderate, but during II the growth in population gave preponderance to the young; we cannot trace exact linguistic consequences of this difference, but we can recognise in it a situation which will increase the momentum with which usages typical of the young establish themselves. And II, like the rest of the NE period, is characterised by a succession of usages rather than the change-by-drift typical of a non-urbanised population of more steady size.

Throughout II literacy was moderately widespread, and something which for linguistic history might almost count as vicarious literacy operated throughout the country, namely, the preaching of educated clerics. There is a danger of thinking of the spread of literacy as following a steady progression, because that has been the pattern since 1870, i.e. in all living memories. While exact figures are unobtainable, it is implied in many sources – book-sales, libraries, and literary references, etc. – that the proportion of literates from 1600 to the Industrial Revolution was far higher than in the early 19c; a reasonable guess might be that the number of literates remained about steady while the population soared. It was the Industrial Revolution which reduced the chances of the poor, especially the urban poor, of learning to read and write. In the early 17c literacy extends pretty far down the social scale, permeating the greater part of the social fabric with the complex kind of relationship between spoken and written English familiar today.

§ 62 By 1770 English had a standard written form almost as invariable as today's. In printed words we should notice a few differences of spelling – for instance, *horrour, terrour, musick, physick, phantasy.* We should observe that alternatives which now distinguish British from American (e.g., *honour/honor, centre/center*), if they existed at all, would not have this function (which largely dates from Webster's 1828 recommendations). A few distinctions now systematic would not, or not regularly, be found (for instance, *flower/flour,* originally the same word, had been distinguished by Cruden in 1738, but the distinction was not recognised by Johnson in 1755, or in the editions of his dictionary which followed up to his death in 1784; *mettle/metal,* also originally the same, were distinguished by Johnson, but not by many other 18c writers). The differences would really be quite trivial. We should, however, be astonished at the gulf between the spelling practices in print and those in manuscript material. The conception of the spelling mistake is largely an invention of period I; before that, wide divergences were customary in the private papers of even highly educated individuals, and the present widespread assumption that handwriting should follow the spelling conventions of printed matter did not hold. Period II is therefore much richer in spelling indications of pronunciation and its changes, though the models for spelling were already so diversified that the evidence must be interpreted with great circumspection.

When we reach as far back as 1570 even the printed word lacks the uniformity we now associate with it. During the early part of II capitalisation practices vary; some use capitals for most or all nouns and to start various syntactic units, not merely, as now, to mark sentence-onset and proper names. Individual words may have variants where now they have none, or be spelt on a different principle, or both. The variations immediately depend on factors in the printer's craft, and only very indirectly on pronunciation; they are slight and often tricky hints to the linguistic historian. Working back from 1770 to 1570 we must distinguish three phases. First the great 18c dictionaries established a level of uniformity approaching our own. But we must not exaggerate our own uniformity, nor, *a fortiori,* that of the 18c. Actually, Johnson proclaims his preference for tradition over consistency (naturally, tradition was not wholly fixed or consistent), and Simeon Potter comments:

> The great one-man Dictionary was not, in fact, entirely free from inconsistencies: *moveable* but *immovable, downhil* but *uphill, distil* but *instill, install* but *reinstal, sliness* but *slyly, conceit* and *deceit* but *receipt, deign* but

disdain, anteriour and *interiour* but *exterior* and *posterior.* Some of these Johnsonian inconsistencies remain as possible alternatives to this day (1950, 72).

Next the 17c witnessed a progressive tendency for printers to reduce *ad hoc* decision-making, each individual or house spelling a given word the same way whenever it occurred, and moving towards uniformity by virtue of a preference for the norms of the early editions of the Authorised Version of the Bible. Then, in the 16c, lacking any sense that a uniform spelling might be desirable:

> Elizabethan compositors vary the forms of words in order to *justify* their lines of type, that is, to make the lines fit in neatly on the page with straight margins. Working with more clumsy types they had less scope than their modern successors. . . . For mechanical reasons, therefore, the Elizabethans printed *the, that,* or *yᵉ, yᵗ: -lesse, -nesse,* or *-les, -nes; manie* or *many*; and so on (Potter, 1950, 71).

There are differences in the functions and distributions of letter-symbols; for example, *i, u,* would be used medially for /ɪ/ or /dʒ/, /ʊ/ or /v/, and *j, v,* initially for the same pairs of sounds: *s* would vary in form according to its position in the word. But the most important difference is one of attitude – the sense that spellings were to be chosen rather than (merely) learnt. Such a situation is inherently unstable; if you choose, you are bound to think about the principles on which you should select, and sooner or later what is felt to be best will become the rule. But while it lasted the attitude gave rise to ideas and practices which have left their mark to this day. Two obvious principles to govern an orthography are the so-called phonetic (i.e. devising spellings to represent the sounds used), and the etymological (i.e. devising spellings designed to reveal what is known or imagined about the so-called origin of a word). It is not always realised (since phonetics is commonly said to be a 19c science) that II was a period of extensive, and often quite sophisticated, phonetic study. Phonetic, or partially phonetic, spellings were proposed, but the British public was no more responsive to the subject then than now. Though we cannot trace the influence of this movement on the subsequent history of the language (except possibly in the origin of such forms as *spelt, learnt,* etc. beside *spelled, learned*), it does have an interesting consequence in Milton's attempt to design, and impose on his printer, a 'sound-suggestive' spelling for *Paradise Lost* (cf. Darbyshire, 1931).

Of course, the vacuum left by the phonetic principle was not entirely filled by the etymological one. Most spellings were determined by factors of tradition and chance. But the etymological principle was extremely influential, for the public has always been willing to heed stories, true or false, about etymology. For instance, *perfit/parfit, verdit, vittles*, all from French, were remodelled according to their ultimate Latin source as *perfect* (contrast the personal name *Parfitt*), *verdict*, and *victuals*; subsequently, it would be hard to say exactly when, the pronunciation of the first was brought into line; similarly, *avantage, aventure*, were turned into *advantage, adventure*; *dette* and *doute* were given a *b* as if from Latin, but this never came to be pronounced. Even the Germanic word *iland* (OE *iegland*) was given an *s* as if from early French *isle*. The *c* unhistorically introduced into *scissors* and *scythe* (as if from L *scindere*) has affected one French-borrowed and one native word. One of the most preposterous changes is the re-spelling of *rime* with Greek *rhy-* to match *rhythm*. Normally, introduction of *h* is due to rather different causes, since in medieval Latin it had a long tradition of 'empty' use after *t, c*. It became established in, for example, *Thames*, where it has not affected pronunciation, in *Anthony*, where it occasionally does, and in *author*, where it has taken over completely. One of the rare instances of evidence for dating the spelling pronunciation occurs when the word *Gothish* (= *Gothic*) is punned with *goatish* in the late 17c; the word was rare, and evidently still kept the old pronunciation. This has no bearing on other words, since as we have seen, they follow individual paths in this matter. After *c* an *h* was introduced in *anchor*, perhaps partly because of association with Greek *anchorite*. Not all such innovations have lasted; *p* unhistorically introduced in *conceipt, deceipt* has been removed, though it persists in *receipt*.

Tradition is closely linked with etymology, especially when knowledge of etymology is in as primitive a condition as it was in period II (cf. the etymology of *Jade* [*sensu* 'a broken down horse'] in the *Gazophylacium Anglicanum*, 1689, 'from the AS *eode*, he went, (i.e.) he went once, but can go no more'); and analogy is closely linked with both. The native word *coud* was altered to *could* on the model of *should, would* (in consequence, any of them might be written with an apostrophe in place of the *l*, which was not normally pronounced). The page generally would be liberally spotted with apostrophes marking real or imagined omissions; the plural of *genius* may be written *genius's*, and *has* may appear as *ha's* as if for **haves*. Possessive pronouns often take the form *her's, our's* etc., (actually required in Lowth's grammar, 1762). On the other hand, certain now obligatory apostrophes might not appear. For the genitive singular of nouns -'*s* became fairly regular by the late 17c, and in the genitive plural -*s*' not till the late 18c. This creates the curious situation that for almost all nouns the two-term system of contrast operative in speech (unmarked form without ending, form marked for case or number with sibilant ending), corresponds to a four-term system in writing.

We should also observe a different expectation about what the relationship between spoken and written should be. For verbs in the 3sg present we have abundant evidence during the 17c that although the old ending -*(e)th* remained common in writing, it was normally (in an age when reading aloud was important) read as -*(e)s*; cf. § 89.

English also looked different on the page, because the modern system of punctuation had not fully evolved. Though it has been used with very different styles, heavy and light, in recent centuries, that system in essentials took shape in the 17c, the latest recruit to it being the comma. England in this followed the European practice set up by Aldus Manutius in the 16c.

§ 63 Meanwhile, spoken standard in notable respects shares the character already examined in period I. London remains a uniquely important centre; contempt for the speech and all other characteristics of rustic and provincial persons has probably never been more forcefully expressed than in Restoration drama. Much has been made of the fact that at the court of Elizabeth, Raleigh spoke with a Devon accent; rather more needs to be made of the fact that such a practice called for comment. As we have seen (§ 61), speech in the metropolis tended to polarise socially, and this always leads to instability. As in period I, inter-variety influence is at the very least as important as linear development within a variety.

It is an oversimplification, but a helpful one, to speak of *a* sound-system at any period. From our analysis so far it emerges that around 1770 standard English must have had a sound-system something like this:

Vowels (a) Long /iː/ (as in PE)
  /eː/ (corresponding to PE /eɪ/)   eː
  /uː/ (as in PE)   not yet
  /oː/ (> /oʊ/>/eʊ/)   oː diphthong
  /ɔː/ (as in PE)
  /ɑː/ (as in PE)

  (b) Diphthongs, as in PE, save for the two exceptions already noted.
  (c) Short, as in PE, but with some movement in the phonetic realisation of /ʊ/.

110

The consonant system was as now in its general structure, consisting of some twenty-five items; as we have seen, the distribution of /h/ and /ŋ/ was phonemic only in stressed syllables, a kind of function not found for consonants in PE; the /w/ :/ʍ/ contrast was less than general, and probably less widespread among standard speakers than today.

§ 64   The most radical changes are those affecting the shape of the system. Among the vowels, the development of /a:/ is most striking. At the beginning of II, uniquely in its history, English had no long vowel in this position; other contrasts were so spaced that we might have guessed the gap would be filled, and so it was, partly as a result of conditioned change, partly by borrowing from an eastern vulgar dialect, probably Cockney. The typical pattern of a borrowed phoneme still shows in the PE distribution – words of the same origin are divided between two different developments, since the adoption has taken place somewhat inconsistently. What happened was that an ME diphthong /aʊ/ (the same sound as in PE *house*, but occurring in words which now have /a:/ or /ɔ:/), developed in some dialects to /ɒʊ/, perhaps especially before certain sounds. Then, at about the beginning of II, the diphthong, in either form, began to monophthongise. In certain dialects this produced /a:/, but in standard, /ɔ:/. In the late 17c, standard was invaded by /a:/ forms. The two vowels remained in competition, and many words had alternative forms (for instance, *sauce, saucy, sausage* have /a:/ variants), but in recent English spelling has taken a hand, so that the outcome has been /a:/ in such words as *dance, half, calm,* and /ɔ:/ in such words as *fault, cause, author*; but with exceptions either way (*aunt, talk, walk* [with loss of *l* cf. § 70]) and some divided usage (*launch*) (cf. Dobson, II, 782–94). The other source of this phoneme is occasional lengthening of /a/ in certain types of syllables, in such words as *blast, casket, gasp, past, path*; here, of course, many dialects do not show the lengthening which has dominated in standard. *Father* develops by this lengthening; its older long form would have given /feɪðə(r)/, which, of course, occurs in some dialects. It seems fairly certain that the /a:/-phoneme was established in standard before a third source contributed to it – the /a:/ arising by loss of post-vocalic *r* in such words as *harm, barge* (see below). In general we may say that by the end of II, but as a result of fairly recent developments, English had an /a:/-phoneme carrying approximately its present load. One curious footnote is that early NE loans of words in foreign /a:/ were normally assimilated to English /ɔ:/ at the stage when standard lacked /a:/, as in the second syllable of *Punjab, Bengal*; but in recent years more direct experience of the people and usages of the Indian sub-continent has tended to establish an /ɑ:/ form in these words.

While the rise of /ɑ:/ filled a gap in the system, the next development is in a sense anomalous, since uniquely in the history it introduces a sound not integrated into the system, a sound involving contrasts which on a world-wide scale are extremely rare. All this goes to make the rise of /ʌ/ one of the most unaccountable things that has happened in the history of English. The vowel we now have in *put, soot*, has always had a place in English (not, of course, always in the same words). At about the beginning of II this vowel began to lose its rounding, except where it was protected by certain labial environments (hence, *put* but *cut*); this is a kind of negative conditioned change – normal conditioned change happens *if*, negative conditioned change happens *unless*. Though foreign observers commented on the new pronunciation in the late 16c, English writers only gradually admit its existence in correct speech in the 17c. We have seen that the sound has been wandering during our own life-time, and is still highly variable from speaker to speaker (Gimson, 1962, 102–4); we may assume that the initial stage of the change was a simple unrounding in the original high–mid back position, and that unrestrained by the normal symmetries and tensions of the system, the vowel has been drifting downwards and forwards ever since.

Closely related was the unrounding of the first element in /ʊɪ/, by which this diphthong fell together with /əɪ/, the source of PE /aɪ/ (cf. § 65). This gave at first /əɪ/ for the sound spelt *oi* in such words as *purloin, boil, toil, oil, join, loin*, which accordingly rhyme with the forms under-lying PE *line, fine*, and share with them the development to /aɪ/. But side by side with this set of forms was a rival set in which the sound was /ɒɪ/, and this, being reinforced by the spelling, has come to prevail. /ɒɪ/ existed throughout in such words as *boy, void*, so the structure of the system has been unaffected by these developments.

The third major change affects both vowels and consonants, and gives rise to a new series of diphthongs. By it /r/ reached its present restricted distribution, one of the exotic characteristics of RP phonology in comparison with other varieties of English or *vis-à-vis* the world spectrum of phonological patterns. In post-vocalic position, finally or precon-sonantally, /r/ was weakened in articulation in the 17c and reduced to a vocalic element early in the 18c. In some cases the change produced new members for existing phonemes, as when the /ar/ of *card* becomes /ɑ:/, or the /ɒr/ of *horse* /ɔ:/. In others the system was affected. Three sequences /ɪr/, /ɛr/, /ʌr/ yielded the long vowel /ɜ:/, which was new, but which contrasted with its neighbours in familiar ways; hence, the PE vowel in *earl, turn, first*. The biggest shock to the system comes from the loss of /r/ after long vowels and diphthongs; it cannot there cause lengthening, but it is kept distinct by developing to /ə/, and creating the series of centring diphthongs now familiar in such words as *mare,* *bear, pair* (from earlier /ɛ:/), *board, more, court, floor* (from earlier /o:/ and with a recent tendency for /ɔə/ to >/ɔ:/). In all these, the habitual tendency of /r/ to lower a preceding vowel is evident. The /ʊə/ diphthong of *poor, moor*, though weakly represented (cf. §34), may be given a place in the 1770 system. The diphthongs /aɪ/, /aʊ/ develop, by loss of /r/, to the triphthongs /aɪə/, /aʊə/, which again do not readily fit the system and have not proved very stable (cf. §34).

Meanwhile, two old de-centring diphthongs had been lost, though the system was adapted to their presence, and their places were soon re-filled. The present homophony between such words as *ail/ale, hail/hale*, originated in the early 17c, when an earlier diphthong (in the words now spelt with *ai*) levelled, and fell together with the antecedent, probably then /ɛ:/, of PE /eɪ/. The exact quality of the underlying diphthong is disputed, but its first element must have been front for it to yield a long vowel which could be identified with /ɛ:/. A similar coalescence has affected the corresponding back diphthong and long vowel, resulting in the homophony of *slow/sloe, grown/groan*. In neither case is PE spelling a safe guide to the underlying vocalisation, since *waist, gait, mail*, originally had long vowels but have been re-spelt to distinguish them from their homophones (actually, the last two are by origin the same word as *gate, male*), and *felloe, throe*, were diphthongal and have again been orthographically distinguished from their homophones.

§ 65 Other changes affected the phonetic realisation of existing vowel phonemes. We have already had occasion to mention that what by the end of II took the form /aɪ/, /aʊ/, had arisen, by increasing the movement between first and second elements of the diphthongs, from earlier /əɪ/, /əʊ/ (cf. §64): the effect was to strengthen the diphthongal character of these sounds, keeping them well away from neighbouring long vowels, and at the same time to distance them from /ʌɪ/, /ɔɪ/. The long vowel /e:/ in such words as *name, hate*, had arisen by raising and tensing of /ɛ:/, earlier /æ:/; and this change restored front–back symmetry with /o:/ in such words as *home, tone*, raised from /ɔ:/ by about 1600. The low short vowel, which had always had considerable freedom of front–back movement, took its present value /æ/ in some standard speakers by 1600, though probably with older /a/ as a variant for a longish time. Movement in this vowel is related to movement in the antecedent of PE /ɒ/, which entered period II with a rather higher value than it now has, and tended to lower. In some speakers this brought the two vowels into conflict, since their /ɒ/ lowered as far as [a]. During the 17c there is some confusion between the two, but generally [a] was felt as a particular way of saying /ɒ/, and by the end of the century it was satirised as an affectation (as it still is in *By Gad*!). As a result of this clash a few originally /ɒ/ words are now standardised in /a/, such as *strap*, *sprat*, (note that the alternative *strop* has achieved independent existence as a separate word).

The /ju/ now found in such words as *neuter*, *beauty*, developed in the 17c by the related processes of stress-shift and raising of the first element, earlier /ɛʊ/. As usual, old and new forms coexisted for about half a century, but by about 1670 the new forms may be considered fully accepted.

§ 66 One of the most puzzling developments requires a paragraph to itself. Generally (cf. §101), the modern spelling *ee* corresponds to /iː/ in 1570, and *ea* to /eː/, in those words where both now have /iː/. But a few words with *ea* spelling, *break*, *great*, *steak*, are out of line, having /eɪ/. Having learnt to look for the lowering effect of following *r*, we might guess (correctly) that *rear*, *gear*, *shear* are of same origin as the /iː/ type, and *bear*, *pear*, *wear* as the /eɪ/ type. In fact, all these words had a similar origin, and differed according to dialect for centuries before period II, in some dialects sharing the development of the words now spelt *ee*, in others making an extra phonemic contrast by having a lower long vowel /ɛː/ or /æː/. Both kinds of dialect were spoken in, or very close to, London, and both have contributed to standard usage. It would seem that the system of long front vowels was too congested when the distinction was made, and generally the dominant system has been that in which no distinction was present. Even in dialects which made it, it has been removed, since the lowered vowel took the form /æː/, and has been overtaken by the antecedent of /eɪ/. Hence the identity of the *break*-type with *name*, *hate*, while most words of this origin have fallen together with *ee* words. The loss of the additional point of phonemic contrast antedates II, but rival forms underlying the /eɪ/ type and the /iː/ type coexisted for a long time before the present distribution was settled (and the distribution still varies in dialects). Pope's rhymes of *tea* with *away*, *obey*, are well known; in the same century the /eː/ (now /eɪ/) form occurred in such words as *conceive, receive, deceive, obscene, feature, supreme, replete*, all with PE /i:/; by the end of the 18c such forms were regarded as Irishisms.

§ 67 The long vowel /ɔ:/ entered II with an abnormally light functional load, but by the end of the period was established in its present distribution. We have already had occasion to refer to it in connection with the rise of /ɑ:/ (cf. § 64). Its modern sources are so complex that they should all be referred to in one place. In the late 16c, as we have seen, one development of /aʊ/ was to /ɔ:/ (cf. § 64); hence, *ball, law, talk*. In certain environments the new sound tended to shorten (PE *want, Waller, laurel, Morris = Maurice*); most words now have a spelling-pronunciation, but some vary, and any of the following may be long or short in the latter part of II: *assault, Baltic, psalter, also, walnut, walrus, false, salt*. We have also seen that in the 17c many words such as *balm, calm, calf*, had /ɔ:/ as well as /ɑ:/ forms. A rather important lost variant is /ʃɔ:l/ for *shall*; in II /ʃal/ was the weak form only, but as has often happened in the history of words with strong–weak forms, we have made a new strong form by stressing the old weak form (whence PE /ʃæl/), re-reduced this to produce a new weak form (PE /ʃəl, ʃl/), and wholly abandoned the old strong (and therefore less common) form. /aʊ/ also became /ɔ:/ in such words as *slaughter* and *fraught* (for the alternative development in /ɑ:/, cf. *laugh*, where the spelling correctly suggests identical origin). In this environment the sound further became identical with ME /oʊ/ in such words as *bought, brought, thought*: these had /ɔ:/ by the beginning of II (it then shortened in *cough*). Some spelling-switches have resulted here too – *daughter* should have *o* and *fought* should have *a*; the idea that these spellings were interchangeable must have been reinforced by the fact that such pairs as *aught/ought, naught* (cf. *naughty*)/*nought*, genuinely had doublet-forms for centuries before the coalescence of the two diphthongs.

By the mid-18c the phoneme had received further reinforcements as the result of loss of post-vocalic *r* in words like *George, horse*. At, or perhaps before, that period, more instances arose by lengthening of /ɒ/ in certain situations, in words such as *off, soft, cloth, moth, frost, lost*. Finally, after /w/ an /a/ or /ɑ:/ rounds to /ɒ/ or /ɔ:/, a change accepted gradually by standard speakers. Some had the rounding by 1500; Shakespeare still rhymes *watch:match, war:afar*, and some speakers had not adopted the new sound over a century later. It seems never to have occurred in such sequences as we have in *wax, wag, swagger*.

§ 68 There are changes of quantity, but their consequences in recent English are so confused that we must believe conflicting analogies have been at work. The short vowels in *good, foot, stood, soot, book, took,* etc., arose during II; all seem to have co-existed with long variants (as they still do in certain dialects), with the result that they were not sufficiently established in standard when /ʊ/ unrounded to take part in that unrounding, though *blood, Monday,* etc., have it, and outside RP it can be found in *foot, soot.* On the other hand, in similar environments, the long form has come to prevail in *brood, food, mood, rood, root.* There was occasional lengthening of the corresponding short vowel in such words as *above, love,* but the short vowel has prevailed.

There is a good deal of shortening in unstressed syllables – in this, and at all earlier periods. Indeed, so much had happened before that some of this late shortening is only possible because of analogical re-lengthenings. *Otherwise* is recorded with /-wɪz/ in the 18c, but that form has been obliterated in favour of one re-modelled on the independent word *wise.* /bɪ/ in *because, beside,* and /mɪ/ in *milord,* must similarly originate in II, though in isolation the old weak forms of *by, my,* have generally been replaced by re-formations in /aɪ/. In other cases there was at the beginning of II alternation of long and short forms as a result of the stronger secondary stress English then possessed. Thus, -*ly* was both /lɪ/ and /laɪ/ till about 1700; for similar reasons shortening in -*hood*, -*lock* (*wedlock*) and in the borrowed suffixes -*ous*, -*our* was late.

At the beginning of II *have* had alternative forms – strong, with a long vowel (the antecedent of PE /eɪ/), and weak, with a short vowel (/a/ or /æ/). Subsequent English has specialised the strong type in the derived verb *behave,* the weak one in the simple verb *have.* A number of our present auxiliary or operator verbs have had a similar history in relation to long and short, strong and weak, forms (cf. § 67). The shortening which accounts for *says, said* (earlier also *saith*), as against *say,* must also date from the early part of II.

§ 69 The consonant-system acquired an additional point of contrast. The story must begin earlier, with a change that did not affect the structure of the system. In the closing years of the 16c there arose by assimilation of earlier /tj, sj/ the sound /ʃ/ in such words as *sugar, sure, secretion, perdition, mission, ocean, special, patience, vicious.* Shakespeare scans such endings as -*tion* with one or two syllables, but the disyllabic form must by then have been pretty old-fashioned. When this change (which merely increased the functional load of an existing phoneme) was fully established, it was followed in the 17c by assimilation to /ʒ/ of the corresponding voiced sequences, e.g., in *vision, collision, disclosure, measure, usual.* This phoneme had never before existed in the language, though the system was in a sense designed to accommodate it, because correlation of voiced–voiceless pairs of consonants was so widespread. At first, because of the circumstances of its origin, it was confined to medial position, but subsequently it has extended to final position in loanwords such as *rouge* (1753, i.e., within II), *beige, garage*: it has never invaded initial position, and its functional load remains abnormally light.

Comparable assimilations produced /tʃ/ from /tj/ in *question, digestion, righteous,* probably in the 17c, and /dʒ/ from /dj/ in the 18c in, for example, *immediately, grandeur, gradual.* Purists have never liked this development, and their influence has to some extent removed it, especially from the voiced sequences. In neither case was the structure of the system affected.

No more than a reminder is needed that at this period the peculiar distribution of PE /r/ arose (cf. § 64). It is a consequence of the 18c losses that linking-*r* can develop, and on linking-*r* in turn depends intrusive *r*: this is first remarked on as a solecism of vulgar speech in 1787.

§ 70 In considering the remaining assortment of consonantal changes we cannot do better than remind ourselves of Wyld's dictum already quoted (cf. § 50); but there are more general trends. Loss of *l* in such words as *talk, walk, balm, calm, Holborn,* belongs here; it went at the same time from *Talbot, Malvern, Colman, malt, salt,* where it has been extensively restored. It did not usually go before *d*, but it was lost in weak forms, *would, should* (consequently, as their strong forms had it, analogically *could* was given an *l* too, sometimes even in pronunciation). The sense that *l*-less forms were weaker partners of words that in a fuller or more correct form had *l* was reinforced by the presence of unhistorical *l* in the spelling of some of them (cf. § 50). A rather different factor explains *l* introduced finally in the place-name *Bristol* (OE *bricg-stow,* 'bridge place'); *l* here was spelt in the 17c but in standard not pronounced even in the 18c. Post-vocalic *l* as a syllable-closer was (and is) characteristic of the local dialect, and – as is likely enough in the case of a major port – the local form of the name seems to have invaded standard at about the end of II.

A History of English

A common dialectal transition, from /t/ to /r/ intervocalically, has found its way into standard in a single word during II, yielding everyday *porridge*, beside older *pottage*, which remains familiar in consequence of its use in the Bible.

Modern spelling rightly suggests that /k/ and /g/ were formerly present before /n/ in such words as *know, gnaw*. The loss took place in the 17c; in 1679 Cooper records that *nave/knave, night/knight, need/knead, not/knot*, are homophones and it is likely that the change was complete some forty years earlier. At about the same time several observers noted assimilation in the place of articulation in the sequences *gl, kl*, giving initial /dl/ in *glory*, /tl/ in *clean*; but this, though it has survived in dialect, has not prevailed in standard. Also at this time *g* and *k* were palatalised before front vowels; in 1653 Wallis records *cyan, gyet, begyin*, for *can, get, begin*; as we have noted (§ 50) this persisted until very recently, and can still be heard, especially from the pulpit.

Among initial clusters, *wr* also indicates a sound once present, now lost. The process seems to have started early in the 17c with reduction of the group to a single component, lip-rounded *r*, which then fell together with originally simple *r* – the result being in most speakers a lingual fricative, but in some a labial scarcely distinct from [w]. The labial type was regarded as an affectation in the 19c and later as childish.

The closing decades of the period also saw a tendency to drop /j/ before /uː/. After /r/ usage varied in the 1760s, but the /j/ has now completely vanished (*rude, crude, crew, fruit*, etc.); elsewhere the change was partial, and accounts for persisting divided usage in such words as *luminous, salute, revolution*. After /s, z/ the results of loss are seen in *Susan*, but more generally the assimilation already described took place (*sugar*). Some words, e.g., *supreme*, developed a /ʃ/ form which has now been ousted by /s/. It is well known that British and American English have followed divergent trends in the matter (which is not surprising for a change inaugurated at such a date).

In general the changes described here substantially altered the permitted patterns of syllable and morpheme onset, and created a considerable number of homophones, without affecting the structure of the consonant system.

§ 71 In 1770 the location of many stresses differed from that now current, but the system was beginning to be, perhaps was, the one we know. Earlier in II this was not so. Secondary stresses were much more marked and behaved more like primary stresses: their presence in many polysyllabic words produced a different rhythm of the kind observable when current American and British pronunciations of such words as *secretary, monastery, voluntary, dormitory,* are compared. The older forms went not only to America, but also to Australia; they can often be traced in the scansion of 18c verse. The new type was established in time for Sheridan to describe it in 1780.

The now familiar level-stress compounds of the type *gold watch, silver plate,* are first noted by Gill in 1621, his examples being *churchyard, outrun, outrage.* This shows that since it came in the incidence of level stress has varied, as indeed it continues to do; this pattern of compounding did not thoroughly establish itself before I and still does not exist for all speakers (cf. § 52). What Jespersen calls *rhythmic stress* (1909, etc., I, 156), i.e., stress developing out of the normal tendency to alternate strong and weak syllables, and coming to be fixed in certain items habitually used in a particular stress environment, has given rise to some alternatives. Thus in early NE ˈthorough, thoˈrough, were stress variants arising from OE *thur(u)h,* and at the beginning of II were not distinguished in function (as is well known from Shakespeare's ˈthorough ˈbush, ˈthorough ˈbrier. It is the pre-nominal or adjectival function that most regularly appears before a stress, and that in later use has been specialised with fore-stress – *thorough,* as in *thoroughfare, thorough worker.* The end-stressed form has been reserved to adverbial and prepositional uses, and its weak vowel reduced to zero, as in *look through, through the passage.* For the same reason we find Shakespeare (as his metre shows) using variant forms of *towards* – with one syllable, two syllables initially-stressed and two syllables end-stressed. The same cause, rhythmic spacing, accounts for some half-stressing of final syllables (now wholly weak) in Elizabethan verse, as in ˈtorch-bearˌers, ˈquicksilˌver, ˈhouse-keeˌper (but in later verse this is what it now seems, mere slovenliness on the writer's part).

Uncompounded disyllables of foreign origin such as *complete, extreme, supreme, obscene, obscure,* also had, for rhythmic reasons, a form with first syllable stress (and consequently with altered rhythm), side by side with their present stress-pattern. The variant is most familiar from Milton's 'clad in ˈcomˈpleat steel'.

In many more derived words (even) than at present we should find alternatives current as a result of conflict between the stress required rhythmically and that suggested by the analogy of the simplex. Throughout the whole period *acceptable, commendable, disputable, rheumatic, splenetic,* etc., may have first or second syllable main stress (initial stress brings in its train half-stress on the third syllable; the final syllable never receives any degree of stress). On the other hand, some prefix-stressing now current was not in use, so that *retinue, revenue*, had second syllable stress; in *importune* the stress was then on the final syllable, but in *persever(e)* on the second. The best way to acquire a wider sense of the old stress patterns is wide and careful reading of 17c and 18c verse.

§ 72　The most important factor for the history of vocabulary during II was the lowering of barriers and broadening of horizons. It is true that the age of exploration by physical travel, and the age of the Renaissance, had begun long before 1570, but enormous linguistic consequences were felt after that date. The most obvious effect was the exposure of the speech-community, at least indirectly, to language and experience from almost the entire inhabited world; but the shock of this exposure seems to have brought in its train an appetite for the exotic. English began to borrow European words from European languages met in the New World as it had not done while both the nations concerned were confined to Europe. This more international atmosphere was not merely an English characteristic; it followed from the circumstances in which Europeans found themselves facing the non-European world (even when they faced it warring among themselves). To a high degree the new vocabulary belonged to all civilised nations and would spread to others as they joined the ranks of the civilised. In II, as in I, there are developments which reduce the old linguistic isolationism, making the concept of English as 'a language' less than clear-cut in the last four centuries of its history (as it was in its first six centuries in England). Jespersen's familiar comment is worth repeating:

> There is, of course, nothing peculiarly English in the adoption of such words as *maccaroni* and *lava* from Italian, *steppe* and *verst* from Russian, *caravan* and *dervish* from Persian, *hussar* and *shako* from Hungarian, *bey* and *caftan* from Turkish, *harem* and *mufti* from Arabic, *bamboo* and *orangoutang* from Malay, *taboo* from Polynesian, *chocolate* and *tomato* from Mexican, *moccassin, tomahawk* and *totem* from other American languages. As a matter of fact, all these words now belong to the whole of the civilised world; like such classical or pseudo-classical words as *nationality, telegram*, and *civilization* they bear witness to the sameness of modern culture everywhere: the same products and to a great extent the same ideas are now known all over the globe and many of them have in many languages identical names (1909, 1919 edition, 150).

I would only dissociate myself from the slightly disparaging tone of Jespersen's references to 'sameness'; the products and ideas are common to the civilised world because we have all been made free of each other's traditions.

The new world was also an intellectual one. The thought and sensibility of the Renaissance likewise carried virtually a single cultural vocabulary across the civilised world. Further, it established the intellectual climate in which insistence on the use of vernaculars flourished. These tongues had to develop, so far as they lacked it, the language of serious literature, of religion, of scholarship – which within the period came to include the new science. The men who in the various speech-communities forged the new linguistic tools were men sharing a classical education; they were at home in Latin, and in at least the vocabulary of Greek. No planning was necessary for them to come up with the same lexical solution to problems facing a wide range of languages. Only German stood somewhat aside from the common development, and at times has been affected by an explicit determination to shape its learned words from native materials; but even German was far from consistent in opting out. In this way a powerful momentum towards convergence comes into being, whose force we feel to this day.

There was a third factor in the mixing of linguistic cultures. The explorers, few in number, opened the channels of communication to many, but these many were not only emigrants and readers. Our period coincides almost exactly with the duration of the Slave Trade, dependent on the opening of the New World for its inception, and legally terminated in 1807. By this means speakers from vast ranges of African territories were transported half way round the world; European actions set off a chain-reaction of suppliers in the interior of Africa and so brought to the west people from lands yet unknown to European explorers. At its height this trade passed about 50,000 persons a year through the port of Liverpool to predominantly English-speaking communities in the west. A great part of the linguistic consequences of this terrible movement is lost for ever, but what can be reconstructed for one area is shown in recent studies of the English of Jamaica (see Cassidy, 1961, and Cassidy and LePage, 1967).

§ 73 We may begin with a round-the-world tour of lexical borrowing, while recognising that it will by no means tell the whole story. From its immediate neighbours in the British Isles English borrowed perhaps a shade less meagrely than at other times. This is a time of a reasonably

121

strong, and strongly England-oriented, English community in Ireland. From Irish come *shamrock, leprechaun, brogue* (the shoe), *ogham, Tory, galore. Tory* meant 'pursuer', and was the name applied to certain Irish bandits or outlaws in the early 17c; it was transplanted to English politics in the latter part of the century, and rapidly took root. It is striking that the popular terms for our two main political traditions are names given from outside, and in a spirit of hostility. Scots Gaelic loans in II are of rather local interest – such words as *ptarmigan, strathspey, ghillie, pibroch*; the outstanding exception is *whisky*. The only important word which may have come from Welsh at this time is *penguin*.

§ 74 To influences from across the Channel we were, as by long tradition, far more receptive. The loans reflect to some extent our continuing naval and military relations with France, but much more our sense of their leadership in social and cultural life (in the broadest sense of those terms). A more detailed study would reveal the extent to which this leadership was based upon the prior absorption by French of elements from the entire world, but especially from other Romance languages (cf. Serjeantson, 1935, and not only the section on French therein). From the closing years of the 16c we have, for example, *cordon, battalion, portmanteau, vogue, genteel* (*gentle* is an earlier borrowing of the same word), *fricassée, cache, moustache, machine.* From the 17 and 18cc, with particularly intensive activity after the Restoration, we have, among many others, *fanfare, fusillade, clique, protégé, chaise, envelope, salon, bouquet, canteen, croupier, roulette, critique, connoisseur, vaudeville* (= 'popular song'), *vignette, denouement, précis, brochure, conservatoire, nuance, silhouette, velours, chenille, pompom, rouge, moquette, chignon, corduroy, casserole, meringue, rissole, tureen, blomange* (with spelling subsequently reformed on the model of French or of the earlier ME borrowing [with a different sense] *blancmanger*), *cuisine, aspic, aubergine, picnic, etiquette, debut, sang-froid, recherché, distrait, gauche, insouciance, encore, hors d'oeuvre, police* (= 'civil administration'), *detour, vis-à-vis, souvenir.* A rather different kind of relationship is shown by the geo-graphical-geological terms, *debris, cul-de-sac, glacier, avalanche, moraine, plateau*; these, like the early borrowing from Swiss-French, *chalet*, reflect the interest in mountains during the latter part of the period. By contrast, our only loan from Channel Island French (at any period) is the word of purely local reference, *ormer.*

The evidence for the chronology of these loans is not merely the date of their first recorded use, which may be later than the date of introduction. In some cases their phonological form indicates that they have or have not undergone certain datable sound changes before leaving their French environment, or after entering their English one. Thus, the *g* of *protégé* is /ʒ/, as a result of a change within French, where earlier loans had /dʒ/ (e.g., *charge*): likewise, the *ch* of *chaise* is /ʃ/, as against /tʃ/ in the earlier loan from the same word, *chair*. In *connoisseur*, the 17c French form in *-oi-* is transmitted, not the more recent *-ai-*. The /iː/ in *machine, cuisine*, contrasts with the /aɪ/ of *delight* (F *délit*, re-formed in spelling through association with English *light*), where the change has taken place in English (cf. §103). These two words, like *canteen, tureen*, have also retained a French pattern of stress, as against earlier loans in which stress has been shifted forward in the English manner, such as *virgin* (with consequent shortening of the vowel of the unstressed syllable). To some extent this is a function of the time the word has spent in English, but there is also in periods II and I a much greater tolerance of alien sounds and patterns in loans, as the present forms of *vignette, conservatoire, nuance*, and variant forms of *salon* and *envelope*, show. As always, the majority of the loans are nouns, but there is an unusually important component from other form-classes, especially adjectives.

§ 75 The debt of English to Low German (Dutch, Flemish, Saxon) is in sharp contrast. At this, as at other periods, it chiefly reflects maritime relations, as in *freebooter* (the cognate word *filibuster* comes from the same ultimate source via Spanish), *stoker, smuggler, smack* (the vessel), *keelhaul, cruise, jib, yawl, schooner, reef, walrus*, and there is also a characteristic admixture of military terms – *beleaguer, blunderbuss, roster, onslaught* (remodelled in English on the pattern of *slaughter*); and a soldier's word *tattoo* (the signal for closing time, '[the] tap [is] to'), whose present military meaning is a development within English. Miscellaneous words reflect the down-to-earth nature of the relationships – *wiseacre, spatter, revel, split, rant, brandy, knapsack, (de)coy, morass, hanker, drill* (v = 'bore'), *snort, shamble, snuff* (v, from which the noun developed in English), *hustle, slim, pea(-jacket)*. The number of familiar verbs in this list is particularly remarkable. There are words originally associated with aspects of Dutch life but now, like their referents, thoroughly acclimatised, such as *skate, geneva* (from *genever*, 'juniper', remodelled in English through erroneous association with Geneva; the short form *gin* dates from 1714). The two remaining groups are, in character, peculiarly of this period. One is the Dutch element in our vocabulary of the fine arts, *easel, sketch, stipple, (land-)scape*. The other reflects the encounters between Europeans in distant places – *monsoon*, which Dutch had borrowed from Portuguese, which had it from Arabic, and *springbok*, the only noteworthy loan at this early date from South African Dutch.

The High German element is relatively small. Apart from geological terms – *zinc, cobalt, quartz, shale* – and terms of local association – *seltzer, landau, pumpernickel* – the words borrowed share the everyday character of other Germanic loans, e.g., *zigzag, drill* (the fabric), *plunder, hamster*. It is, on the positive side, rather surprising that the normal word for a certain dance has come to be the German loan *waltz*, rather than the earlier French loan *valse*. On the negative side, it is a quite staggering demonstration of the power of tradition that in the age of Bach, Handel, Mozart and Beethoven we did not borrow a single musical term from German. This is a salutary warning against naïve inferences about the role of actual cultural leadership in the transmission of loanwords. It should be noted that the phonology of German loans shows a much higher degree of assimilation to English than that of recent French loans; though German is more like English in respect of its sound elements, it is markedly different in its sound-patterning, and this makes the contrasted treatment particularly noticeable.

§ 76   Loans from Spanish and Portuguese played no significant part in English before the 16c, and when they become important it would seem that encounters across the world stimulated the wish to accept words known because of relations in Europe. Trade, warfare, and the linking of the two courts by the marriage of Mary to Philip II accounted for a number of European and Spanish loans from the beginning of II – *sherry, anchovy, rusk, renegade, grandee, bravado, comrade, mosquito, cargo, toreador, matador, duenna, sombrero, garrot, junta, corvette, flotilla, booby, embargo, guitar, castanet, parade, escapade, plaza, corral, albino, stevedore, merino, domino, salver* (re-formed with an English ending, Spanish *salva*; similarly, *cockroach* is made over in English from *cucaracha*). This group naturally divides into words which remain strongly Spanish in form and those that are anglicised; more technically, the English-looking words take the form they would have had if they had been borrowed from French, so strong is that tradition of adaptation. In fact, some items from this list may have come to us via French; we cannot assert the intermediary role of French unless the source-word has been recorded from French, and at the appropriate date.

It is possible that some of the words already listed were really borrowed in the New World, or transmitted from the New World. Those that follow certainly were: *llama, vanilla, pimento, avocado, barbecue, maroon, alpaca, banana, lime* (the fruit), *potato, tomato, cigar* (where Spanish got these words from is a much more complex story, which would take us right across southern and central America, and what is now the south-west of the USA).

Words arriving from Portuguese are rather fewer, but even more cosmopolitan. From the New World, Portuguese brought us *coco-nut, molasses, sargasso, macaw*; from Africa, *madeira, yam, palaver, assagai* (later *assegai*); from the east (the East India Company received its charter in 1600), *buffalo, typhoo* (re-formed later under Greek influence), *joss, cast(e), verandah, emu* (of the cassowary, naturally not of the Australian emu at this period), *tank* (for water-storage) (all Indian), with *pagoda, mandarin* from China and *bonze* from Japan. There is very little sign of borrowing from Portuguese on its home ground; *moidore* (18c) is usually given as an example, but there were plainly other places where the word as well as the thing could have been obtained. This leaves the most famous of all in splendid isolation: *port* (the wine), borrowed in the 17c.

Apart from details such stress placement and occasional retention of /ɑː/, the degree of anglicisation of Spanish-Portuguese loans is extremely high.

§ 77   Borrowing from the last major Romance language, Italian, has had an entirely different character. From this source too loans effectively begin in the latter part of the 16c. This is remarkable in view of the long preceding tradition of cultural relations; indeed, travel to Italy had been an English habit unbroken since Anglo-Saxon times. The list of examples will speak for itself, given these preliminary comments:

1. the words are entirely European borrowings, the Italians having been great travellers, but not (at this time) settlers or colonisers;
2. the element of what may be called Renaissance borrowing – loans in the fields of fine art, music, literature, ideas – is strong, but represents very largely borrowing by travellers rather than borrowing from books;
3. travellers, in a wide sense of the term, also brought back words to do with Italian life (in which I include terms due to Italian leadership in finance and commerce) and resulting from military dealings;

4. the face-to-face mode of borrowing, reinforced by factors mentioned in § 76, accounts for a generally high degree of anglicisation in form, the main exceptions being rather technical words;
5. the French looked up to Italian leadership in the same spheres as the English; many loans (not included in the list) were mediated by French, and others may have been, though the evidence is not conclusive.

The list, then, includes such items as *mountebank, bravo* (a type of man), *madonna* (as a term of address 1584, as a term of art, late 17c [not 1644, as *OED* indicates]), *pedant, bandit, tarantula, belladonna, macaroni, macaroon, vermicelli, volcano, granite, broccoli, lava, casino, bronze, malaria, curvet, escort, musket, parapet, salvo, post* (in the sense 'military station'), *frigate, stucco, portico, villa, grotto, balcony, corridor, pergola, catacomb* (OE had made an earlier borrowing direct from Latin, but it had died out), *dado, rotunda, mezzanine, colonnade, arcade, loggia, vista, model, attitude, pastel, miniature, gesso, fresco, (mezzo-)relievo, intaglio, pieta, catafalque, bust, profile, mezzotint, filigree, chiaroscuro, portfolio, torso, picturesque* (re-formed on English *picture* and a French suffix!), *costume, gala, garb, concert* (not originally in a musical sense), *madrigal, fugue, sonata, solo, pedal, soprano, impresario, trombone, violoncello, pianoforte, cantata, oratorio, concerto, aria, arpeggio* (together with a large number of musical directions, mainly due to Purcell, and introduced through the written word), *stanza, canto* (other literary words were probably mediated by French), *ditto, gusto, pantaloon, mercantile, firm* (a company), *gambit, intrigue,* v, *parasol, umbrella* (a shade from weather; the differentiation of this word from *parasol* by restricting it to use for protection against rain was made under English skies), *manifesto, bulletin* (= health certificate), *stiletto, parry,* v. I have given fuller examples than usual in order to demonstrate the extent of English dependence on Italian in certain areas of vocabulary.

§ 78   Other spoken European languages were not particularly important sources of loans at this period. After Peter the Great's visit to London relations with Russia became a little closer, and we borrowed *mammoth* and *astrakhan,* but *steppe* came to us through French. Basque is the ultimate, but French again the proximate, source of *bizarre, chaconne.* Norwegian gave us *lemming,* which it had got from Lapp, and other Scandinavian loans continue the long tradition of the inflow of homely words – *rowan, rug, slag, kink, skit, snag, scuffle, smug, scrag, scrub, simper, snuffle, oaf, squall, keg, skittles,* (*run the*) *gauntlet* (the keyword remodelled on the earlier French loan *gauntlet*, which has nothing to do with the matter), *smut, cosy, muggy.* *Tungsten* is rather more technical; *rune,* and perhaps *troll,* reflect the interest taken in early northern literature at various times during the period (naturally OE had a word for *rune,* namely, *run*; it would have become **roun,* but did not survive). Again, the non-nominal element in this list should be noted.

§ 79   Direct and indirect loans from the Near, Middle and Far East assume an entirely new importance at this time. Arabic yields *sheikh* and *mufti* (though the current sense of this word is an English 19c innovation), *roc, sash, hashish, fakir, mohair, sherbet, sofa, harem, minaret, henna, genie* – a group which clearly reflects the interests of readers as well as travellers, and involves areas quite different from those in which Arabic had been influential during the Middle Ages (cf. § 110). Hebrew, except for technical words to do with Jewish life, affords very little. Persian is the immediate source of Persian words, *julep, divan* ('council'), *caravan, caravanserai, bazaar, firman, shawl, carboy,* and of others which it had in turn borrowed in India – *cummerbund, lascar, seersucker, purdah, khaki.* Turkish provided *dolman, coffee, caviare, caftan, kiosk,* as well as *jackal,* which it had borrowed from Persian. India gave, from the learned language Sanskrit, *avatar*; from Hindustani (the most widespread IE language in daily use there), *nabob, guru, sahib, pundit, chintz, tussore, dungaree* (but the present sense of the plural is an English development), *mongoose, kedgeree, punch, cot, bungalow, tomtom, juggernaut, pukka, bandana, shampoo*; from the Dravidian languages of the south, *coolie, atoll, cheroot,* and, through Portuguese, *mango, curry, copra, teak.* Tibetan provides *lama*; Chinese, *japan* (lacquer), *ketchup, kaolin,* and through Dutch, *tea* (c1650); Japanese, *kimono, soy, mikado*; the Malayo-Polynesian language family, *kris, paddy, cockatoo, orang-outang, bantam, kapok,* and through other European languages (French, Dutch, Spanish, Portuguese), *bamboo, gong, junk* (the vessel), *gingham, launch.*

   The traceable influence of African languages is only just beginning, with *chimpanzee* from the Sudanese family, *zebra* from the Bantu one, and *gnu* from the Hottentot, together with indirect loans (cf. § 76).

   South, Central and SW North America are represented almost entirely by indirect borrowings, through Portuguese (*toucan, ipecacacuanha, tapioca*) or Spanish (*cacao, canoe, hummock, hurricane, tobacco, guano, tomato, vicuna, poncho, barbecue*) (cf. also § 76). *Ocelot* comes through French; *jaguar, cayenne, tapir* may be direct. The rest of North America naturally shows a predominance of Indian words, the great majority from the Algonquian family in the areas of first settlement – *raccoon, opossum, persimmon, moccasin, terrapin, moose, pow-wow, wigwam, wampum, squaw, tomahawk, skunk, hickory, totem,* and *wood-chuck* (re-formed on English *wood*); these are all, of course, oral loans, and the mode of anglicisation shows a ruthless and haphazard character absent from the adoption of words from literary languages. From the far north we have the one Eskimo word *kayak* at this period. The circumstances of European colonisation of America show interesting parallels with the circumstances of English settlement in this country, notably in the thinness and inferior status of the native population. Yet there is far more borrowing from Indian languages in the 17c and 18c than from Celtic in the 6c and 7c. This must be largely due to the extremely unfamiliar character of the setting of life in the New World; it shows that factors other than the arrogance of the conqueror enter into the English habit of ignoring Celtic sources.

§ 80 Voyages of the mind were no less influential. They were made by scholars and scientists, and their route lay through Latin writings. 'Latin' here means the language of scholarship at the Renaissance; it includes a great deal not found in classical Latin, especially elements from Greek, but also loans from other languages of learning. The linguistic merchandise brought back from these ventures generally differs in content from that of the Middle Ages; older branches of learning had developed their vocabulary, and newer ones now feel the need to do so. Though most of the borrowings are nouns when they enter English, in the source-language they had often not been nouns, or had been nouns in other than the quotation form. What this peculiarity reflects is the borrowers' easy familiarity with the source language; they are at home in its sentences, and can readily snip bits out of them for use as quotation-nouns in English. By contrast, most other borrowing, at all periods, has arisen through a labelling or even glossing use of words. A fairly long list of examples is necessary to show the range of Latin loans at this period:

nasturtium, indecorum, ignoramus, vagary, interregnum, rostrum, codex, compendium, omen, posse, quarto, militia, radius, sinus, delirium, stratum, onus, toga, premium, torpor, equilibrium, specimen, spectrum, series, census, plus, vertebra, amanuensis, tenet, squalor, affidavit, par, arena, apparatus, agendum -a, veto, fiat, curriculum, forceps, query, gratis, formula, crux, impetus, focus, data, insignia, stamen, album, larva, complex, desideratum, pallor, pendulum, nebula, rabies, tedium, minimum, tuber, dictum, serum, fulcrum, calculus, mica, stimulus, lens, lumbago, status, nucleus, cirrus, caret, inertia, propaganda, alibi, auditorium, maximum, insomnia.

Words common by the 16c, to Greek and Latin, are *prima facie* more likely to have Latin as their proximate source. Examples are:

chord, cylinder, prism, basis, sceptic, meander, skeleton, amnesty, climax, comma, acrostic, colon, nomad, critic, epic, trochee, python, chasm, stigma, theory, energy, idyll, archive, enthusiasm, strophe, orchestra, crater, museum, system, hyphen, colophon, clinic, tactics, lymph, dogma, typhus, siphon, disk, pharynx, botany.

In addition, *electric, elastic,* came through modern Latin, and *ode, diatribe, acoustic, disaster,* through French. Direct loans from Greek are *pathos, praxis, larynx, coma, tonic, phlox, bathos, triptych, philander, cosmos.* In nearly all words on these lists the degree of anglicisation is minimal, as is to be expected when scholars take pains over the transference of rather formal words between languages they know and respect.

Greenough and Kittredge make an illuminating comment on the Latin element in the language as a whole, which can be most appropriately quoted at this point:

> Roughly speaking, then, we are safe in asserting that our language has appropriated a full quarter of the Latin vocabulary, besides what it has gained by transferring Latin meanings to native words (1901, 106).

This is also, perhaps, the best point to note that such wholesale borrowing is often misunderstood, as if the real point were that the English language could, at any rate in recent centuries, do so little for itself, and the speakers of it had to get both ideas and words from elsewhere. A more valid inference would be that by its long-standing plunder of other languages, both spoken and learned, it has become uniquely rich in resources – certainly much richer than the major source-languages it has exploited.

It remains to note that from this superabundant wealth English has discarded a number of items picked up, jackdaw-wise, more for glitter than for use. This is particularly noticeable among the Latinate words of the 16c. A few examples from those listed by Sheard (1954, 252–3), are:

anacephalize, charientism, deruncinate, furibund, immorigerous, lapidifical, matutine, oblatrant, polypragmon, suppeditate, temulent, vadimonial.

§ 81 These learned written sources, usually referred to as *Neo-Latin*, are not confined to the donation of whole words. As in recent English (cf. § 21) they also contribute formatives. Among prefixes we may note *crypto-, di-, non-, peri-, post-, preter-, proto, supra-* and *trans-*. Directly or indirectly the following suffixes come from Neo-Latin during period II: *-arian, -iana, -ism, -ist, -ise*. French, mediator of some of these, is also directly the source of *-ese, -esque*. Only one noteworthy development involves a native formative, the use of *-en* to form verbs from the stems of consonant-final adjectives, as in *toughen, widen, broaden, madden, tighten*; this process, originally applied to verbs, has gone so far that we tend to interpret as de-adjectival even the older formations which were actually de-verbal. On the other hand, the suffix *-(e)rel*, previously borrowed, acclimatised, and used to form native words such as *cockerel, mongrel*, ceased to be active around 1600, despite the persistently analysable character of some of the formations using it.

Period II inherited from its predecessor the pattern of formation by zero-morpheme, also called conversion. The process was a most prolific source of new words, especially new verbs, from nouns, particles and interjections, but as the method was not new we need give only a few examples originating in II – the verbs *hint, rival, serenade, guarantee, shoo, encore*, and the nouns *split, contest, grumble*. The conversion pattern of formation was in rather unsuccessful competition with patterns using French or Latin formatives, but tended to oust the older pattern of voiced/voiceless contrast (*advice/advise*); the last new formations on this pattern are *belief* (to contrast with *believe*, and replacing older *believe*, n) and *shelve*, v, formed to correspond with *shelf*; both late 16c. Other types of formation are relatively unimportant at this period – by back-derivation we have *stoke* and *scavenge*. The record (for what it is worth) suggests that ablaut- and rhyme-combinations were not very productive in the 17–18cc though both reactivate around 1800. Clipping created a brouhaha in the latter part of the period, since it came under attack from Swift and others; apart from *mob*, most of the examples that caused such distress have survived at the level of slang or not at all (e.g., *phizz, pozz, plenipo*).

§ 82 After all this, it is natural to compare the vocabulary of 1970 and 1570 in terms of what then could not be, often had no occasion to be, said. Still, losses are apparent too. In this direction also, some change is conditioned by what we no longer have occasion to say; for instance, only in very special kinds of historical discourse do we need to refer to pieces of ordnance called the *basilisk* or the *chamber*. Some old native words have been ousted by borrowings, such as *fere*, 'companion', *clepe*, 'call, name', *clip*, 'embrace'; many, while maintaining a useful existence in dialects, have passed out of standard use, such as *bever*, 'a snack', *bloat*, 'to smoke-dry', *collow* or *colly*, 'to blacken'. One at least has surrendered to an embarrassing homophonic clash arising through the accident of sound change (*quean*, since the 18c pronounced indistinguishably from *queen*).

Other shifts of balance are more subtle, but very important for the correct reading of older texts. Words which now have no special stylistic colour, though some are a little colloquial, were for Johnson 'low', such as *banter, coax, dodge, flippant, fop, frisky, fun, fuss, simpleton*, and writers contemporary with Johnson supplement the list with *bigot, flimsy, budge, dumbfound, enthusiasm, extra, flirtatious, gambling, hanker, humbug, jilt, mob, nervous, prig, quandary, shabby, sham, shuffle, snob, squabble, stingy, tiff, topsy-turvy, touchy*. Even allowing for an inevitable element of personal prejudice in the compilation of such lists, we must take warning that change of tone is extensive.

At the opposite extreme are words, not necessarily lofty words, but glowing words, created under the challenge of translation, especially of the Bible, created often by known writers, from native or borrowed resources that might otherwise have died out, so slender was their tenure. The special quality of such words, powerful for us, does not cling about them in 1570; indeed, the use of some of them in the Bible provoked noisy objections. Examples are *apparel, raiment, damsel, quick* ('living'), *travail, peace-maker, long-suffering, stumbling-block, scapegoat, mercy-seat, broken-hearted, loving-kindness, noonday, morning-star, kind-hearted*; together with certain larger expressions, such as *to die the death*.

§ 83   And, as always, semantic change in established elements accounts for important, and treacherous, differences. The term 'semantic change' suggests an oversimplification, as if we were dealing with a single kind of linear development, A → B, a kind of development which in any case looks arbitrary and implausible – not the kind of thing we would go in for ourselves, or we should never be understood. And, of course, in this simple form, a change from A to B is not what happens. To understand semantic relationships at any one time and through time we need, in fact, several models. There is the radial model, in which points on the circumference are linked mutually with the centre, but not directly with each other. There is the tree-model, in which a common stem or trunk branches and sub-branches in any number of ways we care to think of; and there is the step model in which the progress is A, A + B, B, B + C, C, etc. A diagram should clarify the point:

However, the models will not help us if in turn they are misunderstood; we shall not expect to find *words* which show the radial-type, the tree-type, or the step-type. It will be single stages and processes which are modelled in this way, or small groups of them; only exceptionally, and accidentally, will a single model account for what happens throughout a word. But we are still oversimplifying, because all the movements we have shown are undirectional; in fact various uses cross-fertilise each other in every conceivable way. And this in turn is but one aspect of a wider truth: that relationships and developments are caught up in a network of tensions, influences, checks, provided by the entire linguistic situation. A word may develop a particular sense because a related word in another form-class has it (we may call this grammatical analogy, but it is a special kind of grammatical analogy), or because another which sounds similar has it (phonological analogy) or because a source or related word in another familiar language has it (external analogy). Negatively, all kinds of similarities may impede developments, or cause them to be reversed when they have once taken place. Moreover, in looking at relationships we are accustomed to think of a trunk branching; but in looking at developments we may also need to invert the image, thinking of convergence rather than divergence (for example, with English *fast* in *stand fast* and *run fast*), and for this the flow of tributaries into a river might be an appropriate model. Finally, there is a subtler aspect of the relationships between meanings, for which a mathematical rather than a visual model may serve. There may, among several current meanings, be one which is dominant (there may even be a hierarchy of dominance). The dominant meaning can be regarded as unmarked in the sense that it is at a given time the one intended unless something in the context signals otherwise; the marked uses are the ones that need signalling. But the status of being a dominant or unmarked meaning itself has a history. It is not enough to show when a given sense developed or waned; we also need to know how at a given time it stood *vis-à-vis* other possible meanings.

All this is highly abstract, and perhaps difficult to follow without examples. The examples have been reserved for later discussion precisely because there is no correlation between one word and one model of development, but they must now be considered.

§ 84 The simplest form of semantic change occurs when senses current in II have been replaced by others (which has evidently happened when Kate says 'Then vail your stomachs, for it is no boot', *Taming of the Shrew*, V, ii, 176), or when senses now current have not yet appeared in 1570 (which is the case, though one cannot demonstrate it with a single quotation, for *wit, humour* cf. *OED*). One can draw up lists of words likely to prove a stumbling block to readers of Elizabethan and Jacobean literature, such as *argument, baffle, banquet, awful, blackguard, bodkin, brothel, buxom, carpet, cassock, censure, character, clergy, conceit, danger, distempered, fact, hope* – but before getting very far in the alphabet one would have qualms. How much detail to include? How much explanation? How, above all, to show, from such a starting-point, that Elizabethan Englishmen spoke, as we do ourselves, a language in which the words were interrelated, and dovetailed and overlapping, the whole being natural, workable and of a piece? How, in effect, to show that they spoke their language, not ours peppered with eccentricities? We may well conclude, that having said enough to show that the difficulties are not one but many, we should set about illustrating the changes in quite another way. A sense of how the mind works in these matters is the first requirement, and can be applied to the study of semantic change at any period; it enables us to bring to the reading of older literature the right kind of alertness to concealed differences, and to make understanding use of the *OED*, in checking our suspicions and elucidating difficulties. Such an understanding is shown in Lewis (1960) on a broader canvas, in time, space and languages, than is available here. Some examples analysed by Lewis derive from our period, and illustrate very clearly the kinds of thing that happen, though all need to be read in the knowledge that a rich and complex multilingual history underlies the words and word-families concerned before they reach that point in time. Lewis quotes (4) a schoolboy's misunderstanding of the word *physical* in a passage from *Julius Cæsar:*

Is Brutus sick and is it physical
To walk unbraced and suck up the humours
Of the dank morning?

Physical was interpreted as 'sensible' as a result of reading into it:

    (1) the polarity *mental/physical*

    (2) the sense 'mad' for *mental.*

Both of these are post-Shakespearean developments. (2) is one of those changes that come about in consequence of the syntagmatic company a word keeps. From such collocations as *mental illness, health, institution,* etc., we as it were back-form or clip-form *mental* in the sense 'suffering, diseased, or defective in respect of that which is treated in a mental institution, or classified as a mental defect, etc.' and in this sense we transfer the item to attributive use; once there, it pulls *physical* in its wake in this sense for the simple reason that the two are polar in other senses. Polarity can likewise operate to fill a gap when a sense awaits a form to express it. Lewis demonstrates this from the then new, and still popular, sense of *supernatural,* which is used of the witches and their activities in *Macbeth.* He writes:

Several causes probably contributed to this sense. Whatever such creatures might be in themselves, our encounters with them are certainly not *natural* in the sense of being ordinary or 'things of course'. It may even be supposed that when we see them we are acting above our *nature.* If on these two grounds the experience were vaguely felt to be *supernatural,* the adjective might then be transferred to the things experienced. . . . Again, such creatures are not part of the subject matter of '*natural* philosophy'; if real, they fall under pneumatology, and, if unreal, under morbid psychology. Thus the methodological idiom[1] can separate them from *nature.* But thirdly (and I suspect this might be most potent of all), the beings which popular speech calls *supernatural,* long before that adjective was applied to them, were already bound together in popular thought by a common emotion. Some of them are holy, some numinous, some eerie, some horrible; all, one way or another, uncanny, mysterious, odd, 'rum'. When the learned term *supernatural* enters the common speech, it finds this far older, emotional classification ready for it, and already in want of a name. I think the learned word, on the strength of a very superficial relation of meaning to the thing the plain man had in mind, was simply snatched at and pummelled into the required semantic shape, like an old hat. . . . *Supernatural* in this modern . . . sense does

[1] Note that Lewis has defined this as the use of such terms as *grammar* in the sense 'branch of learning which studies language', while it remains the name of the level of linguistic organisation studied by that subject.

its work quite efficiently. . . . A general term whose particulars are bound together only by an emotion may be quite a practicable word (from pp. 67–8).

On the other hand, the tension of old polarities may slacken; and this tendency, along with others, can be shown in the *sense*-family of words. *Sensible* reached English, as did many adjectives of comparable form, with a grammatical ambiguity preserved from its Latin use; it had an active sense, 'capable of sensing', and a passive one, 'capable of being sensed'. Later English has proved far less tolerant of this kind of grammatical ambiguity than Elizabethan English, and has in most of the words concerned kept only the passive sense – but not consistently, and in some cases greatly weakening the sense that voice-contrast is relevant (cf. *the chair is comfortable, I'm comfortable*). To fill the gap left by the withdrawal of these formations from active senses, it has tended to use other adjectives, e.g., in *-ive, -ful*, which also had both active and passive senses in II. But the analogical extension of grammatical contrasts made elsewhere into the use of derived adjectives has proceeded slowly with *sensible*; passive senses (*sensible*, i.e., *perceptible, objects*) and active senses (*she is sensible (of)*, i.e., 'she feels' or even 'realises'), coexist, but they typically occur in patterns suggesting that the primary difference is between non-human (*sensible object*) and human (*sensible person*); and in the use of language, the suggestion is the fact. It is the personal use which is contaminated from sense = 'judgement', and goes its modern way, as a result of various types of grammatical analogy. Meanwhile the polar form *insensible* was left behind at the stage + human, = 'lacking in sense, i.e., perception, feeling, consciousness'; the polarity is weakened, and one is tempted to think that the now irregular relationship between the positive and negative forms has been a factor in the relative disuse of the negative. The relations in the *sense, sentence, sensible, sensibly, sensibility*, group and their negatives, are, of course, far more complicated than this, but we need use them for only one more point. From *sentence* in an older sense, 'maxim, meaning', *sententious* had in II (as before it) the meanings, 'taking the forms of maxims' *or* 'rich in meaning'; one should *pray sententiously* (Latimer), and the Greek tragedians taught by 'sententious precepts' (Milton). A matrix use for the modern development is 18c 'sententious absurdity' (Fanny Burney), showing the kind of collocation which, once become habitual, colours a word even when it is used in other company. Lewis suggests another possible reason for the development:

The word has also, I suspect, been infected by the phonetic proximity of *pretentious*. A word needs to be very careful about the phonetic company it keeps. The old meaning of *obnoxious* has been almost destroyed by the combined influence of *objectionable* and *noxious*, and that of *deprecate* by *depreciate*, and that of *turgid* by *turbid* (141).

Finally, an example of change in dominance. The dominant meaning of *wit* today is 'that quality which a witty man possesses'. This sense existed in the late 17c, early 18c, but was not dominant. Its older senses were of the groups (1) 'understanding', (2) 'distinction of mind'; and Lewis has shown that external analogy (being treated as the equivalent of Latin *ingenium*) was an important factor in (2). One of the (2) group is 'a man of distinguished mind'; and in personal uses of the word, a generation either way from 1700, this is the sense we must read in unless context warns otherwise. A clear instance of this is the line of descent implied in *wit – poet – critic – fool* in Pope's:

> Some have at first for wits, then poets passed,
> Turn'd critics next, and proved plain fools at last

(Lewis, 94). The modern sense is historically possible, but would be contextually disastrous.

§ 85 We left the prop-word *one* in 1770 (cf. § 58) differing from its present functions only in that it was not used with plural demonstrative or genitive pronoun or with various types of post-modification. Two further uses developed only during II: premodification with singular demonstrative (*that one*) in the 18c, and with *one* (*one good one*) around 1600.

Among ordinary nouns we note a step, an almost final step, in the direction of recognising the *-s* morphophoneme as a sign of plurality. The simplest form this took was the substitution of *-s* plurals for most of the few remaining *-n* plurals; *eyen, hosen, housen, shoon*, already less common than *-s* forms for these words at the beginning of II, die out soon after 1600, leaving only the present *children, oxen, brethren, kine*. By a slightly more complicated process, a final sibilant that was integral to a word might be misinterpreted as a sign of plurality; thus, *richesse* is made over as *riches*, and the new form never develops a singular; *pease* (surviving in *pease-pudding*, where the first element could be interpreted as singular or plural), becomes *pea*, with a new plural *peas*; during the same period *sherry, asset, eave, sash, skate*, are formed in the same way. It will avoid repetition to say here that *cherry* had under-

136

gone the same treatment rather earlier. A yet more remote process was the loosening of the bond between singular and plural in those plurals that did not have -*s*, with the result that *chicken*, old plural of *chick*, comes into use as a singular, develops a regular new plural; *chick* then survives only in a sense more specialised than its old one.

The definite article, as to form, was commonly elided before vowels, in both literary and colloquial style, and the variant *t'*, especially in the double or metanalysed formation *the t'other*, remained in good usage throughout. Its functions have grown steadily in scope and clarity since the beginnings of recorded English, and we should observe in II rather more occasions of hesitation and divided usage than today. Before language-names and subject-names it was used, but far from regularly (though individual writers might make the point into a matter of principle), thus, (*the*) *French*, (*the*) *mathematics*. Today we have residual uses before the names of physical disorders (*the plague*, occasionally still *the flu*), but then such uses ranged much wider – *the toothache*, *the apoplexy*. On the other hand, the last traces of an older pattern in which river names were used without article occur around 1600.

The indefinite article followed in form the same rules as now, but their implementation differed a little because of the relative infrequency with which initial *h* was sounded (cf. § 49); thus, *an hair, an happy end*. Except in cases still obtaining, the only survival beyond 1770 was *an hundred*. The functions of the indefinite were slightly more restricted, since it was not required in structures corresponding to *it's a pity, shame, matter, fact* (corresponding, because the initial structure would be '*tis*, not *it's*), nor after *many* (*many one*, beside *many a one*); and its initial position might be violated in such structures as *so new a fashion'd robe*. *A many* was in perfectly good use; *a good many* was often followed by *of* + noun plural rather than directly by a noun head.

The order of determiners permitted *other some, other two*, beside the present sequence, but this is not simply a matter of arrangement. The order with initial *other* had the meaning indefinite, that with following *other* the meaning definite. We have lost this useful distinction in the process of standardising our sequence-rules. In pro-nominal use *other* might or might not inflect for the plural. *Other* was used much more freely in relation to nouns of non-human reference (i.e., *no other* = 'nothing else' or 'nobody else'; now normally 'nobody else').

§ 86 While in PE adjectives show number distinction only in fossilised instances like *letters patents*, the 16c was familiar with the last authentic distinction, that between *enough* and *enow* (the latter pl or adverbial). This had outlasted its fellows because of the highly anomalous form it took, and for the same reason was doomed to extinction sooner or later. In 1653 it was explicitly taught by Wallis, which shows that it was dying, though not dead. On its origin (in phonological, not grammatical, patterning) cf. § 134: among nouns, *plough/plow* had the same alternation.

The roles of adjectives and nouns were perhaps less sharply distinguished than now; such uses as *better than he* (= better men), *full of poor* (= poor people), and, with a determiner, *in many's eyes*, now require a nominal head. This is related to the growth of the prop-word as a noun-place filler, an aspect of the general sense that there are places that ought to be filled by certain form-classes or certain clause-elements.

Double comparatives and superlatives were perfectly acceptable at the beginning of the period (*more properer*, *most handsomest*), though they came under corrective treatment in the 18c. In certain cases where the forms of comparison had, for phonological reasons, come to be irregular, such as *late, latter, last*, new analogical forms, *later, latest*, had been developed before II, but they were quite recent, and were alternatives in free variation with the historic forms. It is only more recently that the two sets have been differentiated. *Ill*, which is now abnormally restricted to predicative use (except in the fossilised pattern *an ill wind*), was then freely used in attributive function. At the very end of the period begins the shift of participles used predicatively into adjective function, shown by premodification by *very* (*very concerned*, 1760). A new type of attribution, using verb-object compounds (*break-neck* [*speed*]) dates from the beginning of the period; so does the type of adjunct (firs participial, then adjectival), *made-up* (earlier type, *by-gone*). In terms of relationship between the nominal head and its modifiers, the period lacks certain types of transferred attribution, and modification of part of a nominal head, which have since established themselves, and seem to be at present much on the increase (types: *wireless operator, practical joker*).

Secondary modifiers or intensifiers differed considerably. The old forms, *full, right*, were still in general use; newer *very* was known, but not used by everybody even in the 17c. For a more forceful degree of modification, *wondrous* and *mighty* were inherited, but such terms wear out quickly, and changes have been considerable. During II, *pretty, extraordinary, pure, terrible, dreadful, cruel, plaguy, devilish*, take on this role, and most of them have lost it again since. We must distinguish here the built-in obsolescence affecting such items at any time, from the particular factors operating between II and I. These arose from a sense of correctness which prescribed that forms with the appearance of adjectives should not be used in secondary modification. *Very* was all right because it did not have this form; but instead of *extraordinary, terrible, dreadful,* etc., the corresponding *-ly* forms came to be required. In other types of secondary modification we find *what* (PE *how*) before *many, something/somedeal* for PE *rather,* and *nothing* for PE *not at all.* Until the 18c *a great deal* was not restricted as now to use with mass-nouns (*a great deal of timber*) but also occurred with plural count-nouns (*a great deal of pieces of timber*). From the close of the 16c (Shakespeare) we have the still current patterns *these kind of,* on the model of older *all manner of,* which has become somewhat archaic; *these sort of,* a further extension of the pattern, does not appear till the 18c.

§ 87   Changes in pronouns are of considerable importance. In *my/mine, thy/thine, no/none,* the original difference had been purely phonological. The forms with /n/ were used before vowels (cf. *a/an*) and finally (a position closed to *an*). Since the use in final position was pronominal, the distribution could serve as matrix for a new, grammatical, distinction. The now familiar difference of use, +/n/ pronominal, −/n/ attributive, develops from this matrix at the end of the 16c; though in attributive use the old phonological distinction continued in use for a time.

Particularly striking developments affect the system and the forms for second-person pronouns. In 1570 there was still something we could regard as contrast of number in the second person, namely a contrast of *ye* and *thou.* However, it was by no means simply that, since for fully two centuries (cf. § 118) the use of the historically plural pronoun for polite address to a single person had been known. Such a use, once introduced, must snowball, since in all cases of doubt one would rather be polite than risk giving offence, and every precedent widens the range of cases of doubt. From about 1600 the 'plural' was the unmarked or normal form of address to a single person; use of *thou* marked a relationship as not belonging to the central type. It might depart from centrality in the direction of close intimacy, or in the direction of social distancing, as when a man addressed his inferiors (e.g., children) or, in a special case, his superior, God. If this seems an odd assortment, the explanation is that the extremes left over when a central function is carved out of a formerly undivided area generally are ill-assorted;

their relationship is not directly with each other, but only through that which has been removed. In the development after 1611 a special factor enters in, which has been influential in many areas of English usage, but which can be explained here once and for all. Though the Authorised Version of the Bible was published in 1611, its language was almost entirely that of Tyndale, whose New Testament appeared in 1525, almost a century earlier. The intervening years had seen many innovations, especially in areas that were, broadly speaking, grammatical. By 1611 the usage of Tyndale would be in these respects not archaic, but decidedly old-fashioned in flavour; for the most part Tyndale had chosen forms as being normal. Though the use of archaisms in heightened style has been known at all periods, if only as a consequence of the conservatism which poetic form tends to impose, this accident of the history of translation led to a very particular association between antique language and religious subjects or solemnity of tone. The great prestige of the AV led to a growing gap between the familiar expressions of religion and everyday usage as time went on. To return to the point at issue: Tyndale's use of *thou* was not exceptional, but its preservation in AV carried the implication that religious address, especially to the Deity, required special forms. During most of II *thou* could be used between intimates or between superior and inferior, but by 1770 it survived only in dialects, among Quakers, in literary styles as a device of heightening (even in Wordsworth!), and in its present religious function.

It is, naturally, inconvenient to neutralise the major grammatical contrast of number in an area of a grammar that normally expresses it, and various supplementary devices have been introduced to restore the lost distinction. One current in the 17 and 18cc was the contrast of verb concord, *you is* singular, *you are* plural. Already in Swift we find this practice restricted to informal and non-literary uses, and even for this he was rebuked by Lowth in 1762. Unfortunately the purists have succeeded in abolishing it.

Meanwhile, the 'plural' pronoun did not remain unchanged. The old relationship of contrast, *ye*, subject, *you*, object, began, for various reasons, to be displaced. In the late 16c both forms may be used in both functions; by the 18c *you* is the norm regardless of grammatical function, and *ye* only occurs in elevated literary use. And the realisation of *you* has had a history more complex than the written form suggests. Phoneticians indicate that in the late 16c the strong form was /jəʊ/ (= PE* /jaʊ/), weak /jʊ/. While the modern weak form is a continuation of the old one, the strong form is a new analogical creation, by lengthening of the weak one (for other similar developments, cf. § 108). The marked circumstances of use of *thou* have, however, enabled the old strong form to survive, though weak /ðʊ/ has been lost. Evidence of the artificiality of the survival of *thou* since early II is seen in the handling of the associated verb forms. In the 16c the endings showed syncope, i.e., they took the form /st/, which was not normally syllabic; but from the latter part of the 18c poets using the colligation have based themselves on the spelling *-est* and have often made the ending syllabic (/əst/ or /ıst/). These forms were so out of the normal pattern that they had begun to show anomalies even earlier; for instance, even in the 16c we find, beside historic *thou were*, analogical *thou wert, wast*.

We could guess from present usage that the reflexive and intensifying pronouns have had a troubled history; standard has conflicting usage, with genitive first element in *myself*, and non-subject form in *himself*, while vulgar speech has tended to level the genitive type (*hisself, theirselves*). The main formative process was complete by II, but a hint that the grammar has been felt to be changing occurs when 18c printers regularly render *self* as a separate word when the personal element is genitive (i.e., they record their identification of *-self* with the separate word *self*); after the object case this is, of course, impossible. A little further back in the same process is the establishment of the number contrast, *self/selves*, in dependence on the number of the personal pronoun element. This begins in the 16c, but establishes itself gradually.

The genitive *its* now seems so obviously appropriate that we are astonished to find it absent in 1570. Normal at that date, in the function of PE *its*, was the inherited form *his*, i.e., the same form as for masculine concord. But since grammatical gender was as fully absent from the language as it is now, and since the ± personal contrast was otherwise highly systematic in this part of the grammar, speakers felt extremely uneasy about non-personal *his*. Various alternatives had come into tentative use – the most familiar, *it* as in *Lear* (*it had it head bit off by it young*) as early as ME – but usage remained quite unsettled. The first recorded use of *its* is in 1598 (from a foreigner!) and it did not for a time look like a front runner. From the mid-17c it is the norm, and the alternative *his* signifies an element of personification.

§ 88 Relative and interrogative pronouns are also in transition, and the clauses they introduce show change. Like the prop-word, relatives need to be understood in the light of their own history over an extended period, and are not well illuminated by piecemeal presentation. Yet at any one time they have been part of a working language, and their role must be describable, if only in terms of shifts in the balance of probabilities. The recent history of the three main types of relative clause juncture, with *wh-*, *that* or zero (contact-clauses) has been confused by prescriptive teaching, though not by that alone. There are forms in rivalry, and though each has a preferred territory, we cannot describe their present behaviour by clear-cut rules. Four, and even two, hundred years ago there was even more divided usage, because the rivalry was more recent and less resolved. In early NE *that*, which is now virtually confined to restrictive function, was the preferred form even in non-restrictive use. An example showing what was then normal, and now is deviant, is Shakespeare's *Fleans, his sonne, that keepes him compainie*. From about 1700 there is, especially in literary English, a strong feeling for two principles hostile to the extensive use of *that* – for the principle of grammatical explicitness, and for the principle that structures should be self-determining in writing. The first requires that grammatical categories and relations should be specified, not left implicit, if resources existed to make them explicit; and, of course, *wh-* specifies gender (human, non-human) and case (subject, non-subject) as *that* does not. The second principle was well brought out in contributions to *The Spectator* in 1711. Addison (who, like Swift, was as dogmatic as he was ill-informed about the history of the language) presented the *Humble Petition of Who and Which*, their complaint against the recent usurpation (but cf. § 118) of 'the jacksprat *that*'. *That* has the words of a reply assigned to him, but the defence is purely ironic, and mainly serves to play with the possibilities of ambiguity in written English; the punch-line of *that's* defence is:

That that I say is this:
'that that that that gentleman has advanced, is not that, that he should have proved.'

This is, of course, fully disambiguated in speech; the attack is a writer's attack.

The contact-clause was naturally a victim of the same principles, though its decline in written English has no parallel in spoken English. Here the attack began a little earlier, with Dryden's revisions of his own work in the 1680s. It is notable that both Dryden's and Swift's revisions of such structures commonly involve final prepositions too; as Dryden had (so far as we can trace) just invented the principle that sentences should not end with a preposition, it is not altogether certain how far the attack was directed at contact clauses. It is important to realise that contact-clauses are ancient structures of independent origin, not just relatives with pronouns left out. In older English they were indeed more widespread than now, not merely stylistically, but functionally. At the beginning of II, for example, they were still extensively used where the 'relative' had subject function, as in Shakespeare's *I see a man here needs not liue by shifts.* This is ambiguous, and an example from Otway even more so: *to do a deed shall chronicle thy name.* There was good reason for confining the structure to object relations, where there is no ambiguity (as in Defoe, *the same trade she had followed in Ireland*): since the 18c this limitation has been customary in good written usage (on speech, cf. § 43). It is true that Swift's *Polite Conversation* (1738) includes a subject contact-relative, but the point of this work is to ridicule the gauche and uncultured manner of modish conversation; linguistic historians have all too often cited it as by Swift, as if it represented what Swift wrote *in propria persona*, or thought should be said or written. After a disambiguating *that is*, *there is*, and similar expressions the structure has survived even in subject function. This is perhaps the best place to mention the marked restriction of anaphoric demonstrative *that* in relative constructions (as in AV '[sheep] . . . that which is lost'), where *the one* is now preferred; this is the obverse of the development of the prop-word. To this we may relate a use without the *which* we should now require, where it would be hard to say whether *that* was more demonstrative or relative in function, as in: '[handkerchief] . . . that the Moore first gaue to Desdemona'. There are cases where metre shows *that* to be weak, i.e., relative, as: 'I earne that I eate; get that I weare', with which we may compare, in prose, 'I am that I am'. Here, the modern equivalent is *what*.

The feeling for specification of grammatical categories led during II to limitation on the use of *which*. The period inherited the use of *which* in both human and non-human reference, the most familiar example being the Prayer Book and AV forms of the opening of The Lord's Prayer, *Our Father, which art* . . . Except as a deliberate archaism, this use went out in the early 18c, though many were observing the modern rule half a century before that. The feeling for case-specification also played a part here; as early as AV *which* is not used of persons after a preposition (i.e., when use of the personal form enables *whom* rather than *who* to be chosen). In the matter of case the present uncertainties about use of *who* and *whom* are perfectly familiar in the 16c – indeed, they are almost as old as the use of those forms as relatives. *Whose* was inherited as the genitive of *who* or *what*, and continued in that dual role till about 1700, when certain writers deliberately tried to restrict it to uses corresponding to *who*. During the 18c (as earlier) the non-human term had compound formations, *whereof, whereby*, etc., which, though still known, are no longer in daily use. It is curious that they fell into disrepute at the beginning of the 19c as vulgarisms, not as the pedantries we now feel them to be. By way of gain, the first example occurs about 1700 of a highly useful structure in which a relative clause dependent on a preposition is introduced by a relative adverb (Defoe, *near where the thickest of them lay*). As objects of verbs *where/when* relative clauses were formerly in general currency (*hath not where to lay his head*; Milton, *I hate when vice can bolt her arguments*) but they are now restricted to sequence after certain verbs (*find, forget*, in particular); in other cases a normal object (*it*) has to intervene. In other adverbial relative uses, *when* and *where* freed themselves, around 1600, from their earlier co-occurrence with *that*.

There are also differences in the larger structure of the clause. Until the early 18c relatives followed by an iterative pronoun were in good use, but later they have been non-standard, as in Thackeray's, *wanting to fight Tom the post-boy; which I'm thinking he'd have had the worst of it*. But a pronoun is now usual in *that*-clauses after *so, such*, where formerly it was not required (Shakespeare, *no perfection is so absolute, That some impuritie doth not pollute*); the modern pattern has prevailed since the mid 17c.

Derived forms of the relatives have also changed during and since II. *Whoso* was little used and only survives as an archaism; *whosoever* has always been high-flown, and relative *whatsoever* has been archaic since the beginning of the 19c. Jespersen says, contrary to my experience, that *whichever* is not, and has never been, common. At the beginning of II *whosomever, whatsomever*, were still used, but soon died out. The colloquial forms have long been *whoever, whatever*, though usage has never been clear in the genitive. Note, though, that in II the simple relative is common where now either -*ever*, *any(one) who*, or even a conditional clause, would be required (Shakespeare, *Who steales my purse, steales trash*; Pope, *to help who want*).

In certain types of relative sequence there are in PE unresolved conflicts about concord. These result from developments anterior to 1570, but begin to be felt strongly in our period. Colloquial *it (is) me*, literary *it is I*, cannot be satisfactorily matched in a following clause (*who like/likes apples*). The difficulty arises from the conflict between the demands of *it* as overall subject, and *I* as antecedent of the subject relative. The impasse was reached in consequence of a shift in clause-structure during the centuries preceding II. The older construction, *it am I*, meant 'I am the one who'; *I* had subject function throughout, and concord was straightforward. But this order of elements in the clause clashed with the growing sense that immediate pre-verb position is subject position, and that this place must be duly filled. This sense could lead to the use of dummy subjects (*it*, *there*) in sentence-types which had formerly not required a subject (cf. § 123). Or it could lead to a re-allotment of functions to elements in the sentence, as in the type *it am I*, where *it* came to be taken as subject, and *am* therefore to be replaced by *is*. There is as yet no sign that the conflict is moving towards resolution.

Finally on relatives: speakers are no longer at ease with the omission of one preposition in a relative structure that logically requires two. Such omissions had occurred since the earliest recorded English prose, and were probably contrived for the avoidance of clumsiness. In some cases restoration of the preposition may need to be supported by other forms so cumbersome as to make re-writing preferable, e.g., AV *Render therefore ... tribute to whom tribute is due.*

The same *wh-* pronouns are used interrogatively (indeed, this is their older function). Two developments are to be noted. Of *which* Jespersen writes:

> At first it might be used in all kinds of questions, but gradually it was restricted to those in which the question is about a definite number of persons or things. The modern distinction seems to have been carried through pretty much as now from the sixteenth or seventeenth century (1909, etc., III, 130–1).

Further:

> Nowadays the question 'What is he?' always refers to character, office, place in society, or the like, while 'Who is he?' is said when one wants to know the name, etc.; but up till the end of the 17th. c. *what* was used in questions of the latter kind (ib., 131).

Shakespeare's 'Who is Silvia? What is she?' is a familiar example of the older usage.

§ 89 Developments in verbal structures were no less extensive and profound. As one looks at a page, morphological differences most readily catch the eye. Words as familiar as 'It blesseth him that gives' immediately warn us that at the beginning of the period, at least, we shall not find the degree of uniformity in verb-morphology to which we are now accustomed; there is no reason in function or history why *blesseth* and *gives* should differ in ending. The -(*e*)*th* ending was the indigenous southern ending, and had been incorporated into early standard usage. During the 16c a more northerly -*s* form, long familiar to educated London speakers, began to enter their speech; it has finally prevailed. This is another point at which the translation of the Bible has taken a curious hand. The principal momentum of the change was between Tyndale's time and AV; AV preserves the older form, so that this, too, comes quite accidentally to be associated with solemn usage. Great care is needed in interpreting written forms, since there is abundant evidence that one was expected to read -*th* as -*s* during the first half of the 17c. In the 18c. writers who used the -*s* form in speech, and represented it in the conversation of literary characters, would nevertheless prefer -*th* outside dialogue; in two verbs, *hath* and *doth*, the old spellings were particularly tenacious, and there is no reason to doubt that they represented -*s* pronunciations. However, when 19c writers use -*th* as a deliberate archaism, after a period of complete break with the old tradition of representation, they understand by the symbols the same as we do ourselves.

The function of the ending, whatever form it took, also wavered in the early part of II. By northern custom the inflection marked in the present all forms of the verb except first person, and under northern influence Standard used the inflection for about a century up to *c*. 1640 with occasional plural as well as singular value. The tendency did not establish itself, and we might guess that its collapse is related to the climax, at the same time, of the regularisation of noun plurality in -*s*. Though the two developments seem to belong to very different parts of the grammar, they are interrelated in syntax. Before the middle of II there was established the present fairly remarkable type of patterning, in which, for the vast majority of S–V concords, number is signalled once and once only, by -*s* (/s/, /z/, /ɪz/), final in the noun for plural, and in the verb for singular. This is the culmination of a long movement of generalisation, in which signs of number contrast have first been relatively regularised for components of the NP, then for the NP as a whole, and finally for S–V as a unit.

A second morphological difference that meets the eye on almost any page is the use of *be* in the 16c for all forms of the verb *to be* which now have *are*. The older usage is fossilised in AV *the powers that be*, so familiar that we can hardly recognise how far it differs from modern usage; in this instance, too, AV reflects the time-lag between Tyndale and 1611. The new form is again borrowed from northern dialects, and its presence greatly accentuates the anomalies of *be* in comparison with other verbs. It introduces into the present a third form (beside *am*, *is*) which is not the same as, not even from the same stem as, the base (*be*); hitherto, the only real anomaly had been the three-form present as against the normal two-form one. It introduces a major stem-contrast between indicative and subjunctive (*are/be*). From early NE on *be* is additionally unique in having singular/plural, and therefore indicative/subjunctive, contrast in the past tense. The long-standing and deep formal division between *be* and other verbs – now so marked that many linguists have preferred to treat *be* as belonging to a one-member form-class different from the verb – culminates in early II. Since so much of the history of English grammar is a history of levelling and regularisation, this counter-development is all the more remarkable. One is bound to guess that it has some connection with the functional peculiarities of *be*, which had long been in existence, but which assumed a newly systematic role in the language at this time (cf. §91).

Thirdly, we are bound to notice differences in the past tense and participle forms of verbs. In PE the verbs that do not conform to the 'regular' pattern of adding -(*e*)*d* in past and participle are so divergent that it is hardly worth trying to classify them (cf. the large number of classes identified, even though some of the heads of classification are extremely general, in Palmer, 1965). One broad distinction that can be made is between verbs that have two stems, and an alveolar stop terminating the participle (*keep*, *kept*, *kept*), and the rest (though a particular sub-class of 'the rest' will have three stems *ride* – *rode* – *ridden* – and an even more central sub-class will, like *ride*, have a participle in -*en*). We will call the *keep*-verbs Type I and the others Type II; note that in Type I the final stop of the participle need not be an extra (*bleed*, *bled*). These verbs have clear affinities with the regular verbs, and their patterning has been fairly stable. One verb has moved into the regular class since period II (*reach*, *reached*, earlier *raught*), and rather more surprisingly, one has moved to Type I from the regular type (*catch*, *caught*, earlier *catcht*). The big differences are in Type II (which corresponds to what are traditionally called *strong verbs*). There are very few of these verbs in PE (about 60, as against about 360 in OE), and they follow many different patterns of relationship. So although they are mostly very common verbs (it is their familiarity which has kept the remaining ones in this class) we should not expect their patterns to be stable, and we should be right. Not only has there been much change between 1570 and 1770 (the change since is relatively trivial), but also this area of the grammar shows very clearly, by the amount of divided usage, what is meant by saying that the language after 1770 is a regulated language compared with what went before. In Type II verbs we find dozens of alternatives side by side with the forms now standard. There are past forms such as *sate* (for *sit*/*sat*), *spet* (*spit*), *fit* (*fight*), *flang* (*fling*), *stroke*, *strook* (*strike*), *swum* (*swim*), *rung* (*ring*), *drunk* (*drink*), *run* (*run*), *come* (*come*), *writ* (*write*) and participial forms such as *broke* (*break*/*broken*), *held* (= /hiːld/, /hɪld/), *holden* (*held*), *chose* (*choose*), *drove* (*drive*), *drank* (*drink*). Some of these show hesitation between Type I and Type II membership; others move towards the regular type (*understanded* beside *understood*, *shined* beside *shone*); and one goes from the regular type into Type II (*dig*, *digged*, now *dig*, *dug*). It has not been common for the form that in period II was an innovation to prevail, but the pasts *got*, *bit*, came into use in the 16c beside older *gat*, *bote*, and became normal in the 17c. What this confused picture means is the total breakdown of yet older class-affiliations; the restoration of order in more recent English came after a break with tradition, which accounts for the highly arbitrary patterns in many PE verbs.

§ 90   The PE system of contrasts in the verb, and the patterns through which they are realised, are highly unusual; much of this was established before II, but not all. The present modals were used roughly as they are now, but were not so exclusively confined to modal function. Until about 1600 *can* and *will* are current in old uses as full verbs, without following infinitive (*I can no more*; *Ile no gaine-saying*). Similarly with *could*, *would*, which in 1570 preserved more features than now of their origins as past forms of *can*, *will*; and with *might* (= *was able to*, where an element of capacity contrasts with the element of knowing-how in *could*). These differences are fairly subtle, and require great care from us as readers of older texts. For instance, Shakespeare's *she that would be your wife* – 'she who wanted to be' [note also the relative]; that she wants it now or for the future – the natural modern interpretations – is excluded); AV *he would have put him to death* – 'he wanted to', without any conditional element. The use of *would*, the past of tentative wish, (*we would see*) has not in II died out in favour of *would*/*should like to*. Of *would*/*should*, as of *will*/*shall* we need only say that in details the balance of frequency has shifted. The 'rule' quoted by grammar-books for centuries, and drawn up by Wallis in 1653, perhaps had more truth at that than at any other period; it certainly did not hold for Elizabethan

English; it related to a pattern linguistically abnormal, and something steadily rationalised subsequently by dialects and by non-British standards; it is the source of a prescriptive tradition partly responsible for the strange distributions in British Standard. Perfective modals (*would have, should have*) are largely a creation of our period. In Elizabethan, as in older English, *would*, etc. still combined directly with a second participle in this function (Shakespeare, *We should by this . . . found it so*); in clauses of unrealised condition where NE has modal + *have* (Defoe, *I had no compass on board, and should never have known how to have steered*) the norm was *had* (still possible, but rather stiff, and potentially ambiguous). In expression of conditions contrary to fact we find the opposite movement (Congreve, *what a sad thing would that have been, if my lord and I should never have met*, = PE *had never met*).

The distinction between past and perfect was not yet quite so clear-cut as now. Compare Shakespeare's *the time has been*, where (if we can extinguish the effects of familiarity) we should now prefer *was*, with his *I was not angry since I came to France*, where the *since*-clause would now certainly impose the perfect in the preceding verb. This is not to be interpreted as involving a different set of functions, but as reflecting an incomplete stage in the crystallisation of functions which have been emerging with increasing clarity almost since the beginning of recorded English. As to form, the perfect of intransitive verbs is still, in II, quite often formed with *be*, but never to the exclusion of *have*; verbs particularly associated with the *be*-perfect are (*be-*)*come, arrive, get, go*. Passives undergo some development at this period, other periphrastic forms a good deal; thus, at this very time English needs the *be/have* contrast for verbal functions more important than the transitive/intransitive contrast, which is already marked in other ways, and which is itself undergoing remarkable developments (cf. §93). One of the most characteristic British uses, *have got*, often with an essentially present meaning, begins in the late 16c and becomes especially strongly entrenched in questions. Its absence from American English indicates that its hold in the 17c was not very strong (the other distinction often mentioned in this connection, between *got* and *gotten*, reflects independent British and American selection from forms that were in free variation during the 17c; British English has chosen differently in *forgotten*). A fresh extension of perfective forms occurs when the structure *need have* begins to be used where the perfective element really belongs to *need* (*I don't think you need have gone* = had the need to, *have needed); this is common from about 1700. In other ways *need* (and *dare*) show divided usage as they do today, though not in quite the same ways or proportions.

Use in the sense 'have the custom' was current till the early 18c but is now decidedly archaic (*I do not use to* would now usually be simply *I don't* because of the strong habitual element in the bare present; but that depends on the hiving off of the periphrastic present, which must be considered in our next paragraph). The past *use(d) to*, in its modern sense, begins at the end of the 16c, along with perfect and pluperfect forms (*as I haue vs'd to do, I had used to carry*) which are now merely artificial. *Have to* = 'must', but with the full range of non-finite forms which *must* lacks, comes in very slowly; it is recorded in the 14c, has scattered occurrences at the end of the 16c, but is not really acclimatised till the end of II. *Be going to* for the immediate future begins around 1600. With all these, and other forms already mentioned (*am able to, want to*) English developed a repertoire of full verbal paradigms to supplement the defective and functionally restricted modals.

§ 91 We come now to the periphrastic tenses, where the trend has been for rapid growth in use, while at the same time a much clearer functional delimitation of the alternatives has evolved. The general movement is clearly shown by the comparison, quoted in Jespersen (1909, etc.) at IV, 177, between the Gospel of St Mark in AV and in the Twentieth-Century Bible. Twenty-eight instances of periphrastic tenses were common to the two; seventy-eight occurred in the modern version corresponding to simple tenses in AV, and there was only one counter-example. Growth in clarity of functional limitation is shown by the ambiguous form of Polonius's question, *What do you read, my Lord?*, which could now only have *are you reading?* in the sense intended. An apparent counter-trend is explained by the same clarification of function. Elizabethan English permitted the periphrastic form in such imperatives as *Be going!*, but since the meaning is *go (now)* rather than *be a habitual goer* the usage is no longer current.

Growing clarification in the passive notably involved the expanded forms. At the beginning of II *is taken* occurs in functions which are now split between four forms – *is taken, is being taken, has been taken*, and, more recently and colloquially, *gets taken*. There is, for example, a minor misinterpretation in the habitual modern understanding of AV *Blessed are they which* (N.B., relative) *are persecuted*, where the Greek would now have to be rendered *have been persecuted*. The latest stage was the introduction of *get/got*. The matrix (*got acquainted*, predicative which could be taken as a participle) developed in the 17c, but unmistakably mutative passive structures are not found till late in the 18c.

Turning to broader aspects of passive structures, we observe a growing acceptance of transformations with the indirect object of the corresponding active taking subject role. This is one aspect of a yet wider tendency, namely to prefer human, especially first person, subjects where possible. Thus, though we understand them, we would hardly now produce such passive structures as Shakespeare's *attorneys are deny'd me* or *it was told me* or Bacon's *Ther was given us* . . . In each case the normal modern form would use first person pronoun (transformed indirect object) as subject.

It was also at this time that the present, highly unusual, English pattern for clausal contrast of positive/negative, affirmative/interrogative, came to maturity. The evolution of the negation system has continued over many centuries. In 1570, apart from fossilised survivals of the old pattern of pre-negation (*nill* = *won't*), the norm was the use of *not* immediately after any finite verb – *I say not, I know not*, a pattern which remained colloquial till the late 18c. Meanwhile from the 17c, except with such verbs as *know, mistake, matter*, and the current exceptions, a rival pattern, using *do/does/did* as negation-carrier, became increasingly common. Even in the 17c the *do*-forms were not new; what was new was giving them a clearly-defined role, since in Elizabethan and Jacobean English they had been used or omitted indiscriminately, with the sole restriction that they were not used if any other operator was present. A further peculiarity of the PE system is the use of negative operators – *don't, shan't, won't, can't, aren't*, which are in abnormal phonological relationship with their positive counterparts. These contracted forms seem to have developed in speech about 1600, though there is some delay before they appear in writing. It is natural to ask where such very odd forms came from. *Won't* is formed from *wol*, ME alternative to *wil*, but the vowel of *don't* is hard to explain, except, perhaps, if it is modelled on *won't*, or if it is extended from the negative of *does* to the negative of *do*. If its source is the antecedent of *doesn't* it is another instance of early loss of /z/ in a consonant-cluster in a weak form, cf. *isn't* > *i'n't* > *e'n't* > *aint* (/ɪznt/ > /eːnt/ > /eɪnt/). 18c *ha'n't* shows a similar development; modern *haven't, hasn't*, are re-formations from the positive. Note that *ha'n't* would also have agreed in vowel with *shan't, can't*. Modern *aren't* is a simple substitution of a new form from the positive as far as the plural is concerned, and conveniently its termination agrees with that of *shan't*, etc.; with first person singular it is used only in negative interrogation, and not there in all varieties of English; it is in this use probably derived from *amn't*, with the usual loss of the first consonant of the cluster, and lengthening, but its spelling has been borrowed from the type historically descended from *are*.

As regards function, these centuries are those in which the ancient patterns of cumulative negation last appear in the standard language; we still immediately grasp the reinforcing, not contradictory, force of the sequence of negatives in Shakespeare's *And that no woman has, nor never none, Shall mistris be of it*, but by his death this kind of structure has almost passed out of standard use.

Finally, we should note that the new patterning invaded imperatives more slowly than finite constructions. As late as 1700 *let it not* is more usual than PE *don't let it* and to remind us of yet older patterns we have AV (really Tyndale, again) *Thou shalt not kill*.

Closely linked with negatives in PE is the structuring of interrogatives, but here the distinctive patterns are older. Inversion-questions are found at all periods, and the use of *do*-questions in the absence of other operators was already customary by the beginning of II: the only change is that it becomes more sharply defined by the limitation on *do* in its more random uses. Until the early 18c there was a special form *whether* for questions asking *which of two*? Speakers have apparently not felt the maintenance of a special word for this function worthwhile.

§ 92 Among non-finite forms we have to record some shifting in the selection of infinitive forms (*to*-infinitive or bare infinitive), and some in the respective functions of infinitives and gerunds (e.g., *avoid – to*-infinitive, PE – gerund). The infinitive participated in the development of a new type of clause due to metanalysis. What the older function of matrix sentences was is clearly shown by their use in translation. Thus, AV *It is good for a man not to touch a woman* corresponds to an original with the analysis *It is good for a man + not to touch a woman*; but the first part of the first constituent is well-formed as an English clause, *It is good*, and the separability of this led to a feeling that what remained was also a constituent, *for a man not to touch a woman*. On such models a new clause-type arose, with *for + Nom + inf* (*+ Nom*), able to act as subject or complement in sentence-structure.

Absolute constructions reflect the development of periphrastic tenses and of the perfective. That is to say, we now require *being*, or *having been*, to supplement the participle in such late Elizabethan constructions as *his ceremonies layd by . . .* ; *which done, . . .* Also about 1600 a new passive gerund made its first tentative appearance (*who should scape whipping*, now, *being whipped*). In its contrasts and in its functions the gerund has been growing steadily more verb-like, perhaps partly as a result of its formal identity and functional overlap with the *-ing* participle. Jespersen regards as a concomitant of this the growth, since about 1700, of use of a non-genitive nominal in conjunction with the gerund (*I insist upon Miss Sharp appearing, the evil of too much land being locked up*). The same association is held to account for the tendency in early NE, now regarded as vulgar, to use *of* between a participle and its object (*ouer-eying of his odde behaviour*).

§ 93   There have been changes in the verb's relations with other elements of the clause. One group concerns transitivity. There are particular changes, such as the use of *look* as a transitive till the 17c, and *mistake* as an intransitive. Rather more significant is the development in the 16c of the intransitive uses of *get, grow*, which were a prerequisite for the formation of the mutative passive: *go, turn*, followed later. Of most general import was the increasing disuse of reflexives with such verbs as *rest, dress, wash, move*, whence grew the now highly important class of middle or activo-passive verbs. Already clearly established in the type during II are *compare* (= 'be comparable with'), *eat* (+ *short, well*), *pawn, sell, tell, wear* (+ *well, out*). Though there are traces earlier, and the class has grown in membership, its real establishment as a type dates from this period.

We have already seen that the strong sense of pre-verb position as subject position affected the verb's relations with the rest of the clause (cf.§ 88). The use of subject slot-fillers was almost as extensive as now, but there were some exceptions, and the AV's use of Tyndale's patterns kept the old structures familiar (*whosoever hath, to him shall be given*). Expressions with *please – so please you, an(d) please your majesty* – have *please* as subjunctive, while no subject is expressed. The still common *if you please* now has a totally different grammatical analysis from that of 1570, though the form has not changed. Then there was no subject, *you* was indirect object, *please* subjunctive: now *you* is subject, and questions about mood and object would not be raised. Since the use of the subjunctive is governed by the clause and its function, this is the place to mention that the subjunctive in II was used in the same functions as now, but much more consistently, and through a much wider spectrum of styles. The number of occasions when there was a formal distinction between indicative and subjunctive was already very limited, so the seeds of subjunctive decline were already sown.

§ 94 The following passage is taken from the Epistle by E. K. addressed to Gabriel Harvey as part of the prefatory matter of Spenser's *Shepheardes Calender*, 1579:

> And firste of the wordes to speake, I graunt they be something hard,
> /ən(d) fırst əv ðə wɔrdz tə spɛːk, əɪ graʊnt ðeː biː sʊmθiŋ hard/
> and of most men vnused, yet both English, and also   vsed of
> /ənd əv moːst mɛn ʊnjuːzd, jɛt boːθ ıŋglıʃ   ənd aʊlsoː juːzd əv/
> most excellent Authors and   most famous Poetes. In whom
> /moːst ɛksələnt ɔːθərz   ən(d) moːst feːməs poːıts ın h(w)oːm/
> whenas this our Poet hath bene much traveiled and   thoroughly redd,
> /wɛnəz ðıs əʊr poːıtəθ   biːn mʊtʃ træveːld ən(d) θ(ə)ruːleı rɛd/
> how could it be, (as that worthy Oratour sayd) but that walking in
> /həʊ kuːd ıt biː əz ðæt wʊrðı ɒrətɒr seːd bʊt ðæt waʊlkın ın/
> the sonne although for other cause he walked, yet needes he mought
> /ðə sʊn aɫðoː   fər ʊðər kaʊz iː waʊlkıd, jɛt niːdz iː moːt/
> be sunburnt; and hauing the sound of   Poetes still ringing in his eares,
> /bi sʊnbʊrnt ənd ævın   ðə səʊnd əv poːıts stıl rıŋgın ın ız iːrz/
> he   mought needes in singing hit out some   of theyr tunes. But
> /(h)iː moːt   niːdz ın sıŋgın hıt əʊt sʊm əv ðɛːr tjuːnz bʊt/
> whether he vseth them by such casualtye and custome, or of set
> /wɛðər iː juːzıθ əm bı sʊtʃ kæsjʊəltı ən kʊstəm ɒr əv sət/
> purpose and Choyse, as thinking them fittest for such rusticall
> /pʊrpəs əm tʃɔıs   əz θıŋkın əm fıtəst fər sʊtʃ rʊstıkl/
> rudenesse of shepheards, . . . sure I think, and think I   think not
> /ruːdnıs əv ʃepərdz   sjuːr əɪ θıŋk ən θıŋk əɪ θıŋk nɒt/
> amisse, that they bring great grace and, as one would say, auctoritie
> /əmıs   ðət ðeː brıŋ greːt greːs ənd, əz oːn wuːd seː, aʊtɒrıtı/
> to the verse.
> /tə ðə vɛrs/

Naturally, any one transcription involves arbitrary selection between concurrent variant forms, and many words in this passage could have been given alternative representations. Grammatically, we notice features of positional syntax now alien to English (e.g. *of the words to speake*, with the infinitive in final position, already an archaism in the 16c); divergent prepositional uses (notably *of*, NE *by* with passive construction); and morphological divergences (e.g. the *-(e)th* 3sg pres ind, *be = are*; *mought* as a superseded equivalent of *might*; perfect with *be*). *Whenas* exemplifies the old type of compound relative adverb; if

154

think not amisse is a negative clause it shows the older pattern of negation, but the analysis may be *think || not-amisse. Sure* is an old zero-formation adverb which does not survive in standard British English. There is no single word which has gone out of use, but there are important semantic shifts to note, as in *trauailed*, ambiguous between *travail* and *travel* (now distinct words), and *casualtye* = 'chance'. In WF *rusticall* illustrates the earlier free variation between *-ic* and *-ical. Auctoritie* represents the ME loan from French, re-spelled with *-c-* on the Latin model, but the present form, *authority*, has occurred since the 15c; it is not clear when the present pronunciation became established. Other features of spelling and punctuation speak for themselves.

CHAPTER III

1570 – 1370

§ 95   This is, as nearly as any period, the time when Englishmen spoke English and English was the language of Englishmen. Numbers of speakers were small, and although the population grew during the period from perhaps 3m to something like 4½m, it was of the same order of size throughout. The English-speaking population extended from north of Aberdeen to the Devon – Cornwall border, with a few groups of outliers, but not enough to alter the character of an essentially single and homogeneous community in a fairly uniform environment. Only at the very close of the period did the insularity of this community crumble in face of an appetite for the world outside, but even then the major transplantations of the language were still in the future.

Within the community the most important division linguistically was between those with urbanised speech (cf. § 61) and those in pre-urbanised groups, that is, those speaking a variety of English which had had up to a thousand years of more or less undisturbed history in one place. These types are extremes; naturally, people from one village met and married people from another, and sometimes the sharper edges of local peculiarity were worn down by the development of a regional standard language, but the extremes are useful points of reference. When the period began, the process of urbanisation, already under way through the natural evolution of the economy, had been powerfully boosted as a result of the Black Death. A very sharp drop in population-size increased the value of labour and heightened the role of money, and so of urban residence and employment. London was the only major city, not just in terms of size but rather in terms of metropolitan status and range of population-sources. The generation that came to maturity in 1370 saw the last brilliant flourish of regional standard varieties of English. Its more cosmopolitan souls were acutely aware of the state of the language, and the range of varieties, but it is doubtful whether any except those who spoke the London type of Standard recognised that this was a variety already different in kind from any other Standard. By the 15c, London was the only location of a Standard in England (another was, and has continued to be, Edinburgh); so it has remained until the colonies (as they were) started to develop Standards of their own. From a retrospective viewpoint we may draw a pretty direct line from our own educated usage to that of Shakespeare's contemporaries and thence almost to the court for which Chaucer wrote; but for its contemporaries the uniqueness of Chaucerian London English was less evident, and for the first time in our backward path we shall need, as we reach 1370, to see how it compared with provincial Standards.

§ 96   From the close of the 14c there grows in England a class of secular professional scribes who, because they were professionals, might conform to a house-style almost as fixed as that of a modern press, and train their young pupils in the same traditions. In this way the natural tendency of the written language both to regularise and to lag behind developments in speech was greatly increased. There continues, however, to be much documentation produced in a semi-professional way, and further, from the 15c on, a great wealth of personal papers. It would be a mistake to suppose that even personal papers were written in other than a conventionalised orthography, but they are highly likely to include lapses and idiosyncrasies that can be revealing – if we know how to identify and interpret them. At the close of that century Caxton introduced printing to this country (1476). That it was worth printing books in English tells us something about the extent of literacy and the desire for reading in those who were comfortably off without necessarily knowing the languages of learning; and this audience was not new. The extant number of manuscript copies of the major popular long works of the 14c – the *Canterbury Tales, Piers Plowman,* 'Mandeville's' *Travels* – is greater than the extant number of copies of any Caxton edition. But to a printer, unlike a scribe, it is important to find one linguistic form that will be acceptable to any speaker of English who may wish to purchase a copy of the work he has produced; standardisation, across varieties and eventually through time, for the first time comes to be of professional concern to a particular group. Caxton's work stimulates, and articulates, a concern to have it settled that one usage is generally current, and will meet with acceptance everywhere. The *locus classicus* for this concern is his Preface to *Eneydos* (1490, reprinted in W. F. Bolton, *The English Language*, Cambridge, 1966); but it would be rash to take too much at face-value his observations on variation (cf. § 118).

Whatever a printer discovers or decides in the matter will itself become a powerful influence for standardisation and conservation. His successors, especially when printers are still few in number, will not risk failure by making their books look too different linguistically from the exemplars which have already been successful. It is hardly too much to say that the range of devices subsequently used in English spelling was largely determined by Caxton's practice (i.e., his selection from existing conventions); but his practice holds some relation, however complicated and indirect, to spoken English at the close of the 15c.

§ 97 For the first time in our retrogression we need to pay attention to the structure of the alphabet, and we must do it right away in order that quotations may be readable. A general consideration of orthography can, however, wait till Chapter Four. At the end of the 14c the alphabet consisted of twenty-seven single symbols and a number of digraphs and trigraphs; but two of the symbols were dying out of use, and indeed play very little part in the kind of English we are concerned with. Though the manuscript forms of the letters were different, they were, from the beginning of the alphabet to *g*, direct antecedents of our own. While *g* had a form directly underlying modern *g*, it also had an alternative, ʒ, which was used contrastively by some scribes (i.e., medially and finally to represent a palatal fricative, cf. § 128, initially for /j/), but not at all by others; this is one of the dying forms. The next point of difference concerns *j*, which was not in general use, and, if used, was employed as a positional variant of *i*, not to distinguish a separate sound. There are no further differences until *t*, after which we would need to insert þ, a symbol which had been borrowed many centuries earlier from the runic 'alphabet' (cf. § 217), was known by its runic name, *thorn*, and had the value /θ/ or /ð/. I have, for printing purposes, given this letter what may be considered a classical form, but its history in living use belongs almost entirely to manuscript tradition, and letters, like sounds, have a history of continuous formal change. Both depend on human attempts to conform complex muscular movements to what has been humanly conceived as a model. By III the form of this letter had come uncomfortably close in shape to *y*, and if its top closure was carelessly formed, might be taken as a *y*. The clash had a number of consequences. To avoid misreading some took to putting a dot over *y*. But as an alternative was available to replace þ, the now general spelling *th*, it was also natural to concentrate on that to the eventual exclusion of þ. Printers, when their time came, did not wish to have an extra letter for a purpose already met by *th*, and *thorn* went out of use until it was revived for the sole

158

purpose of printing medieval texts. But one function with which *thorn* had come to be closely associated was the fossilised representation of *the*, *that*, *y^e*, *y^t*; these quasi-abbreviations were maintained by early printers, using *y* for the consonantal symbol. It is modern misunderstanding of this convention that has led to the fake antique use of *ye* for *the*: there never was a spoken form in /j/. Meanwhile, the regularisation of the digraph *th* in the repertoire of graphemes (spellings to represent a single phoneme) came after over two centuries of use. It accords with a group of other consonant representations in which *h* has no direct phonological value but serves to signal a digraph. *Wh, ch* were already in regular use as graphemes constructed in this way; *sh* was very common (though *sch* also occurred at the beginning of the period), *gh* was beginning to be, and soon was fully, the replacement for earlier *ʒ, ʒh*. The English alphabet, which was largely Latin in ultimate origin, has never had enough symbols to match English phonemes at any point in history, and the use of digraphs has been one of its common solutions to the problem. In the centuries earlier than III the main deficiency lay in consonants, but as a result of the vowel-changes during III the greatest lack has subsequently been in vowels.

As we would expect (cf.§ 62) punctuation conventions are remote from our own. At the beginning of the period a good manuscript might use a low dot, an inverted semi-colon and a virgule (/) for three grades of either pause or syntactic unit. The devices used by Caxton are virgule, colon and a lozenge-shaped period; these serve to break down the sometimes disorderly and shapeless syntactic stretches that serve him as sentences. Progress towards the modern system (derived from the Aldine Press) was slow; individual practices remained extremely variable, both in degree of self-consistency and in the principles conformed to by those who were consistent.

§ 98   At the close of the 14c writers were acutely and uneasily conscious of the diversity (Chaucer's term) of English, as Caxton the printer was to be at the end of the 15c. Though such remarks became a commonplace with writers in the vernacular, casting an envious eye at the size and permanance of audience afforded by Latin uniformity, there is ample evidence that Chaucer's comment was well founded. But what is very noticeable about the situation is that diversity is a matter for comment (it had existed without attracting much attention for centuries before) and that comment is made from the point of view that one English is the best, while others are inferior, corrupt (*apeyred*), hideous, or at best, laughable. Thus, John of Trevisa, a Cornishman, writing in 1385 in a dialect of marked south-westerly character, ostensibly translating the work of another man, Ranulf Higden, cannot refrain from garnishing the original with remarks of his own about other people's English. His source, which dates from about 1327, shows some such prejudice, but with far less elaboration. John begins by translating quite faithfully:

> Englischmen, þey₃ hy hadde fram þe bygynnyng þre maner speche, Souþeron, Norþeron, and Myddel speche, . . . noþeles, by commyxstion and mellyng furst wiþ Danes and afterward wiþ Normans, in menye þe contray longage ys apeyred, and som useþ strange wlaffyng, chyteryng, harryng and garryng, grisbytting.

> NOTE: ME texts are generally quoted in the form in which they appear in Mossé, 1952. Mossé's principles of editing are not quite those a historian of English might prefer, but his work is indispensable to students and it does not seem justifiable to impose on them two forms of the same text diverging in relatively trivial ways.

But the partly invented and highly onomatopoeic elaborations with which he has concluded the sentence are his own development of the original's contemptuous but laconic *boatus et garritus* (roughly, 'shouts and murmurs'). The same strain enters his rendering of:

> Tota lingua Northumbrorum, maxime in Eboraco, ita studet incondita quod nos australes eam vix intelligere possumus, . . .

to wit:

> Al þe longage of þe Norþhumbres, and specialych at ₃ork, ys so scharp, slyttyng, and unschape, þat we Souþeron men may þat longage unneþe undurstonde.

Not many years from that date Chaucer, who makes no direct value-judgements on the varieties of English he was acquainted with, introduced into English literature the first comic characters who are funny in the first instance because they speak a non-standard, indeed, specifically a northern dialect. The humour, even the humour of character, in the *Reeve's Tale*, is more than this, but it includes this; which has to mean that Standard speakers as a group have achieved consciousness of superiority. Though there had been and still were other kinds of Standard, the sense that there is one variety of English whose speakers are not as other men are, is new. Chaucer was, near enough, a Londoner, and undoubtedly a man of the court; he might be expected to write patronisingly about the likely lads from the north for the entertainment of his courtly audience. These factors do not hold for John of Trevisa, a provincial himself by birth and speech. He belongs to the more generalised but equally strong and persistent tradition of southern contempt for all things northern. It is of some interest that Caxton found Trevisa worth publishing in 1482.

The kinds of variety of English and the social attitudes towards them are familiar to us. They begin at the beginning of III, and despite minor challenges (say, Liverpool in the early 1960s?) continue with little change. Save for the one loss: since 1400 there have not been local standards side by side with the national Standard. From this point there is a colourable excuse for tracing the history of one variety, noting others only as they impinge upon it; in the centuries behind 1370 that would not be possible. In general, even our present sense of the relationship between varieties is fairly appropriate for everything after 1400. The main point of difference is that until the mid-19c spread in geographical range, numbers, size and influence of the public schools, the antecedent of RP was London-based. It was non-localised in the sense that historically it was not the indigenous speech of any area (indigenous London speech, Cockney, was already substantially different). But you learned it by living, at least for a time, among certain circles in London. From the mid-19c the public schools, and the equally regenerated universities, diffused it on a basis that was purely social and non-localised.

§ 99   The rise of this special form of English was a very complicated matter, and, which is rarely true, the more we find out about it, the more complicated it looks. The unique position of London in even earlier centuries had long ago set its speech apart from ordinary dialects, giving it a social stratification that made it vulnerable to changes of fashion, generally considered, and to varying waves of immigrant influence more particularly. What was new in III was a threefold development: first, the evolution of a City of London written standard, which need not imply a spoken one; second, the evolution of a sequence of competing types, of which one (the direct ancestor of PE Standard) dominated from about 1430; third, the rise and spread of a spoken standard (subject to many subsequent variations, but in principle the ancestor of RP) not later than the 16c.

In order to present these events with some semblance of coherence, we must go back behind our period to the beginnings of the rise of (English) London. In Anglo-Saxon times London had been the capital of

Essex, but not of the English kingdom. After the Norman Conquest, as England became part of the 'Channel State' (Barrow, 1956), the national centre of gravity shifted to the Thames estuary. Separated by a couple of miles on the north bank of the river were London proper, ideally placed for trading and the commercial interests that follow trade, and Westminster, already a great ecclesiastical centre with important scriptorial resources, and soon made the home of national administration. Though they were so close, they were in indigenous dialectal development not identical, since they belonged to Essex and Middlesex respectively. From the 12c on, both were subjected to alien influences which began the long history of divorce between indigenous dialect and standard language. In the City of London (henceforth, London) the growth of trade set Londoners moving, at home and abroad, and brought immigrants and temporary residents to London; Professor Barrow writes:

> Trade certainly flourished in Anglo-Saxon times, but during the twelfth century and beyond it grew to such an extent that the country's economy had ceased entirely to be that of a self-contained agrarian society (1956, 87).

York, Lincoln, Exeter, Norwich, shared in this growth, but London's part was substantial. To carry on the affairs of trade, and to supply luxury crafts for the prosperous, strangers, at first from the home counties, poured into London – and incidentally, generated many new needs for written English, and for a class of persons to write it; but in the 13c change of linguistic type remains fairly gradual, since the immigrants were not from far afield. Nevertheless, the foundations of a not strictly localised variety, and therefore of a socially-stratified variety, had been laid. Without such preparation it is unlikely that the rapidity of variety-switches in the following century would have been possible. A standardised written form of English arising out of this phase of London development corresponds to Type II in a classification of late medieval Standards in Samuels, 1963; it is preserved in seven manuscripts originating in the London area, of which the best-known to literary students is the Auchinleck MS. But in the early 14c the pattern of immigration changes. While people continue to come from neighbouring counties, a fresh influx, not necessarily numerically larger, but extremely prosperous and much given to reaching influential positions in City affairs, sweeps in from the East Midlands – notably from Norfolk, but in substantial numbers from Suffolk, Lincolnshire, Northampton and even Yorkshire (Ekwall, 1956). There follows, from the middle of the 14c, a new kind of written English, of strongly Midland character, corresponding to Professor Samuel's Type III, and best known to literary students as the language of Chaucer (according to the consensus of the best Chaucerian manuscripts).

Meanwhile, in the neighbouring City of Westminster, outside influences led to a markedly different development. Henry II (1154–89) transferred the Exchequer from the old capital, Winchester, to Westminster, though 'transferred' is too simple a word for what amounted to the creation of a new institution. It is justified by the linguistic evidence that staff trained in the old West Saxon way of writing were used to man the new establishment. Henry's own Charter of 1155 shows distinct West Saxon (and archaic) features; and that, despite modernisation, the West Saxon tradition persisted, is clear from the Provisions of Oxford issued by Henry III in 1258 (the first State document in English since the early years of the Conqueror). Though Chancery and Exchequer continued in the City of Westminster, we have for a century thereafter no surviving documents to illustrate Westminster English. Since before 1300 one branch of the Chancery had been established in London (Chancery Lane), and from about 1375, when evidence is again available, some London features are found in Westminster written English. Official documents continue to be only exceptionally written in English until 1430, when English becomes the norm and documentation is abundant. It is written in a kind of Standard, Type IV or Chancery Standard, which thereafter reigns supreme. The difference lies in the presence of features of more Central Midland origin than those of Type III, but this does not indicate a fresh wave of migration. East Anglian characteristics were more peripheral and remote, and in particular respects both clarity of communication and a more systematic patterning could be achieved by the adoption of the central type. And so it came about.

Type I has been left to last because it is of quite different origin, and cannot be explained in relation to the history of the London–Westminster complex. It started as a standard for a group of fairly southerly Central Midland Counties – Northamptonshire, Huntingdonshire, Bedfordshire – but was adopted by, among others, Lollard preachers and scholars; it survives in secular as well as religious works, and on a very large scale. How far it was a true Standard can be seen from its use in documents originating in Somerset and Dorset. Professor Samuels considers it to have the best claim to be regarded as *the* literary standard language before the arrival of Type IV, but despite its strength in number and range of manuscripts and geographical spread it could not finally compete with the official standard of the capital, which eventually dominated through sheer bulk. Type I did not wither quickly; far from the capital it was used by the Welsh writer Pecock in the middle of the 15c.

This unavoidable enumeration of types must seem arid in the absence of exemplification. We have not yet had the opportunity of seeing what is meant by a Midland or an Essex type, since we have not yet dealt with a pre-standardised period; yet some introduction to the special circumstances of London-based standards is necessary if we are to understand the complex of forces operating between 1370 and 1570. Our own experience gives us some clue to the situation, in the way that outside forms, especially transatlantic expressions, have crept unnoticed into our own usage; but for us, against centuries of a more or less stable Standard, infiltration is a peripheral phenomenon. At the birth of Standard it was far more central.

There is an inherent contrast in degree of stability between pre-urbanised and urbanised speech, diachronically considered. But since the function of the prestige variety in an urbanised situation is to be the mark of a metropolitan élite, it may seem strange that the source of most innovations proves to be vulgar or dialectal speech. This calls for explanation if the linguistic habits of the 16c are not to seem totally bizarre. First, it is obvious that if change is to come in the élite language by internal borrowing (i.e., from other varieties), it can only come from socially inferior varieties; there are no others. Yet an élite is, by definition, a minority; the preponderant usages must be those of outsiders. The élite will divide into the assured, who will feel no need to resist the influence of other varieties, and the anxious who will want by their language to associate themselves with what they conceive to be a prestige group. They may take over an originally vulgar or provincial usage taken up by those they conceive to be their betters; but even if they do not, we must remember that a use encountered for the first time, at ground-level, so to speak, does not come labelled like a dictionary entry 'colloq' or 'lit'. The listener does not meet it, as we see it from the aerial distance of several centuries, as an item having an overall distribution. He meets it from a particular speaker on a particular occasion, and although it may strike him that the speaker uses it because he is of vulgar or provincial extraction, it may equally well be associated with the speaker's being young, and therefore dashing, or old and therefore sage, or rich and therefore respectable, or a man of the world and therefore sophisticated – or indeed with any number of desirable properties

that can be isolated from the complex and partially-understood phenomenon that is another speaker. Even in this case, then, the origins of a use
may not impede its spread; and overall, any common (in any sense) usage
has a chance of invading Standard. Nor can we expect to find any rationale
behind such invasions. In London circles during the 16c and 17c many
different usages, especially in pronunciation, were jostled together, in one
place and in the same social groups. In that place and those social circles
we find a stupendous amount of divided usage and of the kind of change
we may class as switching rather than development. This was the inevitable form of the rise of a spoken Standard, but equally inevitably it
gave way in the following period to a sense that unity and stability must
be achieved. The guide-line for this normalisation was to be the principle
of correctness, but, as we have seen, the principle was preached long
before it was followed.

§ 100 Bearing in mind these general considerations, let us try to make
sense of the history of sounds. The consonantal changes which can most
readily be brought under a general principle are those of voice, some
of which we have already mentioned (cf. § 50). Voicing after an unstressed
syllable in such words as *desist, resist, dessert, discern, possess*, seems
to have started in vulgar speech; for long voiced and voiceless forms
co-existed, and the present usage is no guide to Elizabethan practice.
The same process accounts for voicing in *knowledge* (14c *knowleche*) and
in the older pronunciation of *Greenwich*; and in the final sound of *curious*,
where we have now restored /s/.

At this, as at all periods, final consonants have tended to unvoice
(that is, speakers have tended to relax the vocal cords rather in advance
of completing an utterance, and the form a word has in final position has
then been generalised). Loss of final -*e* in this period created a new
population of forms to undergo this development; for example, the
/θ/ of *earth, fourth*, arises in this way. Examples are not so widespread
as one might expect, and for a very interesting reason. By older final
unvoicing there had come to be many pairs in which a noun ended in a
final voiceless consonant, and the corresponding verb in a voiced consonant plus -*e* (a pattern reflected in PE in *bath/bathe, advice/advise*.) Now
when final -*e* disappeared, the correlation was often purely one of
voice, and this grammatical patterning was so useful that it survived,
and even extended its range; for instance, a form in final /z/ developed for
sacrifice, v, and one in /s/ for *enterprise*, sb, though neither have persisted
to this day.

There were also widespread tendencies for the loss of consonants. Probably of early 15c date are the loss of /n/ after /m/ and /l/ in *damn, condemn, mill, kiln* (the last restored by spelling-pronunciation in RP but not in craft or dialect use), and of /p/ in *cupboard, raspberry*. Simplification of heavy consonant groups had been going on for centuries, but both loans and new compounds kept up fresh supplies of such clusters, so that the same tendencies can be seen at work during III. At this late date the lost sounds have often been fixed in spellings, and sometimes are now restored under the influences of the spellings. In this way early NE loss of /d/ in *handsome, handkerchief*, of /p/ in *temptation, consumption*, of /t/ in *precepts, often, Christmas, chestnut, pistol, mortgage*, are to be accounted for. What happens is not so much that a sound is dropped as that variations in timing the components of complex articulatory movements will produce or omit a consonant (cf. § 36). Similar variations in timing might cause the introduction of consonants into sequences where they had not previously been. This accounts for the /b/ in *thimble*, the /d/ in *spindle, kindred, thunder, elder* and *alder* (tree-names), and, as early as Chaucer, in *alder* genitive plural of *all* (earlier *aller*). Several factors might have accounted for the tendency to add an unhistoric /t/ as 'finisher' of certain words – *amongst, against, pageant, ancient, parchment*; similarly /d/ at the end of *sound*, etc. This group of changes belongs to about 1400.

As during periods II and IV certain syllable-initial clusters were simplified, with lasting results for the rules of syllabic onset. Initial /wl/ is last recorded in the late 14c (*wlatsom*); it becomes simple /l/, but no words with this original form have survived into PE. The cluster /wr/ was already reduced to /r/ in some speakers by the 15c, but this did not establish itself as Standard usage until much later (cf. § 70). The rare initial cluster /fn/ was absorbed into commoner /sn/ in the 15c; the one everyday word of this origin still in use is *sneeze*.

There was a good deal of instability among the approximants. On the one hand, /w/ assimilated to a following back vowel, and /j/ to a following front vowel. Here, too, we are dealing with a persistent tendency rather than a clear-cut sound-change, and *chaque mot a son histoire*. In a word as common as *two* /w/ might be lost by the 13c, but the principal period of loss seems to have been the 14c before *u* (*such*) and the 15c before mid-vowels (*ooze, swollen, swore, whose, quoth, quote* – as usual, there have been some reversals in later usage). In unstressed syllables loss started even earlier – the 12c in *Canterbury* (*Cant-wara-burh*, 'burh of dwellers of Kent'), and *York* (*Eofor-wic*, 'boar-settlement,

166

-wick'); that it could be heard as late as the 16c in *answer* may be due to the spelling. In parallel we have /j/-less forms of such words as *yet, yesterday, yeast*, but none have survived in Standard.

On the other hand we have the introduction of /j/ and /w/ as syllable-onsets in words that had formerly started with a vowel. From this tendency we have preserved the pronunciation of *one, once* (while our spelling is from the alternative without /w/) and the spelling of *whore* (while our pronunciation is from the alternative without /w/). Words such as *herb* (in which *h* was silent until very recently) and *earth* had variants in initial /j/, but these variants have left no trace in sound or spelling. There is a kind of complementarity about many of these changes, which we meet again in the treatment of (broadly) voiced dentals. It is difficult to interpret the evidence as meaning anything other than a neutralisation of phonemic contrast in a certain environment; what appears to happen is that first, before the following consonant became syllabic, /ð/ before syllables in /r, l, m, n/, becomes /d/ (as in *burden, murder, fiddle, afford*, and in now lost forms of *fathom, farthing, feather*); then, after the 15c development of syllabic /r/, /d/ becomes /ð/ in such words as *father, mother, together, hither*.

I have left till last the one consonant-change that affected the system, loss of /χ/. PE generally derives from a usage in which the consonant was lost, with compensatory lengthening of the preceding vowel, in late ME; but for two centuries at least some speakers pronounced (or affected to pronounce) the sound. Spelling certainly had an influence here, since some late users of /χ/ even followed the spelling in putting the sound into a word where historically it had no place, *delight*. Voiceless fricatives are notoriously difficult to distinguish from one another (cf. /f/ for /θ/ in childish PE, of which there are traces in adult speech during III), and this acoustic property accounts for their liability to undergo changes involving very large articulatory distance. It is in this way that in late ME some northern dialects came to replace /χ/ by /f/ (a change which, just as much as loss, removes one contrast from the system). A number of these forms penetrated Standard, as in PE *enough, cough, draught, draft* (originally the same word), *laugh*, etc.; formerly many other such forms were current.

§ 101 Turning to vowels, it must be evident that reconstruction of a phoneme-system for 1570 will be a very different matter from statements about 1770, or 1970. Something other than the peripheral unclarities of later periods is involved. It is not, of course, that variation was random in any one speaker, but that many conflicting usages coexisted in one centre and among those people who have a claim to be regarded as speaking Standard. In tracing the history of any one phoneme (notably, any vowel phoneme) we may be able to say that at a single time it had one form among advanced speakers, another among conservative speakers, and one that was intermediate; but a man whose speech is conservative in one respect may be advanced in others. This may affect only the phonetic realisation of the phonemes, but it may very well alter the pattern of contrasts he observes. The most we can do is attempt to trace the lineaments of a fairly central type of speech; later we shall see more clearly how variable it was. And this we must do, by way of summary of the changes noted in II, and as a reminder before embarking on the troubled waters of III.

Typically, then, an educated speaker of late 16c London might have the following phonemic system, with roughly the phonetic values the symbols suggest. The long vowels would form a fairly symmetrical group:

/iː/ in such words as *need, meet*;

/eː/ in such words as *read, meat*;

/ɛː/ in such words as *name, hate, bear, tear* (v), and in most speakers, *hail, gay*;

/uː/ in such words as *food, moon*;

/oː/ in such words as *home, goat*, and in most speakers *bold, hold*;

/ɔː/ in such words as *bore, boar*, and in some speakers in *laud, haunt*.

Rather unusually, there is no occupant of the low position; in fact there was a lengthened form of /a/ which occurred in certain environments, (notably before covered /r/ in *barn, card*, etc) but it was probably felt by most as still a conditioned variant (like the long /æ/ of *can* as against *cat* in PE). There was shortly to be a new phoneme in this position (cf. § 64), but probably it was not yet developed in many speakers.

The long, de-centring diphthongs complement this series. The two whose standing is most clear-cut are /əɪ/ in such words as *fine, mite*, and corresponding to it /əʊ/ or /ʌʊ/ in such words as *hour, sound*. There are other de-centring diphthongs, to /ʊ/ in a form /oʊ/ probably employed by some speakers in such words as *bold, hold* (where others have no contrast with /oː/), and probably something like /aʊ/ for some speakers in such words as *laud, haunt*, where others may already have had no contrast with /ɔː/; to /ɪ/ in a diphthong /ɔɪ/ in such words as *choice, joy*; in other words spelt and now pronounced like these, such as *anoint*,

168

cloy, coin, some would use the same diphthong, others would have a contrasting one, /ʊɪ/, or would vary in their usage. Speakers who made a distinction would have an extra contrast in their vowel system, and an abnormally light functional load for the diphthong /ʊɪ/; but both anomalies were likely to be removed by the falling together of this diphthong with the one in *fine*-words (cf. §64; and this is only one of innumerable differences in distribution of phonemes rather than structure of the phoneme-system). Finally, there was a sequence /juː/, which at this date is probably best interpreted as a rising diphthong, in words of rather varied type, such as *use, true, suit, blue, shrew.*

Clearly, speakers, if there were any, who utilised all possible diphthong-contrasts, had an abnormally large range of diphthongs and an unusually large set of long vowels and diphthongs considered jointly. This would be understandable at a period when an old diphthong system was in course of monophthongisation, and a new one being created; and indeed, at the close of III, as at other times in the history of English, this redeployment of the complementary systems was under way. But although it is clear that all these distinctions were made somewhere among Standard speakers, we do not have to believe that they were all made by any one speaker.

The situation among the short vowels is rather simpler – not that usage was more uniform, but that variation affected phonetic realisation rather than phonemic system. The high-mid slack front vowel /ɪ/ in such words as *pin, spit*, had much the same quality and distribution as now, but the corresponding back vowel, /ʊ/ would occur not only in such words as *put, wood*, but also in those like *come, love*; in other words, there would at this point have been one less phonemic contrast (cf. §64) for many speakers, though others no doubt already had an unrounded /ʌ/. With more open articulation were front /ɛ/ as in *men, bet*, articulated much as now and with relatively minor differences of distribution, and back /ɒ/, as in *God, not*. For this last sound, however, many conservative speakers still preferred a higher and more rounded realisation, which had earlier been generally current, while others had not stopped lowering and unrounding at /ɒ/ but had continued to /a/; in the latter case their realisation might or might not coalesce with that of the *hat, man*, words. This is because the older realisation of the *hat*-vowel, /a/, having no forward counterpart, was free to advance and did, but not, it would seem, equally among all speakers; as now, some used /a/, some /æ/. Finally, there was, as now, a vowel /ə/, confined to unstressed syllables. Its approximate long counterpart, /ɜː/, had not yet developed; nor had any of the centring diphthongs.

§ 102 This account might give the impression that there had been remarkably little disturbance of the system and distribution of vowels between 1570 and 1970, but that there had been a tidying up of the areas of divided usage. While the second point is valid, the first is not. We have made the correspondence look closer than it is, because the simplest way into a complicated subject is to illustrate with examples which have had an undisturbed history to the present day, but these examples cannot be generalised, i.e., we cannot say that all PE /iː/-words, like *need*, correspond to 1570 /iː/-words.

The reason for the variations within Standard are connected with the varying pace at which changes were completed or influences from other types of English absorbed. The centuries before 1570 had seen sweeping changes in the realisations of long vowels, and in the length of vowels. So far we have mentioned only the simplest types of divided usage, but they are sufficient to illustrate a principle that will help us to understand a more detailed statement. If a speaker is, say, generally progressive, and uses /æ/ in *hat*-words, he can use /a/ in *God*-words while keeping the two distinct. If he is generally conservative, the same effect results from his retention of /a/ and /ɒ/ respectively. But most people are not that systematic about their adaptation to the diverse forms they hear. For them, the existence of /a/ in *God*-forms can act as what I shall call a *bridge*, provided it has the two banks of /a/-/æ/ identification on one side, and /a/-/ɒ/ identification on the other, to link. By means of this bridge words originally of /ɒ/-type can pass into the /æ/-type (cf. §65). The formation and use of such bridges accounts for much variation in distribution, especially of long vowels, between 1570 and the present day. Further, a situation at once of change and of divided usage will weaken the bonds of correspondence between long and short vowels; speakers have a feeling on this matter, a conviction which can direct their usage, which is not simply dependent on the phonetic facts. For instance, most English-speakers today feel that /ɪ/ is the short partner of /iː/; but the phonetic facts would not necessarily relate it more closely to /iː/ than to /eɪ/. In early NE it is clear that these partnerships were differently structured, and perhaps were less uniformly structured. Thus, movements of shortening, and particularly of lengthening, set up new bridges, by which words came to be affiliated, in respect of their stressed vowels, to a different phoneme.

§ **103** To understand the developments which led up to the 1570 position it is best, first, to distinguish for the vowels three types of system. The system has its fullest realisation in fully-stressed syllables. In syllables with secondary stress the pattern of contrasts is the same, but the phonetic realisations are less marked in character. In PE the system is reduced in unstressed syllables to a two-term contrast, /ɪ/:/ə/; we may suppose that this stage had been reached in principle by 1570, but that the distribution of the weak system was more restricted by the prevalence of secondary stress. The system from which the others can be derived is that of vowels in stressed syllables, which naturally forms our starting-point.

The long vowels have the most complex history, and the one which throws most light on developments elsewhere. Let us begin, apparently in the middle of it, with the vowel of *name*-words, to which we have provisionally assigned the value /ɛː/, and which in II was to reach /eː/, and in I, /eɪ/. This suggests that it was steadily moving upwards; indeed by 1570 it had been moving forward and up for a couple of centuries, its immediate source being /æː/, from /aː/, from /ɑː/. I believe it had this low back quality about 1370, and began its long progress soon after. Thus, in its typical medieval value it was spelt *a*, with a *potestas* general for that letter in Europe; naturally so, since Latin usage is the common source of the spelling conventions. The peculiar modern English value of the spelling is a departure from older common tradition, and it has come about because of the fossilisation of spelling already referred to (cf. §96). There is a widespread correspondence between PE /eɪ/ and 14c /ɑː/ in words now spelt *-a-e*. Now for a vowel to wander thus far through articulatory space is a very strange thing; and it is remarkable that, on the whole, the route did not cross the path of any other phoneme. In other words, if our reconstruction is right, other phonemes too must have been changing, keeping their distance, or they would have been merged with words of the *name*-type. As speakers have no absolute standard of reference for any sound, but identify it by contrasts with others, the preservation of phonemic distance through articulatory change is hardly surprising. As for the timing of the successive stages, we might allow about half a century for each one up to 1570, but we must remember that some speakers might be a stage behind, others a stage ahead, of the sequence we have taken as our norm.

Now it is obvious that this movement of /ɑː/ is a threat to the phoneme next in front of, and above it; and in PE the phoneme in this relationship to /eɪ/ is /iː/, in words of the *need*-type (i.e. most words in which /iː/

is now spelt *ee*, and a number of others). Here, the late 14c antecedent is /eː/, and there is abundant evidence that it completed an upward movement in the 15c (indeed, in the north it had started earlier). We note, therefore, both that it does keep its distance, and that another divergence between PE and general European spelling-values is accounted for.

This may lead us to suspect that PE /aɪ/, in words spelt *-i-e* (e.g., *line, mite*) derives from a medieval /iː/, and must have diphthongised not later than the upward movement of /eː/ in *need*-words, since it has not merged with that phoneme. On both counts we are right. The process is a little more complicated than in the other two cases, but our own experience is sufficient to explicate it. The /iː/ sound requires a substantial amount of energy for tongue and lip movements, and very precise synchronisation of complex muscular activities; if we start it before all the speech-organs are in correct position, we slide into it through a middish, slackish position, which is heard as an /ə/-quality on-glide. Indeed, [əɪ] can often be heard today as the realisation of /iː/, and is general in some varieties of English. Equally, it seems to have become general for older /iː/ in the 15c; thus, a sound which could not go any higher was still kept out of the way of a rising neighbour. Only at a later stage (cf. §64) was the diphthongal character of the sound reinforced by lowering the first element to /a/.

So far, the correspondences seem straightforward, but now the situation alters. For 14c /aː/, in moving forward, had invaded a front-vowel system which already in some dialects had three points of contrast (as 14c rhymes clearly demonstrate); in other words, there was, at least for some speakers, a fourth phoneme which has been submerged as a result of the cyclic movement. This, at the beginning of our period, was /ɛː/, in such words as *read, meat, great, break*. It no longer survives as a point of contrast but has been overtaken by ME /aː/; its reflex in those PE words that survive from forms belonging to this type of English therefore is /eɪ/. Dialects which did not make the distinction have ME /eː/, PE /iː/ in such words, and for the most part PE has conformed to this type (cf. §66). Roughly, SE English made no /eː/ː/ɛː/ distinction, the SW made it in most words, the Midlands in some. London speakers would be aware not only that some people had the distinction while others lacked it, but also that those who made it were far from consistent among themselves about the words it belonged to. Both types coexisted in III, and the present rather fortuitous developments are 18c (cf. §66).

Overall, then, three points of contrast among long front vowels seem to be as many as could be clearly supported; we started with three, and after a period of fluctuation settled down to it again. The intrusion of a fourth item into the pattern led to loss of contrast elsewhere, though the mechanisms of loss were varied, so that items belonging to the lost phoneme have been redistributed, not merely merged into another.

Now, it is remarkable that the cyclic movement we have begun to describe is the only one of its kind in English. The principle of keeping distance, which dominates when such a movement takes place, might be set in action in two ways. As we have seen, /ɑː/, for lack of close neighbours, was free to start drifting, and its movement would set off a chain-reaction, which, since the impetus comes from behind, is called a push-mechanism. Alternatively, we have seen that /iː/ was liable at any time to start diphthongising, and whenever it did would create a gap in its old position, into which, by the principle of distance-keeping, /eː/ might be drawn; this kind of reaction, whose impetus comes from attraction into a gap, is called a pull-mechanism. It is perfectly possible that the forces establishing the new equilibrium should involve both pushing and pulling. One piece of evidence which might throw light on the mechanism is the behaviour of the neighbour of /ɑː/ in the direction it moved away from, namely /ɔː/. If this moves away from /ɑː/ it cannot be dependent on the movement of /ɑː/; and that is what happens. Like its front counterpart, it rises in the 15c, giving /oː/ in such words as *home, goat*; and its neighbour above, 14c /oː/, also rises, to /uː/, in such words as *moon, food*, while 14c /uː/ diphthongises in a way parallel to the corresponding front vowel, becoming /əʊ/, or possibly /ʌʊ/, as in *house, out*.

It is clear that the back-vowel movement cannot result from pushing, and must have started by drift towards a diphthong at the top end of the group, so we may think it most likely that the front-vowel movement was set off in the same way. At the same time, unless /ɑː/ had moved quite a long way independently, it would not have been within the 'magnetic field' of its nearest front neighbour (/ɛː/ becoming /eː/) and would have dropped out of the cycle of movement (this is true, even if you hold, as many scholars do nowadays, that it had already reached /aː/ by 1370). I would regard the movement of the low vowel of *name*-words as caught up in a long, independent movement, lasting over a very extended time. In the course of this progress, I believe, the vowel reached late in the 15c a stage, /æː/ or even /ɛː/, at which it was partly caught up in the pulling movement, partly embroiled in a clash with the vowel of *read*-words. The changes as a whole had the effect of leaving all long vowels mid or high in quality; the low position was for a short time quite unoccupied, though very soon phonetic lengthenings began to invade it, and it was re-established as a phoneme during II. Finally, we should mention that at the beginning of III there was another long vowel, the front rounded vowel /y:/, in such words as *true, blue*. At various times such vowels have entered English, but they have never been very durable; in this case the front quality was soon lost, and an on-glide developed, giving /ju:/ in the 15c, which then lost the on-glide, falling together with /u:/ (the new /u:/ of *moon*-words) in the 16c.

Generally, then, there is a pair of sequences of upward movement, with spin-off of the old high vowels into the diphthongal system, and rogue movements at the bottom (/ɑ:/) and the top (/y:/), thus:

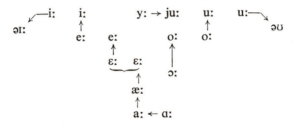

It is this dual raising process which is commonly referred to as the Great Vowel Shift.

NOTE: In general this diagram starts a fresh entry and arrow for each item involved in a movement; in the two dimensions available it is not possible to indicate that at the /ɛ:/ to /e:/ stage both a new movement and continuation of the /ɑ:/ movement are involved, except by the presence of a brace; the diagram does not indicate at all the subsequent switch to an /i:/ vowel in *read*-words, which is not part of the movement of phonemic drift, nor the merging of diphthongal *hail, bold*, types into the then long pure vowels of *name-, home*-words, which is generally later and not part of the pattern.

§ 104 Though the general pattern of raising of long vowels in the 15c can be stated in terms of broad correspondences, the correspondences have often been disturbed, either by changes due to syntagmatic context or by changes of length. Let us look first at the influence of neighbouring sounds. At all times post-vocalic /r/ has tended to cause the preceding vowel to lower, and this effect is very plain in the 15c. A following /r/ inhibits the raising of ME /ɛ:/ in such words as *tear* ('rend,' v, 'rent,' sb), *pear* (ENE /tɛ:r/, /pɛ:r/); the vowel of such words is therefore overtaken by the *name*-vowel, for some speakers in the 16c, for others later; at the same point a following /r/ halted the progress of 14c /ɑ:/, so that *pare: pear, ware: wear*, come to be homophones; and as the former diphthong /aɪ/ falls together with 14c /ɑ:/, that stops at the same point before /r/, adding *pair, hair, fair*, to the homophone lists. They all have /ɛ:r/ until loss of the /r/ produces the diphthong /ɛə/ (cf. §64). For back vowels the development seems to be parallel; the outcome of 14c /ɔ:/ before /r/ is the unraised vowel (as in *bore, boar*, but with /r/ still pronounced); the outcome of /o:/ before /r/ is generally /ɔ:/, as in *hoard, afford, whore*, but in other cases contrary pressures towards raising (see below) prevailed. Sometimes even ME /u:/ is lowered to the same vowel, as in one development of *your, bourn, mourn, floor, pour*, but generally /u:/ remains, to become /ʊə/ at the loss of /r/ in *boor, poor, moor*, etc.; sometimes it diphthongises as in *our, shower*.

On the whole, the weakness of this influence upon the high vowels is remarkable; /i:/ proceeded to /aɪ/ in *fire, mire*, and /e:/·to /i:/ (later /ɪə/) in *fear, hear*; on the other hand, though, retention of the identity of 14c /ɛ:/-words with the *name*-type was more usual than in other environments (in addition to examples already quoted we have *bear, swear, wear*) there are also reflexes indicating identity with 14c /e:/ – *shear, tear* ('lacrima'), and in the 16c many words of this type had both developments. The oddest development is that whereby a few /e:/ words apparently went from /i:/ to /aɪ/, surviving examples being *briar, friar, quire, choir*; these forms are perhaps importations from a dialect in which there had been more general raising of /e:/ to /i:/ before 1400 (i.e., in time for the change of /i:/ to /aɪ/).

The close presence of a labial tended, however, to preserve the quality of 14c /u:/ – not because of the labial position itself, but because of the high tongue position which is a secondary feature of English labials. Thus, ME /u:/ is preserved after /w/ in *wound*, sb (though early NE did have a diphthongised variant, as in the current v form), and before /m/, /p/ in *tomb, coomb, room* (this also with a diphthongised variant, now lost), *coop, croup, droop, hoop, stoop, poop* (the last also diphthongised).

§ 105 The diphthongs /ɔɪ/, /ʊɪ/, must be treated together. They were not entirely distinct in ME, standing in the curious relationship that there was one class of words which could only have /ɔɪ/ e.g., *employ, choice, exploit* (words originating from a particular background in French), while all others (and they were of varied origins) could have either /ɔɪ/ or /ʊɪ/. The reasons for this alternation are only partly clear. It could occur in forms of Anglo-Norman provenance, like *anoint, boil*, v, *coin*, direct

French loans, such as *annoy, broil, oyster, toy,* Dutch *loiter* and *foist,* and the more or less native word (*em*)*broider*. The /ʊɪ/ variety continued during our period, and then shared the unrounding which affected simple /ʊ/. Although that is later, the relationship of /ʊɪ/ to /ɔɪ/ forces us to consider it here, that is, while the variants existed concurrently. Now the unrounded diphthong /ʌɪ/ is hardly distinguishable from /əɪ/, and indeed was quickly identified with it, so that *join* and *line*, *boil* and *mile*, rhyme. But this was not the first time that /ɔɪ/-words had clashed with /aɪ/-words, for the *annoy, oyster* group also had a variant, developed many centuries earlier in Anglo-Norman (cf. § 129), in ME /iː/, early NE /əɪ/. This particular group within the whole /ɔɪ/ class therefore constituted a bridge by which crossing from /ɔɪ/ to /ʊɪ/ and from either to /əɪ/ and back was possible. In consequence, certain forms which historically were of /iː/-type in ME crossed at this time to /ɔɪ/ – *boil*, sb ('ulcer'), *groin, hoist, joist*. No doubt the homophony of *boil*, sb and v, and the association of *groin* with *loin*, helped to determine which items should actually make the crossing. But during III usage remained extremely unsettled. Roughly, any items that had /ɔɪ/ : /ʊɪ/ variation at the beginning of it might have /ɔɪ/ : /əɪ/ variation at the end of it, and the present distribution of /ɔɪ/ forms (which is markedly influenced by spelling) has been fully established for hardly a century. The spelling-conventions which have been so influential on this point were, of course, established during III.

The remaining diphthongs, those decentring to /ʊ/, happily present a simpler picture. Late ME *eu* [which may have been /ɛ(ː)ʊ/, /e(ː)ʊ/ or some range of these possibilities (cf. § 129)] raised its first element to /ɪ/, becoming one phoneme with earlier /ɪʊ/, and shifted stress, becoming the rising diphthong /juː/, giving in such words as *blue, hue, shrew*, /bljuː/, /hjuː/, /ʃrjuː/ from which the /j/ has in most circumstances subsequently been lost (cf. §65): late ME /yː/, usually in French loan-words such as *vertue*, has shared the same development, the two falling together from the 15c. ME *ou* (which, like ME *eu*, is often thought to have had a range of values, but which can hardly have been more than one phoneme by 1400) probably had the value /ɔʊ/, and raised its first element when independent /ɔː/ became /oː/. The /oʊ/ diphthong then tended to monophthongise, again at different rates in different speakers, but with the same outcome /oː/. The /oʊ/ to /oː/, /eɪ/ to /eː/ mono-phthongisations affected some speakers in III, some only in II, cf. §101.

Finally, in words of the *awe, fawn, call* type, late ME had a diphthong

/aʊ/, which monophthongised, in some speakers in III, in others later, and with varying outcome according to date, cf. § 64.

§ 106 Changes in short vowels during III are mainly the result of environmental influences. The recurrent tendency for a following /r/ to cause lowering affected *er*, which often becomes *ar*. This change belongs to the early 14c in the north, and perhaps extended south by internal borrowing, since its results are never consistent in the Standard language. They begin to appear in the late 14c, and some of them were securely enough established to be incorporated into spelling, but there were many alternative forms in the 16c (and even after), and where spelling did not show the change it has acted in favour of *e* forms. Words affected included *hearth, hark, clerk, yard, farm, earl, earn, desert, swerve, serge, heard, servant, varnish, sergeant, arrant, farrier, quarrel, war, far, star*. Note that the double forms *person/parson*, originating in this way, have managed to survive by differentiating semantically (also that many of the forms have been affected by subsequent changes – lengthening when /r/ is lost, and rounding after /w/).

Both /l/ and /χ/ tended to produce diphthongisation of a preceding /a/ or /ɒ/ in late ME; the diphthongs then shared the history of ME /aʊ/, /oʊ/ (cf. §64) (the forms of *half, calf, bold, hold, slaughter, laughter, brought, nought*, are affected by these changes). A following consonant requiring high tongue position tended to cause raising of /ɛ/ to /ɪ/ and /ɒ/ to /ʊ/. The development had generally occurred by the 15c in such words as *England, wing, fling, hinge, singe, mongrel, monger, among, murder* (/d/ influence predominating over /r/ influence here), though for these, and for other words not now showing the change, there were 16c alternatives.

§ 107 The relatively strong value and wide distribution of secondary stress found in II are naturally even more characteristic of III. The vowel-system of secondary-stressed syllables corresponds to that of full-stressed syllables, but the phonetic realisations are weaker – just as in PE the vowel of the second syllable of *follow* is a weak /oʊ/ as compared with the one under full stress in *foal*, but does belong to the full system of contrasts, not to the two-term, /ə/:/ɪ/, contrast of unstressed vowels (as in the second syllable of *collar*, or in non-standard 'foller', /fɒlə/). The highly simplified pattern of contrast in unstressed syllables had taken shape well before III, and it may seem surprising that there can be anything left to report about unstressed-syllable vocalisation at so late a date. There is, for two reasons. One is that the intermediate-grade vowels (as in the second syllable of PE *follow* or the first syllable of PE *obey*) keep feeding new material into the corpus of unstressed syllables. This tendency has to some extent been reversed in I as a result of the new principles of correctness, but until speakers became self-consciously corrective about standards of usage the movement had been pretty consistently from reduced to weak grades of vowel. And as syllables using the reduced vowel system were always being renewed, by new compound formations, and by polysyllabic loans, they did not dry up as a source of weak syllables. The other factor is of a different kind. Sound-changes, though they may not be within the conscious control of speakers, do not operate blindly. A change that will not cause grammatical confusion may proceed rapidly, while under similar phonological circumstances, grammatical utility may prevent it from taking place. We find, in fact, a number of weak vowels with grammatical roles surviving in 1370, where others have gone; meanwhile, the grammar had been evolving new devices, and what we may regard as 'natural' phonological losses were no longer impeded.

In 1370 the system of vowels in fully unstressed syllables was already /ə/:/ɪ/. At first /ə/ seems to have been in free variation with /ɪ/, but not vice versa (cf. PE variation in the third syllable of *ability*, but not in the first); then in syllables with earlier variation /ɪ/ was generalised, perhaps from about 1400 in southern standard usage.

This qualitative change begins to give the language its present air, producing the /bɪ/ of *begin*, *become*, *beside*, the /ɪd/ of *ended*, *hated*, *clouted*, the /ɪz/ of *churches*, *houses*, *bridges*, and many other forms that occur numerous times in every scrap of conversation. Even more far-reaching in effect were the losses, the dropping of a vowel with removal of a syllabic beat, *syncope*. This affects the shape of hundreds, even thousands of words, altering the rhythm of every sentence spoken. The grammatical consequences were also marked, not because the grammar had to change – as we have seen, most of the sounds would have been lost before but for their grammatical function – but because the real mechanisms of modern English grammar now stood on their own feet, and the terms in which the system can be described are therefore quite different.

It is to these losses that we must now turn. Many of the lost vowels continued to be written (as many are to this day), and dating is therefore difficult unless losses are shown in metre; but many lines of verse could be metrical on more than one interpretation, and there is strong evidence that poets for at least a generation drew on pre-syncopated forms if it happened to suit their purposes. The most likely time of onset for the losses in Standard seems to be the beginning of III (which means that the pre-syncopated forms undoubtedly present in Chaucer's verse are a slight archaism), but they were certainly earlier in the north. For Standard we can be sure that our dating is not too early. And we can understand from PE usage that the changes may not have been clear-cut and once for all; for a very long time we have had syncopated and unsyncopated forms side by side in such words as *history, Margaret* – it is not a dialect difference, or an age difference; one simply says the word one way or another from one occasion to the next. The middle syllable of three in words of just this rhythmical structure is precisely one of the locations of early syncope, in words like *every, battery, century, sovereign, poisonous, business.* A variable situation in such words helps us to understand how items have throughout history been fed from the secondary-stressed syllable class into the unstressed class. In a word like *poisonous* a tri-syllabic pronunciation will, by an alternation which is one of the most durable features of the language, have the weakest syllable immediately after the initial stress (the tonic), and the third syllable stronger than the second; if the post-tonic is lost, *-ous* will stand in that position, and will consequently weaken in stress. Loss of post-tonic was much more regular when three syllables followed, in such words as *Salisbury, Bartlemew* (from ˈ*Bartholo*ˌ*mew*); but in other words secondary stress persisted on the third syllable [the *secretary* type (cf. § 52)]. If the post-tonic ended in a vowel and the next syllable opened with one, loss was also regular; *mariage,* /ˈmarɪˌɑːdʒə/ > /ˈmaradʒ(ə)/ > /ˈmarədʒ/ > /ˈmarɪdʒ/ (by the close of the 16c). Similarly, *collier* becomes homophonous with *collar* (the present form being a restoration on the basis of the spelling).

But far more important was the loss of *-e,* /ə/, in final syllables, finally, and when covered by a consonant. This affects the syllable-structure of innumerable nouns and adjectives and verbs and adverbs in their base forms – *love, hate, come, have, take, die, measure, lane, late, fast,* etc. etc. – practically all words now ending with post-consonantal final *-e* and huge numbers of others. This *-e* was often the only surviving formal indication of an extraordinary range of grammatical functions, marks of distinction between form-classes, of the major categories, case, number, person, within form-classes, and of certain types of con-cord within and between clause-elements. The consequences will be seen more fully in the review of grammar at § 118 but we must be clear at the outset that this sound-change does not merely affect phonology, even though in phonology alone its effects are unusually far-reaching.

By this means the present role of inflections in English, small as it is, was achieved. That grammatical function does not impede the losses, shows some 14c inflections were not the true carriers of grammatical meaning. The grammar of the language had come to function by other means, which were sufficient for it when these vestiges of an older mechanism died away. The grammar of modern English was established before 1400; changes after that date merely bring to the light of day what the effective mechanisms really were (cf. § 123).

The loss of final -*e* is phonologically straightforward, that of covered -*e*- slightly more complicated. Loss came first in trisyllables such as *husbandes, northwardes* (note that inflectional syllables have an inherent weakness which takes priority over the tendency for strong – weak alternation). At first disyllables did not lose -*e*-, but there was a natural tendency to identify inflections wherever they occurred, with the result that forms with and without -*e*- came to be treated as free variables after any word; -*es* and -*ed* in particular had the alternative forms. However, the vowel was not lost if the result would have been an unpronounceable or un-English consonant-sequence. This is not a matter of course; the syncope could have occurred, giving no inflection (as in *cut*, present and past, a much older type of formation). The preference for keeping the -*e*- where it was a condition of keeping the consonant indicates how strong was the sense of the grammatical role of such inflections as did survive. This choice is the germ of the later English use of /ɪz/, /ɪd/ beside purely consonantal forms of the morphophonemes, a distribution which became systematic by the end of III (except in verse); it is the only distribution found for the -*s* of verb third singulars, which enter Standard in the later 16c (cf. § 89).

In order to understand this distribution we must also take account of a consonantal change. At various times in the history of English and its antecedents consonants have tended to become voiced if they are not immediately preceded by a main stress. In late ME inflectional -*s* was normally voiced in accordance with this principle, but when -*e*- was lost the principle was no longer relevant, and -*s* (also -*d*) de-voiced if it followed a voiceless consonant. A few forms (*pence, dice*) survive from an alternative sequence of development in which -*e*- was lost before voicing, so that -*s* stood at the close of a stressed syllable and was un-affected by the change. In all discussion of syllable number, sequence and type, it is important to calculate what is the number relevant to the period under discussion, not to assume the present syllable-structure of words.

By a change hardly separable from loss of -*e*(-), post-consonantal -*m*, -*n*, -*l*, -*r*, coming into final position, develop into syllabic consonants, in such words as *bottom, ridden, saddle, keeper,* and non-finally in *student.* Where -*r*- is concerned this may lead to metathesis, i.e., inversion between the consonant and its neighbouring vowel. Metathesis has given the surviving forms *apron, citron, saffron;* in the case of *northern* (and forms from the other compass points) later English has preferred the older form, which, with later loss of post-vocalic -*r*, has given a markedly different outcome. On all these matters early NE usage was divided; and the syllabic consonants seem steadily to have lost ground since the 16c.

§ 108 The indefinite article in late ME was already distinct from the numeral *one*, and had the form *an*, /ɑːn/, weak /an/; loss of final /n/ before consonant onsets develops during III. Although our own strong *a*, /eɪ/ develops directly from the ME form, the Elizabethans had an alternative form by re-lengthening of /a/ (i.e., without 15c fronting and raising). The definite article, in its normal or weak use, has its initial consonant voiced (because the syllable is unstressed, and is often not preceded by a stress). The voicing is 14c, and applies to a number of other forms of similar type. Initial /ð/ does not arise from any other source, so this phonological development comes to be a sign of a, roughly speaking, grammatical class of demonstrative or deictic words (*the, this, that, there, thus, thou, they, though*); some Elizabethan speakers kept old strong forms in /θ/, but subsequently /ð/ has been generalised even in strong use. After an unstressed syllable -*s* will voice (cf. § 100); from 16c alternatives we have selected the voiceless form in *this* but the voiced (which in the particular instance is older) in *these* (*his, is, was,* varied on the same lines). *Their* had strong /θɛːr), weak /ðər/, from which we have a mixed reflex; our *they* derives from the weak form, with later vowel lengthening in final position. *Though* varied in yet another way, since its strong form developed the final consonant /f/ (cf. *cough,* and see § 100); in the weak form post-vocalic /χ/ died away, and like *they* the word has had subsequent lengthening in final position. *He, who, other,* all had variants which have died out. Particles have strong-weak doublets, *as* in /s/, /z/, *if* in /f/, /v/, *with* in /θ/, /ð/; since in certain particles the strong form might be associated with adverbial function and the weak with preposition, the two might separate, as with *of/off.*

§ 109 Changes in the length of vowels are confusing if we look close, at the detail, but clearer if we think in terms of a broader principle, which had begun to operate in ME. A tendency emerges to relate the quantity of a vowel to the structure of the syllable it occurs in. This principle operates fairly widely as far as short words are concerned, but for words of three or more syllables an older principle, of avoiding length in even the stressed syllables of polysyllables, prevails. Both principles are irregular in application, because they conflict with influential analogies; but as guide-lines for the grouping of individual tendencies to lengthen or to shorten it is useful to think of word-structure controlling vowel-length in polysyllables, and syllable-structure in shorter words. In short words the principle divides into complementary branches, requiring that under stress open syllables should have long vowels, and closed syllables short vowels. An open syllable is one ending with a vowel, a closed syllable one ending with a consonant (at all periods in the history of English, as in many other languages, the onset of a syllable is irrelevant to its classification). The application of these statements is clear enough for monosyllables – *die* from 1400 has been an open monosyllable, and *did* a closed one. In disyllables the boundaries are not self-determining, but are governed by the structure of the language. The position in III seems to have been as it is now. Medially, morpheme-boundaries take priority over phonemic composition; where there is no morpheme-boundary a single consonant marks the onset of the second syllable, but a cluster has at least its first component assigned to the preceding syllable. Thus, in PE, *pony, sea-sick, tea-tray*, have open first syllables, but *poultice* and *hat-rack* have closed ones. As a complication we have to note that the distinction between a single consonant and a cluster has at all times been less clear-cut than it might seem. /tʃ/, which for most purposes then and now has been like a single consonant, in this respect functions like a cluster. In medieval English, individuals seem to have varied in sensing *-st-* as single or cluster (hence, NE *priest* but *breast*, though the words are of parallel origin). We might today be doubtful about where the syllable division comes in *-nd-* sequences (e.g., *window, Sindy*), but we would be sure it came after the first consonant in *-dn-* (e.g., *kidney, Sidney*); and this is related to what can and cannot happen in final position (*wind, sinned*, but not **widn, *sidn*).

Quantitative change during IV in accordance with this principle by no means made an end of the matter (cf. §135). In the first place it created many anomalous relationships, since before the loss of inflectional *-e(-)* a monosyllable might have occasion to lengthen when inflected, but not when uninflected; and a disyllable vice versa. Since length-contrast was not a normal way of indicating such grammatical differences there was from the outset a strong pressure to use one length throughout a paradigm – to generalise either the long or the short vowel. And the picture was greatly disturbed when -*e*(-) was lost, after which many words which had the lengthened vowel had come to be closed monosyllables. There was accordingly a new population of forms for the same tendencies to work upon. Early lengthening will show the outcome of 15c raising (as in *waste*); later lengthening will not (as in *master, plaster, father*). Elizabethan English commonly had both forms for such words, but later standard use has dropped one or other.

Similarly in cases of shortening. Elizabethan English had both long and short forms of *death, breath, beneath, deaf, head, bread, stead, spred, shred, tread,* etc.; and for the reflexes of ME /oː/ [long /uː/, with early shortening PE /ʌ/, with late shortening PE /ʊ/ (cf. §64)], *blood, foot, move*; and from ME /ɔː/, *cloth, froth, loaf, road,* etc. From ME /aʊ/ we have the results of early shortening in *laugh* (/a/, with subsequent re-lengthening), and of later shortening in *sausage,* but Elizabethan English also had short forms for *safe, chafe* (beside the forms we have preserved). For ME /oʊ/ there were doublets for *cough, trough, brought, ought, sought* (in addition, these forms had variants in /f/ from /χ/). ME /eː/, whether it shortens early or late, results in /ɪ/; long and short forms were current for *sick, grit, crick, thief, heel,* v, etc.

Such was the inheritance bequeathed to period II, and we shall find that inheritance not much less diverse in grammar and vocabulary than in phonology. An understanding of this diversity may help us to appreciate that those writers and scholars who from the Restoration complained so bitterly of the lack of regularity and ascertainment in English were expressing something more than the bigoted pedantry which motivated such views in later centuries. The apparently irrational confusion of forms and tendencies facing the historian must be understood as arising from urbanisation, the full consequences of which were felt in the Standard language during this period. Yet even this confusion existed against a relatively stable background of consonant structure; once we reach a pre-urbanised stage each variety of the language, by and large, traces its own course, in a way that, so far as we can determine it, is relatively simple and comprehensible. As Chaucer remarked (on a rather different subject) at the very beginning of period III:

Owt of thise blake wawes for to saylle,
O wynd, o wynd, the weder gynneth clere.

§ 110 In vocabulary the first part of the period was probably one of steady but modest gains, and dramatic losses. The later part saw the first stages of that outward-looking behaviour which has characterised English vocabulary ever since. Doubts about the innovations of the early part relate to loans from Romance sources, much the largest group. Literary documentation from 1370 is so much fuller than for the immediately preceding centuries that we are bound to suspect that there will particularly often be a particularly large gap between the introduction of a word and its first recorded instance. Over a thousand French words, for instance, are first recorded in Chaucer's work. No doubt, as a courtly poet priding himself on his elegant French, he did introduce a number of words, but hardly on this scale. Some French words recorded from period III can, for some special reason, confidently be assigned to it. Some are from dialects, encountered in trade, which had not previously supplied English with words – *spigot* from Provençal, *rack* (to draw wine off from the lees) from Gascon, and *chamois* from Swiss-French. Occasionally the phonology of a form will provide a clue; *oblige* seems to have been being domesticated at the time when /iː/ was becoming /aɪ/, and until the 18c had a variant in /iː/ (i.e., a form which must have been accepted after the sound-change, whereas the present form must be from a variant accepted before the change). *Serviette, redeem, Mademoiselle, serge*, are recorded late in the 15c, which, with all reasonable allowance for delay, fairly certainly means that they arrived after 1370. In other cases one is bound to lack confidence, but the following is a brief selection of words first recorded between 1370 and 1470:

abhor, bonnet, casement, desolation, enable, flute, gage, homicide, idiot, jelly, kestrel, loyalty, manoeuvre, nutritive, ordnance, perspective, quinquennial, resonance, separate, transmit, umbrage, virile, waiter, zone.

In the 16c we have entered the international atmosphere of the modern world. If loans are not quite so numerous as in II, they are of much the same kinds – military and naval (*trophy, pioneer, brigantine, pilot, sally, colonel* [with doublet *coronel*, whence the modern pronunciation], *corsair*), trade (*indigo, gauze, grogram, vase, machine*), social (*viceroy, minion, bourgeois*), the arts (*rondeau, scene, grotesque*). The French also played a very important part in the dissemination of words they had themselves borrowed from elsewhere; old-established French words were no doubt felt as no different from other loans from French, but words from the new world of exploration may well have been sensed as exotics.

Very little material arrives at first from Italy – *ducat* at the end of the 14c and *brigand* in the 15c, but travel and trade in the 16c fill out the picture with *traffic, contraband, cartel, milliner, ballot, lottery, scope, doge, nuncio, carnival*; to the military field belong *squadron, cavalier, manage, gambole* (the last two terms in high school, i.e., stylised military, horsemanship); signs of the Renaissance are surprisingly late – we have *cupola, cornice*, towards the end of the period, but the real influence comes in II. At the same time trade, and conflict, with Spain are on the increase; *cordwain* and *cork* come in in the 15c, *cask* (a helmet), *galleon, armada*, in the 16c; encounters outside Europe produce the first of many loans – *tornado, cannibal, negro, iguana, alligator*. Our only early word of Portuguese origin – *marmelade* – came through French; the borrowing of *flamingo* in the New World starts a trend that will grow in II,

Of the whole Romance group, therefore, only French shows anything like the prodigality of later periods, and in this it was continuing the pattern already set up in IV. Meanwhile, shipping and trade interests, as always, channelled Low German words into the language; items from this period include *splint, kit, skipper, firkin, mart, hop* (plant), *pickle, spool, rack*, sb, *sled, selvedge, excise, marline, buoy, deck, hoist, bulwark, boor, loiter, bruin, groove, luck, hawker, scone, isinglass, cambric, dock, splice, yacht, waggon, uproar* (in the sense 'uprising' insurrection'), *snaffle, forlorn hope* (i.e., lost, desperate band, but the present sense had developed in English by 1572). How important the sea was in the transmission of even those words not to do with the sea is evident from the fact that High German, which needed to send words overland, produced (despite important religious links) only *carouse*, sb and v (and indirectly *lobby*, whose proximate source was Neo-Latin). Quite a number of words, mainly everyday words, seem to have come in from the Scandinavian languages – seem, because both the subject-matter and the dialects involved mean that these words could have escaped getting into the record for a very long time. Examples are, from the late 14c, *kilt, ling, rein(deer), scab, scant, skirt, stab, swirl*; from the 15c, *link, silt*; the 16c *batten*, v, *scrag, smelt*. Closer to home Celtic is relatively productive, but again we may suspect that some of the words really belong in IV. Both Scottish *loch* and Irish *lough* are first recorded in the 14c, *clan* in the 15c, *bog, plaid, slogan, garron* from Scots Gaelic in the 16c, *coracle* from Welsh, *gull* and *brill* from Cornish. Against this we may set the larger number of words borrowed at this time from French, but which

French itself had got from Celtic predecessors in what was to become France, including *gravel, lawn, league, marl, quay, skein, truant, valet, javelin*. It is hardly fanciful to infer varying habits of borrowing and of resistance to borrowing.

Words from further afield divide into two groups. The first reflects the ancient overland trade-routes, and the second the newly opened sea-ways to east and west, which supplemented, without replacing, the old routes. Ultimately from Persian come *taffeta, borax, arsenic, musk, mummy, jasmine*; but the words, like the goods, came overland, and were mediated by other languages (*tiara* was perhaps a direct loan). The later routes introduced more Turkish words – *spahi, khan* (also in the form *cham*, through French), *janissary* (possibly through French, as *tulip, horde*, certainly were). The ancient Arabic leadership in mathematics and science is represented (as it had been earlier); words from this period include *alkali, tartar, elixir, almanac, zenith, antimony, ream, cipher*; and in a field that may be broadly designated as arising out of travel and trade-relations, *cotton, caliph, mosque, bedouin, lemon, syrup, apricot, caraway, tarragon, artichoke, calibre, tare, genet, civet* – many of them mediated by French, Spanish, Italian, Neo-Latin, or even more than one of these languages: 16c *rebec, sultan, senna*, are probably direct loans. Russia, too, is at first represented by mediated words, *sable* through French and *siskin* through Dutch, but after the establishment of the English Muscovy Company under Queen Elizabeth some rather locally-oriented words come in direct – *kvass, rouble, czar, verst*. In the 16c Hungarian makes its first direct appearance, with *hussar*, but *coach* had already arrived via French. From India came *sandal(wood), raj, calico, betel*, and many words of more local reference. The first lexical results of exploration in the Far East are Chinese *lychee* and Malay *sago*. The world, except Africa south of the Sahara, lies open to the nations of Europe, and the same movements of exploration have lowered the linguistic barriers between those nations.

§ 111 A rough distinction can be drawn between borrowing as a result of getting to know the world, and borrowing, from learned languages, through written channels. Arabic is a language that might well have been included under both heads, but in most cases the division is clear. Latin learning flourished throughout the period, but especially towards its close. Selecting with extreme caution because we cannot always be certain whether a word is a direct loan from Latin or mediated by French (cf. § 76), and because some loans recorded early in the period might really belong to IV (cf. §74), we may give the following as likely examples of borrowing:

cadaver, arbiter, integer, genius, torpedo (a kind of fish), *pollen, junior, cornea, fungus, vertigo, acumen, folio, alias, mandamus, quondum, area, exit, peninsula, quietus, regalia, abdomen, pus, appendix, miser, circus, aborigines, interim, augur, axis, vacuum, genus, medium, specie, species, terminus, caesura, caveat, corona, hiatus, innuendo, cerebellum, decorum.*

These may be described as partly legal (and therefore of an old type of Latin loan) but predominantly Renaissance, especially scientific. They are much like the period II loans – words of learned original application, some of which have become bread-and-butter words within English, and in their varied forms indicating the ease with which Englishmen could lift a bit of a Latin sentence (*folio, alias, mandamus, quondam*, etc.). Latin is also the main channel through which Greek words reach English; examples of which we may be certain (because they are Renaissance, not medieval) are *irony, alphabet, drama, tome, dilemma, gorgon, idea, trope, enigma, cynic, labyrinth, scheme, anemone, clematis, distich, hyacinth, phalanx, caustic, isthmus, nectar, troglodyte, rhythm, chorus, ambrosia, bulb, nausea.* Although the study of Greek began again in England in the 16c the elements of vocabulary are much less numerous; one has to remember that they can include only those items that users of Latin had not already found occasion to borrow. Examples are: *phrase, rhapsody, crisis, topic.* The borrowing of whole words from the classical languages was less profound in effect than the borrowing of formatives, for which cf. §112.

What we have not encountered previously is a noteworthy contribution from Hebrew. An interesting group of such words apparently belongs here – *nitre, myrtle, jubilee, pasch(al), mammon, babel, leviathan* – but on this subject two caveats are needed. Some, even perhaps all, of these words may be transmitted by French, medieval Latin, or both; though Hebrew, like Greek, was known in 16c England. Moreover, the loans are typically of biblical words, which in superficially latinised forms had been familiar to clerics for centuries. And when clerics expounded the biblical text in the vernacular for laymen they had to have ways, almost certainly standardised ways, of rendering such terms. We do not discover what some of these ways are until complete translations of the Bible appear, i.e., during III; but it would be rash to suppose that in all cases the items listed are innovations as renderings of the biblical text.

§ 112 During III, gains and losses in the material and patterns of WF were of unparallelled magnitude. It is not difficult to see why. Like any other borrowing, this kind presupposes foreign influences and encounters, but while the borrowing of whole words is relatively simple, the borrowing of formatives is a much more complex and indirect process. What we notice in use are words, and if we feel the need, we adopt them; we do not ordinarily, as speakers, review the formative resources of a foreign language and decide upon introducing them to our own (though in recent years, for scientific purposes, academics have done this with learned languages). Formatives work by their generality, and by speakers' sense that words they compose are analysable. Normally, therefore, in borrowing from living languages, and even to some extent from learned ones, the sequence must be that whole words are borrowed; then groups of these words seem to be regularly analysable, or to be in regular correlation with others, so that a morphemic structure is read into them, and its elements treated as formatives that can be combined with other suitable items – sometimes only from the same source language, sometimes from native resources. All this takes time; it requires a heavy impact of homogeneous full loanwords, and an interval of living with them. The most overwhelming experience of homogeneous loanwords came in the centuries following the Norman Conquest, notably in IV. Its backwash in formation-borrowing arrives in III. And the torrent was so great that the language has never again had occasion to borrow formatives on quite this scale.

Let us illustrate the process. English borrowed as whole words from French such composites as *agreeable, comfortable, blamable, comparable, desirable, measurable, damnable, deceivable, profitable, changeable, favourable, passable, serviceable, reasonable, acceptable, commendable,* etc., and English speakers did not fail to infer that -*able* was a suffix which could be used to form adjectives from verbs and nouns (especially those verbs and nouns that were identical in form). They did not have a native suffix that did just this useful thing. And from the later 14c they begin to make their own formations. At least, that is when examples are recorded, though when they appear it is directly with native stems, and also with the native negative prefix *un-*; it is possible, but certainly not necessary, that a stage is omitted from the record. By 1400 there are *understandable, believable, unspeakable, unknowable,* by 1500, *eatable, available, determinable, appeasable, speakable, knowable, unamendable, unbearable, unbreakable* (all from verbs, borrowed and native), and by 1400 *treasonable, seasonable,* by 1500, *meritable, person-*

able, from nouns. Thereafter the rate of increase is enormous, and the type comes to include phrasal verbs, either in the form with particle (*get-at-able*) or without (*reliable* – a class of formation which has continued to be thought a nasty innovation in our own day!). And when formatives are numerous new correlations may develop with further consequences. Thus, English borrowed from French in 14c and 15c a large number of abstract nouns in *-ity*, on a variety of stems – thus, *actuality, agility, captivity, diversity, infirmity, lubricity, singularity*; but one group suggested the correlation *-able/-ability* as a link between related adjective and noun, e.g., *impeccable/impeccability*. The correlation was seized on as a matrix for the formation of new abstract nouns – starting, just after our period, with *capability*, and continuing with formations on native stems (*lovability*), which are not found for any other *-ity* pattern. This instance illustrates both how formative functions can ramify, once established in a language, and how considerable is the time-lag before their patterning properties are isolated and exploited. It is for this reason that the main consequences of the Norman Conquest for WF are felt during III: but this material, once assimilated, provided a mesh of relationships so close-woven that further influence at the Renaissance could be assimilated almost immediately. The two waves strike shore, one heaping upon the other. Professor Marchand writes:

> The system of English word-formation was entirely upset by the Norman Conquest. This does not mean that the present system is due to the Normans, but the Normans paved the way for the non-Germanic trend that language has since taken. It was due to the continuous contact with France that English borrowed so many words from French which, as a matter of course, occasioned the rise of prefixes and suffixes out of these loans. And it is due to this Romanization, through French, of the English vocabulary that Latin words could be so easily adopted. The language took to wholesale borrowing, a method which meant an enormous cut-down on the traditional patterns of word-formation out of native material (1969, 130).

The same scholar draws an important distinction, relevant to the issue of phasing, between two types of formation, both combining native and foreign elements:

> We have to distinguish between two basic groups. A foreign word is combined with a native affix. . . . Just as the introduction of a foreign word is an essentially uncomplicated matter, so is its combination with a native derivative element. . . . This is the reason why native prefixes and suffixes were added to French words almost immediately after the words were introduced. Suffixes such as *-ful, -less, -ness* were early used with French words, so we

find *faithful, faithless, clearness* and others recorded by 1300. The case is different with foreign affixes added to native words. Here, the assimilation of a structural pattern is involved, not merely the adoption of a lexical unit. Before the foreign affix can be used, a foreign syntagma must have come to be familiar with speakers so that the pattern of analysis may be imitated and the dependent morpheme be used with native words. This is much more complicated. When it does happen, formations are found much later than those of the first type. This . . . explains why combinations of the types *sweep-age, utter-ance, yeoman-ry* crop up much later (about 1375 at the earliest) and are less numerous (1969, 210–11).

§ 113 The abnormal influx during III was felt mainly in prefixes and suffixes. Though items in both groups are numerous, their effect is different. The new prefixes ousted the old on a very considerable scale; the suffixes did not. Evidently special factors are involved, as Professor Marchand points out:

> We cannot explain everything through Romance or Latin influence. Surely there are other elements which have played a role, and we are far from being able to solve this problem entirely by pointing out one or two auxiliary elements. Some of the old [prefixes] disappeared because they were practically too weak phonetically, as *æt-, ed-, oþ-* [= *-oth*], *ymb-*. The prefix *for-* had lost its sign character by the ME period. It is suggested that homophony with *fore-* may have played a part. As early as ME, the connection between [prefix] and simple vb was lost in *forget, forgive, forbid, forsake* (OE *sacan* 'strive, contend' had died out) and no common nuance of meaning united *forgo, forswear, forspend*. The intensive meaning was perhaps felt in *forgather, forbear* (still dialectal with meaning 'endure'). The final result was that English lost a prefixal device for expressing the idea of intensity, perfectivity with vbs. This function is now performed by postpositive particles, chiefly *up* and *out* (*finish up, use up, burn out*)(1969, 130–1).

One is tempted to guess at another link in the chain. Marchand points out that prefixes, being first elements, cannot bear the grammatical functions often carried by suffixes. The history of English from III to this day has shown a progressive refinement and clarification of certain generalised, and in a broad sense grammatical, meanings (e.g., in verb-contrasts, duration-habit-instantaneity-perfectivity and the dimension of active–passive contrast symmetrically through the series). There has thus been more scope for rival suffixes to survive by staking a claim to a particular range of contrast. Prefixal meanings are much more of a, broadly speaking, adverbial kind, and in this area the range of distinctions made has been less mutable.

Whatever the reason, many of the old prefixes died, some as active formatives, others without leaving so much as a fossilised trace in the language; for the most part these losses seem to belong to IV, so the old system may have collapsed before the new arrived on the scene. Only some of the more important newcomers can be mentioned; and a mere mention conceals the extraordinary potential for growth and ramification some of the affixes have shown once they were acclimatised. *Circum-* (as in *circumnavigate*, and with some correspondence to older *ymb*) comes into use in the late 15c, flourishes in the 17c and dies back in the 18c; *co-* (as in *co-heir*, and with some correspondence to OE *mid-*) is productive from the 16c; *counter-* (as in *counterblast*, and with some correspondence to OE *with-*, long inactive but fossilised in *withstand*) had a long gestation in loans before becoming an independent formative in the 16c; *dis-* (as in *distrust*, with areas of correspondence to OE *for-*, *un-*) was active from early in the 15c; *en-*, *em-* (as in *enrich*, *emblazon*, more precise than wide-ranging OE *in-*) was also early; *in-* (as in *in-frequent*, corresponding with a different OE *in-*, lost partly as a result of its homophony with the preceding) was active from about 1500; *inter-* (as in *intermingle*, with no recorded corresponding OE prefix) becomes productive a little earlier; *mal-* (as in *maladventure*, with no closely corresponding OE prefix, but in rivalry with a loan from Scandinavian, *ill-*) was active from the 14c; *non-* (as in *nonage*, having some relationship with OE *un-*, but no really close antecedents) is during III active only in its original field, legal terminology, though in II it extends to philosophy, religion, political history, and in I to science; *pre-* (as in *pre-conceive*, with some correspondence to OE *fore-*) is active from the 16c; *re-* (as in *re-enter*, no direct antecedent) becomes active before 1450; *semi-* (as in *semi-circle*, corresponding to OE *sam-*) from the close of the 14c; *sub-* (as in *sub-tenant*, partly corresponding to OE *under-*, which does, or course, survive in similar senses) is active from the early 15c; *vice-* (as in *vice-admiral*, partly corresponding to another sense of *under-*) from the late 15c.

§ 114 Among terminal affixes, Marchand distinguishes between suffixes, which do not occur as independent speech-units, and semi-suffixes, which do (1969, 209–10). Some of the main suffixes which become active are, from the late 14c, *-able* (as in *believable*), *-acy* (as in *delicacy*), *-age* (as in *peerage*), *-al* (as in *rehearsal*), *-ancy/-ency* (as in *vacancy, innocency* but it remains sluggish till the 16c), *-ate* (as in *translate*; rather different from the others, since it is not a matter of adding to a stem, but of choosing one particular stem for the anglicising of Latin verbs), *-ess* (as in *shepherdess*), *-ory* (as in *transitory*, but with few examples till the 16c); from the 15c, *-ance* (as in *hindrance*, but *-ence* is later except in loans), *-ant/-ent* (as in *occupant, resident*, but formations certainly English may be later), *-ate* (as in *affectionate*), *-ician* (as in *geometrician*), from the 16c, *-ise/ize* (as in *epitomise*), and *-let* (as in *armlet*), where the long period of gestation is due to the diversity of the factors underlying isolation of this formative, which has no direct source.

It is not surprising that native prefixes and suffixes are absent from the list of innovations. Nor should it be surprising that they pre-empt the semi-suffix list. The identifying characteristic of a semi-suffix is that it exists as a separate word, yet it is fairly certain to be an old-established word, since as an affix it requires a high degree of semantic generality and a low level of lexical particularity; probably, then, a native word. Moreover, it cannot remain a semi-suffix for long, for the stress-system of English will erode it through the centuries, and separate it from the parent independent word. What, therefore, survives as a semi-suffix in PE (the basis of Marchand's classification) cannot be more than a few hundred years old in that role – certainly not pre-Conquest. In fact we find *-like* (as in *godlike*) in use from the 15c (the same form, becoming an affix in OE, has been reduced to the *-ly* of *godly*); all surviving *-worthy* formations post-date *blameworthy*, 1382, though some earlier formations had had a short existence; *-way/-ways* is a formative from the 14c; *-wise*, in clearly combinative use (as in *crosswise*) is also 14c. The remaining example is marginal: *-monger* was active in OE with the meaning 'trader, dealer' – the morally colourless sense that survives fossilised in such words as *fishmonger*. But Tyndale's 1526 use of *whoremonger*, retained in AV, gave the element, by association, a derogatory meaning, and since then it has been active only in formatives with a strong note of disapproval (these actually belong to II, but the 'fulcrum' use belongs to III).

§ 115 Patterns of compounding show no more than a normal rate of evolution, though there is clear evidence of pressure from foreign patterns. From the 14c are recorded items of the post-modified type *knight-errant*; the order is un-English, and the type never became highly productive, yet it is interesting as showing the complexity of the factors that may make for the appearance of a new pattern. English had long been exposed to familiarity with this order in Celtic (*MacArthur, Kirkpatrick, Coombe Martin*), and encountered it again in incoming

French expressions, such as *falcon gentle*, and in medieval Latin (*sum total*) and Neo-Latin (*gum arabic*); home-products are occasionally structured on this model (*fee simple*), and although they still feel rather alien, we have continued to make them (*consul general*).

At the opposite extreme is the type *lean-to*, 15c, becoming common from about 1550 (*runaway*, *runabout*, belong to the closing decades of III). The type uses native elements, but more than that, it depends on an indigenous, though not very old, development, the type of post-positive (phrasal) verb, e.g., *give up*, recorded from the 12c, and hugely productive during III. Morphologically similar is the type *blackout*, starting in the 15c, but not common till the 17c. A native pattern of formation classed by Marchand as a compound is the type *outlive* (1969, 116); although *out* is an independent word, its semantic function in such formations gives it rather the character of a prefix. Compound verbs of the de-substantival pattern *safeguard* are an innovation late in the 15c (though OE had had similar forms incorporating noun-verb morphological contrast, a type which had died out). A similar break in tradition occurs in the *by-gone* type, whose present origins are late ME. Phrasal units of the type *son-in-law* do not appear to be older than III, though the appearance may be due to lack of earlier evidence.

Zero-derivation is important, as it has been in every period since IV (cf. §31). Marchand gives over a hundred examples from our period simply of the de-substantival-verb type *balance*, *scythe*, *libel* (1969, 365–7, but see the whole section, 359–89). Note that in many cases the type uses loanwords (*balance*, *combat*, *libel*), but even that had been established during IV. Ablaut-combinations of the *flim-flam* type do not seem to be recorded before the early 16c, that is, at about the time when the older grammatical function of ablaut was becoming less clear (cf. §119). Apart from isolated, and perhaps chance, examples, rhyme-combinations begin just before our period (*handy-dandy*, 1362), but are very rare until II, that is, they follow far in the wake of the use of rhyme as a literary device. Clipping seems to begin at the close of III (*coz*, 1559). There are not yet any certain instances of blends or fabrications, though it is conceivable that some of the words of unexplained origin first recorded in III (*fit*, adj and sb, *dad*, *jump*, *crease*, *gloat*, *bet*, for instance) may include some.

§ 116 Though the evidence on such a point is never full or conclusive, it may well be true that during III lexical losses balanced, or even outnumbered, gains; this is certainly not the case during II or I. The subject is not easily defined. We can only look at what was certainly present in that kind of English which, in 1370, was the nearest antecedent to Standard in 1570. Loss from other varieties is one aspect of the submergence of those varieties, and something of its extent will emerge from the lexical study of regional English in Chapter IV (cf. §132).

It is not particularly interesting to list terms for activities that died out or changed beyond recognition, though it is as much a part of the structure to have terms for superseded types of architecture and artillery, arms and clothing, and for exploded sciences, as it is part of the structure of PE to have a vocabulary of nuclear physics and warfare, space-travel and synthetic fabrics. If we disregard all such matters, and set aside all items which remain recognisable though they have been re-formed on new principles, the losses are enormous. A fairly full selection is needed to demonstrate this, but it is only a selection, and as it has certain curious features, I must say that it is a representative selection. It differs from many lists of gains in vocabulary in the size of the non-nominal element, especially the number of verbs, it contains; and the proportion of loanwords, especially from French, is astonishing. Many of these have come into the language quite recently, and none are really old, yet they die like flies. One might have guessed that the main losses would be old native words ousted by newcomers; and in IV that is what one will find. But during III there is a sloughing-off of, on the whole, unnecessary and extravagant borrowings. Since it acquired, in the 12c, the habit of large-scale borrowing, the language has exhibited cycles of indiscriminate borrowing followed by weeding. III is, for the most part, a fining-down period, but towards its end begins a new phase of extravagant borrowing, mainly from Neo-Latin, of items which are still-born or short-lived (cf. §80); yet another such cycle begins after the Restoration, and is purged in and after the 18c. Perhaps we are now in a fourth. Examples are roughly glossed, but for their precise value the *OED* and instances in context must be consulted, and etymologies should also be traced in the *OED*: *abreyde(n)* (start up), *agreyse(n)* (shudder), *alose(n)*, (praise), *amenuse(n)* (diminish), *ancille* (handmaid), *anientissen* (annihilate), *arette* (impute to), *awhape(n)* (amaze), *baude* (lively), *bandoun* (power), *beme* (trumpet), *blinne* (cease; the word has survived dialectally), *bismotered* (spattered), *bitrende(n)* (encircle), *bobaunce* (boast), *bretful* (brimful), *catapuce* (caper-spurge), *cetewale* (a kind of ginger), *chalon* (blanket), *cheeste* (quarrelling), *chi(n)che* (miser, miserly), *clapers* (rabbit burrows; subsequently dialectal), *clergeoun* (pupil), *clote* (burdock; survives dialectally), *colpon* (strip; survives in Scottish), *contubernal* (familar;

194

reborrowed in the 17c in a rather different sense), *corniculer* (assistant), *cuer* (heart), *dagoun* (piece), *decoped* (slashed), *deslavee* (inordinate), *dextrer* (war-horse; disused from 1500, i.e., when there still were war-horses, and revived as a historical term in 18c; survives in dialect), *doutremer* (foreign), *drasty* (filthy), *drovy* (muddy; survives in dialect), *druery* (love), *dulcarnoun* (dilemma), *dwale* (drugged drink), *embelif* (oblique), *engreggen* (weigh down; later in Scottish), *estres* (interior), *fleme(n)* (put to flight; later in Scottish), *forsluggen* (spoil; on the decline of the *for-* prefix cf. §113), *gnede* (stingy person), *gnodde(n)* (rub), *gnof* (lout), *gype* (frock), *gyte* (dress), *halke* (nook), *herbergage* (lodging), *herie(n)* (praise), *heysoge* (sparrow), *helde(n)* (pour out), *hoppestere* (dancing-girl), *howve* (hood; later in Scottish), *jubbe* (vessel, jug), *kechil* (small cake), *kernel* (battlement), *kymelin* (shallow tub; survives in dialects), *lacerte* (muscle), *layner* (strap), *lisse* (sb and v, relief, relieve; survives in Scottish), *litestere* (dyer), *lorel* (wretch), *losenger* (flatterer), *maat* (dead), *mappemounde* (map of the world; to 1560, revived as a historicism in the 19c), *nevene(n)* (name, v), *ore* (mercy), *ostelements* (furniture), *panade* (cutlass), *parentele* (kinship; one later use in a different sense), *pose* (head-cold; later in dialects), *potente* (crutch; obsolete before 1500, but revived by Stevenson), *pouste* (power; survived in Scottish), *pryme temps* (spring, first time), *puterie* (whoredom), *quad* (evil; later in seaman's jargon), *quystroun* (scullion), *rape* (haste), *remuable* (changeable), *rese(n)* (tremble), *ribibe* (lute), *rogge(n)* (shake; later in dialects), *royne* (roughness), *scantilon* (mason's tool), *shode* (parting), *trasshe(n)* (betray), *treget* (jugglery), *trye* (excellent), *trype* (small piece), *vache* (cow), *vekke* (hag), *viritrate* (hag), *wlatsome* (nauseous), *wlonk* (proud), *wonger* (pillow).

Certain groups of words call for special consideration. Complex words involving prefixes that have ceased to be productive show interesting tendencies. The newer pattern with post-positive particle takes over in the class of verbs in *out-*: *out-breke(n), -breste(n), -bringe(n), -drawe(n), -springe(n), -stretche(n), -take(n), -twyne(n), -wende(n)*, etc., drop out of use, and *break out*, etc. come in – even if this means a disjunction within the word-family (sb *outbreak*, participial adjective, *outstretched*). Many verbs with the prefix *over-*, which had formerly had a very wide range of meanings, are replaced by a post-positive particle verb, and this process may tighten the mesh of semantic contrast cf. *overlook*, formerly with the meaning now assigned to *look over*. Division of prefixal territory may, however, come from enlargement of the range of preposed items. *Un-* had an unmanageable spread of functions in the late 14c, and words formerly using it in different ways began during III to be reallocated to some of the newer prefixes in such a way as to make more refined distinctions. The words in brackets after the following examples indicate the lines of this redistribution, and the totality of meanings of the later 'negatives' indicates the excessive scope of earlier *un-*: *uneagreable* (disagreeable), *unapt* (not apt *or* inept *or* disinclined), *unavysed* (unaware *or* unpremeditated), *unbityde(n)* (not happen, fail to happen), *unlove(n)* (cease to love), *unmeek* (lacking meekness), *unneste(n)* (leave the nest), *unsought* (at hand, not requiring a search), *unthank* (a curse, contrary of expression of goodwill), *unusage* (disuse, want of use).

Finally, among words which survive, there are very substantial changes of meaning, or in the dominance-hierarchy (cf. §84) of meanings. This subject requires much space for adequate exemplification, but a search of the *OED* entries for *very, gentle, free, truth, bachelor, harlot, danger, delicacy, pharmacy, girl, honesty, limit(ation), medley, pregnant, textual, sad, kind, gentle, silly, stomach*, will serve as an introduction. The number of adjectives in the list is remarkable; adjectives seem particularly liable to semantic shifts under the influence of the head-words they habitually associate with, and because of the strong value-sense with which they are often charged.

§ 117 Grammatically, the changes we have observed in periods II and I are little more than the final maturation of quite fundamental developments essentially belonging to III; the changes between 1370 and 1570 are profound and sweeping, probably more than at any other time. In a sense we already know this. For instance, when we speak of final *-e* as in many cases inflectional in the 14c, we imply not merely the use of a certain formal index of contrast, but the very existence of a system of contrasts which has been unknown in later English. Other elements in grammar also have to do with phonology. In the many pairs of present–past verb-forms patterned like *lead/led, keep/kept*, there was in 1370 a simple alternation of vowel-length; the alternation of quality has been imposed subsequently, as a result of 15c raising of long vowels. It is largely at this time that lines of distinction between classes of 'irregular' verbs become so complex that classification is of little value. Before this period, we can usefully divide verbs into three types, weak or *-d* participle verbs (now 'regular' verbs), normally without vowel-change, but including some exceptional types; strong or *-n* participle verbs, with vowel change; and anomalous verbs. In many ways we can claim that, just as the late 14c is a watershed between the urbanised and the pre-urbanised in the history of varieties of English, so this is the principal watershed in grammatical history. The metaphor has limits; transition was smooth, and one generation learnt from the preceding, as has always happened. We can see that a great deal happened, and happened fast, and we can see that this was because grammatical patterns had lingered for a long time which no longer carried the most important grammatical information, and were ripe for a sweeping purge by phonological change. Perhaps we should say the period is grammatically Janus-like; at the beginning it can be seen as the conclusion of the Middle Ages, but even this is largely a matter of semblance. By the 16c the system is modern; only a tidying-up operation is required to make the grammar into what we are familiar with.

In this, as in other sections of this chapter, I shall concentrate on what happened in London Standard English within the confines of our period. It is, of course, part of the grammatical history of English that different regional grammars current in the late 14c did not survive in literary use in the 16c or after. But this chapter is already heavily burdened and it will be more convenient to reserve all matters of comparison between London and regional English in the 14c to the chapter devoted to what happened in the centuries immediately before that date.

§ 118 The shape of the declension of nouns was as it is now, save for vestigial remains from very ancient patterns of declension, and for rather more irregular forms in 1370 than in 1570. *Eiren* ('eggs') apparently survived as a variant long enough to worry Caxton (*Eneydos*, Preface), though he does seem to be picking an example to labour a point. Other *-n* plurals and *-ene* genitive plurals are found at the beginning of the period (*lorden, lollarene,*) and there are fossilised uninflected genitive singulars (*oure lady veyle, my fader soule*); but in general, use was close to the 1570, even the 1970 norm. The strength of the correlation between Ø and *-s* for number is shown by the first of the back-derived singulars (cf. §85), *chirie* 14c (from cherise) and *riddle*, 16c (from *redels*).

Among personal pronouns, the second person distinction between *thou* and *ye* was more nearly (or more often) a number distinction at the beginning of the period than at its end (cf. §87); and *ye/you* are still distinguished as subject and non-subject case until the close of the period (cf. §87). Throughout, the third singular masculine has a weak form *a* /ə/, which in literary sources progressively goes underground, but can still be traced in certain formulaic sequences, notably *quotha* ('he said'). The plural pronoun underwent a notable change, since at the

197

beginning of the period the oblique cases were of native origin, *here* and *hem* (source of PE colloquial *'em*) being the common forms; *their, them,* entered the Standard language during the 15c as part of the adoption of a new variety, Type IV Standard (cf. §99). The system of case shows in the late 14c the last vestiges of an old dative–accusative contrast, in the neuter third singular only. For direct object (*h*)*it* (identical with the subject form) is used, but for indirect object *him*; this is the only point in the language at which accusative–dative contrast survived, and naturally it did not last long in such isolation. It is important to recall, in connection with the neuter pronoun, that its genitive was *his* (cf. § 87). There was not as yet any general differentiation between attributive and predicative genitive uses; *youres, oures* (as against attributives *youre(e), our(e)*) have made their appearance by the end of the 14c, but forms with *-n* alternation (*my/mine,* etc.) still use the variation for phonological, not grammatical, purposes. Demonstratives had pronominal as well as attributive use, in reference to persons, and the ones current today were supplemented in late ME by *self,* pl *selven, ilk(e),* which also serve respectively as reinforcers for the personal pronouns and the *this/that* demonstratives. The reflexive use of *self/selves* (plural often *selven* till c1500) developed from the matrix of the reinforcing use, and grew up mainly during the latter part of III, though it was not quite complete by the end of the period (cf. §87). Its progress can be measured by the tendency to introduce genitive forms before *self*; at one point in the *Canterbury Tales* (E108) manuscripts are equally divided between the reinforcing reading *vs self* and the reflexive one *ourself.* In the ordinary way, during the early part of III, reflexive meaning is indicated by repetition of the ordinary personal pronoun after the verb (*ete we and fede us,* 'let us eat and feed ourselves').

The principal relative is *that* (though contact-clauses are freely used). At the beginning of the period (*the*) *which* is just coming into use as a relative. *Who/whom* are still essentially interrogative, but their use in indirect questions constitutes a matrix from which relative use can develop; the oblique case is used first, and *who* begins to appear very gradually from the close of the 14c, not claiming its present territories until II (cf. §88). Indefinite pronouns also change; at the beginning of the period *aught, elles,* have the functions which, by its close, are taken by *anything, something else*; *every, everych,* is pronominal (as well as adjectival) when the period begins, but the present distinction between *each* and *every* is pretty well established by its close. *Many, many one,* also start the period as pronouns; but the second of them normally becomes *many a one* in the latter part of it, as part of the development of the prop-word *one* (which at the beginning of the period had been used in patterns *a/the good one*, and by its end had added plural patterns, (*the*) *good ones*, and inversion patterns, *never a one*, *such a one*, as well as *many a one*). At the beginning of the period *one* = 'someone', but this use shrinks as the prop-use grows; it is contrasted with particularising *som* = 'a certain person', which by the end of the period is rather literary (we now preserve only the corresponding plural, *some* = 'certain people', which formerly partnered it). But much the most important difference in the pronominal system is the survival into late ME of a universally accepted indefinite pronoun *me*, corresponding to 'they, one, people' (as in 1387, *cloþes þar me casteþ yn*, 'clothes that people throw in'). In its earlier form this had had a distinct phonological shape (*man*) but throughout ME it appears in the weak form *me*, which is identical with the weak form of the oblique of the first person singular pronoun, and this clash seems to be responsible for its loss. All speakers are conscious of the gap it has left, but they have not, in the whole NE period, come to any settled usage by way of replacement.

By 1370 the forms of adjectives, many of which occur with or without *-e*, might suggest the persistence of inflectional contrast (cf. §107), but it is doubtful whether this is much more than a metrical device. Certain adjectives of a somewhat learned character, and recognisably of French origin, tend to keep both their French post-nominal position and their French number-contrast in concord with the head; as late as the 1520s we find *weale publyques*. One adjective, perhaps because it was also a pronoun, had a fossilised genitive plural, *aller* ('of all'). Comparison in adjectives and adverbs generally followed the same patterns as now, but there were differences in some irregular forms. At the beginning of the period there was a comparison-set *neigh, neer/nerre, nexte*, whose comparative came to be used as a positive (*near*), and in turn developed regular comparison (*nearer, nearest*), leaving older *nigh, next*, isolated. The mechanism here seems to be that after verbs of motion the comparative would often be used in such a way that positive-comparative contrast was in effect neutralised (*Com neer, draw neer*), and since the formal relationship between the three terms was unusual *neer* in this pattern could readily be taken as a positive. Of the two isolated terms *next* has survived by cutting out for itself a territory somewhat distinct from *nearest*, but *nigh* has passed out of colloquial use. Some forms, which by phonological development had come to have an apparently abnormal relationship between the positive and the other degrees were

199

reformed on the regular model; thus, comparison of *long* with a front vowel (*lenger, lengest*) gave way to forms without vowel-change, and of *great* with a short vowel (*gretter, grettest*) gave way to forms without quantitative variation. Others survived in part, but with a loss of old distinctions. For example, at the beginning of the period *bettre*, adj, is still distinct from *bet*, adv, but by its end *better* is used in both functions; at the beginning *mo* ('more in number') is still sometimes, not invariably, distinguished from *more* ('bigger in size'), and a few 16c examples can be found, but the distinction dies at the close of that century (i.e., before loss of post-vocalic /r/, which cannot be its cause). On the other hand, *lesse, leste*, were at first adjectives as well as adverbs, but *lesser*, was brought into use in conformity with the normal shape of a comparative adjective, and, except in biological names, *least*, adj, has generally been replaced by *smallest*.

Among the numerals processes of regularisation are evident. The only change among the cardinal numerals is that at the beginning of the period *two* has an alternative *tweye* (later *twain*), which is perhaps not much more than a metric device at that date [it had earlier had a distinct grammatical function (cf. §167)]; it certainly soon became merely literary. The ordinals change more. *Forme* was an alternative to *first*, but as it was unlike other ordinals in shape, and functionally redundant, it was made the basis of a new comparative *former*, and lost its earlier role. *Secound* existed, but was an innovation beside older *other*, which in the 14c was still common as an ordinal. All ordinals beyond *third* were remodelled during the period with a common ending *-th*, preceded wherever the cardinal suggested it by *-n-*; in this way traditional forms still in use at the beginning of the period, *fifte, sexte, sevethe, nente, tithe, ellefte, twelfte*, gave way completely to analogical forms, *fifth, sixth, seventh, ninth, tenth, eleventh, twelfth* (which had achieved some currency before the period began). *Tithe*, of course, survived in its nominal role, which had become separated from the general ordinal one.

§ 119 Extensive as these changes are in comparison with any met hitherto, they are less profound than those affecting the verb at the same time. In 1370 three historically distinct types of verb can be distinguished (cf. §154). Two hundred years later, as a result of sweeping phonological, grammatical and analogical changes, there is only a difference between regular (more or less the old weak verbs in type, but not, in many cases, in class-membership) and a wide spectrum of others. Jespersen writes (of changes that are gradual, but whose effect is fully seen by the end of III):

On no other point, perhaps, has the old English grammatical system been revolutionized to the same extent as in the formation of the tenses of the verbs. The old principal divisions of the verb into three classes . . . have no sense if we consider the flexions as found in actual usage, and new divisions must be substituted for them (1909, etc., VI, 23).

Neither this nor other changes in the verb took place suddenly, and therefore they did not take place tidily; that is to say, there is a great deal of divided usage, of overlap of old and new, by the latter part of the period – far more than at any earlier time.

In educated London speech around 1370 the present indicative of verbs made, by means of endings, a threefold distinction, 1sg, 2sg, and all the rest (except in a very few verbs, which had separate form for 3sg). The linking of 3sg with all forms of the plural had no correspondence with what happened elsewhere in the grammar; it blurs the only person-number distinction NE has thought worth-while. In this respect the morphology was abnormal and not illuminating, and we can hardly be surprised that it was ripe for change, and by the time of Chaucer -e(n) plurals, distinct from the sg, were normal. The present subjunctive had one form for all the singular, and one for the plural, though very often the singular form served throughout. If we look at this from a viewpoint internal to the subjunctive, we can say that little or no distinction can be found in the paradigm; if we look at it in comparison with the indicative, we find that the forms contrast at every point except the first person singular, which is the same in indicative and subjunctive. The imperative singular uses the bare stem of the verb without inflection, a form that does not occur in any other use, and the imperative plural is no different from the indicative plural. By 1570 all this has gone, except for a lingering persistence of special forms for concord with *thou*, and the 3sg present indicative in *-th*, about to give way to *-s*. Put like this, the changes of system and form sound complicated. In fact they are profoundly simple, as will appear when the actual forms are set out:

Inf: *-e(n)*

Pres ind	1 *-e*	Subj	Imp
sg	2 *-(e)st*	*-e*	Ø
	3 *-eth*		
pl	*-eth, -e(n)*	*-e(n)*	*-eth*

In all, five forms are involved, Ø, *-e*, *-(e)st*, *-eth*, *-e(n)*, but since *-(n)* is not always used, there is no necessary contrast in any of the positions where -*n* is the sole carrier of it; after that, the system is radically altered by loss of final -*e*. This creates the base form of the verb, used unchanged in infinitive, subjunctive, imperative and first singular present indicative – almost the present position. The -*st* ending is tied to number distinction in the second person, and therefore steadily decreases. The only change originating in the verb is a tendency to drop the indicative plural distinction, extending the base form to that function too; but this is not complete during the period, and, as we have seen (cf. § 89), even when -*s* came in it was still sometimes used for plural as well as 3sg. In the line of descent of the Standard language the first participle underwent no change, though regionally in 1370 it had a number of forms other than -*ing* (cf. § 131).

In the past the superficial grammatical effects are even more far-reaching, but again they derive from the same simple phonological cause. At the beginning of the period strong and weak verbs are distinguished not only in formation but also in inflection. Strong verbs had an ending for the 2sg and another for all persons of the plural in the indicative, one ending for the singular and another for the plural in the subjunctive. All these groups of forms had one stem-vowel (different from the present) as against the 1 and 3sg indicative, which had yet another vowel, but no ending. Comparing the moods, the subjunctive differed from the indicative only in the 1 and 3sg. The contrasts in weak verbs were similar, but did not involve vowel change within the past, nor usually between present and past, and the ending used for 2sg was like that for the present, which in strong verbs at the beginning of the period it was not. Already this system was so far out of touch with the contrasts really needed to make the grammar work that usage had begun to vary; hence the many bracketed elements in the following paradigm:

STRONG	WEAK
Ind 1 Ø	-*ed*/*d*/*t*/(*e*)
Sg 2 -(*e*)	*est*
3 Ø	(*e*)
Pl -*e*(*n*)	(*e*)(*n*)
Subj sg -*e*	(*e*)
pl -*e*(*n*)	(*e*)(*n*)
Part -*e*(*n*)	(*y*) – (*e*)

NOTE: in this paradigm successive brackets are dependent, i.e., (*e*)(*n*) means 'there may or may not be *e*; if *e* is present, there may or may not be *n*'; the weak participle has in free variation presence or absence of prefixed *y*- or *i*-.

It is clear that loss of final -*e* will level person, number and mood contrasts here too, leaving only the vowel change between 1 and 3sg indicative and all the rest in strong verbs, and 2sg concord in weak ones. Once number-contrast had ceased to be general the redundant vowel-variation in strong verbs was doomed; most of them settled for one vowel throughout the finite forms of the past, but this might or might not be the same as the vowel of the participle. Hence later variation between two-vowel verbs (*bite, bit, bitten*) and three vowel verbs (*write, wrote, written*): but before these patterns were established usage fluctuated, and on much the same lines as we have already encountered in II (cf. §89). In weak verbs the second person ending was kept alive by its analogy to the present form, but was on its way out, as *thou* was on its way out, by the end of the period. Thus, by the end of III there was, as now, practically no distinction of person, number or mood in the past of any normal verb (*be* is a special case); past contrast was made in an economical if not wholly orderly fashion by adding a suffix or changing the vowel, with relatively few verbs using both means, or neither.

In addition to these large classes English had, then as now, certain rogue verbs outside the regular order. Taking a long view, we can detect a tendency to let these verbs drop from use except in cases where their peculiarities can be exploited grammatically. The development reached flash point during III. The most important, and at all times the most formally eccentric, of these verbs is *be*, which by reason of its high frequency of use is extremely resistant to change. In fact during III it suffers no more than the attritions common to ordinary verbs [but remember that in Standard *are* is not yet in use (cf. §89)]. The group now sometimes called anomalous finites (because their forms are odd, and they lack non-finite elements in their paradigms) still, at the beginning of III, shared their formal peculiarities with a few other verbs of like history (see below) but, broadly speaking, only those that had found themselves a distinct grammatical niche survived beyond it. *Wot,* 'I know', had an infinitive *wite(n)*, past *wiste*, and contracted negatives *not*, /nɔːt/, etc.; on negation, see §122; *owe*, 'I own, have an obligation, possess', had an infinitive *owe(n)*, and past *aught/ought*; *can*, 'I am able, know how to', inf *cunne(n)*, had a past *couthe, coude*, and a participle/participial adjective *couth*; *tharf*, 'I need', had inf *thurve(n)*, past *thorfte*; *dar*, 'I dare', inf *durre(n)*, had past *dorste*; *shal*, 'I must, am under obligation to', plural *shulen*, had past *sholde*; *mot*, 'I must, can', had regular plural, and past *moste*; *may*, 'I am able to, have the physical capacity to, possibility of', had plural *mowen*, past *might/mought*; *wil(le), wol,*

'I want to, will', had plural *wille(n)*, past *wolde*, contracted negatives. Already these forms are largely defective in non-finite forms (note that where an inf is given and the present plural not mentioned, the present plural was of the same form as the inf).

A great deal happened to these forms during III. In summary, those which had started to develop a grammatical function sharpened it, and often became more peculiar morphologically, as if to signal the special function more clearly; others died out, or adapted to more regular patterns. By 1570 *wit* is almost as completely fossilised as it is today; the formerly distinct meanings *know how* and *know that* have been fused by *know* (which had been used since OE in circumstances where no attention was drawn to the distinction between knowing how and knowing that), and *can* has become largely, though not yet exclusively, modal (cf. §90). *Owe* changes in a very complicated way, splitting into two regular verbs, *owe* and *own*, each with suffixal pasts and a full paradigm, the two surviving because of their semantic differentiation; but *ought* is isolated as a pure modal, without even the semblance of tense-contrast that persists in, say, *can/could. Shall* and *must* differentiate their modal functions and drop other functions, but *must* is left isolated by the decline of its former present, *mot*, as a result of its likeness to *mought* once /χ/ was lost; however, neither *mo(o)t* nor *mought* have quite gone out of use by 1570. *Need* (which earlier had been mainly an impersonal verb) tended to take over from *thurve*, and because of its overlap in function with anomalous verbs started to pattern anomalously itself, setting up divisions of usage that are still not resolved; conversely *dare* has been becoming more like a regular verb, though in it too divided usage is widespread and of long standing.

§ 120 As we turn to the grammatical functions, contrasts, and wider relationships of these formal changes, we find the differences just as great, but more profound in the verbal than in the nominal parts of the sentence.

Case-contrast in the noun depends on the separate identity of the genitive; the *of*-construction is already complementary to it, but the delimitation between the two is (even) less clear than now, and the genitive may be used where, by reason of the inanimate, non-human reference of the noun, *of* would, in NE, be preferred; thus, *handlynge sinne*, "sins' discussion", a structure exemplifying post-position of the genitive, which soon became obsolete. For post-modified structures the period had inherited a pattern of inflecting the head-word concerned (*the kinges sone of Englande*). It inherited this because at an earlier stage genitives had varied in form according to gender and word-class of the head; but by III the structure was inconvenient because it could give rise to ambiguity as to the head of the post-modifier. Speakers gradually came to use the possibility opened to them by the standardisation of the genitive form, by putting the sign of the genitive at the end of the whole group (*the king of England's son*). This *group-genitive* both reflects and strengthens the sense of the unity of the group, which can be treated, in effect, as a word; it is common, but not yet invariable, by 1570; unfortunately it too can be ambiguous, but so far this has not led to any change of usage.

Adjectives in the late 14c could freely be used as head-words in reference to persons or things, singular or plural. But this usage had really become anomalous with the virtual, and in the 15c total, disappearance of adjectival inflections for number, and the growing pronominal distinctions for human/non-human gender. The unease of speakers is shown by the growing use of the prop-word *one* as carrier of at least number-contrast. By the end of the period exceptions can be found (cf. §86), but something approaching the present restrictions on adjectives as head-words is in operation. Adjective intensifiers were varied, as they had been in II (cf. §86). The rapid turn-over in such words (as they become eroded by exaggeration) is shown by the modest amount of overlap between the period II list and that for period III, namely, *ful, swithe, right, moost, wunderly*; during III *very* makes its first steps from being a full adjective ('real, genuine, true') to being an intensifier. One of the intensifiers forms a bridge with the periphrastic alternative to comparison of adjectives: *more, moost*, are used instead of, or together with, inflections, but not in the fairly systematic way that has evolved since III – at least, so it seems; but much of our late 14c Standard evidence is from verse, and it may be that that distorts our impression of how periphrastic and inflectional forms were distributed.

§ 121 Morphology and syntax are at this time particularly closely intertwined, since in the late 14c we see established important new ranges of verb-forms, whose functions are delimited by contrast with the functions of older forms. The raw material for these forms lies in the paradigms we have already examined, but the arrangements have yet to be described.

The tense-system was, as the paradigms have indicated, two-term, present and past. Expression of the future was not provided for in this system, and had traditionally been simply one of the functions of the so-called present form. The traditional usage persisted (indeed, it is not unknown today, but under strict conditions), but there was growing anxiety to mark the present–future distinction. Although this never came to be built into the system by a simple contrast as clear-cut as that between present and past, various devices were available. Though *will* and *shall* still functioned as full verbs (cf. § 170), they were also modally differentiated operators of (among other things) future reference; this pattern existed in II (cf. § 90), and we shall be able to trace it far behind III (cf. § 173). The main indices of futurity in the verb are suspended awkwardly between the modal and tense systems; what is astonishing is that this state of affairs has lasted so long. There is clear evidence in dialects and in American English that the matter would have tended towards resolution by the adoption of *will* as the sole 'uncoloured' future, but in British Standard English this resolution has been resisted, though in the late 14c there are clear indications that it too was tending to the same resolution. For the explanation of this strange state of affairs we may quote Jespersen:

> Here it will be convenient first to mention the biblical use of *shall*, which goes back to Wycliff's practice of rendering the Latin future tense by *shall*, while he uses *will* to translate the present tense of Latin *volo*. The use in the old biblical versions has been carefully investigated by Augusta Björling. . . . 'Except in Bi [i.e., *The holy byble*, 1575] which obviously favours *will*, *shall* is regularly used in all three persons to express futurity. In the Gospel according to St. Matthew in the late Wycliffite Version the Latin future of the Vulgate is, on Blackburn's statement, rendered by *shall* 322 times, and by *will* only twice.' Miss Björling's investigation thoroughly confirms Blackburn's view, which she quotes in full. As, however, Chaucer's practice favours *will* as expression for the future (with inanimate as well as animate subjects), much more than the bibles do, these do not seem reliable witnesses as to the actual usage of those times, but probably show only that it was the practice at school in translating Latin futures always to use *shall*. But on the other hand this biblical usage undoubtedly exercised a powerful influence on literary style, especially in serious and solemn writings (1909, etc., IV, 275–6).

The evidence of 14c original writers is that British Standard was tending in the direction other kinds of English have definitively taken; the evidence of biblical translation is that because of the correspondence of *will* to *volo*, and the lack of any such clear correspondence for *shall*, the schools sharply differentiated the two in instruction, and on lines counter to what can now be seen as the growing trend of spontaneous

usage. The school tradition was powerfully reinforced by its own consequence, the usage of biblical translations, and this twin force was not
spent by the time of Wallis (cf. §90). For prescription to have such power
is rare; the circumstances were in a variety of ways – one cannot say
propitious – at least favourable to a freezing of the rather unhappy state
at which usage was caught.

At the same time other future-ish patterns came into use – *I am to,
I go to*, and the first traces of *I'm going to* (for which see below, on
periphrastic forms). In proportion as *will, shall*, were full verbs, they
retained pasts with ordinary past senses. But *wolde, sholde*, had by III
long been in course of absorption into the modal system. In general,
sholde still retains something of its association with the full-verb meaning
and is rather equivalent to *to be obliged to* (of people), *destined to* (of
things, events); this difference accounts for some uses where in later
English *would* or *was to* might be preferred (Chaucer, *And when this
mayden sholde vnto a man Ywedded be . . .*, Malory, *had it ben any other
than Gawayn he shold not haue escaped . . .*). But still, as in II, the differences in modals are a matter of delicate shifts of balance, not of absolute
and clear-cut differences. Similarly, in the perfect, *have* is in use with all
types of verbs, but for intransitives *be* is its rival – more strongly than in
II, or of course I. The period saw further steps in the process of rendering
conjugations symmetrical, notably the introduction of a perfect participle (*having* + second participle) from the early 16c.

But much the most important was the extension of the periphrastic
forms to match the simple ones. This has been a very protracted process,
and although it appears that period III was definitive for major aspects
of it, there is a possibility that what we are really seeing is a new wealth
of evidence rather than a new wealth of forms and uses. Still, with all
allowance made, this seems the most reasonable point for an account
of what happened.

The use of a periphrastic series, *am taking, was taking,* of more or less
durative aspectual contrast with the corresponding simple forms (*take,
took*) is clearly established in OE, but only in those two series. The
trends that belong to late ME and early NE are twofold – the development
of a much fuller range of patterns, so that the periphrastic forms are
almost fully symmetrical with the simple forms, and an overall increase
in frequency of usage far greater than the introduction of new patterns
could account for. The periphrastic perfect (Chaucer, *We han ben
waityng*) is recorded late in the 14c but does not become at all common
for a century, nor fully current till the 18c. The first instance of the

periphrastic pluperfect is a little earlier in the 14c (*he three dais had fastand bene*) (though it can hardly have developed earlier), and shows its full maturity from the time of the Restoration. Future-referring *shall* and *will* with periphrastic forms are common in the north in the 14c, but were apparently slow to enter the Standard language; they are well established by the 16c, and common from about 1800 (a purely modal *will* makes scattered appearances in even early ME, but is not established until late in the 19c in such uses as *they'll be eating themselves up*); this, and a modal use of *should, would*, with periphrastic forms will require further mention in IV (cf. § 155). The periphrastic first participle comes into use, and the imperative with *let* is recorded from Chaucer (*lat now no heuy thought Ben hangynge* . . .), but other non-finites were already in existence (cf. § 155). In fact, in the active, the periphrastic forms came to be provided with a fairly complete conjugation by III, though much of it was in extremely rare use. The passive, as we know (cf. § 91), is another story. The first phase is the introduction of passive sense into the usual (i.e., PE active) forms. There are traces of a movement in this direction in both OE and ME, but the usage is fully accepted only in the 16c. Meanwhile, from the late 14c, not in literature but in informal and private papers, the use of formally passive types begins; very rarely it surfaces in literature (cf. with the perfect participle, 1590 in Sidney, *shee said it might very well be, having bene many times taken one for another*), but in finite use it does not come into the open till the end of the 18c (cf. § 59), and even then it is a use of young men, and has to face a century of explicit controversy before it is taken for granted. Corresponding to these forms, a periphrastic set for the *go to* future was required; in our period only *am wendyng to* is used at first, but *am going to* creeps in, to become fully established in the 17c.

It is a remarkable thing that the uses of this range of forms were largely established by the beginning of III on the lines they now take; indeed, this was true for OE, though the use of the forms in those functions was much less consistent. The functions that appear to be new in our period are the egressive (i.e., indicating movement out of a phase of activity), as in *þai war all concluding* . . ., which dates from about 1400; and the use of plain modalised forms for subjective duration (hypothesis, etc.) (*if Crist were dwelling here in erþe, men moste ben trauayllynge*) which mainly develops at the close of the 14c. The most important changes are not, however, in range of use but in regularity within the uses (though complete uniformity has never been reached). The rate per 100,000 words roughly doubles during our period; but between the beginning of III and the present day it increases about twenty-five fold, and the sharpest increase is in very recent times (cf. § 59). At all times from OE on, poetry has been notably resistant to the periphrastic forms; the difference in frequency can be seen from the presence of only four examples in Book I of the *Faerie Queene*, and this is typical (except in Wordsworth's *Prelude*) until the 20c.

The increase in *-ing-* forms brought about in this way is only one aspect of a more general phenomenon, for which see § 131.

NOTE: On all matters relating to periphrastic forms I have made extensive use of Mossé, 1938 *a* and *b* (cf. also Nickel, 1966).

§ 122 The subjunctive had distinct roles, first in independent clauses, in the present, to express a realisable wish, in the past, to express an unrealisable one; it was also widespread in various types of dependent clause. But, as we have seen (cf. § 119), by soon after 1400 ordinary verbs did not have distinct subjunctive forms; the subjunctive was from the 15c, as it is now, largely a function of *be*. From this situation there naturally followed a decline in the sense of where the subjunctive should appropriately be used, a decline that has continued to this day, reversed sporadically only by the tendency to hypercorrection in 18c and later teachers and writers.

The infinitive was used in plain and prepositional forms, the prepositional including *for to* as well as *to*; as the range of modals was not very clearly defined a number of verbs could then be used before a plain infinitive, which later came to require *to* (thus *thinke*, 'intend', and *let* in sequences other than fossilised *let go*); that *need* and *dare* were already divided in usage, *need* tending to enter the modal class and *dare* to leave it, we have already observed (cf. § 59).

A causative modal *do* (*do werche* 'have someone work, make . . .') was in common use at the beginning of the period, but declined in frequency in proportion to the growth, towards the end of the period, of the modern special uses of *do* (cf. § 91). In the absence of these uses, negation and interrogation followed markedly different courses from those we have seen developing in II and I. Negation was ordinarily by the particle *ne* preceding the verb, and in certain very common verbs contracting with it [*ne + wil* giving *nil*, *ne + wolde*, *nolde*, etc. (cf. § 173)]. Partly because of the phonetic weakness of this device, and partly because negatives lend themselves to emphatic reinforcement, there was already at the beginning of the period a common use of supporting *nought*, *not*, *nat*, etc. ('not at all'), after the verb (*And he nas nat right fat*). In the common way of reinforcers this tended to become indispensable, and this in turn tended to make the pre-posed particle redundant, so that even at the beginning of the period such negations as *His arwes drouped noght* are common (Professor Quirk draws my attention to a parallel development in colloquial French, *je sais pas*). Naturally negation (cf. §91) is cumulative (*He nevere yet no vileynye ne sayde In al his lyf unto no maner wight*). By the end of the period the pre-posed particle survives only in rare fossilised contracted forms (cf. §91) and the post-posed particle is the norm, though the abundance of unsystematic *do*-periphrases offers the raw material from which the present usage can be evolved. Interrogation is normally by simple inversion (though it is plain that intonation could also serve without inversion); again, it is only at the end of the period that the free use of *do* provides a means which will be exploited for the clausal function of indicating interrogation. The growing use of 'empty' periphrastic use of *do* during the period is at the expense of a similar use, no doubt at least partly metrically conditioned, of *gin*, *gan*, (originally, but no longer, ingressive) and *can* (which also served as modal and as full verb) at the beginning of the period (Chaucer, *Therwith the moones exaltatioun, I meene Libra, alwey gan ascende . . .*, where the co-presence of *alwey* indicates that the use is durative, not ingressive).

§ 123   Of the possibilities for the order of elements in the clause during ME Mossé writes as follows:

The six relative positions that the subject, verb, and its object might occupy were as follows:

SVO   ..   *he takez hys leve* 'he takes his leve'.
SOV   ..   *I hym folwed* 'I followed him'.
VSO   ..   *gaf ye the chyld any thyng ?* 'did you give the child anything ?'
VOS   ..   *Thus taughte me my dame* 'thus my mother taught me'.
OSV   ..   *al þou most sugge* 'you must tell everything'.
OVS   ..   *but hood wered he noon* 'but he wore no hood'. (1952, 122).

Yet it is far from the case that anything goes. The order SVO is normal, as the first example might suggest, in positive affirmative independent clauses, with no introductory word; any departure from it produces a marked effect, as it does today, and the statistical frequency of the pattern is nearly as high as today. The order VSO is equally strongly correlated with interrogation, i.e., a little less strongly than today, by reason of the use of inversion after introductory words. The order SOV functions characteristically in dependent clauses, but without a very high mutual predictiveness, since the unmarked order, SVO, also freely occurred in dependence, and SOV also occurs where O is 'light', i.e a word carrying little information, such as a pronoun. One has the impression in reading late 14c prose that the differences of order over six hundred years are no more than the slight shifting of frequency towards the present unmarked uses of SVO and VSO (with change, here, in the composition of V), with a consequent sharpening of the markedness of VOS, OSV, OVS, when they occur, and total abandonment of SOV, i.e., of a special order for dependent clauses. There is a bigger difference between the balance of patterns in late 14c verse and its contemporary prose than between late 14c prose and present-day prose. One of the forms of poetic licence is the artificial preservation of syntactic patterns, in good use among one's predecessors, but increasingly remote from ordinary speech [we have seen that in the 14c something of the same sort affected phonology (cf. § 107)]. If then, we take prose as our norm, the shifting of balance will be very slight in the two hundred years to 1570.

Not every sentence has the three elements SVO, and the change in frequency of this composition is more noticeable than the change in the regularity of order, though the two are mutually reinforcing. The strong association, in positive affirmative independent clauses (enormously more frequent than other types of clause), between subject and pre-verb position, led to the reshaping of sentences which otherwise would depart from the pattern, as we have already seen in II (cf. §88). The 'empty' use of *there, it,* to fill such positions was well advanced by the beginning of III (cf. *A KNYGHT ther was . . ., It is ful fair to been ycleped 'madame'*) but it was by no means invariable (*Bifil that in that seson . . ., But therof nedeth nat to speke . . .*). It is the 15c that sees something approaching regularisation in the matter of slot-filling of subject-position, and this coincides in effect with loss of inflections to bring about the shift of impersonal to personal verbs in the 16c (cf. §93) (Jespersen quotes in this connection: *the king likede(n) peres,* 'pears were pleasing to the king', later *the king liked pears,* which is the outcome of the old construction, but will be associated, by speakers expecting pre-verb subject, with the SVO pattern, and interpreted accordingly, 1909, III, 209). More generally, reduction in the specificness of person-number contrasts in verb-forms heightens the importance of indicating S–V concord positionally; though we need not question that the positional pattern was fairly well-defined before the loss of inflections. Only the last turn of the screw was needed. And within the elements of the clause, the complex rules of order for noun-phrases, and for verb-phrases, as far as they went, were exactly as now.

Despite the dangers of so large a generalisation, one is tempted to say that in grammar and phonology, and above all because of the relations between them, III is the revolutionary period in which the structure of modern English was established. Much of that characteristic structure has been there since the beginnings of our records, but where change can be detected, it is most fundamental at this time. Since the distinctive pattern of relationships between varieties of English that we have called urbanisation dates from the same period, it is one of unparalleled importance and complexity.

CHAPTER IV

1370 – 1170

§ 124   In the centuries behind 1370, change in the size of population was not directly a major factor in the linguistic experience and history of English people. Period IV was a period of growth, but not of explosive growth. Changes in the distribution and composition of the population however, were of very great importance. The structure of varieties of English, and the relationships between these varieties, were very different in period IV from those of period III. It is true that the foundations of London's unique position as a city had been laid (cf. § 99), but this pre-eminence had not yet extended to a metropolitan variety of the language. Yet the conditions existed which could give birth to such a variety, not only through the development of the capital, but as a result of the mobility of the population and of more general social factors.

It is natural in the 20c, when we are so conscious of the technical facilities that enable us to be more mobile than our predecessors, to assume that in earlier times only exceptional people with exceptional business to conduct did much extensive travelling. Before 1170 this assumption might have some validity, but for the period 1170-1370 it certainly did not. Growing numbers of people, sometimes quite poor people, travelled widely (which necessarily meant long) – to such an extent that we must suppose the affinities of their own speech with its local peculiarities were weakened, and that the need was felt for some sort of *lingua franca*, free at least from the more extreme localisms. We all really know this in connection with the late 14c, when Chaucer's pilgrims, drawn from the middle class in its widest extent, are described as having between them undertaken journeys which must have occupied substantial periods of their lives; and for that very journey they had come together 'from every shires ende Of Engelond'.

But this uprooted way of life was not new, and in earlier centuries it probably extended rather further down the social scale. Not only was pilgrimage, at home and abroad, highly popular, but from 1095 the Crusades had periodically attracted large numbers into arms and the long journey to the Holy Land. We think of knights in shining armour (and it would be interesting to know the effect of long years of campaigning together on *their* speech), but in fact many of the crusaders were extremely humble people from the villages and ports (Barrow, 1956, 100). It is important to remember that much of this travel not only brought strangers into each other's company for months or years, but also created areas of the country which were persistently inundated with waves of travellers. The growth of universities brought young people – again, often of humble background – together from every part of the country – in Oxford from the close of the 12c and in Cambridge from 1229 [not to mention large numbers who studied abroad (cf. § 125)]. Their working language was Latin, but their leisure and conduct of everyday affairs must have been in an English in which local peculiarities were restrained, and this at a time when the students were still at a linguistically malleable age. By the 1330s Oxford alone had about 1300 students at a time; this is a very high proportion, perhaps as much as one in thirty of the relevant age-group of boys. It is not generally appreciated that the proportion of the male population with some experience of university residence was higher than in the first quinquennium of post-Robbins England. Others will have spent part of their youth in the even more cosmopolitan ambience of the Inns of Court, or as pages, or in a religious community of one hundred or more, drawing members from various quarters. These are only a few of the factors leading to the uprooting and mixing of people from their communities of origin. It is natural to wonder how any but great landowners could afford so much wandering. The answer would seem to lie in the feudal system, by which land was held in return for service. The service was fixed in relation to the land, and might, for a single man, be quite burdensome, while for a man with a quiverful of sturdy sons it offered a sinecure. In a time of steady, if not spectacular, population-increase, there was a great deal of leisure-time to be absorbed by travel, and, to all intents and purposes, nothing to be gained by staying home and working harder. The 13c sees the innovation of deliberately producing a surplus for marketing, and as this habit grows, the economy becomes more money-based, and travel becomes the prerogative of the saintly and the well-to-do; but this does not happen at a stroke, and most of our period is one of exceptional mobility among all classes.

People did not just wander, they migrated: and not just, as they must have done since towns began, to the nearest town, but in a much more general movement to London. The growing role of money in the economy made London ever more attractive; many were free to migrate to it, particularly in those parts of the E Mid in which no feudal land-ties existed (cf. §99). Ekwall (1956, passim) has been able to identify by name and locality of origin some 6,000 individuals who migrated to London, largely between 1270 and 1360; these identifiable individuals obviously represent a tiny proportion of the migration that went on. In this particular aspect of the mobility of period IV we have the germ of the conditions for the development of a London-based standard language, and in the principal local sources of the immigrants we have an explanation of some features of the early development of the standard language.

While we suppose these conditions gave rise to some levelling of local speech-characteristics, especially in the form of making all the middle more uniform and the extremities of the country more isolated; and while the period is extremely conscious of English as having divergent forms (cf. §98), we do not see, until IV is turning into III, any of the forms of standardisation in writing. Indeed, the standardisa-tion of writing and speech should be treated as quite distinct at this period, and arising from quite different sources and conditions. Before the rise of a class of secular professional scribes (cf. §96) custodianship of the vernacular written word lay in the hands of clerics, mainly clerics in the scriptoria of abbeys, monasteries and cathedrals (writing for the law, the universities and for national administration was done in other centres, but not normally in English). A young clerk would be trained in his scriptorium; he would derive his spellings from a tradition, but it would be a local, a diocesan, at most a regional, tradition. Very occasionally, an individual would set out to devise a system for some purpose (cf. §133), but he would be aware of doing something exceptional. The normal scribe, who followed the tradition he had learned, might use a form of English with more or less restricted currency; but if his form of writing could be described as following a regional standard, it is still different in kind from a national standard because it has roots in a particular place, and because a trained scribe in that place has no choice of forms available to him. The national Standard, when it arrives, involves preferring a national variety, non-localised in some sense, at the expense of any indigenous tradition.

§ 125 Delay in the development of a national standard language, despite centuries of national unity, is to be explained, at least in part, by the extraordinary position English held in the country during IV,

and for the previous century. In III we saw the reach of English shrunk to
rather less than the shores of England and Scotland; we now see in
addition a politico-social limitation, operating throughout the geographical spread of the country, excluding English from the circles of
power, and from milieux closely dependent upon them. The Norman
Conquest had introduced a ruling class who spoke certain dialects of
northern French – mainly, of course, Norman – and who shared out the
spoils of the new country in such a way that nearly all positions of power
were in the hands of French-speakers. This was done, not, as has sometimes been thought, out of hostility to English, but for the simple motives
of profit and ease – the same motives as made it a matter of course for
the English to continue speaking English when they came to this country
and, over a thousand years later, when they went to India. The newcomers spoke a form of French markedly different from that of Paris,
because their ancestors had quite recently adopted French as invaders
from Scandinavia, and a North Germanic substratum was still apparent
in their speech. In a very short time not only the great secular landowners,
but nearly all holders of bishoprics and major abbacies were French.
Before 1100 virtually all scriptoria were under the direction of French-
speaking authorities, and such business of Church, law, learning and
State as was not conducted in Latin was conducted and recorded in
French. The division inherited by period IV is often referred to as a
class one, and so in a sense it was; but it is easy to misinterpret this
statement. Indeed, with pardonable flamboyance, English writers of
the period have contributed to the misunderstanding by using such
temptingly quotable remarks as that the English language persisted
only among 'feaw uplondysch men' (Higden, *c.* 1327, translated by
John of Trevisa, 1385); this is the exaggeration of bitterness, and is
certainly not meant to convey that English had become the swinish
and half-articulate grunting of a remote and barely human peasantry.
English speakers were lower-class in the sense that they were not great
secular or ecclesiastical landlords. All my acquaintance are lower-class
in this sense, but some of them are rather learned, articulate and sophisticated people. No doubt there were ignorant and churlish people among
the English-speaking community, but there were also comfortably off,
highly educated, widely read and intellectually cosmopolitan people
among them. Because the scriptoria were not generally under English
direction, we know all too little about the literature of English-speakers
during the 12c and 13c, but what we have is as sophisticated, as un-
boorish, as English literature at any period. It still remains true, that

from 1066 to 1200, and in more limited ways thereafter, English was the language of less than the whole community.

Since the extent of currency and the functions of English were not static, we must trace out the course of events, and it will be convenient in this connection to treat the period from 1066 as a unit. The Norman rulers and landowners remained for generations in possession of territories on both sides of the Channel. Their lands have been well designated the Channel State (Barrow, 1956, 146). The continuity of their relations with France after the conquest of England, as well as the wider currency of French as compared with English, may be the explanation of their different behaviour in learning French in Normandy (once there they severed relations with Scandinavia) but not English in England. Their empire was too large for secure management under feudal conditions, and though in the late 12c it was extended south to the Pyrenees its very extension was a weakness, not a strength. The European territories could not be held against Central French power, nor the English borders against the Scots, and to some extent the Welsh. Consolidation was needed, and by a law of 1204 landowners were required to hold estates in either England or France, but not both. Thereafter, those of the aristocracy who opted for English holdings were truly identified with this country, and had the embryo of a motive for learning its language. Their children had to look forward to a future in England, and would naturally learn its language. Bilingualism might persist for a generation or two, but French, on any large scale, was thenceforth doomed as the language of the English, even among the highest classes. As we can see today in Belgium or Wales, very strong cultural motivation will keep alive a minority language, but in the absence of such motivation (cf. Cornish and Manx) decline is inevitable. By the 13c there was, if anything, negative motivation. This came about in the following way. Norman French, as we have seen, was a peculiar dialect of French, and not one of high cultural prestige. This branch of the French language had had a century and a half of independent development within England, by which it had become essentially a distinct language, Anglo-Norman. Apart from its possession of a distinct written form, with a considerable literature in it, its relations with Central French were a little comparable with those of Australian English and RS today; but unsupported by any national sentiment to which pride in that particular variety of language could attach itself. In fine, if, in the 13c and *a fortiori* the 14c, a man wished to show his standing by his command of French (and we have abundant testimony that people did so wish), he would be well advised to adopt Parisian French rather than Anglo-Norman.

Nor was this aspiration a matter of castles in the air. While the beginning of the 13c marks the close of one phase of French in England, the Anglo-Norman phase, it also marks the onset of the next, the Central French. Both political and cultural events contributed to the new linguistic invasion. The centre of gravity of the Channel State holdings shifted when Henry II (1154-89) extended his territories south into France, and John in 1204 lost Normandy; Henry's Court was Parisian-French-speaking, and has been acclaimed as the most splendid and cultivated in Europe. The new culture for which it provided a home was that of a renaissance, starting in Provence and sweeping north through France, which has with some reason been held to dwarf the later movement to which that title is generally given. New themes and forms in literature and music flourished, and their exponents flocked to London. The greatest invention of the new movement was the university, embodiment and stimulus of humanism and intellectual curiosity. Wherever word spread of these new activities the young were swept up as by a whirlwind and deposited at the feet of the great teachers in the universities. There was no academic language-barrier, since Latin was used everywhere. And for English young men, at first, the movement was above all to Paris, though soon Oxford would rival Paris. The liveliest of the young, often poor but intelligent and impressionable, cut loose as perhaps they have not done again on such a scale till the 1960s, to be 'where it's at'. Some stayed to reach eminence as scholars and churchmen in France. But most returned, sooner or later, and in English life they turn up in the oddest places – not merely concentrated in the Court where one would expect to find them, but thinly scattered throughout the country; writers, observers, thinkers, cultured and cosmopolitan, composing the new literary forms in their own language, but seized of the spoils of French humanism.

English in the 13c is thus exposed to a new wave of French influence, of a more Central and cultivated kind. English French is still often Anglo-Norman, and the period of bilingualism will be richer in borrowings than that which preceded, but additionally English is directly exposed to Parisian French sources. The demonstrable effects of these successive and overlapping waves of influence are largely seen in vocabulary, though it is natural to suppose that pervasive, but less definable, grammatical influences were at work.

At a more superficial level, the spelling-system was to be substantially altered (cf. §128), and it would seem that fashionable persons adopted certain features of French pronunciation. The dominant lexical influence could have been predicted. Perhaps the hold French retained in the 13c and 14c on English institutions could not. It remained the regular medium of school instruction (as Latin was of university instruction) until the second half of the 14c, and then the change was gradual. Ranulf Higden, whose comments on the survival of English we have already noted (cf. above), says that French-medium instruction had been customary since the Conquest, but his translator (John of Trevisa) is able to bring the story up to date in an interpolation. He dates the first introduction of English into the schools from the Black Death (1348-9); Johan Cornwall and Richard Pencrych started English-medium teaching, but now (1385) 'in all the gramer-scoles of Engelond children leveth Frensch and construeth and lurneth an Englysch'. It is notable both that this movement begins in the west country, least exposed to Continental influence, and also that at least some Cornishmen not only knew English but taught in it. While he recognises the convenience of this innovation, Trevisa foresees difficulties for those who in future may need to travel; what is important is that in 1385 French is only thought useful in the context of foreign travel. This fits in with another of his modifications to Higden; between 1327 and 1385 it has apparently ceased to be true that those of gentle birth had their children taught French from the cradle (dragging social climbers, needless to say, in their wake). And indeed, it is at this very period, in 1362, that the Statute of Pleading establishes English as the language of the courts, and in the same year that Parliament was opened in English for the first time.

Though French was far the most important language coexisting with English, it was not the only one. That some Celtic speech was used in Cumberland, Cornwall and along the Welsh border is fairly certain, but these areas also had some English, and the proportions cannot be determined. Extensive areas of the E Mid and N were occupied by people of Scandinavian descent (cf. §157); their language was very different from un-Scandinavianised English, but whether they kept up a separate language as late as our period, or whether their speech was different enough to seem like another language rather than a dialect, cannot be determined (cf. §176). The Scottish position is summarised by Professor Barrow. The population totalled about one-third of a million. The area north of a line from Grangemouth to Glasgow was Gaelic-speaking, and even Lothian had a considerable Gaelic element. But English was extending northwards:

By the time of Robert I (1306-1329) a northern version of the English tongue had effectively replaced Gaelic almost everywhere in southern and eastern Scotland, save for Galloway in the south-east, Buchan in the north-east, and the highland parts of those counties which have a coastline on the North Sea (Barrow, 1956, 234);

yet

well into the thirteenth century Gaelic remained the speech of the lowland countryside of Scotland north of the Forth, while in the highlands its supremacy was not challenged until the eighteenth century (ib., 235).

The conquest of Ireland was due to Henry II, but it is not to be supposed that more than a handful of persons spoke English there or in Wales during our period.

§ 126 That there should have been a great and widespread literary movement in the latter 14c might have been predicted as a consequence of the events we have been tracing. Great as he is, Chaucer is not isolated; at only two other points in its history has English produced a group of poets so distinguished and so varied as Chaucer and his contemporaries. Perhaps 'group' is not the word; for these are not people working together or thinking alike; they are not even, in a sense, writing the same language. What is unprecedented, and unparalleled since, is that this tiny nation produced such writers, especially poets, in such abundance, and that they each wrote individually, not merely in style, but in language. The forms of English in which their writings are preserved vividly demonstrate that in addition to the successive varieties of Standard identified by Professor Samuels (cf. §99), there were many other kinds of English which had a rather fixed tradition of writing. Because they conformed to standards and were recognisable as standard, and because their currency was less than nationwide, we might call them cultivated regional, or regional standard. But the areas they represent are not so homogeneous as to give the term 'regional' much sense except in contrast to 'national', as some examples will show. Barbour's *Bruce* (1375) is in Scots, and clearly the linguistic ancestor of later English literature from Scotland; in the early ME period there is a continuous dialect-area from the Humber to the Forth, but since 1157 the eastern end of the border had followed the Tweed, and its presence led to the progressive division, linguistically and otherwise, of an area that had previously been homogeneous. In the late 14c we lack texts from the four northern counties to compare with Barbour's language (unless you count the language of the Northumbrian students at Cambridge

220

represented by Chaucer in the *Reeve's Tale*; on the probable authenticity of this representation see Tolkien, 1934). A further centre of regional standard in the eastern part of the country is Yorkshire (Richard Rolle), and in the next county we have the Lincolnshire work of Robert Mannyng. South of this, any centres of standardisation we know of seem to have been caught up in the rivalry to produce a national standard. But in the western half of the country both foreign influence and the sense of the capital as centre were much weaker. The collection of poems preserved in BM MS Cotton Nero A X (Cheshire–Staffordshire border) is in a highly cultivated form of written language, which differs from eastern English not only on the normal spatial dimensions, but also as preserving remnants of an ancient poetic language not directly comparable with anything in the east. Other western centres can be identified in Malvern, Worcester and Lichfield, etc. The differences from place to place concerned every level of the language – the way graphemes were used, the phonology, the grammar, the vocabulary, the sense of style appropriate to a given kind of writing. There follow selections illustrating these differences; a reading of the tentative transcription will indicate that differences are considerable, but they will be better understood after a reading of § 129, and especially if they are studied in context in Mossé (1952).

(a) Barbour:

> He had bot schort quhill syttyn thare,
> Quhen he saw fra the vode cumand
> Thre men with bowis in thar hand,
> That toward hym com spedely,
> And he persavit that in hy,
> Be thair effeir and their havyng
> That thai lufit hym na kyn thyng.

> /he had bʊt ʃɔrt ʍiːl sɪtɪn θɑːr
> /ʍɛn he saʊ fraː θə wʊd kʊmand
> /θreː mɛn wɪθ boʊwɪs ɪn θar hand
> /θat toʊward hɪm koːm speːdɪliː
> /and he pərsavɪt θat ɪn hiː
> /be θar efaɪr and θar hɑːvɪŋg
> /θat θaɪ lʊfɪt hɪm nɑː kɪn θɪŋg/

(Note the use of *quh*, *v*, *f*, *a* = /ɑː/ = southern /ɔː/, *i/y* in unstressed syllables, final unvoicing in morphemic *-it*, lack of inflection in plural *com*, and first part in *-and*).

(b) Rolle (before 1349, MS *c.* 1400):

> Luf es a byrnand ȝernyng in God, with a wonderfull delyte and sykernes.
> God es lyght and byrnyng. Lyght clarifies oure skyll; byrnyng kyndels
> oure covayties þat we desyre noght bot hym. Luf es a lyf, copuland
> togedyr þe lufand and þe lufed. For mekenes makes us swete to God;
> purete joynes us tyll God; lufe makes us ane with God.

> /luf ɛs ə bɪrnand jɛrnɪŋg ɪn gɔd wɪθ ə wʊndərfʊl dɛliːt and sɪkərnɪs.
> gɔd ɛs lɪχt. and bɪrnɪŋg lɪχt klarɪfiːs uːr skɪl. bɪrnɪŋg kiːndels uːr kʊvaɪtiːs
> θat we dɛziːr nɔχt bʊt hɪm. luf ɛs ə liːf kɔpʊland togɛdɪr θə lufand
> and θə lʊfɪd. fɔr meːknɪs maːks ʊs sweːt to gɔd, pyːrteː dʒɔɪns ʊs tɪl
> gɔd, luf maːks ʊs aːn wɪθ gɔd/

(Note that the underlying type of English is, as far as the two are comparable,
strikingly like the preceding; this, though the geographical distances are
very large. This is understandable as Scottish English is a relatively recent
extension northwards of northern English, while this dialect and those south
of it have had a long period of separate development; time, in this issue,
is a more potent dimension than space. The writing conventions are,
however, more removed from one another.)

(c) Robert Mannyng of Bourne, Lincs, 1338, MS slightly later:

> Of Brunne I am; if any me blame,
> Robert Mannyng is my name;
> Blissed be he of God of hevene
> Þat me Robert with gude will nevene [*name*]
> In the third Edwardes tyme was I,
> When I wrote alle þis story,
> In the hous of Sixille I was a throwe [*time*]
> Danz Robert of Malton, þat ȝe know,
> Did it wryte for felawes sake
> When þai wild solace make.

> /ɔf brʊn iː am ɪf anɪ meː blaːm
> /rɔbɛrt manɪŋg ɪs mɪ naːm
> /blɪsɪd beː heː ɔf gɔd ɔf hɛvən
> /θat meː rɔbɛrt wɪθ guːd wɪl nɛvən
> /ɪn θə θɪrd ɛdwards tiːm was iː
> /ʍɛn iː wrɔːt al θɪs stɔːriː
> /ɪn θuːs ɔf sɪksɪl iː was ə θrɔːʊ
> /dants rɔbɛrt ɔf maltʊn θat je knɔːʊ
> /dɪd ɪt wriːt fɔr fɛlaʊs saːk
> /ʍɛn θaɪ wɪld sɔlaːs maːk/

(Note the form of pronouns *I*, *þai*, the indifference to final *-e* in rhymes and scansion, the northern vowel in *gude* and the south/Midland one in *wrote*, the absence of *-n* infinitives, the regularised past *wild* and the Scandinavian loan *felawes*.)

(d) Cotton Nero A X, poem of *Sir Gawayn and the Green Knight*, written in the closing years of the 14c, contemporary MS, poem and MS from Staffordshire-Cheshire border:

Ful erly bifore þe day   þe folk uprysen,
Gestes þat go wolde,   hor gromez þay calden,
And þay busken up bilyve,   blonkkes to sadel,
Tyffen he(r) takles,   trussen her males,
Richen hem þe rychest,   to ryde alle arayde,
Lepen up ly3tly,   lachen her brydeles,
Uche wy3e on his way,   þer hym wel lyked.

/fʊl ɛrliː bɪfɔːr θə daɪ   θə fɔlk ʊprɪzən
/gɛst(ə)s θat gɔː wɔld   hər groːm(ə)s θaɪ kɑːldən
/and θaɪ bʊskən ʊp bɪliːv   blɔŋk(ə)s to sɑːdəl
/tɪfən (h)ər takləs   trʊsən (h)ər maːl(ə)s
/rɪtʃən (h)əm θə rɪtʃəst   to riːd al araɪd
/leːpən ʊp lɪχtliː   latʃən (h)ər briːdəls
/ytʃ wiː ɔn (h)ɪs waɪ   θeːr hɪm wɛl liːkəd/

NOTE: The language here is more impenetrable. I have not attempted to gloss single words, because the order of elements in the clause is at least as big a stumbling-block. The verse-form is obviously different from those exemplified so far, and unlike them, unfamiliar to us; the more archaic syntax and unfamiliar vocabulary, of which this is an extremely mild example, are associated with this kind of verse. Notice the *-en* inflections of verb plurals, inf in *-e*, the pronouns *þai*, *þem* and *her/hor*, the south or midland vowel in *go*, and Scandinavian loans such as *busken*.

(e) Langland, *Piers Plowman* A-text, composed *c.* 1362 in the Malvern area and copied there rather later:

To preyere and to penaunce   putten heom monye,
For love of ur lord   liveden ful harde,
In hope for to have   Heveneriche blisse;
As ancres and hermytes   þat holdeþ hem in heore celles;
Coveyte not in cuntre   to cairen aboute,
For non likerous lyflode,   heore licam to plese.
Bote japers and jangelers,   Judas children,
Founden hem fantasyes   and fooles hem maaden,
And habbeþ wit at heor wille   to worchen, 3if hem luste.

/to praɪɛr and to pɛnaʊns   pʊtən əm mɔnɪə
/fɔr lʊv ɔf uːr lɔːrd   lɪvədən fʊl hard(ə)
/ɪn hɔːp fɔr to haːv   hɛvənəriːtʃ(ə) blɪs(ə)
/as aŋkrəs and ɛrmɪts   θat hɔːldəθ əm ɪn ör sɛl(ə)s
/kʊvaɪtə nɔːt ɪn kʊntreː to kaɪrən abuːt
/fɔr nɔːn lɪkəruːs liːflɔːd   ör lɪkam to plɛːz
/bʊt dʒɑːpərs and dʒaŋglərs   dʒuːdas tʃɪldrən
/fuːndən əm fantasiːs   and fɔːləs əm maːdən
/and (h)abəθ wɪt at ör wɪl   to wʊrtʃən jɪf əm lyst(ə)/

NOTE : This is in the same metrical tradition as [d], but although its language is more remote from our own than [a], [b] or [c̄] – let alone Chaucer – it is much more straightforward than the language of [d]. Notice the verb-forms, *-en* in past plurals, *-eþ* in present plurals, and variable *-n* on infinitives, variable *-v-* / *-bb-* in *have*; pronouns *hem, heore*; Scandinavian loan, *cairen*; south Midland phonological features, *-ch* in *Heveneriche, worche*, westerly in *monye*, and south-westerly in *luste*.

More areas could be illustrated, but this will suffice to show the variety of concurrent kinds of English, and the number of centres which had a recognisable form of written English associated with them. There were other kinds of English designed for more narrowly local circulation, but these will come under review later (cf. § 133).

§ 127   This wealth of cultivated varieties seems to be a new phenomenon of the 14c, and we can see why this might be so. But we should not accept appearance for reality without looking deeper. Time may be a distorting factor; when documents are produced a copy at a time the later ones have simply a better chance of survival than the earlier. Moreover, scholarly investigation of such records as do survive is incomplete. Some of the findings incorporated into the past paragraph have been published only in the last few years (notably McIntosh, 1963, Samuels, 1963), and much more of the same kind awaits publication. Other topics have not yet been investigated; on them we can say nothing, but a closer look at the work of Professors McIntosh and Samuels must be our next concern.

ME is, *par excellence*, the dialectal phase of English, in the sense that while dialects have been spoken at all periods, it was in ME that divergent local usage was normally indicated in writing. It was preceded by a phase in which the language had one kind of written standard (cf. § 179), and followed by a phase in which it had others. It stands alone as having a rich and varied documentation in localised varieties of

English, and dialectology is more central to the study of ME than to any other branch of English historical linguistics. Yet although there were studies of individual texts and areas, overall knowledge of ME dialects (and it is a subject in which each part depends on the whole) remained more or less static from 1935 to 1952, and very little of the work begun in 1952 is yet available. This was not because the state of knowledge was satisfactory, or even as satisfactory as it could be made. The classification of ME dialects generally used was that set up by Moore, Meech and Whitehall (1935), though it was clear that their findings were both impoverished and distorted by the small number of texts they analysed, the small number of criteria they employed, the discarding of much evidence, and, above all, the use of the written data simply as clues from which phonemes and morphemes in the spoken language could be reconstructed. It was as if medieval scribes were taken to be concerned with setting up a speech-encoding device for us to break, rather than a means of communication to be interpreted by fellow-speakers with a knowledge of the same writing conventions. Finally, the work covered such a large time-span that no accurate distinction was possible between strictly diatopic (place-to-place) variation, and diachronic (time-to-time) change.

These criticisms are summarised from a statement by McIntosh in his 1963 paper, in which he describes the genesis and planning of a new investigation, begun in 1952. First he limited his enquiry to approximately a single century, and chose the one richest in documentation (and most interesting in every way), c. 1350-1450. He secured the co-operation of Professor Samuels, who is investigating a large body of texts from the southern half of the country, while he himself is investigating those from the northern half. It has been necessary to make an inventory of the documents from the chosen century that could be exactly localised on non-linguistic grounds, and to plot on maps the isographs (i.e., the boundaries of variant representations) of every graphemic variable except the very rarest. In other words, graphemic information was not discarded simply because it did not seem to represent a difference of pronunciation. They thus came to operate with a battery of about two hundred and sixty items, each of which may yield anything from two variables to three dozen variables. In this way they are able to cover at least a very considerable part of the map of England with a fairly close-meshed reticulation of isographs.

It is at this point that the investigation becomes not merely more exhaustive, but different in kind from its predecessors, because from

225

here on the work is cumulative in its findings. The graphemes of MSS not localised on non-linguistic grounds can be superimposed on the initial plotting. Sometimes they will 'fit' (quotes, because 'fit' henceforth is a technical term in the investigation) in only one location, and every new manuscript located by the 'fit'-technique adds to the data for local- ising others. The validity of this method of extension was corroborated in a test whereby workers in the Linguistic Survey of Scotland (also directed by Professor McIntosh) were asked to 'fit' the characteristics of written data for dialects whose identity was concealed from them on to partly completed maps. In this case the results could be checked, and the success in terms of deducing the correct location was over- whelming. Since all the major literary works of the century (other than those in a variety of Standard) are non-localised in the relevant sense, and many of them are both extensive and of high graphemic regularity, there is abundant material for progressive localisation, and the results will be as important for literary as for linguistic history.

The small amount of material already published has fully justified Professor McIntosh's claim: 'The results of the work are, I think, likely to be fairly revolutionary' (1963, 10). They are going to affect our understanding of what happened as early as the 12c and as late as the 16c; they vividly point the need for a similar approach to material from other periods. The history of ME, and more than ME, is shortly going to be rewritten.

The inadequacy of our dialect-classification is partly mitigated by the fact that in the early part of IV, before linguistic urbanisation began, the situation must have been simpler than at its end. Nevertheless, much of what must now be said is merely provisional. Furthermore, the nearer we come to a time when, for the average person, the limits of his linguistic experience were set by the community of his own village, the more do we need to speak in terms of the speech-characteristics of very small areas. We do not have the material to do this, and the custom has grown up that characteristics of a text we know to be, say, Mid, are described as Mid, though all we know is that they fit somewhere in that huge territory. As we come to the use of such sweeping labels they will need careful glossing, but properly understood, they serve a purpose in enabling us to discuss diatopic differences. They must not be taken to imply that a particular usage was standardised throughout a region, though in grammar this is more likely to have happened than in phonology.

With this caution, we may look at the phonology of the period, and

226

we can only do so by taking account of local differences, which hitherto we have seldom needed to do. The attempt to reconstruct the pronunciation of this period is no more disreputable than the attempt to reconstruct that of later periods; as always, some parts of the reconstruction are more convincing, even more certain, than others. What is disreputable is to treat the written evidence as if its only value lay in its implications for phonology. There is no doubt that improved reconstructions will follow from Professor McIntosh's work, but research has always led to such advances, and this is no reason for keeping silent about what now seem our best inferences from the evidence so far brought under contribution. As we turn to this subject we have also to remember that dialects are artefacts, fictitious entities invented by speakers, in which, for limited purposes, linguists suspend disbelief. In reality, there are not dialects, but dialect-criteria. Each criterion has its own boundaries (isoglosses), and each isogloss (which may be as specific as the form of a single word) has its own history. When a group of isoglosses bunch together we regard them as forming a dialect boundary, and may speak of the speech in the area they enclose as a dialect. But this is secondary and it is exceptional; most of the time most isoglosses go their own individual ways. With all these cautions in mind we must turn to the written data, and to what they seem to tell us about speech, in various parts of the community between 1370 and 1170.

§ 128   We have first to consider the alphabet and what can be reconstructed of its use. Its structure in 1370 has already been given (cf. §97). In 1170 the forms ʒ and þ were in much more widespread use, and three further symbols were current, æ (called *ash*), normally used for the vowel in RP *at* (very occasionally, just at the beginning, for the equivalent long vowel); ð, corresponding to later *th*, by some used indifferently with þ for /θ/ and /ð/, by others distinguished positionally, þ being used initially and ð medially and finally, and by some not at all; ƿ (called 'wynn' = 'joy'), in the value of *w* (which, indeed, was already beginning to replace it). On the other hand, *g*, *q*, *v*, and to a large extent *w* and *z*, were not current. The alphabet therefore had twenty-five symbols at the beginning of the period, compared with twenty-seven (of which two were rare) at its end. The symbols which died out had been current in the OE alphabet, and those which were brought in followed Continental, more specifically Norman-French, custom. *W* (in early use also *u*) was a simple substitution for ƿ, and *q(u)* for insular *cw*, rarely *kw* (it was also used, in the north, in symbols for /hw/), but the other changes involved more complex relationships. In effect *g* was needed beside ʒ to make a phonemic distinction, and *v*, *z*, beside *f*, *s*, to make other (recently developed) phonemic distinctions; but *æ* could go because the short sound it represented was no longer distinguished in any dialect from /a/, represented by *a*. In its long value it was replaced, on the French model, by *e*, later also *ea*.

Certain important innovations had nothing to do with phonological developments but were adjustments, made possible by exposure to an independent spelling-tradition, to aspects of English spelling which had always been unsatisfactory. The first writing down of English around 600 had been accomplished by missionaries trained in Latin; briefly, the problem facing them was to make an analysis of the phonemes of a language foreign to them, and to make the best possible deployment of the alphabetic symbols designed for writing a different kind of language. Their solution was a very considerable achievement (cf. § 198). But the incompatibility remained: as a result of their Latin training they assumed that the basis of a writing-system should be phonemic, and the English phoneme-system was a square peg in the Latin alphabet. Some incompatibilities eased, others grew worse, by 1170, and in the ME period a number of conventions were developed to solve the remaining problems.

One obvious area of difficulty was the family of palatal consonants, highly elaborated in English, small in Latin. The voiceless stop had the value of /k/; this had traditionally been spelt *c* (rarely and unsystematically *k*), and now with progressive regularity appeared as *k* in environments where *c* might be misread. ME forms such as *kene*, *knave*, look more like NE *keen*, *knave*, than like OE *cene*, *cnafa*; but this is misleading, since in pronunciation they were alike, /keːnə/ for both as against PE /kiːn/, OE /knava/, ME /knɑːvə/ as against PE /neɪv/; medially and finally *-kk-*, which has not survived, and *-ck-*, which has, were used beside *-k-*. Before *a*, *o* and *u*, where it was not liable to misreading, *c* continued in use (OE *can(n)*, ME *can*, PE *can*, modal verb, OE, ME, NE *corn*, 'grain', OE, ME *cum*, /kʊm/, PE, *come* /kʌm/, imperative 'come'). In the vicinity of front vowels *c*, in the French manner, was given the value /s/, as in *service*. OE had also used *c* for /tʃ/, but henceforth the French spelling *ch* took its place; ME *chese* looks like PE *cheese* but sounds like OE *cese*, /tʃeːzə/. For /ʃ/ (derived from a palatal cluster /sk/) the old spelling *sc* is still found at the beginning of the period, but it rapidly gives way to *s(c)h*, again under French influence; OE *scip*, ME, NE *ship*, are all pronounced /ʃɪp/, but ME *shook* looks like NE *shook* and sounds like OE *scoc* /ʃoːk/. For the voiceless palatal

fricative the old spelling *h* survives at first but soon gives way to *ch,
ʒ, ʒh, gh*. There is less difference of pronunciation between OE *liht* and
ME *light*, /li(:)χt/, than between both of them and NE *light*, /laɪt/.
Of the voiced sounds in the palatal group, the stop /g/ was increasingly
represented with 'Continental' *g* to distinguish it from the fricative
/ɣ/, for which the symbol ʒ, which had formerly served both purposes,
came to be reserved; but early in the period this voiced fricative dropped
out of the sound-system (cf. §134). The complex consonant /dʒ/ had
originated from a palatal (cf. §161), and at this period was commonly
represented by 'palatal' letters, *gg* (as in *wiðseggen*, 'withsay'), or *g*
(especially after another consonant, as in *chalenge*); French practice
was to use *g* as well as *j* with this value initially (cf. *gentil, geste, juge*),
which made for ambiguity, since in a few words *g* had the value /g/
before front vowels. For this minority use the graph *gu* was devised
(thus *guest*, distinct from *geste*, 'feat'); this is a new application of an
old principle of using vowel-letters as diacritics for consonant-values,
rather than directly as vowel-symbols. The last of what had been palatal
consonants was now the initial approximant /j/; early in the period
it was spelt in the traditional way with ʒ, later, in the French manner,
with *y* (OE *ʒeond*, ME, NE *yond*, pronounced /jɔnd/ 'throughout'.

The other most important areas of difficulty persisting as a result of
the incompatibility between OE sounds and Latin letters, were those of
vowel quantity and diphthongs. In fact, at the close of OE one diphthong
system died out and another took its place, so we need not concern
ourselves with this until we look at phonological history; the traditional
equations between sound and symbol were broken, though it is important
for ME spelling that certain graphs were thus liberated from use. In
the matter of contrasting vowel length, Latin had long and short vowels,
but as their values, unlike those of OE vowels, could be read off from a
knowledge of the structure of the word as a whole, there was no need for
the orthography to represent the difference. For lack of this differentiation OE words in isolation, rarely in context, could be ambiguous, but
the difficulty does not seem to have been felt as serious until the language
came to be written by Norman-trained scribes. They use whatever
devices come to hand, but neither then nor later has any one system
established itself in English. Occasionally OE scribes had doubled a
vowel to show that it was long, and in ME, especially after 1350, much
more use is made of this custom, whence many PE spellings, such as
foot, feet (though with other vowels this has not survived, contrast ME
caas, 'case'). Note once again that though ME spellings in such cases look

like modern ones, the sounds they represent are like OE ones: OE *fot*, ME *foot* /foːt/, NE *foot* /fʊt/; OE *fet*, ME *feet*, /feːt/, NE *feet*, /fiːt/. A counterpart was the doubling of a following consonant to show that a vowel was short, as in *pibble* (earlier *pibol*), 'pebble'. Loss of diphthongs liberated old diphthongal spellings for length-contrast, *ea* with the value /ɛː/, as in *read*, (mainly in the latter part of the period), *ie* (from Anglo-Norman) with the value /eː/, as in *chief*. Towards the end of the period northern writers used *i* after a vowel to indicate length (preserved in PE *raid*, and the spelling, though the pronunciation is from a variant form, of *build*; cf. also Scottish *guid*).

But not all innovations were related to the solution of ancient problems. The Norman-trained scribes used symbols as they were accustomed to, without considering the theory and history of English orthography. For instance, some dialects of OE had a sound /y(ː)/, spelt, *y*; Norman-French had such a sound, spelt *u*; throughout our period the French practice is followed. Partly the reason was that, except in the South-West, the sound in IV occurred only in French loanwords. But the French usage was advantageous in another connection. The symbol *y* was liberated to fulfil the same function as in French, namely, to be a graphic alternative to *i* (which was not yet dotted) in environments where it was liable to misreading. Such environments were common, since minims (down strokes) were used for the components of many other letters, notably *m*, *n*, *u*; the word *minim* itself, for instance, would have appeared as ıııııııııı, which might be read many ways, whereas ıııyııyııı would be fairly unambiguous. Similarly, when *v* was introduced, it was used as a positional variant of *u*, and not to represent a consonant-vowel contrast.

Another consequence of the restriction of *u* to /y/ value was that an alternative was needed for the representation of /ʊ/, /uː/, and naturally French practice was adopted. Increasingly *o* is used for /ʊ/, especially in the vicinity of minim-letters (whence such modern spellings as *come*, *love*, *son*), and, incorporating the previously unrepresented length-contrast, *ou* for /uː/ (as in PE *hound*, *sound*; towards the end of the period also *ow* as in *gown*); ME *mouth* looks like PE but sounds like OE *muð*, /muːθ/.

However, it would be quite wrong to imply that a solution was found for every problem, and all spellings were unambiguous. As we turn the subject the other way round, looking at the phonological system and its realisation, we find that even in somewhat normalised spellings from a highly standardised variety there is much scope for variable reading.

§ 129 In reconstructing a phoneme-system for 1370 we can only take as our basis the Type III Standard used in Chaucer's work. Though it is not the direct antecedent of later RS in all things, it is extremely close to it in phonology; and Type IV is too late for our purpose.

The long vowels were:

/i:/   in *ryden, shire*

/e:/   in *sweete, nede*

/ɛ:/   in *heeth, lenen, reden* (but most, possibly all, words in this class had variants in /e:/; whether we should count a man as speaking Type III Standard who used /e:/ regularly in all the words is doubtful)

/ɑ:/   (possibly [a:]) in *name, caas*

/ɔ:/   in *holy, rood,* 'rode'

/o:/   in *good, bote,* 'remedy, advantage, boot'

/u:/   in *fowles, houre.*

The short vowels were apparently unusually few in number:

/ɪ/   in *this, thyng*

/ɛ/   in *tendre, men*

/a/   in *can, that*

/ɔ/   in *oft, lot* (the symbol is chosen as a reminder that the vowel was probably rather higher and rounder than PE /ɒ/, but it occupies the same place in the system, and has largely the same distribution.)

/ʊ/   in *but, yong, songen,* '(they) sang'

/ə/   in unstressed syllables only, as in the first syllable of *aboute*, and, probably only in poetry, in final syllables such as *croppes*.

The diphthong-system is rather more controversial. If we look at it historically, we can see that diphthongs arose from the conjunction of long or short vowels with a following /ʊ/, and of /a/ or /ɔ/ with a following /ɪ/. However, not all the originally distinct vowels in the /ʊ/-series can have resulted in different diphthongs, and I am not convinced that there were two series of diphthongs contrasted by length. Without being too positive about the exact phonetic values, I should postulate a sub-series (a), decentring to /ʊ/, /ɪʊ/, /eʊ/, /ɛʊ/, aʊ/, /ɔʊ/, /oʊ/, but within which the differences at mid-height were at least on the point of resolution, giving one /e/ and one /o/ diphthong in place of the paired /ɛ/:/e/, /ɔ/:/o/ types; and a sub-series (b) decentring to /ɪ/, /aɪ/, in *faire, sayle, wey*, and /ɔɪ/ in *coy, joye*.

The consonants differ systematically only in the regular presence of /χ/, restricted to medial and final position, which in 1570 was at most sporadic in a few speakers. The distribution of the items, especially as regards their patterns in syllabic onset, was strikingly different. Fortunately for us, the older patterns are still incorporated in spellings, and the simplest way of describing the situation is to say that the clusters spelt *wr, gn, kn, ng, mb,* are to be given the full value their component letters suggest; in reading it is important to sound *l* and *r* wherever they appear (e.g., in *folk, arme*), and to distinguish (using PE pronunciation as a guide) between the /dʒ/ and /g/ values of *gg*.

The stress-system was in principle as it had been in 1570 but in the distribution of stresses there is some need to distinguish between native and borrowed words. Native words were, as at all times, accented on the first lexically meaningful (root) syllable – that is, the first syllable unless a prefix was present, thus, ˈ*ofte*, 'often', but *of*ˈ*taken*, 'taken away'. Many Romance words had been borrowed with stress later in the word, and were in some measure of progress towards the native pattern. There was accordingly much divided usage in words which by 1570 had settled to initial stress (though many words were still not settled then, or, for that matter, now). To illustrate this, Mossé (1952, 15), quotes Chaucer's line: *In* ˈ*divers art and in di*ˈ*vers figures* (note that this word, by sense-differentiation, has kept alive both patterns). Many trisyllabic words, such as *miracle*, could have first or second syllable stress. Chaucer was perhaps conservative in his treatment of stress, but such patterns as *pre*ˈ*sence, ma*ˈ*tere, co*ˈ*rage, ser*ˈ*vice, ho*ˈ*nour(en), go*ˈ*verne(n),* ˌ*parle*ˈ*ment,* ˌ*gener*ˈ*al,* ˌ*glori*ˈ*ous,* are normal with him.

NOTE: The reconstruction here is possibly conservative throughout, but for many reasons it is based on Chaucer's apparent usage, and there is abundant evidence that, at least in verse, he preferred a highly conservative kind of English.

§ 130 Only the broadest indication can be given of some outstanding local differences from this phonology – contemporary differences both in system and distribution. The south-eastern area, centred on, but not confined to, Kent, was and had long been, characterised by an extraordinary concentration of vowels into the phonemes /e(:)/. In addition to having this long–short pair in such words as *sweet, men* (as everybody else did), Kentish had them corresponding to earlier /y(:)/, which was preserved in the south-west, but elsewhere became /i(:)/, in such words as *mes*, 'mice', *pet*, 'pit'; the *e*-type sometimes labelled 'Kentish' in fact extends over several southern counties (cf. the place-name *Petworth* in Sussex) and well into East Anglia. It also had /eː/ corresponding to what in Type III Standard was /ɛː/, as in *heeth*, *lenen*; and it had /e/ corresponding to Standard /a/, in *wes*, *et*, etc. And like all the E and N, it had /e/ in such words as *herte*, 'heart', where the SW and W Mid used *eo* /ö(ː)/. Pure Kentish, and to some extent other counties which shared the same features, had, accordingly, reductions in the number of vowel-contrasts, which might be quite considerable. On the other hand, Kent (probably only the actual county in this case) preserved the distinction of OE long diphthongs, while all other parts of the country had lost all trace of all OE diphthongs. The sound values are uncertain, but the existence of contrast is clear; for the old long diphthong written *eo*, which in Standard was levelled with /eː/, Kentish has spellings *ye*, *ie*, which are never used for *e*-words, thus *byen*, 'be'; for the old long diphthong *ea*, which elsewhere fell together with /ɛː/ (occasionally /eː/), Kentish has distinct spellings *i(e)a*, *ea*, *y(e)a*, as in *dyad* 'dead'. For reading purposes these diphthongs might be reconstructed as [iə], [ja] respectively.

In its consonants the SE shares certain characteristics that are common to the S – a term which, when not otherwise specified, means south of the Thames–Severn line. Two features are important – neutralisation of the /w/:/ʍ/ contrast under /w/, so that *Wat*, personal name, and *wat*, 'what', become homophones; and the voicing (which in the W swings N to meet the Welsh border at the mid-Wales level) of the initial fricatives /s/, /f/ to /z/, /v/, and no doubt also of /θ/ to /ð/, though the spelling can never show this (cf. *ze*, 'sea', *velaʒe*, 'fellow'). Initial voicing of fricatives was still a general southern feature in the 16c, and has left its mark on RS in a few forms, *vane*, *vat*, *vixen*, *Vauxhall*, but otherwise it has receded westwards with the spread of RS in the southeast. The phonemic implications of this voicing are quite important; the areas affected by it only retained voiceless fricatives in a few words in final position, since these sounds had always been voiced medially. It should perhaps be said at this point that though we know the voicing was in existence during our period, we are unable to say how old it is; if it existed in the OE the orthography would not have been able to represent it.

In vocalic characteristics the SW needs to be treated as a continuum with the SW Mid counties. In this area the features are the preservation of /y(ː)/, written *u* (SE *e*, elsewhere *i*) in the *mus*, 'mice', *put*, 'pit', words; not only is this found nowhere else, but under the same phoneme are classed the reflexes of an OE diphthong which itself was confined to this area, as in *huren* [London *here(n)*], 'hear'. The area also had the widest range in the country of forms with /ɛ:/ – which occurred, not only in the *heeth* words which had it in Standard, but also in such words as *beren*, '(they) bore', *meten*, '(they) measured', where the rest of the country had /e:/ (on the sources of these differences, see §212). S and W of a line from about Chester to Southampton, a mid-front rounded vowel-pair /ö(:)/, spelt *eo*, represented an OE diphthong which elsewhere had fallen together with /e(:)/ except for the long form in Kentish (see above); this is spelt *eo* or *o*, and at the end of the period, *u*, as in *beon*, *heom*, *hom*, *eorthe*, 'be', 'them', 'earth'. On the whole, the SW has rather more vowel-contrasts than elsewhere. It shares one feature with the whole of the west, which does not affect the structure of the sound-system, namely the use of *o* corresponding to eastern *a* before nasals, as in *mon*, *bonkkes*, 'banks'. One very striking difference in a restricted environment calls for notice – that typified by the modern place-name difference *weald* (S), *wold* (Mid). In common words PE development is from the Mid type, as in S *helden*, Mid *holde(n)*, 'hold', *belde*, *bolde*, 'bold'. The difference here between the S and the Mid is due to an ancient dialect distinction (cf. §163), but in ordinary environments the S and Mid go together in showing an *o*, /ɔ:/, vowel, where the N has /ɑ:/ (cf. §134). The correlation can sometimes be shown by linking the ME forms with forms still known in PE: thus, N *mare*, S, Mid *more*, 'more, Sc mair'; *hale*, *whole*, PE *hale* beside *whole*; *stan*, *stone*, PE *stone*, but N names *Stainmore*, *Stanegate*. In all these, ME /ɑ:/ corresponds to PE /eɪ/, /ɔ:/ to PE /əʊ/. Otherwise, the N is most notable for its consonantal features – the preservation of stops, /k/, where the rest of the country has /tʃ/ (*church*, *kirk*), /sk/ (occurring only in loanwords) where the rest of the country has /ʃ/ (PE *shirt*, *skirt*), /g/ where the rest of the country has /dʒ/ (*ridge*, N and Sc *rig*). The N also had very strong aspiration of /ʍ/, probably [hw], spelt *qu(h)*, *qw(h)*. Along the east coast from Scotland to Kent there was modification of certain words in earlier /ʃ/, which Scottish spelling indicates as a falling together of /ʃ/ and /s/, e.g., in *sal*, 'shall'; the SE uses *ss* in such words as *vissere*, 'fisher'.

In unstressed syllables vowel-contrast was normally between /ə/ and /ɪ/, but the N neutralises this residual contrast by using /ɪ/ in final syllables before a consonant, as such spellings as *walkys*, *merkyd*, show, and this development, though not represented in spelling, was beginning to spread southwards, to become the source of PE /ɪd/, /ɪz/, in such inflectional endings as are preserved in *hated*, *chooses*, etc. Indeed, in the N syncope of such vowels, except in the positions where they now survive, was well under way by 1370. In final position the N had dropped *-e* centuries before, and this accentuates the differences due to another development, which, in itself, may not have been altogether local. This is the unvoicing of final consonants (neutralisation of voice in final consonants, as in modern German). Because of vowel loss, many consonants were final in the N that were covered in the S, so we find such differences as N *luf,* Mid and S *love, ris, risen* (/riːs/, /riːzən/). In one respect the N was more conservative. It retained /l/, adjacent to another consonant, in circumstances where the S lost it (a difference which depends on different treatment of the adjacent consonant), thus N *ilk,* S and Mid, *eche,* N *quilk,* S and *Mid w(h)ich,* N *mikel,* S and Mid *muche.*

Even in this summary treatment I have tried to emphasise two aspects of the distribution of dialect-features. They do not, as I have said, necessarily run in bunches, demarcating areas, so that we are able to say that there is a given number of dialects with such and such boundaries. They also have their individual distributions in terms of phoneme-correspondences. It is not always the case that phoneme x is realised by one sound in one area and another in another area; one class of words with phoneme x may have one kind of correspondence, and another class another kind of correspondence. In such cases the classes may be determined either by the origin of a phoneme in a particular word, or by its phonetic environment in the word. To put the point in more practical terms, what has been said so far does not enable one to give a plausible reading aloud of a ME text; for that, much more knowledge about the earlier history of words is still needed.

§ 131 The popular assumption that dialect-differences are primarily a matter of accent is erroneous. In ME particularly, the importance of non-phonological, especially morphological, features, is very great indeed, and morphology and phonology are so intertwined that certain differences, which might be regarded as differences of pronunciation, can only be understood in the light of morphological patterning. We have already analysed the morphology of Type III Standard (cf. §129). Against this background we must now set out some of the major local variations. Among nouns the S used a number of common case plurals in *-en* not found elsewhere, such as *dyevlen*, 'devils', and genitive plurals in *-ene*, as *lollarene*, 'of Lollards', *knavene*, 'of lads or villeins'; this is the last remnant of a fondness for *-n* plurals which had been widespread in the S (cf. §142). Pronoun differences were much more striking. Notably, where Standard in the third person plural combined a subject-form of Scandinavian origin, *they*, with oblique forms of native origin, *here, hem*, the N and NE Mid also had Scandinavian oblique forms, *their, them*, or similar forms starting in *th-*. The S had only *h-* forms in all cases, and the SE continued to make a distinction between accusative, *hi, hise* ('them') and dative *hem* (with other variants, all in *h-*). Gender was only distinguished in the singular, and the most variable form was the feminine. Very broadly speaking, *heo* was used in the SW and W Mid, and the unrounded equivalent, *he or hi* in the SE, the E Mid had *sche*, and the N Mid, between a line about from the Wash to the S Lancs border and the Humber to the N Lancs border, had *sche* or *ho* in the E, *ho* or *scho* in the W. The far N, so far as it is documented, had *scho*. How much more complicated the picture really is can be seen from the map (*see* Appendix, p. 420). It is clear that the forms for the primary grammatical elements, *they* and *she*, have been profoundly disturbed, and as this is a very unusual thing to happen in a language, we must examine the reasons.

From OE times the masculine singular pronoun had everywhere been *he*, but as a result of phonological change considerable areas of the S had come to have the same form for the feminine singular, and almost all the country except the SW and W Mid to have it also for the plural. Yet the distinctions between *he, she*, and *they* were then, as now, fundamental to the working of the language (when, in one of the best-known ME love-poems, the lover says of his lady 'He may me blisse bringe', the danger of misunderstanding is evident). Now the N and the E Mid had available, as a result of heavy Scandinavian settlement in those areas, a solution of the *he/they* problem by adoption of the Scandinavian form *they*. It is noticeable that in areas of dense Scandinavian settlement the whole set of forms, *they, their, them*, is taken over; elsewhere, this solution would be known as a result of the extensive population movements (cf. §99), especially movement by people belonging to primary Scandinavian areas. The pronoun *they* was thus spread, southwards, and into Standard, not by direct borrowing from Scandinavian, but by internal borrowing, i.e., borrowing from another dialect of English; this secondary adoption does not immediately lead to the borrowing of *their, them*, but by the time of Type IV Standard (cf. §99) the whole paradigm has been regularised under the Scandinavian forms. The new element in the feminine pronouns is presumably to be explained by a similar disambiguatory process, giving rise to /ʃ/ forms; the source of these forms is not really known (cf. most recently Clark, 1958, lxiii, and

Mustanoja, 1960, 130); they may have arisen as phonetic variants rather than as new words, borrowed or otherwise. What is clear is that a similar structural weakness in the southern forms of the language led to the spread of the E Mid forms southwards by internal borrowing.

Adjectives, which in Standard only inflected by adding an *-e* (except in comparison, which does not vary dialectally), had long lost all trace of inflection in the N.

Verbs showed differences of a much more complex and substantial kind. In the pres ind the N drew only one contrast, between 1sg, usually without ending, and all the rest, which ended in *-is*; there was a tendency to extend this ending even to 1sg (cf. PE non-standard, 'I says to her . . .'). The subj had normally no ending, and therefore was clearly distinct from the ind in all persons except sometimes the 1sg. In this respect, phonological progressiveness has led to the retention of a grammatical distinction almost obliterated in the S (cf. §119). The imp was in *-is* and the first part in *-ande*. For strong verbs N had no person–number contrast in the past, while Standard still distinguished 1 and 3sg, on the one hand, from 2sg and the whole of the pl on the other; nor did the north vary the stem-vowel within the past. It thus heightened the polarity of tense-contrast, which in strong verbs was far less clear-cut in the south. For *be* it had alternative forms throughout the present, *am/be, ert/es/bes, es/bes*, pl, *ar(e)/, es/, bes*; past *was*, sg, *war(e)* pl and all persons subj. Mid forms show a strong likeness to Standard ones (naturally, since they are the chief source thereof), but the NE Mid has a first part in *-ende*. In general, the Mid which cover a very large area, approximate in morphology to the extreme dialects as they approach them geographically. In the S verbs are characteristically conservative, keeping the old inflection *-e* for 3sg and all persons of the pl in the pres ind – an accidental conjunction, quite out of relation with the real grammatical alignments of the language. Such patterning was naturally vulnerable to the more meaningful distribution of forms characteristic of Standard.

There is a quality of redundancy about many forms of S and SE 14c English. For instance, in second part *y-* is often retained, though the form was sufficiently distinct, and functioned perfectly in the N without prefix; and in the numeral *two*, the variant *twey(ne)* is kept, though it no longer has a grammatical function distinct from that of more usual *two*. This quality of redundancy is a natural result of the conservatism of speakers not brought up against a positive reason for change (as speakers in the N and in the E Mid were) (cf. § 188). The conservatism may make for positive grammatical anomalies. For instance, where a verb-stem ended in an alveolar, the S had long ago developed a syncopated form of 2 and 3sg pres ind, so that the forms for *binden* would be *bin(t)st, bint*; these forms were kept in the late 14c, quite counter to the general movement of regularisation in grammar. Other anomalous forms kept alive were 2 and 3 sgs with vowel change as well as ending, for *do(n)*, 'do', for instance, *dest, deth*, instead of regular *dost, doth*. For the verb *go* all areas had a suppletive past, but the S kept the historic one *ȝede*, even though this could not be related to any other verb-forms; the N introduced *went*, past of *wend*, 'turn', a verb otherwise used in the language, and, of course, the form that has prevailed in later English. The S was also conservative in its first part form, *-inde*, which is thus kept apart from the verbal noun; in the Mid they fused in *-ing(e)*, producing a multiple-purpose form which is one of the most striking features of NE (cf. § 121).

The same quality appears in the treatment of certain sub-classes of verbs. We may sum it up by saying that in the S phonological developments took their course, whereas in the Mid and the N certain minor and anomalous types were radically re-cast in conformity with the major classes. There is a sub-class of weak verbs which puts an *-i-* between the stem and the ending of certain parts of the present in its conjugation; the overall distribution is explicable historically, but as a working structural pattern the result is simply a mess. Thus, the verb *make* will have the forms: inf *makien*, pres ind sg, 1 *makie*, 2, *makest*, 3, *makeþ*, pl *makieþ*; subj sg *makie*, pl *makien*, imp sg *make*, pl *makie* (past always without *-i-*); the S not only retains this pattern, but absorbs some borrowed words into it. The N and Mid cut out the *-i-*, so that this minor group conjugates like any regular weak verb. Even more remarkable is the survival in the S of a type of conjugation that in OE affected only four verbs, one of which was extinct by ME. In the same distribution as the presence or absence of *-i-* in the *makien* type, these verbs had consonant alternation, in two of the three surviving cases accompanied by stem-vowel alternation. The verbs concerned are those for *say, have, live*. While the N and Mid re-shaped them, the S (especially SE) kept the conjugation for *say, ziggen, zigge, zayst, zayþ, ziggeþ; zigge, ziggen; zay, zigge* (past, *zayde*, etc.); for *have, habben, habbe, hest, heþ, habbeþ; have, habbeþ* (past, *hadde, hedde*, etc.); *live* had infinitive *libben*, and *b/v* alternations, without vowel alternation or syncope.

In the N, as in PE, the rationale of pattern and useful contrast took precedence over direct phonological development; the Mid were intermediate, but one could almost say that to be exposed to the N system was to prefer it. As this happened, the Mid transmitted to Standard those features which sharply differentiate it from the indigenous S type which might have been expected to play a major part in the formation of a London Standard, but signally failed to do so.

§ 132   In some respects vocabulary, as far as we can trace its history, was common throughout the country to a degree unknown in phonology or morphology. Naturally, because of the high degree of particularity in lexical items and the fragmentary nature of our records there is greater loss of information at this level than at any other. And there are two exceptional fields, one concerning loanwords, one concerning native words, in which areas of divergence are extremely marked.

Among loanwords there is a sharp difference between Romance words (both Latin and French) and Scandinavian ones. The Romance words are found equally throughout the country, but more in certain social and educational classes than in others. Scandinavian loans are oral, non-literary and everyday in character; they are distributed geographically in the first instance where there was a Scandinavian community to transmit them. The old Danelaw, N and E of a line from London to Chester and as far as the Tees, is a primary area for 'Danish' settlement, and therefore for Scandinavian loan words, sometimes of a distinctly Danish character. The three NW counties, Lancashire, Westmorland, Cumberland, are another, but mainly Norwegian. The central and southern Mid, inland from East Anglia, are progressively derivative areas, with many loans, but loans by internal borrowing rather than direct from Scandinavian speakers. Finally, in the SW Mid there is a secondary area, colonised by Scandinavian farmers in the early 11c; here, borrowing is direct, but as it occurs late it is relatively superficial in character. Only the S, notably the SE, remains untouched by these various types of influence. By internal borrowing Type III Standard already has a Scandinavian component almost commensurate with that in PE; the picture is completed in Type IV Standard. The kind of words involved in this influx will be discussed at § 139.

Local survival of native words is a less clear issue. To some extent it is complementary with the adoption of Scandinavian loans. Clearly the native word *nimen* had a better chance of survival in areas which did not adopt Scandinavian *take(n)*, 'take', native *weorpen* in areas where

Scandinavian *caste(n)* was not current. But other factors are involved. As we have already noted (cf. §126), the W used a form of poetry, indigenous to English culture, which in the E had been replaced by forms of French origin. For use in this poetry OE had had a very rich vocabulary of words not used in prose. These special words were not merely decorative; they were used to suggest emphases and associations, and to select the aspect under which what was mentioned was relevant to the context. Yet these refinements were luxuries, and the everyday language managed without them. Such an elaborate, as we may say, non-utility, vocabulary, unsullied by diurnal use, can only be kept alive in a culturally close-knit society, with an unbroken tradition of corporate enjoyment of the poetry using the special words. If there is a break in the tradition of composition or the habit of public performance, only the everyday words will survive. In much of the country the Norman Conquest clearly led to such a breach, but in the W the form of the poetry persisted, and in the NW Mid, a good deal of the special vocabulary endures even in the late 14c (cf. §126; and for examples of the words concerned, §141).

§133   What can we trace of the history of these complexly-varying forms? In addition to the problems of reconstruction at every period, there is a special difficulty in period IV because it is the dialectal phase of the language (cf. §127). We need, at most periods, continuous evidence about a single variety; in period IV we need continuous evidence about all varieties. And this we are very far from having. For a generation either side of 1200 the language is much less fully documented than towards 1400. There are longish MSS, whose meaning for the spoken language we have some confidence in interpreting, from the S, SE, SW, SW Mid and W Mid. None of them are author's autographs; their regularities as written material are due to mature scribal traditions – in the W, traditions descended from those of OE, in the E and centre more strongly influenced by Anglo-Norman conventions. The presence of an Anglo-Norman component provides some check on our interpretation of spellings; that is, we can generally assume that graphemes are used with the value they had in the source-language (if we can reconstruct that). The E also has the advantage of rhymed verse; if we have general reason to believe a poet is an accurate rhymer, we can tell from his rhymes what his sound-contrasts were, though we cannot identify, from that evidence alone, what phonetic realisations the phonemes had. The W poetic tradition does not use rhyme, and when we get back behind this period we are everywhere deprived of the extremely valuable evidence rhyme has produced hitherto.

The areas so far omitted from our inventory of those for which there is anything like adequate documentation around 1200 include the areas of primary Scandinavian settlement. But there are two other kinds of documentation, and a third just outside our period, which leave us not entirely in the dark about the Mid, though our knowledge of the N depends on inference from what happened before and after. One kind of evidence is copying of OE literature. A consequence of the sharp break usually made in histories between the OE and ME periods is that the continuity in copying OE literature is underestimated. For a linguist, copies of ancient works are not evidence of the highest order, but they are important all the same. Serious OE prose works of exposition were copied in the 11c and the 12c, and in considerable abundance, to judge from the wealth of extant MSS surviving against very powerful odds. We must be clear about the meaning of this practice; a scriptorium undertook to copy a major work at great expense of time and money. Instructions for such work would not be given lightly. The existence of a 12c copy does not simply mean that some scribe somewhere could still read and reproduce the old language, but that some superior in a religious house knew that a costly decision would justify itself in terms of the education of clergy in his care; they, in sufficient numbers, would have to be able to read the text, and perhaps to transmit it intelligibly to the laity. 'Mere' copies are therefore important evidence of continuity of literary tradition, and of a general capacity to understand the old language when read aloud. We must not exaggerate the break effected by the Conquest.

Very important evidence for the language of Peterborough exists in a document written just before IV. Since the late 9c, England had had a national system of enshrining the record of events in chronicles. Each local archive was expected to combine a record of local events with central national reports issued at intervals to all of them (cf. § 179). Needless to say, much happened in many parts of the country to disrupt the execution of this neat plan. Nevertheless, even of the seven Chronicle versions we now know about, some were kept up after the Conquest, and the Peterborough one, renewed in 1070 after the presumed earlier version had been lost or destroyed, is kept up, from a variety of local and national sources, until 1154. The document will be of primary use to us for period V, but it is close enough to be used for the illumination of the E Mid usage in early IV.

241

We now turn to the second kind of documentation lying within our period. This is the work of men who set out to devise a form of writing that should accurately suggest, for those capable of interpreting it by reading aloud, the English of a given place and time, quite narrowly defined. This is an activity quite different from using a standard written form on the one hand, or writing by whim within an ill-defined tradition, on the other. Well done, it can carry a great deal of information about the contemporary spoken language not only to the readers it was designed for, but also to the 20c linguist; it is in many ways our most direct source of information, but in each instance it illuminates a variety of very limited currency. In period III there are two large documents of this kind, both preserved (understandably enough) only in the author's autograph. The first comes from the Stamford area (cf. § 145), and the hand can be dated to about 1200. The author gives his name as Orm (Scandinavian, = OE *wyrm*, 'dragon, serpent'); he is an Augustinian canon, and his brother by birth and as a member of the community is Walter (Norman-French) – a name which must make us hesitate to infer, as we otherwise might, that he came from a household still Scandinavian-speaking. Belonging to a community with parochial responsibilities, Orm was concerned that while the truth required for salvation was enshrined in the Bible, many parishioners had no access to it, since they could not read it themselves, and had no one to preach it to them in a language they could understand [there is abundant evidence of priests ignorant of English holding English livings at this time (cf. Moorman, 1945)]. What Orm seems to have done is to have hit upon a method for converting a priest who did not speak English (or a kind of English understood by his congregation) into a 'megaphone' for the Bible's message – an instrument whereby it could reach the people, even if the instrument remained uncomprehending. He translated and expounded in English the readings prescribed throughout the Church's year, and set them down in something approaching a phonetic script. This script assumes a reading knowledge of Latin. To a man so equipped, the quality of vowels will present no difficulties, but quantity will; this problem Orm solves by doubling consonants after short vowels; consonants, especially palatals, are not entirely straightforward, but he retains all available differentia and invents an extra g symbol – $\bar{g}$ – to help out. He seems to have revised his text, and to have found the system was in need of support when English length conflicted with a major rule for Latin quantity; in such cases he added breves ($\cup$) or accent marks (' – sometimes three-strong) to underline what the letters indicated. Stress is attended to by putting the whole composition into a familiar Latin hymn metre. Though, even in so extensive and painstaking an exercise, the interpretation of the spellings is not free from doubt and difficulty, Orm's work does tell us a very great deal about an area otherwise not well represented; and since many developments seem to have been common to the country, about the language generally around 1200.

The only other comparable document is considerably distant in time and space, the *Ayenbite of Inwit* (*again-bite of in-knowledge*, a calque of *re-morse of con-science*), written in 1340 by a religious who tells us his name and purpose in a preface rather like Orm's. He is Dan (master) Mich(a)el of Northgate, Canterbury, and his purpose is to instruct the simple people of his locality, using their own variety of English. Though he lacks the fanatical orthographic single-mindedness of Orm, his long work does show a high degree of graphemic consistency. It is particularly valuable since it stands at the culmination of a long tradition of linguistically fairly reliable documents from Kent, and enables us to check the authenticity of what their spellings suggest about Kentish usage. Up till 1340 Kentish has the most continuous written records of any English dialect; thereafter, it virtually passes from our knowledge until around 1800, when self-conscious dialect-recording begins.

No doubt much more could be discovered about early ME if the McIntosh–Samuels techniques were applied to documents from the two centuries before their present survey. At the moment we have to confess that our identified materials are neither rich nor evenly spaced. Here, to conclude, are some specimens of the kinds of English discussed in this paragraph; a tentative transcription is given in the line below the text, and a word-for-word gloss in the line below that.

(a) Peterborough Chronicle for 1140 (which cannot have been composed before 1154, but probably belongs to that year):

Þa   ferde   Eustace þe kinges sune to France ⁊   nam þe kinges
/θɑː feːrd(ə) ɛʊstas θə kɪŋgəs sʊnə toː frans   and nam θə kɪŋgəs/
then went   E.   the king's son to F.   and took the king's

suster of France to wife; wende   to bigæton Normandi þærþurh.
/sʊstər ɔf frans toː wiːvə weːndə toː bɪgɛtən nɔrmandɪ θeːrθʊrh/
sister-of-France to wife; thought to get   Normandy thereby.

Oc he spedde litel ⁊   be gode rihte, for he was an yuel man; for
/ɔk heː spɛdə lɪtl and beː goːdə rihtə fɔr heː was an iːvəl man fɔr/
But he sped   little and by good right for he was an evil man; for

warese he com he dide mare   yuel þanne god: he reuede   þe
/waːrsə heː koːm heː dɪdə maːr(ə) iːvəl θanə goːd heː rɛːvədə   θə/
whereso he came he did more   evil than good; he plundered the

landes ꝥ læide micele geldes on. He brohte   his   wif to
/laːndəs and laɪdə mɪtʃlə geːldəs ɔn heː broːht(ə) (h)ɪs wiːf toː/
lands   and laid large   taxes   on. He brought his   wife to

Engleland, ꝥ dide hire in þe castel on Cantebyri.   God wimman
/ɛŋgləland and dɪdə hɪr(ə) ɪn θə kastəl ɔn kantəbɪrɪ   goːd wɪmən/
England,   and put her   in the castle in Canterbury. Good woman

scæ wæs, oc scæ hedde litel blisse mid him.
/ʃeː was ɔk ʃeː hɛdə lɪtl blɪsə mɪd hɪm/
she was but she had   little bliss with him.

NOTE: Wherever possible, glossing is by the formally nearest word in PE even if it is not the most appropriate that could be found. Each line of transcription is enclosed in slant lines so that the eye can pick it out, but it is important to read continuously, as there may be elision between words. I have taken a rather conservative view of how far inflectional -e was preserved, but Peterborough is not very far north. That the text is highly traditional in certain respects can be seen by comparing it with material almost two hundred years older (cf. §166). Note the preservation of S and Mid /aː/ in *mare*, etc., though we know that this must have been distinct from /ɑː/ in borrowed words by this date; and southerly *w* in *war-* = *where*. The verbs conform to their OE classifications; this passage does not show many of their forms, but is chosen for its inclusion of the new *scæ* = *she* pronoun.

(b) Orrmulumm:

Icc hafe samneddo þiss boc
/ɪk haːvə samnəd ɔ θɪs boːk/
I   have collected in this book

Þa goddspelles neh   alle,
/θɑː gɔdspɛləs neːχ al(ə)/
the gospels   near(ly) all

Þatt sinndenn o þe messeboc
/θat sɪndən ɔ θə mɛsəboːk/
that are   in the mass-book

244

Inn all þe ȝer att messe
/ɪn al θə jeːr at mɛs(ə)/
in all the year at mass

Annd aȝȝ affterr þe goddspell stannt
/and aɪ aftər θə gɔspel stant/
and aye after the gospel stands

Þatt tatt te goddspell meneþþ
/θat at tə gɔdspɛl meːnəθ/
that that the gospel means

Þatt mann birrþ spellenn to þe follc
/θat man bɪrθ spɛlən toː θə fɔlk/
that one should narrate to the folk
  (impersonal, it behoves one to)

Off þeȝȝre sawle nede
/ɔf θeɪrə saʊlə neːd(ə)/
of their soul's need.

(Note here the normalisation of -v- in the verb *have*, the absence of participial prefix *y-* before *sammnedd*, the loss of final -n in weak forms, (*o*), the unchanged form of *boc* (it has neither vowel-change nor ending to indicate case). In the plural definite article *þa* seems to be contrasted with case-invariable singular *þe*, but its use in line 2 would make sense as a demonstrative; the relative is *þatt*, whereas in the Peterborough Chronicle (no examples in our passage) it had normally been the indeclinable particle *þe* (as in OE), which is now used for the article; *sinndenn* = *are* (weak and preserving an OE form) is typically E Mid, but the syncopated third singular *stannt* is here at its northernmost reach; there is good evidence of sandhi (inter-word assimilation) in *þatt tatt te* = *that that the*; the old impersonal pronoun *mann* is used in its strong form; the impersonal verb *birþ* and the personal pronoun *þeȝȝre* are Scandinavian loans).

(c) *Ancrene Wisse*, a version (not just a copy), written in the W Mid in the early 13c, of an older guide to conduct for anchoresses. This text illustrates the unbroken development, in a sheltered area, of a cultivated regional variety of written English established in OE (cf. § 197). Its manuscript, Corpus Christi College Cambridge, 402, and the MS, in a different hand, of a collection of religious texts, Bodley 34, are consistently written in exactly the same variety of English, though not all works in them are by the same author, and they cannot be alike because they are both autographs by the same author. They embody a regional written standard, and one remarkably unchanged since OE. We cannot tell how long this kind of English persisted; there is simply no evidence after the date of these two MSS:

Nim nu ȝeme hwet uvel beo i-cumen of totunge; nawt an uvel
/nɪm nuː jeːmə ʍɛt yːvəl böː ɪkʊmən ɔf toːtʊŋgə naʊt ɑːn yːvəl/
take now heed what evil be come of looking; not one evil

ne twa, ah al þe wa þet nu is ant eaver ȝete wes ant eaver
/nə twɑː aχ al θə wɑː θɛt nuː ɪs ant ɛːvər jeːt wɛs ant ɛːvər/
nor two, but all the woe that now is and ever yet was and ever

schal i-worðen al com of sihðe. Þet hit beo soð, lo her preove:
/ʃal ɪwʊrðən al koːm ɔf sɪχθə θət hɪt böː soːθ lɔː heːr pröːv/
shall become, all came of sight. That it be truth, lo here proof:

Lucifer þurh þet he seh ant biheold on himseolf his ahne
/lysɪfər θʊrχ θɛt heː seːχ ant bɪhöːld ɔn hɪmsölf hɪs aχnə/
L. through that he saw and biheld in himself his own

feiernesse leop into prude, ant bicom of engel eatelich
/faɪərnəsə löːp ɪntoː pryːdə ant bɪkoːm ɔf ɛŋgəl ɛːtəlɪtʃ/
fairness leaped into (ran) pride and became from angel deadly

deovel.
/döːvəl/
devil.

NOTE: The number of words transmitted into NE is striking here, but the word *engel*, which might be taken for an antecedent of PE *angel*, is not that, but represents a very early OE loan from Latin (cf. §214) which was subsequently ousted by *angel* from French. The spelling and morphology are highly conservative, so that the passage has in appearance more affinities with OE than with 14c English; note particularly the preservation of /ɑː/ in *twa*, though the text is not northern. The westerly character is very marked in the use of *u* = /y/ in native words (*uvel*), and of *eo* = /ö(ː)/; use of *e* in such words as *þet*, *wes*, ties the text to a particular OE tradition (cf. §197). The orthographic distribution of *þ* initially and *ð* medially and finally is a professional detail observed by only the most careful OE scribes, and most unusual in the 13c.

(d) Dan Michel of Northgate, Canterbury, *c.* 1340:

Nou ich wille þet ye   y-wyte
/nuː ɪtʃ wɪl(ə) θɛt jeː wɪtə/
Now I   wish that you should know

Hou hit is   y-went
/huː hɪt ɪs   ɪwɛnt/
How it has come about ('went')

Þet þis boc   is y-write
/θɛt θɪs boːk ɪs ɪwrɪtə/
That this book is written

Mid Engliss of Kent
/mɪd ɛnglɪʃ ɔf kɛnt/
With English of Kent
(In)

Þis boc is y-mad vor lewede   men,
/θɪs boːk ɪs ɪmaːd vɔr leʊwəd(ə) mɛn/
This book is made for lewd   men
                        (ignorant)

Vor vader and vor moder, and vor oþer ken
/vɔr vaːdər and vɔr moːdər and vɔr oːðər kɛn/
For father and for mother and for other kin

Ham vor to berʒe vram alle manyere   zen,
/ham vɔr toː bɛrjə vram al(ə) manjɛ(ː)r(ə) zɛn/
Them for to protect from all   manner (of) sin,

Þet ine hare   inwytte ne bleve   no voul wen.
/θət n (h)ar ɪnwɪt   nə bleːv(ə) nɔː vuːl wɛn/
That in their conscience remain no foul wen.

(Note that I have indicated in brackets elements about whose presence I am uncertain; I have taken the grapheme *-ss-* as /ʃ/ and the first sound in *Engliss* as /ɛ/, not /ɪ/, though I regard both realisations as doubtful. Initial voicing, Kentish *e* for /a/, /ɛ(ː)/, /y/ are well represented, and there is a good range of pronoun-forms – *ich, ye, hit, ham, hare*; not only participles, but an infinitive, have prefixed *y-*.)

§ 134 The local peculiarities of stressed vowel quality noted in § 130 are all older than 1170, though they are not all clearly indicated in writing. For example, the S and Mid development from /ɑː/ /ɔː/ in such words as *mara, more,* must have been so far advanced when the earliest French loans entered the language that their stem-vowel was not identified with the /ɑː/ in French words. The loans, as we can see from such examples as *dame, save, grace,* with modern reflexes in /eɪ/, do not undergo the change. While French loans do not pour into the language the moment the Norman Conquest is completed (cf. §137), they must have been familiar to some English speakers not later than the early 12c. We must conclude that OE /ɑː/, even if it was not yet /ɔː/, was so far changed by 1100 that the sound of the new words could not be identified with it, though borrowers allow a very wide latitude in making such identifications.

In general, then, period IV is one of exceptional stability as far as vowel quality is concerned. At the beginning it was apparently, in all localities (except for long diphthongs in Kent), entirely without phonemic diphthongs (though there were no doubt conditioned glides, components of phonetic diphthongs). If this reconstruction is correct, we have a state of affairs unique in the history of English; at any rate, it is not surprising that a new diphthongal system rapidly emerges. The new diphthongs arose primarily by vocalisations of the approximants /j/, /w/, in post-vocalic position. In this way were created two parallel series, decentring to /ɪ/ and /ʊ/ respectively, at first orderly and symmetrical, but increasingly disrupted ever since. With /ɪ/ as final element we have /aɪ/ (in *day, dai,* earlier *dæg*), /ɛɪ/ (in *wei, wey,* 'way', earlier *weg,* also as I believe, from an original long vowel, in *grey,* earlier *græg*); these two fairly soon fell together (as the confused modern spelling tradition might suggest), most probably under the form /aɪ/; and at some time in the period further classes of vowel join this phoneme as a consequence of what had at first been conditioned development of a glide, as in *ehta>eiȝte>eight(e).* The /ɔɪ/ diphthong was very slightly represented among native words, and would not have established itself as a phoneme without an influx of loans (cf. *join, boil,* etc., §105). With /ʊ/ as second element we have the same sources – /aʊ/ by vocalisation in *strawes,* by glide-development in *tauhte,* /ɔʊ/ by vocalisation in *soule,* by glide-development in *douhter* (there may at first have been a contrasting diphthong /oʊ/, as in *glowe,* but if so it soon merged with /ɔʊ/), /ɛʊ/ by vocalisation only, in *lewed, treuthe* (possibly also with distinct /eʊ/ at first, soon merged with /ɛʊ/), /ɪʊ/ in *stiward.* Thus was created the system we have described for 1370 (cf. §129). As a footnote to these developments we should note what happened in words of the type OE *fugol,* PE *fowl.* In the first place intervocalic /ɤ/, early in the period, develops a labial element [ɣw], and then this loses its palatal component, giving /w/ (cf. OE *draʒan*, *draw*; *laʒu*, *law*; *boga*, *bow*). Note that when /w/ follows /ʊ/ it still vocalises, but to form (naturally) a long vowel, not a diphthong; ME *fowl*(*e*), /fuːl(ə)/, PE *fowl* /faʊl/.

§ 135 In vowel quantity too there were changes notable in extent and in implication. In disyllabic words the vowels /a/, /ɛ/, /ɔ/, lengthened to /aː/, /ɛː/, /ɔː/ in open syllables (cf. § 109). This is not generally apparent in spelling at the time of occurrence, but that there has been lengthening, and in ME, is clear from the modern reflexes of *faren*, 'fare', v, *spere*, 'spear', v, *boren*, 'born(e)'; we do not have to wait till NE for evidence of the lengthening, however, since its presence is demonstrated by rhymes. This lengthening has to be later than the rounding of /aː/ to /ɔː/ (since the new /aː/ is not rounded), but probably followed close upon it, say, during the late 12c. For completeness it may be added that the remaining vowels, /ɪ/ and /ʊ/, were affected by lengthening under similar conditions, but later, and mainly in the north; moreover, in lengthening they were identified, not, as we might have expected, with /iː/ and /uː/, but with /eː/ and /oː/. Very little evidence of this later lengthening enters the Standard language, but a few forms show it, such as OE *wicu*, PE *week*, *bitol*, *beetle*, *wifol*, *weevil*; it is just possible that PE *door* also shows it.

However, the lengthening of /a/, /ɛ/ and /ɔ/ has had considerable effect, and in rather complicated ways. Many nouns and adjectives (in particular) are monosyllables which become open-stemmed disyllables in their inflected forms; others are open-stemmed disyllables which become trisyllables in their inflected forms. In either case, vowel alternation in nominal inflection is anomalous, and at a time of paradigmatic regularisation, has little chance of survival. Normally, one grade of vowel would be extended to all forms of the word, and since the sum of uses of inflected forms was greater than the uses of the one uninflected form, it was most often the lengthened grade which survived in monosyllables, and the short one in disyllables. Hence, *lat*, *late*, has given PE *late*, *whal*, *whale*, PE *whule*, *met*, *mete*, early NE *mete*, 'measure', but *fader*, *faderes* generalised the short vowel, which has only later lengthened to give PE *father* (the ME lengthening would have given /feɪðə(r)/). Sometimes variants survive in different functions, as in *small* (from the ME short vowel), personal name *Smail* (from the ME long vowel). The alternatives certainly came into existence in ME, and are the first of a series of independent developments running counter to what seems

249

to be a persistent tendency from the 13c to deploy long vowels in open syllables, short ones in closed syllables (except in polysyllables, where the tendency – again never fully realised – has been towards the abolition of long vowels). Hard upon this lengthening came the loss of final *-e* as a result of which many words which had lengthening ceased to be either open-stemmed or disyllabic.

§ 136 The consonants during period IV are relatively stable as to system and distribution. The one loss from the system is the sound /ɤ/, which had become /w/ (cf. §134) by 1200 in most places, though not till the late 14c in Kent.

Changes in distribution take much to rehearse, but do not really add up to very much. Assimilations account for the /m/ (earlier /n/) in such words as *comfort, noumpire* (later metanalysed as *umpire*). The closely-related process of simplification of consonant-groups results in loss of /w/ in *so* (OE *swa*), *two* (OE *twa*); of /v/ in *hadde* (OE *hæfde*), *lord* (OE *hlaford*,) *lady* (OE *hlæfdige*); of /t/ and /d/ in heavy clusters, *best* (OE *betst*), *gospel* (OE *godspell*); of /ð/ in grammatical words, *wher, sin* (OE *hwæðer, siððan*); occasionally of /k/, *made* (OE *makede*). All these changes probably belong to IV, though the conservatism of spelling makes the *terminus post quem* uncertain.

The initial sounds /hr/ (OE *hringan*), /hl/ (OE *hleapan*), /hn/ (OE *hnutu*) fall together with /r, l, n/, giving such forms as *ringen, lepen, nut(e)*, and starting the reduction in the inventory of permitted types of syllabic onset that continues in III and II (cf. § 70,100). /h/ (which is only initial) is lost in all weak positions (as PE *it* shows, though in less common words there has been widespread restoration on the basis of the spelling standardised from strong forms). And in final position there are many losses which are dealt with under morphology (cf. §142, 150, 152).

§ 137 In terms of lexical history this period most notably demonstrates the impact of the Norman Conquest, above all in direct loans, but incipiently also in WF. English had been exposed to French influence and had made a few borrowings even before the Conquest. For a surprisingly long time after the Conquest a rather modest rate of borrowing continues. Yet the time-lag is understandable, because borrowing requires more than contact between two speech-communities. It requires bilingualism, at least in some measure. And Anglo-French bilingualism, on any significant scale, was slow to develop (cf. §125). Once it did, the sluice-gates opened, and there poured into English the greatest flood of loans from a single source by which the language has ever been inundated. The early loans were transmitted from Anglo-Norman, and often show this by their form; the later ones are from Central French. The effects of this influx are, as has always been understood, far-reaching in many ways. In the first place there are simply so many new words that old habits of WF tend to atrophy, though they never disappear, and some later revive (cf. § 54). In the second place, the change of emphasis from WF to borrowing as a source of new words established what Jespersen (1919, 142) has called the 'undemocratic' quality of cultivated English vocabulary. While derived and compounded words are transparent to those who know the common elements from which they are made, and the patterns by which they are composed (i.e., to all mature speakers), borrowed words are opaque, and have to be learnt separately, one by one. To a considerable extent (though appearances can be deceptive in the matter) the speaker of modern English needs more education to be enfranchised of a fair range of English vocabulary than the German-speaker to reach a similar level in his own language. The gap has certainly widened during the last six centuries, but the habits that created it were largely the product of period IV. Important as all this is, there is probably nothing so widely misunderstood in the history of English as the true meaning of the influx of French words. It is often, quite wrongly, supposed that English borrowed items it lacked, and that inferiority, in vocabulary and culture, can be detected where borrowing occurs. In fact, hordes of the French words which swept into the language in period IV were synonymous with perfectly good words already long established in English (see below); and when we realise that our records of OE vocabulary are more imperfect even than our records of ME vocabulary, we realise that this 'redundant' borrowing was on a very substantial scale indeed. In the latter part of the period, borrowing from Central French was indeed borrowing from a language of high culture into one of lower culture – both because the French had advanced, and because the English, as a result of the Conquest, had retrogressed; gaps were made good, and the English-speaking community was given access to the modern world. At the time of the Conquest the English were superior to the Normans in all aspects of civilised life except those directly dependent on an advanced stage of military sophistication (such as castle-building); to a large extent the early loans reflected what it was convenient or expedient to borrow, not what gaps needed to be filled.

When our period begins English is by no means merely insular in vocabulary; even the records we have show it to have contained many hundreds of loans from Latin and Old Norse. But by that same date barely fifty French loans have been recorded. In the early part of the period the pace increases, but remains moderate. Typical loans are *baptist* (corresponding to OE *fulluhtere*, originally a transparent word meaning 'one who completes the rite of sanctification'), *dame* (OE *hlæfdige*, 'lady'), *grandame* (OE *eald-modor*), *meister* (OE *mæʒester*, an earlier loan from Latin), *prince* (OE *æþeling*), *prophete* (OE *fore-cwedere*, 'sayer forth or in advance'), *seint* (OE *halig*, 'holy', adj and noun), *sire* (OE *hlaford*, 'lord'). In some cases, naturally, the correspondence is less simple – OE had several words covering between them the meaning of the borrowed word, or vice versa; but it is pointless to multiply examples. In almost every case these early loans were not 'needed' in the sense that they expressed concepts for which OE had no expression, even no word. At the same time these examples show something of the rate of loss from the native vocabulary (not all of it immediate), a subject to which we shall have to return (cf. § 141).

Other loans which reflect Norman areas of dominance, and the nature of Norman relations with the English are *curt*, 'court', *castel*, *rente*, 'income from land', *poure*, 'poor', and *rich* (a word which in OE had meant powerful, but which acquired its present meaning from Norman-French, in which the shift from *mighty* to *wealthy* had not uncharacteristically taken place; it is ironic that both languages have the word by borrowing from Celtic), *chapel*, *prisun*, *tur*, *crune(n)*, v and n, *place*, *serven*, *warant*, *grace*, *merci*, *lei* ('law'), *miracle*, *parais* ('paradise'), *ymage*, *aromat*, *oil*, *rose*, *marbre*, *cachen*, *changen*, *mantel*, *purpre*, *palefrei*, *sacrament*, *lechur*, *barun*, *waiten*, *prove*, etc. Well over two hundred loans are recorded in the first generation of our period, though the number of texts available is not large. Words are borrowed repeatedly in only slightly different forms, as one expects when borrowing is oral and the dialect of the source and even of the borrower may cause variation; through time the superfluous forms were generally weeded out.

In the 13c and 14c the tide is at the flood; to some extent Anglo-Norman is still a source, but Central French is now the major one, and because of its cultural standing the loans (though they still represent the old areas of contact) cover new fields. There are so many excellent lists of such words (and on the whole the educated Englishman can fairly easily learn to spot them for himself), that it seems pointless to produce another; details can be found in Serjeantson, 1935, 136 ff. The areas of interest are often overlapping, but they include names of people, with their kinds, classes, ranks, temperaments and offices, terms for finance, property and business, for building and for the equipment of homes, for law and social organisation, religion, war, the arts, clothing and food, entertainment, hunting, animals, especially foreign, science and medicine; nouns are dominant, but there are many verbs and adjectives, and some other forms.

There are some half-dozen main points of French dialect-differentiation in the words English borrowed. Curiously enough (at first sight, anyway) such differentiae may appear quite often in words which French itself had borrowed from Germanic, the language-family to which English belonged. In fact this is readily understandable, for where the phonology of such words conflicted with indigenous French phonology it was re-worked by Central French-speakers but accepted by those French-speakers (the Normans) whose original language was Germanic (cf. §125). Thus initial /w/ was adapted to /gw/, then /g/; our early loans reflect Norman retention of /w/, but from the 14c we have /g/ forms, and sometimes the two survive side by side through differentiation of sense. *Werre*, 'war' corresponds to French *guerre* (not found in English) and there are doublets for *wile/guile, ward(en)/guard(ian)*, the personal name *Wawayn/Gawayn*, etc. An indigenous French change is that of /k/ to /tʃ/ before /a/, which occurred in Parisian French, but did not reach all the north, i.e., most of Normandy or Picardy (a district from which many of the invaders of England came); from the northern dialects we have *carpenter, caudron* 'cauldron' (beside Central *chaudron*, now disused); from Central French *chair, charity* (beside northern *cariteþ*, now disused); but we have both types, differentiated in meaning only in England, for *cattle, chattel, catch, chase*. This last example illustrates in its final sound a further difference, the reduction in Central French of /tʃ/ to /ts/, later /s/. Further examples of the Norman type in English are *chisel, cherry* (cf. later *cerise* from Central French), and of the Central type, *wince, celle, citee*. Similarly, Norman French has /ʃ/, Central French /s/ in words borrowed into English as *punish, nourish, anguish, cushion*, as against *rejoice*: and /g/, Central /dʒ/, represented in English *garden* as against *joy, jest*; in *gaol/jail* the first spelling represents the Norman type, the second the Central, but only the Parisian pronunciation persists. The differentiae strikingly affect consonants, which in English we can usually regard as the stable framework within which vowels vary, but there are one or two points to note about vowels, especially the development of the Old French diphthong *ei*, which in Anglo-Norman was levelled under *ai*, the development reflected by many English loans – *obey, air, fair,* etc., while in Central French it became *oi* in the 12c, a type from which English has *esploit* (later *ex-*), *poise; real, royal, leal, loyal,* reflect both types.

§ 138   Latin borrowing, also extensive during IV, rested on a much older and broader tradition, but in type many of the words are similar to those culture-words borrowed from Central French, and in form they are so similar that in many cases a word could be from either source (and, of course, many are borrowed more than once, and from both sources). The form may give a clear indication of Latin origin, as with such religious terms as *credo, dir(i)ge, ipocrisis* (later replaced by French *hypocrisie*), *requiem, limbo, pater(noster)*, and a dozen others; and legal terms such as *client, arbitrator, conviction, exorbitant, extravagant, pauper*, etc.; and terms of the schools, such as *allegory, cause, desk, index, item, library, major, minor, scribe*; and scientific terms such as *diaphragm, digit, orbit, ligament, dissolve,* and many more. But there were also many non-technical terms, including a remarkable proportion of verbs and adjectives, such as *adoption, collision, colony, conflict, depression; accede, adjure, combine, commend, discuss, expend; aggregate* adj, *alienate*, adj, *complete, imaginary, immortal,* etc.

There was no knowledge of the other languages of learning in England during this period. Words ultimately deriving from them were adopted, but through the medium of Latin or French. In the examples already given, *diaphragm, allegory, hypocrisy,* are ultimately Greek; additionally a few Hebrew words are recorded for the first time (*alleluia, sabbat,* but cf. § 111); in words from Arabic and Persian sources learning, trade and gracious living are so interconnected that it is best to disregard the usual distinction between orally-transmitted and literary loans, e.g., *saffron, admiral, algorism, camphor, lute, alchemy, scarlet, azure,* and a number of chess terms.

§ 139   Entirely different in kind are English loans at this period from other branches of the Germanic-speaking world – simple everyday words borrowed orally between members of similar cultures in fairly similar physical environments. From the Low German group of languages come *poll* ('head'), *dote(n),* v (later, with a French suffix, *dotard), luff* (in sailing), *bounce, snatch, huckster,* etc. In kind and quantity this group is akin to what we have found at every period; if the supply seems to dry up in periods yet to be treated, two points must be borne in mind:

English documentation will henceforth be much fuller than that for other languages in the same group, and before 970 English and Frisian, if not the whole Low German group, were so alike as to be mutually comprehensible and to make loans almost indetectable.

Borrowing from the North Germanic (Scandinavian) branch is on quite a different scale. There were certainly Scandinavian-speaking communities in England in 970, and quite probably in 1170: and the languages were mutually comprehensible up to about the time of the Norman Conquest. Even after that there may have been an Anglo-Scandinavian retaining this property, but we lack records of its existence, let alone its nature. As we examine the record of borrowing from Scandinavian it is very important to remember that we come to know of it only when English texts appear in Scandinavianised areas, or from place-names, which in these areas are often recorded long after they must have come into use. The words to be considered here are recorded in period IV, but it seems most likely that most of them, at least, entered the language in period V; we cannot tell which.

The closeness of the source-language leads to much uncertainty about whether words are really loans or not; northern English, in which most direct borrowing is to be expected, is particularly close in form. Moreover, there is evidence that speakers learnt to make 'phonemic translations' from one language to the other, i.e. to render a word into a familiar phonological form and treat it as a native one. Many of the items that can be identified were current in dialects which have not contributed much lexically to later Standard (hence the need to gloss), and the close fusion of the two communities is reflected in the grammatical range of the following examples: *bulle* ('bull'), *gape(n)*, *caste(n)*, *wante(n)*, *gra* ('grey'), *hap* ('luck'), *stor* ('great'), *wandraþ* ('suffering'), *fro*, *ill(e)*, *þoh* ('though'), *skenting* ('amusement'), *skill*, *wing*, *egg*, v and n, *skin*, *take*, *they*. Though these are a handful of examples out of hundreds, they illustrate certain points of interest. Even more than Anglo-Norman loans these words are taken, as it were, over the heads of existing English words, words of a most basic kind, and even including primary grammatical elements. Another thing that quite often happened was that a word formally like but semantically different in the two languages would simply come to be used in its Scandinavian sense; this was already known in V but an example from IV seems to be *dream* (OE 'music, joy'), used from the 13c in its present sense, as a loan from Scandinavian (though Chaucer has the native word *swevene* as late as the close of the 14c). The converse of this is a relatively minor formal modification in the direction of Scandinavian usage in words sharing a meaning in the two languages; thus OE (*ge*)*byrd* comes to be replaced by *burth*, and that in turn by the specifically Swedish form, *byrþ*, ME, NE *birth*.

The problems of distinguishing Scandinavian from native forms are dwarfed by the problems of distinguishing which variety of Scandinavian speech an item comes from. Speakers from the West Scandinavian branch (chiefly Norwegians) seem to have predominated in what is now Yorkshire and the NW Counties (but we have no reason to think much English was spoken in Cumberland at this date, and the heights of the Lake District were little inhabited by speakers of any language); East Anglia and Lincolnshire were mainly settled by East Scandinavians (Danes and some Swedes), and in these areas there was a considerable antecedent English population. Words which appear to be distinctly W Scand are *bole* (as against *bulle*, 'bull'), *bon* ('boon'), *bu* ('stock of cattle'), *bu* ('inhabitant'), *bun* ('bound [for]'), *busken* ('to prepare'), (intr; note that this, like *bask*, is an old reflexive), *lire*, ('face'), *weng* ('wing'), *þreue* ('bundle'), perhaps *gill* ('ravine'), which has become important in place-names. Probably E Scand are *boþe* ('booth'), *bulle*, *wing*; it is natural that when both forms were borrowed, the E Scand, because of its geographical distribution in this country, should be the form to spread into Standard and survive in general use.

The scope of the Scandinavian invasions and settlement can best be appreciated if we consider that over seven hundred place-names in -*by* are still known, more than two hundred of them in Lincolnshire; yet this was an area by no means deserted before the Scandinavians came and seized and settled. Enormous numbers of places are named with -*thorp*, -*toft*, -*thwaite*. If every Scandinavian place-name represented no more than the presence of a Scandinavian head of household (which is certainly not the case) the influx would still account for a considerable proportion of a population as small as England's then was. And naturally the vast majority of settlers would have been men. The mothers of their children must often have been English, so that children in several counties would in at least one generation have grown up in a bilingual household. In many areas this phase was past before our period, in others it comes in the period; either way, the consequences of such a phase naturally last some time. The scale of both destruction and settlement indicated by Scandinavian place-names is in sharp contrast with the fairly meagre crop of place-names of French origin. In one case the impact depends on numbers and proximity of relations, in the other on power, wealth and authority.

As we know (cf. § 131), the Scandinavian element in RS is due to internal borrowing. For a sample of the size of the influx we may consider that initial *sk-* or *sc-* (but not *sch-*), pronounced /sk/, in a word is a practically certain sign of Scandinavian origin; if we turn from a dictionary of the Standard language to the *English Dialect Dictionary* we find that the now common words of this form are supplemented by over 1,100 of purely dialectal currency.

§ 140   The abundant loans of this period provided data from which new patterns were inferred, and thus had secondary consequences in WF – most of them in III (cf. § 112), but some already in IV. English coinages on foreign suffixes precede those on prefixes, and include some on *-ard* (*shreward*), *-ery* (*husbandry*), *-ment* (*chastisement, eggment*), *-ous* (*gluttonous*). Of a more domestic kind is *-kin* from Low German, used in names (*Tomkin, Perkin, Malekin*) from the 13c. The extension of native suffixes to borrowed words is a matter of course (as *-ness* in *gentleness*) (cf. § 112) and does not require further illustration. Many English formatives were dying out, but these developments are merely the completion of major trends which got under way in V; they should be studied in the light of new borrowings (cf. § 113).

Compounding, often thought to be in decline at this period, does show new developments. At this time appears the type in which the first element is a verb, which in full syntax would be predicate of the nominal second element (*goggle-eye, leap-year*) as do sex-denoting compounds in *he-, she-* (*he-lamb, she-ass*); this no doubt takes the place of the declining sex-denoting derivational patterns. These are endocentric i.e., the head is of the same kind as the whole. Exocentric compounds produce a new type exemplified by *trailbastoun, spilltime, spurnwater* (cf. PE *cutpurse*) at the beginning of the 14c. It is also in ME that we first find nominal bahuvrihi compounds (such as *white-thorn, court-mantle*); these are exocentric compounds meaning one who or that which is characterised by what is expressed in the compound. In OE the type had been restricted to adjective formations, and these, by contrast, almost die out during IV (though *barefoot* survives as an individual word, and *bareback* appears to be a 16c formation). A marked feature of the period is the persistence of patterns, though all the old words made according to them die out. Thus, there were predicate-object compounds in *-ing/ -ung* in OE, but they all went out of use, and a new series on the same pattern begins with *backbiting* (1175), *blood-shedding*, etc. A similar story of loss and replacement underlies the type *heartburn, sunshine*, in which the second element is a deverbal noun; the type *wire-drawer*, *man-slayer*, in which the underlying theme is a verbal phrase; and that with a locative particle, as in *after-telleres*, 1340 (modern type-word *onlooker*): also the adjective type, *new-born*. The development of formations in *down* (*downcast*, *downfall*) from 1300 is interesting, because a pre-condition is the isolation of *down* as a particle; it was originally a noun, and the matrix type of construction for the particle was *a-dune*, 'off the down/hill'. It is also at this time that many originally locative particles come to be used figuratively in compounds (as *overking*, *overlord*, from about 1200).

§ 141   To set against our general uncertainties about the chronology of losses among old native words we have one very striking piece of evidence. The rather south-westerly text of Lawman's *Brut* survives in one version in a MS of *c.* 1200 and in a revised form in a manuscript about fifty years later. The later text is not just a copy, but a re-working to suit contemporary taste and usage. Some of the old words removed in the revision, and the French words which replace them, throw interesting light on the processes of change in the early 13c. Thus *here-toga* gives way to *chieftain* (*cheueteine*), *hireden*, 'company of military followers', to *rout*, *æhte* to *tresur*, *gauel* to *truage*, 'tribute', *munucclif* to *abbey*, *chireche* to *chapel*, *quarcerne* to *prisun*, *munstre* to *nonnerie*, ʒ*ette* to *grant*, v, ʒ*isles* to *hostages*, *heren* to *serve*, *milce* to *grace*, *axe* to *gisarme*, *here-marken* to *pensiles*, 'standards', *hauweres* to *spiares*, 'spiers, spies', *friðe*, 'protected place', to *parc*, 'hunting reserve', *marmon-stane* to *marbre*, 'marble', *wisen* to *atyr*, 'attire, guise', *bolle* to *coupe*, 'cup', *at-breac* to *ascapede*, *hoʒien* ('consider') to *aspien*, 'see', *liðen*, 'go', to *pass*, *boc-runen* to *lettre*, etc. Occasionally the word removed is a Scandinavian loan, as *husting*, which gives way to *conseil*, 'council'. Not all of these are exact 'translations', and the presence of *church* and *axe* in the list warns us that factors other than obsolescence may enter into the revisions, but most of the words replaced are unfamiliar to the general reader today, and were equally so in the 13c.

NOTE: It should be recorded before we leave lexis that this is the period at which the giving of second-names becomes normal. For the great, names in 'of x' had been used, largely since the Conquest, but in the 12c it became usual for humble people to be known by one or more second names, usually derived from their occupation (it is often said that the trades with humbler customers are typically English, as *baker*, *miller*, and those with grander customers typically French, as *tailor, souter*), or locational, often using the place-name directly after the Christian name, as *Simon Chikesonde* (but in Latin *de Chikeshand*), from Chicksands in Bedfordshire, or patronymic, as *Godwinson, Williamson*. The OE patronymics have largely disappeared before the onset of surname-giving, and the *-son* type is purely Scandinavian.

§ 142   Outwardly and in their import, the grammatical changes between 1170 and 1370 are enormous. Let us first look at the system for 1170 and then consider how, and to what effect, it changed.

Among nouns, Mossé (1952) distinguishes in early ME three types of inflection:

    I. having Ø in nom-acc sg, *-e* dat sg, *-(e)s* gen sg and all cases of the plural;

    II. being identical with I except that the stem itself ends in unstressed *-e*, to which nothing is added except the *-s* of the gen sg;

    III. having *-e* throughout the sg, and a variety of forms with *-n(-)* (never *-s*) in the plural.

In nouns as a whole, therefore, the primary distinction is one of number, and except for a few anomalous cases (unchanged and mutated plurals, commoner than today, but of roughly the same types), the number-contrast is unmarked in the singular, marked in the plural, and by one of two forms, according to which a broader classification of nouns will be into *-s*-plurals and *-n*-plurals. The secondary distinction is one of case, made only (again with a few exceptions) in the singular, only by the *-s*-plurals, marking off the gen from other cases, and identifying it with the marked number-sign. In addition, some nouns mark the form corresponding historically to a dat, but the marking is phonetically feeble, and with many nouns does not exist at all. No inflection in *-e* survives in the N. But this is not just a phonological difference. More generally, adding the dimension of dialect-variation, we can say that the N shows only Type I; the Mid Types I and II; the S all three. This pattern arises from a levelling under dominant types of formerly much more divergent declensional patterns; it involves a high degree of regularisation, but much more in the N and Mid than in the S, which did not merely preserve old *-n*-plurals but extended *-n*-pluralisation to nouns of other types, thus creating two rival dominant types. Not only did historic *-n*-plurals such as *eye, eyen, fa, fan* ('foe'; by 1370 the form was *fo(o)n*) preserve their traditional patterning, but other forms such as *sho, shoon, deouel, deoulen, sunne,* *sunnen* were newly adapted to it. Clearly the southern trend is less progressive, and weaker because less consistent. But the S nominal declension generally incorporates a good deal that serves no purpose (the N already gets along without it), and the system is ripe for further development. The levelling achieved by 1370 in all essentials (cf. §118) represents the present state of affairs. This levelling is not only a matter of simplification; in the matter of representing the gen sg it involved the extension of a form of marking that had proved its value. The loss of oblique-case contrast was the easier because of the progressive fixing in earlier centuries of the placing of object-forms, and of the relative order of direct and indirect objects, which jointly had rendered it superfluous. Moreover, prepositions, long used with inflected nouns, diversified in ME to such an extent as to make the oblique-case inflection a very blunt instrument by comparison (cf. §153). Nevertheless, in the Mid and S it remained customary in period IV to combine the two methods; a text using *child, wif, lif*, as subject – object forms would commonly use *to childe, to wiue, of liue*.

As to 'irregular' plural forms, a few -*r*-plurals surviving at the beginning of the period had been made over to the regular type by its end, namely *lomb/lomber*, 'lamb', *calf/calure*, 'calf'; this left *child/childer* so isolated that it was given a second plurality sign for good measure, establishing the still current 'double plural' *children*. The native word for egg, *ei* was treated in the same way, giving the double plural *eiren* (cf. §118). Other double plurals which have persisted to some extent are *brethren* and *kine*, both of which are based on original mutated plurals of the *foot/feet* type (OE *broðor/breðer, cu/cy*); it is curious that later English has retained the -*n*-plural almost solely for these inherently anomalous forms. A few other mutated forms found in the 12c, such as *gat/get*, 'goat', *hand/hend*, 'hand', are also regularised during the period. The great numbers of loanwords assimilated during this, as during the preceding, period were pluralised according to the dominant patterns, and constituted a powerful reinforcement to that dominance. Very occasionally, for example if a loan ended in a sibilant, there were exceptions, such as the assigning of *caas*, 'case' to the unchanged plural type.

This type was, indeed, notably stronger in ME than later. Many old unchanged plurals, such as *word, thing, leaf*, were regularised during IV, and the tendency was to use the unchanged plural less according to historic word-class membership than according to function. On the analogy of *year* (which by class-membership did have an unchanged plural), many other words preceded by cardinal numbers in measure-expressions were left unchanged in the plural, e.g., *syx myle, fourty fadme length*, etc. The association with number-attributives suggests that the old genitive contributes to the forms (cf. § 167). Distinctive function had a preservative, even developmental, value. The pattern has persisted to some extent, though increasingly in recent decades it has been felt as a vulgarism, and therefore has been receding. Similarly, some unchanged plural words were animal names, and from this coincidence a distinctive function has tended to evolve, mainly in NE. On the whole, ME here still represents historic word-class membership. *Neat* 'bovine animal, cattle', had an unchanged plural; *horse* kept one until III; *swine*, once, as an animal term, singular and plural, has in NE become so general in collective plural function that it no longer has a singular.

Nothing in the form of nouns, even at the beginning of the period, indicates their division into three genders grammatically determined. Nevertheless, their concord with articles and to some extent with pronouns indicates that in the 12c this ancient classification still persisted to some degree (cf. § 145 and § 167).

The classification and forms of nouns in ME are normally set out to help modern readers learn ME in order that they may read it as a mildly foreign language. This makes them look, especially as early as 1170, very different from those now current. Yet the sinews of the system were already those which today provide its real power, and in the N they were manifestly working independently of traditional grammatical supports. Language is so much a matter of habit that redundant, even confusing, traces of outgrown patterns and contrasts can, and in this case did, survive for many centuries.

§ 143 Changes in pronouns go deeper. In principle, the personal pronouns had, in 1170, a four-case, three-number system, but this was much eroded, since only the third singular masculine had distinct forms for all the cases; only the first and second persons had, and they rarely used, the dual (in addition to singular and plural) number.

In the first person the asymmetries between singular and plural are inescapable, since they depend on the nature of human identity; the dual is in this, of course, like the plural (i.e., it means *I and another, not two I's*); both dual and plural can be inclusive or exclusive (i.e., the 'other person(s)' may or may not include the addressee). In the absence of an acc–dat contrast we identify an object-case. Thus the forms are:

Subj S, Mid, *ic, ich*, /ɪtʃ/; N, strong, *ic, ik*, /ɪk/, weak before consonants
i, /ɪ/.
Obj *me*, strong /meː/, weak /mɛ/
Gen *min*, /miːn/

DUAL	PL
Subj *wit*, /wɪt/	*we*, strong /weː/, weak /wɛ/
Obj not recorded, ? survived (cf. § 168)	*us*, strong /uːs/, weak /ʊs/
Gen *unker*, /ʊŋkər/	*ure*, /uːr/

NOTE: The dual is recorded only in the first two generations of the period,
and is naturally rare. With its loss in the early 13c (possibly earlier in the
N), the structure of the first person pronoun becomes virtually what
it is today. In the subj sg the difference of final consonant in the N
reflects a general phonological dialect difference. The N took the lead
in dropping the final consonant in unstressed use, to give a weak form which
by 1370 had extended into Standard. A form of this, re-lengthened under
stress, /iː/, then developed, to become the basis of the present form. It
existed in time to undergo the shift to /aɪ/, but not much earlier. The sg gen
soon developed a form without final consonant for use (though not yet
consistently) before consonants. This alternative, *my, min*, provided the
formal contrast which was later to be exploited grammatically, i.e., to
distinguish possessive adjectives from pronouns. Otherwise, modern usage
does not differ from that of 1170 save as a result of straightforward phonological development – a very different picture from that we shall find for the
second and third persons.

§ 144 In the second person the forms were:

SG	DUAL	PL
Subj *þu, tu* /θuː, tuː, θʊ, tʊ/	*ȝit*/jɪt/	*ȝe*, /jeː, jɛ/
Obj *þe, te* /θeː, teː, θɛ, tɛ/		*eu, ou, ȝow*
	(ȝ)inc(er)/(j)ɪŋkər/	
Gen *þin*, /θiːn/		*(ȝ)(o)ure*

NOTE: The dual dies out in the early 13c, and probably only belongs during
this period to the most conservative dialects; even where the form is used
its historic function has been forgotten. The singular forms are used in all
address to one person; the 'polite' use of the plural is found very occasionally
in the 13c, but is not an important factor in usage till period III. The
initial *þ* is still unvoiced (cf. §108). It shows a strong tendency to assimilate
to a preceding homorganic ('articulated in the same position') consonant.
This tendency is shared between pronouns and other forms inclined to be
weak, notably articles; effectively they become enclitics. Typical sequences

are *art þu > artu, and þe > and te, and þat > and tat*. This tendency existed
earlier, though it comes through in writing most strongly in period IV; it
continued later, but a growing sense that writing should be ideographic,
i.e., that a single form should stand for each word in all circumstances, has
increasingly removed it from the written record. In transcription, weak
forms follow strong ones. From the 13c an additional sg weak subj form,
þe, enclitic *te*, came into use and from the early 14c *you* sometimes appears
in subject-function, *ye* as object. These usages must have added to the
confusion about the case-role of the *e/u* distinction in second person pronouns, which became acute after the polite plural was established (cf.
§87). The gen needs no comment additional to that made in the last paragraph. Omission of transcription from the plural obj and gen forms is not
accidental. Almost certainly many variants were current; there must have
been obj forms /juː/, /jʊ/, strong and weak, and with /rə/ added in the gen,
but it would not be wise to guess how many others there were. The opening
diphthong had been falling, /eo/ in OE; at some point it became (as initial
and occasionally other diphthongs tended to) rising, presumably at first
/jo/, but the following /w/, no doubt vocalised to /ʊ/, has then tended to
dominate. At just what stage what variants were current it would be rash
to claim to know.

Between 1170 and 1970 the second person pronoun undergoes a
sorting-out of the various alternative forms. The polite plural was
established, and a number of old weak forms, relengthened, were
substituted for original strong forms (cf. §87). Otherwise the differences
can be accounted for by straightforward phonological development.

§ 145   The third person is quite another matter. Here it is necessary
at all periods to distinguish three genders in the singular, none in the
plural. It is during period IV that this threefold gender distinction
becomes isolated – that is, it does not appear anywhere else in the
grammar, and as a counterpart to this change, its value is transformed.
The forms for the singular are:

M	N
Subj *he*, /heː, hɛ/	*hit*
Acc *hine*/hɪnə/	
Dat *him*/hɪm/	*him*
Gen *his*/hɪs/	*his*

F

Subj SW *heo*/hö(ː)/, SE *he*,/heː, hɛ/, E Mid *sche*/ʃeː, ʃɛ/, Orm *ho* (cf. also §131)
Obj (acc/dat) *hire*/hɪrə/
Gen   *hire, here*/?hɪrə, hɛrə, hər(ə)/

NOTE: The four-term case-system of the masculine is isolated in the language and cannot be expected to endure much longer – as indeed it does not; in the N we cannot be sure it lasted this long. The general movement of case-reduction had been by extending the old dat at the cost of the acc, and even in the masc sg pronoun this has happened by the end of the period. In the neuter the simplification has followed different lines, because already in OE there was no nom–acc distinction in it. While that was a perfectly normal situation in OE it had become anomalous in ME, where, in addition, a three-term case contrast was confined, after the very earliest documents, to person-referring words. This led to a tendency, which establishes itself in period III, for extension of (h)it (the dominant form because it had both subject and direct-object function) to indirect-object function which, in this instance, is less common than the other functions. These and other pressures (see below) brought about a situation in which human/non-human gender-contrast was foregrounded, and as a result, identity in the gen between masc and neuter *his* was felt to be anomalous, and was dealt with in ways already described (cf. §87).

The only one of the three forms with a case-structure conforming to the type which would be regular in subsequent English is the feminine. The forms of this, especially the subject forms, indicate a disturbed state of affairs of another kind. Actually, they are an oversimplification as shown, since they include nothing for the N, which was soon to develop a *scho*-type [we have no indication whether this existed in the early part of our period; it was fully established by its end (cf. §131)]. It is plain that such diverse usage for so central a form cannot survive any movement towards standardisation; the picture given here is limited to the 'dialectal' phase of English. It is also natural to ask how such diversity can have arisen. We can break it down into diversity of initial consonant, and of closing vowel. The closing vowel is in principle simpler to explain, though we may have some doubt about its phonetic value. In a fairly SW area ME has /ö(ː)/ corresponding to /e(ː)/ in the rest of the country as a reflex of what in OE was spelt *eo*, and was probably a diphthong; in some cases the reflex of this sound has stress-shift and further develops from /jo/ to /oː/ in certain environments (hence PE *choose* from OE *ceosan*). The outcome of straightforward phonological development will therefore leave a large part of the country with a form for 'she' which is identical with its form for 'he' (as a further complication, part of that area would also have the same reflex for 'they'; hence the introduction of new forms, cf. §131).

The gender distinction in 1170 is completing its transition from OE functions to those it has had ever since. The earlier language had a two-tier gender system, dependent partly on the properties of the antecedent's referent, partly on the gender-classification of the noun used as the antecedent. Under the old system nouns belonged to one of three grammatically determined genders, established to a very limited extent by nominal form, but largely by agreement with determiners. Even in OE grammatical gender in the noun conflicted with, and was largely subordinated to, natural gender in the personal pronouns. That is, the selection of third person pronoun depended primarily on answers to the ordered questions, (1) is the referent human? (2) if human, male or female? (3) if not human, by what gender of noun is it designated? Within the relatively close-knit structure of the noun phrase grammatical gender lasted better than in the remoter range of pronoun-selection. By 1170 it was broadly true that if reference to a person was involved, natural gender took priority; if not, either system might prevail. By 1370 the conception of grammatical gender is hardly relevant to English; departures from natural gender involve personification. Once again, the more advanced stage had been reached in the north before the beginning of our period; elsewhere evidence for the chronology of the change to a consistently natural system is scrappy, but some grammatical gender can be traced in the SW in the early 13c (Lawman repeatedly uses the pronoun *he* in reference to a lake, *mere*, a word which is historically masc: but when his work was revised half a century later such *he*-forms were replaced by *hit*). There are very rare traces of grammatical gender in pronouns in the stupendously long Ormulum (*c.* 1200, Stamford, cf. McIntosh, 1963), but in Kent it is still quite common in 1340. As so often happens, what strikes us as a historical change turns out to be distributed at first diatopically rather than diachronically. Once again it is important that somewhere the language was already in 1170 functioning in what has become the modern way; the change, once started, was irreversible. As we have seen, what happens in the pronoun is only one aspect of a general fore-grounding of ± human gender, which in turn had (and is still having) repercussions on other pronoun-forms.

In the second person the shifts of distribution between original subject and object forms looked primarily formal in origin. The third person shows us that other forces were at work. In syntax (cf. §123) periods IV and V are those of the full establishment of pre-verb position as subject position in unmarked affirmative sentences. The identification of this position has a decided effect on pronouns, which are the only forms distinguishing subject and object cases. In most cases no conflict arises; but where there is a clash between function and position we can see that a slight shift of distribution has taken place. Position can now override subject-object function in determining form-selection, and from the early 13c we find such uses as *Him þat is Laverd of lif* . . . *þe is ilevet* ('he who is Lord of Life is granted to you'). The 3rd plural pronoun began to follow the same course in the 15c and the 1st person in early NE (cf. § 123).

§ 146 The 3rd plural makes no distinction of gender and a threefold one of case. The forms vary so importantly and widely that they require discussion rather than tabulation. Here we are dealing, in certain areas, with one of the rare cases in the history of any language of the borrowing of a primary grammatical item. Where the native form survived it had forms beginning with *h-*, - *hi, hy, he, heo, ho*, and this was mainly in the S, with the rounded vowel-forms being more westerly. Late in the period there is a weak form *ha*, but earlier weak forms simply had the short equivalents of the vowels used under stress. Just before our period begins the east-ish Midlands (Peterborough, 1154) had *hi*; just afterwards (Stamford, *c.* 1200) *þeȝȝ*. Scandinavian forms certainly soon became widespread in Scandinavian areas, but we lack documents to tell us whether they were normally in use at the beginning of the period. In the second half of the 13c *þai* can be found in the SW Mid; it penetrates the Standard language late in the 14c, but is absent from Kentish. As we have seen, the assimilation and spread of this form is greatly helped by the multiple ambiguity of *he/hi* in certain areas; the whole *þ*-paradigm is not usually borroved at once.

The S had a distinct *-s*-form for the accusative [(*h*)*is*(*e*), *es*] often enclitically attached to a preceding verb. Not only is a distinct accusative form anomalous (which makes it even odder that the south invented this form; it did not occur in OE), but this particular realisation of it blurs the number distinction, which in the pronoun is primary. We are not surprised that nothing further is heard of this form.

Everywhere else the reflex of the old dative extended its reach into the accusative. The usual forms were *h*(*e*)*om* in the W and *hem* in the E, with a weak variant *ham* (/əm/ as in PE). This did not clash with any other form, and was the slowest to be replaced by *þ*-forms. In Orm *þeȝȝm* is known, but is in a minority compared with *hem*. The spread of *þ* outside Scandinavian areas is extremely retarded, and even in Caxton *hem* is still more frequent than *them*. It is, of course, the only native plural form to have left a trace in PE.

The genitive takes very varied forms, at first mainly of *he(o)re, hire, hare* types. The first evidence of *þ* is found in Orm's *þeȝȝre*, which he uses more often than *h*-forms. The Scandinavian type spreads quicker than in the oblique case, slower than in the nominative, and enters the Standard language as one of the defining features of Samuel's Type IV (1963, 89).

§ 147 At this period mention must be made of the indefinite pronoun of personal reference. At the very beginning of ME it had the form *me(n)*, but since it was almost invariably weak in use the *-n* was soon completely lost. Modern readers often have difficulty in distinguishing it from the oblique form of the 1st person pronoun; confusion in ME must have arisen from its homophony with the weak form of *me* and it may also have been analysed as plural of *man*. It continues in use throughout the period, but with a great decline in frequency. And just before the beginning of the period we find recorded one of the forms that later substituted for it, the 2nd person pronoun in the sense 'one'. The Peterborough Chronicle, 1154, has both *na gode ne dide me* ('people did no good') and *þu myhtes faren all a dæis fare* ('you could go a whole day's journey'); the translations here, with 'people' and 'you', indicate a distinction between a generalising and a non-generalising sense. In the generalising sense 'the people' began to replace it from the 13c, but 'people' is not found till the 15c. In the non-generalising use 'a man', 'one', begin to take over in early NE, but *me* is occasionally found as late as Elizabethan English. No satisfactory all-purpose substitute for it has ever been found.

§ 148 The definite article, which had arisen out of pronominal forms, was by 1170 only marginally related to the pronoun-system, but the connection is sufficient to justify treating it next. It had two distinct types of realisation throughout the period. In most parts of the country it was indeclinable *þe*, later *the*, or at the very most it varied between singular *þe* and plural *þa*. However, in the S and SW Mid it was declinable, with three genders in the singular and up to four cases. Where it had declinable forms they were the same as those for the 'further'-demonstrative, *that*, since, in fact, they had originated in a special use of that form. This section will therefore take the demonstratives as part of its subject. The forms set out below were in some parts only demonstrative, in others they had double function; they are presented for reference-purposes, but they tend to suggest far more differentiation than most speakers knew. In the masc sg there were four forms: *se*, subj; *þene, þane,* acc; *þan, þene,* Kt *þa,* later *þo,* dat (i.e., some speakers reduced the case-system to three even here). The fem sg usually had three forms: *seo, si* (SW and SE) subj; *þa,* later *þo,* enclitic *to,* oblique; *þer, þære,* gen. The neuter (like the 3rd person pronoun) had the same form for subj and direct obj *þet* or *þat* (according to dialect, but *a* tended to invade *e*-areas, as a weak form, or by internal borrowing, or both); the dat was usually *þan,* the gen *þes* or *þas.* In the plural all genders had subj–obj *þa,* later *þo,* dat or oblique *þan,* gen *þere.* We have here all the signs of a paradigm in transition. The number contrast is already stronger and more clear-cut than case or gender contrasts, and changes elsewhere in the grammar were to widen the gap in the course of our period. Gender, as a grammatical system, can hardly survive the transformation of the personal pronoun-system already described (cf. § 142), and it was partly as a consequence of the same changes that the three-term case-system came to be associated solely with person-referring pronouns. After the very beginning of our period, and outside Kt, case and gender distinctions, in article or demonstrative, occur only patchily, and then in circumstances showing that their historical functions have been forgotten. A few, more or less formulaic, sequences have left traces in later English (OE *æt þam ende,* ME *atten ende,* PE *at an end,* where the indefinite article makes no sense; *for then ones* metanalysed as *for the nonce*). Otherwise, except for some persistence of plural *tho,* the definite article has become fully indeclinable by the end of the period.

In the N, where early levelling of *þe* for the article had already separated it from the demonstrative, the demonstrative had extended initial *þ-* to all cases; it only remained, early in ME, to level them under invariable *þat* in the sg, and this was done very early in ME, first in the N, and then everywhere except Kt. Only in special patterns in which the dem was stressed were there exceptions, and curiously one of them survives in a reflex now having the form *the*; this is an old instrumental or measure case, *þy, þi,* persisting in PE *the more, the merrier* (where *the* has the value 'by so much', and does not make sense as a definite article). In the dem, too, the important and most clear-cut distinction was that of number. By historic development the N had the plural *þa,* the Mid and S *þo.* From the early 13c the regularising N uses an analogical plural in *-s*; only in the 15c do we find the S adopting this, in the form *thos(e),* whence the PE form. What is really significant at this period is, then, that out of a rather tangled range of initial uses there comes a clear-cut distinction between article and demonstrative, in one dialect after another, and that from the muddle of inflectional distinctions originally occurring with both there comes an uninflected article and a demonstrative variable for number only, and using a unique pattern for the distinction.

The 'hither'-demonstrative (*this*) also goes back to forms with number, gender and some case distinctions, but its history as a functional unit is simple. The form which during this period came to be used throughout the sg was originally a neuter subj–obj form, *þis*; at first only the E Mid and N used it, the S levelling the masc form *þes*, but as usual the S form gave way. The old plural for all genders was *þas*, which in the N went out of use before 1200; new plurals adding *-e* to the new regular singulars were developed (whence PE *these*) – otherwise both the N and S forms would have fallen together with the analogical plural of *that*.

§ 149   The interrogative pronouns were *hwa, hwæt, hwich* (N *quhilk*), *hweþer*, but the lines of distinction between them were not wholly settled. *Hweþer* was traditionally used to ask 'which of two?' (and to some extent as a marker of direct questions without inversion), but it declined in frequency, without yet dying out, during the period. Both its functions ceased to have special word-forms as it went out of use. *Hwich* was originally a qualitative interrogative (asking 'of what kind?'), but side by side with this function in period IV it develops its modern value of enquiring about a definite number, and the newer sense predominates, again without any replacement for the dying one. *Hwæt* and *hwa* (late *what, who*), functioned, as they had in OE, as the human/ non-human gender forms of a single pronoun. They have always been number-invariable. At the beginning of the period there are traces of a five-term case-contrast in the human-gender forms; but the old accusative was soon merged under the dative, and the old instrumental, *hwy*, became dissociated and began its career as a distinct interrogative. This left the three-term system with which English has since been familiar, and a general levelling of case-contrast in the non-human after the loss of grammatical gender, though some non-human *whose* forms are used in early NE.

So familiar are the forms that it is easy to overlook the absence of two later functions. At first the *who/what* interrogatives are used only in direct questions; in predicative use *what* appears first, and is at first preferred even in reference to persons. In indirect questions *who* is often followed by *that*, which enters into a great many quasi-compound relational forms; from 1300 *who* is found alone in this function, but it is not in undisputed use till the 17c.

The second missing use is as a relative, which, as we have seen (cf. § 118) is rarely a *who*-form even in III. In 1170 the inherited relative form was indeclinable *þe*, but down to the 13c, as in OE, *þe* was very often combined with a form of the demonstrative, which acted as a case-number-gender distinction carrier (thus, *se þe* = '[he] who'). But the original neuter form, *þat*, was also used in all functions. The links between *þe* and *þat* forms in other functions have already been discussed; in relative function *þat* tends to replace *þe* from the 13c (*þe* is common in the first version of Lawman, rare in the second), producing by the end of the period a relative new, but like the old one uninflected. There were also, as there had been at all periods, contact-clauses, with no relative pronoun, and they occurred in subject as well as object function.

The modern introduction of *who*, *which*, in relative function runs counter to the normal tendency, since it involves inflectional grammatical differentiations additional to those not merely of ME, but also to those of OE.

§ 150 Adjectives, in the Mid and S, are inflected during period IV, on a twofold system relating them to their head-word. This pattern survives the period in Type III (Chaucerian) Standard, but for general purposes period IV can be taken as marking the disintegration of an old system of adjective concord. The system had already gone out in the N, and the following account does not apply to that region.

Though there is, as in the pronouns, some additional differentiation in the earliest texts and in Kt, in general the system is that after a defining word (article or demonstrative) monosyllabic adjectives add -*e* throughout, but in the absence of such a word they have Ø in the sg and -*e* in the pl. Longer adjectives do not generally inflect. The difference in those that do inflect does not lie in the class of adjective, but in its syntactic function. The two patterns of inflection had formerly served a purpose, when the subordinate parts of a noun-phrase were marked throughout for concord with its head, and, the defining words being already fully marked, adjectives following them could afford to make fewer distinctions than those not so supported. From this older function the two patterns are given the names strong (i.e., independent of a defining word) and weak (i.e., dependent on a defining word). Even in OE the strict positional rules now current for the premodifiers of a noun were regularly followed, so that for attributives the inflections had little use. But with the decline in grammatical gender and of case-distinctions on one hand, the sharpening of number-contrast on the other, neither the strong-weak distinction, nor any concord-inflection of adjectives served any purpose. The inertia of habitual use was sufficient to keep them in general use with the shorter adjectives until the phonological loss of unstressed *-e*, but since then speakers have found no call for such distinctions.

The only area in which these developments led to some consequential re-adjustment was in the use of adjective forms in noun-function. As long as adjectives were fully inflected this was a matter of course. With the decline of adjective inflection, there was some tendency to use nominal-adjectives with the *-s*-plurals now generalised in nouns, e.g., *to knawe . . . þe preciouses vram þe viles*; except in well-defined cases where we now tend to recognise de-adjectival nouns this gave way to a tendency to use of *thing* or *one* as number and gender carrier. This is in line with the foregrounding of the human/non-human distinction. In the latter part of IV, accordingly, the first clear instances of the prop-word *one* occur. Though matrix-patterns are earlier, the first certain example is in Robert Mannyng (Lincolnshire, 1338), *a moche felde; so grete one never he behelde.*

Naturally, the one place where the adjective does preserve inflection is comparison, but throughout the period periphrastic comparison (with *more, most*, instead of, or as well as, inflections) is found. The difference between the two patterns is not clear-cut, but there is some tendency, contrary to modern practice, to prefer the periphrastic form with monosyllables. The growth of periphrastic constructions is very marked during this period, notably in verb-forms and prepositional phrases (cf. § 153).

§ 151 In OE the first three cardinal numbers had differed from the rest, morphologically, since they were inflected, and syntactically, since they were adjectives in concord with their head, whereas the higher numbers were commonly pronouns governing a genitive plural (i.e., one spoke of *two sheep*, but *twenty of sheep*). By period III this system has disappeared; in this, as in so much else, IV is a period of transition. The details, and the dialect-divergences, need not be traced (for the OE forms, from which, in the framework of developments already established, the pattern can be inferred, cf. § 167). A point that does call for attention is the evolution of the indefinite article, originally a form of the first cardinal numeral. Functionally, this was rather more advanced in OE than the definite article, yet it did not stand out clearly because the function was divided between two forms, *an* and *sum*. Early ME begins to drop *sum* as a sg article, and thus the role of *an* is more clear-cut. Mustanoja (1960, 261–2) calculates that the Ormulum shows an increase in *an* of *c.* 135% as compared with late OE, the ratio being *an* 10, *sum* 1. The change is not merely formal; *an* had been used to focus attention on an individual, *sum* on the individual's being one of a class. Speakers have preferred to drop this as a distinction made lexically, and now have to use some such phrase as *a certain* in the role of *sum*. The formal consequence of the specialisation of *an* in article-function was the differentiation of a strong form, *an*, later S and Mid *one*, /aːn, ɔːn/, in numeral function, weak *a(n)*, /a(n), ə(n)/, in article function.

As in all earlier periods, the composite numerals from twenty to ninety-nine had units before tens (e.g., *nyne and twenty*). The modern pattern originates in late ME. Among ordinals the only major change is that *oþer* is replaced by *second* (from French); this was clearly an improvement in view of its wide range of functions (then as now).

§ 152 Superficially, the development of adverbs is not very striking during the period, and yet it is during IV that essential aspects of modern adverbial formation take shape. Certain important features were inherited from OE. In the first place, all adverbs save a few notable exceptions were derived; in the second, many of the derivations were by specialisation of inflectional forms belonging to other form-classes. Most commonly, adverbs were specialised uses of an old adjective case-ending in *-e* that we can best call dative-instrumental (it is concerned with means and thence with manner). A very common type of adjective with which this method was used was that which itself was formed with the semi-suffix *-lic* ('shape, form, body') added to a nominal stem, as in the series *freond - freondlic - freondlice* ('friend, friendly, friendlily'). Indeed, such forms were so familiar that *-lice* came to be isolated as a formative and thought of as 'the' way of making adverbs. It is added even redundantly, and to forms where *-lic* would not fit; for instance, we have *eornoste*, adj and adv ('earnest(ly)'), but a new adverbial form *eornostlice* is created to keep the Ø : *-lice* correlation. Although the formations in *-e* and *-lice* are in origin identical, by 1170 they were felt as distinct, *-e*, though familiar in many common words, having become inactive, while *-lice* was highly productive. This was the situation in the S and Mid. The N, having already lost -*e*, will have types in Ø and -*lik*, which in weak (i.e., normal) use, will become -*li* (cf. *ik, i,* §143). This is clearly the pattern we have inherited in PE. In *run fast, go slow,* adverbs of unchanged type survive; in *prettily, happily, noisily,* the -*li* type survives. It is likely that the ON suffix -*lig,* which also became -*li,* gave support, but native tradition is sufficient to account for it. By the end of our period the S was reaching the same stage in respect of loss of -*e,* but its reflex of -*lice* was -*lich,* which cannot be the source of the modern forms. The sense of unease about adverbs homophonous with an adjective, which led to the development of the *eornostlice* type, has been felt at all periods, and there has been a steady progress from plain to -*ly* forms; even the very tenacious close-knit phrases I quoted as evidence of plain adverbs are now felt by some speakers to require re-formation in -*ly.* The history of adverbial forms demonstrates very well both how long linguistic processes can take, and that a factor in them is speakers' analyses of the patterns of their language, right or wrong!

Adverbs were also formed as specialised uses of the case-forms of nouns, mainly the dative-instrumental and the genitive. Because of the loss of final -*e* the dative-type has hardly been detectable in later English except where fossilised in such structures as *otherwise, nowise;* actually, in early NE the -*wise* suffix became isolated as an adverb-formative exactly as the -*lice* suffix had formerly been, and although British English allowed the formation pattern to lapse, American English kept it alive, and has recently lent it back to us. A dative plural formation surviving into ME and somewhat beyond is *whilom* ('at times'); apparently on the analogy of this the very strange formation *seldom* was built in early NE, *seld* being already an adverb, 'seldom', to which the ending -*om* has been analogically added (though on an adverb it can hardly be interpreted as a dative plural). Very common in OE was the genitive type, and many examples survive into period IV, though it is not certain that the type was still productive. It mainly belongs in rather set expressions, such as 'wintres and sumeres', 'daies and niʒtes', just as it does at the present time, 'Tuesdays she goes to the hairdresser', etc.).

As we have seen at all periods, adverbs are a frequent source of intensifiers. Very common in period IV, and almost entirely new in this function, was the use of *al,* with adjectives (*al milde*), participles (*al singinge*), and adverbs (*al prively*). We have also seen that the rate of turnover for intensifiers is high, so we are not surprised that after period IV *al* is no longer active in this function, though it survives fossilised in *all right.* The other main intensifier in IV, *ful,* had a much longer history in the role (to the 19c). There is the usual wealth of minor intensifiers, and the usual rapid turnover among them. Some of the most familiar are, *clean, enough, faire, fast(e), fele, ferly, muche, right, swithe, utterly, well, whole, wonder*.

§ 153   The role of prepositions is of interest and importance during period IV. In OE the catalogue had been relatively short, and the functions restricted. During ME, prepositions flourish in both respects. Their number increases in various ways, by compounding and analogical formation, and by borrowing from French and Scandinavian. Neither process is common in a language, nor is there much evidence of either in earlier or later English. It is not possible to break down the ME developments into an exact chronology, but period IV is the central one to allocate them to, even if they spill over both edges of it. The matter is well put by Mustanoja:

> The large majority of English prepositions are native in origin. Very little has been obtained directly from Latin. *Except* is the Latin ablative absolute *excepto*, but *per* is possibly only a Latinised form of French *par*. There are a number of other prepositions – not many – taken as such from French (*countre, maugre, sans*, and *save*); some of these are absolute participles (e.g., *touchant*). In addition to these there are some which are disguised under a partially anglicised form (*according to, considering, during, excepting, saving*, and *touching*). A few native formations are calques on OF prepositions: *lasting* (cf. OF *durant*), *notwithstanding* (cf. OF *non obstant*), and *outtaken* (cf. OF *excepte* and L *excepto*).
>
> Apart from these direct and indirect loans, foreign influence has affected several native prepositions by enriching or otherwise modifying their uses. Thus – to mention only some of the most common English prepositions – *at* seems to have acquired some new meanings and greatly increased its phrasal power under the influence of OF *a*, L *ad*, and obviously also of ON *at*. The use of *by* seems to have been influenced by F *par*. . . . It is also highly probable that F *en* and L *in* have influenced E *in* and strengthened its position, with the result that this preposition has encroached upon the domain formerly held by *on* (cf. *in a book*, OF *en un livre*, and L *in libro*, while OE [West Saxon] has *on bec*).
>
> Old Norse has also played a part in the development of English prepositions. It has obviously strengthened and enriched the use of certain prepositions, like *at* and *with*, and a few prepositions, such as *fro*, are Scandinavian loans (1960, 348–9).

Not counting minor variants, Mustanoja is able to list some hundred ME prepositions, and this number, larger than any before or since, represents a good deal of experimental exuberance. In spite of the large number of items available, it is at this period that the great diversification of functions for the most favoured prepositions is centred. An example is the instrumental use of *by*, known in OE, but more frequent by far in ME, where it develops the role of expressing agency with passive verb constructions. *In*, in early OE chiefly characteristic of Mid dialects and having a literal local or temporal meaning, extends its range in many figurative uses (*in short, in common, in distress, in exchange, in sight, in vain*, etc.). *Of* makes a major innovation as a periphrastic alternative to the genitive case, and the rivalry between these two modes of expression to this day leaves some areas of unclear usage. In OE the preposition had had the meaning *from*, but it shows in ME a tendency to encroach in various ways on the territory of *on*. *To* extends its ancient use with infinitives (cf. § 170) and, like *for*, invades the domain formerly held by the dative case. In OE *mid* had been used for 'accompaniment', *wiþ* for 'against'. From about 1200, though *mid* continues in its old functions, *wiþ* begins to compete with it, and in late ME supplants it; *mid*, like *on*, is an instance of shrinking in an age generally of expansion.

It is not easy to understand the complex of forces which led to these shifts of balance, and perhaps we shall never have the knowledge to penetrate them completely. But one factor is clearly of the highest importance, though itself of complex and not wholly understood provenance. This is the development of the verb–particle combination (phrasal verb), in which the particle may be preposition or adverb. Such combinations were virtually unknown in OE, which used particles with verbs in separable prefix form (as does modern German). The separable use gave rise to many patterns in which the particle followed the verb, and for some reason this arrangement came increasingly to be preferred. In early ME it does not make great headway in merely numerical terms. Kennedy (1920), in the standard work on the subject, traces in two early 13c texts proportions of fifty-four compound verbs to 15 verb–particle combinations, and fifty compound verbs to six verb–particle combinations. He suggests that the arrival of the type just at the time when loans were pouring new compounds into the language caused it to make slow headway against the older type, so that it is not really dominant till the 15c. This may well be so. The crucial fact is that by the mid-12c verb–particle combinations already have so specialised a lexical sense (*give up* = 'surrender', 1154) that we must suppose the type to have become deeply entrenched even before period IV. This is one of many points in which the progress of syntactic developments may be obscured from our view by stylistic restraints in the kind of writing chiefly preserved. The verb–particle combinations seem always to have had the the air of colloquiality that still often clings about them. Though not quite new in IV, they became then, as they have been ever since, extremely active as formative types, and since we have chosen to locate here an account of the medieval flowering of prepositions, we must at the same point treat of this highly characteristic and closely related phenomenon.

§ 154 The rationale of the scheme of verb-classification presented in Chapter III is even clearer in IV, and will be progressively so as we go back in time. In 1170 relatively few French verbs had been absorbed, and although some dialects had borrowed many Scandinavian verbs, the likeness of verb-classification between ON and English was so close that these loans fitted and reinforced both the strong–weak–anomalous classification and the balance between the two main types. In the course of period IV the large influx of French verbs, almost all conformed to the weak type, completely altered the balance. Weak verbs became so far the norm that they attracted more and more old strong verbs into their mode of conjugation.

In 1170 we find for the first time in our backward course enough strong verbs to reveal a clear internal classification. In their traditional forms these verbs had four principal parts – that is, forms from which, by applying a knowledge of inflectional formation rules, we can derive the entire conjugation of the verb. The four forms are the infinitive, the past singular, the past plural and the second participle. Since it is characteristic of strong verbs to form these parts by vowel-change, we shall find it convenient to speak of the infinitive vowel or grade of vowel, the past singular vowel, the past plural vowel. We only need to identify three grades of vowel, because in their origins these vowel-series usually had only three distinct terms; when the vowels of the third and fourth principal parts differ the difference, though often old, is not in most cases original.

Class I, which in medieval and modern English is the most entrenched, had the vowel-series, *i* /iː/, *a* /ɑː/ (later in the S and Mid *o* /ɔː/), i /ɪ/, as in *writen, wrat, writen, (y-)writen*. About twenty verbs belonged to class I in period IV, and nearly half of them have more or less continued to do so. Others, *stryken, gliden, sliden, wriþen*, stayed in it till period III, and then developed alternatives which have come to prevail. The rest went out of use altogether, and it cannot be coincidence that one of them had a prefix which died (*umstride*, 'stride about, bestride'), and the others all had consonant alternations which gave their conjugations a somewhat irregular shape (*stien*, 'climb', *wrien*, 'cover', *lipen*, 'go'). Not only have losses from this well-defined class been few, but the association between it and an /iː/ infinitive was so strong that, contrary to the normal usage, it attracted loans to itself, notably *strive*, which has lasted, and *fyne*, which has not. It is true of all strong verbs that they have begun, even in IV, to get rid of the vowel change between past singular and plural. They may level one vowel or the other; they may develop regional or even idiosyncratic doublets. A process of levelling is already at work which will grow far stronger in later centuries, thus creating a phase of divided usage, marked in III, declining in II and I, still not wholly eliminated. When we speak of survival it does not necessarily mean any more than that alternation of the infinitive vowel with one of the past vowels is still to be found.

Class II had the vowel series, *e* /eː/ (SW *eo* /öː/), *e* /ɛː/, *u/o* /ʊ/ and /ɔ/ later /ɔː/. Perhaps a dozen verbs could be assigned to this class in 1170, but for a number of reasons it was much less secure than class I. Some of the commonest verbs belonging to it share the consonant alternations already referred to, e.g., *chesen*, (*ches*, *curen*, [*y-*]*coren*) 'choose', similarly *lesen*, 'lose', *fresen*, 'freeze'; in the case of *chesen* there is alternation of initial consonant as well as final stem consonant, and a variant in which the infinitive vowel is replaced (as a result of shifting stress on an original diphthong) by *o*. An even more disturbing consonant-alternation affected the verb *fleʒen* 'fly', which was already confused with *flen*, 'flee'. And several verbs had a quite different present, in *u* (e.g., *buʒen*, 'bow'). Such accidental factors meant that the identity of the class was easily lost sight of. Former members of the class were treated in divergent ways. *Chesen* had its consonants levelled as in the infinitive, and numerous divergent vowel patterns established themselves, by the verb rather than by the class. A number of verbs began to drift to the weak type of conjugation (e.g., *buʒen*, *greten*, 'weep', *crepen*, 'creep'), or died out (e.g., *beden*, 'order', *unlouken*, 'open'). The disintegration of the class leaves many verbs isolated and subject to fluctuation in later centuries, but that disintegration must be placed in IV.

Class III, as it is traditionally called, has a larger membership, but its identity really belongs to the pre-English phase of its development. In English its unity has always been fragmented. Type III a(i), whose stem ends in a nasal plus another consonant, has the vowel-series *i* /ɪ/, E *a* /a/ but W *o* /ɔ/, *u* /ʊ/, as in *drinken*, *drank* (*dronk*), *drunken*, (*y-*)*drunken*. As other rather common verbs ([*bi-*]*ginnen*, *ringen*, *schrinken*, *singen*, *springen*, *stinken*; also in IV [*y-*]*limpen*, 'happen', *swyngen*, *swinken*, *wynnen*, *rinnen*, 'run') followed the same pattern the type was well preserved, and today is the only close rival of class I. Generally, the latter part of the period witnesses a tendency to extend the vowel of the past singular into the whole of the past, but in the past and participle forms there has been much divided usage to this day. Several verbs of the type have a stem ending in *-nd*, and those tended to have a lengthened vowel in the past singular, and thus to form a transition to Type IIIa(ii), which was characterised by a lengthened vowel in all positions. This lengthening had arisen during OE (cf. §189) and had continued the disruption of the class. However, the verbs with lengthening were fairly common ones, and the type maintained itself well in period IV, and for the most part later. The verbs involved are *finden* (*fand*, W and later S and Mid *fond*, *funden*, [*y-*]*funden*) *grinden*, *winden*, *climben*. Levelling has generally been in favour of the past plural-participle type, except in *climb* (early NE *clomb*), which eventually went over to the weak type.

Type IIIb had a stem ending in a liquid (*l* or *r*), and this difference of stem-formation had resulted in a highly divergent development even in OE. The vowel series in 1170 was *e* /ɛ/, *a* /a/, *u* /ʊ/, *o* /ɔ/, as in *helpen*, *halp*, *holpen*, (*y-*)*holpen*. Most verbs of the type, such as *berȝen*, 'protect', *werpen*, 'throw', *werþen*, 'become', did not survive the period at all, and those that did, such as *helpen*, *bresten*, 'burst, break', *ȝelden*, 'give, yield', *sterven*, 'die', developed irregularities and then progressively went over to weak conjugation. On the other hand, Type IIIc, a one-member class, with a stem ending in *-ȝt*, and the vowel-series *i*, *au*, *ou*, was able to maintain itself owing to the high frequency of occurrence of its sole member, *fight*. We know from dialects that it tended to go over to class I (*fit*), but in Standard it has levelled the vowel of the past singular and so survived.

Class IVa consisted of verbs whose stem ended in a single consonant, usually a liquid (*l* or *r*), and its vowel-series was *e* /ɛː/, *a* /a/, *e* /eː/ in most areas but /ɛː/ in others, *o* /ɔ/ but later /ɔː/, as in *stelen*, *stal*, *stelen*, (*y-*)*stolen*, and similarly *beren*, *teren*, *helen*, 'conceal'. Though few, these verbs were common, and the type was strong enough to attract into itself a number of verbs, with similar infinitive-forms, originally belonging to class V, e.g., *breken*, *speken*, *treden*, *wreken*, *weven*. The PE reflexes show how well class IV, thus strengthened, has maintained itself. The vowel of the second participle begins during our period to move first into the past plural, then into the singular, so that an *e/o* alternation is the mark of surviving class IV verbs. A number of subsequent changes have, however, disturbed the regularity of the correspondences. Moreover, in Scandinavian areas the *a*, /ɑː/ vowel of the Norse cognates tended to invade the past, as in *iafen*, 'gave', and this has sometimes provided the form standardised in PE.

Type IVb is a very small group, fragmented already in OE, of verbs of similar origin, but having a stem ending in a nasal instead of a liquid. One, *nimen*, 'take', had the forms (unsupported by any analogy) *nom(en)*, *(y-)numen*, and in period IV found itself at a disadvantage with its synonymous rival, the Scandinavian loan *taken*; it survived into NE, living longest as a term of thieves' cant. The other is similar except in the vowel of the infinitive grade, *cumen*; this begins to be invaded, like *give*, by the Scandinavian form of the past grade of vowel, and in that form is regular throughout NE.

Class Va was closely related to IVa. It had a stem ending in a single consonant other than a liquid or a nasal, and its vowel series was the same except in the participle, which had *e*, /ɛ/. An example is *meten*, 'measure', *mat*, *meten*, *(y-)meten*. By losses to IV or to the weak verbs, or the extinction of certain of its members, this class is lost almost without trace by the end of our period, though *eat/ate* preserves its memory. A class with much smaller membership, Vb, had *i*, /ɪ/ in the infinitive, and a long consonant closing its infinitive stem, as in *bidden*, *bad*, *beden*, *(y-)beden*, also, as in class IV, *(y-)boden*; *bid*, *sit*, and in an indirect way, *lie* ('be recumbent'), have preserved the class in PE. The divergences characteristic of *lie* were carried even more marked in *sen*, 'see', which varied widely according to dialect. Historically it belongs to class V, but descriptively, at every period in the history of English it needs to be treated as a one-member class.

Class VIa had the vowel-series *a* /a/, *o* /oː/, *o* /oː/, *a* /a/ (both *a* components had lengthened by the end of the period). It was, and is, quite a secure type (though later developments have obscured its original regular patterning). *Forsaken, schaken, schapen, waken, waxen, draʒen* (later *drawen*), *laʒen* (later *laughen*) belonged to it. Some of its members have gone over to the weak type since, but none have been lost altogether. A very ancient variant is the type with infixed -*n*- in the present, *standen* (which for quite other reasons is also eligible for lengthening of *a*). Class VIb had *e* in the present [combined in the S, as it had been in OE, with other differences of present stem formation (cf. § 131)]. In period IV *sweren, heven*, 'heave, raise' etc., belonged to VIa, but only the first has lasted into PE. *Slen*, /slɛːn/, was of similar origin, with consonant alternation of which we see a reflex in PE *slay, slew, slain.*

There remains a class of verbs conventionally identified as VII. These are put together because of a similar origin in pre-English usage, where they were all verbs with reduplicating pasts. This principle of unity left almost no traces in OE, and for that stage of the language we would not descriptively class them together. However, they do have some semblance of adventitious unity in ME, since those that survived did so by grouping into related types. We can recognise an *o/e* variety, as in *blowen, blew* (also *growen, knowen, throwen, mowen, sowen*). Others, diverse in their infinitives, were alike in having a past in *e*, /eː/ (sometimes raised to *i*, /iː/), e.g., *hewen, fallen, leten, halden* (later S and Mid *holden*), *fon*, 'seize' (also *fangen*), *hon*, 'hang' (also *hangen*), *lepen, hoten*, 'call, command', *wepen, dreden*. But the unity of the class was naturally frail, and many of these verbs had alternative weak forms as early as period IV.

§ 155 A verb pattern not new in this period, but assuming in it a function which was to grow into one of the most characteristic features of NE syntax, is the durative-periphrastic with forms of *be* + first part. Such patterns were used in OE, part as calques of Latin (cf. §193). But the aspectual contrast they now realise was then carried by a difference of form in the verb itself: simple verbs were inherently durative, derived ones, especially those formed with the prefix *ge-*, ME *y-, i-*, were perfective or determinate – at any rate, non-durative. The decline of the old system belongs to Chapter VI (cf. §193); we may note the preservation of the old prefix, especially in the S, as a ME sign of the second ('perfective') participle. But, as we have seen, the old prefixal system generally declined (cf. §113); early in our period the S may keep aspectual contrast (it is found, for example, in the Essex *Poema Morale, c.* 1200), but in general the language has lost the capacity to make this grammatical contrast by grammatical means. At this point the formerly rather artificial patterns of periphrastic formation are taken up in genuine English usage, and become optional markers of durative aspect. In the 13c the new usage is characteristic of the SE, but towards the end of the century, when texts are available from the N, it is well established there. In the 14c it is in general use all over the country (the W Mid keep a low rate of use), but the evidence is mainly poetic, and the periphrastic forms have never been (still are not) widely used in poetry. The first participles used in these forms (PF) are variable according to locality, but will eventually settle as -*ing* everywhere. Closely connected with the rise of the PF is that of -*ing*, as a verbal form ranging in function from participle to gerund; it too takes its rise during the 13 and 14cc, and becomes one of the outstanding peculiarities of NE. The distinctive forms and functions of the type *I am/was coming*, though they have traceable antecedents, really exist as *signes* from period IV; in this period, too, we find extensions of the PF into modal and passive constructions, though such uses remain infrequent until NE.

§ 156 In the long run the morphological developments we have studied prepared the way for syntactic changes. To a large extent morphological decline came first, inflectional contrasts fading with an ease that showed they had no real function. We may guess that this laying bare of the real articulation of the grammar came first in the N because of its long exposure to bilingualism. Those of us who have tried, as adults, to fit into a new language-community know that in such circumstances one does not retain any more of the morphology of the new language than is strictly necessary to make oneself understood. Where a community is unilingual, old patterns remain from inertia, regardless of their functional obsolescence. In this indirect way, far more than through direct syntactic borrowing, the presence of a Scandinavian community affected the syntax of English.

No detailed study of the developing positional syntax of this period has yet appeared. It seems clear that all the patterns known in the 10c can still be found in IV, and even early III, but the shifts of frequency are very marked. By the end of the period, in unmarked positive affirmative independent clauses the factor of first importance is that subject-finite verb should form a cluster in that order, but this factor is not yet so dominant as to cause the re-structuring of sentences, as it would in later centuries (cf. §123). There are no important developments of negative and interrogative patterning. In dependent clauses an older order, with finite verb in final position, exists side by side with a new one in which there is no order-difference between independent and dependent clauses. In short, many things are possible, but we lack detailed knowledge.

CHAPTER V

1170 – 970

§ 157   In 970 England was a divided country. The Danelaw (cf. § 132) together with substantial parts of north Lancashire, Westmorland and Cumberland, was settled largely by Scandinavians, and predominantly Scandinavian in speech (other parts of Cumberland spoke a Celtic language, Cumbric). The Scandinavian settlements were about a century old, and had been preceded by almost a century of viking raids, but during all that time links with Scandinavia had not been broken. Fresh waves of raiders or settlers poured into the country, and those already settled sided sometimes with them, sometimes with the English. These Scandinavians did not (except with runes, cf. § 217) write their own language; if they became literate it was in English. Our knowledge of them as a speech-community is therefore inferential, but certain points are clear. Those of the E were predominantly Danes, those of the W predominantly Norwegians (usually coming indirectly, from Ireland, the Isle of Man or western Scotland, rather than directly from Norway). Danish and Norwegian were not widely separated linguistically at that date, nor would either have been mutually incomprehensible with English. Our evidence on this is literary, but it is strong and inherently plausible. At the time when the English migrated to England the Danes were their close neighbours and they must have spoken much alike. At the time of the early Scandinavian settlements in England the period of separation had only been slightly longer than between British and American English today, and the two communities had been in touch with one another for much of the time. Once the Scandinavian settlements began, one might expect movements of convergence rather than divergence.

Politically, the English and Danish groups were united by the accession of Cnut in 1016, but after his death in 1035 further hostilities arose – not simply on an English–Danish alignment but also among the English. It was while dealing with these troubles at the Battle of Stamford Bridge in 1066 that King Harold received news of the landing of Duke William. William the Bastard entered England not simply to plunder, but at least in part to claim what he had some reason to think was his due. His victory resulted, where an English one might not have done, in the reunification of England. This was above all because the Normans, unlike the English, were castle-builders, and that art made those possessed of it in the 11c virtually invincible. The tranquillity and unity imposed by Norman rule were not the first the kingdom of England had known, nor were they unbroken; but at least the Norman Conquest seems to have stopped the inroads of the other vikings, and to some extent to have kept the established population under control.

At first William left the native judiciary and administration untouched, but within three years continued disturbances convinced him that a nation-wide show of Norman power was needed. This, combined with the need to reward his helpers in the invasion with grants of land, resulted in the establishment of a Norman land-owning aristocracy throughout the country. Bishoprics and major abbacies were treated in the same way. By the time of William's death in 1087 the native secular and Church leaders were largely dispossessed. The consequences of this for the English language have been sufficiently considered in Chapter IV.

Four speech-communities have to be distinguished. That longest established is the Celtic. The far north-west was brought under English rule in 1092, but it would be foolish to assume that all use of Cumbric immediately ceased; it would, however, tend to recede, as did Celtic speech along the Welsh and Scottish borders. The Scandinavian-speaking community was increasingly cut off from its countries of origin, and progressively became assimilated to the wider community of English-speakers. The French-speaking aristocracy looked towards Europe, where many of its members held land and spent much time; they had as yet no reason to feel that their interest lay with the community of their new country. The English were, in geographical and social space, hemmed in by the other three.

While it is important to appreciate these limitations in size and importance, we must not assume a parallel between externals and cultural standing. In the years immediately following 970 the parts of England where English was regularly and generally spoken constituted a tiny community of high culture. It was currently producing a magnificent prose literature, and works of high scolarship in both English and Latin. Both lay and religious patrons were having collected and recorded the ancient vernacular poetic literature, much of which had been handed down for centuries in oral, and partly in written, tradition. The first stirrings of drama in Europe since the degradation of the theatre in post-Classical Rome were going on in England. There was a written standard language current throughout the community. There was a great school of manuscript illuminators, and one of embroidery (whose main surviving monument is the so-called Bayeux tapestry). Anglo-Saxon civilisation was not at its highest peak in the late 10c and early 11c, but it doubtfully had any contemporary superiors in the Western world. To this shrinking and beleaguered, but civilised, community, came, in 1066, that fresh wave of barbarian vikings, the Normans. How they destroyed English culture we have seen – not of deliberate intent (as medieval Englishmen were neurotically inclined to suppose), but as an accidental by-product of other activities. It is perfectly true that when Central French influence came to the depressed English of the post-Conquest era it came as a higher culture to a lower, and it is perfectly true that the English were oriented towards Europe because of their experience of Norman rule; but we must not transfer these truths back to the 11c situation, or think of the Normans as a kind of Frenchman, and therefore civilised. They were a kind of viking, and therefore (except in military architecture) barbaric. Culturally, period V is broken-backed; 1066 marks the division between an age that, if not Golden, is Silver, and one that if not Dark, is Twilight. These changes are vividly reflected in the kinds of English used, and the kinds of evidence we have about them.

§ 158   The written standard language of the late 10c was derived from the practices of West Saxon scholarship a century earlier. How this standard arose, and came to be diffused throughout the country will therefore be a subject for Chapter VI. After the Norman Conquest the major scriptoria pass out of English control, and the kind of document for which a standard language is used largely ceases to be written in English. Yet continuity can be traced. In the west, in such centres as Winchester, Worcester and Lichfield, the tradition of this writing was actively maintained. And when in the 13c new works are produced in English from this same westerly area, their line of descent, in language and style, is perfectly clear. Very occasionally a scriptorium in the east would be under sufficiently enlightened direction for the tradition to persist there. The outstanding example is Peterborough, with its Chronicle kept up till 1154 (cf. § 133).

We move in this period from a phase of westerly-based standardisation to one without standardisation. Except for regional movements flourishing and dying out, we reach a time when all local dialects are on a par. At the close of the 14c, as we have seen, the return to standardisation is based on the usage of quite different parts of the country. In the 10c the language we have most fully recorded is not that which will later be the norm. In treating of the intervening period it is therefore necessary to try to see through the veil of standardisation in the early records, and to bridge the gaps in the later ones, in an attempt to provide some sketch of English in all parts of the country. This is our best hope for relating an obscure period to what goes before and after it.

§ 159 In 970 the mode of writing English was that established by Christian missionaries nearly four centuries earlier, with minor modifications to the alphabet. By 1170 the first, though not yet the complete, impact of Norman-French modes of spelling had been felt (cf. § 128). At the beginning of our period twenty-three symbols were in regular use, *a, æ, b, c, d, ð, e, f, ȝ, h, i, l, m, n, o, p, r, s, t, þ, u, ƿ, y; k, x, z,* were rare and none of these three had a distinct function. Of this repertoire *æ* and *ð* had almost dropped out by 1170, but others had come in.

However, the number of phonemes in the language was considerably greater than twenty-three; a consistently phonemic use of the letters was not possible. Nevertheless, spelling, especially in stressed syllables, was highly systematic, and to a considerable extent its phonemic and phonetic implications can be recovered.

We can most practically take as our starting-point for analysing the graphemes of late OE the use of WS in stressed syllables. The pure vowels offer few problems. There are two parallel series, long and short, and members of the series are felt to be correlated. Thus the symbol *i* represents a long vowel /iː/ in such words as *līf, mīn, drīfan* (PE *life, mine, drive*), and a corresponding short vowel in *scip, bringan* (*ship, bring*). We do not know whether this was phonetically /i/ or the lowered, slack /ɪ/ that has been current since at least later ME. There is no direct evidence when the qualitative difference between long and short generally made its appearance, or why. Since speakers in the OE period seem to have perceived the long–short pairs in quantitative terms it is usual to regard that as the only difference. For the most part we can avoid transcribing (and thus committing ourselves on unsolved problems); OE spelling, supplemented by diacritics generally used amongst editors, conveys all that is needed.

Coming down the series of front vowels, the next item is written *e,* and is taken to represent /eː/ when long, as in *gēs, mētan* ('geese, meet'), and a corresponding short vowel (whether /e/ or /ɛ/ we do not know), in *helm, west.*

The letter *æ* represents a long, low, slack front vowel /æː/ in *dǣlan,*

285

tæcan ('share [deal], teach'), and a corresponding short one (/æ/) in *sæt, mæsse* ('sat, mass'). In its long form it is in phonemic contrast with the back vowel written *a*, /ɑ:/, as in *bāt, stān* ('boat, stone'). In its short form it has a corresponding back vowel, /a/, as in *faran, daʒas* ('go, [fare], days'). Are short *æ* and *a* to be regarded as separate phonemes? In origin they were allophones of one phoneme, *a* occurring before a back vowel in the next syllable, and *æ* elsewhere; in the late OE of our period *æ* sometimes occurs analogically in *a* positions, but as neither earlier nor later were they separate phonemes it seems best to regard *a* as merely a conditioned variant throughout. There is, however, another problem about the phonemic analysis of the short low back vowels. The letter *o* represents /o:/ when long, as in *sōð, mōna* ('truth, [sooth], moon'), and a short sound (/o/, /ɔ/ or /ɒ/) in *on, open*. But *o* is also used in alternation with *a* in environments where an original short /a/ occurred before a nasal consonant, as in *mann, lang* ('man, long'). It seems likely that the sound in question must have been nasalised /ã/, and that those who devised the writing system were uncertain whether to interpret it as /a/ or /o/. By the late OE period we are here concerned with the most likely situation is that in the E the sound, even if phonetically distinct, was treated as a member of the *a*-phoneme (which is no other than the *æ*-phoneme), while in the W it had fallen together with /o/. However mixed the written evidence, and however intermediate the phonetic quality, we cannot speak of this sound as having been phonemically in no man's land.

The letter *u* represents a high back tense vowel, /u:/ when long, as in *hūs, tūn* ('house, farm town'), and a corresponding short vowel (/u/ or /ʊ/) in *sunu, cuman* ('son, come'). Finally, there is a central or even front rounded vowel, spelt *y*, long /y:/ in *fȳr, brȳd* ('fire, bride') and short in *cyning, pytt* ('king, pit').

Thus we have under the qualitative series, *i, e, æ, o, u, y*, six pairs differentiated by length, with an additional long vowel *a*, whose short partner is present phonetically if not phonemically. OE script does not distinguish length differences (except very occasionally). Our knowledge of length-differences derives from comparative study and from analysis of verse; but our belief that quantity is meaningful in verse depends on reconstruction. The knowledge is therefore inferential – in most cases quite certain, though sometimes, especially where there is a change, the evidence for a particular form at a particular time is inadequate. Our biggest uncertainty in the material studied so far relates to the quality of short vowels.

§ 160 The simple vowels have already stretched the resources of the Latin alphabet, but there was more to cope with. OE had, at the time of its first writing, and still in 970, a series of diphthongs treated as part of the long vowel system. In WS at this date there were only two, *eo*, as *bēon, frēosan* ('be, freeze') and *ēa*, as in *ēac, frēas* ('also [eke], froze'). These are normally falling diphthongs (i.e., the stress is on the first element); though there has been doubt about the details of the phonetic value, it seems fairly safe to regard *ēo* as ǀ*e* + *o* and *ēa* as a simplified writing for ǀ*æ* + *a*. In both cases the second element would be weakening by, or soon after 970, and moving towards /ə/, so that the important distinction is between the first elements, lower and slacker in *ēa* than in *ēo*.

The solution in this case, then, to the shortage of vocalic symbols, was the use of digraphs. Similar digraphs are also used in other circumstances, and this leads to difficulties of interpretation. For instance, there are also not enough consonant symbols to go round, and a vowel letter is sometimes used as a diacritic of consonant value; to distinguish, say, *c* = /k/ in *cuman* from *c* = /tʃ/ in *tæcan* the scribe may write *tæcean*, in which *e* does not have vocalic value at all (cf. *u* in later *guest*). If that were all, reconstruction and reading would not be too difficult. Unfortunately, there is a third class of digraph uses, and there has been considerable dispute as to whether they belong to the diphthong-type or the diacritic type. These are digraphs used for what historically correspond to short front vowels occurring before certain consonants of back quality. Do *ea* and *eo* then indicate the development of a glide between a front vowel and a back consonant, or are they merely a reminder to the reader of how to pronounce the consonant? And if they do indicate a glide, have we a phonetic variant of *æ*, *e*, or a pair of separate phonemes? I shall take the view that they do represent a glide (i.e., that we have short diphthongs *ea*, *eo*), and that for most parts of the country there is no point in asking whether these diphthongs were phonemically distinct. Examples are *earm*, *healf* ('wretched, half'), *eorðu, beorn* ('earth, warrior').

In late WS, therefore, we have identified fifteen to seventeen vowel phonemes, to which we must add one confined to unstressed syllables, written with a variety of letters, usually *a, o, u, e*, namely /ə/. This is a system of the order of size English has generally had. And although the history of vowels in stressed and unstressed syllables continues to be markedly different, this is near the end, in our retrograde course, of the need to identify a special vowel /ə/ for unstressed syllables.

§ 161 Consonants in OE are written to be pronounced (this is another reason why for general purposes transcription can be avoided). *P, t, b, d,* have the same values as in PE (except that they are always to be read if present, thus *lamb* = /lamb/ not /læm/). The symbol for the /w/ sound is *þ*. *L, m, n* have their present values, but when they occur with syllabic value they are written alone, thus *æpl* = /æpl/ as in PE *apple*. *R* is to be pronounced wherever it is written; it constitutes a single phoneme, with conditioned variants, probably tongue-trilled before vowels and retroflex elsewhere. Fricatives did not have phonetically-contrasted voiced–voiceless series, but were voiceless in initial and final position, voiced medially. Being sub-phonemic, the difference was not represented in spelling; *s, f,* are therefore to be read /s/, /f/, initially and finally, but /z/, /v/, medially, thus *stānas*, 'stones', /stɑːnəs/, but *frēosan*, 'freeze', /freozən/, *fīf*, 'five', /fiːf/, but *lifde*, 'lived', /livdə/. The same difference of distribution affected the /θ/ : /ð/ pair, but in this case either spelling may be used with either value, as in *þis, ðis*, /θis/, *āþ, āð*, 'oath', /ɑːθ/, but *ōþer, ōðer*, 'second, other', /oːðər/.

As we know from the innovations ME scribes found necessary (cf. § 128) the group least suited by the Latin alphabet is that loosely called palatal. There is a phoneme /k/, usually represented by *c* (rarely *k*), occurring often near back vowels, and always (as against /tʃ/) before consonants, as in *corn, weorc, cnēo* ('corn, work/deed, knee'), and one /tʃ/, also spelt *c*, often found near front vowels, as in *cirice, cȳse* ('church, cheese'). As we have noted (cf. § 128) a following front vowel may be used as a diacritic of the quality of *c*, especially in environments where it might be ambiguous. Speakers of modern English can almost invariably by guided by whether PE has /k/ (or zero), or /tʃ/, but for beginning readers the modern editorial device of marking *c* = /tʃ/ with a dot, *ċ*, is useful. Remember, however, that the dot is not found in MSS. The combination *sċ* has the value /ʃ/, as in *sċip, sċeal* (ship, shall' – the pronunciation of the modern counterpart can safely be used, though the vowel quality may not be quite right in *ship*). *C* also occurs in a digraph *cȝ*, but this digraph represents a variety of original voiced palatal, and will be treated below.

In 970 the only symbol available for the voiced palatals was *ȝ* (called 'yogh' or 'open g'). In the neighbourhood of back vowels initially, and of consonants more generally, it is to be pronounced /g/, as in *gōd*, 'good', /goːd/, *hrinȝ*, 'ring', /hriŋg/, *ȝnornian*, 'lament', /gnorniən/ (it is the uses before and after consonants that are liable to trip modern readers; note, too, in this connection that /ŋ/ only occurs before palatal stops, and is therefore a conditioned variant, not a phoneme). Elsewhere in a back environment ȝ is /ɤ/, as in *laȝu*, 'law', /laɤu/, *draȝan*, 'draw', /draɤən/. Generally in a front environment it is /j/, in which case it may be given a front vowel as diacritic, *i* more often than *e*, as in *ȝyfan*, 'give', /jyvən/, *dæȝ*, 'day', /dæj/, *heriȝean*, 'praise', /herijən/. Unfortunately, as the examples show, it is not so easy to read back the /g/:/j/ distinction from modern practice, so the editorial device of using ȝ when the symbol = /j/ is especially helpful. In the combination *cȝ*, which has the value of a long consonant, the sound is /dʒ/, as in *ecȝ*, *hycȝ(e)an*, 'edge/sword, think'; this sound did not occur initially until French loans introduced it.

/h/, written *h*, is a single phoneme, with approximately its modern value when used initially (but it is always to be pronounced), and the value [χ] medially and finally, as in *hand*, *dohtor*, *cniht*, 'hand, daughter, boy, [knight]', /hand, doχtər, kniχt/; note that [χ] is front or back in quality (as in German *ich*, *ach*) according to the preceding vowel. *H* also occurs in digraphs before consonant letters, *l*, *r*, *n*, *w*, as in *hlāf*, 'bread [loaf]', *hring*, *hnutu*, 'nut', *hwilc*, 'which'. There has been some doubt whether in this case it is to be pronounced as a separate consonant or is a diacritic of voicelessness in the following consonant; by 970 the diacritic interpretation is the more likely, though originally there must have been a consonant-sequence.

This yields a system of from fifteen to nineteen consonant-phonemes. But just as there is a difficulty about establishing certain details of the long–short series among the vowels, so with the consonants. For in 970, as we have already implied, English had long and short consonants, the long ones being written in the simplest cases by doubling the symbol for the short, thus *cwelan*, 'die', /kwelən/, *cwellan*, 'kill', /kwellən/. This is again difficult for speakers of PE to remember, but as the example shows, it is a matter of some moment. We might be inclined to ask whether a long consonant counts as a different phoneme from a short one, or as a sequence of two phonemes. There are indications in both directions, and there was probably no clear-cut structural feeling on the question. A complication is that long consonants do not always have short ones corresponding to them. For instance, as we have seen, there is no medial [s], but there is a medial *ss*, *hyssa*, 'of the young men'; we have already noted /dʒ/ as a long sound with no short 'partner'. Another class of uncertainty arises with consonant-clusters opened by *s-*, which poets may require to alliterate on the same cluster, not just on *s-*, as if somehow the cluster functioned as a single unit; this is to be related to the uncertainty in ME about whether *-st*, *-sk* are a consonant or a cluster in cases of possible shortening (cf. § 181). There is no simple solution to the problem of interpreting the OE long consonants; they are distinctive, but there are difficulties about treating them as segmental phonemes. Such difficulties are usually evidence of a system in transition, and this is probably no exception. The concept we need to handle our evidence is that of a phonemic time-unit or *mora*; distinctiveness at the lexical level may be carried by one or more such units.

§ 162 Stress-accent, as at all periods, was placed on the root-syllable, but in practice this principle has a different meaning in 970 than in later centuries. This is because the proportion of loanwords was very much lower, and the rule therefore applied to almost the whole vocabulary. Prefix formations were an exception, but then only if they were verbal, not nominal (as in ˈæfþunca, 'cause of offence', ofˈþyncan, 'displease'). Since the language is also relatively highly inflected it will have a strongly falling pattern overall, which has been less general in later English because of the increase in pre-posed weak particles. With this pattern, however, goes a general rhythmical structure which has undergone little, if any, change.

There was a secondary stress on the second element of compounds (possibly elsewhere); we may well suppose that in sequences of unstressed syllables there was, as there has been later, a sub-phonemic alternation of stronger and weaker.

As in later periods secondary-stressed syllables had the same vowel-system as stressed ones, though we may suppose that the quality was a little less strongly marked. Unstressed syllables had an alternation of much simpler type. Just before our period began, vowels in unstressed syllables had largely been reduced to a two-term system, one term representing former front vowels, the other all back vowels, but this was on the way to being reduced to the single item /ə/, representing former front and back vowels. For late 10c transcription I have assumed this further stage of levelling, though it may only have obtained in rather informal speech. In very restricted environments there was also an unstressed /ɪ/, surviving only where development of the vowel and loss of stress were of recent origin, as in *hāliʒ*, 'holy'. The levelling of vowels in unstressed syllables meant that distinctions of spelling which had had phonological (even grammatical) meaning when the writing of the language was standardised a century earlier were now meaningless. Careful writers make distinctions that others ignore – indeed, this is our most important evidence for assuming that levelling has taken place. Readers must therefore beware of reading late OE texts as if the phonological distinctions implied by letters in stressed syllables could be carried over into all uses. Not only the phonology, but also the orthography, has at this date a distinct system for the two types of syllable.

§ 163 Dialectally, variation in 970 is most noticeable among stressed vowels; in unstressed positions, though its form is phonological, its function is often morphological, and it can best be treated under grammar.

What in WS appears as $\breve{y}$ is of two distinct origins. In the SE ('Kentish') the corresponding sound is always $\breve{e}$, as in *mȳs/mēs*, 'mice', *pytt/pett*, 'pit', *cȳse/cēse*, 'cheese', *ȝyfan/ȝefan*, 'give'. In the rest of the non-WS area we generally find *ī* for words of the *mȳs/pytt* type, $\breve{e}$ for those of the *cȳse/ȝyfan* type. In other words, differences familiar from ME dialects are already, on this point, in existence. The ways of representing them orthographically are different – first because the symbol $\breve{y}$ now represents a distinct phoneme, whereas later it was a spelling-variant of *ī*, while *u* took over its phonemic role; secondly because the influence of standard WS writing is so strong that dialect variations are often not directly shown in writing. We are at least as likely to find *y* spellings in 'Kent' as *e* spellings. But more than this. If a Kentish trainee scribe finds his models using *y* and *e*, for all he can see indifferently, for what to him is a single sound, he will start following the same practice, and vary *e*'s with *y*'s, regardless of the origin of the sound, which naturally he does not know. In other words, inverted spellings, e.g., *y* for *e* in districts suspected to be *y*-less, are as revealing as direct *e* for *y* spellings. The differences of $\breve{æ}/\breve{e}$ distribution found in ME also exist at this period, and indeed may well go back to the period of the settlement of England. The WS diphthong *ēo* represents a conflation of two formerly distinct diphthongs, *īo* and *ēo*, which tend to be kept apart elsewhere, but with many differences of detail; by late OE the second element was weakening everywhere, and there is some evidence in both 'Kt' and Northumbria that it had become *a* in both diphthongs. The most widespread, and the most controversial, differences relate to the 'short diphthongs'; even those who agree that short diphthongs exist may dispute the precise value of the corresponding sounds from dialect to dialect. Since the detail of variation is confusing, and rarely has any reflection in later English, only one feature need concern us. WS and 'Kt' *ea* before certain consonant clusters correspond to *a* in the Mid and N (whose dialect is known jointly in relation to OE times as Anglian). Early in the 10c the sounds had lengthened before the clusters in question, to *ēa* and *ā* respectively, and the new *ā* was in existence when the S and Mid rounded *ā* to /ɔː/. In ME and after, words of this vocalism have therefore shown very different developments in later English – S /ɛː/, with a PE reflex /iː/, Mid /ɔː/ with a PE reflex /əʊ/, and far north /aː/ with later reflex (not in Standard) /eɪ/. So strong is the Mid character of NE Standard that in all common words we have the *o* reflex, as in *healdan/ haldan*, 'hold', *beald/bald*, 'bold', but in a place-name of local character we have the Kent-Sussex *Weald*, but the *Cots-* and Yorkshire *wolds* (cf. § 212).

As far as consonants are concerned, the main feature differentiates the N from the Mid and S. Instead of the affricate values /tʃ/, /dʒ/ the N retained the older distinction by which front and back *c* and *cʒ* were both stops, differing only as do front and back /k/, /g/, in English *keen, cool, give, good*. The front–back pairs should be regarded as each constituting one phoneme.

§ 164 Between 970 and 1170 changes in the vowels of stressed syllables were less important than those in unstressed syllables. But to this period we must assign S and Mid rounding of /aː/ to /ɔː/ (cf. § 130), which must follow lengthening before consonant groups (OE *căld* > NE *cold*) and precede the introduction of French loanwords (cf. § 134), although it is slow to be reflected in spelling. Somewhere here belongs the apparent retraction of *æ* to *a*, in all words (and areas) that had it, giving, for example, *was, sat* for earlier *wæs, sæt*; we find one form in late OE, another in early ME, but we cannot date the change more narrowly, and some would question whether there is a change or merely a simplification of spelling convention. At any rate, the letter *æ* does drop out in ME; the fact that it is replaced in its short value by *a* and in its long value by *e(a)* suggests that more than a spelling change is involved.

The biggest qualitative change is the almost total loss of the OE diphthongal system. We have already referred to the weakening of the second (i.e., unstressed) elements of diphthongs (cf. § 160); somewhere between late OE and early ME this process was completed, and everywhere except in 'Kent' monophthongs result. For *ēo* the smoothing is generally to *ē*, but in the SW the *eo* spelling remains, with value /ö(ː)/ (cf. § 130, p. 234; on the 'Kentish' development, ib, p. 233). Thus, a pair of distinct phonemes is retained in the S (though the forms are very different in the SE and the SW) which in the rest of the country is levelled under /e(ː)/; PE development is always from the *e*-type, as in *bēon, leornere* ('be, learner'). Short *ea* smoothes to *æ* early enough to share in its retraction to *a*, as in *earm*, 'wretched', ME *arm*. Long *ēa* also smoothes to *ǣ*, though the spelling is often retained, as in *chē(a)s*, 'chose'; in 'Kent', however (where there was no *ǣ*), it became a diphthong, probably rising in quality (cf. § 130).

Certain quantitative developments appear as tendencies which may become active at almost any time, rather than as sound-changes that can be precisely dated. The preference for a short vowel before consonant-clusters (except in special circumstances, cf. § 189) may have been active just before this period, and certainly continued to be so. The general pattern was that two or more consonants following a vowel would inhibit lengthening or cause shortening. One might suppose that once this tendency had come into force there would be nothing left for it to continue operating upon. But this was not so. Like later quantitative changes (cf. § 135) this tendency was disturbed, impeded or reversed in its effects, because they separated forms that speakers felt belonged together. For instance, the adjective *clǣne*, 'clean', would stay long, but the verb *clǣnsian* would shorten, the adjective *wīs*, 'wise', would stay long, but the noun *wisdom* would shorten. Shortening in *wisdom*, in fact, could be caused not only by the consonant-cluster, but because it was a compound. Similar shortening is found in *haliʒdæʒ*, 'holiday' but formally corresponding to the name 'Halliday', beside the simplex adjective *hāliʒ*. The double modern reflexes of *haliʒdæʒ* illustrate the tendency to re-lengthening on the analogy of related words. The modern surname reflects early shortening; but the compound was re-formed on the model of the simple form, stayed long during the change of /ɑː/ to /ɔː/ and has re-shortened, once again because it is a compound, at some later date.

A group of words showing successive shortening is that with OE *ǣ*. There are very many weak verbs with this vowel which will keep it in their present forms, but undergo shortening in the past, when a *-de* suffix is added; and there are many compounds, some of the best known being place-names in *strǣt*, which will stay long in the simple form and shorten in the compound. In all such cases, early shortening will give *æ* in time for the retraction of *æ* to *a*, thus *rǣdan*, 'read, advise', *radde*, *drǣdan*, 'dread', *dradde*, *strǣt*, *Stratford*. Speakers will then tend to restore a vowel to match their sense of the norm for a particular word, but later the same tendency to shortening catches it, after retraction has taken place. There is then no exactly corresponding short vowel, and instead of shortening in such a way as to create a new phoneme, the vowel fits into the nearest short phoneme, which by then is /e/, giving *redde, dredde, Stretford, Streatham,* etc. Therefore, in all dialects which originally had *ǣ*, shortening to *a* or *e* is respectively early and late shortening. Of course, the SE had no *ǣ* at all, and its shortening is to *e*, in all cases; the rest of the country had it in some, but not all, situations where WS had it. It is notable that in all common words PE has standardised the *e*-type.

One further point: as we have seen, what constitutes a consonant-cluster in OE is not always self-evident. Some speakers seem to have felt *-st* as one sound, others as a cluster; it may or may not cause shortening. In exactly parallel OE forms, *prēost* and *brēost* ('priest, breast') both developments can occur, and later usage will standardise one or other – in this case, one of each type.

Consonants undergo the usual simplifications of heavy groups, and developments of parasite sounds familiar at all periods. They do not, in stressed syllables, require special discussion.

§ 165   During this period grammar and the phonology of weak syllables are so interrelated that we must next consider morphology and syntax. In 970 the language as it is preserved in most writings shows elaborate morphological patterning, almost the same as that of 770, and differing in little more than superficialities from that of 570. Indeed, the account we are now to give will save the necessity of any detailed morphological description for the next two periods. Yet if we turn to writings not in the Standard language, we find in Northumbria a phase of grammatical development almost as far advanced towards modernity as the Standard language of the 15c. And by 1170 these developments are far advanced everywhere except in 'Kent'. The pace of change is extremely variable, but probably not so variable as the written record would suggest. Indeed, the fidelity with which 12c copies of 10c works preserve obsolete grammatical distinctions must serve to warn us against too literal an interpretation of standard spellings even in the 10c. Let us, without falsifying the written evidence, attempt to reconstruct the grammatical contrasts on which speakers really depended for daily communication.

The noun, in the late 10c, showed grammatical gender as far as its relations within the NP were concerned – that is, dependent words, such as adjectives and articles, had to fit one of three patterns of inflection, patterns to which modern grammarians give the names masculine, neuter, feminine. This was a covert patterning, that is to say, there was hardly ever anything in the form of the noun itself to indicate which pattern it would require from its concomitants. Where wider concord with pronouns was involved there was a mongrel system of natural and grammatical gender (cf. § 145).

In its overt patterning the noun is usually described as having four cases and two numbers. In practice, no nouns, and no dependent words in NPs, made any distinction between nominative and accusative plural, and few kinds of nouns, but more dependent words, made a distinction of nominative and accusative singular; none had more than three distinct forms in sg or pl, many had less. We can clearly see in the entire history of OE the weakness of the accusative that led to its absorption into the dative in ME. Historically, if we set out the paradigms of OE nouns, we find the number of declensions to be rather large. On the other hand, many distinctions between declensions are minimal in practice. The declensions varied widely in the case-number contrasts for which they had formal indices, and this tended to weaken the sense of any particular case-number form's identity. But since one declension often differed from another in only trivial respects the identity of each declension was also weakened. In other words, the system was ripe for change, for simplification and levelling.

The most basic distinction of declensional types was between weak nouns, which had a base-form ending in a vowel, and added an -n (partly with further modifications) in their inflected forms, and strong nouns, whose inflections were mainly vocalic. The weak nouns are also known as -n stems; they are not, as the weak verbs were, Germanic innovations, but are of IE origin (the parallel between L *homo, homin-*, OE *ʒuma*, *ʒuman*, words of the same origin and meaning, is self-evident). Weak nouns occur in all three genders. Strong nouns are also known as vocalic (a term which reflects their origins, rather than their form in OE); the main varieties were m and n *a*-stems (corresponding to L *-us*, *-um* declensions), and f *ō*-stems (corresponding to L *-a* feminines), *i*-stems (of all three genders, and corresponding to L *-is* nouns), and *u*-stems (originally of all three genders, but with only m and f surviving; they correspond to L fourth declension *-us* nouns). In addition there were many sub-varieties of these main types, and five minor declensions.

The details of the declensions are set out in any grammar of OE, but if we draw up a chart, necessarily simplified, of the main forms and variables, we shall see where the system worked well, and where it was ineffectual. This will help us to understand the directions of change. At the same time we must remember that the whole story is not told by the noun; the dependent words have a role of great importance.

		STRONG			WEAK		
	M(a)	N(a)	F(o)	MF(u)	M	N	F
Sg N	-(e)	-(e)	-(u)	-(u)	-a	-e	-e
A	-(e)	-(e)	-(e)	-(u)	-an	-e	-an
G	-(e)s	-(e)s	-e	-a	-an	-an	-an
D	-(e)	-(e)	-(e)	-a	-an	-an	-an
Pl NA	-as	-(u)	-a, -e	-a		-an	
G	-a	-a	-(en)a	-a		-ena	
D	-um	-um	-um	-um		-um	

The brackets here signify, as usual, that an element may or may not be present; but they do not have the same value as in ME paradigms (cf. § 142). For OE they almost invariably imply sub-classes of words, not variable usage among speakers. If we read the paradigm in this understanding, the first point to strike us will probably be the comparison between strong and weak types. The weak type is much more clear-cut in its forms, but those forms make extremely few distinctions; in particular, what we may call the base-form of the plural, the common NA form, is indistinguishable from the inflected cases of the singular. Since, in the absence of an effective NA distinction, number concord with the verb is an important way of distinguishing subject from object, this is an inefficient type of noun-declension. The only case-number form that is uniform across the board and distinct from anything else is the dative plural. Otherwise the strongest forms in 970, and the only ones that can maintain themselves phonologically as weak vowels reduce in the coming centuries, are the m and n Gsg in -(e)s and the m NApl in -as; the vocalic distinction between these two has already been pretty well obliterated, and will shortly be completely lost, leaving /-(ə)s/ as the marked form in contrast with the base. The dative, though usually written as in the paradigm, usually lost its final lip closure and became /ən/; thereafter its history is connected with the progressive refinement of prepositions used to discriminate the various functions formerly lumped together under the dative; being redundant, it goes into decline. Now it is true that m *a*-stem nouns were a very common type, and that by 970 they had grown stronger by the virtual absorption of the *i*-stems, which previously differed from them only in using an -e plural in place of an -as plural. But the extent of the switch by 1170 to a noun-declension derived from that type, in which the central fact was the marking of Gsg and most plural forms by -s, is something more than can be accounted for by numerical frequency. The type spread because it worked; it made the distinctions that the grammar as a whole required to have made. It made them clearly and unambiguously, and did not blur the issue with a lot of unnecessary variants. While all areas kept minor types, generally the S retained two major types, strong and weak, distributing nouns of most types between them, the Mid and N kept only the strong major types.

At the same time, the transition to ME saw the establishment of a principal minor type, that with unchanged plural, while the other minor types were hardly more than 'irregular nouns'. The core of the unchanged plural class was the old neuter nouns, formerly with plurals in -(*u*), which in either form would give Ø in ME. But it will both demonstrate the sources of other unchanged plurals, and also show more clearly the dispersion of contrasts in the OE noun, if we spend a little time on the OE minor types. The first type is called the mutated declension, because in certain of its forms the stem-vowel changed [*mutated* (cf. §212)]. There were few words of this type, but they were common words, even more importantly, words coming early in the language-acquisition process, and those that had survived till 970 have mostly remained for the following thousand years. Not, however, with the full range of mutated forms they then had. The masculines were *fōt*, *tōþ*, *mann*, differing from *a*-stems only in the NApl, in which they change vowel and add no ending; all that has happened to them is the extension of the mutated form to all plural uses. The feminines were *gōs*, *mūs*, *cū*, *bōc*, *burg* and *sulh* ('plough'). The feminines have mutation and no inflection in the Gsg as well as the NApl; their rate of survival can be seen from the list, and in the survivors mutated forms are made a general sign of number-contrast, but removed from the domain of case-contrast. Another group has some affinities with this type, the *r*-stem nouns of relationship, *fæder*, *brōþor*, m, *mōdor*, *dohtor*, *sweostor*, f. These originally had no inflection for Gsg or NApl, but *fæder*, except in formulae, had largely gone over to the *a*-stem type, and the rest of the group were to follow suit. Their greatest peculiarity was that any pure back vowels fronted in the Dsg (thus, *brēþer*, *mēder*, *dehter*, but *fæder*, *sweostor* unchanged); since this pattern was not common to the whole group, or even in line with its gender distinctions, it had little chance of survival. But the greatest weakness was that it highlighted case-contrast above number-contrast, and the whole economy of the language was working in the opposite direction. Four *ð*-stems (e.g. *mōnað*, 'month') were beginning to go over to dominant types, -*s* plurals or unchanged plurals, and so were *nd*-stems (originally participles), such as *frēond* ('friend, one who loves'). A small group of neuters (original *as-/is-* stems; on

$s > z > r$ cf. §219) added -r- between stem and ending in the plural; of these *čild/čildru* proved durable, and *æ̃ȝ/æ̃ȝru* kept its -r- plural into early NE. Note that these two were so isolated in ME that their plural forms were felt to need reinforcing by a more usual form, whence the 'double plurals' in -n.

The same processes as operated in strong verbs (cf. §170) were at work among minor types of nouns. There were many lexical losses, and it may be that grammatical idiosyncrasy played a part in some of the losses. But to a very large extent the nouns that survived, their numbers swollen by the first influx of French loans, 'regularly' declined, followed in 1170 essentially the pattern they do today.

§ 166 The rules of order within the NP were already, and had been throughout OE, almost identical with those followed today (cf. §58). The rules about what had to be included were far less rigid. That is to say, the article, if present, stood first, except possibly for predeterminers, such as *eall*, 'all', but phrases without article were fairly common. By the end of the 10c prose used the definite article in much the same functions as we do today, but very much less consistently; in poetry both articles, then as now, were less frequent than in prose. Since both articles arose as special uses of forms which had other functions, there would come, during our period, to be differentiation of a strong (demonstrative or numeral) and weak (article) form (cf. §148, 151), but in 970 this differentiation has not begun, and functionally items may be ambiguous. What we may call the demonstrative article had full declension in three genders in the sg, three cases, with forms common to all genders, in the pl. It distinguished in the sg one more case than the noun, the instrumental used for means/agency/comparison and the like; almost everywhere else in the NP, functions of this case had been absorbed into the dative. In comparison with its ME counterpart (cf. §148) this paradigm will strike us by its regularity; the blurring of unstressed forms which was to come in the following centuries coincided with a period of dialectal fragmentation, and so had highly diversified results here, as in the personal pronouns.

SG	M	N	F	PL COMMON
N	sĕ	ðæt	sēo	ðā
A	ðone	ðæt	ðā	ðā
G	ðæs	ðæs	ðǣre	ðāra, ðǣra
D	ðǣm, ðām	ðǣm, ðām	ðǣre	ðǣm, ðām
I	ðȳ, ðon	ðȳ, ðon		

By contrast with the noun forms, this has a phonetically strong and regular differentiation of the grammatically contrasted forms; the point is particularly clear in relation to the masc Asg, which strong nouns never distinguish. On the other hand, the two forms with initial *s*- are anomalous, and as regularisation proceeds we should expect them to be lost – as by 1170 they very largely are. The frequency and uniformity of the contrasting forms protected them against losses as rapid as those in nouns, but in ME inflected forms are sporadic and mainly southern and westerly in distribution (cf. § 148).

Of the use of the demonstrative article it may be said that long stretches of late 10c, early 11c, prose may be read without any sense either that articles are missing or that they are oddly used; but at other times gaps will be felt, and no doubt they should be felt more often because some uses are really demonstratives rather than articles. Here is an example:

Ōsþold cyninȝ his   cymes fæȝnode, and hine ārþurðliċe onfēnȝ
O.   king   of his coming rejoiced and him honourably received

his folce   tō ðearfe, þæt heora ȝelēafa þurde āþend   eft   tō
his people to need   that their faith   might be turned again to

ȝode fram þām þiþersæċe þe   hī   tō ȝeþende þǣron.
God from that/the enmity which they to turned   were.

(Oswald [the] king [*or* King O.] rejoiced at his coming, and received him honourably for [the] need of his people so that their faith might be turned again to God from the?/that? hostility to which they had turned.)

If we look at a scrap of verse from the same decade (the closing one of the 10c) the sense of something missing is more marked:

Đā þǣr Byrhtnoþ onȝan   beornas trymian
Then there B.   began   warriors to encourage

rād and rǣdde,   rincum tǣhte
rode and counselled   warriors taught

hū hī   sċeoldon standan   and þone   stede healdan.
how they must   stand   and that/the place hold.

(Then B. there began to exhort [the] warriors, [he] rode and instructed [the] men how they must stand and hold the?/that? place.)

The definite article, so far as it existed, was not yet in clear, one-to-one contrast with an indefinite. As we saw in IV (cf. § 151) there were two forms, *ān* and *sum*, with different emphases. The *ān*-article evolves from a numeral, and in the late 10c it is still fairly unusual, in poetry unknown. Which is to say that when *ān* occurs it generally has a numerical meaning. Both are fully declined as adjectives. A short passage will illustrate some differences from later usage:

Ōsþold . . . bæd ðā   hēafod-menn þæt hī . . . him sumne lāreoþ
O.   bade the/those head-men   that they him a   teacher

senden. . . . Hī   sendon þā . . . sumne   ārþurðne bisċeop, Aidan
send.   They sent   then a (certain) reverend bishop, A.

ȝehāten. Sē þæs mæres lifes man.'
called.   ⎰That one was of noble life (a) man.
         ⎱Who

(O. asked the head-men that they should send him a teacher. Then they sent a certain reverend bishop, called A, who was a man of glorious life.)

In this passage the first *sumne* can only be translated as *some* teacher or other. The second may be *a* or *a certain*; it is now in principle particularised, and may mean, in its context, 'He wanted one and they sent him one', or, 'He wanted one, and the one they sent him was . . .'. In the final phrase, NE 'a man of glorious life' must have an article, but in OE it must not, because there is no idea of contrasting his oneness with any other possible number, nor his particularity with a class; it is a simple characterising phrase. Thus discussion of the rise of articles is bedevilled by complexities; by the making of one set of distinctions in OE and another set later. We may say that the indefinite article is beginning to develop, and that by 1170 *ān* will be overtaking *sum* in frequency; but the process is not one we can understand simply by counting examples. As late as the closing entry of the Peterborough Chronicle (1154-5) the functions of the indefinite are much as they were in OE; we have *in an ceste*, 'in a chest', but *he milde man was*, 'he was [a] mild man'.

The articles, then, are differentiated from ordinary adjectives mainly by their relatively fixed position and generalised meaning. They by no means function as markers of the onset of a NP, nor, indeed, will they fully come to do so during the medieval phase of English.

Finally, it must be said of the forms discussed here, and of all others which can be attributive within the NP, that as long as they remained highly inflected they were free to act as heads. Demonstratives, numerals, adjectives, are all really pronouns as well; the traditional labels do not imply the distinctions we are now familiar with. During ME, as the inflectional distinctions weakened, these uses struggled on, but grew ever less frequent, until in NE very stringent limits were placed on the operation of pre-modifiers as heads (cf. §86).

§ 167 Adjectives in 970 show the differential types of declension, strong and weak, whose syntactic functions were described at §150. Strong adjectives show the same measure of grammatical differentiation as the definite article (realised by much the same inflections). Weak adjectives made much the same distinctions as weak nouns, and by means of very similar inflections. In the differentiation of the two types a principle of economy was at work; so long as a preceding word carried the full differentiae the adjective could appear in less highly differentiated form. Gender in adjectives was purely a concord phenomenon, and could not survive the loss of grammatical gender in nouns, which got under way in this period. But whereas in nouns case belonged to declension, and had a function independent of gender, in adjectives the two were inter-dependent (-*re*, for example, was a dative form, but specifically a dative feminine). By the 12c adjective inflection, at anything more than the level of Ø versus -*e*, was sporadic and confined to the more conservative dialects. The plurality distinction, it is true, was gender-independent, but since it was the distinction most clearly marked by nouns, it was in most adjective uses redundant. Though our period does not see the end of adjective concord-inflections, it sees the last of their functioning as part of an integrated working system.

Inflection for comparison, of course, remains. The regular inflections, the source of those still used, had in 970 the forms -*ra*, -*est* (also -*ost*). There were, however, many variant formations – those which have survived as 'irregulars' and quite a number of others. One group of forms which only straggles into period IV is that in which the comparative and superlative have mutated forms, e.g., *brād*, 'broad', *brǣdra*, *brǣdest*, *ēaðe*, 'easy', *ȳðra*, *ȳðest*, *ȝeonȝ*, 'young', *ȝynȝra*, *ȝynȝest*, etc. *Gōd*, 'good', in addition to *bet*(*ra*), *be*(*t*)*st* had alternatives, *sēlra*, *sēlest*, but in ME generally, most speakers found one irregularity enough. *Miċel*, 'much', had comparative *māra*, 'more', superlative *mǣst*; *mā* was used adverbially and to mean 'more in number'; on the fusion of *māra* and *mā* in late ME, early NE cf. §118.

Periphrastic comparison (antecedent of the modern forms with *more*, *most*) was known, but extremely rare; it was not an indigenous pattern, but occurred only in close imitation of Latin constructions. The pattern remained dormant until the sweeping experimentation with a variety of periphrastic constructions which characterises periods IV and III (cf. § 121).

The first three cardinal numerals are primarily adjectives and decline as singular or plural strong adjectives respectively. It should be noted that the masculine of *two* is *twēgen*, 'twain', while the neuter and feminine agree in the NA form *twā*, which is therefore the dominant form, and becomes the norm in unmarked use. Numerals above three are primarily pronouns governing a genitive plural of the item numbered. The ordinals regularly end in -*a* and decline as weak adjectives, with the exception of *ōðer*, 'second', which is always strong.

Among NP modifiers, *fela*, translated 'many', requires special mention. It functions as an indeclinable pronoun, requiring the governed word to be in the genitive plural (*fela husa*, 'many of houses'). On the other hand, *maniʒ*, an adjectival word of similar meaning, was already in use, and progressively took the place of *fela*, perhaps because it fitted a more familiar grammatical pattern. *Sum*, in the 10c, was adjectival (but predeterminer), even where we would now require a pronoun, thus *sume þā tēð* – 'some those teeth', i.e., 'some of those teeth'.

§ 168   On the first and second person plural there is very little change to report as compared with 1170, though the full range of dual forms, if rare, was still known in 970. The third person shows forms of much greater regularity than hitherto, and of sufficient historical interest to be quoted in full:

SG	M	N	F	PL COMMON
N	hē	hit	hēo	hȳ, hí (Mid hēo)
A	hine	hit	hi(e), hȳ	hȳ, hí (Mid hēo)
G	his	his	hi(e)re	hiera, heora, hara
D	him	him	hi(e)re	him

In every column the third person pronoun agrees with the adjective–pronoun type in distinguishing the accusative from the dative, even though it does not always distinguish the accusative from the nominative. On this point, in 970 (and throughout OE) as in 1170, the first and second persons put the dative and accusative together, distinguishing them from the nominative. On the whole, the distinction subject/non-subject was the primary one the language needed, and in ME it prevailed. Separate accusative forms only trickle into ME in the more conservative dialects. Already in the Mid there is a clash between the feminine singular and the common gender plural, and simple phonological change in the transition period will produce the further clashes that made this pronoun so vulnerable to innovation in ME. But quite early in OE the genitive plural had variants, more or less dialectally distinct, whose reflexes will have diversified further, and increased their clash with the feminine genitive singular, by 1170.

From the genitive forms were derived fully declined possessive adjectives, used where the possessor was one other than the subject. Subject-referring possessives were formed from the stem *sīn*. Thus, *John took his book* would have distinct forms in OE according to whether *his = his own* or *another man's*. This useful distinction has had since ME to be rendered in more long-winded ways; it is possibly one of the grammatical casualties of a period of bilingualism.

The demonstratives were, as we have said, pronouns as well as adjectives. The further-demonstrative has been described. The hither-demonstrative had full strong adjective-pronoun declension, using a stem *ðis* in the great majority of forms, but *ðes* in the Nsgm, *ðeos* in the Nsgf, and certain other forms not predictable from a simple inflectional process. During the period the dominant *-i-* form came to prevail, and such declension as remained in ME was based on *ðis* (cf. §148). *Ilċa*, 'same' (which was always weak), and *self* (which was always strong), were also used both as demonstratives and as reinforcers.

By inheritance OE had no relative pronouns, and at first seems to have made comparatively sparing use of relative constructions. As the passage quoted in §166 shows, clauses may be linked by the article-demonstrative in a way that leaves us uncertain whether or not the second clause is relative. One particle does, however, develop a clear relative and subordinating force, the indeclinable particle *þe*, which by 970 is quite common. Contact-clauses were also used; and for emphasis, or where a carrier of case-number-gender contrast was required, the complex relative *se þe* could be employed. If we look simply at the forms, we might suppose that by early ME the old relative and the old article had switched forms. In fact, the two seem to have coalesced, at least in certain functions, in a weak form, *þe*, to which *þæt* was felt to be the corresponding strong form. Then, when strong and weak forms polarised according to the two functions, pronoun and article respectively, both pronoun functions, demonstrative and relative, stayed with *þat*. The whole process must have been eased by the strong association already engendered by the *se þe* pattern.

303

The interrogative had (as it always has done) a two-gender distinction, animate (*hƿā, hƿone, hƿæs, hƿǣm,* sex and number indifferent) and inanimate (*hƿæt, hƿæs, hƿǣm/hƿām,* with an instrumental *hƿȳ* or *hƿon*). A yet older instrumental *hū* was no doubt already felt as a distinct interrogative, *how*? Nothing of importance happens to this system until *who(m)* begins to move into subordinating and relative functions at the end of IV. The other common interrogative, *hƿelc/ hƿilc,* asks 'of what kind?'. This sense begins to be invaded by *what* in ME, and at the same time *which* begins to develop its present role of asking about a definite number. Another trace of the dual is found in *hƿæðer,* asking *which of two?* a sense it retains, though progressively less frequent in use, throughout ME.

There is a great wealth of indefinite pronouns, including, but not confined to, the antecedents of those discussed in IV (cf. § 147).

§ 169 Since we have reached in 970 a phase in which all nominals and their modifiers conform regularly to a case-structure more elaborate than that of later English, this is the point at which the functions of the cases should be reviewed. What is said here will hold equally for earlier OE.

The nominative was the case for the subject and its appositions, and for the vocative function. The primary use of the accusative was for the direct object (although certain verbs required a genitive or dative in this function); conversely, it was used with some impersonal verbs (*þeȝnas ȝelyste,* 'it was pleasing to the thanes'), though most such verbs required a dative. It had two other important uses, for measure (*þone þinter,* 'during (throughout) that winter') – a usage inherited from IE – and with certain prepositions, such as *ȝeond,* 'throughout', *oð,* 'until', *for,* 'because of', *fore,* 'in front of', *þurh,* 'through, during'. The genitive retains two extremely ancient functions, adnominal (*þæs cyninges þeȝnas,* 'the king's thanes'), and partitive (*þrītiȝes mīla brād,* 'broad of thirty miles, thirty miles broad', *fēowertiȝ sċipa,* 'forty of ships, forty ships', etc.), and develops a newer one, adverbial (cf. § 152) (including government by certain verbs), cf. *his cymes fæȝnode,* quoted in § 166 and *dæȝes,* 'by day'; it is used in various related functions that may be loosely classed as adverbial, and with a few prepositions. The prepositional role, though limited, can be important; it serves, for instance, to distinguish *þurh* = 'through, across' from *þurh* with the durative meaning it has with an accusative. The central role of the dative is that of attribution, *þū ofslōȝe him fætt ċealf* 'you slew a fat calf for him', but from it derives very commonly a dative of possession, as in *him on þæt hēafod*, 'to him on the head, on his head', and cf. *his folce to ðearfe*, 'for the need to (i.e., of) his people', quoted at §166. There is also a closely related adnominal dative, as in *ūs lēofre*, 'dearer to us'. The dative of time-space was strictly distinguished from the accusative of measure by designating 'within which' rather than 'throughout which', as in *sume dæӡe*, 'on a certain day'; and the great majority of prepositions governed a dative. The attributive dative also gave rise to an adverbal use (*him folӡode miċel folc*, 'to him followed a great host') and an adverbial use already discussed (cf. §152). The roles of the instrumental have already been mentioned (cf. §166).

§ 170   The verb in its inflectional forms has ordinarily only the active voice, but the verb to name, *hātan*, uniquely preserves an inflectional passive (*hātte*, 'I/he am/is, was called . . .'). Everywhere else, the passive has to be formed periphrastically (cf. §155). As always we find in 970 two tenses, past and non-past, but the non-past more generally includes future-referring functions, and periphrastic forms are reduced in range and frequency. The moods are as we have already encountered them; the clearest distinction within each tense-mood form is that of singular and plural; the plural always has a single form common to all persons, the singular may vary according to person. The non-finite parts of the verb present features not found in later centuries; the infinitive is normally plain, and has the characteristics of a noun, inflecting for the dative (its only recorded case) in *-ne*. The inflected infinitive is used after prepositional *tō*, usually with a marked implication of purpose; it might be considered a gerund rather than an isolated inflected infinitive. There are two adjectival forms of participles, both inflecting. They are the formal antecedents of those we have already had to do with, but their function is to distinguish aspect rather than tense – the first or 'present' being primarily durative, the second or 'past' perfective. These, too, are entering into periphrastic forms, and in this use are not inflected in period V, though the perfective one was in VI. In most other respects the system described here will hold good for VI, and in fact, back to the period before the arrival of English in England.

Verbs can still be classified as strong, weak, and anomalous, but the relations between the types are rather different. The strong verbs are primary, that is, they were formed as verbs, and nearly all of them were inherited by OE, though a few loans were conformed to the strong type in OE as in ME. The weak verbs were secondary or derivative, that is, they were formed from other words of various form-classes, including other verbs, often with a causative sense. In a very considerable number of cases the relationship between primary form and weak verb was still apparent. As we have seen, aspectual (perfective) meaning was widely present in prefixed verbs, especially those in *ȝe-*, which also served as a prefix for the perfective participle (cf. § 193). The anomalous verbs were in the main special cases of strong verbs, used without special syntactic value, though for the beginnings of modal periphrasis cf. § 173.

The strong verbs were considerably more numerous than in 1170, but already the seven classes were considerably fragmented. The main type of class I verb was much as in 1170 (*drīfan, drāf, drifon, ȝe-drifen*). But it included a considerable number of verbs that had more or less died out by 1170, such *hrīnan*, 'touch', *nīpan*, 'grow dark', *wīȝan*, 'fight'. During the OE period it had been strong enough to attract alien verbs to its type, such as *rīnan*, 'rain', and the loan *scrīfan* (L *scribere*). It had minor variants with consonant-alternation (*hnīȝan*, 'bend', *līðan*, 'go') which have not proved durable, and a type combining consonant-alternation with contraction (cf. § 199) (*lēon*, 'lend, *lāh, liȝon, ȝeliȝen*) which was so different that its affiliation to the class can hardly have been felt. That, too, has been lost.

Class II is typified by *bēodan*, 'command', *bēad, budon, ȝeboden*. It too had a larger membership, from which some items, such as *brēowan*, 'brew', *ċēowan*, 'chew', were lost by transfer to weak conjugation, and others by dying out of use (e.g., *brēoðan*, 'perish', *nēotan*, 'enjoy, use'). It had, as in 1170, members with various types of consonant-alternation, together with some half-dozen verbs with *u* in the present, most of which did not survive (cf. § 154).

Class III already had in OE the six sub-types we have traced in ME., and further sub-divisions in certain dialects. Though it was a very large class, with common and important verbs among its members, it was vulnerable because of its fragmentation. The types are:

bindan, bānd, būndon, ȝe-būnden	In which vowel-lengthening would be very new in 970; in earlier OE, before the lengthening, this pattern would not be different from that of such verbs as *swincan*, 'work', which did not undergo lengthening.
helpan, healp, hulpon, ȝe-holpen	WS forms; the Mid and N would have past sg *halp*, keeping the type nearer to the *bindan*-pattern.

beorȝan, bearȝ, burȝon, ȝeborȝen, 'protect'

In most of the country this would be a type identical in patterning to *helpan* by 1170, but in the SW it would continue to have a distinct set of infinitive-present forms.

ȝȳldan, ȝēald, ȝūldon, ȝe-ȝōlden, 'pay, yield'

This type differed from the *helpan* type only in WS; like *bindan* it had recently undergone vowel-lengthening, which separated it from another type, *ȝylpan*, 'yelp', which it formerly resembled. Note that in WS it will branch off again in the transition period, since its past sg will remain /ɛː/ while that of *bindan* will become /ɔː/).

murnan, mearn, murnon, ȝemurnen

Clearly, even in OE the class is recognised by linguists for historical reasons, and cannot have been felt as a unity by speakers.

Class IV has only one common type, illustrated by *beran*, 'bear', *bær*, WS *bǣron*, NWS *bēron*, *ȝe-boren*, which, contrary to the normal movement had more members in ME than in OE, because it attracted a number of class V verbs. Its variants were each represented by one common verb, *niman*, 'take', *nam* or *nōm*, *nōmon*, *ȝenumen*, and *c(þ)uman*, 'come', *c(þ)ōm*, *c(þ)ōmon*, *ȝe-cumen* (in which the *þ* represents the early OE form, and had been assimilated to the following lip-rounded vowel by 970).

Class V was also much sub-divided. The type nearest to the original pattern of formation is seen in *etan*, 'eat', *æt*, *ǣton*, *ȝe-eten*. Here, as in class III, there were sub-divisions in WS where other dialects recognised a single type. There were many forms with consonant-alternation, sometimes combined with contraction. The most aberrant formation of this type was the verb *sēon*, 'see', *seah*, *sāwon*, *ȝesewen*, with many inter- and intra-dialectal variants. Another type had *i* and a long consonant in the infinitive (e.g., *biddan*, 'ask'), but normal patterning elsewhere. This type maintained itself well except where consonant-alternation was superimposed on its other oddities, as in *þicȝan*, 'partake', which after some flirtation with class I forms died out altogether.

The main type of class VI verb is exemplified by *faran*, 'go', *fōr*, *fōron*, *ȝe-faren*. Its membership is much the same in 1170 as in 970. It also had a sub-type with special infinitive-present forms, which partly survived into ME (cf. §154); the strength of the *faran*-type is shown, however, by the making over to it of one of the sub-type verbs, NWS, *sċeppan*, WS, *sċyppan*, ME *shape(n)*, PE *shape*. Verbs with consonant-alternation tended to be regularised (e.g., NWS *hlehhan*, WS *hlyhhan*, later *laughen*, with weak past). OE had a considerable body of contracted verbs in this class, of which only *slēan*, 'strike', with its compounds, and *flēan*, 'flay', survive into ME.

Class VII, as we saw in ME, is from an English point of view a rag-bag, recognised by historians because all its members shared a mode of past-formation by reduplication in a pre-English phase of the language. Such unity as they have in OE must be put in much more general terms than we have used hitherto; they were alike in having one vowel in the infinitive and second participle, and another, always *ē* or *ēo*, throughout the past. There are minor exceptions even to this statement, and the infinitive vowel varies so widely that we need to recognise some ten different patterns. Yet so common were many of the verbs in the class that its membership is fairly well maintained (cf. §154). One thing met in OE but not in ME is the fairly rare, usually early and poetic use, of some past forms preserving traces of the original reduplication, as in *hātan*, 'command', *heht* beside *hēt*, *rǣdan*, 'advise', *reord* beside *rēd*. These forms were certainly not in general use in 970, but must still have been familiar to the cultured from their use in the writing of ancient poetry; it is possible that in the N and Mid they kept a more everyday currency.

To these verbs should be added those, belonging to most of the strong classes, which shifted the two grades of vowel characteristic of the past into the present, and formed new pasts, in appearance, though not necessarily in origin, like those of weak verbs. These, no doubt, had only lasted into OE because they were extremely common verbs, and their survival-rate into ME is remarkably high. On the origins of the specialised uses that enabled a selection of them to continue into NE cf. §121.

§ 171   The regularity of formation which played a large part in the progressive dominance of weak verbs from ME on was not present in OE. There were three main types, with a number of sub-divisions, depending on the formations preceding inflection. These formations need to be divided into two parts, a stem and a vowel (theme) between stem and inflection; both varied under somewhat complex conditions, and the variation could include total loss of the vowel. Regularisation largely took the form of extending a single stem-formation throughout the whole of a given conjugation; to a considerable extent it followed from normal phonological change, loss of distinctive consonant-length and blurring of unstressed vowels under /ə/. These routine developments produced so large a measure of uniformity that by 1170 all but the most conservative dialects analogically levelled the remaining differences.

If we disregard these differences of stem and theme-vowel formation, we find the inflections of strong and weak verbs to be in agreement in the present. In the following list (V) indicates that some vowel may be present, according to verb-type or stem-formation, between the stem and the inflection; in a work of this kind it is not possible to indicate all differences of stem-formation, but they mainly affect the 2 and 3sg present indicative in both strong and weak verbs:

	Ind	Subj	Imp	Part
Sg 1	WS -e, NWS, -o			
2	-(V)st	-e	-(V)	
3	-(V)þ			
Pl	-aþ	-en	-aþ	-ende

There are over-simplifications in this chart; in particular, it does not clearly show one important point, namely, that in any given verb the form of the 3sg pres ind will differ from that of the plural. Thus, the sg–pl contrast is the dominant one made by the verb, and in relation to both the declension of nominals and the positional syntax of the period, this is an important point (cf. §165). From the ME development it is clear that while the S has let phonology take its course, the Mid have blended a new set of forms, part ind, part subj, in origin, while the N has innovated completely in the form and distribution of its present inflections.

The past formations are even less uniform. They vary in the ways already mentioned. In addition, the strong verbs use in 2sg the vowel of the plural, with the ending -e; the sg grade of vowel is used in 1 and 3sg only, which have no ending. Weak verbs add -(V)d- or -t- between stem and ending. The following list of inflections then belongs to the weak verbs, but is shared by strong verbs save where exceptions are stated:

	Ind	Subj	Part
Sg 1	-e		
2	-est	-e	
3	-e		
Pl	-on	-en	Ø (strong -en)

Thus in addition to the number distinction, which we have seen to be clearly marked, the tense distinction is almost always clear, and so, as long as weak vowels are distinguished, is mood distinction. But in the plural, present and past, mood distinction is vanishing in 970, and will soon disappear completely; from about A.D. 1000 the subjunctive will only be distinguished in the 2 and 3sg of the pres, the 2sg of weak verbs and the 1 and 3sg of strong verbs. The re-shuffling of personal endings in various dialects in early ME will throw the distinction further into disarray, so that we are not surprised to find that by late ME, as in NE, it survives only in the highly anomalous verb *be*.

One group of weak verbs formed its past with what in OE appears as vowel change (it originates from a difference of formation in the pre-English phase of the language). These verbs, like the verbs that shifted the past vowels into the present, had survived this far because they were very common, and their later survival rate was again high (cf. § 89).

Finally it should be noted that inflectional *-n* was lost in the N by the time of the earlier texts. The picture of contrasts in the verb, and to some extent in nominals, is thus greatly simplified even before the blurring and loss of unstressed vowels.

§ 172 Finally there is a group of very common verbs, each of which is wholly idiosyncratic in formation. The verb *be* (like Latin *esse*) preserves an old type of conjugation with *-m* in 1sg present indicative, in OE as in NE; also, like its Latin cognate and IE source, it is suppletive, that is, fills out its conjugation with forms drawn from more than one stem. It has alternative infinitives, *bēon*, from a root originally implying process, becoming, growth, and *wesan*, from one originally implying habitation, staying, dwelling. *Wesan* already in OE supplied the only past forms, but, unlike them, it hardly survived into ME, perhaps because by then *bēon* had lost its special emphasis, which left *wesan* redundant. The present forms of the verb are doublets, having *be*-forms and *is*, etc., forms, the latter implying simple *is*-ness, with no special emphasis. Something of this original distinction between the two sets of forms can be seen in OE, where the *be*-forms are preferred for future reference, or wherever a statement involves some implication of coming to be.

It is not surprising that such a pattern gave rise to many local divergences, still preserved in ME, and that our present forms for the verb should not finally have settled into shape until the 16c.

The verb *do* was originally of the same *-m* type; in the Mid and N it retains a first person singular present indicative *dom*, but in the S it has a regularised form *dō*. Otherwise its main peculiarity was in the formation of its past, *dyde*, which has survived, with only regular phonological changes, to this day. A rather similarly anomalous pattern of past formation occurs in *willan*, *wolde*, and again has survived. The verb *go* had a suppletive past *ēode*, later replaced by the more familiar but equally suppletive form, *wente*.

§ 173 At the heart of the categories central to the verb is the two-term tense contrast realised within the verb's own form. As we know, the non-past serves for durative and non-durative present and future reference; in OE the past covers not only simple past but also meanings that are now distinguished as durative, perfective and pluperfect. It is evident that speakers were not satisfied with so grossly simple a system, and they were beginning to use supplementary patterns. The perfect is mainly formed with a *have*-auxiliary, though quite often *be* is used with intransitive verbs, as in *ic cūðlice ʒeleornad hæbbe*, 'I have learned for a certainty', *is nū sǽl cumen*, 'the time has now come'. These forms occur from the earliest times, but they remain optional, and when they are used they highlight the aspectual contrast to a marked degree. A sense of the novelty of the pattern comes through in a common 9c variant in which the verb *have* is treated as a transitive, and the participle made accusative in concord with the object, as in *hī hæfdon þā heora stemn ʒesettenne*, 'they had then completed their term of service', literally, 'they possessed then their term of service in a state of having been sat out'.

The durative aspect with forms of *be* + first participle, which was to achieve such importance in later English, is found sporadically in OE, but is at first something of an alien, a calque of Latin. It is used in V very much as in VI, and its origins will be considered in § 193.

It is possibly also under Latin influence that the need for a distinct future came to be felt. At any rate, the earliest examples of modal periphrases are those in which an element of tense is combined with modality, those using *will*, *shall*, *would*. In a very common kind of use we have a bridge between the lexical meaning of *shall* ('must') and its tense-modal function, e.g., *Hpæt sċeal iċ singan*? 'What am I to sing?' In the late 10c the following seems to be clearly modal, *feallan sċeolon hǽþene æt hilde*, 'the heathen shall/must/are to/will fall in battle', *Hī þillað ēoþ tō ʒafole ʒāras syllan*, 'They wish to/will give you spears as tribute'. The beginnings are slenderly evidenced, but they are there. The process of elaboration will go on steadily for centuries; indeed, it shows no sign of having reached a point of equilibrium now.

The function of mood-contrast is more traditional; this, indeed, as we have seen from a study of its formal history, is a distinction on the way out, not on the way in. The indicative is the unmarked term. In independent clauses the subjunctive is used for the unreal – for hypothesis, wish, advice, command; it has a similar general value in dependent clauses, including cases of 'unreality' involving goal, wish or doubt, but it also occurs in indirect speech, concession, and sometimes in relative, temporal and other clauses. What we find in later centuries is less the replacement of this system by another, than its general decline as other forms become available to make the contrast of mood.

Finally, negation is, as in ME, primarily by the pre-verb particle *ne* (contracted with the verb in certain cases); reinforcement occurs, but is not yet the norm as it was to become in ME.

§ 174 The scraps of OE quoted so far have plainly demonstrated how much the language has changed in its positional syntax. None of the patterns exemplified would be impossible in ME, but some, which had died out by NE, were becoming abnormal. It is often said that order in OE was free, but this is not the case. As we have seen, within the NP it was as it is today, though within the VP both finite and non-finite parts of verbs might find themselves in positions that surprise us. The more important differences concern the placement of elements of the clause relative to each other, rather than that within the elements. This is a complicated subject for several reasons. The system was in transition, and we shall have to consider its antecedents in later chapters. Partly the transition is due to factors we may regard as accidental and evolutionary: that is to say, a pattern might come to predominate through a series of coincidences, and then to be felt as a norm, and so extended further. Partly it is due to what is happening in quite diverse fields of morphology. We have observed that quite often not only a noun, but a NP, would contain no mark of distinction between nominative and accusative; other means of distinguishing subject and direct object were therefore of high importance. In quite a lot of cases S–V concord would serve this purpose; and this is why the number-distinction of verbs was crucial. But this solution worked only haphazardly. Some norm for the placing of subject or direct object (or both) relative to the verb was also required. A complex of forces worked together to foreground the S–V order and relationship after A.D. 1000, whereas the central issue before that date had been object-placement.

In the late 10c the picture that can be discerned has at its centre a norm or unmarked pattern for affirmative sentences. Departure from the norm was a means of obtaining emphasis or focus, but it did not follow any simple rules, since various classes of elements had their own patterns of emphasis displacement. The governing principle in ordering was a mixture of the syntactic and the rhythmical, 'light' and 'heavy' elements having different positional rules; an ornate stylist might make intricate use of the various ordering possibilities.

With these cautions, we may formulate the norm as follows: in first position there may, but need not be, (0) a pre-head, that is a short function word, unstressed, such as *ȝyf*, 'if', *and*; this will be followed by the direct order (1–2), i.e. S–V (but S need not be expressed), followed by other elements in terms of progressive 'weight', of which six grades can be distinguished. Naturally they will not normally all occur in a single clause, but the relative order will be preserved. The six classes range from (3) light function words only stressed in contrastive conditions (such as personal pronouns), to (4) medium function words commonly stressed (such as adverbs), to (5) non-finite verbs, to (6) heavy, simple or compound non-verbal full-words and endocentric phrases, to (7) exocentric phrases (e.g., prepositional phrases), to (8) dependent and finally (9) independent clauses. Elements (3) to (9) may jointly be labelled T (*tail*), since in the normal structure they follow the pre-head and S–V nucleus, and the formula for the maximum possible structure will be

$$(0)\ [(1)\ 2]\begin{pmatrix} T \\ 3\text{–}9 \end{pmatrix}$$

covering such diverse examples as:

Ic can þē be naman, 'I know thee by name', 1237
God cþæþ þā sōþlice: Bēo nū lēoht, 'truly God then said, "Be now light",' 12349.
Þone hē ȝenemde Gerson, 'that he named G.', 0226

The most important departures from this normal order are by placement of the verb extra early, especially in the pattern 2–1, or late (often with splitting of its finite and non-finite parts). These are always to be read as having some kind of marked or contrastive meaning.

§ 175 OE is well known as a period when WF, by derivation and compounding, was extremely active. We can trace a range of types active in OE but not in its antecedents, a range of types inherited from the antecedent stages of the language but no longer productive, and a range that failed to survive the migration to England. Within OE, however, it is much more difficult to say what changes belong to each two-century period, and in general the subject will be postponed for treatment in later chapters.

The revival of learning which characterised the late 10c brought with it a very large influx of Latin loans; something like one hundred and fifty new ones can be traced by the end of the OE period. Most of these words, however, remain very much on the surface. They were borrowed from books by scholars, and remained, while they lasted, rather technical terms. This, after all, is not surprising, for the wealth of direct and indirect borrowing from Latin in previous centuries had been very extensive indeed; only rather specialised words were now needed. On the other hand, some of the late OE borrowing is unnecessary and pedantic, reeking of the study. For example, Aelfric uses *cuppe*, when earlier loans, *cupp* and *copp*, had already been assimilated. Other loans, though confined to specialised uses, were the words that had to be used for those purposes, such as *talent, synaȝoȝe*. The change from earlier practice is that these words are taken over whole and undigested; as we shall see, in the missionary age normal practice was to introduce Christian and other Latin concepts by calques and imitative native formations, with a rather low proportion of direct borrowing (cf. §204). In the 10c, religion, and the civilisation it brought in its train, have established the vocabulary needed by the common man, and the gaps that remain to be filled are those mainly relevant to the concerns of the educated professed man of religion, for whom linguistic concessions do not need to be made. But though as a whole the Latin loans of this period have a scholarly tone, they are not all to do with religion; many reflect growing curiosity about branches of learning and about distant places and their products, such as *camell, cēder, cucurbite*, 'gourd' (earlier *cyrfet*), *persič*, 'peach', *polente, plaster* ('medical plaster'), *scrōfel*, 'scrofula', *bibliođēce, philosoph*. Notably few of these loans have survived; to some extent this is because older borrowings held their ground, but very much more it is due to the replacement of most scholarly vocabulary by later borrowings from French. This group of loans is important for the light it throws on the sophistication of cultivated late Anglo-Saxon society, rather than for its contribution to the resources of later English.

§ 176 Nothing could be more strongly contrasted in character than the other main type of borrowing which got under way in the 10c, that from Scandinavian languages. Our study of the delayed entry of French loans after the Norman Conquest will have taught us to be patient in seeking linguistic evidence of the contacts between viking and English settlers. In this case there are additional delays in the record, since most documents are from non-Scandinavian areas. The main apportionments of land to Scandinavians belong to period VI, and we shall in that period consider the contribution of ON to English place-names. But borrowing of common words was apparently slow, and largely confined to rather technical items for which there was no corresponding English word, as long as a Norse-speaking community maintained itself in England. When the full flow of loans appears, its exact extent is not ascertainable, both because the languages were so much alike that many forms might be accounted for by English or Norse transmission, and also because it is natural to suppose that during the bilingual period many English words entered the Norse of settlers in England, and will have become Scandinavianised in phonology. In a way, then, the situation is clearer in V than in IV. Eric Björkman writes:

> A careful examination of the Scandinavian elements found in English before the M.E. period will prove these elements to be of quite a different character from the main part of the traces of Scandinavian language found after, say, the year 1200. Such words as *barda* 'beaked ship', *cnear* 'small warship', *fylcian* 'to collect, marshal', *hā* 'rowlock', *hold* 'freeholder', *huscarl* 'one of the king's body guard', *liþ* 'fleet', *ōra* (Danish monetary unit), *orrest* 'battle', *rān* 'rapine, robbery, *sceʒð* 'a vessel' and many others which are, for the most part, not found in M.E., had been borrowed from the Scandinavian language chiefly to denote things closely connected with the life and institutions of the invaders. . . . The Scandinavian element found in Middle English, on the other hand, is for the most part of quite another stamp. Such words as *hānum* 'him', *þaþen*, *þeþen*, 'thence', *heþen* 'hence', *wheþen* 'whence', *þeʒʒ* 'they', *summ* 'as', *oc* 'and' etc. . . . cannot be otherwise explained than as depending on a very intimate blending of the two languages. Instances of such a blending may, of course, have existed very early (the word *hānum* appears about 1050) at several points where the Northmen were in very close connection with the English, especially on the borders of the Scandinavian colonies, and thus gave up their nationality earlier than in other districts (1900, 5–6).

Björkman's examples of early loans (some of which are recorded before 970) illustrate, in addition to the points he makes, the extent of lexical loss between O and ME; it is very striking that even the ME loans that show closest fusion of the two languages have almost entirely passed out of use. It is certainly towards the end of our period that those linguistic conditions arose which made for the maximum influx of Scandinavian loans; accordingly, the subject has received more attention in Chapter IV than here. However, it would be quite wrong to pass over in silence the outstanding exception to the generalisation we have quoted. The word *laʒu*, 'law', with a number of derivatives and compounds based on it, was one of our earliest Scandinavian loans; it first confined the native synonym, *ǣ*, to use of divine, not secular law, and finally took its place in all senses.

§ 177   It should not be supposed that borrowing from French is merely due to the Norman Conquest. The cultivated and outward-looking society of late Anglo-Saxon times already had relations with France, and in accordance with the late tendency to borrow rather than form calques a number of French words had been taken in even before the Conquest. Examples are *prūd*, 'proud', *sōt* 'foolish' (which seems to have been borrowed in slightly different forms from both Latin and French before the Conquest), *tūr*, 'tower' (which had also been borrowed very early in the form *torr*, from L *turris*), *capun*, 'capon', and a few others. Before 1100 we have (and now the subject-matter of the loans is highly significant), *arblast, serfise, prisun, castel, market, cancelere* (a Norman form). Between 1100 and 1170 some thirty others, including *abbat, capelein* (Norman), *cardinal, clerc, cuntesse, duc, legat, prior, curt, rent, tresor, iustise, miracle, standard.*

Naturally enough, the carving out of great Norman estates left its mark on English place-names. Compared with earlier elements in English onomastics this component is small, but it deserves mention. *Richmond* (first in Yorkshire), and *Pontefract* ('pont freit', 'broken bridge'), and a number of names in *Beau-* (reflecting the choice of a seat for scenic rather than utilitarian reasons), belong here. Some originally French names no longer declare their source so plainly, e.g., *Devizes* ('divisas', 'boundary lands'), *Butterby* ('beau trouvé') and *Haltemprice* ('haut emprise', 'great undertaking').

CHAPTER VI

970 – 770

§ 178 In 770 the English occupied most of what is now England, together with SE Scotland to the Forth, and a little of SW Scotland. There were few, if any, English-speakers in Cornwall; certainly pockets of Celtic-speaking people remained in Cumberland, and in areas of English occupation, as they had done in the preceding centuries. On the other hand, though English was felt as a distinct language, it was mutually comprehensible with a range of Germanic languages on the Continent of Europe, with whose speakers the English in the 8c had much to do. The English community was small, but it did not set the bounds of the world to which the Englishman's language gave him access.

The English were already conscious of themselves as a people, especially as a people identified by church organisation and language (cf. §196), but they did not yet constitute a political unity. The chief English kingdoms were those of North and South Northumbria (Bernicia and Deira respectively), running from wherever the frontier currently was in the north and west to the Humber on the south; Mercia, extending over the whole of the Midlands; Kent and Wessex in the south. At various times one power or another had established supremacy over the others, and when our period begins the longest and most effective dominion yet known was in force, the supremacy of Mercia established during two successive reigns lasting eighty years, and ending with the death of King Offa in 796.

Need one say that in this society there were elements of the violent, the barbaric, the harsh and the corrupt? As in all societies these elements were present, yet dominantly it was a prosperous, cultivated and pious society, a society that we might think rather lightly took stability for granted. In its primary form love of piety and learning filled the monasteries with men and women; in a secondary form it showered upon these defenceless establishments the most lavish patronage. What could be more attractive to a viking than an undefended treasure-house seated, for isolation, on an island or lonely shore? The attacks started with a small inroad on the Wessex coast in 787; in 793 and 794 the two greatest monasteries of the Northumbrian coast were sacked.

The onslaught was not followed up immediately, and this is not to be wondered at. The Danes were a small community, perhaps half-a-million strong; the Norwegians perhaps 200,000. They were not one nation or alliance attacking another. Their enterprise has been compared to that of a joint stock company, in which a group put up the resources to equip and carry out a raid, and then share its profits on some agreed basis. The whole of coastal Europe was in their range, and for any single group the proceeds of one expedition, in the early days, might render further travel superfluous for quite a time.

Within England, the death of Offa was followed by a period with no clear overall lordship, until in 825 Egbert of Wessex defeated the Mercians, annexed the whole southern territory, then Northumbria, and became overking of a region even more extended than Offa's domain. From then on we may think of England as a monarchy, within which a conception of national policy can sooner or later be expected to emerge. Nevertheless, sub-kings remain, and some national kings will have a greater authority than others; the idea of political unity is, in any case, very new to the English. In 835 viking attack enters a new phase. Peter Hunter Blair writes:

> The first major attack against southern England took place in . . . 835, and was directed against Sheppey. It marks the beginning of a series of raids which were of almost annual occurrence during the next thirty years and which ranged along the south coast from Cornwall and Somerset to Portland, Southampton, Winchester, Sandwich, Canterbury, Rochester and London. Their scale varied, according to contemporary English estimates, from about 30 to as many as 350 ships (1956, 68).

We know so much about these attacks for reasons that will soon emerge (cf. §179), but it would be folly to imagine that areas other than the south coast were free from attack at this period. During these thirty years the vikings begin the practice of wintering on an offshore island – Thanet or Sheppey – to be at hand, in spring, for the next season's campaign.

Clearly, such a sequence of coastal raids soon exhausts its own prey, and in 865 the attacks enter a third phase, requiring, and displaying, large-scale organisation amongst the attackers (who, indeed, can now be called invaders). What an English chronicler calls the Great Army landed in East Anglia, and began a systematic series of campaigns lasting fifteen years, occupying parts of the country and devastating the rest. In 866 the Danes (as they are called, and predominantly, but not exclusively, were) left their East Anglian base, marched over two hundred miles and sacked York, which held, among other things, one of the greatest libraries of the Western world and a school of something like university status. Exactly at the same time a predominantly Norwegian force from the Western Isles, the Isle of Man and Dublin, took Dumbarton, capital of Strathclyde in the north-west. The following year they marched into Mercia and occupied Nottingham, but were met by a Mercian–West Saxon alliance, and withdrew, as they preferred to, without open battle. In 870 they moved on Wessex, taking up headquarters in Reading, and despite heavy opposition were able to advance westwards. This campaign was still in progress at Easter 871 when the West Saxon king Æthelred died, and his brother Alfred succeeded to the throne. In one year Alfred fought nine major battles and what the chronicler describes as innumerable forays, but at the end of it he made terms – not good terms, but the Danes left Wessex for London, and time was bought. For the next five years the campaigns continued across Northumbria and Mercia, but Wessex was left in peace. At the end of 874 the Danish army split into two, and a fourth phase begins. One section:

> led by Halfdan, moved north from Repton to the Tyne and after a year spent in harrying attacks against the Picts and the Strathclyde Welsh, it returned to southern Northumbria and settled down to permanent homes in what, as later evidence shows, corresponded broadly with modern Yorkshire (Hunter Blair, 1956, 73).

In 876, the chronicler records, Halfdan 'dealt out the lands of Northumbria, and they began to plough and till them'. The other section of the army was not ready for settlement. They moved south to Cambridge, and from that base renewed their attack on Wessex. Alfred had used his breathing-space well and the Danes were driven back to Mercia, where another large contingent, under Guthrum, decided to turn to settlement, and occupied the Five Boroughs, i.e., Lincoln, Nottingham, Derby, Leicester, Stamford, and the surrounding lands. In 878 the remaining Danes, soon reinforced by a new fleet which attacked Devonshire, made a third attack on Wessex, driving Alfred back to Athelney in the Somerset marshes. For some weeks the English defence was reduced to operations on guerilla scale, till in May Alfred advanced, met forces assembled with careful planning from several counties, and won a decisive victory. The Danes left Wessex, and in 879 occupied the lands of East Anglia.

Alfred next set about establishing himself in the eyes of the remaining English powers as leader, not merely of Wessex, but of them all, and in 886 he was able to occupy London (north of the Thames), the first step in the re-conquest of the Danelaw. For some years the new generation of vikings found it more profitable to plunder Continental Europe, but whenever this situation changed the English would be faced by the additional danger that a fresh wave of invaders could find support from the Danes in England. In 891 the vikings suffered heavy defeat in France and returned, in two fleets of two hundred and fifty and eighty ships, to Kent. At first Alfred tried to negotiate, but in 893 the English Danes threw in their lot with the newcomers and a hectic series of fresh campaigns began. Besides inland forays there were sea-attacks on north and south Devon; the Danes went up the Thames and Severn to Buttington, where they were besieged and defeated. At harvest-time they made a dash for Chester, were frustrated by a scorched earth policy, ravaged North Wales, and returned to base. In 895 they rushed across to a place near Bridgenorth on the Severn and wintered there. Next year they recognised that no more was to be gained in England; some returned to East Anglia, others to the Seine.

§ 179 Thus matters stood at the death of Alfred, probably on 26 October 899. This was not the end of viking attacks, nor of their relevance to the history of English, but it is a convenient breaking point. In 770, England (if the term is not too misleading) led the Western world in scholarship, scholarship which reached its highest level, as it had done for nearly a century, in Northumbria. Of the situation at his accession in 871 Alfred wrote:

Sᵽǣ clǣne hīo   þæs oðfeallenu on Angel-cynne ðæt sᵽīðe
So   cleanly it (learning) was declined   in   England   that very

fēaþa   þǣron behionan   Humbre ðe   hiora ðēninᴣa cūðen
few (there) were on this side of H.   who their missals could

understondan on Enᴣlisċ, oððe furðum ān ǣrendᴣeþrit of Lǣdene on
understand   in English, or   even   one letter/epistle from Latin to

Enᴣlisċ āreċċean; ond iċ þēne ðætte nōht moniᴣe beᴣiondan Humbre
English translate; and I think that not   many   beyond   H.

nǣren.   Sᵽǣ fēaþa hiora þǣron ðæt iċ furðum ānne ān-lēpne
(there) were (not). So   few of them (there) were that I even one single

ne mæჳ ჳeðenċean be-sūðan Temese, ðā-ðā iċ tō rīċe fēnჳ.
one not can think of south of (the) Thames when I to (the) kingdom
succeeded.

(So completely had learning declined in England that there were very few on this side of the Humber who could understand their missals in English or even translate a single letter from Latin into English, and it may be supposed there were not many beyond the Humber. There were so few that I cannot think of a single one south of the Thames when I succeeded to the kingdom.)

For nearly a century attack had centred on the only places from which education could proceed. Alfred is a southern king, and can speak explicitly for the illiteracy of even the clergy among his own people; Northumbria he does not know at first hand, so he will not make assertions about it; he makes a bitter supposition, but none of his contemporaries can have had imagined this supposition to be too gloomy.

In 878, under a lesser leader, the English would have been defeated, successive waves of vikings would have occupied territories further and further west; the English language would perhaps have been driven back into the mountains of Wales, as the English in their day had driven back Celtic-speakers, but more probably, being so like Danish, it would simply have been absorbed and submerged. Nothing like the preceding chapters could have been written about it. There may be some who would have found themselves at full stretch with Alfred's political and military responsibilities on their shoulders. Alfred was not such a man. He had long brooded on other needs of his kingdom, and no sooner had he taken London than, approaching the age of forty, he set himself to learn Latin in order to supply what had seemed superfluous to the secure scholarship of the 8c, a set of translations of the basic materials of education into English. He was not so rash as to suppose he could do this single-handed. He wheedled into his team of colleagues and advisers the best scholars available who could address themselves to an English-speaking public. In England scholarship survived only in western Mercia; from there, from Wales, from the Germanic peoples of Europe to whom the torch had been handed by English missionaries of the 8c, he drew his recruits. Together they set about the work of translating, editing, compiling, even composing, the basic texts. As an incidental they forged the first European post-Classical vernacular prose, whose very first document is the letter prefaced to his earliest translation, from which we have already quoted. They were also responsible for a national history in the form of a chronicle, compiled from all available written sources and kept up from personal knowledge of events within living memory.

The work of this school of prose-writers is of the highest importance for the history of English in the later part of the OE period. Alfred's method, clearly stated in his first preface, is to have each diocese sent a copy of new works as they become available. By its aid the bishops are to re-educate themselves and train their clergy, and the clergy to teach the laity. The plan is that all free-born boys with sufficient means should be made literate in English (given a primary education), and those destined for clerical training should then continue with Latin studies (receive a higher education). It would be almost exactly a thousand years before the English public was again offered education on such a scale. Naturally, Alfred's scheme was a two-generation process, and he died before the second stage reached fruition. For the first half of the 10c his successors were not able to advance his educational policy. When more tranquil conditions were established under Edgar (959-75) scholarship in England did indeed move forward again, but not from the broad base Alfred had envisaged.

For linguistic history the importance of his scheme does not depend on its total success, but on the completion of the first phase, the circulation of documents from Wessex to the rest of England, and the use of these documents in teaching a new generation to read and write. Literacy did not extend much beyond the clergy, but the clergy, whatever their spoken dialect, knew and learned to write a written English derived from Wessex. The production of the documentary material was a huge undertaking. While we know quite a lot about the team who assisted Alfred at the scholarly level, we do not know about the scribes who made the copies. One thing is clear: even if they were Wessex men, their training must have been at the hands of scholars who were not West Saxon (since there were no literate West Saxons to speak of). It is probable enough that they would have been trained as a group, and we should expect to find, as we do, that the documents they produced share a common character. This character is not necessarily purely West Saxon; indeed, elements of inconsistency within these early documents may suggest that the writers were using conventions not consonant with their speech-habits. The standard written language with which they familiarised the whole country is known, and for good reason, as early or Alfredian West Saxon, but it should not be taken as a written 'picture' of spoken West Saxon. By and large the standard written forms used by writers of the late

10c renaissance derive from this tradition; but there is some evidence of change not due to the passage of time so much as to those sudden switches in convention we have seen standard languages to be subject to (cf. §99). The evidence of ME would associate with the West Saxon area the kind of language embodied in late or classical West Saxon writing, rather than that of early West Saxon. The principal difference is that in forms where late West Saxon shows *y* corresponding to *e* in other dialects, early WS had *ie*. The continuing issues of national material to be incorporated in the chronicles maintained locally would ensure that all local centres would be kept up to date with their WS in later generations.

§ 180 Only in the far north, notably in Northumberland, do writings of the late OE period escape the influence of WS standard. Yet we seem to be able to discern through the coating of WS the existence of an alternative, and older, standard language of quite a different kind, and spoken rather than written. This kind of OE was the variety used for poetry. Poetry, however composed, was designed for oral performance, and needed to be in a variety of English free from such localisms as would limit a listening audience. It was true in the OE period, as John of Trevisa observed of the 14c, that a Midland dialect commanded the widest understanding, and such a variety, Anglian rather than Saxon, seems to have been the medium of poetry, wherever composed. Most poetry survives in copies made in the late 10c under the influence of the then general WS written standard, but something of its Anglian character comes through. Some of the poetry that is datable comes from period VI, some from V and some from VII. The great bulk of it is undatable, but in large part is most likely to have originated in VI, certainly to have been transmitted through VI. The poetic language illustrates so fully certain characteristics of OE and is of so special a nature that it requires separate attention. Without implying that the poetic language belongs more to this period than to the ones before and after it, we may conveniently locate an account at this point.

§ 181 There are several reasons in the nature of OE verse why it should, to a greater extent than later poetry, develop a language distinct from that of prose. The most radical is not often mentioned, and is difficult for readers accustomed to later literature to grasp. It is that OE had a straightforward distinction between metre, which had a single, unique, form, and non-metrical writing, i.e., writing not in this form. This is indeed a situation rare in any literature; normally, if one decides to write in verse, one can also decide which verse-form to write in. In ME, though forms derived from OE metre survived, the essential of the situation was changed, for the poet always had a choice of metres open to him. His verse might be alliterative or rhyming; the lines might contain any number of feet, of various types, uniform or in mixed patterns; they might be arranged in stanzas of various types, or not in stanzas at all. Before 1100 these alternatives did not exist as choices. There was one metre; you used it or you did not. You might compromise and conform to some but not all of its rules, writing a kind of semi-verse, and you could add patterning of your own selection to the basic form; but you could not write a verse of a different form. This characteristic English shared with other ancient Germanic languages. Before our period there had been many centuries of exploring what could be done in the one metrical form. Its properties, resources and limitations were well known, conventions in its use well established. Its long and unique history distanced it in a very particular way from everyday usage, while as poetry for speaking it was preserved from artificiality.

When we look at the form of this metre we find that while its status is the root cause of the distinctness of poetic language, its particular characteristics account for the nature of the differentiation. Certain essential qualities of OE can best be revealed by examining those characteristics. The unit of the verse is a two-part line; there is no higher structural unit. Even on the very rare occasions when lines are grouped in sequences the grouping does not correspond to a structural unit such as we would call a stanza. A major structural break within the line, which we may call a caesura, divides it into two parts, *a* and *b*, which in principle are the same in structure, but which are subtly differentiated in effect. Each half-line contains a double unit, which we may, not altogether satisfactorily, describe as two feet, and the rules for *a* and *b* half-lines are the same. But every permitted pattern has a range of possible realisations, and in a good line the halves must be paired in such a way that *b* is not heavier than *a*; usually it will be lighter. There is no single determinant of 'weight', but the various factors constituting it will emerge from analysis of the half-line patterns. First, however, the notion that there are paired half-lines, rather than sequences of short lines, must be justified. The half-lines are linked in pairs by initial rhyme or alliteration. Alliteration depends on likeness of initial sound – normally membership of the same phoneme, but with additional conventions that could not be inferred from phonemic analysis, notably that all vowels alliterate together.

Each half-line contains two stresses, with other material disposed about them. We need to be able to distinguish stronger and weaker elements in metrical patterns from stronger and weaker syllables, since there will not necessarily be a one-to-one relationship between them. We shall speak, as usual, of stressed, secondary or half-stressed, and unstressed syllables, and reserve the terms lift (/), half-lift (\), drop (x), for the three grades of metrical component. Of the various patterns which two lifts and their related drops might form, five, with variants, are accepted in OE verse, and are usually symbolised thus:

A / x / x
B x / x /
C x / / x
D / / \ x *or* / / x \
E / \ x / *or* / x \ /

Any half-line starting with a lift can be preceded by an extra drop (anacrusis) and half-lines may be preceded by an extra foot of A or B type (/ x *or* x /), in which case they are said to be lengthened. The norm for each half-line will be four components, but five or six are possible.

These patterns are a selection from those used in ordinary speech; indeed, the effect of OE metre is that of rhythmically stylised speech. That it has a rhythmical effect as read by speakers of modern English is of considerable importance, for what we have described are not rhythmical patterns, but stress patterns, patterns of intensity rather than patterns in time. The rhythm is there because the temporal patterning we impose from our experience of PE corresponds to the temporal patterning of OE. For a description of this patterning as it now occurs see §40. In both OE and NE we need to distinguish syllable-quantity from time-patterning. Syllable-quantity, then as now, was two-term; the essential difference was between a long syllable, containing a long vowel or ending in more than one consonant, and a short syllable lacking either of these features. Time-patterning has always had more than two terms.

The lifts and drops are realised in syllable-sequences, some determinate, some free. A lift must be realised by a stressed syllable, normally long, or if short, followed by another short syllable which also belongs to the lift; but these restrictions do not apply if one lift follows directly upon another (i.e., to the second lift of a C or D type half-line). A lift spread over two short syllables is said to be *resolved* (here the distinction between lift and stress is clearly needed; the stress obviously is not spread over two syllables). In most cases a drop consists of any number of unstressed syllables (their length is indifferent) between one lift and the next. This rules out some patterns that look theoretically possible, such as */ x x /; in such a sequence the unstressed syllables, being un-interrupted, would coalesce as one drop, and the half-line would have only three components instead of the required four. Since the half-lines can combine in any order it is clear that this coalescence does not happen at the boundary between half-lines (or, say, A + B would give */ x / x/ x /, with seven components instead of eight). That is to say, there is between half-lines a break, or line-end marker, corresponding to the central type of line-end marker in later English. And as in later English, there is more than one feature which acts as a line-end marker. The end of a half-line is always determinate in syllabic structure; if it is occupied by a lift this goes without saying, but if it is occupied by a drop there is the special restriction that the drop must there be monosyllabic. Now if we use the symbols — for syllable-length, and ◡ for shortness, we can amplify our formula for the five types in the following way:

$$A \ / \ x \ / \ x$$
$$B \ x \ / \ x \ /$$
$$C \ x \ / \ \ / x$$
$$D \ / \ \ / \ \backslash \ x$$
$$E \ / \ \backslash \ x \ /$$

NOTE: ◡ are used here for syllable-quantity; vowels are not necessarily long in long syllables.

The incidence of stresses is no different from that in ordinary usage. There are three types of syntactic element, in which we can recognise distinctions made in the discussion of late OE positional syntax (cf. §192). The root syllables of words normally stressed, notably nouns and adjectives, will carry lifts; the second elements of compounds and certain other syllables will carry half-lifts; a class of elements can carry a lift or half-lift when given special emphasis, and displacement will be the sign of this emphasis – here belong, for example, finite verbs, adverbs, oblique cases of pronouns, prepositions; and some particles will never be stressed.

Half-lines so constructed are linked in pairs, which, accordingly have four lifts. The alliterative link between them gives added weight to certain stresses – the first, second or both in the first half-line with the first in the second half-line. Here is one specific ingredient in the elusive 'weight' of which the second half-line should have less than the first; only in rare patterns of double alliteration can its second lift enter the alliterative pattern. Thus, with the symbol α for alliteration, adding β if a second alliterative element enters, the four lifts in the total line may be represented in this way:

(a) norm   1 2 3 4   (b) special effect, 1 2 3 4   or   1 2 3 4
         (α)(α)α   α β β α   α β α β

In terms of the variable realisations possible for each of the five types the poet has many other resources for 'weighting' or lightening a half-line.

The system is so complex to verbalise that it may seem artificial and remote; in fact long stretches of prose from any period, and of PE conversation, scan according to these rules (cf. Daunt, 1946). The main restriction is that we do not regularly speak in nothing but two-stress units. Because these patterns are selected from normal speech, and because we know OE to be an inflected language with root-stress, we can predict that much the commonest pattern will be A, and that certain grammatical forms, certain incidences of word-boundaries, will characteristically go with certain half-line types. Let us look at a short extract to see how these matters arrange themselves:

A   /   x   /   x   /   / \ x   D

1. Secge ić þē tō sōðe   sŭnŭ Ecʒlāfes
    /ˈsedʒə itʃ   θeː toː ˈsoːðə   ˈsunu ˈedʒˌlɑːvəs/
    say   I to   you as truth   son of Ecglaf

B   x   /   x   /   /   x /   x   A

2. þæt næfre ʒrēndel sþā fĕlă   ʒrȳrĕ ʒefrĕmĕde
    /θæt næːvrəˈgrendəl swɑːˈfelə   ˈgryrə jəˈfremədə/
    that never Grendel so   many horrors had performed

D   /   / \ x   /   x   /   x   A

3. ătŏl   ǣʒ-lǣća   ealdre þinum
    /ˈatəl   ˈæːjˌlæːtʃə   ˈæːəldrə ˈθiːnum/
    deadly monster (against)   prince   yours

A	/	x	/ x		x	/	/ x		C

4. hȳnðo on Hĕorŏte ʒif þin hĭʒĕ þǣre
/ˈhyːnθo onˈheərətə jif θiːn ˈhijə ˈwæːrə/
humiliations in Heorot if your spirit were

A	/	x	/	x			/	/ x		C

5. sĕfă sþā sĕarŏ-ʒrim sþā þū self tălast.
/ˈsevə swɑː ˈseəro ˈgrim swɑː θuː ˈself ˈtaləst/
courage so battle-grim as you yourself consider

(Son of Ecglaf, I tell you as a certain truth that G., the deadly monster, would never have inflicted so many horrors, shames in Heorot, upon your prince, if your spirit and courage were so terrible in battle as you personally consider them.)

The short passage calls for a good deal of comment and explanation. First it must be said that the pronunciation transcribed represents one that may be supposed to have been current when our extant copy was made, in the late 10c. The poem itself was composed in the 8c, and there is extensive but unsystematic evidence about what the poet's pronunciation might have been. Just as we would normally read aloud the work of Shakespeare in a modern pronunciation except where metre showed us to be wrong, so it seems best to read OE poetry according to the pronunciation of our extant manuscripts, restoring older forms where metre requires. It is not a consistent procedure, but there is no satisfactory all-purpose way of reading either Shakespeare or *Beowulf*. Turning to the scansion, we see the frequency of A exemplified. In line 1a it occurs with a long first drop; in 3b in its most basic form; in 4a with a disyllabic first drop and a resolved second lift; in 2b and 5a with both lifts resolved (the latter half-line ends in a syllable that could take a half-lift, so it is quite a weighty specimen). Type B, with its pure rising pattern, is generally, and predictably, the rarest type; this passage, which being short cannot be representative in everything, distorts the frequency-picture, since it includes no E. In 2a we find B with a trisyllabic first drop and a short second lift. Type C is common, and the examples here illustrate two different realisations – 4b has a disyllabic first drop, a resolved first lift and a long second lift; 5b has a disyllabic first drop, an unresolved first lift and a short second lift. The two D's 1b and 3a, are alike in resolving the first lift.

Alliteration in 1 is on /s/, linking both lifts in the first half-line to the first in the second half-line (the head-stave); *sōð, sunu*, are nouns, *secge* a finite verb heightened by displacement. In 2 the structural alliteration (as the head-stave shows) is on ʒ in the first lift of each half-line (on the alliteration of these sounds, phonemically different in the 10c but not in the 8c, cf. §189); there is extra or decorative alliteration in /f/ on the second lift of each half-line, giving an αβαβ pattern. Line 3 has vowels alliterating together, linking its first three lifts, an adjective and two nouns. Line 4 has alliteration on /h/ across its first three lifts, all nouns, and line 5 on /s/ on noun-adjective-noun. The negative distribution is almost as striking as the positive; no adjective or noun is omitted from the alliterative schemes. Only lifts enter into patterns of alliteration; first sounds in drops are not structurally relevant (cf. *spā* in line 4, not part of the alliteration although it begins with /s/).

So much for the phonological patterning. What is sometimes called the grammetrics (i.e., the relation of syntactic to metrical units) is not less remarkable. Each half-line is filled by one or more elements of the clause; no major syntactic break occurs within a half-line. And both metre and syntax are related in a rather special way to the 'doling out' of meaning by lexical items. In a sense the positional syntax is perfectly regular, in terms of the norm versus marked order patterns we identified in Chapter V. Yet this outline order is interrupted and broken by repeated and resumed clause-elements. Thus the main stressed element of 2a, ʒrendel, is resumed by the whole of 3a, the main stressed element of 2b, ʒryre, by the whole of 4a, the main stressed element of 4b by the whole of 5a. These are very simple examples of the devices of repetition and variation, which may be carried to much greater length. They may well remind us of the resumptive structure of many spoken sentences, and of course this passage is part of a speech. But in a sense all OE poetry is part of a speech, for it is designed to be spoken to an audience, and this characteristic is by no means more marked in dialogue than elsewhere.

The paying out of information as the sentence proceeds typically carries to extremes a characteristic noticeable at all periods in English. Stylistically and semantically nominal elements are elaborated and foregrounded, while verbal elements are relatively weak. All the elements we have watched the poet dwelling on are nominal, and nominal elements as they are introduced are presented under diverse aspects; repetition and variation show them to us in the round, make us attend now to one aspect, now to another. None of the verbal elements are highlighted in this way, and frankly, they do not deserve to be. The first is a verb of *saying*, which, in the course of a speech, is low in information, the second a verb of *doing*, also highly general, the third the verb *be*, and the fourth the verb *think* completing a frame in which its information-value is extremely low.

Though our passage is so short, it illustrates the two main resources used in this characteristic nominal elaboration: the grouping of near synonyms (*hiȝe, sefa*) and the modification of a noun by determination or compounding (*ȝrendel, atol ǣȝ-lǣċa*, exemplifies both types of modification). In interpreting this tendency we must be cautious about assigning cause and effect; presumably this kind of poetry developed because the language was already of what is sometimes described as a nominalising inclination. But once the poetic form existed, it provided a huge stimulus for futher nominalisation. In so far as the nominalising tendency exploited synonyms, it depended on keeping alive a wealth of items that in ordinary prose usage would have died out. One cannot invent synonyms; on the other hand, everyday language will not retain them if they are redundant, as true synonyms are. In this sense, then, the language of poetry was inherently archaising. As far as modification and compounding were concerned interest would necessarily centre on innovation and the avoidance of cliché. The patterns of formation naturally would be traditional, the realisations of them constantly renewed. Here, then, lay the counterbalance to the archaism of synonyms. The two resources, jointly, both almost entirely nominal in character, provide OE with a poetic vocabulary of astounding richness and variety. Yet the resplendent luxuriance of vocabulary was not a falsification, but only an exaggeration of the natural habit of speakers. If we study OE lexis mainly from poetic materials, the chief reason is that they bring out so clearly the essential quality of the language. Eventually this most characteristic featue brought the poetry to an end. Writing within such a convention is only possible so long as the social sharing of spoken poetry is a daily part of life for poet and audience. In most parts of the country such conditions ceased to exist after the Norman Conquest. Though alliterative poetry survives in the west, it is written by men familiar with European forms of verse, and accustomed to the sparer styles that go with them. As we shall see a few, but remarkably few, of the old poetic compounds survive into ME; but in their earlier existence they had not functioned as handed-down words, since what mattered was the pattern of formation within which the poet's inventiveness could work. For the most part the items, many of the patterns, and the style they characterised, came to an end at the Conquest.

§ 182   The wealth of modes of WF, and the abundant productivity of many of the types, must be one of our main concerns in this chapter. We may begin with nominal compounding, which illustrates the process at its most elaborate. The types are, for the most part, common to the language as a whole, but are most active in poetry. In order to save fragmentation and repetition it will be convenient to consider here all types current in OE, explaining their antiquity, origins and survival rate as we go along.

The predominant type in OE, shared by English with all Germanic languages, is the determinative, e.g., *ēarhrinʒ*, 'ear-ring'. Even with our very limited records, over one hundred of these can be shown to be of Common Germanic origin; and so can a number of others with first elements which are not nouns (*middanʒeard*, 'middle-yard, earth') a type of later origin, but growing in OE. The way in which such patterns were productive is shown by the relationship of inherited *undernmete* ('meal taken at mid-morning') to the OE coinages *morʒenmete*, *æfenmete* ('morning, evening meal'), or of old *rūnstæf* ('runic letter') to the coinage *bōcstæf* ('letter written in a book, letter of the Roman alphabet'). In many examples (such as those given) the two elements each contribute a distinct meaning, but in many others the second element is of such generality as to be barely translatable, e.g., *fācenstæf* ('treachery stave, treachery)', *foldþeʒ*, *eorðþeʒ* (with synonymous first elements, 'earthway, earth'). This type of formation can be used so carelessly that it reveals a writer choosing it for nothing but its shape; but we should beware of assuming that because we cannot assign a translation meaning to both elements they did not have any function. By speaking of the *earth* as *fold*, simply, one indicates that it is to be considered generally; by calling it *foldþeʒ*, one invites attention to that aspect under which the earth may be seen as traversed by the means of communication, as having traversable spatial extension, rather, than say solidity, gravity, universality, etc. Post-Conquest English has indeed kept many of the formative patterns of OE, but this capacity in using the patterns it has lost. Here is a difference elusive and not easily defined, but of profound importance.

In a second way these compounds may be untranslatable, namely, if their second element is a specific rather than general word, but, as we say, synonymous with the first element; in *holtþudu*, both elements are translated *wood*, and the second is often said to be redundant. But *holt* is a representative of the family 'wood, copse, -*holt* [in place-names], forest'; it is not quite like any of them, for in this compound it certainly is not specific as to the size of the tree-plantation, as the PE words are.

þudu is of the family 'woods, wood, timber, tree', but not quite like any of them because it does not necessarily distinguish live from dead, growing organism from material, as PE words do. The closer in meaning two components of a compound come the more readily can one reverse their order without changing the referent, as is done with *holtþudu, þuduholt*. This facility is again one which can be abused by incompetent metrists, but in itself it is of interest and value, because the determinative relationship of the elements differentiates the meaning while the referent remains the same. Thus, in OE a spider is both *ʒanʒe(l)þǣfre* and *þǣferʒanʒe*, 'a going-about, i.e., swift-moving, flickering one' and 'a flickering swift-mover'. (Is it any wonder that periphrasis became a favourite grammatical device?) Now this word for *spider* raises another point, one of the rare clues to what happens to WF within the history of OE. The reversal of elements shows plainly that speakers associated the element *ʒanʒe(l)* with the meaning *go*; but in origin the first element was quite different, having the sense *web*, while the second was *weaver*. Compounds are more subject than simple words to such reinterpretations while the form remains unchanged.

Also very common, and surviving in large numbers from a Common Germanic stock, are noun-adjective formations, such as '*ʒærsʒrēne*, 'grass-green', *lofʒeorn* 'praise-eager', including many participial formations, e.g., *ʒold-hroden*, 'gold-adorned'. By contrast, copulative compounds are extremely rare and the type is not productive. The two surviving nominal examples are relationship terms used in the oldest poetry and probably misunderstood by, at least unfamiliar to, the later copyist from whom we have the text (e.g., *aþumsþerian*, 'son-in-law and father-in-law'). The copulative type, therefore, may be taken to have been extinct in OE, so that later formations, of the *king-emperor, fighter-bomber*, types start a new tradition in ME.

Exocentric compounds are also much less common, though not extinct. The type participle + noun = adjective, as in *bolʒenmod*, 'angered mind', is dying out; almost all the examples are in the earliest poetry. In later English it is represented only by extended formations of the *broken-heart(ed)* type. The type *bærfōt*, 'barefoot' is very ancient, but did not have many representatives because speakers since CG had sensed the discrepancy between nominal form and 'adjective meaning', and had tended to replace the formation with one manifestly adjectival in character (as we also use *barefooted*); an OE example of such extension is *dēophȳdiʒ*, 'deep-minded', where the adjective suffix *-iʒ* has been added to an originally exocentric formation 'deep-mind'. The only fairly common formations of this type are those with a numeral as first element, as *ānhende*, 'one-hand(ed)'. A type initiated just before the migration to England, and found very sparely in OE, is that formed with verb–noun, such as *hþetestān*, 'whetstone'. Many first elements were in base form, and could be nominal or verbal; these forms constituted a bridge to formations of purely verbal type.

An innovation within OE is the use of triple compounds, such as *ʒodspellbōc*. These were not used in pre-OE, are very rare in the earliest texts, but from the 9c seem to be established.

§ 183 The part compounding plays in the total vocabulary of OE can be seen from a glance at any OE dictionary, but this will not demonstrate the way in which the compounds are used. C. T. Carr, in a brilliant study of nominal compounds in Germanic, from which all material in this treatment is drawn, has shown that in poetry there are in long poems rates from two in just over three lines to two in just over eleven lines; as the lines are composed of few words (four to six being most usual), and as the number of words per line is reduced where there are many compounds, this is an extraordinarily high rate. Even more striking is the originality of the compounds. If we count only the occurrence of different compounds, the rates begin at 2 for every 3·8 lines; in other words, they are hardly changed. In *Beowulf*, which has over 3,000 lines, only 233 out of 1,069 compounds are repeated.

It is this fecundity which is lost in ME. Though in some areas the alliterative metre survives, and with it whole formulae which had established themselves as half-lines, the diction is conspicuously changed. The only poet at all close to the OE tradition is Lawman, but in over 32,000 lines his rate of compounding is only 1 : 40 lines; he uses twenty-six of the old compounds (e.g., *balusiðe*, 'deadly journey', *feðerhoma*, 'feather-coat, plumage'). Outside his work only nine examples (some the same as Lawman's) survive. In all OE topics we have discussed, examples of words dying at about the Conquest period have arisen; but nowhere is the loss so sharp and extensive as in the compounds. Many of the types, and some of the formations, survived, but the role of compounding in the language was changed for good. In OE it is rather as if the manner of Gerard Manley Hopkins belonged not to an individual, but to a whole speech-community.

§ 184 Occasionally borrowing can be traced between the Germanic languages. One of the most interesting cases is *here-toʒa* (literally, 'one who draws the army [after him]', 'a general', also used to translate L *consul*). This is first used by Alfred, then in later poetry (where it is one of the survivals into ME). The source of this is WG, and it may have been brought to England by one of Alfred's Continental aides. In turn, WG got it from EG, where it was used in the Gothic Bible as a calque of Greek *strategos*, 'army leader'. Having adopted it, OE characteristically used it as a model for a new formation, *folctoʒa*, in which the first element is translated as *people* (*folk*) or *army*, and means 'the whole people considered in its capacity to form a (national) fighting force'.

A group of loans occurring in a more restricted context illustrates the closeness between WG languages not only in materials but in patterns of formation. At the time of Alfred's educational revival an Old Saxon working in England 'translated' an OS religious poem into English. His idiom was not perfectly native, and he retained, with superficial anglicisation of form, a number of compounds which were not actually English, such as *ʒebodsċipe*, 'command', *hyʒesċeaft*, 'mind'; yet the subsequent manuscript history of his work shows that it was cherished and absorbed into the corpus of standard poems, not regarded as an outlandish freak. There is ample evidence that at sea and by settlement the Anglo-Saxons were always in close contact with the Frisians, whose language was the closest of all to their own, and one compound, *īeʒland*, 'island', appears to derive from that source.

Naturally, in later OE, many compounds as well as simple words were borrowed from Scandinavian. It is more surprising that the earliest datable evidence of loans – the only evidence that can clearly be placed in period VI – involves compounds. Two such loans appear in the Alfredian recension of the Chronicle, completed in the year 891-2, namely *sumorlida*, 'summer traveller', i.e., one who joins a summer expedition or raiding trip, and *ðēnestmann*, 'retainer'; neither have survived as common words, but *Summerlid* could recently be found as a family name in the London telephone directory.

The chances of our being able to detect an inter-Germanic compound borrowing are extremely slender; the amount of evidence we have indicates that these words must have wandered about a good deal between the various Germanic languages. Throughout the period, English contributed at least as much as it received in this matter.

§ 185 Prefixal formations are extremely numerous, and are not specially characteristic of verse usage. They belong largely to compounding, though there is some tendency to derivation. The reason for this mixed character is that, except in nominal formations, they are unstressed. They started as elements that could exist independently as words, but in unstressed position some of them have developed weak forms that do not occur as independent words. There are some thirty-four of them, and many (cf. §113) did not survive into, or did not remain active in, ME. *Ā-* (weak form of *or-* which occurs in noun and adjective formations) originally has the meaning *away from*, but in combination with verbs of certain lexical meanings this easily passes over into an intensive force, and this in turn comes to be used alone, with no sense of distancing (*ā-þendan*, 'turn [aside]', *ā-brecan*, 'break [up]'). *Ǣ* is privative (*ǣ-mynde*, 'forgotten'); *æf*, weak form of *of*, 'from', has already been mentioned (cf. §162). *Æfter* involves continuation in time or space (*æfter-fylȝian*, 'pursue', *æfter-ȝenȝa*, 'successor'). *An-* is the strong equivalent of *on-*, 'in, on' (*an-bryrdnes*, 'inspiration', *on-bærnan*, 'inflame'; many figurative uses, as *on-cnāþan*, 'understand'). *And-* is the strong equivalent of *on(d)-*, 'against' (*and-sþaru*, 'answer' sb, *on-cþeþan* 'reply' v). *Be-*, 'around, on, near' (*be-hindan*, 'behind, back'), corresponds to strong *bī-* (*bī-leofa*, 'material to live by, sustenance'). *Ed-* is 'again' (*ed-lēan*, 'recompense'). *For-* has an apparently odd range of meanings, but like those of *ā-* they can be seen to be bridged by certain verb-formations; we may identify elements of completion, intensity, destruction, pejoration, cf. *for-bærnan*, 'destroy by fire', *for-þeorðan*, 'perish', *for-bod*, 'interdiction'. *Fore-* is 'before', locally, temporally, figuratively (*fore-ȝanȝan*, 'precede', *fore-scēaþian*, 'foresee', *fore-spreca*, 'one who speaks on another's behalf, guarantor'). *Ful-*, 'completely', appears in *ful-þiht*, 'baptism', literally 'completion of the rite of sanctification [i.e., after prime-signing], and already in a weakened sense in *ful-nēah*, 'nearly'). Probably the commonest of all, and purely derivational, is *ȝe-* which has a double value as collective and completive (perfective). In addition to its use in verb-formation and to make participles, it is freely employed in noun and adjective formations (*ȝe-fēra*, 'companionȝe', *-mǣne*, 'common'). *In-* is 'in(to)', as in *in-ȝanȝan*, 'enter', and *mis-* has its present value with nouns, adjectives and verbs. *Ofer-* is used both literally and figuratively (*ofer-fēran*, 'cross, traverse', *ofer-cuman*, 'overcome'), *Oð-* is 'far, away', as in *oð-beran*, 'carry away'; and *sām-*, 'half, semi-', (*sām-þorht*, 'half-made, finished'). *Sin-*, 'perpetual', is used very generally as a heightening or intensifying element (*sin-ȝal*, 'incessant', *sin-snǣd*, 'huge piece cut or torn off, mouthful'). There are two clashing *tō-*forms; the less frequent in OE is the one that survived, as in *tō-becuman*, 'arrive (at)', but more frequent *tō-*, 'asunder, to destruction' (which, of course clashes with the meaning of *tō* as an independent word) died out (cf. *tō-berstan*, 'burst, break in pieces', *tō-ċeorfan*, 'cut (carve) up'). Đurh- with verbs has both a directional meaning, 'through', and an intensive one 'thoroughly', as in *ðurh-brecan*, 'break through', but *ðurh-smēaʒan*, 'understand, consider profoundly'. *Un-* is used within its later range, negating adjectives and giving a pejorative sense to nouns; the reversative *un-* with verbs (*un-lūcan*, 'unlock, open') is of distinct origin, but was also in use; *under-*, *ūp-*, and *ūt-*, having survived, hardly call for comment. *Þan-* has a negative or pejorative meaning (*þan-hāl*, 'sick'), and *þið*, as in independent use, means 'against', as does the extended form *þiðer-* (only surviving in *widdershins*). *Ymb(e)-* is used with verbs and nouns in the literal and figurative sense 'around'.

§ 186   In derivation proper we have once again primarily to do with nominal formations. There were over twenty noun-forming suffixes, ranging over six distinct functions. There is necessarily much duplication of function, and we can hardly be surprised that some suffixes have died out altogether, while rather more have remained in fossilised formations. For masculine agent-nouns OE had four formation-types, in *-a, hunta*, 'a hunter'; in *-(e)nd* (originally from the first participle); in *-bora, mundbora*, 'protector', literally 'protection-bearer', and *-ere* (probably borrowed by the Germanic languages from L *-arius*). Of these the first survived till late ME, but was already then subject to confusion with verb-forms, and with loss of *-e* became quite obscure and died out; *-bora* does not survive OE; the participial formations last only in fossilised form, in *friend, fiend* (they cannot be active in ME when *-end(e)* ceases to be a participial ending and the formation-pattern is obscured); leaving *-ere* to hold the field – which it has more than succeeded in doing (it was also reinforced by many French loans of parallel formation). An agent-formative which may have been originally feminine in reference is *-estre*; some of its formations survive from OE to PE in names, *bæcestre*, *Baxter*, *webbestere*, *Webster*, and it remained somewhat active in ME (whence *spinster*). There were competing concrete-noun suffixes (all masculine), *-ing, -ling, -(o)l, -els*, all of which survive fossilised (*king, staple, bridle*, etc.) but had ceased to be active by the end of the OE period. Competition between abstract-noun formatives has largely been resolved in favour of originally masculine *-sċipe* and originally feminine *-nes(s)*, but traces of several other formatives have survived (*-dōm* in *Christendom*, *-hād* in *maidenhood*, *-ð(o)* in *mirth*, *-ing* in *reading*, *-rīce* in *bishopric*, *-lāc* in *wedlock*). The rest, in *-en, -ung, -o, -et(t)* have

died out – indeed, hardly passed into ME. The fifteen adjective formatives include those which have remained alive, even active – (*-en, -fæst,
-erne, -feald, -ful(l), -iġ, -isċ, -lēas, -līċ, -sum, -weard*) and remarkably
few that did not survive the Conquest (*-bǣre*, 'bearing', *-cund*, 'kind',
-ol, 'disposed', *-wende*, 'turning towards'). The glosses for the archaic
formatives are based on their etymological meanings, and are more
literal than their force in many OE formations. Adverb formation was
largely dealt with in §152; the most important addition is *-an*, suffixed
to indicate direction from; this useful element was a victim of obscura-
tion resulting from lack of stress.

Verbs which have the appearance of being compounded (other than
those formed with prefixes) are in fact derived from nominals, as
ēað-mēdan, 'humiliate oneself', from *ēað-mōd*, 'humble'.

A peculiarity of OE WF was that suffixes related in etymological
origin were largely, perhaps wholly, interchangeable. We may sometimes
suspect that one dialect generalised one form, another another form, but
we do not have sufficiently representative evidence to do more than
observe that doublets exist. Some of the doublets involve suffixes still
active in WF in our period, others involve earlier suffixes whose role
remained clear, but which were no longer active except in the limited
sense of being transferable by the principle of interchangeability. In
earliest OE there had been alternative adjective-forming suffixes, *-ul, -il*,
both containing vowels that will have a particular effect on the vowel of
a preceding syllable (cf. §199, 212). A stem might be extended by either or
both, and be modified accordingly; then in periods VI and V the endings
would remain interchangeable, and could occur with either form of stem,
until redundancy led to loss of one of the forms. Thus, the forms in
standard use, *dīeʒol*, ('secret'), *hetol* ('hostile, given to hating'), have
stem-vowels which could only have developed under the influence of
suffix *-il*, later *-el*, but the variants in *-ul*, later *-ol*, have not only come into
use, but actually ousted their predecessors, historically developed. It is
more usual to be able to detect the alternation because regular doublets
are recorded; in early Nhb we have the word *hefæn*, corresponding to
WS *heofon* ('heaven', literally, 'that which is heaved up, the vault of the
sky'). The noun-formatives here are *-an*, later *-æn*, and standard *-en*, as
against *-un*, later *-on*. This may be a case in which for the given word
different dialects levelled each a distinct form, and that would seem to be
the case generally for one of the abstract-noun formatives, for which WS
prefers *-nes*, Mercian and Nhb *-nis*, while 'Kentish' goes from an earlier
preference for *-nes* to a mixed later usage. In all these cases, and others

like them, the interest of the variation is confined to OE, since the different forms produce the same or similar reflexes in later English. But one alternation which is of importance for later developments is that between -*ung* and -*ing* in feminine abstract-noun formation; here one form or another might be specialised according to the type of stem to which it was added, or the dialect in which the formation was made. WS preferred -*ung*, NWS -*ing*, which eventually established itself as the ME norm, and so extended its range as to become one of the most important formatives, lexically and grammatically, throughout the history of late ME and NE.

§ 187　Up to a point borrowing can be studied within the confines of the period, though not all loans can be dated accurately. In particular, words which are primary to Christianity will be assumed to belong to period VII, even if, in the nature of the records, they are not recorded till VI. But a considerable number of Latin loans of a more learned character are first recorded in work of this period, such as *apostol, cālend*, 'month', *mūr*, 'wall', *fenix, pēa*, 'peacock', *plant, citere*, 'cither', *chōr*, 'chorus, choir', *sācerd*, 'priest', *balsam, canōn*, 'canon of scripture', *regol*, 'rule of religious life', *cometa* (glossed as *feaxede steorra*, 'haired-star', and shown by the context to be felt as an alien). In fact, after about 650 the form of a word does not give much indication of when it was borrowed, and the first recorded instance is only evidence of a *terminus ante quem*. But since the period begins at a time of high scholarship, and ends with one of painstaking re-education from Latin sources, we may reasonably suppose that considerable numbers of words do date from this era. To its close may belong certain Scandinavian words we are not certainly able to place earlier than V.

§ 188　What is quite certain is that the bulk of Scandinavian place-names in England must belong to the period of first settlement in the Danelaw (i.e., the second half of the 9c) and to the rather later Norwegian settlements in the north-west. Some reference has already been made to this in connection with the size of the Scandinavian influx (cf. §139) but the subject now requires fuller treatment. Fresh territorial divisions, administrative arrangements and coinage demonstrate the importance of the Norse settlement in official life, but our central concern must be with the number of settlement names, which shows the density of habitation. The huge numbers of -*by* and -*þorp* forms have been mentioned (cf. §139). *Booth*, 'a hut', *lathe*, 'a barn', *garth*, 'an enclosure', *thwaite*, 'a clearing, meadow', are clearly Scandinavian, as are many nature-names, *bank*, *breck*, *fell*, *how*, *rig*, *holme*, *scar*, *skerry*, *gill*, *car*, *beck*, *force*, *tarn*, *crook*, *gate*, 'way', *wath*, etc., of whose use all can supply familiar examples. Of these, *thorp* and *booth* indicated specifically Danish, *breck* and *gill* specifically Norwegian origin.

The names formed with such elements are not all of the same type. Some are purely Scandinavian, as their inflections, for instance, may show. There are a good many names preserving a genitive in -*ar*, -*er* (e.g., *Borcherdale*, *Borrowdale*), which, as we know, was never an OE inflection. On the whole, place-names reflect not so much the usage of the original occupants as that of the surrounding neighbourhood, the people who needed to refer to the new settlement. One or two pure Scandinavian names could have established themselves merely by chance, but a considerable survival indicates Scandinavian settlements in an area in which already the dominant language was Scandinavian, and the numbers involved certainly are considerable. Other names combine Scandinavian and English elements or features. We see one form of this in *Scalford*, Leic, 'the shallow ford'; the /sk/ onset is Scandinavianised, but there is no Norse word corresponding to OE *sceald*, 'shallow', so the origin of the form must be English. Another form of it is shown by the history of *Eamont*, Cumb, OE *æt ēaʒemōtum*, 'at the meeting (moot) of the rivers, (many OE names are preserved in locative forms); the medieval form (probably the source of the modern form; the OE should give *Eye*-) is *Amot*, in which Norse *á*, 'river', has replaced OE *ēa*. Such blends indicate heavy Scandinavian infiltration into areas populated by English settlers – infiltration on such a scale as to make the Scandinavian forms normal currency in the area. There are also hybrids clearly made by Scandinavians, e.g., those using pre-Scandinavian material inflected in a Scandinavian way, such as *Allerdale* (valley of the Ellen), and hybrids clearly made by English-speakers, such as those using a Norse personal name and English second element, e.g., *Grimston*.

From all this it should be clear that place-name evidence about Scandinavian settlement is obtained not from the isolated name, but from such a grouping of names as indicates something of the character of the neighbourhood. Often, from localities in which personal names have been recorded, we can establish that the amount of Scandinavian settlement is much greater than place-names tell us. What can be reconstructed is therefore an irreducible minimum. It shows settlement to have been heavy in Yorkshire, South Durham, Lincoln, Nottingham, Leicester, Derby, Northamptonshire, Rutland, east Norfolk (less in the rest of East Anglia), all predominantly Danish. In Cumberland, West-morland, northern and coastal Lancashire and the Wirral peninsula of Cheshire the names are chiefly Norwegian, and Norwegians moved over the Pennines into western Yorkshire. While no certain figures can be given for either the Scandinavian or the English population at this period, it seems unlikely that Norse settlers were much inferior in numbers to Englishmen; if immigration had not been checked by military means the numbers would certainly have grown substantially further. As it is, one can see, from the blend of peoples and from the scale and penetration of linguistic fusion, why some scholars have preferred to speak of an Anglo-Danish language, rather than of English with high absorption of Scandinavian elements. On balance, however, the historical justification for the name English seems to me sufficiently established.

§ 189   With fuller evidence we might conclude that much more happened phonologically in period VI than we are at present able to do. The two preceding centuries and the two following centuries are times of enormously more phonological change. Perhaps our dating is inaccurate; the earlier changes must really be early, but some that seem to be later may really belong here. That is mere guesswork, on which in any case we cannot act, since we have no idea which changes might be involved. On the other hand it may really be the case that after the very extensive changes of the migration period the phonology settled to a time of equilibrium.

Whatever the truth of this, the fact is that there is less than usual to record under phonology. Among consonants we can detect a group of phonetic changes resulting in phonemic split. In the 8c the sound written ȝ has back and front values, which are allophonic; thus in *Beowulf* ȝār, 'spear', alliterates with ȝēar, 'yore'. In the 10c the back variant, originally fricative, has become a stop, /g/, and the two sounds no longer alliterate. The same happens to the corresponding voiceless sound; originally /k/ with front and back qualities according to context, its front variant becomes an affricate /tʃ/, and is no longer felt to belong to the same phoneme. We may naturally suppose that the cluster *sc* developed from /sk/ to /ʃ/ at the same time. This creates a new phoneme; the few remaining /sk/ sequences, as in *tusc*, 'tooth', must thenceforth have been felt as clusters. Here, too, must belong the affrication of the long voiced stop /gg/, also front, to /dʒ/, one of the factors in distancing long consonants from their short counterparts.

Distributional changes in consonants – additions and losses – are of much the same kinds as we have met at other periods. In particular it is to this period that we must date simplification of the initial cluster in *sprecan*, 'speak', *sprǣċ*, 'speech'.

In vowels we detect the 10c WS substitution of *ȳ̆* for *ĭ(e)* in words in which it corresponds to NWS *e*, as in *ȝiellan, ȝyllan,* NWS, *ȝellan,* 'yell' (cf. §163). Most other dialect-variation of a phonological kind is pre-770 and can best be dealt with at one blow in Chapter VII. One change, in the 10c, is common to the whole country, namely the lengthening of all vowels (including diphthongs) before certain consonant-clusters, usually liquids or nasals followed by a voiced stop, though occasionally another following voiced consonant will have the same effect. To this, as we have seen (cf. §170) we owe the development of many sub-types of strong verbs; *bindan* becomes *bīndan, band > bānd, bundon > būndon,* and so on. Subsequent developments in both ME and NE have affected long vowels more than short, and have continually widened the gap. The lengthening was immediately followed by a process of shortening before all other consonant-clusters; indeed, though we have treated the shortening under period V, it may even have been simultaneous with, complementary to, this lengthening. The truth is that we have more precise information about the relative chronology of the lengthening.

§ 190 Of greater interest are the developments in unstressed syllables. It was around 770 that the distinct front vowels (*æ, e, i*) levelled in unstressed syllables to a single sound, written *e*, and at first no doubt of /e/ quality; in course of time it faded to /ə/, a further development that cannot be closely dated, though it had certainly happened by the end of period VI. This reduction of contrast levelled in a single form a number of formerly distinct inflections, and serves as evidence that the language was able to function without those distinctions (cf. §200).

The back vowels remained distinct. The height and rounding of /u/ require considerable energy. The sound survived at the beginning of the period; in medial position it seems to have been identified with /o/ by the early 9c, when texts begin to show wavering spellings. Hesitation between the spellings *u* and *o* in unstress does not indicate a sound midway between the two phonemes, as is sometimes claimed, but that the new sound has been reached, and sometimes appears in spellings, while at other times spelling-habits prevail. Both in final position, and when 'protected' by a high neighbouring sound (notably /u/ in the preceding syllable, or a nasal following), /u/ lasts till the close of the period (as in *sunu,* 'son', *-um,* dat pl). A very large number of /u/ forms occur in grammatical endings in OE, but as none of them were in grammatical contrast with /o/ forms no great consequences followed from the weakening of /u/.

Quite early in the 9c we find in 'Kentish' documents that the remaining distinction, between /o/ and /a/, has gone; evidence is scrappy, and we cannot assume that the loss proceeded at the same rate throughout the country. By around 900 it seems to have been general. At that stage the language has a single front unstressed vowel, and a single back one, exact quality unknown, though something like /a/ seems most likely. This further reduction levels a number of earlier grammatical contrasts in both verbs and nominals, as can be understood from a study of the forms in §171 and §165. The grammatical distinctions kept or blurred when the unstressed vowels are reduced to two are a matter of chance; the reduction of vowels is a sign that these formal distinctions were no longer functionally important, and their progressive ineffectiveness becomes a stimulus to the further losses of the transition and ME periods.

Since the traceable dialect differences of OE are above all a matter of vocalism, it is not surprising that the unstressed syllables, with their greatly simplified vowel-system, have little to offer in the way of phonological dialect material. But inflectional syllables belong at least as much to morphology. There is a particularly important dialect difference which cannot be explained phonologically, but must involve substitution of morphological endings. In WS the first person singular present indicative of verbs had the ending -*e*. In almost all NWS texts it has in early use -*u*, later -*o*. The innovator is WS, which has replaced the historically developed ending, presumably with one borrowed from the subjunctive. Such a substitution seems abnormal to modern readers, who think of the indicative as the usual form, and the subjunctive as rare and in danger of loss, rather than as strong enough to influence the indicative. In OE, on the other hand, the subjunctive was a somewhat dominant form, both because it had a very wide range of functions in which it was required or permitted, and because its singular, unlike that of the indicative, was common to all three persons, and therefore of more frequent occurrence than any one indicative singular form. The traditional, NWS, form, raises another point of some importance. We were able to compare the -*m* of *am* and of L *sum* as isolated survivals, but now we have a whole class of endings, OE -*u*, L -*o*, which look comparable. From now on as we go back in time, such comparisons will become more frequent. They will not necessarily be with Latin, but that is, of all non-Germanic IE languages, the one whose morphology is most likely to have some familiarity for English readers. All such comparisons involve common descent; the English does not come from the Latin, but both descend from a common source. The model is not *A→B, but

B $\overset{\nearrow A \searrow}{\quad}$ C. In such a case B and C are said to be cognate languages, or the forms under consideration to be cognate forms; it is important to distinguish the cognate relationship from both the borrowing relationship and the descent relationship. It is also important to understand that while the arrows indicate that B is later than A, and C is later than A, they do not imply anything for the relative chronology of B and C.

Turning to the consonants in morphological development, we find a marked peculiarity in Nhb. This had lost final inflectional -n wherever it occurred – in the oblique forms of weak nouns (e.g., *sefa*, 'heart', gen sg), in infinitives (*ʒistiʒa*, 'climb, mount'), past indicative plurals (*cþomu*, 'came'), etc. In fact these developments are already in evidence in the earliest written records, i.e., before period VI begins. They continue to characterise Nhb till the end of the OE period, and they establish its character as a 'progressive' dialect from the very earliest times. By the 8c its phonology and morphology are such that as soon as loss of unstressed vowel contrast occurs it will have lost practically all grammatical distinctions dependent on inflection. In fact this gives rise to very little ambiguity; the remaining /ə/ serves little or no purpose, and itself is lost by the close of OE. What Nhb puts in place of the older patterns is a broad contrast between nominal and verbal forms, by extending to other persons of the singular the old second person present indicative ending -s; almost all other verb-forms are distinct from nominals in other ways. What Nhb had focused upon around A.D. 1000 has come since ME to stand at the heart of modern English grammar, though the means used are not always the same.

It may be added that in its loss of final inflectional -n, as in other features of its morphology and lexis, Nhb exhibits striking parallels to the Scandinavian languages at a time antecedent to the first viking raids (cf. § 208).

§ 191 For modern English we assume that punctuation will afford substantial evidence on syntactic interpretation, but for late medieval English we found it to be of little assistance (cf. § 97). In OE it is even less illuminating. For instance, MS A of the Chronicle, which is one of our best pieces of evidence for Alfredian WS, uses only two symbols. The normal one is :√, which occurs at the end of each yearly entry, perhaps equivalent to a single sentence, perhaps pages long and consisting, on any

definition of sentence, of many sentences. Within entries there are twelve
instances of the use of a point, either the same one, or one roughly like
a semi-colon. Clearly the rarer point marks some kind of lesser break,
but there is no obvious syntactic significance in the placing of either kind
of internal point. In general, what we encounter is pointing derived
from liturgical chant rather than syntactic structure; the two are related,
but not identical. From the 8c on, a well-pointed manuscript may contain a single point for intermediate pause, and more than one point
(various numbers, variously arranged) for a main pause; this system is
still widespread in verse and prose manuscripts of Alfred's time. Verse
and prose are also alike in lineation; except for major sections, in both
the lines are written continuously across the page (from which it follows
that our knowledge about the metre of OE is inferential).

The 8–9c system was followed in the 10c by a down–up system, in which
a low point was used for intermediate pause, and a high one for main
pause. At the same time, a more elaborate system was introduced into
homiletic writing (it occurs, for instance, in Ælfric's sermons). This
used four symbols, taken from the pointing used to distinguish the
melody of final cadences in chanting; perhaps the texts written with it
were meant to be chanted. The occurrence of any cadence (hence, any
symbol when the system was transferred to literature) marks the end of
what is musically called a phrase, a unit to which corresponds some sort
of syntactic unit, not always one of the same rank. The choice between
cadences was symbolised by signs for voice-lowering, *punctus circum-
flexus* (rather like a question-mark in one form, a raised dot in another)
or *punctus versus* (rather like a semi-colon in one realisation, a low dot
or full stop in another). These correspond syntactically to sentence-
ends; for suspension at a medial pause there is the raised point or
punctus elevatus, and for rising tone in questions *punctus interrogativus*,
⸳. There is, thus, a transfer from chant to literary composition, from
melody to intonation and so to syntax. These transfers proceed gradually,
in such a way that it is difficult to judge how far symbols have linguistic
meaning in a given manuscript. From homiletic writing the system
extended to all careful script and became general in the 12c. It persisted
in the 14c, but then had to compete with rival modes of pointing which
finally replaced it at the Renaissance (cf. §62). In so far as PE makes, in
intonation, a primary distinction between rising and falling tones, the
use of pointing in OE suggests that the distinction is of extreme antiquity; but whether the distribution was exactly the same (for instance,
whether the use of a question-word resulted in falling intonation for a

344

question), and whether the refinements of the broad rise–fall distinction were alike, we cannot say.

We are so habituated to a syntax-oriented punctuation-system that we might expect to find many syntactically ambiguous passages in OE. There are some, particularly in poetry, but they are the exceptions. In the great bulk of surviving records the boundaries and internal structure of clauses are clear and unambiguous; further, features of order and verb-selection indicate, almost always unambiguously, the relations between independent and dependent clauses. We are in a position to speak confidently of OE sentences, and do not have to limit ourselves (as has sometimes been claimed) to clause-analysis.

§ 192   The degree of morphological reduction in Nhb is evidence that already means other than morphology carried the main burden of indicating syntactic function. The most important was order, and it is not surprising that the whole OE period shows rapid and complex evolution of its positional syntax. It is not simply that various orders succeed one another, but more importantly, that the determinants of order, and the elements whose ordering is of prime importance, themselves change swiftly and profoundly.

The pioneer in the study of historical change in ordering factors was Fourquet (1938), and an example he uses clarifies the problem of historical study of positional syntax. He points out that the common assumption that there is the same order in French *il vint* and German *er kam* is wrong. The likeness between these structures is secondary, and if we describe them both as instances of S–V then our syntax as a whole will be a muddle. If we look at each of them in the contexts of the other sequential patterns with which they coexist and correlate in the two languages, we find that the correct description of the French sequence is S–V, while the crucial fact about the German sequence is that the verb is in second position. If, while keeping to the same clause-type, we expand both structures by means of an initial adverbial, we have for French *hier il vint* and for German *gestern kam er*; French retains S–V order, German retains the verb in the second position. This factor in the positional syntax of the two languages is primary; it establishes a nucleus, about which other elements can be grouped in dependent ways. From this it follows that historical study of syntax cannot be pursued by counting examples of one pattern and then of another. If our statements are to have any general validity, we must first determine whether, at a given time, a language has a nuclear positional rule, and then look at the ordering of elements whose placing is dependent on the integrity of the nuclear rule. In the latest OE the nucleus, positionally speaking, was already the S–V sequence, as in all later English, though dependent ordering rules took forms which have since been superseded. As we go further back, we find that even the primary or nuclear rules are different.

Fourquet shows that on the eve of period VI the nuclear structure was that of the verb with its nominal determinants, i.e., objects and complements; this, indeed, had been the case for a very long time. Even in early OE the subject of a verb is not always expressed, and at a yet earlier phase, when verb-endings had been fully distinct for the three persons of the plural as well as the singular, non-expression of the subject had been common. Historically, then, we should not expect subject-placement to enter the primary rules; nor does it. The verb–object nucleus (as we may roughly call it) had two chief orders in independent, affirmative clauses: in the unmarked form the order is nominal-verb, and any displacement involves marking or highlighting of the clause or of the element displaced. Since there may be more than one nominal, secondary rules govern their order relative to one another, normally dative, genitive, accusative; this secondary order assumes particular importance within OE because of the large measure of loss of distinct accusative forms. These verb-determining nominals will lead, in the order given, to the verb they relate to, and since the whole sequence is nuclear the subject will not interrupt this order, which leaves it, if unmarked, in initial position. But in early OE its being there is entirely consequential. Contrast, from the 8c poem *Beowulf*, presumably written just before our period, an unmarked sequence: *hē him ðæs lēan forʒeald* ('he to him in respect of that a reward gave', 'he paid him back for that'), with the marked sequence: *iċ hine cuðe cnihtþesende* ('I him knew boy-being', 'I used to know him when he was a mere boy'). In both the subject comes first in unmarked position; the fact that this is so common is going to have great consequences for future positional syntax, but in the 8c it is a contingent, not a primary, fact of sentence-organisation. There follows in the unmarked sentence the sequence of object-nominals leading up to the verb; which, indeed, is in final position, but contingently so. The marked sentence splits the object, placing it, in so far as its relation to the verb is normal, before the verb, but reserving for displaced position, and therefore for prominence, the apposed adjective which gives the sentence its point.

Already in the 8c there existed side by side with this ancient ordering principle a newer one exploiting the contrast between light and heavy elements – in the first instance, elements that except under contrastive stress would not fill a lift in verse, and those that regularly would. By the new principle all light elements are transferred to initial position in the clause, preceding even the subject, as in the sentence (from the same poem): *him þā Scyld ʒeþāt tō ʒescæphþīle* ('himself then Scyld took off at shaped/destined time', 'then S. departed at the time ordained'). The new principle is indirectly syntactic, since we know that metrical and rhythmical weight in OE depended largely on form-class membership (cf. §181), but the differences are great, both because the relationship between weight and form-class intervenes, and further because form-class membership is not the same kind of syntactic consideration as clause-element function; a personal pronoun will commonly be light as subject or object, a noun heavy in either function. Though the two systems exist side by side, we can tell by comparison with other Germanic languages that the weight-principle is the innovation, and belongs especially to OE. One very important implication of the weight-principle is seen in the classification of verbs. Verbs of full lexical meaning are heavy, but the verb *be*, and other verbs used in what we may recognise as something like auxiliary sense, are treated as light elements. Although there are few occasions when the old meanings of *sceal, þille, sceolde, þolde*, in particular, would be impossible in OE, we can sometimes distinguish the old full meaning from the new auxiliary meaning by the weight-classification of the verb, and we can certainly see that *be* is already being treated distinctly from normal verbs. For example we find in *Beowulf: him þæs ʒeōmor sefa* ('to him was sad heart', 'his heart was heavy'), in which the light copula is placed with the other light element *him* before the lexically full elements of the sentence.

Now by the new principle of ordering, sentences with light elements (and such sentences were, naturally, numerous) were unable to show marking by traditional means, and had to develop an alternative. The new type of marking involved putting the verb in initial position, as in: *niston hīe dryhten ʒod* ('not-knew they Lord God', 'they were wholly unaware of the Lord God'). Really what is highlighted is the clause-type, and perhaps a better translation would begin 'what they were ignorant of was . . .'. This function of drawing attention to clause-type made the pattern particularly suitable for interrogative sentences, in which it has persisted, though its more general origins are no longer evident. But equally, in OE, it was used in justifying or intensive clauses, and of this too we have some traces in such colloquial structures as 'like it you may

347

not, but the fact is . . .'. In relation to later usage the pattern is often, and not inappropriately, labelled *inversion*. This term should not be used in relation to OE, since what the pattern involves there is marking by use of set, initial position for the verb, while unmarked sentences do not have a fixed position for the verb as such.

The rivalry between two systems of marking in early OE necessarily constituted an unstable state of affairs. For the early 9c we lack evidence in normal continuous syntax to show how and when the rivalry resolved itself. By the end of the 9c, when evidence is once again abundant, the new type of ordering has quite displaced the old. In itself this process leaves a gap, for originally the new ordering made no special provision for the ordering of sentences beginning with heavy elements. To fill this gap a new pattern develops in which the nominal determinants of the verb are grouped at the end of the clause. Thus in the part of the Chronicle, MS A, written in the year 891-892, we find the sentence: *Sē Ecȝbryht lǣdde fierd tō Dore þiþ Norþanhymbre* ('this E. led [an] army to D. against [the] Northumbrians'). The opening element is heavy; the direct and prepositional objects come at the end; this leaves the verb in a position that might be described as medial, second, post-subject or pre-object. The point is that given the phonological weight of the opening, the remaining nominals will have end position, and the position of the verb is purely contingent. A co-ordinate sentence having one clause opening heavy and one opening light shows the new contrast very well: *C. ꒐ C. ȝefuhton þiþ A. ꒐ hine in Cent ȝeflīemdon* ('C. and C. fought against A. and him into Kent put-to-flight'). The first clause has a heavy (noun) onset, and its prepositional object is in final position; the second has no subject expressed, and the two dependent nominals (*hine, in Cent*) are pre-verbal. By the late 9c this alternation according to weight of sentence-onset characterises unmarked sentences, while marking is by initial placement of the verb: *hæfde hine Penda ādrifenne* ('had him P. driven away', 'P. had got him banished' 'he was taken care of, as far as P. was concerned, by banishment').

The primary determinants in such a system give great prominence for weight, but they do not include any ruling for the position of the verb *per se*. Yet a variety of factors brings about the result in practice that a great many sentences do, for one reason or another, have the verb in second position; and that unmarked clauses commonly do have the subject in initial position. Since speakers plan their sentences according to what they sense as a norm (and not, of course, by principles histori-cally worked out), the situation is once again unstable. Speakers of a new generation, extrapolating from the sentences they hear, will govern their usage according to different norms. The Chronicle MS A is written in a single hand for a substantial period lasting from 894-925. We may take this scribe's usage as typical of the generation that was in full maturity in the first third of the 10c. There are now two dominant patterns of clausal order, both characterised by fixed positions for the verb. The old expressive type with initial verb position persists. The unmarked type has two patterns, the normal one with second position for the verb, and another, without fixed position for the verb, which (for reasons we have seen shaping) attaches itself to contrast of clause-type. In unmarked sentences it is now usual for independent clauses to have the verb in second position, dependent clauses to avoid fixed position for the verb. But this too is unstable. For if verb-position has a meaning, distinguishing either marked clauses or dependent clauses from unmarked independent clauses, it will be natural to regularise the pattern by making the verb of dependent clauses avoid the initial and second positions, which have meanings of their own. It therefore comes to be a mark of dependent clauses that the verb is placed at or near the end; at the same time, the formal distinction between independent and dependent clauses becomes sharper than ever before.

In this way was the scene set for the type of patterning we have already encountered in the late 10c (cf. §174); equally, the ingredients of the present scheme came into being, though they were far from forming the fairly regular system they were later to become. To a large extent the dynamism of the change is clear – each stage was necessarily unstable and led to another, though we cannot wholly explain why the movement should have followed quite the lines it did. At no other time in the history of English has such profound syntactic change occurred in so rapid and complex an evolution. The primacy of syntactic evolution at this time explains why such disruptive processes could affect the morphology. Certain of the morphological patterns were largely superannuated, and had no function sufficient to check the decline naturally consequent upon root-stress. Moreover, though in details of syntactic usage dialect-variation can be traced, in the broad lines of positional syntax the sweeping changes occurring from the 8c to the 10c affect all dialects in exactly the same way. For all of them we must postulate a dynamism resulting from common features of the language as the English first brought it to their new homeland, though the movement took several centuries to exhaust itself and to produce a new equilibrium.

§ 193 Discussion of positional syntax has drawn attention to an extension of the distinction between heavy and light. Originally phonological, and partly associated with form-class membership, it easily shifted into territory shared between grammar and lexis. A pronoun is lighter than a noun because of its habitual lack of stress, but this difference is closely associated with a semantic one: the pronoun has a general or grammatical meaning, the noun a specific or lexical meaning. It is to this aspect of the differentiation that the embryonic contrast between full and empty verbs associated itself. In other words, positional syntax is closely linked not only to morphological developments, but also to the growth of periphrastic forms, in the verb and elsewhere. We should be rash to claim that we can distinguish cause and effect in this area; the two, apparently, are interdependent. For our knowledge of periphrastic development, as of positional syntax, in this period, we are largely dependent on European scholarship; the following account leans heavily on Mossé (1938a, b, 1945).

With very rare exceptions, usually capable of more than one interpretation, periphrastic verb forms may be said to begin in the 9c. They soon attain quite high frequency of occurrence, but their distribution indicates that they are not fully at home. The use of forms of *be* (*bēon, þesan*) with the first participle is in the first instance to show simultaneous activity having duration; it is much commoner in the past (*he þæs bodiende*, 'he was preaching, went on preaching, used to preach') than in the non-past (*þū eart rīxiende on þīnum uuldre*, 'you are reigning, reign perpetually, in your glory'). The sense of duration, especially in the past, passes imperceptibly into that of stating a characteristic (*þæs ðe hy þonne þylniʒende þæron*, 'in respect of what they then were desiring, what they wanted at that time'). Barely distinct is the sense of indefinite duration (*sē man þæs þēldōnde [prospere agens] on eallum*, 'that man was well-doing/successful in everything'), and close to this is the sense of permanence or unlimited duration (*sylfa sette þæt þū sunu þære | efen-eardiʒende . . .*, 'he himself appointed that you (a) son should be dwelling in parity [even-dwelling] . . .'). The last strand in the close-woven bundle of meanings is description (*ælc buruhþara þæs būʒende to him*, 'each of the citizens [borough-dwellers] was under submission [bowing, obedient] to him').

While this nexus of uses forms a unity and may have evolved to some extent under Latin influence, the pattern also develops independently in OE. A use apparently quite original is that for limited duration, often with a special sense of persisting through the period in question, of keeping on, not giving up. Frequently the words *oð* or *oððæt* ('until') signal the limit of the duration/persistence, as in *he þæs heriende and feohtende fiftiʒ þintra, oð he hæfde ealle Asiam on his ʒeþeald ʒenȳd* ('he harried and fought [kept on harrying and fighting] for fifty winters/years until he had compelled all Asia into his dominion'). This usage is common with temporal expressions, and practically requires the presence of an adverbial of time. Closely related to it is the use of the formation for repeated action and for insistence.

Similar forms were seen as a means for distinguishing future from present, since there was no formation within the verb which would render this distinction in Latin originals. Translators were often concerned to render not merely the sense but also the grammatical articulation of their models. For example, *dicturi* is rendered by a PF in *bi ðǣre þē nu syndon sprecende* ('about that we are now [about to be speaking]', 'that is what we are going to discuss next'). Such renderings are experimental, and by no means invariable. Future and ingressive meanings are shared with other auxiliaries, *onʒinnan* (as a full verb, 'begin'), and *þeorðan* (as a full verb, 'become'). Increasingly *(on)ʒinnan* comes to be associated with the past, first as an ingressive ('began to') and, from the 10c to at least the 15c, as a simple auxiliary of the past. *Þeorðan* never established more than a marginal role as an auxiliary, and in ME died out in all functions. This is one of the mysteries in the history of English, for this verb, whose cognate *werden* has come to be so important in the grammar of German, could be used for distinctions not briefly shown in any other way. In English too it might have taken over the role of expressing futurity; instead, English has preferred the double forms *will* and *shall*, in which tense is inextricably linked with modality. And it might have assumed the role of a mutative as contrasted with a static or descriptive passive, distinguishing *he was wounded* (*þearð*), i.e., 'from having been unharmed he came to be a casualty', from the descriptive *he was wounded* (*þæs*), i.e., 'he was in a wounded condition'. The loss of *þeorðan* at the Conquest blocked initiatives in this direction. Though NE has used *get* as a mutative passive, the pattern has not established itself above the colloquial level of usage.

Summing up the origins of the *be* periphrases, aspectually considered, Mossé points out that the study of the PF is essentially the study of duration in the verb. In OE the pattern could remain peripheral because verbs were durative unless a prefix marked them as non-durative (cf. §155). In ME the loss of most OE verb-prefixes (cf. §113) destroyed this ancient index of a contrast speakers were accustomed to make.

It was only then that they turned to the rather learned and artificial periphrastic pattern as a means of filling the vacuum. In ME the pattern was from the beginning inherited, not imitated, and this was the pre-condition for its remarkable efflorescence in later English.

By period VI the *be*-passive was already in use; in its course the *have/be* perfect, and the modal use of certain anomalously formed verbs, get under way. All these patterns are still peripheral and relatively rare, but the foundations of their future roles have been laid.

CHAPTER VII

770 – 570

§ 194   By 570 English had been in England for just over a century. We must not think of the English as acting or invading as a nation, nor of the territory they invaded as being a nation State. In quite small bands they attacked and settled according to their needs and according to their military capacity to seize and hold. Sometimes they were repulsed, or had to kill for what they wanted, but the enemy they fought was organised, like themselves, on a small scale and for local engagements. There was no national British defence of any area they attacked. Very often the occupants fled in advance of their arrival. In other cases, whether or not they had first given battle, the British stayed alongside the English – either in the sense that they occupied higher and lower lands in the same districts, or in the sense that they were absorbed into English settlements. No single formula will cover what happened to either group or to the relations between them during this early period.

The English, by 570, had made their way inland, mainly by river, from various entry points along the south and east coasts. They had long occupied Kent, Surrey and Sussex (except for the Weald, which for some time remained quite uninhabited), Middlesex, Essex, East Anglia, Lincolnshire, South Yorkshire, and, further along the south coast, the Isle of Wight and the part of Hampshire facing it. Advancing along the Thames, they had reached the beginnings of present Berkshire and Oxfordshire by about 500, and turned north towards Worcestershire. For about half a century they were halted, but near the beginning of our period they felt the need for further advance. This land-hunger seems to have had a double source – the continued arrival of new settlers from the Continent, and the population-growth of early English settlements. Both new settlement and colonisation from old settlements took place, though there is much expansion that cannot be identified as of one type or the other, nor can we do more than guess at the linguistic implications of the two types. Further advances during the generation which closed about 600 brought the English a boundary running from the Dorset coast through Selwood to the Severn estuary, then almost due north

353

on a line west of Worcester, skirting the west of Cannock Chase, then swinging east, and north again on roughly the present western boundaries of Lincolnshire and eastern Yorkshire to a point well north of the Tees, where it cut across to the east coast. The Durham uplands were ignored; but cut off from the main territories the English held land along the Tyne and the Northumbrian coastal strip. Maps for the 550 and 600 extent of settlements are given in Hodgkin (1935, facing p. 155) and Jackson (1953, 208-9). What appears on a map as English territory contains deserted areas, pockets of British settlement, and large holdings not yet fully settled; the boundaries show more clearly where the English were not, than where they were. Long after the settlement the English did not form a political unity, nor, indeed, though they shared a language, do they seem to have felt themselves to be any sort of unity; they were as ready to fight each other as to fight the British. They perhaps appeared from the outside as a unity, because of common features of their culture, especially their heathenism, but in themselves such a feeling was absent. Until the close of the 6c they were in a minority, and it was by no means obvious that they would come to be the dominant people in the country. On the other hand, since long before our period they had come for land, and with the intention of becoming permanent occupants of the new territory; though they undoubtedly formed a common speech community with Germanic peoples left on the Continent (cf. §207) they did not regard Continental Europe as home. We must suppose that, arriving in the course of more than a century, and from diverse tribes of origin, they arrived with different dialects, and slight traces of these ancient differences can be recovered. But settlement in a new country to which the settlers feel a lasting commitment is usually accompanied by a process of linguistic convergence to a norm for the new community (cf. §44). We do not know whether the early English shared in such a process, but the reasonable supposition is that they did. If so, however, the size of the community within which the norm was established must have been extremely restricted – more often the village or the estate than the kingdom, which itself, in most cases, would be of approximately the size of a modern county.

To all intents and purpose the settlers were illiterate (cf. §195), and such limited knowledge as we have of their linguistic situation, especially in its sociolinguistic aspects, is inferential and indirect. At the close of the 6c the arrival of Christian missionaries led to a fairly rapid conversion. Linguistically the effects of this can hardly be overestimated. The world of letters accompanied the new religion; it transformed what the English had to talk about, how they talked about it, and their capacity to keep records from which we can recover information on all aspects of their life. Less obvious, but linguistically relevant, is the organisation of the Church on a basis by which the English were treated as a single and distinct people; they became a unity in religious organisation long before they constituted one politically. These matters will require fuller treatment in the next paragraph, but the story of expansion cannot be continued as if the 7c were simply an extension of the 6c.

During the 7c the south-western border was pushed back to the line of the Blackdown and Quantock Hills in Somerset, the mid-western to approximately the present Welsh border (but excluding Herefordshire west of the Severn), while in the north the Mersey–Ribble area, the flat land round the Solway Firth on the west, and Scotland up to the Forth on the east, came under the dominion of English kingdoms. This and later expansions seem to have involved the conquest and holding of territory in which considerable alien populations remained, not necessarily confined to the moors and fens as they typically had been in the earlier phase. Late in the 7c the English occupied the Exeter area, and in the 8c the rest of Devon (thinly populated since the Britons made their exodus to Brittany in the 5c and 6c). Still, British was spoken in the south-west, in Dorset and Somerset, as well as Cornwall, certainly to 700, though we cannot tell how much later except in the case of Cornwall. British survived locally in other regions too. In the 7c and 8c English conquests begin to assume a national character; by then there can be no doubt that the settlers mean to occupy the whole country, and will succeed.

§ 195   In 570 the only writing known to the English was the runic 'alphabet', secret to initiates, neither well adapted nor commonly used for recording and communication. It is to the conversion that we must look for the introduction of a system of writing having the functions we now associate with that medium. The well-known date for the arrival of the first missionaries, 597, has probably assumed excessive importance, and distorted popular understanding of what happened. Augustine and his colleagues were well received in the kingdom of Kent, where not only the king but 10,000 (we are told) of his people were baptised by the end of the first year. The missionaries turned their attention north of the Thames, and the bishopric of London was founded under Mellitus to serve the people of Essex. But Mellitus was ejected in 617, and for a decade Kent was the only Christian English kingdom; even there

Christianity was not fully established till 640, and preaching in Essex was not resumed till 654.

Augustine's group were urban, Mediterranean men. They pleased the Court, and apparently were reasonably at home with its people, but they did not greatly fraternise with ordinary men. Their anxieties about having their message interpreted in a language they did not know almost led them to turn back before they reached the country; we do not know how these initial difficulties were overcome, but we do find the missionaries giving offence sixty years later by the inadequacy of their English. Two Roman churches in Canterbury were brought back into use and a monastery founded, but one of the main concerns even in Augustine's church-building was to provide a mausoleum for the kings of Kent and archbishops of Canterbury. Since such religion as preceded can hardly be called a faith, and offered little to either mind or emotion, conversion was not difficult, but Christianity as received from Augustine's teaching was not likely to go very deep. It may well be that the success of the new religion depended far more on a later, but more searching, mission of quite another kind. There remain, however, points of interest in Augustine's work. His churches laid the foundation of book-based education, and his mission saw to it that English was committed to writing after the Roman fashion. In particular, he was worried that the code of law as orally handed down provided for men according to their ranks, but had no place for clerics, who were unknown in earlier English society. He persuaded King Ethelbert of Kent (?560-616) to have the traditional code written down and to enlarge it with articles designed for the protection of the clergy. This code survives only in much later copies; we do not know what its writing was like, or whether it should be regarded as founding the tradition of writing that has come down to us.

In 625 Paulinus travelled to the Northumbrian Court as escort and chaplain to the Kentish Christian princess betrothed to King Edwin of Northumbria (regnal dates 616-32). In due course he was able to convert the king and his council, and to baptise many others. He is said to have spent thirty-six days at the royal vill of Yeavering, which lies on the banks of the Glen at the foot of the Cheviots, baptising from morning to night in the river. Although again this account indicates that many beyond the Court were reached, we do not know how many were English or were true converts. Yeavering, which has recently been excavated, shows strong British influence in position, lay-out and structure, and it may well be that many who flocked to hear Paulinus were of British origin. The policy of Edwin, as of Ethelbert, was not to impose the new religion on his people, but in both cases it seems likely that many followed the king's example with little idea of what the new religion was supposed to mean. Edwin is one of the earliest kings to establish wide dominion within England, becoming overlord of all English kingdoms up to the Forth, together with the British kingdoms of Strathclyde, Cumbria, Elmet, and the equivalent of Wales and Cornwall (map in Hodgkin, 1935, 275); yet when he fell it was to a Mercian heathen, Penda. From a Christian point of view there followed an interregnum, which, if prolonged, could still have spelt the end of the faith in England. That it was terminated was due to action not from the Roman but from the Celtic Church.

One might have supposed that a Roman mission was unnecessary for a people settled amongst the Britons, who were Christian. The Britons did not on any substantial scale choose to convert their invaders; indeed, the wisest of the Anglo-Saxons (though in this matter he perhaps exaggerated) took the view that the Britons found their only consolation in the thought that if no one converted the Anglo-Saxons they were all heading for hell-fire. The Irish, who were less closely affected by English onslaughts, took the view that even the English had souls worth saving. They took this view in a form sufficiently moderate to wait till they were sent for before they began their missions. The Irish and the Scots at this time belong together, the Scots being those Irish who had emigrated to Scotland, where they found themselves in rivalry with the British and the Picts, and, in the southern parts, with the English. A member of the Irish royal house, Columba (521-97), established on the Scottish island of Iona a monastery, which, in the Irish fashion, was also a centre of scholarship. There, at the beginning of Edwin's reign, two brothers belonging to the royal house of Bernicia (North Northumbria), Oswald and Oswiu, who might have been considered Edwin's rivals for the throne, took refuge. Oswald's training in Celtic Christianity during his years on Iona was the final guarantee of England's conversion. In 633 he brought the pagan interregnum to an end by defeating Penda, and as king of Northumbria invited Bishop Aidan from Iona to preach to his people. The king, at first, personally acted as Aidan's interpreter, though it is implied that as soon as possible Aidan learnt the language; and he gave the missionaries an island monastery, of the kind they favoured, on Lindisfarne. There, of course, they set up a school. By perambulating the country, by educating (not merely instructing in the faith), by recruiting new missionary-teachers who in turn passed on both faith and learning, the Iona missionaries reached the populace as the Romans had not. They moved gradually, being a small band unable to conduct operations on a grand scale, but their converts were led to understand that the new faith was something of a different order from what had gone before. When, in 640, Oswald was killed by Penda, there was no return to paganism. Perhaps Penda himself took a fresh view, since he allowed Oswiu to send missionaries into Mercia. He still regarded Oswiu as a dangerous political rival, and attacked him, but was defeated and killed in 655. Thereupon Oswiu became overlord of Northumbria and Mercia, and lost no time in sending further teachers into Mercian territory. A frequent visitor at his court was King Sigeberht of Essex, who became Christian, asked for teachers, and was sent Bishop Cedd, who had been working with the Middle Angles; it is particularly notable that instead of sending across the River Thames to Canterbury he turned to Northumbria for a teacher.

The third independent strand in the conversion is the despatch by Pope Honorius, *c.* 635, of Bishop Birinus, charged with a mission to the West Saxons. The WS king was baptised in the presence of the king of Northumbria, and the diocese of Dorchester was set up in communion with Rome, but not under the authority of Canterbury. By 654 every English kingdom except Sussex and Wight was more or less Christian; the organisation of bishoprics was largely related to the structure of the kingdoms, so that some centre of learning existed in almost all of them. But both missionary zeal, and association with a dominant secular power, combined to make Northumbrian–Celtic Christianity a greater force than southern-English Roman Christianity. Within ten years that position would be reversed at the Conference of Whitby, largely through the actions of an ambitious and aggressive Northumbrian aristocrat–cleric, Wilfrid, dedicated to the Roman party. Because the Roman missionaries arrived first in time, and their party prevailed in the end, it is often supposed that the Celtic mission was no more than a peripheral episode. From the point of view of religious history this is almost certainly a mistake; without the Celts Wilfrid might not have had a church to be prince of. For linguistic history it is misleading in the extreme, since the generation in which the Northumbrian Church led in religion and scholarship is crucial for the establishment of the tradition of writing English. OE orthography can better be explained as derived directly from Irish traditions, and only indirectly from their source in the writing of Latin, than directly from Latin.

§ 196   Though in some quarters and some respects the issues between the Celtic and Roman traditions decided at Whitby left great bitterness, on the whole the following generation is one of rapprochement between the two traditions. For five years after Whitby there was no archbishop of Canterbury, and widespread plague came near to wiping out clergy and episcopate, on whom the maintenance of literacy depended. The arrival in 669 of two very great men, the Asian Theodore as archbishop, and the African Hadrian as his aide, marks the beginning of a secure, organised Church, fountain-head of learning, in England; when Theodore died in 690 the Church was united throughout the country, and indeed constituted the only national organisation of any kind. He and Hadrian were good scholars in Latin and Greek; they established a great school and library at Canterbury, and attracted to it another two men of the highest distinction. The first, Benedict Biscop, was another Northumbrian nobleman devoted to the Church, determined to learn all he could, in matters of religion, art and scholarship, from Rome. Three times he made the pilgrimage to Rome, and on his return in 669 he was invited to be abbot and to direct the school at Canterbury until Hadrian should be free to take charge. He then made a fourth visit to Rome, and returned with a magnificent collection of books; he so impressed King Ecgfrith of Northumbria that he was granted a large estate in County Durham, where he founded in 674 the monastery now known as Monkwearmouth. He imported stonemasons and glaziers from Gaul to make a building unlike any previously known in the north, and set off to Rome again, for more books, paintings, musicians. The king was sufficiently pleased to give him a second estate, at Jarrow, in 681, and lived just long enough for the dedication of the church there in 685. Benedict set off to Rome again for more equipment; on his return he gave precise instructions for the maintenance of the library he had assembled with such devotion, and in 690 he died. In under a lifetime Northumbria had passed from barbarism to being the leader, almost, indeed, the sole surviving representative, of learning in a tradition combining classicism and Christianity. Monkwearmouth–Jarrow flourished to the extent of attracting a community of six hundred in a short time, to an extent, indeed, that gave rise to some anxiety as to the execution of secular duties in the running of the kingdom. Just before the foundation of Monkwearmouth there was born, on land which was to form part of its endowment, a child who at the age of seven entered the community, and there spent all the remaining years of his life. There, teaching and writing his thirty-four books, in Latin and English, Bede became in his own lifetime a legend throughout Europe. There, by standards of historical scholarship that would not be matched for over a thousand years, he completed in 731 what now seems his greatest work, the *Historia Ecclesiastica Gentis Anglorum,* in which for the first time the concept of an English people is given verbal expression, long before the term has any national or political reality. Yet it must not be assumed that the new foundation eclipsed the old in artistic and scholarly work. A monk of Lindisfarne named Eadfrith illuminated a copy of the gospels now known by the name of Lindisfarne, and kept in the British Museum: possibly the greatest work of visual art ever produced in this country. Throughout Northumbria a school of stone-carvers produced the great crosses, of which the most notable surviving examples are those of Bewcastle and Ruthwell; for our purposes this achievement is of special importance by virtue of its combination of the pictorial with the verbal, and specifically for the employment of runes for purposes of Christian teaching and worship. A similar combination of traditional and Christian themes, pictures and runes, is found on the carved whalebone box from Northumbria, also in the British Museum, the Franks Casket. Few things better illustrate the diffusion, breadth and humanity of the Northumbrian tradition of learning and literature than the fact that King Aldfrith of Northumbria (685-705) wrote verse in Gaelic and scholarly letters in Latin. For many centuries thereafter a majority of English kings would be illiterate.

We reached Northumbria through Benedict, the first of the great men associated with the Canterbury school. We must now turn to the second, Aldhelm, born 639 or 640, a member of the royal house of Wessex, who had received his primary education from an Irishman at Malmesbury, and turned to Canterbury for higher education. Like Bede, he combined love of native literature, and skill in the composition of English poetry, with a passion for Latin learning. The reign of King Ine of Wessex (688-725) was a period of conquest (cf. §194), as a result of which it became necessary to set up a new diocese at Sherborne, to serve the people west of Selwood. To this Aldhelm was appointed. Later he moved to the great bishopric and school of Winchester, where one of his pupils was Wynfrith (better known by the Latin translation of his name, Boniface), born *c.* 675 to a prosperous family living near Exeter. Though he had been placed in the local monastery at the age of six, Wynfrith was dissatisfied with the education he received there, and at the age of about twenty-five migrated to Winchester, to sit at the feet of Aldhelm. In 716 Wynfrith set off, not the first, but the best educated and the best organised, to convert the still heathen Germanic peoples of the Continent of Europe. Setting up monasteries and schools in one province after another – Thuringia, Frisia, Hesse, Bavaria – he became Metropolitan of Germany, and in extreme old age was martyred (754). If faith and learning had not thus been established in Germany it is doubtful whether Alfred could have found sufficient associates for the restoration of learning in the almost totally illiterate England of the late 9c (cf. § 179).

For a century after its full establishment the Church in England experienced a Golden Age of sanctity and scholarship. In one generation it moved from hungry assimilation of the learning, arts and crafts of the Mediterranean to absolute leadership. There is no need to find reasons why this splendour did not last; there are few moments in history when human beings have achieved so much, and decline is the normal aftermath. Bede died in 735, and the rest of the 8c is a time of more routine achievement, rich in self-criticism, some of it justified. Yet the schools and libraries flourished till the shocks that began in 793. English ecclesiastics, oriented towards Rome, had been struck, in the course of their southward journeys, by the plight of the Germanic peoples in Europe; they had neglected the far more threatening Germanic tribes across the North Sea. It would shortly be their turn to suffer what they, three centuries before, had inflicted on the British. Here, as evidence of the mutual comprehensibility of English and Continental Germanic, are a few lines from a catechism used with Wynfrith's Continental Saxon converts:

> Forsachistu diobolae? R. Ec forsacho diabolae.
> End allum diobolgelde? R. End ec forsacho allum diobolgelde.
> End allum dioboles uuercum? R. End ec forsacho allum dioboles uuercum end uuordum, thunaer ende uuoden ende saxnote ende allum them unholdum the hira genotas sint.

> ('Do you forsake the devil?' 'I forsake the devil.'
> 'And all idolatory (devil-worship)?' 'And I forsake all idolatry.'
> 'And all works of the devil?' 'And I forsake all works and words of the devil – Thunder (Thor), and Woden and Seaxneat and all those faithless ones who are their companions.')

The spelling conventions differ, but this would be no problem for an Anglo-Saxon to understand, and little more for him to learn to speak.

§ 197 Now we must survey the documentary evidence surviving from the period, having escaped the viking ravages of the time immediately following, and the hazards of a further millenium. The principal contemporary records are available in a single volume (Sweet, 1885). They include runic material (one Northumbrian inscription is in both roman and runic script), and scraps, mainly isolated words, in roman letters, together with two copies of the nine lines of verse ascribed by Bede to Caedmon (who has a part-British name), the first English Christian poet. Copied just after the period, but perfectly representing the forms of the earliest Northumbrian, are two other short poems, Bede's *Death Song* and a riddle.

In the south, almost the only evidence is from charters. There are scattered English words in predominantly Latin Kentish and Saxon charters from the closing years of the 7c, in Mercian ones from 736. Cautious use may be made of Mercian glosses, in a later hand, but apparently preserving 8c forms. Extended texts are not found till the 9c. Of WS we know practically nothing until the time of Alfred; the main documentation for early Kentish and Mercian is early 9c, and for Northumbrian very early, and then again at the close of the OE period.

However, for the study of syntax, and to some extent of WF, we may supplement the evidence of contemporary records by that of later copies, especially of poetry, whose form is more fixed than that of prose. Late copies may even tell something, by virtue of their metrical patterning if not by their spelling, about the phonology of their period of composition. The most important work thus brought into limited consideration is *Beowulf*, extant in a late 10c copy, but plausibly assigned to an 8c origin, though it cannot be dated more closely. We are also able to make extensive use of inferential knowledge about what earlier and later stages of the language must have been like, and by what transitions during our period the second stage could have evolved out of the first. In the account that follows conclusions are drawn from all available evidence, but the discussion of the runic 'alphabet' is postponed to Chapter VIII, covering the period when it was introduced to England.

§ 198   The earliest known orthography differs in some respects from that described in § 159. Mainly the differences are in consonants, which presented most difficulties to those devising a written form based directly or indirectly on Latin tradition. The voiced labial fricative, later spelt *f*, had evolved from a bilabial ($/\beta/$), and we do not know when it became a labio-dental. In early spelling it is generally represented by *b*, which shows its bilabial but not its fricative quality; since the later spelling accorded with the sound's phonemic membership (though still not with its phonetic quality) it was an improvement. In the 8c and 9c *b* and *f* alternate with this value. Similarly, *d* was used for a fricative (later *ð*, borrowed from the Irish alphabet, or þ borrowed from the runic 'alphabet') as well as a stop. The voiceless dental or alveolar fricative was in this early orthography kept quite distinct from its voiced counterpart, and was normally spelt with the digraph *th*; this represents a phonetic difference, but the later custom of not distinguishing voiced from voiceless fricatives was in accord with their phonemic membership. For the voiceless palatal fricative *ch* was used, as in Irish, but later the spelling was with *h*, and again the later spelling gave priority to phonemic grouping over phonetic representativeness. It is notable that though Latin used the *th*, *ch* digraphs it gave them the values /t/, /k/ respectively, and cannot have been the source of early OE practice. At first for /w/ *u*, *uu* ('double *u*') were used, but around 750 we have the first instances of the runic symbol þ in this value; it did not regularly take the place of *u* for a very long time.

Early English scribes exploited the vocalic symbols *oe*, *ae* or *æ* which in Latin had been mere variants for /e/, and *y*, which had been a variant for /i/. The sounds so represented were all new in English (i.e., did not belong to the Continental antecedents of the settlers), and they were reflected in specifically English developments of the runic 'alphabet'. The symbol for *u*, ᚾ , had an *i*-stroke added to indicate its fronted counterpart /y/, thus ᛗ ; the old *o*-rune, since original /o/ had changed (cf. §223), could be used for *oe*, thus ᛨ ; the *a*-rune split into three, the original form, ᚠ , being used for /æ/, the normal reflex of older /a/ (cf. §212), a modification, ᚥ , for /a/ preserved before a back vowel (cf. §212), and a further modification, ᚦ, for the *o*-like sound used before nasals (cf. §212). At the same time, in roman orthography there developed the use of vowel-digraphs for original diphthongs, and probably for new ones (cf. §160), and the use of vowel-symbols as consonant-diacritics, which certainly had a precedent in Irish orthography.

§ 199 Only at the very end of the period can phonological change be traced from orthography. For most of it we are dependent on inferences about what must have happened since the English migrants left their Continental speech-community, and the order in which developments must have happened if they were to leave the results they did. The settlement period seems to have been one of unusually intense sound-change, and the completion of the processes then inaugurated belongs, fairly certainly, to period VII.

A change common to the whole country is loss of /χ/ either between vowels (in which case the loss was compensated by lengthening, if it was not already long, of the preceding vowel) or between a liquid and a vowel, in which case no accompanying change took place. 8c poetry, no doubt displaying the conservatism we have seen to characterise medieval and later poetic language (cf. § 59), uses in a single work half-lines which require the /χ/ to be present and others which require that it should have been lost (the 10c spelling of the poetry naturally gives no clue to this difference). We must conclude that in normal usage the change had taken place by the 8c, but that the older form was not so remote as to be unusable in the declaimed or chanted formal language of verse. Thus in lines 511b and 528b of *Beowulf* we find: *belēan mihte* ('could dissuade') and *nēan bīdan* ('wait near'). The first must be Type C, x / / x, i.e., -*lēan* must have one and only one syllable; it is one of the verbs called 'contracted' because this loss of /χ/, with syllable-contraction, has taken place (cf. § 170), and the line only scans on the assumption that loss is completed. The second must be Type A, / x / x, but *nēan* as it is written constitutes one syllable, not the required two; for the line to scan we have to 'de-contract' to **nēahan*. From extensive evidence of this kind we conclude that the change had taken place in or by the 8c, but was not far past. The change brought about extensive disturbance of morphological patterning. Within the classes of strong verbs it dissociated the contracted verbs from the patterns of the class to which they historically belonged. Within single paradigms it created various anomalies; generally they were levelled out in later English, though not always in the same direction; an extreme case being the difference between the common word *high* and the end of the name *Alphege*, OE *hēah* and *Ælfhēah*.

A change which may have belonged to the same or a slightly earlier time was known in all dialects, but took different forms, and proceeded to varying degrees, from one dialect to another. This was the tendency to diphthongise a front vowel under certain conditions involving the presence of a back vowel in the following syllable. Apparently a glide of back-quality developed, so that, for instance, *ʒeolu*, 'yellow', and *ʒeoluc*, 'yolk' have a diphthongal symbol, *eo*, corresponding to a sound that had earlier been the simple vowel /e/. The example is one in which this change, technically known as back-mutation, has had some effect on the later history of the language; by a shift of stress Standard (though dialects have a form *yelk*) has developed a reflex *yolk* which presupposes back-mutation. Except in such cases the sound-change has no effects beyond the OE period. It affected only short vowels, and short diphthongs did not survive into ME. The main importance of the change is not for general linguistic history, but as a guide to the localisation of OE dialect-texts. We do not, therefore, need to describe it in detail (cf. Campbell, 1959, 85–93).

A change restricted to a single, but extensive, area has been of importance for later history; this is the smoothing of diphthongs before palatal consonants, giving in Anglian (i.e. Mercian and Northumbrian) *līht*, 'light', where WS has *lēoht*, 'Kentish' *līoht* (and other diphthongal forms). However, most of the differences separating Anglian from the southern dialects, and later reflected in Standard, arose in period VIII, and will be considered in the next chapter (cf. §212).

§ 200 Extremely far-reaching changes affected unstressed syllables at this time, of which we may single out for mention those that had a bearing upon morphology. Again our chronology is relative, not absolute, but we need to distinguish three phases, of which the first may belong in our period or before, while the last is traceable in recorded spellings and certainly belongs to this period.

In the first of the three phases, final *u* and *i*, the only then current short final vowels, were lost after certain types of stem-structure but kept after others. The loss took place when the stem consisted of one long or two short syllables (here we see an equivalence which also functions metrically, cf. §181). It is conditioned phonologically, but its effects are felt in grammar. In general it is one more cause of the fragmentation into different types of forms once alike. More particularly, since both final vowels served in the inflection of nouns, it creates new patterns of declension. Of these the most important in both immediate effect and durability have been new plurals. Regular (*a*-stem) neuter nouns formed their plural in -*u*, and by this loss a large group of them came to have no change in the plural. Thus, by a phonological accident, is created the pattern of unchanged plural, which in ME came to be associated with special functions, and which as a property of certain nouns and to mark certain functions stays with us today (cf. §142). Of the various ways in which loss of -*i* affects morphology, probably the most important has been that certain nouns, which because of the presence of -*i* had vowel-change in the plural (cf. §212), now lost the -*i* and showed pluralisation only by vowel-change (e.g., *fōt/fēt*). There thus comes into being the pattern in which vowel-mutation is felt as a sign of plurality, a type which has lasted, though it has never become productive.

The second phase is generally described as later than the first; in fact, all we know is that it cannot have been earlier, and there is reason to suppose they may have been simultaneous. In it, all remaining long vowels in unstressed syllables became short; among other results, this created a new -*u* and -*i*, and their survival is our evidence that the change cannot have been earlier than that of phase I. This change produced an unstressed vowel system containing five terms, *a, æ, e, i, u*, a system very poor by comparison with that operating in stressed vowels, which had long and short vowels and diphthongs, and included *ŏ, ǣ, ў*, which do not appear at all in the unstressed system. Since the great majority of inflections had already lost all consonantal components, these five items had to shoulder a vast burden of grammatical differentiation. As their distribution was governed by historical chance they were not even used economically. For instance, all genitive plurals were formed with -*a*, but so were some nominative plurals and some genitive and dative singulars. There is no need to multiply examples; we are on our way to the confusion shown in the paradigms of later OE (cf. § 165) and every step in that direction makes the inflections less satisfactory and more liable to accidental erosion.

Whenever it came into being, this system lasted till a little after 700. During the 8c the movement towards blurring all front vowels under a single sound, written *e*, gets under way. In the very early Northumbrian texts *æ* and *i* are generally used in a historically accurate way, but there are already indications of their being confused with *e*. By the end of our period the loss of those two points of contrast is complete, and OE morphology has reached the state set out in § 165.

§ 201 The syntactic patterns illustrated from *Beowulf* belong to this period, and may be taken as representative of it. They seem to have persisted into period VI, and for that reason were described there. Our evidence does not enable us to go behind that as far as OE is concerned. The element of innovation in the mixed positional syntax of *Beowulf* – the special treatment of elements according to their weight – is more likely to have had an English than a pre-English origin, but nothing more can be said about it.

§ 202 As regards vocabulary, the aspect of language most immediately sensitive to social change, the central issue in this period is the exposure of the English to Christianity, and to all its cultural consequences. We do not find that the earliest Latin–Christian words in English date from this period. Many words, chiefly to do with Christianity as an institution, were borrowed much earlier, even before the migration. But the conceptions of Christianity as a faith pour into English from this time on, and study of them is of particular interest for the light it throws on the methods of the missionaries and on the adaptive habits of the language. Once again it is not possible in every case to date items exactly to this period.

The simplest way of transmitting a new concept is, from a linguist's point of view, by lending the word for it, and the clearest starting-point for our study will be loanwords. Loanwords entering the language from the close of the 6c on escaped the action of the important sound-changes which swept through English at the migration period, and so are, in many cases, easily distinguished from those that arrived earlier (not in all, since not all words would include sounds subject to the changes). As we have little documentation from the early period it is not so clear which of the loans belong to this period rather than to VI. Fairly certain are *mæsse*, 'mass' (and various derivatives from it), *abbod*, *abbudesse*, *nōn*, 'ninth hour [as a time for saying the office], noon', *ælmesse*, 'alms', *nonn(e)*, 'monk', *pāpa*, 'pope', *(a)postol*, *cumpæder*, 'godfather', *sācerd*, 'priest', *sanct*, 'saint', *culpe*, 'guilt, fault', *offrian*, 'offer, sacrifice', *bæzere*, 'baptist' (also in the form *bæðzere*, through mistaken association with the word for *bath*). The last example shows how frail is the demarcation between loans and other modes of adaptation to the new ideas. In fact it has been estimated that only 5% of the new words resulting from the Christian missions were actually loans (Keiser, 1918, 3); while exact quantifications must be suspect, and while the importance of the loans exceeds their actual numbers, we may agree with all who have written on the subject that the most striking feature of this great cultural change is the small part played in it by loanwords. The cultural change does not only consist of the introduction of religious concepts; in other aspects of its impact loans do play a greater part. Thus, fairly certainly from period VII, we have *ferele*, 'rod', *pīc*, 'pike', *fers*, 'verse', *fiðele*, *orgel*, 'organ', *cōc(ere)*, 'cook', *fenester*, 'window', *plætse*, 'open place in a town', *alewe*, 'aloe', *bēte*, 'beet', *fēferfuʒe*, 'feverfew', *lilie*, 'lily', *laur*, 'laurel', *menta*, 'mint', *rōse*, *temprian*, 'temper, mix', *tīriaca*, 'medicine', *scōl*, 'school', etc.

We can easily understand why preachers should try to introduce the basic tenets of their faith through some more homely medium than the loanword, and why such considerations should be less important for the cultural concepts which are merely consequent upon the faith. The use of native resources for expression of new ideas is central only to the concepts of the faith itself. What we have loosely termed adaptation of native resources, as opposed to borrowing, is a complex and highly varied group of processes. The most important sub-divisions distinguished in the most recent study (Gneuss, 1955, 3) are loan-formations and loan-translations. Under loan-formations he classes formations made from native material in imitation of a foreign model – they may be exact renderings, component by component, paraphrases, or independent new formations triggered by the model; loan-translations or semantic loans render analogically, or by substitution, the meaning of foreign items. It is to such resources as these that OE turns for the core of its Christian vocabulary in the generations of, and just after, the conversion, but it must not be supposed that every new formation exploits one principle and one alone.

The best term to start with is the word *god*. This is an old neuter noun, the meaning of whose stem has been disputed. It may mean 'that which is invoked' or 'that to which libation is poured' (in which case, it represents the same stem as we find in the name of the Goths and the Geats, cf. §207); OE shares the form with other Germanic languages, which have formations from the same stem with the same meaning. In its inherited form the noun has a plural, since the monotheistic idea was unfamiliar to the Germanic peoples. The missionaries need to convey to the English the conception of a single Deity, a Person, One of the Persons of the Trinity, the Father, the Creator of the Universe, etc. They have a choice of explaining all this, and adding that the word for it is *Deus*; or of saying that the English have hitherto misunderstood the nature of *god* – not *it*, but *He*, not *many* but *One*, etc. They choose the latter course, and their usage, as well as their belief, prevails. The noun acquires a new meaning, or rather, the whole complex of Christian meanings, though it is still the term for the old gods. From this development follows a curious grammatical change, akin to the modern use of the capital letter. When singular the word becomes masculine; when plural (therefore pagan in reference) it remains neuter. Thus, even syntax enters into the pattern of adaptation.

Among analogical semantic loans we find instances of specialisation of meaning, as when *þrōþunʒ*, the general abstract noun from *þrōþian*, 'suffer', is used for the passion of Christ (and of the martyrs); and transfer of various types of figurative meanings, as when *ʒetimbran*, literally 'build', is used to render Latin *aedificare* in the transferred sense 'edify'. The substitution-type is seen when OE *cniht*, 'boy', is used to render L *discipulus*, 'pupil', in the technical sense 'disciple'. The difference is that the analogical type depends on an underlying common meaning, from which transfers are made, but in the substitution-type there is no such underlying common meaning.

The abundance of WF resource in OE makes loan-formation a simple matter. In such correspondences as *eft-ārīsan* we have element-for-element rendering of L *re-surgere*; a looser type of paraphrase appears in *mild-heort* for L *miseri-cors*; new formation is seen in the word 'baptise', *fulþian*, literally, 'complete the rite of sanctification'.

§ 203 Rather than multiply examples out of context we can demonstrate the pattern of adaptation by looking at two short extracts which are as representative as short passages can be of the blend of adaptational modes. The first item is the short *Hymn to the Creator*, ascribed by Bede to Caedmon, composed between 657 and 680, and recorded in many copies, of which we shall use one dating from the beginning of the 8c. It shows in particular the value of the traditional poetic modes of diction in presenting to the English the multiple aspects of a complex concept, in this case, the nature of God:

Nu sċylon herȝan	hefaen-rīċaes uard
Now (we) must praise	(of) heaven-kingdom (the) guardian
metudæs maecti	end his mōd-ȝidanc
(the) Maker's powers	and his mind-thought
uerc uuldur-fadur	suē he uundra ȝihuaes,
(the) works of glory-father	as he of wonders each
ēċi dryctin,	ōr āstelidæ,
eternal Lord	(the) beginning established,
hē aērist sċōp	aelda barnum
he first shaped	of men for the children
heben til hrōfe	hāleȝ sċepen,
heaven as (a) roof	holy Maker,
thā middun-ȝeard	mon-cynnes uard,
then middle-yard	mankind's guardian,
ēċi dryhten	æfter tīadæ
eternal Lord	after created
fīrum foldu	frēa allmectiȝ.
for men of earth	Lord Almighty.

(It is now our duty to praise the Guardian of the Heavenly Kingdom, the powers of the Creator and His intelligence, the works of the Father of Glory, since He, the Eternal Lord, instituted the beginning of every wonder. First the Holy Creator made heaven as a roof for the children of men. Then the Guardian of mankind, Eternal Lord, Almighty God, subsequently made this world for the men of earth.)

As in later poetry, the verbal element is semantically and formally minimal. The nominal concentration is upon Christian concepts, this being not only the first English Christian poem, but actually one composed at the behest of an angel. God appears in it as guardian (*uard*), where the double aspect of keeping under control, ruling, and keeping in good order, protecting, is intended: as Guardian of the kingdom of heaven He represents the greatest conceivable power, and this power is to be used in fatherly protection, as the phrase *Guardian of mankind* suggests. In the second line *maecti* follows up the theme of power, but the genitive *metudæs* introduces another aspect of the Divine Being; it is derived from the verb *to measure*, hence *to create*, with a special emphasis on the planning, almost the 'cutting out' or 'tailoring', which went into creation. Especially, He is to be praised for His *mōd-ȝidanc*, where *mōd* has a complex of meanings not rendered by any one NE word – mind, spirit, courage, intellect, feeling, pride – the totality, or almost any part, of the inner or spiritual being; *ȝi-* is a collective prefix, *-danc*, 'thought, idea'. The whole expression means something like intelligence, inspiration, insight, vision. We are invited to praise God not merely for the excellence of His craftsmanship in the creation, but for having such a splendid idea to put into practice. To His credit are not merely powers, but achievements (*uerc*, 'deeds'); He is Glory-Father – the compound does not distinguish 'He is a Father, who is glorious' from 'He is the father, i.e., source, of all glories'; and this second meaning divides into 'He is responsible for all the splendours we are contemplating' and 'If you want glory, it can come only from Him'. Once again, the concept of glory follows from what has been said, the concept of fatherhood is newly introduced. In sum, He is *a* or *the Eternal Lord*, where *dryhten* is the regular word for lord, leader, given a special application to the Deity, who unlike the tragically mortal lords who protect one humanly, is eternal. He *sċōp* and is *sċepen*, both forms derived from the root 'shape', i.e., He is the bringer of form out of chaos; and He is *hāliȝ*, 'holy', derived from the word for *whole*, and having the implications inviolate, inviolable. In sum, He is *frēa allmectiȝ*, where *frēa* is again a specialisation of a word for a human lord or ruler, the difference being that This One has no peers, but is omnipotent. Thus in nine lines we have eight expressions, seven of them different, for aspects of the Deity, all formed from native sources and interwoven with complex subsidiary themes for praise. All the resources used are native, and since the formations are typically poetical we may assume that they are here used for the first time.

Of the many other aspects of this poem's language that might detain us we must stop for only one. The word *middun-ʒeard* signifies 'yard, garth, enclosure, in the middle'. It is a term from pre-Christian cosmogony, used for earth as intermediate between the home of the gods and the realm of shades, the hidden domain of the goddess Hel. Its sense is therefore extremely appropriate for transfer to the Christian concept of the world as intermediate between heaven and hell; accordingly, the word is taken over with this slight shift of sense. Unlike all the terms previously discussed, it is, as a unit, antecedent to Christianity. *Hell*, derived from a root meaning 'conceal', was anciently used for the world of the departed, hidden from mortal experience, and it did not imply a place of punishment for the departed. The adaptation of this word to Christian use involves a subtle and very sharp semantic shift; in its old sense it is a general term standing for any hidden realm, and can therefore be (and in OE often is) used with the definite article or demonstrative. In its Christian sense it is unique, and cannot be modified in this way. Only for the upper realm of the three-tiered structure did the Christian English have no truck with the ancient word. In pre-Christian thought this upper world was the home of a particular family or group of gods, called in ON *Æsir* (OE sg *Ōs*, gpl *Ēsa*). Unlike the more general term *god* this name was perhaps felt to be too specific in its pagan sense to be retained. Very rarely it occurs in independent use, but it is only common as a first element in personal names (cf. *Ōswald*, 'God-power', etc.); in this value it may have remained current because of the saintly reputation of the early converts bearing such names, notably King Oswald of Northumbria.

§ 204   While poetic language best illustrates how the English mind was bent to an understanding of Christian devotional concepts, we shall learn more about technical theological terminology from prose. This can be illustrated from the account following Bede's quotation of Caedmon's *Hymn*, in which he catalogues the poet's other work (which, so far as we know, does not survive). The passage is given here in the OE translation made at Alfred's behest; we cannot guarantee that the actual terms used are those introduced at the Conversion. Probably most of them are, but their value for us is as a demonstration of the adaptive patterns:

Sonʒ hē ǣrest be   middan-ʒeardes ʒescēape ond bi   fruman mon-cynnes
Sang he first about middle-yard's   shaping and about origin   of mankind

ond eal þæt stǣr   Genesis, þæt is sēo ǣreste Moyses booc; ond   eft
and all the story of Genesis, that is the first   of Moses book; and again

bī   ūtʒonʒe Israhēla folces of   Ǣʒypta   londe ond bī   inʒonʒe
about Exodus of Israel's people from Egyptians' land and about   entry of

þæs   ʒehāt-landes,   ond bī   ōðrum moneʒum spellum þæs   hālʒan
(into) Promised Land and about other many stories   of the Holy

ʒeþrites canōnes bōca; ond bī Cristes menniscnesse ond
Writ's   canon's books; and about Christ's humanity/incarnation and

bī   his ūpāstiʒnesse in   heofonas; ond bī þæs   Hālʒan ʒāstes
about his Ascension   into heavens; and about of the Holy Ghost

cyme   ond þāra apostola lāre;   ond eft   bī   þǣm dæʒe þæs
coming and of the apostles doctrine; and again about the day of the

tōþeardan dōmes   ond bī   fyrhtu þæs   tintreʒlican þiites
future   judgement and about terror of the tormenting punishment

ond   bi sþētnesse   þæs   heofonlecan rīces   hē moniʒ lēoð
and   about sweetness of the heavenly   kingdom he many songs

ʒeþorhte;   ond sþelċe ēac   ōðer moniʒ be   þǣm ʒod-cundan
/poems composed; and likewise also other many about the   divine

fremsumnessan ond dōmum   hē ʒeþorhte.
favours   and judgements he composed.

Analysis of the religious diction of this sentence will illustrate not
only innovations in OE but also subsequent changes, losses, and substitutions (words are quoted in the form they have in the text). For
ʒesceape, 'shaping', transparent in itself, and as a religious term supported
by many other 'creation' words from the same stem (cf. § 203), we now use
the non-transparent loan *creation*; and for *fruma*, related to the familiar
OE word for *first*, we have the loan *origin*. *Stǣr*, 'narrative', is a loan,
but not from Latin (cf. §205); the name of the first book of the Bible
is given in alien form, but is immediately glossed. *Ūtʒonʒe* is a trans-

parent formation, 'out-going', for which we use the more technical *Exodus*, cf. *in-ʒonʒe*, 'in-going', correlating with it to make a point that escapes in the NE pairing of *Exodus* and *entry*. Where *Promised* is a specialisation of a loan, *ʒehāt* uses the stem of the common native verb of promising in OE. *Spellum*, (dpl) 'message, story', is both a common word and a component of the technical *ʒodspell*, which is thus linked with everyday usage in a way that modern *gospel* is not. None of the words now current for message, story, narrative, are of native origin. The stories are (in a rather complex sequence of genitives) 'from the books of the canon of Holy Scripture'. In this structure the rather specialised word *canōnes* (gsg) is borrowed, but the term *ʒeþrit* is a collective, 'writings', in every-day use; it is true that we can still speak of Holy Writ, but the effect is not the same, since the word is not now in common use for literature. The name of *Christ* is naturally enough borrowed, but curiously enough we do not know for sure whether its source is Latin, in which case the vowel should be marked long, or Greek, in which case the vowel in OE would be short, and the modern long form would depend on fresh borrowing from French or Latin in ME.

Consider the problems for the missionaries in explaining the incarnation. The essential is that God became man; so the concept is explained by the transparent formation, *-nesse*, abstract noun formative, 'state of being', added to *mennisċ*, 'human', 'man-like'. If we compare this with modern usage, the OE loses the element, present in *incarnation* (the Latin text at this point reads *incarnatione*), of the uniqueness of Christ's state; it is undoubtedly a great deal easier to explain. That *Passion*, as a term in religion, was rendered by *þrōþung*, has already been mentioned (cf. §202). For *ascension* the term is again composed of native elements, *ūpāstiʒnesse*, 'up-to-mounting-ness'. *Holy Ghost* with us exists only as a specialised pattern, but in OE (like *ʒeþrit*) it brings common words into religious function, as does *lāre* (dsg), 'teaching, lore' doctrine'. The more technical *apostola* (gpl) does, however, appear in loan form. *Dōmes* and *þiites* are the common words, in legal and general use, for judgement and punishment. *Fremsumnessum* renders Latin *beneficiis*, and would be translated in PE by such borrowed words as *graces, favours*; in OE it is a transparent native formation, meaning 'acts of advancing (someone else)', derived from *fram*, 'forward'.

§ 205 A small group of words reflects the Irish contribution to the conversion, and must be of 7c introduction into English. Most are words which the Irish themselves borrowed from Latin, such as *stǣr*, 'story' (cf. §204), and probably *ancor*, 'anchorite', *æstel*, 'bookmark' (ultimately a double diminutive of *hasta*, 'spear', a tiny spear-shaped object'), *cros*, 'stone cross'. Two are actually Celtic words, *drȳ*, 'magician' (singular of the word which later gave us *druid*), and *clucȝe*, 'bell'. Of these the only one to survive the Norman Conquest was perhaps *cros(s)*; at any rate this form, originally only used of carved stone crosses, has entirely replaced the usual OE word for cross, *rōd* (except in *rood-screen*). However, the weak hold which Irish loans had on usage may make us doubt whether even this is really an exception. There are two sources from which OE could have borrowed this particular form, Irish and Scandinavian, and the second must have played at least some part in its rise to frequent use, which did not occur till *c.* 1200. The poverty of the Celtic contribution to English vocabulary even in this area, and at a time when Celtic cultural influence was enormous, is very remarkable.

§ 206 There remains a small but central group of words whose status raises many problems. They seem to be Christian terms which were diffused within Germanic, and this can only mean that they were borrowed by some route from Gothic, since no other Germanic people were converted before the English. The form of certain words shows that they have long been in English or another Germanic language, yet their content is such that we cannot imagine their being learnt, as terms for the great visible (i.e. sack-able) institutions of the faith were. All but one are from Greek, the language through which the Goths learned the new faith. *Enȝel*, 'angel', is a specialisation of a Greek word meaning messenger; it is very common in OE in the specialised sense, and only once has the meaning 'messenger', in a literal biblical gloss. On the other hand, the normal OE word for messenger, *ār* (whence *ǣrend*, 'errand'), is used for 'angel' as well as in its general sense. In ME *enȝel* found itself in unsuccessful rivalry with the new French loan, *angel*, which soon replaced it completely. The other three words in the group have survived: *dēofol*, 'devil', *ċiriċe*, 'church', and *prēost*, 'priest'.

The remaining word in this group is not from Greek, but appears (though its history presents various problems) to represent a calque of L *paganus*. The Latin word, originally meaning 'countryman', developed its religious sense in the 4c, when Christianity was characteristically the faith of townspeople. Gothic uses *haiþnō*, derived from *haiþi*, 'heath', apparently in imitation of this semantic extension, and cognate forms are found in North and West Germanic languages, including OE, though the 'literal' sense, '[man] of the heath, countryside', is unknown.

CHAPTER VIII

570 – 370

§ 207 It was during this period, from about 450, that English-speaking peoples first settled in the British Isles. They were people of diverse origins and affiliations, and the chief thing they had in common was language. People of similar speech occupied extensive territories in Scandinavia and Continental Europe; they did not form any kind of political unity, but were organised in numerous tribes and small bands. As a whole, they and their language may be designated Germanic. Then, as later in England, when they occupied territory they did not usually claim it as a geographical block, but simply took over the parts it suited them to live in – coasts, river valleys, lowish country that was neither fen nor forest. This type of occupation is very extravagant of land-resources, and in a time of rising population leads to constant expansion. In the early centuries of the Christian era the population of the Germanic peoples apparently did rise continually, and perhaps even sharply. For this, and probably for less immediately practical reasons, those centuries were a time of movement, of a long and complex pattern of raiding and settlement known as the age of migrations. Germanic territories in Scandinavia gave little scope for expansion; as population rose settlers could only move south, east or west. Already before our period one great wave of southward expansion had carried the Goths from southern Scandinavia to the Mediterranean. The early separation of this group led to the development of their speech (East Germanic or Gothic) on lines different from those followed elsewhere in the Germanic world – just how different it is hard to say, since our principal evidence for Gothic is confined to a date earlier than that of most other Germanic records; we cannot altogether compare like with like. Within the Germanic family of languages, the threefold division into North, East and West, with a rather close relationship between the first two, is the primary grouping, but another line of division has come to intersect it. After the early migrations, the Germanic peoples were geographically distributed in two linguistically significant groups. There are inland Continental peoples – those around the Mediterranean, and east of it, and those in

376

what is now central and southern Germany; and there are coastal peoples, those of Scandinavia, the North Sea coasts, etc., who remain sea-goers, and thus, to some extent in touch with each other. The dialects of the inland peoples will predominantly develop divergently, while those of the coastal peoples will in some respects converge. Though we have spoken of the Germanic languages as forming a family, the metaphor must not be pushed too far. In particular it will mislead if it makes us think of a single, unidirectional line of descent. The relationships between the Germanic dialects are by no means simple, and one reason is that after initial movements of divergence on one pattern, some dialects are caught up in movements of convergence, on quite a different pattern. The complexity of relationships in such a small and homogeneous language-group as this must be remembered when we try to find a model by which we can understand the much more complicated and heterogeneous situation from which Germanic itself evolved.

At the beginning of our period the Germanic peoples were united by a common heritage of heroic (oral) literature, a fund of themes and stories from all parts of the Germanic world, which would still be 'their literature' to the English until at least the 10c. Linguistically there was mutual comprehensibility between North and East Germanic, North and West Germanic. Speakers of East and West Germanic would have less to do with one another, though the evidence of loanwords is that the groups maintained some kind of contact. How much they would understand of one another's speech it would be rash to guess.

§ 208   The settlement of England came from the coastal groups. There has long been uncertainty about just who the settlers were, and some preliminary explanations are needed. In name-giving, as is natural in unsettled conditions, the names of groups of people were prior to names of places. Names of peoples were not all alike; some were what we should ordinarily understand by tribal names – that is to say, a man born to a given tribe describes himself as a member of it. This seems to be the case with the Angles, whose name enters the compound Anglo-Saxon. Others were the names of bands gathered *ad hoc* under a particular leader, and had, in origin, nothing to do with birth except in so far as the family might form a nucleus for the band; thus the name *Hastings* in England signifies 'men of Hæsta'. Such a leader might found a dynasty, in which case the men so designated would begin to make the transition towards being a tribe, and their name towards being a tribal name. Thirdly, bands would find it convenient to associate themselves in confederacies for defence or, more likely, large-scale operations, and the confederacy would give itself, or come to be known among its neighbours by, a name derived from some characteristic. The Saxons formed such a confederacy, named from the *seax*, or knife of a special kind. It was a fighting confederacy, known from the weapon it favoured. Thus, being a Saxon is a matter of belonging to a confederacy, not of birth. An Angle by birth may be a Saxon by association. The two names are not on a par, and not necessarily mutually exclusive.

Local names are secondary; they arise when a group has stayed for some time in a place, either because the group came to settle and has given the property a name stating their claim to it, or because they have in fact remained in occupation, and the district designates the property from its inhabitants. Thus, the southernmost part of Denmark probably received the name Angeln from its Angle occupants; that the practice continued in England is shown by the name Hastings.

The Saxons, from a base just south and west of the Angles, in the Eider–Ems–Weser coastlands, had been expanding westwards during the migration period, across Frisia to the Rhine and even as far as what is now Normandy. There were certainly both Angles and Frisians among them. Leaving aside for a moment the special case of Kent (said to be settled by Jutes), we can see that the geographical origins of the Angle and Saxon settlers will account for the geographical distribution we find in England. Those who came in via the Thames and the south coast were known as Saxons, and this is the way one would come in from the north coast of Continental Europe. Those who came in via the east coast rivers between the Thames and the Tees were known as Angles, and this is the way one would come in from southern Denmark. But the differences were not as sharp as they are now, say, between, a Scot and an Englishman; nor were they symmetrical, since the Angles may well have had a cultural homogeneity the Saxons lacked. At the beginning of the 8c Bede refers to all Germanic peoples in the country as *gens anglorum*, and he does it without explanation, as if merely rendering into Latin the normal term for his people. The first person recorded as giving the name of the vernacular language in the vernacular is Alfred; though a West Saxon he calls it, again without explanation, *enȝlisċ*; finally, when a name for the whole country is required, much later, it is, as a matter of course, *Englaland*, 'England'.

Some further light may be thrown by bringing Kent into the picture. The name of Kent is pre-English; it reminds us that for generations before the settlement the south-east coast had been the scene of both raiding and mercenary service for members of Germanic tribes. The major place-names were familiar to the Germanic peoples while they were still based in Europe. Germanic settlement in Kent was very early, and for centuries Kent remains more distinct in culture, law, land-tenure, coinage and language than any other part of England. Bede said the settlement was carried out by a third Germanic people, the Jutes. The Jutes are a mysterious people, and even Bede may have been mistaken about their separate origins; the label is, however, useful for the Germanic people of Kent, and the areas colonised from it (primarily Wight and the neighbouring coast of Hampshire). Whatever their origins, they deserve to be regarded as distinct within England. Their early presence will perhaps throw some light on the early kingdom names and later regional names in England. The structure of the Saxon names is odd – Essex, Middlesex, Sussex, Wessex. These are all people-names, not place-names, so they must be, as historical documents confirm, early formations (they mean 'East-Saxons', etc., not 'Land of the East Saxons', etc; contrast the later type *Englaland*, which is a true territorial name). But they cannot be original names given by the Saxons themselves. While Sussex, which was settled early, is indeed south of Essex, which is also settled early, and Middlesex is in between, the position of Essex during this phase of settlement is not east but north; it becomes east only by a later expansion of the settlers west along the Thames. In any case, first-generation names are isolated, like Hastings, not correlated. The names look like external, secondary names, i.e., names given by the established Germanic people of Kent to the newcomers who came in past their shores. It may well be that *Seaxe* was the name the Kentish people used for Germanic settlers without the intention of distinguishing one group from another (as the English later called all vikings *Danes*), but that *Angle* was a name all felt entitled to use of themselves.

There are linguistic as well as other differences between the Angles and the Saxons in England; and it is certainly the case that not all settlers arrived speaking alike. But it would be unwise to seek the primary explanation of recorded dialect-differences in the Continental background of the various groups of settlers.

Finally, the Northumbrians, alone among the early English kingdoms, retained the British names of their kingdoms, Deira in the south, a horse-shoe shaped settlement of the Yorkshire lowlands, and Bernicia, a secondary settlement, apparently from Deira, a right-angle shaped northern settlement along the Tyne and up the Northumberland coastal strip. The language of Northumbria, especially of Bernicia, shows,

before the viking invasions, such extraordinary parallels with North
Germanic that one may wonder whether its people did not originate
from somewhere north of Angeln.

§ 209 By 370 footloose Germanic coastal bands were well acquainted
with the south-eastern shores of Britain, but not until the mid 5c did they
decide to settle there in substantial numbers. The settlement must not
be thought of as a concerted movement or invasion. Some of the settlers
apparently came as mercenaries and turned on their masters. In some
cases groups of perhaps three ships, each bearing probably forty men,
would arrive to seize land sufficient for their wants. As we have seen
(§ 194), relations between settlers and old inhabitants could take many
forms.

The English came in boats that were costly and laborious to build.
Crossing the North Sea was an enterprise which required a powerful
driving force, yet the political organisation of the Germanic peoples was
such that it could be undertaken only by small groups at a time. Since
the English came for land, and the British population was small and
politically disorganised, it was not difficult at first for the English to
settle by infiltration along the valleys, edging their predecessors into
the uplands, without bringing the issue to any large-scale conflict.

But around 500 the pattern changed, whether because the British were
alarmed at the danger of further losses, or because a leader arose capable
of uniting them, we cannot tell. At any rate they did succeed in joining
forces to repulse the barbarians, who were defeated soundly at the battle
of Mons Badonicus (location disputed). By that time the English
held such lands as suited them in Sussex, Kent, Surrey, East and Middle
Anglia skirting the Fens, and the flat lands of southern Yorkshire. They
were on the brink, at least, of a new wave of expansion, taking them into
Wight and Hampshire, Middlesex, up the Thames to Oxford, into Essex
and Lincolnshire. The timing strongly suggests that a new generation
was determined to seek estates for itself, without waiting for, or sharing
with brothers, the family patrimony; in other words, that the Germanic
population was still rising. Some of the movements of the early 6c are
demonstrably from older English settlements, some are certainly due to
new waves of immigration from Europe. No wonder the Britons grasped
that a new policy of resistance was needed. Somewhere, probably in the
Berkshire–Wiltshire area, the advance was halted, and there was stability
for about half a century.

Ironically, it may have been the capacity of the British to unite which doomed them. Hitherto the Germanic settlers had operated band by band, with no sense of community towards other similar bands. But the unity of the British made further progress for the English dependent upon a similar capacity to work in unison. In the second half of the 6c they begin to advance again, and for the first time on a systematic territorial basis; they will fight for an area, put in a governor to control it, but leave it largely to British occupation. They are thinking of themselves as a community, and they are thinking of the general security of that community. As, around the mid 6c, they move west to the Gloucester–Worcester area, occupy the whole of central England, nibble at the rest of lowland Yorkshire, and pour into the flatter parts of Northumberland, we begin to detect a sense of nation aligned against nation. Politically this is still far from being true; but the feeling of the settlers has been channelled, as it eventually always is by land-tenure, into an us-against-them pattern. Since the British are without reinforcements, while the English are both helped and pushed by new waves from Europe, only one outcome is possible once this pattern develops. Why the Germanic peoples should have been marked by such a long period of population-expansion when the British clearly were not, is unknown.

§ 210   We do not know how large either the British or the English population was. Jointly, around 570, they are most unlikely to have amounted to as much as a million; half that is more probable. Communities among the new settlers would typically be very small, and in most areas very scattered. There are few cities in which urban life has been continuous, and in the rare cases where the newcomers did settle on the site of an old town their life apparently was not urban in any relevant sense. The main waves of migrations to England may have lasted a century or more, but before and after that people were continually coming – and going. The Germanic peoples of the North Sea littoral must have felt themselves very much one culture, and there are close links, in excavated material, between East Anglia and places as far east as Sweden.

We cannot suppose the settlers all spoke alike before the migration, since that is not the way of human beings; but we know little of the differences. One OE criterion does divide Saxons on one hand from Anglians and Jutes on the other, but separation after the settlement could account for this just as well as divergence before it. Settlers leaving over the course of a century or more would not all have brought the same form of speech with them, even if they had been from a single place of origin, as they were not. Once they were in England they may or may not have made a point of conforming to the speech-norms of their new community (as 'new chums' were later to do in Australia, cf. §44). Any convergence can only have been towards a narrowly local norm, perhaps still a war-band (as the name Hastings might suggest) or a *tun* with a hall and half a dozen buildings within a palisade. How inward-looking these tiny settlements were is suggested by an article of the earliest laws, those of Ine of Kent (*c.* 600), by which a traveller who gets off the road as he approaches a settlement is to shout or blow a horn, or he will be taken for a thief. It is true that this article is repeated in the West Saxon laws, but by then there were other reasons for fearing strangers. Convergence, if we accept that hypothesis, cannot have produced anything like even a regional standard. More widely valid norms can only have developed as a phenomenon of writing, diocese by diocese, as new bishoprics were founded in the wake of still small, but growing, kingdoms. The formation of these norms, as we can trace them, must have depended more on where each new scriptorium recruited its scribes than on how the people of the surrounding countryside actually spoke. We know from the settlement of the American west that even in conditions of relatively easy communication a century's separation can produce very marked divergences, but we can only guess how far this pattern of development characterised the early English communities as they settled more and more of the country. The dialect-differences within OE as we can detect them are remarkably superficial. We are bound to suppose that the relative homogeneity of the language, through space and time, is deceptive, and results from the conditions for the spread of writing.

Comparison between the English and the later 'Danish' settlements naturally comes to mind. The places of origin were much the same; the cultural level of the invaders was much the same; the methods of entry, both the routes and the sequences of raiding and settlement, were much the same. The shift from private enterprise to organised invasion followed the same pattern. The two movements are really successive phases of the same wanderlust arising under the same pressures. The vikings found the approachable south-east rather strongly held and concentrated on the east coast further north; they added the western approaches, which the English had not used. The viking movement at its peak was certainly larger and better organised than anything in the English settlements, and viking attacks went on longer. We are mistaken if we think of ourselves as essentially an English population with a few Danish accretions, now well absorbed. If we tend to conceive of the 'English settlement' and the 'Viking invasions' as quite distinct in kind and in their impact on 'English' history, we are to some extent being misled by secondary differences. Of these the chief is that the British were wholly distinct from the English in language, and have remained so to this day; the English and the Scandinavians spoke closely related dialects, which, within RS, have largely fused. Nevertheless, the English who fought the vikings were not the English who fought the British. Their own comunity by the 8c was built on an altogether larger scale; relative to the residents, the successive waves of invaders were comparable in size. Probably the most important difference was cultural. By the time of the viking raids the English were not merely literate, but in many ways highly civilised; the vikings were illiterate. When the outcome of the fusion of the two languages was written, it was written in an extension of the English tradition, and so appears as a variety of English. Culturally it was; a modern reader must beware of reading national meaning into such a claim.

§ 211 During period VIII we are almost without direct evidence about the language we may still find it convenient to call 'English'. There are, from England, brief runic inscriptions towards the close of the period (there are more, and earlier, inscriptions from the North Germanic area); there are scattered words preserved in quotation in other languages (e.g., Gildas, a Roman-Briton born *c.* 500, records *cyula* as a latinised form for the name of the ships the English came in – this corresponds to OE *cēol*, with earlier *-iu-* diphthong, later *keel*). But even more than in period VII we are dependent on comparison and reconstruction, which, in fact, tell us quite a lot. The inferences are, in particular, well-founded, because they can use rather extensive material preserved from 4c Gothic, that is, from a language not far separated from the common antecedent that must underlie the three branches of Germanic. The Gothic bishop Wulfilas translated substantial parts of the Bible from Greek into his own language; the surviving manuscript, the Codex Argenteus, is of 6c date, but as a sacred text preserves in detail the forms of the original translation. This document, written in silver letters on purple vellum, richly but chastely decorated in gold and silver, should be seen (in the library of the University of Uppsala) by all who use the term Goth as a synonym for barbarian. Such is the perfection of its script that it was once thought to require explanation by the postulation of an early mode of printing, subsequently lost.

In trying to delineate the speech of the first English settlers we are concerned with the West Germanic branch of the once common language. The principal division within West Germanic is between the speech of those who turned south into 'Germany', and those who stayed in touch with the North Sea and Channel coasts. The southerly branch, High German, is chiefly characterised by a consonant shift, which seems to have originated between about 500 and 750, and whose effects are still apparent in Standard German. By this group of changes, /t/ becomes /ts/ (cf. English *ten*, German *zehn*), /p/ becomes /pf/ in some positions, /ff/ in others (cf. English *pipe*, German *Pfeife*); /d/ becomes /t/ (cf. English *do*, German *tun*), and /b/, /p/ (cf. English *bolster*, German *Polster*; /k/ becomes /χ/ only finally (cf. English *book*, German *Buch*), /θ/ becomes /d/ (cf. English *three*, German *drei*), and /β/ (which in English becomes /v/, cf. §198), /b/ (cf. English *love*, German *Liebe*). There are some further modifications, and not all the developments are equal in extent, but by and large they can be taken to delimit the High German variety of WG. The effects are very obvious to us, but they cause very little disturbance to the phonological system, and it is doubtful if they were much of a barrier to communication. We may compare the tendency in non-standard PE to develop stops in a similar way – for 'Oh dear! I told you!' we may hear /ɒʊdzɪə aɪ tsɒʊldʒuː/ and be aware of the difference from RP in social, not linguistic terms.

Of the coastal peoples the Frisians and the English, especially those of Kent, seem to have been closest in speech, and to have undergone little differentiation for centuries after the settlement. We have already seen that English Saxon and Continental Saxon remained close enough for comprehension in the 8c and 9c (cf. §196), and even in some measure N and W Germanic after that (at least in Northumbria).

§ 212   When we go back so far behind the written records our chronology is bound to be relative rather than absolute. Yet on archaeological and historical grounds it is reasonable to think of our period as covering the Anglo-Frisian phase and the changes typical of English proper but antecedent to the earliest written documents. The only part of the language we can reconstruct with any clarity is its phonology; of word-formation we can trace some aspects, namely those which persist, but of those which are not Common Germanic we cannot always say how far the differences are due to innovation or to loss. Some other aspects of lexical history can be traced, and some inferences can be drawn about syntax from agreement between Gothic and the earliest OE.

Three phonological developments must be mentioned as specifically

Anglo-Frisian. Before nasals *a* develops to *o*. In its short form this change gives rise to the phonemically anomalous vowel of such words as *mann/monn*, which was to give so much trouble to OE scribes (cf. §159). In its long form the change accounts for the stem-vowel of such words as OE *mōna*, OHG *mano*, PE *moon*, and for the disintegration of class IV of strong verbs. One group of these had stems ending in a nasal, and their past forms became so out of touch with the normal development that the unity of the class was progressively lost (cf. §154). Before fricatives a nasal consonant was lost and the preceding vowel lengthened (perhaps we should say, nasalisation was transferred from segmental to prosodic realisation); hence such forms as OE *ūs*, 'us', *fīf*, 'five', as against German *uns, fümf*. Rather later, probably after the settlements had begun, is the monophthongisation of one of the Germanic diphthongs, *ai*, giving OE *ā*, OFris *ǣ*, in such words as OE *stān, hām, dāl*, where Gothic (*ai*) and Norse (*ei*) retain diphthongs.

Later again, indeed specifically English, is the fronting of *a* to *æ* unless protected by a following sound. We already know that a following nasal afforded 'protection'; it was also given by a back vowel in the following syllable. In this way was set up an alternation in certain words, such as *dæ ʒ*, where all forms of the singular had *æ* and all forms of the plural had *a* (*daʒas, -a, -um*). Even if this change were not confined to English we would know it was later than the smoothing of *ai* to *ā*; *a* as the first element of a diphthong fronted at the same time as independent *a*, thus *au* > *æu*, and by weakening of the second (unstressed) element, *æa*, written *ea*, cf. Go *hlaupan*, OE *hlēapan*, 'run, leap'.

Now it is very noticeable that no 'protection' is afforded by a following *r, l, h*, in themselves. From this we must conclude that their quality (which can be that of any vowel) was not fixed according to position (as that of, say, PE /l/ is), but variable according to phonetic environment, as that of, say, PE /k/ is. Nevertheless, very shortly after the settlement that quality did come, in certain sequences, varying by dialect, to be positionally fixed. Like the /l/ of fixed back-quality post-vocalically in PE (cf. /mɪlk/), this fixing tended to lead to the development of glide vowels. In certain combinations (broadly, when *r* or *l* was followed by another consonant and with *h* regardless of the presence of another consonant) these sounds developed post-vocalically a fixed back quality, and therefore back-glides were produced after any stem-vowel of front quality – /a/ if the vowel was low, /u/ (later /o/) if it was mid or high. As a whole the development is common to England, but in detail its incidence varied. Not surprisingly, dialects varied in their treatment of

Germanic *a*. Speakers who were slow to accept the fronting to *æ*, or quick to fix the quality of post-vocalic liquids, will have retained *a* throughout, instead of going from *æ* to *ea*; whether or not such speakers were originally distributed on a local basis, the *a* form before *l* plus consonant came to be the norm in Anglian dialects. There were other local differences, but this is the one which has had consequences for the subsequent history of English (cf. § 130). The sound-change is commonly known as 'breaking', which is a convenient label as long as one does not interpret it too mechanically. Because of the almost total loss of the OE diphthongal system at the Conquest its importance for the general history of English is far less than its interest for the OE dialectologist.

In certain areas the fronting process which had already affected *a* continued further, though perhaps not as a single process, since 'breaking' seems to intervene between the two stages of fronting. In its full form the 'second fronting' involves the development of *æ* to *e* (actually a raising) and of such *a* as survived to *æ*. This pattern is found in SW Mercian, in such forms as *deʒ*, *dæʒas*, 'day, days'; 'Kentish' has the change to *e* but does not consistently show *æ* for *a*.

We now come to the most, and most multifariously, puzzling change of all. In the first place, it is shared by the whole North and West Germanic world, yet there is conclusive evidence that it followed the specifically English change of 'breaking'. In the second place it is very difficult to conceive of any mechanism which could account for it. What happened, in general terms, can be stated as follows: if, in one stressed syllable, or a succession of two syllables of which the first was stressed, there was a vowel (or vowels) disparate in quality from *i*, and an *i* (or its approximant partner, /j/) followed in the next syllable, then the disparate vowel(s) would be attracted towards the quality of *i* by fronting or raising, and certain concomitant changes would take place. Since it is a change or mutation, and appears to be caused by *i* or *j*, this development is known as *i/j*- (pronounced /iː jɒt/) *mutation*; it must be thought of in terms of sounds, not letters. Let us consider examples before looking any closer:

a (only before nasals) > *æ* (later, by independent change, *e*), **manni* > **mænni* > *menn*, 'men';

ā   > *ǣ*, verb **hāljan* > *ǣhlan*, cf. adj *hāl*, 'whole';

o   > *œ* (later, by independent change, *e*), dat sg **dohtri* > **doehtri* > *dehter*, nom *dohtor*, 'daughter';

ō   *ǣ* (later, by independent change, *ē*), verb **dōmjan* > *dēman*, cf. noun *dōm*, 'doom';

u	> *y*, verb *fulljan > *fyllan*, cf. adj. *full*;
ū	> *ȳ*, verb *tūnjan, 'enclose' > *tȳnan*, cf. n. *tūn*;
æ	> *e*, weak verb *sættjan > *settan*, cf. past sg of strong verb, *sæt*.

The diphthongs were also fronted, but with very different results according to dialect. 'Kentish', with no *ǣ*, had *e* in such words as *hǣlan*, and later unrounded *ỹ* to *ĕ* (cf. §163). The unrounding of *æ* to *e* proceeded at different rates throughout the country. I/*j*-mutation not only created a huge range of new lexical forms, many of which survive in PE, but laid the foundations for new grammatical alternations; it not only redistributed phonemes but created several new ones, though none of them proved to be long-lived. Indeed, OE shows, with its many phonetic changes, a remarkable stability of phonemic system.

So far we have taken no account of the concomitant changes. In certain circumstances it is clear that an intervening consonant is palatalised as part of the change; perhaps this always happens, but cannot always be indicated by the orthography or by later pronunciation. At any rate it is clear in such forms as infinitive *hyċȝan*, 'think' (cf. the noun *hyȝe*, earlier *huȝi, 'mind') compared with past *hoȝode*. This is also a good example of how far related forms could be separated as a result of this and roughly contemporary changes. The consonant-plus-*i*/*j* sequence was affected in other ways. Medially, after a long syllable, a /j/ simply dropped (cf. *dēman*); after a short syllable, except one ending in /r/, the sequence becomes a long consonant without *j* (cf. *settan*); after a short syllable ending in /r/, /j/ became /i/ without the preceding consonant being affected (as in the verb *nerian*, 'defend'). Elsewhere, the causal sound remains for a bit, to become *e* or drop altogether at a slightly later period, and not as part of the mutation.

For all our uncertainties about the meaning of these developments, and for all the complexity they show when set out analytically, it is clear that we are dealing with a process not to be understood in terms of segmental phonemes, but affecting syllable-stretches. Ordinary processes of physical or mental anticipation do not seem to account for it, especially as the causal sounds are invariably in syllables weak by comparison with the syllables affected. It has been explained as due to vowel harmony; this could operate from a weak syllable back to a strong one, but is not very likely to do so, and in any case vowel harmony does not explain the odd treatment of the syllable-closure. Perhaps the most plausible suggestion is that distinctions formerly conveyed segmentally were transferred to a prosody of frontness, operating right across the stressed syllable (even, in many cases, affecting its onset). The advantage of this view is that it can be related to a common cause affecting all Germanic languages even after the separation of the various component speech-communities. All of them were still adjusting to their common adoption of root-stress (cf. §226) and it is conceivable that the distinctions dependent on *i* and *j* in weak syllables were felt to be too feebly represented by segmental phonemes, and that some representation must be transferred to the preceding stressed syllable, not as a segment, but as a prosody. Whatever the cause, the penetrative effect on both phonology and morphology was so great that it can only be compared with that of the loss of final *-e*.

Several other changes in this period which find a place in grammars of OE did not have sufficiently lasting effects for discussion in a general history. However, it is probably at this period that there arose a difference between WS, which keeps original $\bar{æ}$, and the rest of English, which raises it to $\bar{e}$ (the sound occurs most notably in the past plurals of class IV and V strong verbs). The dialect-distribution of the reflexes of this sound is thus different from that of $\bar{æ}$ arising by *i/j*-mutation, and that difference has had lasting effects.

§ 213 We might guess that a good deal was going on in unstressed syllables, and therefore in morphology, at this time, but nothing can be dated more finely than to the West Germanic period, and discussion will therefore be reserved till the next chapter. Much the same is true of gains and losses in WF from native resources. But this period of geographical movement naturally brought the pre-English and English into contact with other languages, and quite a lot can be said about loan-words at this time. All borrowing is through oral channels, and loans from Latin are from the vulgar spoken language, not from classical Latin. Relationships are primarily of a military and commercial nature, as the loans reflect, but Germanic awareness of visible institutions and officials, especially of the Roman Church, is evident.

We must deal here with borrowing of two periods, and in two environments, Continental and settlement. The Continental loans go back well before the beginning of our period – it has been reckoned that four hundred traceable words from Latin were already in Common Germanic (Streadbeck, 1966, 92). Occasionally the form they take shows clearly that they are very old, and their presence in two or three branches of Germanic points in the same direction; but in many cases it is not possible to determine just how old. Words are assigned to England of the settlement period if, in the form in which they are borrowed, they do not appear in other Germanic languages, and if they show signs of having undergone the English sound-changes of the time, but no earlier changes. These mixed criteria clearly leave many cases undecided. To the Continental period (not necessarily post-370) belong *camp*, 'field, open space, battle' (but NE *camp*, with a different meaning, is from the French development of the same word), *scrīfan*, 'allot, decree' (the ecclesiastical sense of *shrive* being a later development), *strǣt*, 'paved road', *cēap*, 'goods, price, market', *mangere*, 'merchant', *mīl*, 'mile', *pund*, 'pound (weight or money), pint', *toll, mynet*, 'coin' (whence *mint*), *cealc*, 'chalk', *coper*, 'copper', *ʒimm*, 'gem' (also borrowed in late OE in form *ʒemme*, while the PE form is borrowed later again from French), *belt, pilece*, 'fur garment' (PE *pilch*), *pylwe*, 'pillow', *sioluc*, 'silk', *socc*, 'shoe' (= PE *sock*), *sūtere*, 'shoemaker' (now only personal name), *candel, pīpe, seʒne*, 'fishing net', *spynʒe*, 'sponge' (the PE a later loan from French), *butere*, 'butter', *cēse*, 'cheese', *wīn*, 'wine', *binn*, 'manger, bin' (from Latin *benna*, itself borrowed from Celtic), *cetel*, 'kettle' (the NE word being from ON, which also borrowed the word from Latin), *cuppe*, 'cup', *scrīn*, 'chest' (PE *shrine*), *ceaster*, 'city' (represented by (-)*chester*, -*caster*, -*cester*, in modern place-names), *cycene*, 'kitchen', *cylen*, 'kiln', *tīʒle*, 'tile', *weall*, 'wall', *wīc*, 'dwelling, village' (cf. -*wīch*, (-)*wick* in modern place-names), *ynce*, 'inch', *box*, 'box-tree' or 'box' (= container made of box-wood), *cesten*, 'chestnut', *ciris*, 'cherry (for these two the modern forms come from French), *mealwe*, 'mallow', *minte*, 'mint', *nǣp*, 'turnip' (the second syllable of the PE word preserves this form, which is from L *napus*, probably ultimately Egyptian), *pise*, 'pea' (back-derivation in NE, cf. §85), *culter*, 'coulter', *mylen*, 'mill', *plante*, 'plant', *pytt*, 'pitt', *sicol*, 'sickle', *pēa*, 'peacock', *turtle*, 'turtle-dove', *fefor*, 'fever'.

In selecting examples I have for the most part concentrated on cases in which a form survives or has a recognisable relative in PE. This is misleading, in so far as a majority of words have left no such trace. However, the number of words which have been re-borrowed, again from Latin, or, more often, from French, is very considerable, so that even from these examples many have no direct reflex in post-medieval English. The semantic changes are also very striking.

Some words showing the effect of sound-changes which help to date them are those in which (1) an unstressed *e* has been raised to *i*, and (2) *i/j*-mutation has followed, such as L *moneta*, OE *mynet*, PE *mint*, L *balteus*, OE, PE, *belt*; or, with *i/j*-mutation only, L *uncia*, OE *ynce*, PE *inch*. In other cases we can see a re-working of the Latin material

389

in a way not dependent on general phonological developments. Thus L *causa*, 'cause, reason, business, judicial process', appears in OE as *čēas* (on *au > ea*, cf. §212) but as this is not a typical shape for a noun the word is given an excrescent final -*t*, *čēast* (it also develops semantically, having in OE the meaning 'strife'); such re-shapings of the ends of words are well known in later times (cf. §50) L *margarita*, 'pearl', itself borrowed from Greek, is re-shaped in OE by folk-etymology as *mere-ȝrēot* or -*ȝrota*, in which the first element is mere, 'sea, lake, stretch of water', and the second means 'grit, gravel'.

§ 214   What was the language-situation in Britain when the English reached it? This is a complex problem, to which many answers have been given; it is clearly of crucial importance for our understanding of early English lexical history. Kenneth Jackson (1953, Chapter III), in a detailed review of the evidence, concludes that in the first half of the 5c Latin was still the official language of Britain, as it had been under the Roman administration, which ceased in the years following 410. For everyday purposes ordinary people used British, which was still at this date a single language. In the second half of the 5c and during the 6c (i.e., during the period of English settlement) Latin survived chiefly among the upper classes and rulers of the Highland zone, to which the Britons were progressively confined, and at the same time British, as its speech-community was split up by the new settlements, began to separate into dialects which eventually became distinct languages. Very many Latin words passed into OE at this stage, but large numbers had already passed into British. It is not certain how far the early English loans from Latin represent direct borrowings from Latin-speaking Britons who remained among them, how far they are words which have passed through British to enter OE, or even how far they are really Continental loans resulting from the close contacts the English still maintained with Europe (under which the arrival of later settlers may be included). From one source or another, however, many words were taken in, such as *cyrtel*, 'garment, kirtle', *stropp*, 'strap', *ancor*, 'anchor', *punt*, 'punt', *oele*, 'oil' (itself a later loan from French), *čest*, 'chest, box', *mortere*, 'mortar' (for grinding), *pæȝel*, 'pail', *pott*, 'pot', *tunne*, 'cask, tun', *čæster* (cf. earlier *ceaster*), *čerfelle*, 'chervil', *coccel*, 'corn-cockle', *petersilie*, 'parsley' (the modern form is essentially from F *persel*, but its ending probably shows the influence of the early loan), *fann*, 'winnowing-fan', *forca*, 'fork', *catt(e)*, 'cat', *cocc*, 'cock', *truht*, 'trout', *muscelle*, 'mussel', *lǣden*, 'Latin, a language', *munuc*, 'monk', *mynster*, 'monastery, minster', *nunne*, 'nun', *sætern-*, 'Saturn' (in *Saturday*).

Even larger numbers of words borrowed at this period have not lasted into post-medieval English. In several cases there are re-borrowings of words already taken in in the Continental period, such as early *sinoð*, 'council, synod', later *senoð* in the same sense; early *sinop*, 'mustard', later *senap*; in both cases neither word has survived. The effects of sound-changes taking place before and after borrowing are visible as at the earlier period. L *monasterium* must have developed to late **munastirium* to be taken into English in a form that, by *i/j*-mutation, would become *mynster*.

At this point it is appropriate to return to a problem raised in the previous chapter (cf. § 106). The words which may have come into Germanic direct from Greek include two, *enʒel* and *ċiriċe*, which show *i/j*-mutation (Gr *aggelos, kuriakon*); for the former, indeed, though it is usually said to come direct from Greek (Serjeantson, 1935, 51) the probability of Latin transmission is high, since late Latin, by the change of *e* to *i* in the second syllable, had the form **angilus*, which would account for mutation. While the word *church*, being used both for the building and for the assembly of the faithful, is a likely enough word to have been borrowed before the conversion, *enʒel* would seem to be a word with a function only in relation to the faith. It is thus difficult to see where it can have been when *i/j*-mutation took place. If it came from Gothic the change did not affect it there, since it did not take place there, and no other Germanic-speaking people was Christian at the end of the change. Here, then, is another mystery connected with *i/j*-mutation; though various explanations are conceivable, there are objections to all of them.

§ 215 Having allowed that Latin loans of the settlement period were largely transmitted by Britons, and may sometimes have been transmitted through British, we must now consider the borrowings of words which are actually Celtic. As always, the numbers are extremely small. *Bannoc*, 'a piece (of a cake or loaf)', occurs once, and other probable loans are *dunn*, 'grey, dun', and *brocc*, 'badger'; *ʒafeluc*, 'small spear', is less certain. Other words are found, not surprisingly, only in Northumbrian texts, such as *bratt*, 'cloak', *carr*, 'rock', *lūh*, 'lake'.

The extensive influence of Celtic can only be traced in place-names, though a few place-name elements also seem to have been used as common words, such as *torr*, 'rocky peak', *cumb*, 'valley', *funta*, 'fountain' (cf. also *carr* and *lūh* above).

The study of place-names of Celtic origin is fraught with difficulties, not least because of the haphazard way in which the English analysed and adopted into their own speech forms meaningless to them, and beset with alien sound-patterns. Some British names for regions were known to the English before settlement and retained thereafter, such as *Kent*, and perhaps *Thanet* and *Wight*, but others must have become familiar to them on arrival, such as *Lindsey* (*Lindesse*), which combines the old Roman name of *Lincoln*, *Lindon*, with a British suffix *-is*, also found in *Loidis*, *Leeds*. The Northumbrian kingdom-names are further examples, *Deira* (cf. Welsh *deifr*, 'waters') and *Bernicia* (Br *Briganticia*, from the tribal name *Brigantes*). The British kingdom in the Yorkshire Pennines, *Elmet* (in which Leeds was situated), remained independent till late in the 7c and the region continued to be known by its British name. OE *Defnascīr* has as its first element the old tribal name *Dumnonii*, *Cornwealas* ('the Cornubian Welsh') preserves the first syllable of the British name, and *Cumberland* is 'land of the Cumbri, British' (cf. Welsh *Cymri*); all these are areas of late settlement.

A second important group is that of major towns, some known before settlement (e.g., *London, Dover, Lympne, Reculver, Richborough*), others after it, such as *Winchester, Salisbury, Dorchester, Exeter, Cirencester, Gloucester, Worcester, Lichfield, Lincoln, Doncaster*. Many of these are really hybrid formations or re-shapings involving an element of folk-etymology. For instance, *York, Eboracum*, was anglicised as *Ebor – *wīč*, i.e., 'boar-settlement'; the $\beta > v$ (which in ME is lost intervocalically as in *lady*, cf. §136), the *e* develops a glide before the back vowel of the following syllable (*eofor*), the diphthong shifts stress in initial position (*Yo-*); and thus *York* develops.

It is thus clear that many British towns survived as features of life and landscape, even if urban living as such was interrupted. Continuity of another kind is shown by the place-names which have developed out of the names of other notable structures, such as *Eccles*, alone or in compound, meaning 'church' (cf. Br *eclēs*, from L *ecclesia*, and modern Welsh *eglwys*; the stress has naturally been shifted in English). Other names involving human products are rare except in the counties settled very late.

Where British elements are really common is in the names of major natural features, rivers, hills, forests, in particular. The pattern of distribution of Celtic river-names is of singular interest. A map in Jackson (1953, 220) divides England and Wales into four areas. Area I includes everything east of a line from the Yorkshire Wolds to Salisbury

392

Plain and the New Forest, and is in striking correspondence with the boundary of English holdings by 600. Within this area Brittonic names are rare, and are confined to large rivers, such as Trent and Thames (from *Tamesis*, with *i/j*-mutation, which shows, as would be expected, its early adoption); there is also in this area a very large number of names of doubtful origin. Area II lies to the north and west of this, its boundary, starting from the north, running east of Cumberland and Westmorland to the Ribble, and from Chester along the valleys of Dee and Severn to the Bristol Channel, then, skirting Somerset, through Selwood and down the Hants–Dorset border. Here the number of British river-names is much larger and more certain, and many small rivers are included; examples are Dove, Leddon, Dee. This corresponds to the area settled by the English at the close of the 6c and the beginning of the 7c. In Area III, lying to the west of this, in Cumberland, Westmorland, west Lancashire, the Welsh border counties and south-west England to the Tamar, the proportion is yet higher, and includes even stream-names (examples are all the *Avons*, and *Usk, Exe, Axe* -names); and in IV (Wales and Cornwall) the whole character of the nomenclature is Celtic. These areas also correspond to the westward movement of the English, with their language, and to the halting of that movement.

§ 216 It would not be right to conclude without some mention of the English names of early formation, though the subject is far too large for such incidental treatment. As we know (cf. §208), an early stratum consists of names which were really personal and tribal, and not truly place-names. Some of these, the names in personal-name + -*ing*(*s*), particularly, are very early, and contrast with later forms in -*ingham*, -*ington*, which are genuinely by origin names of places; but the person-type in other cases persisted, as *Somerset* (*sumer-setan*, 'settlers of the Somerton district') shows. Those names which do by origin denote places are mainly of two types, descriptive and personal. In the first class the elements used show a very keen eye for the features of the landscape, and a detailed classification of them according to their natural and exploitable characteristics, and are not easily rendered into PE. Since these elements may be presumed to be drawn from vocabulary in use for general purposes, they evidence a wealth of material which has now been lost, or suffered from the blurring of fine distinctions. Thus, for 'small wood or copse' we find such elements as *bearu* (the source of some modern *Barrow* names), *bysc (in *Bushey*, etc.), *fyrhþ(e)* (cf. *Firber*,

Chapel-en-le-Frith), *grāf(a)* and *grǣfe* (*Grafton*, *Griff*), *hanȝra* (*Oak-hanger*), *hearȝ* (*Harrow*), *hēse* (*Hayes*), *holt* (*Knockholt*), **hylte* (*Navant*), *hyrst* (surviving in some obvious forms, and some very greatly transformed ones, such as *Hartest*, *Titness*, *Staplers*, *Copster*, *Horsebridge*), *lēah* (*Lea*), *sċeaȝa* (*Shaugh*). The list excludes terms which are used for large areas of woodland. It includes some terms whose special meaning we can discern, such as *hanȝra*, which is specifically a wood on a slope, *hearȝ*, used of a grove regarded as sacred, *hēse*, used rather of land covered with brush or small trees than of the extent of copse itself, *lēah*, used specially for woodland regarded as a site for clearing, and later developing the sense 'land cleared for cultivation' and *sċeaȝa*, originally 'wet land liable to be overgrown with alders', whence 'alder copse', later 'copse'. Even so, the number of what strike us as synonyms is high. The list could be increased by the addition of two or three dozen terms used of thickets, or of land covered with, or for copses of, brushwood and trees of specific kinds. A number of these words seem to have passed out of active general use during the OE period, and their early abundance is perhaps a development we should expect of a people who for some centuries had been eyeing the countryside with a view to settlement, and who had developed their usage in conditions likely to give rise to divergences from group to group. Smith (1956) provides abundant material for the wealth of terms for related features – types of hill, of valley, of clearing, enclosure, and so on. The rise and fall of this rich vocabulary is a fine example of linguistic adaptation to a phase of life making particular demands. It is yet another warning against the supposition that the additions to vocabulary we trace in later centuries are all gain, and that early English made do, in its fumbling way, with a small number of words, each of which was of necessity a very blunt instrument. The English Place-Name Society has now completed its survey of the place-names of most counties (map in Smith, 1956, Part I, back-pocket, shows the position in 1954, since when much more has been published), and only now do we appreciate the extent even of what is still traceable of the early place-name vocabulary. While the Society's list of the chief place-name elements is not confined to OE material, a comparison of length between its 1924 list of elements (67 pp.) and its 1956 list (305 + 283 pp. in two volumes) is a guide to the quantity of material that has been brought to light in recent years. There is probably not much more to be discovered but much more must have been in use.

It is clear from the *hearȝ* names that this material represents a pre-Christian stratum of English to which we hardly gain access by other means, and this is confirmed by a number of forms using the names of Germanic gods and other supernatural beings, especially the quite frequent ones based on *Woden* (*Wednesbury, Wansdyke*, etc.). The place-names also show dialect-divergences in lexis, for which our literary evidence is rather shaky. For instance, the word *ćert* is common in Kent and Sussex, used in Surrey and Essex, unknown elsewhere, for a particular kind of rough common land (cf. the modern *Chart* names in Kent). Dialect-evidence may be combined with evidence about the progress of colonisation, as in the *-denn* names of the Weald (e.g., Tenterden, Biddenden). Originally the name for an animal's lair, *denn* came to be specialised in the sense of a place where swine lived. The first opening of the Weald to human residence seems to have been the stationing of swine-herds in charge of the pigs feeding on Wealden mast, and when their huts became the focus of a new settlement the settlement was given a determinative first element and kept *denn* as the second.

The value of place-name material cannot be adequately summarised; only study of the EPNS volumes can reveal the diversity of illumination it brings to language, history, social life, culture and literature.

§ 217   The PE words *write* (originally, 'carve, engrave, inscribe') and *read* (with various earlier senses, of which the relevant one is 'interpret, decipher') have their first discernible uses as technical terms relating to the use of runes. The Anglo-Saxons distinguished sharply between the two types of letters, *rūn-stæfas* and *bōc-stæfas*, but transferred the related verbs from their older runic use to use for the inscription and interpretation of the alphabet. There are many unsolved problems relating to this mode of writing, whose very name means 'secret, mystery', but it is quite certain that the English brought it with them at the settlement.

All known European alphabetic writing systems originate in the Mediterranean, and there is no reason to suppose that future discoveries will change that picture. The first evidence of writing of a Germanic language comes from the early years of the Christian era (probably A.D. 6-9), and is found on one of a hoard of helmets from Negau in Styria; the characters, written from right to left, are North Etruscan, and closely similar to runes in form – closer than the common epigraphic function of the two scripts can account for. Runes proper are found from about A.D. 200, and the very early examples centre upon Denmark. The Danish aristocracy in the 1c and 2c was wealthy and cosmopolitan, with a keen appreciation of luxury objects from the Mediterranean. It seems, therefore, that two phases can be distinguished: first, that a Germanic tribe on the middle Danube learns the use of writing from southerly neighbours, and adapts the symbols for the writing of its own language; second, that someone re-structures the available symbols into runes, whose use begins nearly two centuries later in Denmark. All the evidence is that the new system was conceived at a stroke by a single mind, and was not the result of a gradual evolution or transfer. But whether the invention took place in Denmark or further south is not clear.

For our purposes, Denmark is the home of runes, and from it they rapidly spread to Norway, Sweden and the Continental Germanic peoples. Whether the Goths knew them cannot be decided on present evidence. In their original form they formed a set of twenty-four symbols with a fixed order (the source and meaning of which are inexplicable). Since this order has nothing to do with that of Greek or Latin it is correct to say that runic writing is alphabetic rather than an alphabet (i.e., it approximately embodies the principle that one symbol corresponds to one phoneme, but not in A-B order). From the values of the first runes the whole set of symbols is known as the *futhark* for Germanic as a whole, but (because of the change of *a* to *o*), as the *futhork* when it is used for or in English. In the forms of the letters, by comparison with any possible antecedents, the most striking change is the removal of curves in favour of angles; the purpose must from the outset have been epigraphic, and the futhork never developed a cursive form.

In early use it was typically employed for necessarily brief inscriptions – often without discernible meaning – on small objects. Formerly its purpose was thought to have been magical; now we see that though, like our own writing, it could be used for spells, charms and curses, these purposes were not specially associated with runes; its functions, within the limitations of space, were those of any script. Runes developed in an aristocratic environment, and were often carved on luxury objects; their forms and meanings were presumably at any time known only to a few. As a script they have one inexplicable feature, namely that no style evolves through something like eleven centuries of use; there are individual differences in form, but the shape of runes does not have a stylistic history as any other script does.

Not only the order, but the acrophonic names of the runes, are Common Germanic, though the English series shows Christian expurgation (for example, the third rune is called *þorn*, not by the OE reflex of the original name *þursis*, a supernatural being). The acute ear for linguistic analysis shown by the first deviser of runes seems to have been characteristic of later users, at any rate in England. The English followed the changes in phonology after the settlement, adding four symbols reflecting the new vocalism. The English futhork of twenty-eight symbols, devised some time after the settlement, remained in use till the mid-7c, and occasionally later, but thereafter further symbols were developed to represent the elaborated velar consonant-system of the English, making a total of thirty-three. But most extant English runes are subsequent to the knowledge of the alphabet, and show its influence in a number of ways, notably, regularity of writing from left to right. English runes are concentrated in three areas, central Mercia, Kent and Northumbria; there are none from Wessex. Much the most important collection is that from Northumbria, where the runes were used for public and private Christian objects on a considerable scale. The link with Denmark is again noticeable here. One may also suppose that Irish influence, since the Irish had their ogham script independent of Latin, would have supported the use of indigenous forms of writing. In the end, however, Latin script, which could do all the futhork could, and more, completely replaced the use of runes, as, in about the 2c, it had swamped the Etruscan alphabets which seem to have been their source.

§ 218   The move the English made in their settlement was not a very large one in terms of distance, or change of environment; for some it no doubt represented a changed way of life, but others must have been farming, or seeking land to farm, before their arrival. They did not form a political unity before or after they came, nor had they a written form of language in either phase. In fact the extent of the shock to the language-system is surprisingly great. The century after the settlement sees a series of major sound-changes and further progress in the decline of inflections, paving the way for a new syntax. Of course, to each generation the change was gradual to the point of imperceptibility. The growth of the self-image of the English as a distinct community was, likewise, prolonged. The settlement is the crucial fact in the history of English to us, as we look back and trace its consequences; to contemporaries the transition must have seemed relatively slight.

CHAPTER IX

Before 370

§ 219 We have now reached a point at which the designation *English* can be used of the language we are studying only in the rather forced sense that some of the speakers of it were Angles. The story cannot be dropped abruptly, since there was no sudden shift in the habits of speakers; nor can it be traced in the detail appropriate for English proper. Very briefly we must survey three antecedent phases of development: the WG which lies behind Anglo-Frisian, the CG lying behind that, and the IE family, which is the furthest we can trace any relative of English. To do this, we change our pace from even steps of two hundred years, to one of about a thousand followed by one of perhaps two thousand. The truth is that we are going more and more into realms of relative rather than absolute chronology, and the time-scale becomes not only larger but a great deal vaguer than it was before.

It will be most convenient to take the Germanic phase as our focus, both to trace the separation of WG from it, and also to look at its relationships with the wider IE family. The emergence of Germanic as a distinct family must be not later than the 10c B.C. The earliest traceable home of the Germanic peoples is in the region of the Elbe, and the expansions which led to the break-up of the speech-community started in the 2c B.C. by the northward movement into Scandinavia and the eastward movement of the Goths to the Vistula, leaving a range of tribes in the old central area, who also redistributed themselves geographically while remaining central *vis-à-vis* the new northern and eastern groups. Much information about these tribes (though it needs careful interpretation) is preserved in the *Germania* of Tacitus, and to some extent in other classical sources. In the early centuries of the Christian era the westward movements of certain of the old central tribes, already to some extent linguistically distinct, took them into territories from which the designation Western derives (cf. § 207); as these movements continue till the 6c there is progressive differentiation into dialects, and eventually languages.

WG is sometimes like NG, sometimes like EG, sometimes unique.

From the outset, the characteristic phonological changes are such as to disrupt the old pattern of morphological relationships. *I/j*-mutation is common to NG and WG; both lose (except in a single verb) the distinct forms of the passive, and eventually have to make good the want by periphrases; both lose almost all trace of the old reduplicating past, so that class VII of strong verbs no longer has a perceptible identity. The features WG shares with EG are grammatical: the development of a pre-posed definite article out of the same original *þ*-demonstrative (NG uses a post-posed form derived from an *-n* pronoun), and the prominence given to the verb *have* (OE *habban*, Go *haban*) as against NG *eiga* (OE *ā3an*, 'own'). The characteristics peculiar to WG are chiefly phonological. The WG languages are characterised by a free development of diphthongs – perhaps we may say, by an early phase of that tendency to vocalise post-vocalic /j/ and /w/ which was to be evident throughout the history of English; thus OE has a diphthongal form *3lēaw*, 'wise' where cognate words in EG (Go adv *glaggwo*) and NG (ON asm *glöggvan*) do not, and in general greatly increases, as do all the WG languages, the functional load of the long diphthongs (all diphthongs arising before the OE phase are long). Two voiced consonants underwent changes of quality, which separated them from their voiceless counterparts, and so obscured previously clear grammatical alternations: /z/ become /r/, and thus in conditions for voice-alternation /s/ alternates with /r/, a sound having no obvious relationship with it; /ð/ became /d/, which to a lesser extent obscured relationship with /θ/. Hence the fragmentation of a considerable number of verb-paradigms which had a voiceless consonant in the present and past singular, the voiced counterpart in the past plural and participle (*cēosan, curon; weorðan, wurdon*). The origin of this voice-alternation will be traced in §226. WG also shows in certain environments a tendency to lengthen consonants; the results appear in OE long consonants, and can still be traced in some PE double-consonant spellings though phonemic length was lost centuries ago (cf. *apple, bitter*).

§ 220   If we turn to the dim period of perhaps a thousand years we speak of as Germanic, it is clear that it must contain, in many dimensions, lines of differentiation. The term Common Germanic is used for the common features of those forms of speech from which the three branches diverged; it obviously does not mean that for so long a time speech remained stable and undifferentiated throughout the Germanic community. We are not, for instance, following a course similar to the tracing of branches from twig-tip to common trunk. The language is no more Common in the sense of uniform than English has been during the last thousand years.

In speaking of the relationship of Germanic to a wider group of languages designated Indo-European, it has long been customary, and is still illuminating, to use metaphors of family or genetic relationship. The point of a metaphor is to bring together things like in certain respects and unlike in others. When we use metaphorical language in academic study it is important to limit our applications to those aspects in which there is genuine likeness; accepted uncritically, a metaphor can mislead more than it illuminates. Some aspects of the comparison between language-relationships and family-relationships are so obviously irrelevant that they do not mislead; for instance, no one supposes that a language has a mother and a father. Other differences are sufficiently obscure to be harmful. Notably, family relationships are unidirectional and divergent, and the terms related are absolute and distinct individuals. A son cannot reverse relationships with parent or cousin, and once born he is for ever himself and no one else. Language relationships can be both convergent and divergent; because languages are not clear-cut entities like individuals they may re-shape their relationships, growing like that from which they formerly diverged, or moving into a new family with which they are not genetically connected, and so on. A diagram in the form of a family tree may show some truths, but it must not be read in so simplistic a way as to obscure other truths, which might be expressed in terms of ripples spreading out through disturbed water, or of the making up of trains from carriages previously combined in different ways in different places on different journeys. There are few things in our experience so complex as language, and no single one that forms a perfect image for its functions, structure and history.

A fortiori, when we speak of Common Indo-European (more usually, simply of IE) we refer not to an undifferentiated language, but to a combination of features which can be shown to have been common to the antecedent of sub-families of the level of Germanic, and of the recorded members of such families. From the stage of differentiation recorded for about 2000 B.C. we are forced to place the end of this Common phase well back into the third millennium B.C., and we do not know how much further back it stretches. Now the term IE is used in two ways: as a designation for sub-families and languages of IE origin, and for the sum of features common to their antecedent. In the second sense, the one with which we are primarily concerned, IE does not have to be a designation for a language at all, let alone an undifferentiated one. To collect evidence about underlying features is not to show that they all coexisted at one time in one speech-community, and can therefore be spoken of as a language, or as fragments of a language. It is likely enough, to judge from sub-families whose 'parent' is recorded (notably the Romance languages descended from Latin), that what we can reconstruct is part of a language; but this is a working hypothesis, not a proven truth.

From this hypothesis it is tempting to try to work out something about the location and culture of the earliest speakers of the assumed language, and much ingenuity has been expended on this study. Certain points are obvious: these speakers did not come from Africa, Australia or America, but from the European-Asiatic landmass. What can be traced of their common vocabulary suggests that they came from neither a tropical nor an Arctic nor a mountainous region. They were nomadic and pre-agricultural. This still leaves much scope for speculation, and no conclusive association with any part of Europe has been shown. Even more speculative are questions about who the early speakers were; from the time of the earliest material we know IE languages are spoken by many races, tribes and nationalities, from India to the Aegean, with diverse cultures, all (since they are so early documented) of an advanced nature. That nomadic life spread these languages is understandable, but their extent must involve conquest and invasion as well. Needless to say all these considerations strengthen the *a priori* case against uniformity within IE. Moreover, this unsettled mode of life led not only to differentiation, but to the emergence of dominant groups, with the absorption of minor ones and a fresh pattern of divergences. After speaking of the disintegration of the postulated original speech-community, Prokosch (1939) writes:

> In the course of time, many of them re-integrated, being absorbed by leading groups, and these new, larger units in turn again split up into sub-divisions – a process which is illustrated most clearly by the Romance group: The Italic group was absorbed by one of its members, namely Latin. This formed a number of dialects, in France, in Italy, in Spain, in Rumania. The rise of the dialect of the Isle de France as 'Standard French' super-imposed a new standard upon the numerous sub-languages of French – and the process still continues (23).

This almost cloud-like process of splitting and re-formation can only be observed in relatively recent times, but it would be rash to suppose that in pre-history the pattern was simpler. What we can trace of the relationships between sub-families does not suggest a single line of divergence, and our evidence is very incomplete. The dates from which different sub-families and single languages are recorded differ widely; of ten sub-families now identified, two only came to light within living memory; both those, and individual members of other sub-families, are extinct; one IE language (Manx) has become extinct since the Second World War. We do not know how many missing links are concealed from us.

The IE phoneme-system which is taken as a starting point from which CG may be traced, and which might be placed in something like the third millennium B.C., is not the oldest that can be reconstructed. Lehmann (1955) is able to identify a succession of radically transformed systems underlying it. Without going into details of the sound-systems, we should note that changes in segmental structure can be related to prosodic evolution. The earliest detectable phase (A) is one before the development of phonemic stress; this is followed by B(a), in which phonemic stress is introduced, and B(b), in which syllable-structure is affected by the innovation. In C stress becomes non-distinctive, and the shifting distribution of phonetic material between phonemes continues. In D pitch becomes distinctive, and certain vowels differentiate under divergent pitch-conditions. E sub-divides, into E(a), in which pitch becomes non-distinctive, and the vowels developed earlier under contrastive pitch-conditions evolve from allophones into phonemes, and E(b) in which certain sounds following the new vowels are lost, leaving divergent vowel-development as the only sign of their former presence. Finally, in F, we reach the system from which the sub-families can be shown to have evolved.

This brief summary has, by itself, little meaning. It is included as evidence that the successive phases involve changes which go very deep in the structure of the sound-system, and must extend very far behind the dates we have been considering. For those who wish to follow the subject more closely in a standard work on IE it will become clear that the sound-system of each phase can be reconstructed rather fully and with considerable confidence. No room is left for vague speculations about the possibility of linking IE with other language-families. Speculation of this kind has been pursued in many detailed studies involving a number of possibly cognate families. No convincing positive results have been achieved. A negative cannot be proved, but in this case it begins to look extremely promising.

The astonishing worldly success of IE speaking peoples has given rise to a popular supposition that when relationship has been traced so far, between such divergent communities, and between languages having no or few obvious points of resemblance (as English-speakers who have tried to learn Russian, Sanskrit or even Gothic must have noticed), then it can only be one step further to prove the kinship of all languages in the world, and their common origin. There are many fallacies in the supposition. One is the unidirectional theory of development – the giving of a quite false priority to divergent development within IE. Who knows how many Manxes or Cornishes were lost by the spread of a single dominant language in pre-history, as English has spread in recent history? But this growth in uniformity has also reduced the variety of non-IE languages in the world. The last two centuries, even the last two decades, have seen the extinction of various Amerindian languages in favour of English, and it is quite clear that the spread of IE must have been at the cost of extinguishing many non-cognate languages in the past while others, such as Basque, survived in a fringe situation. It is inconceivable that we should ever know the range of languages that has existed in the world. Then, too, guesswork about origins involves severe distortion of the time-scale on a distant perspective. Late common IE may be 5,000 years old, and early common IE can hardly be twice that. This leaves nearly half a million years of human evolution unaccounted for. Since there is no human community without language it would be rash to assume that anything recognisable as man evolved independently of the origin of language. Of the time unknown to us compared to that within our powers of re-construction we may say, as King Edwin's counsellor said in 627 of life in the world we know, that it is:

tō þiðmetenesse þēre tide þe ūs uncūð is, sþylċe þū æt spǣsendum   sitte
by comparison with that time that to us unknown is, as if you at feast should

mid þīnum ealdor-mannum on þinter-tīde and sīe   fŷr   onǣled
be   sitting with your elders in   winter-time and there should be fire kindled

and þīn   heall ȝeþyrmed and hit rīne and snīþe and
and your hall   warmed,   and it   should be raining and snowing and

styrme   ūte; cume   an spearþe and hrædlīċe þæt hūs þurhflēo,
storming out; should some a sparrow and quickly that house through-fly

cume þurh ōðre duru in, and þurh ōðre ūt ȝeþite.   Hþæt, hē
should come through one door in, and by the other out depart. Lo,   he

on þā tīd   þe   hē inne bið, ne bið hrinen mid þy storme þæs þintres;
in the time that he inside is, not is touched by the storm of the winter;

403

ac þæt bið ān ēaȝan bryhtm and þæt læste fæċ,   ac he sōna of
but that is an eye's winking/flash and the least time but he straightway

þintre on þone þinter eft cymeð, . . . hþæt þær   foreȝanȝe, oððe hþæt
from winter into winter back comes, what thereto may precede or what to

þær fyliȝe, þe ne cunnen.
it may follow, we do not know.

The reconstruction of IE is one of the great achievements of the human intellect in the last century and a half. There is no call to twist it into evidence about the origin of language, a subject which remains totally obscure.

§ 221 The sub-families of IE now known are the following. Indo-Iranian, the furthest east in location except through recent transplantations of European languages, has two branches: Indic, represented by a classical language, Sanskrit, which, with texts from about 2000 B.C. is the first recorded language in the family, and by over a dozen modern languages; and Iranian, also recorded early, and having some ten modern descendents. Thraco-Phrygian, represented by Old (7c B.C.) and New (Roman period) Phrygian, and Old (from the 5c A.D.) and Modern Armenian, is centred in Asia Minor; Thraco-Illyrian has ancient representatives extending widely over Europe from the Balkans to the Mediterranean, from Western Europe to Asia Minor, and one modern representative, Albanian, recorded from the 14c A.D. Balto-Slavic has a southern group of Slavic languages represented from the Middle Ages on, an east Slavic group whose largest representative is Russian, and a Baltic group whose main modern member is Lithuanian. These four easterly sub-families are associated by certain phonological likenesses, but other groupings cut across the east–west one. The westerly sub-families include Hellenic, represented by various ancient and later forms of Greek dialects, recorded from about 850 B.C. Probably Hittite should be mentioned next, the language of a people who flourished in Asia Minor and Syria in the second millennium B.C. and whose language and culture were destroyed in the 12c B.C. Its grammar and phonology are IE, its vocabulary largely of different origin, so the exact relationship it bears to IE is a matter of dispute. Provisionally, it may be regarded as a further sub-family. The next is the Italic, consisting of three subsidiary groups, of which the Latin one, from which the Romance languages are descended, came to overwhelm and absorb the others. Particularly close to the Italic is the Celtic, dividing into Continental, represented by Gaulish, which died out in the 6c A.D. (i.e., gave way to the descendant of Latin), and Insular, of the Cumbric (Cornish, Welsh, Breton) and Goidelic (Irish, Gaelic, Manx) branches. Before coming to Germanic we should mention the sub-family most recently discovered, Tocharian, evidenced in two languages of Asia Minor in documents going back to the 6c A.D., and sharing the phonology of the western group of sub-families. Finally, there is the sub-family with which we are most closely concerned, the Germanic, whose Eastern branch is represented by Gothic, Burgundian and Vandal, all extinct; its Northern branch has given rise to Icelandic, Swedish, Danish and Norwegian; its Western branch to High German and Low German, the latter including certain German dialects, Dutch, Flemish, Frisian, and English in all the forms it has taken throughout the world. At any rate it is clear that, genetically, this is where English stands. Typologically the developments of the last fifteen hundred years have so distanced it from its closest relatives that the question 'Is English a Germanic Language?' has been seriously raised (Zandvoort, 1956). Genetics is not everything in the grouping of languages, and if it were there comes a point – as with the tracing of Romance languages to Latin – at which diversification has gone so far that the founding of a new family has to be recognised. Typically this happens when a great empire has spread use of a single language far beyond its original home. The parallel hardly needs underlining.

§ 222 Having established the context of related languages, let us consider what can be discovered of what IE was like at the stage antecedent to the separation of Germanic. There would seem to have been a system of thirty-two phonemes, forming four classes or sub-systems. The first class consists of those sounds which cannot function as syllabics (syllable-peaks), called obstruents. These form a close-knit and symmetrical system, within which we are certain of the patterning of contrasts, though some have doubts as to phonetic values. The usual view, embodied in the spellings generally employed to represent these phonemes, is that there are four positions of articulation, labial, dental (used in a broad sense, not excluding the possibility that the sounds were really alveolar), velar, and labio-velar. At each position of articulation there are three modes of articulation, voiceless stop, voiced stop, and aspirated voiced stop. The first sub-system can thus be represented in the following way:

$$p \quad t \quad k \quad k^w$$

$$b \quad d \quad g \quad g^w$$

$$b^h \quad d^h \quad g^h \quad gw^h$$

The second sub-system consists of those sounds which can only function as syllabics, the vowels, in a short series which, giving the symbols their slack values, we may represent as *e, a, o*, and a weak form *ə*; and a long series *iː, eː, aː, oː, uː* (nine vowels in all). The third sub-system consists of resonants, i.e., sounds which may or may not have syllabic function (thus corresponding to approximants, liquids and nasals in PE): there are six, *w* (syllabically *u*), *y* (syllabically *i*), *r, l, m, n*. The fourth group consists of sounds, not evidenced in any recorded language, but postulated to have existed in order to explain certain developments that are found; it is most likely that there were four of them, and they are known, evidently, from their contrasting effects rather than in their inherent qualities: they are called laryngeals. There were many diphthong-like sequences, but they are best interpreted as constituting a cluster of vowel plus resonant, or vice versa; if each one were taken as a diphthong they would add another thirty-two phonemes, producing a wholly abnormal type of sound-system. Quite a lot can be inferred about their allophonic realisations, and it must be remembered that at this phase there was also non-phonemic accent-variation.

§ 223 Unless special environmental conditioning intervenes, these phonemes develop into Germanic in the following way. /a/ remains, IE *agros* 'field', Go *akrs* (OE *æcer* shows the usual fronting of *æ* to *a*, thereafter the vowel lengthens in the open stem syllable of a disyllabic word, ME *aker*, the /aː/ undergoes the 15c shift to /eɪ/, and post-vocalic /r/ is lost; the meaning persisted unchanged till OE, and the modern central sense of *acre* dates from before A.D. 1000). /e/ remains, I E *bhero*, 'bear', OE *beran* (inf); in this the vowel has lengthened for the same reason, and has diphthongised at the loss of /r/, but the meaning has never changed. /i/ remains, IE *widhewā*, 'widow', OE *þiduþe* (there are other spellings), in which the only change has been the development of a diphthong in the second syllable. In Germanic (as in Lithuanian) /o/ becomes /a/, IE *okto(u)*, 'eight', Go *ahtau*; here, we have fronting to *æ* followed by breaking, further ME diphthongal developments and finally loss of /χ/. IE /u/ generally remained, *yugom*, 'yoke', Go *juk*, but OE has a different development, since in WG the sound lowered to /o/ unless 'protected' by a following sound (it is this development which accounts for the widespread alternation in strong verbs between *u* in past plural, where the ending in *-un* does give protection, and the second participle in *o*, where the following *-en* gives none). Everywhere except in Indo-Iranian *ə* becomes *a*, as IE **pətēr*, 'father', Go *fader*, OE *fæder* (with later retraction to *a*, modern English lengthening and loss of /r/). /ɑ:/ remained in most sub-families, but in Lithuanian and Germanic became /o:/, IE **mātēr*, 'mother', OE *mōdor*, with 15c raising to /u:/, followed by shortening and unrounding, and intervocalic /d/ > /ð/. IE *ē* (slack) remains in Germanic (where it is customarily transcribed *ǣ*); its reflex is also *ǣ* in OE (WS, but elsewhere *ē*, as in Go), but the evidence seems incontrovertible that in WG it became *ā*, and then in WS reverted to its former value; the history of the non-WS sound is doubtful. Compare IE **dhē-*, 'put, place', with Go *ga-dēþs*, OHG *tāt*, WS *dǣd* NWS *dēd*, PE *deed* (by the 15c vowel shift). IE *ī* remains, as in **swīno*, 'pig', OE *spīn*, PE *swine* (by the 15c vowel change); so does *ō*, IE **bhlō-*, OE *blōsma*, 'blossom' (with shortening before consonant-cluster). Of the 'diphthongs' we need only observe that any *o* element shared the development of single *o* to *a*, so that *oi* becomes *ai* (OE *ā*), *ou* > *au* (OE *ēa*). The syllabic consonants 'fill out' to *-ul, -um, -ur, -un*. The conditioned changes chiefly involve raising of *e, o*, under typical raising conditions (a following nasal or high vowel) and lowering of *i, u*, under typical lowering conditions (a following *r*).

The laryngeals, of course, are lost. But so far the modifications of the phonology are extremely slight, and, laryngeals apart, do not affect the system.

§ 224 The development of the IE vowel-system seems to have taken place largely under successive accentual developments, and the conditions are highly relevant to important features of Germanic. Lehmann (1955) postulates an early system in which the only true vowel was /e/ (though resonants might have syllabic function). At the stage when stress accent was phonemic this vowel remained, or in certain conditions was lengthened under stress, giving rise to the vowel /e:/, which in turn became phonemic when stress was lost; otherwise it became /ə/ or was lost. At the stage when pitch accent was phonemic at least three grades must be distinguished, and under secondary accent /e/ > /o/, /e:/ > /o:/.

Members of this vowel system functioned within roots, which had commonly a structure of vowel preceded by obstruent or resonant, and followed by either or none; the root could be extended in various ways. Alternations of accent upon the words formed from these roots

were related to grammatical function. The consequent patterning of
vowels in series (ablaut-series) is seen most clearly in what we know as
the strong verbs, which had primary accent in the present, secondary
in the past singular, and typically the lowest grade, with zero vowel,
in the past plural and participle. Ablaut-variation also appears in nominal
formations, but having watched in English the disintegration of the
strong-verb system, we now concentrate on its origins.

In its simplest form the series can be seen in OE verbs of class III.
Here, since the stem always ends in a reflex of a resonant, the series
consists of strong *e*, weak *o*, and zero developing to *u* + resonant:

IE	*wert-	*wort-	*wrt-̩	*wrt-̩
Gmc	e	a	u	u
OE	þeorþan, 'become'	þearþ	þurdon	þorden

(Here OE shows breaking in the first two grades, and lowering of *u* to
o in the participle; all the sub-classes of this type developed as a result of
sound-changes in Gmc and later).

In class I we have the same series, with the vowel followed by *i*, combining
to give the diphthong *ei* in the present, *oi* weak, and with *i* alone in
the past; the strong grade diphthong smooths to *ī*, and *oi* becomes *ai* in
Germanic, thus:

IE	*steigh-	*stoigh-	*stigh-	*stigh-
Gmc	i	ai	i	i
OE	stīȝan, 'climb'	stāh	stiȝon	stiȝen

(The verb has not survived, but formations on the same root can be seen
in *stile* and *stirrup*; again, sub-divisions of the class arose only in Gmc
and later).

In class II we have the same series, with the basic vowels followed by *w*,
realised as *u* after vowels and with syllabic consonants. Thus:

IE	*geus-	*gous-	*gus-	*gus-
Gmc	eu	au	u	u
OE	ċēosan, 'choose'	ċēas	curon	coren

(OE has its normal development of the diphthongs, and lowering in the
participle; sub-divisions arise in Gmc and later).

In Class IV the structure of the series is modified, since the past plural
has the lengthened grade, thus:

IE	*bher-	*bhor-	*bhēr-	*bhr̩-
Gmc	e	a	ǣ	u
OE	ᴜeran	bær	bǣron, bēron	boren

(OE has the normal fronting of *ā*, in the past plural divergence between WS and the rest of the country, and lowering in the participle; as usual, sub-divisions are Gmc or later).

Class V is like IV except for a different grade of vowel in the participle, but VI belongs to a distinct and later ablaut series, originally in *a-ā-ā-a*, Gmc *a-ō-ō-a*).

§ 225   In all examples quoted so far the vowels have been notably more stable between IE and Germanic than the obstruents, whose progress must now be traced. They undergo, as a system, a topological change, that is to say, every item changes, but they all keep their distance relative to one another. The dramatic nature of this shift has attracted much attention, but it does not go very deep, since it leaves the system unchanged.

The first series of obstruents, the voiceless stops, pass through a phase of aspiration from which they become fricatives, thus:

p > ph > f, IE *phor-, 'travel', OE faran, NE fare;
t > th > θ, IE *treyes, Go þreis, OE þrēo, PE three;
k > kh > χ, IE *peku Go faihu (/feχu/), OE feoh (all = 'cattle'), PE fee (but in initial position this χ > h, IE *km̩tom, Go and OE hund, 'hundred');
kw > khw > χw, IE *kwod-, OE hþæt, PE what (in rather different grammatical function; note the same initial development to *h* as with the reflex of simple *k*).

The second series, the voiced stops, loses voice, thus:

b > p (this sound, a new phoneme, is rare in IE, and few clear instances with wide range through various languages can be found), cf. Lithuanian *bala, OE pōl, NE pool;
d > t, IE *dem- (cf. L domus, 'house'), Go timrjan, OE timbrian, 'build', cf. PE timber;
g > k, IE *geus-, Go kiusan, OE ċēosan, PE choose;
gw > kw, IE *gwem-, Go qiman (/kwiman/), OE cwuman, PE come.

The third series, the aspirated voiced stops, loses aspiration, thus:

bh > b, IE *bhū, 'be', OE bū(a)n, 'live', and with different grade bēon, PE be;
dh > d, IE *dhur-, OE duru, PE door;

409

gh > g, IE *ghostis, 'stranger' (cf. L hostis, 'enemy'), Go gasts, OE (with
  i/j-mutation) gest, cf. PE guest.
gwh > gw, *IE *sengwh-, Go siggwan (gg = /ŋg/), OE singan, PE sing.

Clearly, these three series could have changed in a certain order or
simultaneously. They could have occurred in the order of exposition,
but not in other orders, since if the aspirated stops had lost aspiration
first, they would have fallen together with the voiced stops, and shared
their development; manifestly, they do not. And if the voiced stops had
lost voice before the voiceless stops changed they too would have coalesced into a single series; but they did not. When a whole system mutates
in so tidy a fashion there is a *prima facie* case for the view that the change
was a single process, affecting all parts of the system at once. For a
long time the treatment of loan-words seemed to make this natural
supposition unworkable. But Fourquet (1948) showed that there was no
serious obstacle, and we may conclude, with him, that the consonant-
shift, in all three phases, happened at one time. This, then, is a change of
very great generality – far greater than the 15c vowel-shift. It is not
merely sounds that change, or even sub-systems of sounds; the shift
lies in the correlation between series of sub-systems. It may be stated and
diagrammed thus: before the shift the three series were correlated, 1 and
2 by voice, 2 and 3 by aspiration; at the end of it, 1 and 2 were correlated
by plosion, 2 and 3 by voice:

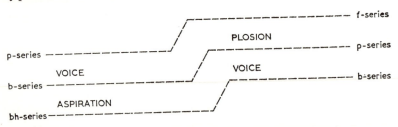

During the transition period (indicated by slant-lines) the three series
must have been kept apart by correlations of mixed character – such as
can be heard today in the renderings of English consonants by those
whose speech had a Gaelic or Erse sub-stratum; it suggests a carry-over
of speech-habits from another language in an adult population trans-
ferring to an IE language, presumably as a result of conquest. But such
a shift can also occur spontaneously, and the general pattern of development in Germanic is against the sub-stratum hypothesis.
  This correlated group of changes is usually known as the First

Germanic Consonant Shift (contrasting it with the Second, which affects only High German, cf. §211); but out of piety to the great scholar who first formulated it (not quite in the terms we have used) it is also called Grimm's Law; linguists now feel some squeamishness about the use of the term *law* in linguistics, though in the 19c it had a considerable vogue.

§ 226 The First Germanic Consonant Shift is the first of a series of characteristics differentiating Germanic from IE. It does not affect consonants in every environment, but happens unless there is anything to prevent it. A clue to the dating of it is provided by the loanword *hemp*; knowledge of *hemp* was spread to the Western world by the Scythians in the 5c B.C., and the Greek word, *kannabis*, was borrowed into Germanic, where it appears in OE as *hænep*. From this form it is clear that the word has undergone the shift ($k > h$, $b > p$), which must have been operative at or after the 5c B.C. The change, may, however, have been extremely gradual, and there is no reason why it should not have started earlier.

For a long time scholars were puzzled by certain apparent exceptions to the shift, instances in which it has, indeed, taken place, but in which the resulting consonant has been voiced. The explanation of this voicing was furnished in 1877 by Karl Verner, and is consequently known as Verner's Law. Though Verner's Law has few direct reflexes in PE it has played an important part in the development of the language, both through its operation in Germanic, and because it formulates a tendency which has been operative fairly consistently at all periods (for later operations, cf. §38). The voicing depends upon the evolution of the second major characteristic of the Germanic languages, namely a new system of phonemic accentual stress, which eventually comes to be located on the root-syllables of words. This has remained a constant feature of the sub-family (unlike the consonant-shift, a once-for-all change), and has played a greater part than any other single element in the history of English – its grammar as well as its phonology. Its first detectable consequence, Verner's Law, is quite simple. At the closure of a weak syllable articulation is weak, and this weakness typically shows in two ways; voicing present in the preceding and following syllabic elements is not discontinued, and the slack articulation typical of voiced consonants takes the place of the more energetic articulation typical of voiceless consonants. In other words, a consonant not immediately preceded by a main stress becomes voiced; for the persistence of the tendency in later English cf. §100, §108. Typically, and certainly in Germanic, the voicing affects fricatives only; it is noticeable that fricatives in Germanic do not correlate with a voiced series, and the changes were probably at first sub-phonemic, 'strong' and 'weak' allophones of the same phoneme.

The incidence of this voicing in Germanic can be given a relative chronological placing. It is after, since it works upon the results of, the Consonant Shift; it is after, since it is caused by, the development of accentual stress. But its incidence shows that it is antecedent to the fixing of that stress on root syllables. It reflects a stage at which stress is 'free'. 'Free' is a technical term; it does not mean that speakers could put stress anywhere, but that stress did not have a fixed place in the syllabic structure of all words; its position was determined word by word, or, more usually, grammatical function by grammatical function. In strong verbs, for instance, it was on the root in the first two grades, and on the suffix in the past plural and participle; in other words, it reflected what IE had once distinguished by pitch. The voicing therefore occurs in those last two parts of the verb (as in other structures); by it $s >$ z, $\theta > \delta$, $\chi > \mathfrak{z}$. As we know (cf. §219), $z > r$, $\delta > d$, and in OE -χ- is lost intervocalically; we see some direct traces of the change in OE, but very few by ME; the most important consequence of the developments is their weakening of the pattern-integrity of strong verbs. In other parts of speech the changes can be seen by comparisons outside Germanic, as in the difference between IE *bhrāter*, L *frater*, OE *brōðer*, PE *brother* (in which *bh* and *t* undergo the consonant shift, but since the stress precedes it *ð* does not have any further change till it is voiced intervocalically in OE) and IE *pǝtēr*, L *pater*, Go *fadar*, OE *fæder*, PE *father* (in which *p* and *t* undergo the shift, and the resulting /θ/ is then voiced and made plosive, /ð/, then /d/; PE /ð/ is a later development cf. §100).

Finally, after the completion of this phase, comes the fixing of stress on root syllables, which has among its many effects that of obscuring the causal conditions for the operation of Verner's Law.

§ 227 The remaining characteristics are grammatical. The first is the introduction of a new type of verb-formation, the weak verbs, formed from existing parts of speech by the addition of a -*jan* suffix (sometimes separated from the root by a vowel formative), and characterised by a dental suffix formation in the past. There is nothing comparable in any other IE sub-family. The weak verbs undergo 'Verner's Law', but as that was not a once-for-all change it does not give useful information about when the type originated within the CG phase. It should be noted that their relatively short history before the OE period is one reason why these

412

verbs maintain their class-identity better than the OE strong verbs; but, as we know (cf. § 170), the principle of formation meant that they could become more numerous than strong verbs (since they could be formed from all strong verbs as well as other parts of speech), while, since the causal conditions for ablaut-variation had been lost, the strong type was no longer active.

Germanic introduced the syntactically distinct form of adjective declension, the weak adjectives, thus reducing the number of points in the NP at which grammatical information was specified. The conditions for survival of this pattern did not exist in post-medieval English, but it continues to play an important part in German.

Finally, Germanic underwent a drastic simplification of the system of grammatical contrasts within the verb, resulting in the two-term, non-past/past, system still operative throughout all Germanic languages as far as their inflectional forms are concerned. This development cannot be understood in terms merely of tenses. IE distinguished six aspects, certain of which had tense-implications, originally secondary, but easily able to evolve into tenses. The *present* expressed action in progress; its central meaning was durative, and it did not necessarily imply any time-specification. The *imperfect* placed an action with duration in the past. The *aorist* placed a momentary action in the past. The *perfect* expressed a completed action (and thus was often, but not necessarily, past in reference; cf. the time-reference of *I have finished* in PE). The *future* expressed actions to come. Even so bare a statement shows the delicate balance, easily upset, between primary aspectual meaning, and secondary, but often crudely obvious, temporal implications. So finely balanced a system could readily shift one way or another; the reduction made by Germanic preserves both aspectual and tense features. The single remaining contrast was between a tense-oriented past form, combining all previously distinguished past-referring aspects, and an aspect-oriented present, which is always durative and can as well be future-referring, or non-time specified, as actually present in reference. Functionally, it is an asymmetrical contrast; formally it employs the old perfect as its marked term, the old present as unmarked. The so-called two-tense system has the air of a pidgin reduction of contrasts, and raises again the possibility of substratum influence. Since both a two-tense system and initial stress characterise Finnish, with which the Germanic-speaking peoples had long been in contact, this may be the source. By the end of the migration period speakers in the various Germanic communities felt the need to refine it by the development of periphrastic forms; as they had much the same resources available to them they met the same problem in very similar ways, but they did so independently. One of the main peculiarities of English in the steady growth – still in progress – of periphrastic forms is the loss of *þeorðan* from the 'auxiliary' system (cf. § 193). For all the elaboration which has been brought about in this way, the basic forms of the English verbs, the so-called present and past, remain difficult to describe because they retain the asymmetry of function which Germanic evolved out of the IE resources.

The verb-system was simplified in other respects. The three voices – active, middle and passive – were largely reduced to one, the active. IE had five moods – indicative, subjunctive, optative, imperative, injunctive. Of these Germanic retains the indicative more or less intact, but subsumes under the optative (originally used for wish or possibility) the subjunctive (for the expression of will), and the injunctive (for the expression of unreality), and some uses of the imperative. In mood too, then, a two-term system develops, essentially (though these one-word labels are always half-truths) concerned with the contrast between actuality (indicative) and non-actuality (formally optative, but often referred to in studies of Gmc and OE as subjunctive). It does retain a separate imperative, but so reduced in form and function that it ceases to be felt as a mood on a par with the other two. English has since gone exceptionally far in confounding the indicative and subjunctive-optative, restoring the contrast in some cases by periphrasis.

Further simplifications, dropping the dual so as to reduce the number-contrast in the verb to two, and levelling all persons of the plural in all cases and moods, followed in WG.

§ 228   Detailed comparison between IE and Gmc morphology would take us far afield, and would be useless without close annotation because of the important functional shifts that accompanied formal changes. Yet certain general observations can be made, and illustrated by a single set of forms. Meillet (1921, 7 ff.) points out that the developments from IE in the many descendant languages differ widely as to their material realisations, but are identical in general direction. This pattern shows us later languages resolving independently and divergently the tensions and disequilibria inherited from the common antecedent. For instance, the structure of roots undergoes rather little change, but endings, though they differ differently, are subject to sweeping changes everywhere, and this brings in its train severe modification of the old morphology and the devising of new syntactic signals for grammatical function (not necessarily in that sequence). Inflection was extremely complicated, and showed the relations between elements on many morphological dimensions; order was, so far as we can tell, purely subjective and stylistic. All descendant languages have reduced the importance, the roles and the complexity, of inflections, and have found devices of one kind or another for relating sentence-elements independently of inflections. Almost everywhere order assumes some sort of structural function. Inflections may be regularised or they may be replaced by prepositions; really this comes to much the same thing, pre-position or post-position. What has happened in Germanic is not unique in kind, but through the early fixing of root-stress it has gone particularly far, especially in English. In many central grammatical areas English now has enclitic (post-posed) forms, which might be interpreted as a step towards a new era of inflections (cf. *won't, I'll*). Such forms introduce us to a further principle. The most used forms in a language have a history different from that of less frequent forms; we are not able to quantify this so exactly as to state a formula (though some have tried to do so) but a general correlation between frequency and peculiarity of development can be observed. This is another factor in the 'wear and tear' on grammatical forms; in another area of high-frequency use, the numerals, evolution has been so complex that many puzzles remain – we need only illustrate by the comparison of IE **kwetwōres*, OE *fēower*, PE *four*, IE **penkwe*, OE *fīf*, PE *five*, to show how great the differences are.

Let us then consider one paradigm, that of a common type of noun, in illustration of the processes of simplification, without looking in detail, at the course of the sound-changes involved. IE had eight noun-cases, represented in Germanic by only four. We do not know that the reductions came about all at once; indeed, that is most unlikely. Probably, then, the earliest Germanic had a richer system, which we cannot recover. Our reconstruction can only be based on the indications from surviving reflexes:

SG	IE	Gmc	Go	OE
N	*dhoghos	*ðaȝas	dags	dæȝ
A	*dhoghom	*ðaȝ(an)	dag	dæȝ
G	*dhogheso	*ðaȝes(a)	dagis	dæȝes
D	*dhoghoai	*ðaȝ(a)i	daga (inst)	dæȝe
PL				
N	*dhoghoes	*ðaȝōz	dagōs	daȝas
A	*dhoghoms	*ðaȝanz	dagans	daȝas

| G | *dhogheom | *ðaʒōn, -ēn | dagē | daʒa |
| D | *dhoghomos | *ðaʒomoz | dagam | daʒum |

NOTE: The Go forms are included as showing the closest recorded evidence to Gmc, but of course are not antecedent to the OE ones in a direct line, as Gmc and IE are.

Here OE has not only reduced the content of surviving contrasts, but reduced the number to three, and, as we know, erosion has continued into NE, though the unmarked /deɪ/, marked /deɪz/, system has now been stable for a long time and further reduction does not seem likely.

§ 229 It was once thought that a substantial part of Germanic vocabulary was non-IE, but further knowledge of IE has progressively reduced the residue. However, not all IE words in Gmc are of direct descent. There are borrowings, notably from Latin (cf. §213) and from Celtic (the Germanic and Celtic peoples having been in constant touch since about 400 B.C.). The vowel of Go *reiks*, 'king' (OE has the related abstract noun, *rīce*, 'kingdom', now in the suffix -*ric*) can only be explained by Celtic transmission, but, as the Celtic form *rigs* shows, the word reached Germanic early enough to undergo the consonant shift. Not quite so old, but still very ancient, are words the Goths borrowed from the Slavs in Russia, and transmitted to the other Germanic peoples, such as Slav *chleb*, Go *hlaifs*, OE *hlāf*, 'bread' (the formal reflex being *loaf*. There are still many words of unknown origin.

As far as WF goes, certain types existing in IE did not last through Germanic, such as copulative adjective compounds of the *bitter-sweet* or exocentric verb-compounds of the *pick-pocket* type; exocentric adjective formations of the *bare-back* type were already in decline. But in general both determinative and exocentric compounds are of very early IE origin.

Conclusion

§ 230   The writing of linguistic history is a systematically misleading activity. One writes in the hope of being read. Therefore one gives a false impression. No one would read a history which set matters out as they really are – nine hundred and ninety-nine features the same in every generation for every one that changes. The implication of a historical study is, 'Everything remained the same except the things I now describe'; but what it conveys is that that to which most attention is given is the most important. The purpose of this Conclusion, accordingly, is not to draw conclusions, but to try to redress the imbalance. Hopefully some examples, especially those of Chapter IX, have already given rise to reflections on continuity as the necessary background for change.

§ 231   Thus, the IE short vowel system is remarkably well preserved. It underwent considerable disruption in certain environments in OE, but not in all, and even in those environments it largely returned to something like its ancient state in ME. The only important Gmc change was of *o* to *a*, and though OE fronted *a* the sound was restored in ME and has had wide dialectal currency ever since; *u* remained till its unrounding in certain environments in very recent times. The long vowels (except *ō*) remained from IE till the 15c vowel shift; and though diphthongs have been subject to successive cycles of change, the pattern has been remarkably homogeneous – absorption of old diphthongs into the long vowel system and creation of new diphthongs from vowel plus approximant sequences. Since IE the obstruents have undergone only one major shift, and that did not affect the system; since CG they have remained constant in their functions as syllable-frames, while undergoing minor adjustments of distribution, again and again on the same lines – development of parasitic sounds and simplification of heavy clusters. Most constant of all have been the resonants, essentially unchanged since IE. Words whose stem consists of certain types of sound have remained unaltered for thousands of years; IE **su-* 'pig', OE *sū*, PE *sow*, stable until the 15c

417

vowel shift; similarly *mūs*, unchanged from IE to the 15c, now *mouse*, and the oblique case of the pronoun *me*, which has had eddies of minor variation, but which in the direct line of descent has changed by no more than final lengthening in Gmc and the 15c vowel shift. Even obstruents, in positions which protect them from the consonant-shift, can show this continuity, as in IE *sper-, OE *spere*, PE *spear*. IE *wes-, *wos- persists in OE *þesan*, *þæs*, PE *was*. In this case, of course, the sound /wɒz/ has changed more than the spelling suggests (cf. IE *swino-, OE *swīn*, PE *swine*); the many cases in which this holds indicate that there was no substantial change till the 15c vowel shift and other developments of that time, whose effects are not represented in the orthography. These examples also show semantic stability.

Similarity does not always mean direct and unchanged descent. For instance IE *kaput, 'head', has reached English very indirectly through Latin and German (and with marked semantic change). A large group of imitative words show very great stability, but have reached English immediately as loans from French, such as IE *mā, *māmā, *pap(p)a, *murmur. Suspected cases must be examined with the aid of a scholarly dictionary, whose etymological notes will not be comprehensible without careful reading of the introductory explanations.

Accentual patterns underwent much early change, but from CG on have remained essentially the same. Even the huge influx of non-Germanic loanwords has been in large measure assimilated to the stress-patterning English inherited from Germanic, though it remains responsible for the greater degree of diversity in English than, say, German. Many related features of rhythm and pace have remained unaltered since the Germanic period.

§ 232 In vocabulary the types of WF were largely established in IE, and have undergone relatively minor expansions, losses, and shifts of emphasis. As far as whole words are concerned, while English has shown universal voracity in the consumption of loans, the rate for the last nine hundred years being unlike anything in earlier history or in other IE languages, the overwhelming majority of the borrowed items are also IE in origin. This must, however, be regarded as an area of immense and highly accelerated change.

For grammar the main period of alterations was the Germanic one; what has followed, and is still in progress, is a sequel to that, preserving some old categorical contrasts, restoring others by new, largely syntactic means, removing yet others for good: here change is most extensive and penetrating, but it shows a common trend from morphology to syntax.

Aspects of continuity once we have reached English proper are well discussed by Gordon (1966). On vocabulary he points out the centrality in function of the inherited lexical material:

> The wealth of our available vocabulary tends to obscure an even more important truism: without using our inherited Germanic vocabulary we cannot express ourselves at all (13).

Continuity can be looked at not only from the viewpoint of where our words come from, but also, in reverse, from the viewpoint of how much survives from the past; Gordon estimates that four-fifths of OE prose vocabulary is still in use, and that the importance of these elements is consistently obscured. How central to the language our stress-patterns are he shows from various considerations – speakers can distort almost anything else and be understood, but not stress; English children never need correction in it as they do in many other aspects of pronunciation and usage; and it is difficult to learn for all foreigners except speakers of other Germanic languages, who have kept closely similar systems since the CG period. The segmentation and internal order of minor syntactic groups, NPs and the like, have remained unchanged since OE, and larger syntactic structures have had, except for object-placement, which in its present form dates from the 14c, the same shape in prose since the 10c. In assessing the import of these continuities, their fundamental nature is more relevant than mere numbers. In sum:

> The history of the English language is almost invariably conceived as a history of continuous change. Such an approach is accurate – if one looks only at the changes. But there is a remarkable group of features in the language that have never changed (13).

In our end is our beginning; the nature and role of change, the interplay of change and stability, are exactly the same through the centuries as they are across the community at any one moment. If we did not know that what is common is the heart of the matter, we should not speak of the English language.

Appendix

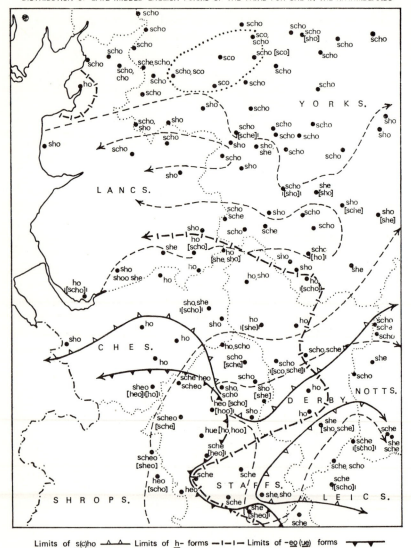

This map was drawn by Mr. G. W. Leslie, cartographer to the *Linguistic Survey of Scotland*, from material collected, analysed and interpreted by Professor Angus McIntosh, who has generously allowed me to publish it.

Bibliography

This Bibliography is intended to serve two purposes: to give particulars of works referred to in the text, and to suggest further reading.

ABERCROMBIE, D. (1965), *Studies in Phonetics and Linguistics*. London.

ALSTON, R. C. (1965, etc.), *A Bibliography of the English Language from the invention of Printing to the Year 1800*, 8 vols. London.

BACQUET, P. (1962), *La Structure de la Phrase verbale à l'Époque Alfrédienne.* Strasbourg.

BARBER, C. L. (1964), *Linguistic Change in Present Day English*. Edinburgh and London.

BARROW, G. W. S. (1956), *Feudal Britain*. London.

BAUGH, A. (1959), *History of the English Language*, 2nd edition. New York.

BENSE, J. F. (1926, etc.), *A Dictionary of the Low-Dutch Element in the English Vocabulary*. The Hague.

BJÖRKMAN, E. (1900, etc.), *Scandinavian Loanwords in Middle English*. Halle.

BLISS, A. J. (1966), *A Dictionary of Foreign Words and Phrases*. London.

BOLTON, W. F. (1967), *A Short History of Literary English*. London.

BOSWORTH, J. and TOLLER, T. N. (1898, etc.), *An Anglo-Saxon Dictionary.* Oxford.

BRADLEY, H. (1904), *The Making of English*. London.

—— (1928), *Collected Papers*. Oxford.

BRATLEY, P., DEWAR, H., and THORNE, J. P. (1967), 'Recognition of syntactic structure by computer', *Nature*, **216**, 969 ff.

BROOK, G. L. (1958), *A History of the English Language*. London.

BRUGMANN, K. and DELBRÜCK, B. (1897, etc.), *Grundriss der vergleichenden Grammatik der indogermanischen Sprachen*, I–II, 2nd edition. Strassburg.

BRUNNER, K. (1950, etc.), *Die englische Sprache: ihre geschichtliche Entwicklung*, I–II. Halle.

BRYANT, M. M. (1948), *Modern English and its Heritage*. New York.

BÜLBRING, K. (1902), *Altenglisches Elementarbuch*, I. Heidelberg.

CAMPBELL, A. (1938), 'An OE Will', *Journal of English and Germanic Philology*, **xxxvii**, 133 ff.

—— (1959), *Old English Grammar*. Oxford.

CARR, C. T. (1939), *Nominal Compounds in Germanic*. Oxford.

CASSIDY, F. G. (1961), *Jamaica Talk*. Kingston, Jamaica.

—— and LE PAGE, R. B. (1967), *Dictionary of Jamaican English*. Cambridge.

CHAMBERS, R. W., and DAUNT, M. (1931), *A Book of London English* 1384-1425. Oxford.

CHOMSKY, N., and HALLE, M. (1968), *The Sound-Pattern of English*. New York.

CLARK, C. (1958), *The Peterborough Chronicle*. London.

CLARK, J. W. (1957), *Early English*. London.

CLEMOES, P. (1942), *Liturgical Influence on Punctuation in Late OE and Early ME. Mss.* Cambridge.

COLLINGWOOD, R. G. and MYRES, J. N. L. (1937), *Roman Britain and the English Settlements*, 2nd edition. Oxford.

CRAIGIE, W. A. (1927), *English Spelling, Its Rules and Reasons*. New York.

—— and HULBERT, J. R., edd., (1938, etc.), *A Dictionary of American English on Historical Principles*, 4 vols. London.

CURME, G. O. (1931, etc.), *A Grammar of the English Language*, I–II. New York.

DARBISHIRE, H., (1931), *The MS. of Milton's Paradise Lost Book I*. Oxford.

DAUNT, M., (1939), 'Old English sound-changes reconsidered in relation to scribal tradition and practice', *Transactions of the Philological Society*, 108 ff.

—— (1946), 'OE. Verse and English speech rhythm', *Transactions of the Philological Society*, 56 ff.

DAVY, D., and QUIRK, R., (1969), 'An acceptability experiment with spoken output', *Journal of Linguistics*, 5, 109 ff.

DICKINS, B. (1959), *Studies Presented to Bruce Dickins*. Cambridge.

DOBSON, E. J. (1968), *English Pronunciation* 1500-1700, 2nd edition. Oxford.

—— (1962), 'ME. Lengthening in open syllables', *Transactions of the Philological Society*, 124 ff.

EKWALL, E. (1928), *English River Names*. Oxford.

—— (1947), *The Concise Oxford Dictionary of English Place-Names*, 3rd edition. Oxford.

—— (1956), *Studies on the Population of Medieval London*. Lund.

ELLEGÅRD, A. (1953), *The Auxiliary Do*. Stockholm.

ELLIOTT, R. W. V. (1959), *Runes*. Manchester.

ENGLISH PLACE-NAME SOCIETY (EPNS.), Publications from 1924. Cambridge.

FISHMAN, J. (1966), *Language Loyalty in the United States*. The Hague.

FÖRSTER, M. (1921), *Keltisches Wortgut im Englischen*. Halle.

FOURQUET, J. (1938), *L'Ordre des Éléments de la Phrase en Germanique ancienne*. Strasbourg.

—— (1948), *Les Mutations consonantiques du germanique*. Paris.

FRIES, C. C. (1940), 'On the development of the structural use of word-order in modern English', *Language*, **16**, 199 ff.

FRY, D. B. (1947), 'The frequency of occurrence of speech sounds in southern English', *Archives Néérlandaises de Phonétique Expérimentale*' xx 103 ff.

GELB, I. J. (1952), *Writing*. Chicago (also as paperback).

GIMSON, A. C. (1962), *An Introduction to the Pronunciation of English*. London.

GIRVAN, R. (1932), *Angelsaksisch Handboek*. Haarlem.

GNEUSS, H. (1955), *Lehnbildungen und Lehnbedeutungen im Altenglischen*. Berlin.

GORDON, I. A. (1966), *The Movement of English Prose*. London.

GREENBAUM, S. (1969), *Investigating Collocations*. The Hague (in press).

GREENOUGH, J. B., and KITTREDGE, G. L. (1900), *Words and their Ways in English Speech*. New York.

GREIN, C. W. M. (1912), *Sprachsatz der Angelsächsischen Dichter*. Heidelberg.

HALL, J. R. CLARK (1916), *A Concise Anglo-Saxon Dictionary*, 2nd edition. New York.

HALL, R. A. (1943), *Melanesian Pidgin*. Baltimore.

HARRIS, Z. S. (1952), 'Discourse analysis', *Language*, **28**, 1 ff.

HIRT, H. (1921, etc.), *Indogermanische Grammatik*, I–VII. Heidelberg.

HODGKIN, R. H. (1953), *History of the Anglo-Saxons*, 3rd edition. Oxford.

HOLTHAUSEN, F. (1934), *Altenglisches etymologisches Wörterbuch*. Heidelberg.

HOPE, T. E. (1962-3), 'Loanwords as cultural and lexical symbols', *Archivum Linguisticum*, **14–15**, 111 ff and 29 ff.

HORWILL, H. W., (1935) *A Dictionary of Modern American Usage*. Oxford.

HUCHON, R. (1923, etc.), *Histoire de la langue anglaise*. Paris.

HUDSON-WILLIAMS, T. (1935), *A Short Introduction to the Study of Comparative Grammar (Indo-European)*. Cardiff.

HUNTER BLAIR, P. (1956), *An Introduction to Anglo-Saxon England*. Cambridge

JACKSON, K. (1953), *Language and History in Early Britain*. Edinburgh.

JESPERSEN, O. (1909), *Growth and Structure of the English Language*. Leipzig. (On some points the 8th edition, 1935, is to be preferred.)

—— (1909, etc.), *A Modern English Grammar*. Heidelberg.

JONES, D. (1917, etc.), *An English Pronouncing Dictionary*. Successive editions show changes during the last generation. London (13th edition, 1967.)

JONES, R. F. (1953), *The Triumph of the English Language*. Oxford.

JORDAN, R. (1934), *Handbuch der mittel-englischen Grammatik*. Heidelberg.

KEISER, A. (1918), *The Influence of Christianity on the Vocabulary of OE Poetry*. Illinois.

Bibliography

KENNEDY, A. G. (1927), *A Bibliography of Writings on the English Language*. Cambridge, Mass. and New Haven.

KINGDON, R. (1958), *The Groundwork of English Stress*. London.

KÖKERITZ, H. (1953), *Shakespeare's Pronunciation*. New Haven.

—— (1954), *A Guide to Chaucer's Pronunciation*. Stockholm.

KRAPP, G. P. (1925), *The English Language in America*, I–II. New York.

KUHN, S. M., and QUIRK, R. (1953), 'Some recent interpretations of the Old English digraph spellings', *Language*, **29**, 143 ff.

LABOV, W. (1966), *The Social Stratification of English in New York City*. Washington.

LEHMANN, W. P. (1955), *Proto-Indo-European Phonology*. Austin, Texas.

LEWIS, C. S. (1968), *Studies in Words*. Cambridge.

LINGUISTIC BIBLIOGRAPHY (1939, etc.), Permanent International Committee of Linguists (C.I.P.L.). Utrecht and Brussels.

LLEWELLYN, E. C. (1936), *The Influence of Low Dutch on the English Vocabulary*. Oxford.

LOCKWOOD, W. B. (1969), *Indo-European Philology*. London.

LONG, M. M. (1944), *The English Strong Verb from Chaucer to Caxton*. Menasha, Wis.

LUICK, K. (1913, etc.), *Historische Grammatik der englishen Sprache*. Leipzig.

MACGILLIVRAY, H. S. (1902), *The Influence of Christianity on the Vocabulary of OE*. Halle.

MCINTOSH, A. (1963), 'A new approach to ME. dialectology', *English Studies*, **44**, 1 ff.

MCKNIGHT, G. H. (1928), *Modern English in the Making*. New York. (Paperback, 1968, with title, *The Evolution of the English Language*. New York.)

MARCHAND, H. (1969), *Categories and Types of Present-Day English Word-Formation*. 2nd edition. Munich.

MARCKWARDT, A. H. (1942), *Introduction to the English Language*. Oxford.

—— (1958), *American English*. New York.

MARTINET, A. (1962), *A Functional View of Language*. Oxford.

MATHEWS, M. W. (1951), *A Dictionary of Americanisms*, 2 vols. Chicago.

MAWER, A. and STENTON, F. M. (1924), *Introduction to the Survey of English Place-Names*. Cambridge.

MEILLET, A. (1921, etc.), *Linguistique historique et linguistique générale*, I–II. Paris.

—— (1927), *Caractères généraux des langues germaniques*' 3rd edition. Paris.

—— (1937), *Introduction à l'étude comparative des langues indo-européénnes*. 8th edition. Paris.

—— (1950), *Les Dialectes indo-européénnes*, new edition, revised. Paris.

—— and COHEN, M. (1956), *Les Langues du Monde*, 2nd edition. Paris.

MENCKEN, H. L. (1956, etc.), *The American Language*, 4th edition and two supplements. New York.

MENNER, R. J. (1945), 'Multiple meaning and change of meaning in English', *Language*, 21, 59 ff.

MIDDLE ENGLISH DICTIONARY (1953, etc., in progress), ed. H. Kurath and S. M. Kuhn. Ann Arbor.

MOORE, S., MEECH, S. B., and WHITEHALL, H. (1935), *ME Dialect Character-istics and Dialect Boundaries*. Ann Arbor.

MOORMAN, J. R. H. (1945), *Church Life in England in the Thirteenth Century*. Cambridge.

MORSBACH, L. (1896), *Mittelenglische Grammatik*, I. Halle.

MOSSÉ, F. (1938a), *La Périphrase verbale ÊTRE + PARTICIPE PRÉSENT en ancien Germanique*. Paris.

—— (1938b), *Histoire de la forme périphrastique, ÊTRE + PARTICIPE PRÉSENT en anglais de 1200 à nos jours*. Paris.

—— (1945), *Manuel de l'Anglais de Moyen Age*, I, 1–2. Vieil Anglais, Paris.

—— (1947), *Esquisse d'une histoire de la langue anglaise*. Lyons.

—— (1952), *A Handbook of ME*, translated by J. A. Walker. Baltimore.

MUSSET, L. (1965), *Introduction à la Runologie*. Paris.

MUSTANOJA, T. (1960), *A Middle English Syntax*, Part I. Helsinki.

NICKEL, G. (1966), *Die Expanded Form im Altenglischen*. Neumunster.

OAKDEN, J. P. (1930, etc.), *Alliterative Poetry in ME*, I–II. Manchester.

ONIONS, C. T. (1905), *An Advanced English Syntax*. London.

OXFORD ENGLISH DICTIONARY (*OED*) (1888, etc.), ed. A. H. Murray, H. Bradley, W. A. Craigie and C. T. Onions. Oxford.

PALMER, F. R. (1965), *A Linguistic Study of the English Verb*. London.

PEDERSEN, H. (1931), *Linguistic Science in the 19th Century*, translated by J. Spargo. Cambridge, Mass.

POKORNY, J. (1959, etc.), *Indogermanisches etymologisches Wörterbuch*. Bern.

POPE, J. C. (1942), *The Rhythm of Beowulf*. New Haven.

POTTER, S. (1950), *Our Language*. London.

POUTSMA, H. (1904, etc.), *A Grammar of Late Modern English*, I–IV. Groningen.

PRAZ, M. (1929), 'The Italian element in English', *Essays and Studies*, XV, 20 ff.

PRICE, H. T. (1910), *A History of Ablaut in the Strong Verbs from Caxton to the end of the Elizabethan Period*. Bonn.

PROKOSCH, E. (1938), *A Comparative Germanic Grammar*. Philadelphia.

QUIRK, R. (1960), 'Towards a description of English usage', *Transactions of the Philological Society*, 40 ff. (No. 7. in *Essays on the English Language, Medieval and Modern*, 1968, London, is based on this paper.)

—— (1965), 'Descriptive statement and serial relationship', *Language*, 41, 205 ff. (= No. 16 in *Essays on the English Language, Medieval and Modern*, 1968, London.)

—— (1966), 'Acceptability in language,' *Proceedings of the University of Newcastle upon Tyne Philosophical Society*, I, 7, 79 ff. (= No. 17 in *Essays on the English Language, Medieval and Modern*, 1968, London.)

—— and SVARTVIK, J. (1966), *Investigating Linguistic Acceptability*. The Hague.

—— and WRENN, C. L. (1960), *An OE Grammar*, 2nd edition. London.

REANEY, P. H. (1958), *A Dictionary of British Surnames*. London.

RESZKIEWICZ, A. (1966), *Ordering of Elements in Late OE Prose*. Warsaw.

ROBERTSON, S. revised CASSIDY, F. G. (1954), *The Development of Modern English*. Englewood Cliffs, N.J.

RYNELL, A. (1948), *The Rivalry of Scandinavian and Native synonyms in ME, Especially* taken *and* nimen. Lund.

SAMUELS, M. L. (1963), 'Some applications of ME. dialectology', *English Studies*, 44, 81 ff.

SERJEANTSON, M. S. (1935), *A History of Foreign Words in English*. London.

SHEARD, J. A. (1954), *The Words We Use*. London.

SHELLY, P. van Dyke, (1921), *English and French in England*, 1066-1100. Philadelphia.

SIEVERS, E. (1893), *Altgermanische Metrik*. Halle.

—— and BRUNNER, K. (1951), *Altenglische Grammatik*, 2nd edition. Halle.

SISAM, K. (1950), *Fourteenth Century Verse and Prose*. Oxford.

—— (1953), *Studies in the History of Old English Literature*. Oxford.

SKEAT, W. W. (1891, etc.), *Principles of English Etymology*, 1st and 2nd series. Oxford.

—— (1911), *English Dialects*. Cambridge.

SMITH, A. H. (1956), *English Place-Name Elements*, I–II. Cambridge.

SMITH, L. P. (1912), *The English Language*. London.

STANLEY, E. G. (1966), ed. *Continuations and Beginnings*. London.

STENTON, F. M. (1947), *Anglo-Saxon England*, 2nd edition. Oxford.

STERN, G. (1931), *Meaning and Change of Meaning*. Gothenburg.

STOCKWELL, R. P. (1964), 'On the utility of an overall pattern in historical English phonology', *Proceedings of the Ninth International Congress of Linguists*, 663 ff. Cambridge, Mass.

STRANG, B. M. H. (1966), 'Some features of S–V concord in present-day English', *English Studies Today* (Proceedings of the Sixth I.A.U.P.E. Congress), 77 ff. Rome.

—— (1967), 'Swift and the English language', in *To Honor Roman Jakobson*, 1947 ff. The Hague.

STRATMANN, F. H. and BRADLEY, H. (1891), *A Middle English Dictionary*. Oxford.

STREADBECK, A. L. (1966), *A Short Introduction to Germanic Linguistics*. Boulder, Colorado.

SWEET, H. (1885), *The Oldest English Texts*. London.

—— (1888), *A History of English Sounds*, 2nd edition. Oxford.

—— (1892, etc.), *A New English Grammar*. Oxford.

THORNLEY, G. C. (1954), 'Accents and points of MS. Junius 11', *Transactions of the Philological Society*, 178 ff.

TRNKA, B. (1930), *On the Syntax of the English Verb from Caxton to Dryden*. Prague.

TURNER, G. W. (1966), *The English Language in Australia and New Zealand*. London.

ULLMANN, S. (1951), *The Principles of Semantics*. Glasgow.

VISSER, F.Th. (1970, 1972, 1969, 1973), *An Historical Syntax of the English Language* (three volumes in four, the first two being corrected reprints). Leiden.

WEBSTER, (1961), *Third International New English Dictionary*. Springfield, Mass. and London (Merriam–Webster Co.).

WEEKLEY, E. (1957), *The English Language*, revised edition. London.

WHITELOCK, D. (1952), *The Beginnings of English Society*. London.

WILSON, R. M. (1943), 'English and French in England 1100-1300', *History*, **28**, 37 ff.

WRENN, C. L. (1952), *The English Language*, corrected reprint. London.

—— (1968), *Sound and Symbol*. London.

WRIGHT, J. (1896, etc.), *The English Dialect Dictionary* (including in Volume VI 'An English Dialect Grammar'). Oxford.

WYLD, H. C. (1913), *The Historical Study of the Mother Tongue*. London.

—— (1923), *Studies in English Rhymes from Surrey to Pope*. London.

—— (1927), *A Short History of English*. London.

—— (1936), *A History of Modern Colloquial English*. Oxford.

ZANDVOORT, R. W. (1956), 'Is English a Germanic language?', *Durham University Journal*, N.S. **XVIII**, 83 ff.

Index

This *Index* is intended to complement the *Analytical Contents* as a guide to material in the book. It is reasonably detailed, within the following limits. Related items are found under a single head unless a point of linguistic significance is involved in the distinction. Thus, *Phonemic(ally)* will be subsumed under *Phoneme, Adverbial* under *Adverb;* but *Adverbal* is distinct. Topics receiving extended discussion are given a reference even where the word listed does not occur on every page, except in cases where the *Analytical Contents* makes this unnecessary. Terms used on more than 100 pages evenly spread throughout the text are not listed in detail (e.g. *Grammar, Word*) and terms only marginally technical in sense (e.g. *Element, Item*) are excluded. Negatives are listed separately from positives only where they are of fairly frequent occurrence (thus, *Non-human* is entered separately, but *Asymmetry* is subsumed under *Symmetry*). In alphabetisation, items are ordered in their totality regardless of word-boundaries (thus, *Functional load* precedes *Function word*). In many cases, clarifying material is added in parentheses; parenthetic material is not taken into account in alphabetisation (thus, *Middle (verb)* precedes *Middle English*).

Index

Addison, J., 142

Adjective (Adj), 23, 32, 59, 69, 84, 89–91, 119, 123, 130, 134–5, 137–9, 179, 188–9, 193, 195–6, 199–200, 205, 237, 249, 252–4, 257–8, 262, 270–3, 293–4, 300–3, 305, 326, 329, 332, 335–7, 346, 386–7, 413, 416

Adjunct, 138

Adnominal, 304–5

Adverb(ial) (Adv), 23, 32, 36, 55, 69, 84, 119, 138, 144, 155, 179, 181, 190, 199–200, 272–3, 275, 301, 304–5, 313, 326, 337, 345, 350

Adverbal, 305

Aelfric, 314, 344

Aethelred, King of Wessex, 319

Affirmative, 151, 210–1, 265, 281, 313, 346

Affix, 26–7, 88, 189–192

Affricate, 292, 340

Africa, 18, 76, 94, 121, 125, 127, 186, 401

Agent, 275, 336

Aidan, Bishop, 357

Air-column, 7

Albanian, 404

Aldfrith, King of Northumbria, 360

Aldhelm, Bishop, 360

Alfred, King of England, 16, 67, 319–322, 334, 343–4, 361–2, 371, 378

Algonquian, 128

Alien (elements), 28, 46, 52, 93, 123, 193, 338, 372, 392

Alliteration, 289, 324–5, 327–30, 333, 340

Allophone, 49, 80, 286, 340, 402, 406, 412

Alphabet, 158–9, 227–8, 285, 287–8, 331, 355, 362–3, 395–7

Alternation, 138, 175, 179–80, 196, 198, 238, 249, 277, 279–80, 290, 306–7, 337, 348, 385, 387, 399, 407

Alveolar, 51, 147, 238, 363, 405

Ambiguity, 99, 135, 142, 150, 155, 205, 229–30, 266, 288, 297–8, 343–4

America, 104–5, 127–8, 382, 401

American English, 18, 24, 29, 31, 35–8, 40–4, 58, 61, 73–8, 84, 86, 90, 92–4, 98, 105, 107, 118–19, 149, 206, 273, 282

Amerindian, 19, 38, 94, 120, 128, 403

Anacrusis, 325

Analogy, 15–17, 25, 29, 42, 53–6, 78, 83–5, 103, 109, 116–17, 119, 132, 135, 138, 140–1, 182, 200, 203, 268–9, 233–4, 279, 286, 293, 309, 368

Analytic, 59

Anaphora, 143

Ancrene Wisse, 245

Angeln, 378, 380

Angle, 377–9, 398

Anglian, 291, 323, 365, 381, 386

Anglicisation, 28–30, 36, 38, 124–6, 128–9, 192, 274, 334

Anglo-Danish, 340

Anglo-Frisian, 384–5, 398

Anglo-Norman, 175–6, 217–18, 230, 240, 251–3, 255

Anglo-Saxon (AS), 19, 109, 125, 161–2, 284, 314, 316, 334, 357, 361, 377, 395

Anglo-Scandinavian, 255

Animal cries, 5–6

Animate, 97, 206, 304

Anomalous, 141, 147, 169, 182, 196, 203–5, 238, 249, 259–60, 264, 266, 276, 299, 305–6, 310–11, 352, 364, 385

Antecedent, 144, 265

Anticipation, 485

Aorist, 413

Aphetic, 103

Apodosis, 68

Apostrophe, 109

Apposition, 304, 306